HNC HND BUSINESS

Optional Units 17-20

Business and Marketing

Course Book

BPP PUBLISHING

EDEXCEL HNC & HND BUSINESS

First edition February 2001
ISBN 07517 7042 6

British Library Cataloguing-in Publication Data
A catalogue record for this book is available from the British Library

Printed in Great Britain by Ashford Colour Press

Published by
BPP Publishing Limited
Aldine House, Aldine Place
London W12 8AW

www.bpp.com

CONTENTS

BPP PUBLISHING

INTRODUCTION

The HNC and HND qualifications in Business are very demanding. The suggested content, set out by Edexcel in guidelines for each unit, includes topics which are normally covered at degree level. Students therefore need books which get straight to the core of these topics, and which build upon the student's existing knowledge and experience. BPP's series of Course Books have been designed to meet that need.

This book has been written specifically for the optional pathway in Business and Marketing (Units 17 to 20). It covers the Edexcel guidelines and suggested content in full, and includes the following features.

- The Edexcel guidelines
- A study guide explaining the key features of the book and how to get the most from your studies
- An index

Each chapter contains:

- An introduction and study objectives
- Summary diagrams and signposts, to guide you through the chapter
- Numerous activities, topics for discussion, definitions and examples
- A chapter roundup, a quick quiz and answers to activities

At the end of the book, you will find two assignments for each unit, with answer guidelines.

You will notice that in the book Unit 19, Marketing Planning, precedes Unit 18, Advertising and Promotion. This is because of the inter-relationship between the content of the Units. The content of Unit 19 bears close relation to that of Unit 17, and therefore it is logical to link the two units together.

BPP Publishing are the leading providers of targeted texts for professional qualifications. Our customers need to study effectively. They cannot afford to waste time. They expect clear, concise and highly-focused study material. This series of Course Books for HNC and HND Business has been designed and produced to fulfil those needs.

BPP Publishing
February 2001

Titles in this series:

Core Unit 1	Marketing
Core Unit 2	Managing Financial Resources
Core Unit 3	Organisations and Behaviour
Core Unit 4	Organisations, Competition and Environment
Core Unit 5	Quantitative Techniques for Business
Core Unit 6	Legal and Regulatory Framework
Core Unit 7	Management Information Systems
Core Unit 8	Business Strategy
Option Units 9-12	Business & Finance
Option Units 13-16	Business & Management
Option Units 17-20	Business & Marketing
Option Units 21-24	Business & Personnel

For more information, or to place an order, please call 020 8740 2211, or fill in the order form at the back of this book.

If you would like to send in your comments on this book, please turn to the review form on the last page.

EDEXCEL GUIDELINES FOR UNIT 17: MARKETING INTELLIGENCE

Description of the unit

The aim of this unit is to enable students to learn about different types of information needed for planning and monitoring in a competitive environment. Students will examine and apply techniques used in marketing to identify sources of information, trends in customer demand and the wider competitive environment. This unit gives the student the opportunity to develop further skills, knowledge and understanding of the concepts of marketing research.

Summary of outcomes

To achieve this unit a student must:

1 Identify and evaluate models of **buyer behaviour**.

2 Identify and evaluate **market research techniques**.

3 Carry out a **competitor analysis**.

4 Identify and apply methods of establishing **customer satisfaction** levels.

Content

1 **Buyer behaviour**

Customers and behaviour: approaches used to understand buyer behaviour and evaluate their contribution to marketing practice.

Buyer behaviour: stimulus response models, models of purchase behaviour, diffusion and innovation, model unitary and decision-making units.

Buying motives: psychological factors, socio-psychological factors, sociological factors, economic factors and cultural factors influencing customer behaviour.

Branding: relationship between brand loyalty, company image and repeat purchase.

2 **Market research techniques**

Market research: issues relating to the use of primary and secondary data sources and methods, existing sources of primary and secondary market research, internal sources, external sources, competitor data and sources and customer data.

Market research companies: benefits and limitations of use, cost, reliability and types.

Research techniques: use of qualitative and quantitative methods, use of surveys, sources of information, value and interpretation of data.

Types: face-to-face, telephone/postal, electronic, focus groups, depth interviews, omnibus surveys, psychological research, mystery shoppers, sales, price and distribution research.

Reliability of research: sample size, sample and interviewer bias, methods of recruitment.

Researching developing and established markets: issues associated with researching developing as well as the established consumer, industrial and service markets.

3 Competitor analysis

Measuring: estimating total market size, value and volume, growth and trends.

Competitive analysis: competitor analysis – market/product profiles of competition, brand and market share, characteristic of the competition – market innovator/follower, objectives of the competition, strategies of the competition, strengths and weakness of competition, future behaviour of the competition and their strategic intent.

4 Customer satisfaction

Measuring customer satisfaction: post-sale surveys, guarantees, complaint handling, product placement, and service agreements, customer follow-up.

Customer care: customer care programmes, objectives, use and value in data collection, customer care as a means of adding value and influencing purchase/repeat purchase behaviour.

Outcomes and assessment criteria

To achieve each outcome a student must demonstrate the ability to:

Outcomes	**Assessment criteria** **To achieve each outcome a student must demonstrate the ability to:**
1 Identify and evaluate models of **buyer behaviour**.	• identify approaches and theories of buyer behaviour in terms of individuals and markets. • evaluate the relationship between brand loyalty, corporate image and repeat purchasing. • explain the factors that affect buyer behaviour.
2 Identify and evaluate **market research techniques**.	• review and evaluate differing types of market research techniques. • identify and use sources of secondary data in two marketing contexts. • assess the reliability of market research findings. • propose a marketing research plan to obtain information in a given situation.
3 Carry out a **competitor analysis**.	• identify market size, growth and trends within a given market. • plan and carry out a competitor analysis for a given organisation. • evaluate an organisation's opportunities and threats for a given product or service.

NOTES

Outcomes	Assessment criteria To achieve each outcome a student must demonstrate the ability to:
4 Identify and apply methods of establishing **customer satisfaction** levels.	• identify and evaluate techniques of assessing customer response. • design and complete a customer satisfaction survey.

Guidance

Generating evidence

Evidence of outcomes may be in the form of written or oral assignments or tests. The assignments may focus on real problems or case studies. Learning and assessment can be across units, at unit level or at outcome level. Evidence could be at outcome level, although opportunities exist for covering more than one outcome in an assignment.

Links

This unit is part of the HN marketing pathway, and forms a direct link with other marketing units in the programme. The unit is also linked with core 'Marketing' (Unit 1), 'Quantitative Techniques for Business' (Unit 5), 'Advertising and Promotion' (Unit 18), 'Marketing Planning' (Unit 19) and 'Sales Planning and Operations' (Unit 20).

This unit offers opportunities for demonstrating Common Skills in Communicating, Managing Tasks and Solving Problems and Applying Design and Creativity.

Resources

Access should be available to a learning resource centre with a good range of market research texts. Texts should be supported by journals, company reports and government statistics. Case studies, videos and documented examples of current issues should illustrate the topical nature of this unit.

World Wide Web sites can be useful in providing information and case studies (eg http://www.bized.co.ac.uk which provides business case studies appropriate for educational purposes).

Delivery

This unit builds on 'Quantitative Techniques for Business' (Unit 5) and is designed to enable students to apply quantitative methods and research techniques in developing marketing research. It can be delivered as a stand-alone package or in combination with the marketing planning unit. Wherever possible a practical approach should be adopted with the use of case studies or the collection and evaluation of primary and secondary data for a given organisation, product or service. The use of outside speakers and visits to organisations could be used where appropriate to support delivery. Efforts should be made to ensure that students gain a good understanding of the marketing knowledge they gain and can apply it to real-life situations and case studies.

Suggested reading

Adock Dennis et al – *Marketing Principles and Practice* – 3rd Ed. (Pitman, 1998)

Davies Mark – *Understanding Marketing* (Prentice-Hall, 1998)

Marketing (BPP, 2000)

Stokes David – *Marketing: A Case Study Approach* (Letts Educational, 1997)

Woodruffe Helen – *Services Marketing* (M&E Pitman Publishing, 1995)

NOTES

EDEXCEL GUIDELINES FOR UNIT 18: ADVERTISING AND PROMOTION

Description of unit

This unit is designed to provide students with an understanding of key areas of advertising and promotion and to develop student's ability to select and apply appropriate communications tools within a strategic and tactical framework. It is a broad-based unit covering theoretical concepts as well as current promotional practice. It provides the basis for career choices in this field as well as for further study for professional qualifications.

Summary of outcomes

To achieve this unit a student must:

1 Analyse the **communications environment.**

2 Explain the role and objectives of **advertising.**

3 Explain the role and objectives of **below-the-line techniques**.

4 Prepare a **promotion strategy.**

Content

1 Communications environment

Organisation of the industry: advertising agencies, media owners, advertisers, triangle of dependence, types of agency – full service, à la carte, media independents, hot shops, concentration in buying and selling, media sales houses, other supporting services – PR, sales promotion, marketing research.

Regulation of promotion: Sale of Goods Act, Trade Descriptions Act, Consumer Credit Act, Data Protection Act etc. Statutory authority – Independent Television Commission and Radio Authority, self regulation – Advertising Standards Authority, consumerism, ethics and public opinion as a constraint.

Current trends: media fragmentation, micro-marketing, media costs, increasing use of sales promotion techniques at the expense of advertising and its effect on branding and awareness, new media, eg payslips, till receipts, petrol pumps etc, role of IT, Internet, computerised home shopping.

Communication process: model of communication process, adoption process and adopter categories, consumer buying decision-making process, influences on consumer behaviour – personal, psychological, social, response – hierarchy models.

2 Advertising

Role of advertising: definition, purpose and objectives of advertising, remind, inform, persuade, advantages and disadvantages, role of advertising within marketing mix, within promotional mix, characteristics of advertising media – press, TV, radio, cinema, posters/outdoor etc.

Branding: definition, purpose and objectives of branding, benefits, concepts, branding strategies – blanket, family, individual, multi-branding, brand

BPP PUBLISHING

extension, own brands, situations when branding is inappropriate, brand equity, brand evaluation techniques.

Creative aspects of advertising: positioning, messages, message-appeals, ad design and testing, copy writing, visuals, creative briefs, impact of IT on advertisement design.

Working with advertising agencies: structures, role of account handler and account planner, process and methods of agency selection, agency appointment including contracts and best practice guidelines, remuneration – commission, fee, results, evaluation of agencies.

3 Below-the-line techniques

Primary techniques: sales promotion, public relations, sponsorship, direct marketing, packaging and merchandising. For each of the above techniques detailed consideration of role, characteristics, objectives, advantages/ disadvantages, appropriate uses, evaluation measures.

Other techniques: an overview of the role and uses of corporate identity, exhibitions, word-of-mouth, personal selling, miscellaneous and new media.

4 Promotion strategy

Budget formulation: methods – percentage of sales, per unit, competitive parity, task, executive judgement, overview of media costs, guidelines for budget allocation, relative costs of various promotional techniques and low-and high-budget campaigns.

Developing a promotion plan: situation analysis, objectives, target audiences, creative strategy, promotional strategy and tactics, media selection, scheduling, budget allocation, evaluation measures, inter- and intra-media decisions, burst versus drip.

Integration of promotional techniques: benefits, methods, role of positioning, importance of PR, corporate identity and packaging in aiding integration, barriers to integration – eg company and agency organisation structures, cost etc, methods of overcoming these barriers, levels of integration, award-winning campaigns.

Measuring campaign effectiveness: customer response, recall, attitude surveys, sales levels, repeat purchases, loyalty, cost-effectiveness, degree of integration, creativity, quantitative and qualitative measures.

Outcomes and assessment criteria

Outcomes	Assessment criteria **To achieve each outcome a student must demonstrate the ability to:**
1 Analyse the **communications environment.**	• explain the structure, role and relationships between parties in the communications industry. • identify current trends in advertising and promotion and evaluate their impact. • use models to assess the impact of advertising and promotion on customer behaviour.
2 Explain the role and objectives of **advertising**	• explain and demonstrate how advertising can be designed to stimulate customer response. • discuss appropriate uses and applications for advertising in two given situations. • discuss the role and organisation of agencies in the advertising process.
3 Explain the role and objectives of **below-the-line techniques**	• differentiate between the characteristics and objectives of the various techniques. • recommend the use of individual techniques in three commercial situations.
4 Prepare a **promotion strategy**	• explain the principles and process of campaign management. • combine appropriate techniques into an integrated and cost-effective campaign. • present promotion recommend-ations in the form of a promotion plan. • suggest appropriate measures for assessing campaign effectiveness.

Guidance

Generating evidence

Evidence of outcomes may be in the form of written or oral assignments or tests. The assignments may be on real problems or case studies. Evidence produced at outcome level can maximise flexibility of delivery although tutors may find implementation using the framework of a promotion plan, of the unit as a total package better suited to the needs of students. A portfolio of evidence generated through work placement could provide evidence against outcomes, although it is more likely that evidence will be generated by a combination of tutor-led assignments or tests.

Evidence could include:

- A group brand tracking study conducted across the academic year, which observes, records and analyses campaign techniques used by a major brand.
- Individual assignment which appraises and compares individual advertisements to evaluate their likely impact, audience and effectiveness.
- Time-constrained assessment which requires a student to devise a promotion plan against a case study scenario.

Links

This unit is part of the HN marketing pathway and forms a direct link with other marketing units in the programme: 'Marketing' (Unit 1), 'Marketing Intelligence' (Unit 17), 'Marketing Planning' (Unit 19), 'Sales Planning and Operations' (Unit 20).

This unit offers opportunities for demonstrating Common Skills in Working with and Relating to Others, Communicating, Managing Tasks and Solving Problems and Applying Design and Creativity.

Resources

Texts should be supported by tracking of latest developments within the communications industry from trade journals (*Campaign, Marketing Week, Marketing, Incentive and Marketing Business* could be used) and *Trade Association Monthly Bulletins* (ASA). Case studies, videos and documented examples of current practice should illustrate the topical nature of this unit. Access to media statistics and cost information, BRAD and media research reports eg JICNARS is desirable. Where appropriate, guest speakers from the industry should be invited to contribute.

World Wide Web sites can be useful in providing information and case studies (eg http://www.bized.co.ac.uk. which provides business case studies appropriate for educational purposes).

Delivery

This unit can be delivered as a stand-alone unit or as a part of the marketing pathway. Wherever possible, an integrated approach of academic and practical skills should be delivered. Emphasis in this unit should be towards an observational approach to promotional practice necessitating involvement in documentary and analytical studies based on current or case study marketing activities and the practical application of the communications mix for a given product or service.

NOTES

Suggested Reading

Black Sam – *The Practice of Public Relations* (CIM/Butterworth-Heinemann, 1997)

Fill Chris – *Marketing Communications* (Prentice Hall, 1995)

Smith P R – *Marketing Communications, An Integrated Approach* (Kogan Page, 1993)

White R – *Advertising (What it is and How to do it)* (McGraw Hill, 1993)

Wilmshurst J – *Below the Line Promotion* (CIM/Butterworth-Heinemann, 1997)

EDEXCEL GUIDELINES FOR UNIT 19: MARKETING PLANNING

Description of unit

This unit will consolidate previous knowledge and understanding of marketing and enable students to select, analyse, apply and evaluate marketing planning models and theories to marketing planning. Upon completion candidates should have the ability to evaluate an organisation's ability to develop and launch a new product, and present a credible marketing plan

Summary of outcomes

To achieve this unit students must:

1 Carry out **marketing audits.**

2 Prepare a **marketing plan** for a product or service.

3 Examine **ethical issues** in marketing.

Content

1 Marketing audits

Changing perspectives: changing perspectives in marketing planning

Assessment of capability: evaluate issues relating to the aspects of competing for the future and balancing strategic intent and strategic reality

Organisational auditing: evaluating and coming to terms with organisational capability: balancing strategic intent and strategic reality, the determinants of capability, managerial, financial, operational, human resource and intangible (brand) capability, approaches to leveraging capability, aspects of competitive advantage.

Environmental auditing: approaches to environmental analysis, the identification and evaluation of key forces using the PEST framework, the implications for marketing planning of different environmental types, identifying the organisation's competitive position and relating this to the principal opportunities and threat, market, product and brand life-cycles

2 Marketing plan

The strategic alternatives for new product development: an overview of the marketing planning process, SWOT, objectives in differing markets, products and services, product modification through to innovation, evaluation of product and market match, use of Ansoff matrix in NPD and meeting customer needs, product failure rates and implications for screening ideas against company capabilities and the market, product testing, test marketing, organisational arrangements for managing new product development, unit's costs, encouraging an entrepreneurial environment, the importance of celebrating failure

Pricing policy: policy taking versus price making, the dimensions of price, approaches to adding value, pricing techniques: cost-based versus market-oriented pricing, the significance of cash flow, the inter-relationships between price and other elements of the marketing mix, taking price out of the competitive equation

NOTES

Distribution: distribution methods, transport methods, hub locations and distribution centres, choice of distribution medium to point of sale, distribution and competitive advantage

Communication mix: evaluation of promotional mix to influence purchasing behaviour, media planning and cost, advertising and promotion campaigns and changes over the PLC, field sales planning

Implementation: factors affecting the effective implementation of marketing plans, barriers to implementation and how to overcome them, timing, performance measures: financial, non-financial, quantitative, qualitative

3 Ethical issues

Ethical issues in marketing: ethics and the development of the competitive stance, different perspectives on ethics across nations, ethical trade-offs and ethics and managerial cultures

Ethics of the marketing mix: management of the individual elements of the marketing mix

Product: gathering market research on products, identification of product problems and levels of customer communication, product safety and product recall

Price: price fixing, predatory pricing, deceptive pricing, price discrimination

Promotion: media message impact, sales promotion, personal selling, hidden persuaders and corporate sponsorship.

Distribution: abuse of power – restriction of supply

Counterfeiting: imitation, faking, pre-emption, prior registration

Consumer ethics: warranty deception, misredemption of vouchers, returns of merchandise, recording of music and videos, software copying, false insurance claims

Outcomes and assessment criteria

Outcomes	Assessment criteria **To achieve each outcome a student must demonstrate the ability to:**
1 Carry out **marketing audits**	• explain the purpose of marketing audits • apply organisational and environmental auditing techniques in a given situation.
2 Prepare a **marketing plan** for a product or service	• explain the need to be innovative in the market or services • identify and assess techniques for developing products.
3 Examine **ethical issues** in marketing	• investigate two different organisations' responses to ethics in marketing • make recommendations for pricing, distributing and communicating a product or service • specify measures to monitor and review marketing performance • present a marketing plan for a product or service • identify ethical issues in marketing • describe the implications of ethical issues on the marketing mix for an organisation.

Guidance

Generating evidence

Evidence of outcomes may be in the form of written or oral assignments or tests. The assignments may focus on real problems or case studies. Learning and assessment can be at unit level as an integrated unit or at outcome level. Evidence could be at outcome level although opportunities exist for covering more than one outcome in an assignment.

Links

This unit is part of the HN marketing pathway and forms a direct link with the marketing units in the programme: 'Marketing' (Unit 1), 'Marketing Intelligence' (Unit 17), 'Advertising and Promotion' (Unit 18), and 'Sales Planning and Operations' (Unit 20). This unit is also linked with 'Organisation, Competition and Environment' (Unit 4).

This unit offers opportunities for demonstrating Common Skills in Communicating and Managing Tasks and Solving Problems.

Resources

Access should be available to a learning resource centre with a good range of market research texts. Texts should be supported by use of journals, company records and government statistics. Case studies, videos and documented examples of organisations and their marketing, auditing and planning techniques should illustrate the topical nature of this unit.

World Wide Web sites can be useful in providing information and case studies (eg http://www.bized.co.ac.uk. which provides business case studies appropriate for educational purposes).

Delivery

This unit can be delivered as a stand-alone unit or as a part of the marketing pathway. It is designed to be linked to the marketing research unit and can be delivered and assessed in the form of an integrated case study on a real or tutor-devised organisation, product or service. Efforts should be made to ensure that students gain a good understanding of the theoretical underpinning and practical application of marketing planning and produce credible responses.

Suggested Reading

There are a large number of textbooks available covering the areas contained within the unit. Examples are

Doyle P – *Marketing Management and Strategy* (Prentice Hall, 1998)

Firfield P – *Marketing Strategy* (Butterworth-Heinemann, 1997)

McDonald M – *Marketing Plans* (Butterworth-Heinemann, 1995)

Wilson and Gilligan – *Strategic Marketing Management* (Butterworth-Heinemann, 1997)

EDEXCEL GUIDELINES FOR UNIT 20: SALES PLANNING AND OPERATIONS

Description of unit

The aim of this unit is to develop a critical awareness of sales planning and operations. The unit will evaluate the sales process in both domestic and international contexts and the various situations in which sales techniques are applied. It will consider the role of sales management in achieving sales, marketing and corporate objectives and enhancing the output of the sales function. This unit is designed to provide the basis for career choices in this field as well as for further study for professional qualifications.

Summary of outcomes

To achieve this unit a student must:

1 Explain the role and objectives of **field selling**

2 Assess the role of the **sales manager** in enhancing sales performance

3 Evaluate techniques for **controlling sales output.**

4 Explain the implications of operating in different **sales environments**

Content

1 Field selling

Promotional mix: personal and impersonal communication, objectives of promotion activity, push-pull strategies, integrating sales with other promotional activities, evaluating promotion, allocation of promotion budget

Understanding buyer behaviour: consumer and organisational purchase decision-making processes, personal, psychological and social influences on consumer purchase behaviour, environmental, organisational, interpersonal and individual influences on organisational buyer behaviour, purchase occasion, buying interests and motives, buyer moods, level of involvement, importance and structure of the DMU, finding the decision-taker, distinction between customer and users

Role of sales force: characteristics for personal selling, product and competitor knowledge, sales force responsibilities, information gathering, prospecting, stock allocation, sales reports and records, liaison with sales office, sales force communications and the role of IT in improving communications

Sales process: preparation and objective setting, opening remarks, techniques and personal presentation, need identification and stimulation, presentation, demonstration and use of visual aids, handling and pre-empting objections, techniques and proposals for negotiation, buying signals and closing techniques, post sale follow-up

2 Sales management

Sales strategy: setting sales objectives, relationship of sales, marketing and corporate objectives, importance of selling in the marketing plan, sources, collection and use of marketing information for planning and decision-making, role of sales forecasts in planning, quantitative and qualitative sales forecasting techniques, strategies for selling

Recruitment and selection: importance of selection, preparing job descriptions and personnel specifications, sources of recruitment, interview preparation and techniques, selection and appointment.

Motivation, remuneration and training: motivation theory and practice: financial and non-financial incentives, salary and commission based remuneration, induction and ongoing training, training methods, preparation of training programmes, the sales manual

Organisation: organisation of sales activities by product, customer area, estimation of call frequency, territory design, journey planning, allocation of workload, team building, creating and maintaining effective working relationships, sales meetings and conferences

3 Controlling sales output

Sales budget: purpose of budgeting, the role of the sales budget within the overall budgetary process, importance of sales forecast, top-down and bottom-up approaches to budgeting, allocation of sales budget

Evaluation and appraisal: purpose of evaluation, setting standards of performance, sources and methods of gathering information for evaluation, quantitative and qualitative measures of performance, ratio analysis, estimation and allocation of expenses, preparing and conducting appraisal interviews, improving individual and team performance, self-development plans

Quality and customer care: creation, maintenance and development of long-term customer relationships, Just-In-Time delivery, Total Quality Management, partnerships between buyers and sellers: handling complaints, after-sales service, supply commitments, setting standards for customer care, designing and implementing systems and procedures for customer care, customer care as a source of competitive advantage, corporate hospitality and customer entertainment, corporate gifts

Database management: importance of database building, sources of information, updating the database, use of database to generate incremental business and stimulate repeat purchase, use of databases control mechanisms, importance of IT methods in database management

4 Sales environments

Sales settings: sales channels – retailers, wholesalers, agents, importance of segmentation, industrial selling, selling to public authorities, selling for resale, telephone selling, selling services, pioneer selling, systems selling, selling to project teams or groups

International selling: role of agents and distributors, sources, selection and appointment of agents/distributors, agency contracts, training and motivating agents/distributors, use of expatriate versus local sales personnel, role, duties and characteristics of the export sales force, coping in different cultural environments

Exhibitions and trade fairs: role, types and locations of trade fairs and exhibitions, principles of stand design, setting objectives for exhibition attendance, audience profile and measurement, qualification and follow-up of exhibition leads, evaluation of exhibition attendance, financial assistance for exhibition attendance

Outcomes and assessment criteria

Outcomes	Assessment criteria **To achieve each outcome a student must demonstrate the ability to:**
1 Explain the role and objectives of **field selling**	• explain and provide two examples of the roles and relationship between objectives of different elements in the communication mix • illustrate how an understanding of buyer behaviour can be used in field selling • analyse the stages in the sales process.
2 Assess the role of the **sales manager** in enhancing sales performance	• explain how sales strategies are revised in line with corporate objectives • devise appropriate recruitment and selection procedures • explain the role of motivation, remuneration and training in enhancing sales performance • use given information to recommend appropriate organisation structures and procedures.
3 Evaluate techniques for **controlling sales output**	• explain the role of the sales budget as the basis for directing sales activities • suggest evaluation and appraisal techniques designed to improve sales performance • prepare proposals for customer care and quality control as a basis for competitive advantage • suggest how database management can improve business and customer relationships.
4 Explain the implications of operating in different **sales environments**	• identify and give three examples of the differences in the nature of sales tasks and skills in a variety of contexts • explain the role of sales staff operating in an international environment • explain the purpose of trade fairs and evaluate their contribution

NOTES

Guidance

Generating evidence

Evidence of outcomes may be in the form of written or oral assignments or tests. The assignments may focus on real problems or case studies. Learning and assessment can be at unit level as an integrated unit or at outcome level. Evidence could be at outcome level although opportunities exist for covering more than one outcome in an assignment.

Links

This unit is part of the HN marketing pathway and forms a direct link with the other marketing units in the programme: 'Marketing' (Unit 1), 'Marketing Intelligence' (Unit 17), 'Advertising and Promotion' (Unit 18), and 'Marketing Planning' (Unit 19).

It also offers opportunities for demonstrating Common Skills particularly in Communicating and Managing Tasks and Solving Problems.

Resources

There are numerous textbooks covering sales planning and operations. It is important that students are directed to a balance of comprehensive theoretical texts and the more readable 'how to' books which exist and provide an excellent source of practical exercises.

Marketing and sales journals are a good topical source of field sales and management activities. Over the years a number of videos have been produced demonstrating good (and bad) sales techniques. Many of these form part of sales training programmes which can be purchased. Throughout the course of an academic year, topical programmes often appear on television.

There is also a good source of topical video material available from:

The Open University

Tel: 01908 858785

E-mail: ouwenq@open.ac.uk

World Wide Web sites can be useful in providing information and case studies (eg http://www.bized.co.ac.uk. which provides business case studies appropriate for educational purposes).

Delivery

This unit is designed to have a variety of theoretical and practical delivery mechanisms. The use of case studies and sales organisation evaluation could be used to develop upon theoretical knowledge. A data bank of sales figures relating to number of customers, number of sales visits, number and value of orders for a number of sales staff could be analysed to evaluate sales force performance against a variety of criteria such as profitability, new business generation etc. The use of outside speakers and visits to organisations could be used where appropriate to support delivery. Efforts should be made to ensure that students gain a good understanding of the marketing knowledge they gain and can apply it to real life situations and case studies.

Suggested Reading

There are a large number of textbooks available covering the areas contained within the unit. Examples are

Lancaster G and Jobber D – *Selling and Sales Management* (Pitman, 1994)

Allen P – *Selling* (Pitman, 1993)

Johns T – *Perfect Customer Care* (Century Business, 1994)

STUDY GUIDE

This text gives full coverage of the Edexcel guidelines. This text also includes features designed specifically to make learning effective and efficient.

(a) Each chapter begins with a summary diagram which maps out the areas covered by the chapter. You can use the diagrams during revision as a basis for your notes.

(b) After the main summary diagram there is an introduction, which sets the chapter in context. This is followed by learning objectives, which show you what you will learn as you work through the chapter.

(c) Throughout the text, there are special aids to learning. These are indicated by symbols in the margin.

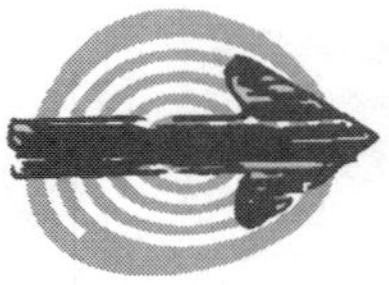

Signposts guide you through the text, showing how each section connects with the next.

Definitions give the meanings of key terms.

Activities help you to test how much you have learnt. An indication of the time you should take on each is given. Answers are given at the end of each chapter.

Topics for discussion are for use in seminars. They give you a chance to share your views with your fellow students. They allow you to highlight holes in your knowledge and to see how others understand concepts. If you have time, try "teaching" someone the concepts you have learnt in a session. This helps you to remember key points and answering their questions will consolidate your knowledge.

Examples relate what you have learnt to the outside world. Try to think up your own examples as you work through the text.

Chapter roundups present the key information from the chapter in a concise format. Useful for revision.

(d) The wide **margin** on each page is for your notes. You will get the best out of this book if you interact with it. Write down your thoughts and ideas. Record examples, question theories, add references to other pages in the text and rephrase key points in your own words.

(e) At the end of each chapter, there is a **chapter roundup**, and a **quick quiz** with answers. Use these to revise and consolidate your knowledge. The chapter roundup summarises the chapter. The quick quiz tests what you have learnt (the answers refer you back to the chapter so you can look over subjects again).

(f) At the end of the book, you will find two assignments for each unit. Each assignment allows you to put your knowledge into practice. Answer guidelines for the assignments are after the assignments.

(g) At the end of the book, there is an index.

PART A: UNIT 17

MARKETING INTELLIGENCE

Chapter 1 :
BUYER BEHAVIOUR

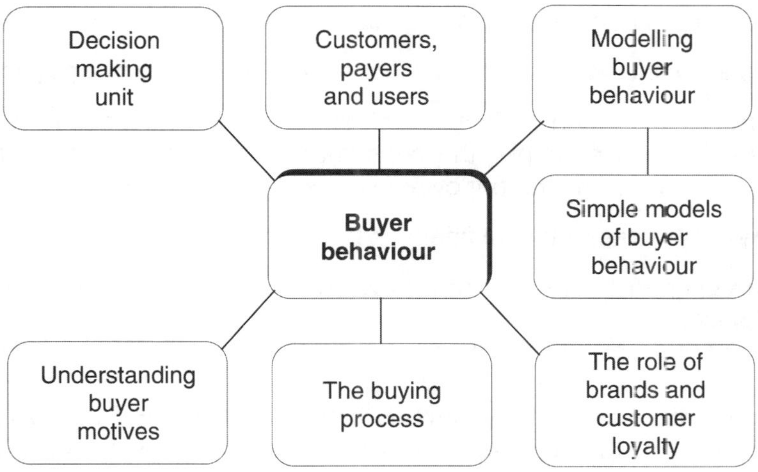

Introduction

The aim of this chapter is to introduce the basic principles of buyer behaviour. The first section offers a number of useful definitions and explains the concept of role specialisation. Section 2 gives on to discuss the modelling approach to buyer behaviour by looking at how models can be applied and evaluated. Simple models of buyer behaviour such as the black box and personal variable models are explained in the following section. A simple decision process model is used to illustrate the buying process and this includes references to the Engel, Blackwell and Miniard model.

The rate and extent of diffusion are then elaborated on with emphasis on the variability of diffusion using the adopter categories to illustrate this.

In practice, many different people can be involved in decision making both at a personal and organisational level. The different roles within the decision making unit are discussed with reference to the personal influences of gender and children. The decision making roles and processes within a personal and organisational context are compared.

The penultimate section is concerned with providing the reader with an understanding of the consumer's motivation mix. Psychological influences such as attitudes, loyalty and personality are assessed along with roles, reference groups, culture and sub-culture. This first chapter ends with a discussion regarding the role of brands and customer loyalty. Aspects which are covered include customer retention, relationship marketing and imagery.

Your objectives

In this chapter you will learn about the following:

(a) an overview of buyer behaviour
(b) the function of modelling in buyer behaviour
(c) a range of simple models of buyer behaviour
(d) the importance of the decision making unit
(e) the principles of buyer motives
(f) the role of brands and customer loyalty

NOTES

1 CUSTOMERS, PAYERS AND USERS

1.1 Customers and users

Ted Johns (*Perfect Customer Care*) makes the distinction between **customers** and **users**.

Definitions

- **Customers** are people who use goods and services and **pay** for them.
- **Users** are people who use the product or service, but **do not pay** for it.
- A **consumer** is the end user of a product or service who may or may not be the customer. For example, the consumer of a tin of cat food will be the family pet, while it was the pet owner who was the customer.
- The **payer** is the person who finances the purchase.
- The **buyer** participates in the procurement of the product from the marketplace.

Not all organisations accept this distinction between '**customer**' (the person who **pays**) and '**user**' (the person who **consumes**). In particular, **not-for-profit organisations** such as local authorities, libraries and schools often have a diversity of people and groups interested in the products and services they supply. These people and groups may be variously described as 'clients', 'users' or 'customers'.

The roles can be combined in many different ways:

User's role		*Example*	
Payer	Buyer	Business	Consumer/domestic
No	No	• Furniture, eg equipment used by employees but procured	• Cat food • Car purchased by parents for sole use of child • Health insurance policy paid by the company
Yes	No	Office manager may buy and pay for stationery for use by others	• Stockbrokers are agents who buy shares on behalf of the user
No	Yes	Consumer-based examples: the driver who selects a car breakdown service with the costs reimbursed by an insurance company; the bride who specifies prospective wedding gifts from a 'list' maintained through a retail operation.	Business-related examples: corporate sponsorship can mean that universities can select a building contractor and enjoy the subsequent benefits of the builder's work (in the form of, say, a dedicated business school or residential conference centre) without having to meet the costs.
Yes	Yes	Consumer-based examples: most consumers purchase and pay for products intended for their personal use, such as clothing, watches, airline tickets, haircuts, and so forth.	Business-related examples: small-business entrepreneurs often combine all three roles when they acquire office equipment, furniture, and the services of an accountant.

NOTES

1.2 Reasons for role specialisation

Users are unlikely to play other customer roles when the:

User lacks:

- Expertise/knowledge to make a choice
- Time to evaluate choice
- Buying power
- Access to the product

Product is:

- Unaffordable
- Subsidised (eg staff canteen)
- Free (eg public library)

Distinctions between user, payer and buyer are important because their clarification of the buying process helps potential product/service suppliers to **focus their marketing efforts** to optimal advantage. On the other hand, these same distinctions, even when clarified, do not necessarily show where (or how) power and influence are exercised, and by whom.

FOR DISCUSSION

In the arena of **children's toys**, for example, is it straightforward to argue that the child is **user** and the **parent is payer**. However:

(a) Who is the buyer, ie who is it who chooses which toy will be purchased?

(b) Does the fact that the parent is payer does not mean that **power** automatically resides with the parent.

Activity 1 **(10 minutes)**

Try to think of some more examples where the distinction between customer and user is significant.

2 MODELLING BUYER BEHAVIOUR

2.1 Rationale and objectives

The 'modelling approach' is based on the idea that any phenomenon or process can be **simplified**, by leaving out of the 'picture' any aspects or variables that are not of interest to the modeller, while still portraying something **meaningful** about the real phenomenon or process. This is particularly true of **consumer behaviour models**.

Because a model is a simplification of reality based on the modeller's interests, different models may be developed to describe the same phenomenon or process, **showing different aspects of the same thing.**

2.2 Objectives

(a) **Help researchers to develop theories**. Models provide a simplified framework within which research can be directed to confirm or refute/modify hypotheses about the relationships between variables and about the nature of the 'invisible' intervening variables.

(b) **Describe and explain behaviour and aid prediction**. Models which have been substantially confirmed by research and practice offer a useful tool to the marketer who wishes to understand the consumer decision process, and to predict consumer reactions to a marketing strategy based on the manipulation of stimulus and intervening variables.

2.3 Applications

Micro versus macro	A micro-model deals with the **individual** or other small unit, while a macro-model deals with a **wider environment**.
Descriptive, diagnostic, predictive	Descriptive models **describe** historical or current phenomena, while diagnostic models set out to find **causes** - to explain - and predictive models try to show what **outcomes** will result from given inputs in given circumstances.
Low-level, medium-level, high-level	These terms denote the complexity of the model and the number of variables included.
Static or dynamic	A static model is a '**snapshot**' of a phenomenon at a **particular point in time**, while a dynamic model can take account of **variations over time**.
Qualitative and quantitative	Qualitative models do not make explicit variable **measurements,** while quantitative models do, weighting the variables according to importance and so offering a more accurate predictive model.
Data-based versus theory-based	A data-based model is based on logical analysis of **available data,** while a theory-based one is developed by means of logical **extension of existing theories**, often of marketing but sometimes of psychology or sociology.
Behavioural versus statistical	A behavioural model is based on **stimulus response theories**, that is on how people are expected to behave, while a statistical model uses numerical analysis without prior assumptions about motivation.
Generalised versus ad hoc	A generalised model is constructed to apply to a **wide range of markets,** while an *ad hoc* one applies just to one market or brand.

2.4 Evaluating models

(a) **Validity**. We **should be able to verify** the model, that is **test** its proposed relationships.

(b) **Factual accuracy**. Is the model consistent with known facts (even if it is an admittedly intuitive or theoretical model)?

(c) **Rationality**. Is the model logical and internally consistent (not contradicting itself or requiring irrational 'leaps')?

(d) **Completeness**. The model may by definition leave out aspects of the phenomenon/ process, but are all assumptions explicitly stated? Are the exogenous variables identified?

(e) **Simplicity**. Is the model accessible? Are the relationships portrayed as direct and easily-perceivable as possible?

(f) **Originality**. Does the model include new elements, or put elements together in a new way, which will further our insight or knowledge?

(g) **Effectiveness for its purpose**, whether that be:

(i) **Explanation**. Does the model show causal relationships which explain how and why the phenomenon occurs?

(ii) **Prediction** - does the model enable the behavioural response/output to be predicted, given knowledge of the relevant input/stimulus and intervening variables?

(iii) **Heurism** - does the model identify gaps in our knowledge, and so suggest new or further areas of research?

3 SIMPLE MODELS OF BUYER BEHAVIOUR

As examples we shall discuss some of the lower-level forms of modelling.

(a) Black box models leave out the **internal** variables, the mental processes of decision making.

(b) Personal variable models leave out the **external** variables, concentrating only on the mental processes of decision making.

3.1 Black box models/stimulus-response

Black box models assume that **observable behaviour** is the only valid object of study. Concentrating as they do on environmental factors, such models in the context of consumer behaviour are **market models** which may be used in market research to identify, for example, the following.

(a) The **decision environment**. Factors external to the individual which influence his buying behaviour, are shown - but the individual is a black box.

(b) The **marketing distribution process**. The 'flow' of products, or information, or influence, is plotted - from producer to salesforce to retail outlet to consumer to other consumers. Competitors can be similarly plotted on the model.

(c) The **buying process** - taking into account only inputs and outputs.

Black box models

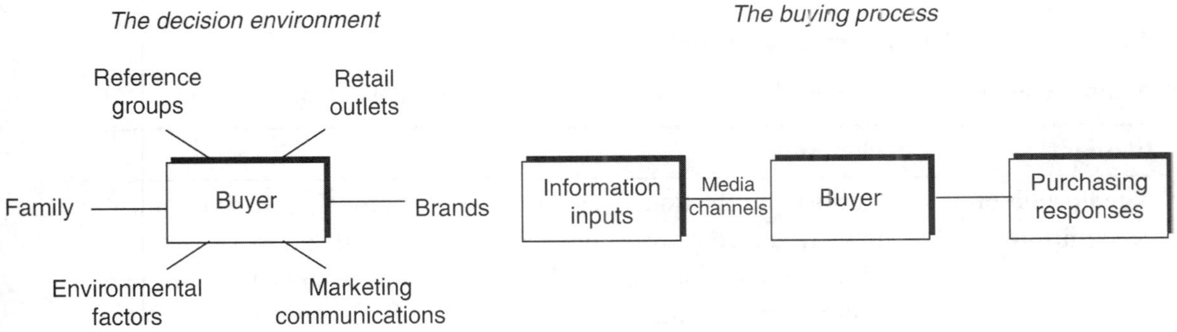

Why are Black box models useful?

(a) They include **observable, quantifiable variables** which are easier to measure and to manipulate

(b) They concentrate on a **manageable number of relevant input variables**, on which a strategy can be based - without 'analysis paralysis' from speculating about all the possible intervening factors.

NOTES

(c) **Stimulus variables** such as price, quality, availability, service, or advertising, can be identified by models, and the results of each - in terms of product/brand or supplier choice, quantity and frequency of purchase - set out in a simple, direct way. If a model indicates that decreased price results in increased purchase quantity, the marketer is able to respond accordingly: it does not matter, to an extent, why the phenomenon occurs.

(d) Black boxes are, however, limited to **simple, unambitious functions**. They do not attempt to predict behaviour in a wide range of circumstances, nor to explain behaviour.

Activity 2 **(5 minutes)**

Analyse a simple regular purchase that you make - a pint of milk, say, or a chocolate bar - in terms of the black box model depicted above.

3.2 Personal variable models

Personal variable models are simple models of **internal processes** - beliefs, intentions, motives, perceptions etc - without any of the **external, environmental influences**.

Examples of personal variable models

(a) **Compensatory or trade-off model**. When faced with a choice between products composed of certain attributes or benefits in different proportions, a consumer will **compromise** on his image of the 'ideal' product, and accept less of one attribute in return for more of another. This is a judgement about which combination of attributes offers the highest overall utility, or value.

(b) The **threshold model**. For each perceived attribute of a product, there is a perceived threshold of acceptability, below which the product will be rejected. Each attribute is assessed, until the product falls short on one (usually, price) and is discarded.

4 THE BUYING PROCESS

4.1 A simple decision process model

A simple descriptive model of the decision process consists of these elements.

Element	Comment
Need/problem recognition	Leads to motivation. (In a more complex model, would be shown to be triggered by psychological, physiological and social factors.) Marketers can identify needs/problems for the consumer, through product positioning
Pre-purchase/ information search	In a more complex model, would be affected by sources, attitudes, perceptions. Marketers can provide product information, tailored to need
Evaluation of alternatives	Marketers can make products available for evaluation and provide comparative information about competing products: the important thing, though, is to get the product onto the short-list of options

Element	Comment
The purchase decision	(In a more complex model, would be affected by situational factors: intention is not everything)
Post-purchase evaluation	Experience 'feeds back' to the beginning of the process, providing positive or negative reinforcement of the purchase decision. If the consumer is dissatisfied, he will be back at the problem recognition stage again. If the consumer is satisfied, the next decision process for the product may be cut short and skip straight to the decision, on the basis of loyalty (or, in a more complex model, expectations and learning constructs)

Such a model provides a useful descriptive framework for marketers, with indications of strategy requirements at each stage. It is still, however, too simple to be predictive, unless a large number of extra social, psychological and cultural variables are added or assumed.

4.2 Engel, Blackwell and Miniard model

This model was originally developed in 1968 by Engel, Kollat and Blackwell but has since undergone several revisions. The 1990 version considered is here.

The basis of the Engel-Blackwell-Miniard model takes the simple process of consumer behaviour described above as its basis.

The *influencing variables* are divided into four main categories.

- Stimulus inputs
- Information processing
- Decision process
- Variables influencing the decision process

Step 1.

The starting point of the process is the customer's perception of a want or a problem which must be satisfied.

Step 2.

This stimulates the start of the next stage, information search, which can be divided into two further stages. First, the customer searches his **internal memory** to ascertain what is known about potential solutions to the problem. If insufficient information is found through this course of action, the customer will begin the process of **external search**. The likelihood of external search is also affected by environmental factors, such as the urgency of the need, and also the individual characteristics of the customer. For example, individuals who are low risk takers will tend to seek more information before making a decision.

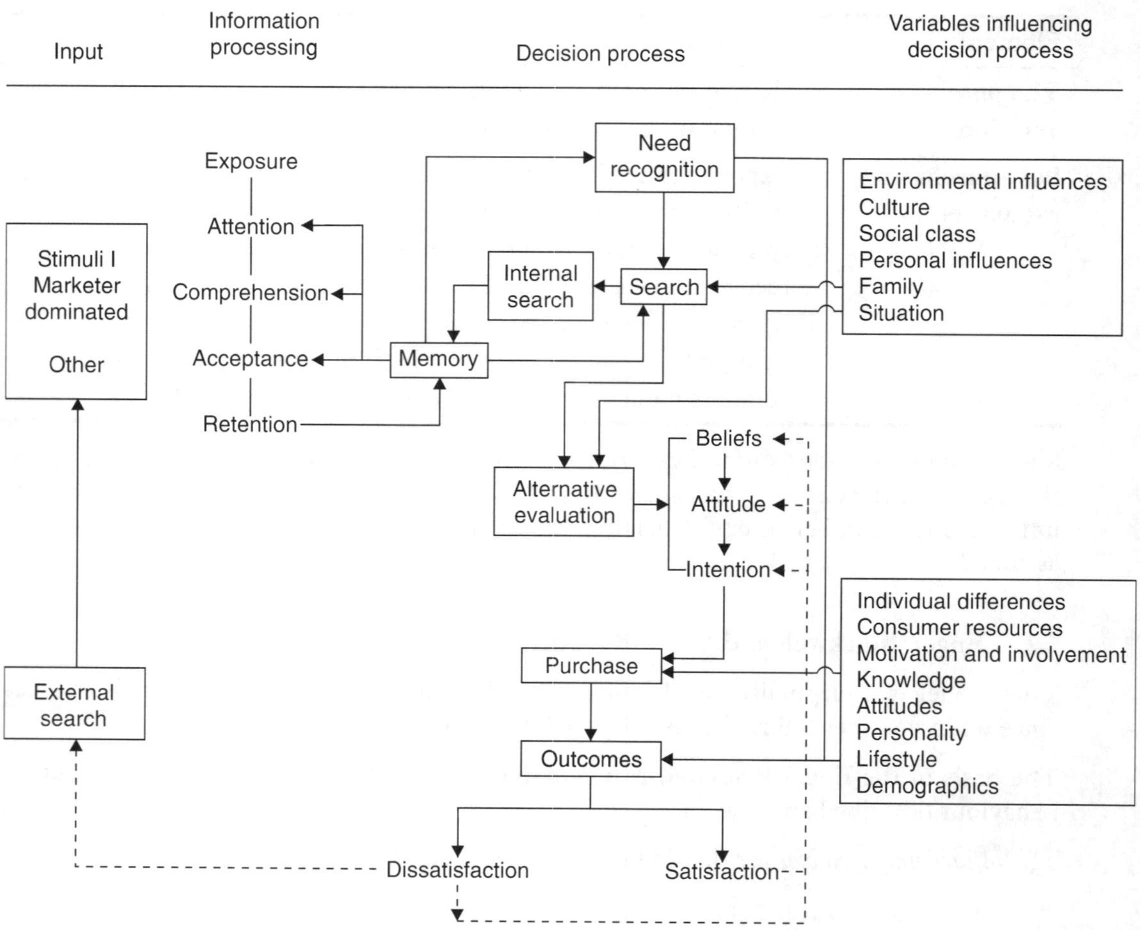

The Engel-Blackwell-Miniard model

Definition

> **Attention** – the process by which consumers select information in the environment to interpret.

Step 3.

This search process identifies the various ways in which the problem can be solved. Those various ways are then evaluated. The *alternative evaluation* stage involves comparing the alternative brands against evaluative criteria, which are 'product judging standards that have been stored in the permanent memory'. This evaluation process may lead to changes in beliefs regarding the brands, which, in turn, leads to changes in attitudes and intentions to purchase.

Step 4.

The process of **alternative evaluation** leads to an **intention** to make a purchase of the most favourably evaluated brand.

Step 5.

This intention will be translated into action unless unforeseen circumstances intervene to postpone or prevent the purchase.

NOTES

Step 6.

Once purchased, the customer will use the product and will continue to evaluate the product by comparing performance against expectations. If the product chosen does not meet expectations, the result is dissatisfaction and this may lead to further search for information about the brand and/or changes in beliefs.

The overall process can, therefore, be seen as a continuous one, especially given the desirability of repeat purchase.

Activity 3 **(10 minutes)**

Read the following information and decide **who are the customers** that Delta Dental need to care for?

Delta Dental is a non-profit service corporation that was created in 1998 to provide high quality dental benefits programs for employee groups throughout the state. Delta Dental's programs are available to employee groups of 10 or more people. Groups can choose managed fee-for-service, preferred provider and HMO-type programs.

Delta Dental is a growing administrator of dental benefits programs in Indiana, covering more than 170,000 people in more than 200 groups.

The satisfaction of our customers is evidenced by our contract renewal rates, which exceed 97 percent each year.

Delta Dental annually pays approximately $20 million for dental treatment.

Some groups with Delta Dental coverage include the Indianapolis Public Schools, Indiana State University, and Kimball International Corporation, plus numerous other businesses, public schools, city and county governments, hospitals and universities throughout the state.

Additionally, Delta Dental Plan of Indiana offers dental benefits programs to people nationwide through our DeltaUSA program. Companies that are headquartered in Indiana and have employees located outside the state can provide quality consistent benefits to employees nationwide.

Delta Dental Plan of Indiana is a member of the Delta Dental Plans Association and is affiliated with Delta Dental Plan of Ohio and Delta Dental Plan of Michigan.

Delta Dental Plan of Michigan has a proud history of community service, which its employees enthusiastically support every year.

4.3 Diffusion of innovation model

New products represent a significant opportunity to both **consumers** (who may find a better means of satisfying their needs) and **marketers** (who may find a new source of profit or competitive advantage). The **first buyers** of a product are the **most important,** since there is no established frame of reference within which the product will be considered: no experience, association or reference group adoption to build on.

Definitions

An **innovation** is anything new (product, service, practice or idea) from the point of view of:

(a) The organisation ('We've never done this before').
(b) The product ('It hasn't been done quite like this before').
(c) The market ('You may not have seen this before').
(d) The consumer ('I don't think I've seen this before').

Everett Rogers' definition of innovation is: 'any idea or product perceived by the potential innovator to be new.' This is the essence of the customer-focused approach to innovation.

Diffusion of innovation is the 'macro' process by which the innovation is spread or disseminated from the source to the consuming public.

Adoption is the 'micro' process by which a consumer makes the decision to accept or reject an innovation.

4.4 Diffusion of innovation

You may have noticed that some new ideas 'catch on' suddenly, while others take a long time to gain acceptance, and others never get beyond the fringes. The **rate and extent of diffusion** of an innovation depend on:

- The **characteristics** of the innovation/new product
- The **channels of communication** used
- The **social system** within which communication takes place
- The **stages of the adoption process** reached by members of the social system

4.5 Product characteristics that influence diffusion

(a) **Relative advantage**

Relative advantage is the degree to which potential consumers perceive the product innovation to be better than previous or competing products.

(b) **Compatibility**

Compatibility is the degree to which potential consumers perceive the product innovation to be comparable or consistent with their existing values, attitudes, needs and practices.

(c) **Complexity** is the degree to which potential consumers find the product innovation **difficult to understand or use**.

(d) **Trialability**

Trialability is the degree to which potential consumers can test or sample a product innovation before committing themselves to adopting it.

(e) **Observability**

Observability, or 'communicability' is the degree to which a product innovation's benefits or attributes are visible to the potential consumer - by his own observation, or imagination, or the descriptions of others.

Fashion items, for example, have high 'social visibility' and are more easily disseminated than products for private use, which are 'shared' less with other people.

Activity 4 **(10 minutes)**

Whenever you see a product or service which claims to be 'new' in some way, apply the tests of relative advantage, compatibility, complexity, trialability and observability to it.

EXAMPLE

'It is an uncomfortable dilemma for a company. If you do not innovate, old products will be overtaken by new technology. If, on the other hand, you introduce a new range it can cannibalise the old product. Even more likely, sales of an existing model can dry up overnight once word gets out that a new product is imminent.

Yet companies must innovate. If you are Microsoft introducing Windows 95, this is less of a problem. Its marketing muscle and industry dominance are such that it could endure a fall in sales of Windows 3.1. When BMW announces a new 7-series, it has at least got sales of the 5-series and 3-series to tide it over should old 7-series sales slow down.

This is not the case if you are a small one-product company, as SDX Business Systems was in 1991. When the management team, led by Frank Bretherton, bought the Welwyn Garden City-based company from Northern Telecom of the US it realised its digital telephone exchange had a limited life. But because the company had only one product Bretherton knew he would have to 'bet the company' when introducing the new exchange called Index.' *Financial Times*, 23 January 1996

4.6 Rate of diffusion: 'adopter categories'

Diffusion research has indicated that diffusion of an innovation follows a normal distribution (a **bell-shaped curve**) over time, and that consumers can be classified according to the time they take to adopt an innovation, relative to other consumers.

Five adopter categories have been identified (by Rogers and others). (Note that although they are 'adopter' categories, we are still looking at 'diffusion', not 'adoption' as a process: we are still at the 'macro' level of society and the whole life of the product innovation.)

(a) **Innovators** (2.5% of the population that eventually adopts the product).

Innovators are the first people to adopt an innovation. Their main characteristic is said to be 'venturesomeness': they are not averse to risk, are eager to try new ideas, are varied and extensive in their social networking.

(b) **Early adopters** (13.5% of the population that eventually adopts the product).

Early adopters are next to adopt the innovation. Their main characteristic may be called 'respectability': they take fewer risks than innovators (watching to see how they get on before themselves adopting the innovation), and are integrated into their social system and culture. They have the highest number of opinion leaders and role models, and so are important in the communication process.

(c) **Early majority** (34% of the population that eventually adopts the product.)

The early majority are the first of the general mass of the population to adopt a new idea: just before the 'average' adoption time. Their main characteristic is said to be 'deliberation'. They are slightly above average in education, age and income, but tend to be followers, seldom holding leadership positions, and relying heavily on information from others.

(d) **Late majority** (34% of the population that eventually adopts the product.)

The late majority are the last of the general mass of the population to adopt a new idea: just after the 'average' adoption time. Their main characteristic is said to be 'scepticism': they are cautious about new ideas and tend to adopt only as a result of economic necessity, or social pressure.

(e) **Laggards** (16% of the population that eventually adopts the product).

Laggards are last to adopt. Their main characteristic is said to be 'traditionalism': they tend to be oriented to the past and custom, parochial in their social outlook and suspicious of anything new.

Remember that these are **not stages** people go through: they are '**types**' or categories of people. The stages refer to the **diffusion process over time**, and the points in it at which the different categories of people adopt the innovation.

Adopter categories: average adoption time

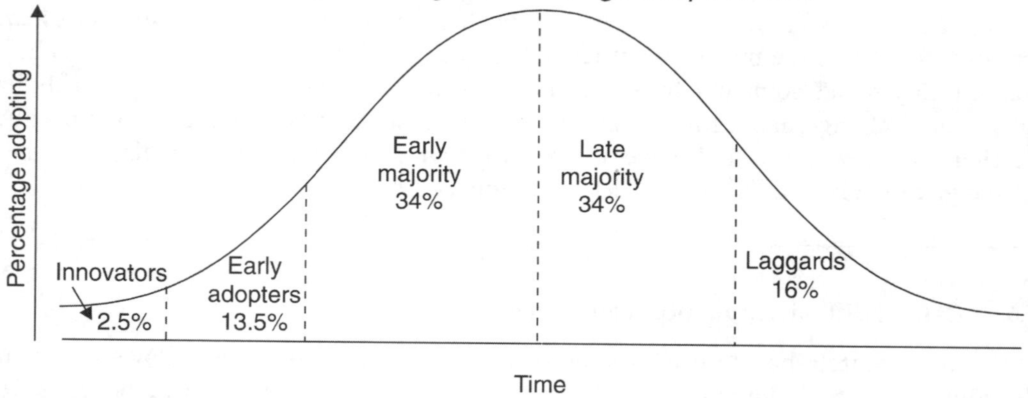

The main problem with using this model is that the categories appear to add up to 100% of the social system - the target market. This is not a reflection of marketers' experience, since some potential consumers do not adopt/purchase at all.

4.7 The adoption model

Definition

> **Adoption** is the process by which a consumer arrives at a decision to try (or not to try) and - having tried - to continue using (or discontinue using) a new product.

Based on the premise (not universally accepted) that consumers tend to engage in fairly extensive information search and problem-solving in order to reach a purchase decision, a five-stage model of product adoption has been proposed.

(a) **Awareness**. Consumers have been exposed to the product innovation, and are aware that it exists, but their attitudes to it are neutral at this stage.

(b) **Interest**. Consumers become curious about the innovation or aware of its potential to fulfil a need or want of theirs: they become interested in it to the extent of seeking out more information.

(c) **Evaluation**. Consumers use the information they have gathered in order:

  (i) To decide whether more information is necessary: delayed decision.

  (ii) To establish a positive or negative attitude (favourable or unfavourable evaluation) of the innovation.

  (iii) To decide whether to purchase/try or reject the innovation.

  The perceived product characteristics discussed earlier will influence this stage.

(d) **Trial**. Consumers try out the innovation, if possible on a limited, low-risk basis: their experience then provides them with the decisive information to adopt or reject.

(e) **Adoption** (or rejection). Based on evaluation ('mental trial') and physical trial of the innovation, consumers decide to continue to use it on a full committed basis - or to reject it.

Some researchers suggest that following trial, there are **two intermediate stages** (direct product experience and product evaluation: confirmation) before rejection or adoption.

4.8 Value of the adoption model

The adoption model offers a useful framework for marketers.

(a) To concentrate on **relevant aspects of the consumers' state of mind** at each stage. The most important goal, initially, will be to get attention, in competition with other stimuli. The next will be to arouse interest by suggesting motivations. The next will be giving information relevant to evaluation, then making the product available for trial etc;

(b) To study **which information media are most effective at each stage**. Awareness is best served by mass media, but in later stages, especially evaluation, mass media influence declines in favour of more personal sources: salespeople, opinion leaders and so on.

Definition

> **Opinion leader** – person who is knowledgeable about a product and is frequently able to influence others' attitudes or behaviours with regard to a product category.

However, the traditional adoption model has been **criticised** for:

(a) **Leaving out the problem/need recognition stage**, which may have to precede awareness if the message is going to be perceived

(b) **Suggesting that the stages are distinct and in sequence**. In practice, evaluation may take place throughout the decision-making process. Trial may occur before evaluation or interest - or not at all

(c) **Leaving out the possibility of post-adoption discontinuance**, because of further experience, post-purchase dissonance, forgetting and competing innovations

5 DECISION MAKING UNIT (DMU)

In practice, many different people are involved in taking the buying decision. We hinted at the various different roles – the consumer is not necessarily the person who pays for the good.

Definition

> **Decision making unit** - all people influencing a buying decision – could be just one person.

Role	Comment
Initiator	Suggests the idea of buying a particular product
Influencer	Provides information about a product/service to other members of the DMU.
Gatekeeper	Controls the flow of information about a product/service into the family (for example by 'giving the gist' of a consumer article, or selecting the advertising message that is relayed to the family).
Decider	Has the power to determine whether to purchase a specific product/service
Buyer	Makes the purchase of the product/service
Preparer	Makes the product into a form suitable for family consumption (by preparing food, say, or assembling DIY furniture)
User	Consumes or utilises a particular product/service
Maintainer	Services or repairs a product so that it continues to satisfy
Disposer	Initiates or performs the disposal or termination of the product/service

This model can be used in a number of contexts. We now discuss two of these, the family and organisational DMUs.

5.1 The family DMU

Within a family group as a decision-making unit various members may occupy these roles. Morden gives the examples of the purchase of a child's toy and a family car.

Toy		*Car*	
Initiator:	Child	Initiator:	Main earner, salesperson
Influencer:	Parents	Influencer:	Homemaker
	Relatives		Family
	Friends		Friends/colleagues
	Salesperson		Salesperson
Decider:	Parents	Decider:	Father, mother
Buyer:	Mother	Buyer:	Main earner
User:	Child	User:	Father, mother

Marketers will be interested in reaching each of these roles: to make the product attractive to the initiator (if it is not a product automatically bought), **influencer** and **decider** in particular. They would need to make the product readily **available** for the **purchaser**, and satisfying enough for the user to initiate future repurchase.

These roles - and the number and nature of the individuals who adopt them - will **vary from product to product, and from family to family**.

If the **buyer** of a product is a **different** person from the **decision-maker**, the marketer would need to **redirect promotional effort** from packaging and point of sale (attracting the buyer in-store) to advertising and promotional activity outside the store (where the decision-maker would be reached). If powerful influencers can be identified, they can be targeted as a way of getting to decision-makers.

Media which are designed for **sharing by the whole family** unit like television, Sunday newspapers, or cinema (when 'family' films are showing) offer marketers the opportunity of reaching influencers, decision-makers, buyers and users at the same time, facilitating discussion and influence within the decision-making unit.

5.2 The influence of gender

The pattern of decision-making roles has also **varied in society generally**, over time, particularly in relation to **gender roles**. The relative influence of male and female partners is of particular interest to consumer researchers, who commonly classify decisions as being male-dominated, female-dominated, joint, equal or 'syncratic', or unilateral or autocratic.

The relative influence of male and female partners, and the extent to which decisions are shared, may vary according to a variety of factors.

(a) The **family's attitudes to gender roles**.

(b) The **surrounding culture's attitudes to gender roles**.

(c) The **product or service**. Car purchase is a particularly interesting example: several decades ago, it was strongly male-dominated, while now, although still mainly male-dominated for the purchase of the main family car, the female car-buyer forms a rapidly expanding market segment (for second cars, cars for single and/or working women etc). The reverse trend is true for products like food and household items.

As the couple's education increases, more decisions are likely to be made together.

Activity 5 **(20 minutes)**

(a) Look out for car advertisements featuring women buyers and drivers, stressing independence and equality.

(b) Look out for advertisements in which the male partner (or even child) is 'sent out' shopping for food, washing powder and other such items: note how some choices they make change the female partner's mind and the family purchase pattern ('Well done. We'll be getting your brand from now on. Won't *you*?')

(c) Look out for advertisements which, on the other hand, reinforce traditional gender-related buying patterns: 'You're not a 'real'/'proper' mum if you don't buy/give them X.' 'Real men buy x.'

5.3 The influence of children

Children also have (or attempt to have) an influence on purchase decisions, not only those which are **relevant** to their particular wants ('I want toy X', 'I want chocolate bar Y') but also those which - **however irrelevant to them personally** - they relate to attractive messages they have seen and heard on television, or at friends' houses (a brand of dishwashing liquid marketed as having lots of soft bubbles, a car that a friend's dad has etc).

Definition

Parental yielding – when a parental DM is influenced by a child's request and makes a purchase.

Television. There is still controversy over whether pre-school children are able to distinguish between television programmes and advertising: the impact of television in general, however, is undeniable, because of its **power of creating associations** which become part of child learning. Older children are able to recall slogans and recognise symbolism in TV advertising.

Activity 6 **(20 minutes)**

For each of the following five product categories – groceries, cars, holidays, furniture and domestic appliances – describe the ways in which you believe a married couple's choices would be affected if they had children.

5.4 The DMU within organisations

All **organisational buying decisions** are **made by individuals or groups of individuals,** each of whom is subjected to the same types of influences as they are in making their own buying decisions. However, there are some real **differences** between personal and organisational buying decision processes.

(a) Organisations buy because the products/services are **needed to meet wider objectives**: for instance, also to help them to meet their customers' needs more closely. (However, as individuals also do not buy products and services for themselves but for the benefits they convey, it could be argued that both are forms of derived demand.)

(b) A **number of individuals are involved** in the typical organisational buying decision. Again, a personal buying decision may involve several family members, for example, and so may not be very different in some cases.

(c) The **decision process may take longer** for corporate decisions: the use of feasibility studies, for example, may prolong the decision process. Tendering processes in government buying also have this effect.

(d) Organisations are **more likely to buy a complex total offering** which can involve a high level of technical support, staff training, delivery scheduling, finance arrangements and so on.

(e) Organisations are **more likely to employ experts** in the process.

There are many examples of different types of organisational buying behaviour ranging from simple reordering (for example, of stationery supplies) to complex purchasing decisions (such as that of a consortium to build a motorway with bridges and tunnels, for example).

One system of categorisation for corporate buying decisions, devised by Howard and O'Shaughnessy, is based on the **complexity of organisational behaviour**. They identify three types:

Routinised buyer behaviour	This category is the habitual type, where the buyer knows what is offered and is buying items which are frequently purchased. It is likely that the buyer has well-developed supplier preferences and any deviation in habitual behaviour is likely to be influenced by price and availability considerations.
Limited problem solving	This category is relevant to a new or unfamiliar product/service purchase where the suppliers are nevertheless known and the product is in a familiar class of products, for instance a new model of car in a company fleet.
Extensive problem solving	This category relates to the purchase of unfamiliar products from unfamiliar suppliers. The process can take much time and effort and involve the need to develop criteria with which to judge the purchase. For example, the construction and refurbishment of new offices where previously buildings were looked after by managing agents.

5.5 The DMU in organisations

The **DMU is a particularly useful concept** in marketing industrial or government goods and services where the customer is a **business or other organisation**. The marketing manager then needs to know **who** in each organisation makes the effective buying decisions - this might be one person, or a group of people - and the DMU might act with formal authority or as an informal group reaching a joint decision. Many large organisations employ **buyers** - but the autonomy of the buyers will vary from situation to situation.

Purchasing decisions may be influenced by several people in the consuming organisation.

(a) **Employees or managers** in operational departments might make recommendations about what type of supplies should be purchased.

(b) A **junior buying manager** might decide what he would like to buy, but **submit his recommendation** to a superior for approval.

(c) In large organisations, there will be **several buying managers**, who might work independently, but might also work closely together, either formally or informally.

(d) Technical specifications for component purchases might be provided by **engineers or other technical staff**.

(e) **Accountants** might set a limit on the price the organisation will pay.

(f) Large items of purchase might require approval from the **board of directors**.

The relationships between **members of the DMU** are also important.

The **user** may have influence on the technical characteristics of the equipment (and hence the cost) and on reliability and performance criteria, and so on.

Activity 7 **(15 minutes)**

Whenever you have the chance - when visiting clients, when browsing in the newsagents, at the dentist's or hairdresser's - browse through the trade magazines that you find (*Campaign, Farmer's Weekly, Banking World, Engineering Today* or whatever).

What do you notice about the way products and services are marketed in such publications? Is more technical language used? Are the ads less 'glossy'? What do you learn about price and place?

6 UNDERSTANDING BUYER MOTIVES

6.1 The consumer's motivation mix

Customer behaviour is determined by **economic**, **psychological, sociological** and **cultural** considerations. The reasons for buying a product may vary from person to person, or product to product, or the reasons may be the same, but the weighting given to each reason in the mind of the customer may vary. These reasons make up the motivation mix of the customer.

The **motivation mix** leads a customer to choose:

- The type of goods or services he wants to buy (food or a new hairstyle, say)
- The brand
- The quality
- The quantity
- In what place
- From whom
- At what price
- By what method of payment (cash, cheque, credit card)
- The timing of his purchase

The motivation mix of a customer for **consumer goods** will be different from that of a buyer of **industrial goods**.

(a) The **domestic buyer** might buy on impulse, attracted by the branding, packaging or display of an article, as well as to meet the family's needs within the shopping budget. The homemaker has a variety of demands to satisfy, within the limits of the family budget.

(b) An **industrial buyer** might be expected to give more emphasis to rational motives for purchasing - a clear need for the article, its price and quality, delivery dates and after-sales service.

Motives sit between **needs and action**. Motives are derived from needs in that a need motivates a person to take action. The difference between needs and motives are as follows.

(a) Motives **activate behaviour**. Being thirsty (need) causes (motivates) us to buy a drink (action). If the need is sufficiently intense, we are motivated to act.

(b) Motives are **directional**. Needs are general but motives specify behavioural action. A general need to belong may lead to a specific motivation to join a badminton club.

(c) Motives serve to **reduce tension**. If we are too cold, we are motivated to reduce the tension in our bodies that this causes by seeking a source of warmth.

Although we know that motives arise from needs and can lead to purchase actions, motives do not tell us **how** consumers choose from the options available to satisfy needs. Other influences are clearly at work.

6.2 Psychological influences on buyer behaviour

Attitudes. Some writers have suggested that a buyer's attitude towards a product is an important element in the buying decision. However, there is no empirical evidence to link a favourable attitude directly with consumer purchases. Attitudes are discussed in more detail later.

Loyalty. A consumer may demonstrate a loyalty towards a particular company's goods or to a brand, or even to a particular shop or retail chain. It is not clear, however, that marketing efforts can be successful in trying to increase customer loyalty. Although it is an important phenomenon, it may well be outside the sphere of management influence or control.

Personality. Inevitably, a consumer's buying behaviour will be influenced by his or her personality. For example, the latest computer might be purchased by a customer whose personality traits include self confidence, dominance and autonomy. Coffee producers, on the other hand, have discovered that heavy coffee drinkers tend to have sociability as a principal personality trait.

DISCUSSION

Why is it that it is accepted practice to haggle about the price of some purchases (a house, or a second-hand car, say, in the UK) but not others?

6.3 Attitudes and behaviour

An **attitude** is a **relatively consistent, learned predisposition** to behave in a certain way in response to a given object.

(a) **Relative consistency**. Attitudes are not permanent: they can be changed, as we will see later. However, they tend to be reasonably well established, and to lead to behaviour with a reasonable degree of predictability. (If someone prefers coffee to tea, he is likely to choose coffee over tea fairly consistently.)

(b) **Learned**. Attitudes are 'learned' or conditioned, formulated with experience as a result of learning factors such as motivation, association and reinforcement.

(c) **Predisposition**. Attitudes are a predisposition to behaviour: they do not imply that a given behaviour will *necessarily* follow.

(d) **An object**. Attitudes relate to some aspect of the individual's environment: it may be a thing, person, event, concept or whatever.

Definition

> A technical definition of **attitude** is: 'a mental and neural state of readiness, organised through experience, exerting a directive or dynamic influence upon the individual's response to all objects and situations with which it is related.'
> (Allport)

There is no automatic, direct relationship between attitude and behaviour. Insofar as attitudes and behaviour are inter-related, the process may be portrayed as a **tendency** for an individual to behave in a given way: not a **prediction** of how he will behave.

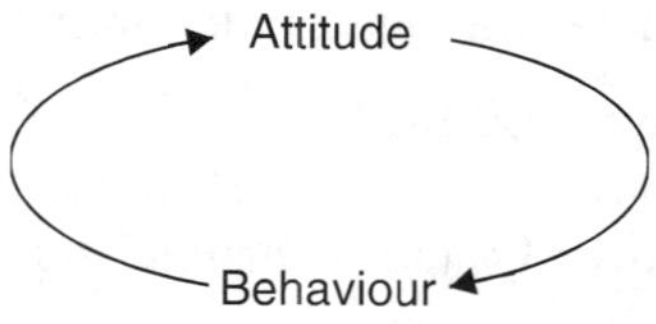

Situational factors affect our behaviour: attitudes are not the sole variable involved.

(a) An individual's **behaviour** may be influenced by the **situation,** to contradict his attitudes. For example, you may have a strong liking for organically-grown produce (you believe it is 'right' to buy such produce, and you intend to buy it) - but it is more expensive in the supermarket, so for economic reasons you do not buy it every week.

(b) An individual's **attitudes** may also be influenced by the **situation**. People who generally avoid chocolate for health and figure reasons may feel differently in situations where they are physically exhausted and need a boost in blood sugar, or where they are in a festive mood and sharing a bar/packet/cake with friends -especially if told that 'A Mars a day helps you work, rest and play!'

6.4 Attitude formation

Attitude theories are based on the premise that individuals seek **cognitive consistency**.

(a) Consistency between the attitudes they hold

(b) Consistency between their attitudes/perceptions and their experience of reality

(c) Consistency between their behaviour and their self-image

When **discrepancies or inconsistencies** occur (and are perceived) the individual experiences **tension**. In order to alleviate that tension, the individual has to change one or more of the factors creating the inconsistency: to **change one of his conflicting**

attitudes to 'fit' the other, to change his attitude to 'fit' his behaviour, or to change his behaviour to 'fit' his attitude.

Balance theory is simple, which is useful when it comes to application. However, it has been **criticised** as too simple to adequately portray the complexity of attitude systems and conflicts, particularly since it **uses only the dimensions 'positive' and 'negative'** without taking into account the **strength** of positive or negative feeling, which would allow us to predict which way people would choose to resolve an unbalanced situation.

An application of balance theory

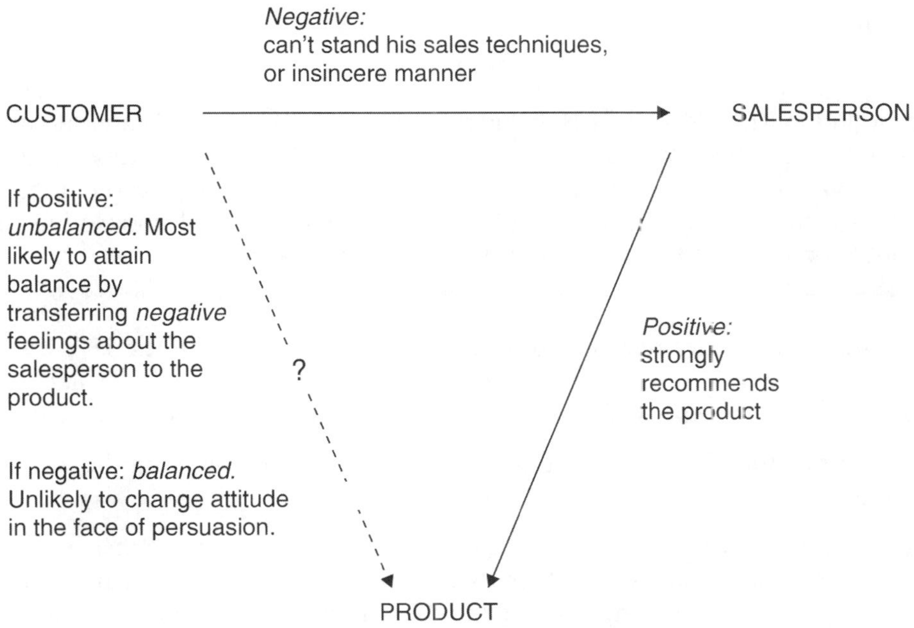

Definition

> **Balance theory** – considers relations among elements which a person might perceive as belonging together, and people's tendency to change relations among elements in order to make them balance.

6.5 Cognitive dissonance theory: Festinger

Cognitive dissonance is the discomfort experienced by an individual when he receives **new information which appears to contradict a belief or attitude he holds**. The theory is particularly concerned with **decision-making**.

(a) In making a decision - for example, to buy a product - individuals frequently have to **weigh up positive and negative factors** and compromise on that basis. Post-purchase dissonance occurs when somebody regrets or feels anxious about a choice they have made.

(b) He may also find himself acting in a way that appears to contradict a belief or attitude he holds: he has chosen a foreign-made car because of a special financing deal or promotional campaign, when he has previously always believed in 'buying British'.

The individual may experience psychological discomfort as a result.

Marketers can use dissonance theory in several ways.

(a) To persuade people to **try or buy first** and develop a **positive attitude afterwards** (eg money back if not satisfied).

(b) **To reinforce purchase decisions**. The consumers will only be able to convince themselves they like the product if you *tell* them in your advertising they've done the right thing!

(c) **Be careful to avoid disappointing your customers.**

6.6 Socio-psychological influences

Definition

According to Keith Williams (*Behavioural Aspects of Marketing*), **socialisation** is 'the process by which the individual learns the social expectations, goals, beliefs, values and attitudes that enable him to exist in society'. In other words, socialisation is the process by which he acquires sufficient knowledge of a society and its ways to be able to function and participate in it.

The **learning** of gender-related, consumer and occupational roles is part of the socialisation process: what it means to 'be' or 'behave like' a girl or boy, what money is for, what 'buying' is, what 'work' is and what sorts of work different 'sorts' of people do.

We can therefore identify a number of agencies who are instrumental in the socialisation of individuals.

(a) The **family** is probably the most enduring and extensive source of influence, because it is here that the dependent child learns from his or her parents and siblings. The family is a particularly strong influence on the child's perception of appropriate roles and on his or her self-esteem, which in turn affects aspirations.

(b) **School** is an important source of values, particularly as they relate to other people.

(c) **Peer groups** exert influence on social groups which can control a person's social and emotional satisfactions, say by appointing a person unelected leader or by 'sending him to Coventry'. As a person grows, peer groups become more of an influence, eventually superseding the family.

(d) The **mass media** is extremely pervasive and has a profound effect on all of us.

'**Consumer socialisation**' is the process by which children acquire the skills, knowledge and attitudes that enable them to **function in society as consumers.**

(a) **Children** observe the consumption behaviour of their parents or older siblings (while pre-adolescents), or their peers (once adolescents and teenagers), and model their own behaviour accordingly.

(b) **Parents** use consumption-related events to socialise children generally: promises of gifts or shopping expeditions are used as incentives to behave in a desired way; withholding of money for self-directed purchases is threatened as a deterrent to undesirable behaviour.

(c) **Children** are socialised into attitudes, values and motivations which are indirectly related to consumption: products or particular brands are means of satisfying socialised needs and wants. Socialisation creates consumer motivations.

6.7 Reference groups

Definition

> **Reference group** theory was formulated in the 1940s by Herbert Hyman, to describe the way in which **an individual uses groups as a point of comparison** or 'reference' for his own judgements, beliefs and behaviour.

A reference group is an actual or imaginary individual or group perceived as having significant relevance upon an individual's evaluations, aspirations or behaviour.

Groups can serve as a benchmark for:

(a) general behavioural norms.
(b) specific attitudes or behaviour - such as 'fashionable' product purchases.

An individual may be influenced by a non-contactual or secondary group, as well as a primary one with which he is intimately in contact. Note, too, that the individual **does not need to be a member of a group** in order to measure his behaviour by it.

(a) An **aspirational group** can impel an individual to act as it does, or to wear the same 'badges', in order to feel closer to attaining actual membership.

(b) A **dissociative group** can impel an individual to disown any behaviour or object associated with it.

Reference groups influence a buying decision by making the individual **aware** of a product or brand, allowing the individual to **compare** his attitude with that of the group, encouraging the individual to **adopt an attitude consistent** with the group, and then **reinforcing and legitimising** the individual's decision to conform.

EXAMPLE

Group membership has entered cyberspace as 'netizens' around the world rapidly form virtual communities. Members are linked to one another via their computer modems, and all of their interactions are digital. This electronic anonymity opens up exciting new opportunities for many, especially those who have difficulty interacting in face-to-face settings (eg the Internet has made a dramatic difference to the lives of many disabled people who can now interact with others around the world without having to leave home.) New technologies allow people to chat about their mutual interests, to help one another with enquiries and suggestions, and to get suggestions for new products and services.

It has been suggested that we adopt **different reference groups** for **different areas** of our lives and consumer choices. Miles carried out a study of adolescent girls, and found that the **peer group** was most influential in, for example, the choice of clothes and books, while in matters such as the choice of boyfriends, their **parents**' opinions were more valued. **Youth**, however, is the stage at which we are most **personally insecure**, and at which the reference group has the most power: consider the market for training shoes or music, for example.

DISCUSSION

Discuss some factors that influence whether or not membership groups will have a significant influence on a person's behaviour.

6.8 Roles

Definition

A '**role**' is the sum or 'system' of expectations which other people have of an individual in a particular situation or relationship. Role theory is concerned with the roles that individuals act out in their lives, and how the assumption of various roles affects their attitudes to other people.

An example may help to explain what is meant by 'roles'. An individual may consider himself to be a **father** and **husband**, a good **neighbour** and an active member of the **local community**, a **supporter** of his sports club, an amateur **golfer**, a conscientious **church-goer**, a man of certain **political** views, a **professional** and a **marketer**.

The other individuals who relate to him when he is in a particular role are called his **role set**. At work, he will have one role set made up of colleagues, superiors and subordinates, and any other contacts in the course of business: at home, he will have another role set consisting of family members.

Roles are **shaped** by:

(a) The **expectations** of other people as to how a person in a given role should or usually does behave.

(b) **Norms** - the customs and informal 'rules' of behaviour which society has formulated.

We learn, growing up in society and experiencing different role sets, **what is expected of us**, and what the '**rules**' are in given situations.

(a) We learn, for example, the '**appropriate**' **behaviour for our gender**

(b) When we start a **new job** - or first become a student - we are confronted with a whole new set of expectations and norms, and have to 'learn the ropes'

Individuals give expression to the role they are playing at any particular time by giving **role signs**. One example of role signs is **clothing or uniform**. A **white coat** indicates that an individual is performing his role as a hospital doctor, a certain shirt indicates that an individual is acting in the role of a **football team** supporter, and a **college scarf** is a sign that a person is in the role of student.

Note that **role signs** can be embodied as **particular products**. Many products are purchased because they reflect or reinforce social roles. Clothing and accessories are bought as symbols of role, for example; people buy gifts for each other which reinforce the nature of their role relationship (intimate and familial or formal and professional).

The nature of roles is not dependent on the particular people who fill them: people fit into roles. Roles are therefore valid units of analysis, in themselves. Knowledge of roles can:

(a) **Enable marketers to predict the kind** of role signs people will want to buy, for a wide range of roles.

(b) **Suggest role models** - ideal figures who embody the highest expectations of particular roles - who can be associated with a product (through licensing, advertising or promotions) in order to appeal to the aspirations of people in those roles.

(c) Offer the basis of **market segmentation** and product positioning: categories such as executives, or young mothers, carry with them a range of role expectations, norms and signs which can be appealed to or catered for.

Since roles depend on learning and perception, and since an individual occupies multiple roles, there are situations in which **problems** occur.

(a) **Role ambiguity** is a term which describes a situation when the individual is not sure what his role is, or when some members of his role set are not clear what his role is.

EXAMPLE

Role ambiguity is perhaps inherent in the way certain complex financial services, such as pension plans, have been sold. Is the person that sells the pension a 'financial advisor' or 'an insurance salesperson'?

The difference is important - a financial advisor is required to offer 'best advice' to the customer but, at the same time, may be required to meet sales targets.

Role ambiguity might sometimes emerge as 'conflict of interest'.

(b) **Role conflict** occurs when an individual, acting in several roles at the same time, finds that the roles are incompatible. A businessman who receives a telephone call from his wife, who wants him to leave work and go home, will experience conflict in his roles as businessman and family man. Similar conflict might be experienced by a working woman, who must reconcile her roles as a businesswoman and a mother. A trade union member may be reluctant to obey a strike call, because he disapproves of its reasons.

EXAMPLE

Ratners was a jewellery chain famous for its 'cheap and cheerful' products. Its managing director told an audience of investors that the products were 'crap', to explain its market position. This suggests role conflict between:

(a) The MD's role as being responsible to investors, explaining the business strategy.

(b) The MD's role as spokesman for the company as a whole to its other publics, including its customers.

6.9 Secondary groups: the social environment

If we are to understand our customers we need to have some idea of how far the individual's cognitive processes and behaviour, including his/her decision whether to become our customer, depend on his/her perception of and interaction with **other people**. In this section we will cover two particular ways in which we see ourselves, and behave, **in relation to others**.

Some roles are perceived as **superior or inferior** in relation to others. The roles of employer and employee, or parent and child, have this connotation in traditional Western societies. One role may be superior to another because it is perceived that a person in that role has power or authority.

A combination of such factors - power, wealth, expertise, position - determines 'where' a person is in relation to other people, or in the framework of society as a whole. This relative position of superiority or inferiority is called status.

Definition

> **Status** has been called 'a kind of social identification tag': as such, it is the basis of the determination of social class, or social stratification. It also forms part of the individual's self-image.

Status may be:

(a) **Ascribed**, or attributed to someone by society, on the basis of perceived factors such as their sex or age, intelligence or race. Improved status comes automatically with seniority in some cultures - such as the Japanese - while the male has traditionally had higher status than the female in Western cultures.

(b) Achieved by **deliberate effort** on the part of the individual. Professional and occupational status are *achieved*.

Status may be achieved by **acquiring appropriate roles and behaviours.**

DISCUSSION

It is suggested that people play different roles and that their consumption behaviours may differ depending on the particular role they are playing. Do you agree or disagree with this perspective and can you give examples to illustrate?

Some cultures are 'status-conscious', while others are not.

Marketing, as well as management, will need to take into account the extent of status-awareness. **Low-status** individuals, in a status-conscious society, may **aspire to achieve higher status**: products can be positioned accordingly. **High status** individuals may wish to be '**congratulated**', or to emphasise the exclusivity and power of their position in society: premium quality (and price) products frequently appeal to this sense. Status symbols are products that are purchased and displayed to signal membership of a desirable social class.

6.10 Social class: stratification of UK society

However, in practice, class strata or divisions are commonly derived from the specific **demographic factors** of:

- **Wealth/income** - economic resources
- **Educational** attainment
- **Occupational** status

From a marketer's point of view, it is also possible to infer **shared values, attitudes and behaviour within a social class**, as distinct from those of a higher or lower class: some research has been able to relate consumption behaviour to class standing. This makes social class an attractive proposition for market segmentation.

6.11 Class distinction and mobility

Social class tends to perpetuate itself, **where people are highly class-conscious: they do not tend to move between classes**, or indeed to interact socially with members of other

NOTES

classes. Sociologists note that some societies have a very rigid class system, while others do not.

Social mobility has several **implications for marketers**.

People aspire to upward mobility, given a reasonable expectation of success, and will exhibit purchase and consumption patterns suitable to the class to which they aspire. (Consider the boom in products for 'yuppies' - by definition 'young upwardly mobile' people in the late 80s - and in demand for owned homes, foreign holidays, private education and health clubs, all of which used to be considered 'exclusive' to the upper middle class.)

The **'lower' classes will become a less significant proportion of the population** (and therefore target market), as people move up out of them - assuming that the country's economy can support a widespread increase in per capita income.

People are **afraid**, in a society of increasing inequality, of **downward mobility**.

DISCUSSION

What consumption differences might you expect to observe between a family characterised as under-privileged versus one whose income is average for its social class?

6.12 Education and achievement

Social Trends (1998) reports that 16% of the UK's male working age population and 21% of the UK's female working age population have **no qualifications**. However, it is likely that more and more people will become qualified.

(a) *Social Trends* reports that the workforce is becoming **increasingly well qualified**, with an increase (1975 - 1997) in the proportion of adults with GCSE grades A - C or equivalent rising from 27% to 62%.

(b) The number of people leaving school without qualifications is lower than the past. Women are doing increasingly well. In fact, fewer girls leave school without educational qualifications than boys. Overall in the UK, **girls outperform boys**.

There is also a definite correlation between an individual's academic attainments and their socio-economic group. The following comparisons may be made for 1991/2 and 1998/9.

EXAMPLE

People participating in Higher Education

	91/92	*92/93*	*93/94*	*94/95*	*95/96*	*96/97*	*97/98*	*98/99*
Professional	55	71	73	78	79	32	79	72
Intermediate	36	39	42	45	45	47	48	45
Skilled non-manual	22	27	29	31	31	32	31	29
Skilled manual	11	15	17	18	18	18	19	18
Partly skilled	12	14	16	17	17	17	18	17
Unskilled	6	9	11	11	12	13	14	13
All social classes	23	28	30	32	32	33	33	31

Source: www.statistics.gov.uk

BPP PUBLISHING

The changes could be attributed to:

(a) the expansion of higher education after World War II;
(b) government policy, which has been to extend the scope of education;
(c) removal of maintenance grant entitlements.

6.13 Buying patterns

Demography and the class structure are relevant in that they can be both **behavioural determinants** and **inhibitors** of household buying behaviour.

(a) **Behavioural determinants** encourage people to buy a product or service. The individual's personality, culture, social class, and the importance of the purchase decision (eg a necessity such as food or water, or a luxury) can predispose a person to purchase something.

(b) **Inhibitors** are factors, such as the individual's income, which will make the person less likely to purchase something.

Socio-economic status can be related to buying patterns in a number of ways, both in the amount people have to spend and what they spend it on. It affects both the quantity of goods and services supplied, and the proportion of their income that households spend on goods and services.

EXAMPLE

Let us compare, for 1995-6, household expenditure of the poorest 20% to that of the wealthiest 20% (*Social Trends* 1998).

Item	*Bottom 20% % of total purchases*	*Top 20% % of total purchases*
Housing	15	18
Fuel, light, power	7	3
Food	24	15
Alcohol and tobacco	7	5
Clothing and footwear	5	6
Household goods and services	13	14
Motoring and fares	11	16
Leisure goods and services	13	18
Other	5	5
(After rounding)	100 (£158 per week)	100 (£477pw)

As you can see the wealthiest households spend less of a **proportion** of their total income on food and more on leisure, than do the poorest. This does not imply they spend any less in absolute terms of course: they just have more available to spend on other things.

6.14 Secondary groups: cultural issues

Culture is a concept crucial to the understanding of buyer behaviour and can be thought of as the collective memory of a society.

Culture embraces the following aspects of social life.

(a) **Beliefs** are perceived states of knowing: we feel that we know about 'things', on the basis of objective and subjective information.

(b) **Values** are the comparatively few key beliefs which are:

(i) Relatively enduring.

(ii) Relatively general - not tied to specific objects.

(iii) Fairly widely accepted as a guide to culturally appropriate behaviour - and therefore as a 'standard' of desirable and undesirable beliefs, attitudes and behaviour.

(c) **Customs** are modes of behaviour which represent culturally approved ways of responding to given situations: usual and acceptable ways of behaving.

(d) A **ritual** is a type of activity which takes on symbolic meaning, consisting of a fixed sequence of behaviour repeated over time. Ritualised behaviour tends to be public, elaborate, formal and ceremonial - like marriage ceremonies.

(e) The different **languages** of different cultures is an obvious means of distinguishing large groups of people.

(f) **Symbols** are an important aspect of language and culture: the symbolic nature of human language sets it apart from animal communication. Each symbol may carry a number of different meanings and associations for different people, and some of these meanings are learned as part of a society's culture. The advertiser using slang words or pictorial images must take care that they are valid for the people he wants to reach - and up-to-date.

(g) Culture embraces all the physical **'tools' or artefacts** used by people for their physical and psychological well-being. In our modern society, the **technology** we use has a very great impact on the way we live our lives, and new technologies accelerate the rate of social change.

(i) **Appearance and dress**
(ii) **Food and eating habits**
(iii) **Gender roles**
(iv) **Mental processing and learning styles**
(v) **Time and time consciousness**

DISCUSSION

Culture can be thought of as a society's personality. If your culture were a person, could you describe its personality traits?

6.15 Characteristics of culture

Having examined the areas included in the definition of culture, we can draw together some of the underlying characteristics of culture itself.

(a) **Social**. Culture exists to satisfy the needs of people. 'It offers order, direction and guidance in all phases of human problem solving, by providing 'tried and true' methods of satisfying physiological, personal and social needs'.(b) **Learned**. Cultural norms and values are taught or 'transferred' to each new member of society, formally or informally, by socialisation. This occurs in institutions (the family, school and church) and through on-going social interaction and mass media exposure in adulthood;

NOTES

(b) **Shared**. A belief or practice must be common to a significant proportion of a society or group before it can be defined as a cultural characteristic;

(c) **Cumulative**. Culture is 'handed down' to each new generation, and while new situations teach new responses, there is a strong traditional/historical element to many aspects of culture;

(d) **Adaptive**. Culture must be adaptive, or evolutionary, in order to fulfil its need-satisfying function. Many factors may produce cultural change - slow or fast - in society: eg technological breakthrough, population shifts, exposure to other cultures, gradual changes in values. (Think about male-female roles in the West, or European influences on British lifestyles.)

Activity 8 **(30 minutes)**

Schiffman & Kanuk (*Consumer Behaviour*) give the following summary of American core values and their relevance to consumer behaviour. Consider how far they are applicable to your social culture.

Value	*General features*	*Relevance to consumer behaviour*
Achievement and success	Hard work is good; success flows from hard work	Acts as a justification for acquisition of goods ('You deserve it')
Activity	Keeping busy is healthy and natural	Stimulates interest in products that are timesavers and enhance leisure time
Efficiency and practicality	Admiration of things that solve problems (eg save time and effort)	Stimulates purchase of products that function well and save time
Progress	People can improve themselves; tomorrow should be better than today	Stimulates desire for new products that fulfil unsatisfied needs; ready acceptance of products that claim to be 'new' or 'improved'
Material comfort	'The good life'	Fosters acceptance of convenience and luxury products that make life more comfortable and enjoyable
Individualism	Being oneself (eg self-reliance, self-interest, self-esteem)	Stimulates acceptance of customised or unique products that enable a person to 'express his or her own personality'.
Freedom	Freedom of choice	Fosters interest in wide product lines and differentiated products
External conformity	Uniformity of observable behaviour; desire for acceptance	Stimulates interest in products that are used or owned by others in the same social group
Humanitarianism	Caring for others, particularly the underdog	Stimulates patronage of firms that compete with market leaders
Youthfulness	A state of mind that stresses being young at heart and a youthful appearance	Stimulates acceptance of products that provide the illusion of maintaining or fostering youthfulness
Fitness and Health	Caring about one's body, including the desire to be physically fit and healthy	Stimulates acceptance of food products, activities, and equipment perceived to maintain or increase physical fitness

6.16 Micro-culture

Culture is a rather broad concept, embracing whole societies. It is possible to subdivide (and for marketers, further segment) a macro-culture into **micro-cultures** (or **sub-cultures**) which also **share certain norms of attitude and behaviour**.

Definition

> A **micro-culture** is a distinct and identifiable cultural group within society as a whole: it will have certain beliefs, values, customs and rituals that set it apart - while still sharing the dominant beliefs, values, customs and rituals of the whole society or 'mainstream' culture.

The main **micro-cultures relevant to the UK** are defined by the following factors.

(a) **Class** (discussed in detail earlier).

(b) **Nationality**. Nationality refers to the birthplace of one's ancestors. The UK is home to many nationalities. The key issue for marketers is whether these offer segmentation opportunities.

(c) **Ethnicity**. Ethnicity refers to broader divisions. There are identifiable differences in lifestyles and consumer spending patterns among these groups, but it is only relatively recently that attention has been given to reaching and serving ethnic minority market segments, as distinct from mass marketing which would 'also reach' the racial minorities.

(d) **Geography or region**. Even in such a small country as England, there are distinct regional differences (eg lifestyle), brought about by the past effects of physical geography (poor communication between communities separated by rivers or mountains, say) and indeed its present effects (socio-economic differences created by suitability of the area for coal-mining, say, or leisure, or urbanisation). There is talk of a 'north/south' divide.

EXAMPLE

Just as marketers have discovered that it is a mistake to group together all members of racial minorities, the same principle can be applied to Caucasian consumers. In the US, there are significant differences in income levels among subcultures of various European extractions. These differences often reflect the length of time members of a subculture have been settled in the US. This is because groups who have been there longer have had more time to develop business networks and amass wealth. French-Americans are the most likely to be affluent – almost 42% have a household income greater than £50,000, while Polish-Americans have the lowest income among these segments.

(e) **Religion**. Adherents to religious groups tend to be strongly oriented to the norms, beliefs, values, traditions and rituals of their faith. Food customs are strict in religions such as Judaism, Hinduism and Islam. Values and lifestyle are also likely to vary according to the teachings and customs of the religion.

(f) **Age**. Age micro-cultures vary according to the period in which individuals were socialised, to an extent, because of the great shifts in social values and customs in this century. (You may have seen specially branded products for 'Baby-boomers': those born between 1946 and 1964 in the post-war birthrate explosion.)

(g) **Gender**. We have already discussed gender roles in family buying behaviour, and their gradual erosion - despite which, marketers make frequent appeals to gender-linked stereotypes. The Working Woman and the New Man are perhaps the most important current micro-cultural markets segmented on this basis.

Marketers also need to **avoid exaggerating the exclusivity of micro-cultures**. Promotional strategies need not target a single micro-cultural membership, since each consumer is **simultaneously a member of many micro-cultural segments**. (You do not need to sell cornflakes specifically to a ethnic minority, when its members are also Protestants, women, young people, living in the West Midlands - and part of the mainstream UK culture, as far as cornflake consumption is concerned.)

Activity 9 **(30 minutes)**

(a) Find at least one example of marketing targeted at a segment of each of the above micro-cultures. You do not have to confine yourself to commercial enterprises or to TV advertising. The Metropolitan Police, for example, recently ran a recruitment drive using a poster that featured a white man chasing a black man - or so one concluded until one read the copy. Actually both men were policemen chasing an unseen villain.

(b) Visit shops or look through magazines that are not targeted at the micro-cultures into which you happen to fit. Make a note of the differences that you perceive.

6.17 Economic influences

Economic man

Economists have believed that the consumers make *rational decisions*, that is:

(a) They are aware of all product alternatives;

(b) They are capable of correctly ranking the alternatives having assessed their merits and disadvantages; and

(c) They are able to identify the best alternative.

This probably sounds pretty far-fetched to you and indeed the theory has been roundly criticised on a number of grounds.

(a) People do not have perfect information;

(b) People tend to act in accordance with their existing values and goals, and are limited by existing habits, skills and reflexes.

Passive man

(a) The objections to the economic man model give rise to a second model, the passive man. Such a person is irrational and impulsive, and is therefore entirely prey to the aims and strategies of marketers. The model suggests that the consumer can be manipulated at will.

(b) It is a simplistic model and ignores the fact that consumers can and usually do seek some information about product alternatives (even if the information is not perfect) and then make a choice which gives *them* satisfaction, not the marketer (even if the choice is not perfectly satisfying).

Cognitive man

Cognitive man is a thinking *problem solver* who seeks information on which to base consumption decisions from a range of choices. He is aware of the risks involved in making a choice, and will use various strategies to handle them.

RISKS 'the uncertainty that consumers feel when they cannot foresee the consequences of their purchase decisions'	STRATEGIES FOR HANDLING RISK
Functional risk: will the product do what 'they' say it will, and what I want it to do?	Seek information Brand loyalty ('I was happy before')
Economic risk: will it be worth the cost? Am I getting a good deal? Ought I to be spending this money?	Brand image (expert opinions reduce perceived risk)
Physical risk: is it difficult or dangerous to use? Is it environmentally friendly?	Store image ('it's M&S, it must be good') Pay more for premium quality
Social risk: will the Jones's be jealous or contemptuous?	Seek reassurance (warranties etc)
Psychological risk: will I feel good about it?	
Time risk: is this all going to be a waste of time as the product doesn't work?	

Emotional man

This model confirms what many of us instinctively know - that our feelings and emotions play a large part in our purchase decisions. Many people buy impulsively, without any information search, because it makes them feel good at the time. In fact, buying something because it affords emotional satisfaction is a rational thing to do because it satisfies a need, the need to feel good. This is in many instances a more important need than the need for food or for a particular shade of lipstick.

6.18 Scarcity

It is a fact of life that there are limits to available resources. For the individual (often called the *consumer* or deemed to be collected together in *households* by economists), the scarcity of goods and services might seem obvious enough. Most people would like to have more: perhaps a car, or more clothes, or a house of their own. Being physical commodities, these are called *goods*. Most people would also like to have more *services*, which can be defined as things which can be consumed only at the time of production. Examples of services include live theatre performances, public passenger transport and child-minding.

Since resources are scarce and there are not enough goods and services to satisfy the total potential demand, choices must be made. Choice is only necessary because resources are scarce.

6.19 Opportunity cost: the cost of one use for resources rather than another

Choice involves sacrifice. If there is a choice between having books and having butter, and a person chooses to have books, he will be giving up butter to have the books. The cost of having books can therefore be regarded as a sacrifice: not being able to have butter.

The cost of an item measured in terms of the alternatives forgone is called its *opportunity cost*. Thus the opportunity cost of buying six eggs can be measured as the two pints of milk or the one bus ride that could have been bought instead. Similarly, at a national level the opportunity cost of a country having a nuclear missile could be measured in terms of the number of schools that could have been built and staffed with the same amount of resources.

6.20 Income levels

Disposable income (also known as discretionary)

Whether a customer will buy, and what he buys - his demand - depends to a very large extent on whether he has the disposable income available to make the purchase. His disposable income will be considerably less than this total income since a large part of that will be committed elsewhere (to his mortgage, basic food bills, electricity bills etc). In economic terms, demand is affected by disposable income levels.

Change in household income

More income will give households more to spend as their disposable income rises (the necessities form a smaller percentage of the total), and they will want to buy more goods at existing prices. However, a rise in household income will not increase market demand for all goods and services. The effect of a rise in income on demand for an individual good will depend on the nature of the good.

Demand and the level of income may be related in different ways.

(a) A rise in household income may increase demand for a good. This is what we might normally expect to happen, and goods for which demand rises as household income increases are called *normal goods*.

(b) Demand increases up to a certain point and then remains unchanged as household income continues to rise. Examples are basic foodstuffs such as sugar or bread for which demand can reach a maximum level because there is a limit to what consumers can or want to consume.

(c) Demand may rise with income up to a certain point but then fall as income rises beyond that point. Goods whose demand eventually falls as income rises are called **inferior goods**: examples might include tripe and cheap wine.

6.21 Change in price

Two things happen when the price of a good falls.

(a) Firstly, the fall in price raises the real income of the consumer, thus increasing the demand for normal goods, but decreasing the demand for inferior goods. This is called the *income effect*.

(b) Secondly, now that the good is cheaper, it will tend to be substituted for other goods by the *substitution effect*, leading to a rise in demand for the good. For normal goods, the price fall thus results in greater demand for the good because the two effects work in the same direction.

6.22 Change in fashion and expectations

A change in fashion will alter the demand for a product.

EXAMPLE

Bottled water was once rarely purchased in the UK, but has come into fashion since the early 1980s, as a result of clever marketing and public concern – unjustified according to the water industry – about tap water.

If consumers believe that prices will rise, or that shortages will occur, they may attempt to stock up on the product, thereby creating excess demand in the short term which will increase prices. This can then lead to panic buying. Examples include the petrol crisis in the UK in September 2000.

In one instance some years ago, a rumour was spread that the Siberian salt mines were closed and this caused panic buying of salt in the UK to the extent that most shops ran out of supplies - even though salt for the UK is supplied from enormous deposits in Cheshire and not from Siberia at all!

6.23 Elasticity of demand

Where demand is **inelastic**, the quantity demanded falls by a smaller percentage than price, and where demand is elastic, demand falls by a larger percentage than the percentage rise in price.

EXAMPLE

Salt has a very low price elasticity of demand. We spend such a tiny fraction of our income on salt that we would find little difficulty in paying a relatively large increase in price. In contrast, a major item of expenditure has a much greater price elasticity of demand. If mortgage interest rates rise (the 'price' of loans for home purchase) people may have to cut down substantially on their demand for housing, being forced to buy somewhere much smaller and cheaper or live in rented accommodation.

Activity 10 **(5 minutes)**

Do cigarettes have elastic or inelastic demand? What about curable products?

For most commodities an increase in income will increase demand. The exact effect on demand will depend on the type of product. For example the demand for some products like bread will not increase much as income rises. Therefore, bread has a low *income elasticity of demand*. In contrast, the demand for luxuries increases rapidly as income rises and luxury goods therefore have a high income elasticity of demand.

6.24 Elasticity of supply

The elasticity of supply indicates the responsiveness of supply to a change in price. Where the price of goods is fixed, for example in the case of antiques, vintage wines and land, whatever price is offered, the elasticity of supply is zero.

7 THE ROLE OF BRANDS AND CUSTOMER LOYALTY

Branding is covered in detail in Chapter 13 as part of Unit 18. Here we simply cover what you need for Unit 17 – in other words the relationship between brand loyalty, company image and repeat purchase.

7.1 'Customer loyalty is the same as customer retention'?

There are differences between loyalty and retention.

Definition

> Properly understood, **customer loyalty** can be defined as **voluntary, profitable repurchasing and referral**.

It is voluntary in the sense that it is not a result of so-called 'incentives' like loyalty cards. In other words, customers are genuinely loyal when they return to a product/service supplier of their own accord and not merely (or principally) because if they do so they will collect 'points'.

It is **profitable** because it generates financial advantage for the product/service supplier (plus, presumably, a sense of 'value' for the customer).

It involves **repurchasing** and not merely window-shopping.

It includes **referrals** and recommendations to others - again without any financial or material 'consideration' being expected or offered.

Customer retention, on the other hand, may occur for a variety of reasons which have little to do with loyalty.

(i) Some customers may be '**tied in**' to the purchase of 'software' which is essential for the effective operation of previously-acquired 'hardware'. Thus, for example, users of a proprietary type of shaver may find it essential to buy razor blades which are only manufactured by a single source. Their frequent re-purchasing can scarcely be defined as genuine customer loyalty, as it arises from the realisation that **switching costs** are prohibitive.

(ii) Customers may continue to use a particular product/service supplier through **inertia**: perhaps the supplier's performance, whilst not impressive, is not yet bad enough to justify a switch.

(iii) **Switching costs** may also be prohibitive, literally so, in cases where customers have benefited from temporarily lower prices whilst accepting a long-term contractual commitment. This applies particularly with house mortgages: 'special [lower-interest] rates' are almost always linked to the existence of penal redemption charges where mortgages are redeemed within, say, five years.

'**Customer satisfaction produces customer loyalty**'. Many organisations still claim that one of their strategic goals is the achievement of exceptional levels of customer 'satisfaction'. However, customers can be 'satisfied' and still defect to alternative suppliers, if apparently better deals suggest themselves.

(a) Most customers now **expect** to be satisfied: they are not surprised when they buy something and it works.

7.2 Relationship marketing

Relationship marketing helps them to do this. Technology is the key factor. Software developments have made **databases** flexible and powerful enough to hold large amounts of **customer specific data**. While the corner shop of old recognised customers visually, companies today can recognise them electronically.

Definition

> **Relationship marketing** can be seen as the successor to mass marketing, and is the process by which information about the customer is consistently applied by the company when developing and delivering products and services. Developments are communicated to the customer, for example via specially targeted promotions and product launches, in order to build a 'partnership' with him and encourage a long term relationship by paying attention to his specific needs. It stresses the long-term, human side of buyer/ seller interactions.

EXAMPLE

Affinity cards

Affinity credit cards such as those issued by the Bank of Scotland, Beneficial Bank and the Co-operative Bank on behalf of non-profit organisations such as the RSPCA, are taking an increasingly prominent role in the credit card market. Credit card issuers see the affinity route as a means of establishing and maintaining relationships with customers, that they would otherwise not have the opportunity to contact. Charities, as one of the earliest affinity partner groups, are also forming an increasing number of relationships with credit card issuers, as these issuers seek out more affinity partner groups.

The **rewards from effective relationship marketing** are potentially impressive (and are linked to the whole exercise of **customer retention**).

(a) One credit card company calculated that a 5% increase in customer retention would create a 125% increase in profits.

(b) American Express believes that by extending customer lifecycles by five years, it could treble its profits per customer.

(c) According to Coca-Cola, a 10% increase in retailer retention should translate to a 20% increase in sales.

In a **relationship approach**, 'smart marketers try to build up long-term, trusting, win-win relations with valued customers, distributors, dealers and suppliers ... it is accomplished by building strong economic, technical and social ties with the other parties.'

The justification for relationship marketing comes from the **need to retain customers**. There are five different levels of customer relationship.

Level	Comment
Basic	The salesperson sells the product without any further contact with the customer.
Reactive	The customer is encouraged to call the salesperson if there are any problems.
Accountable	The salesperson phones the customer to see if there are any problems and to elicit ideas for product improvements.
Proactive	The salesperson contacts the customer on a regular basis.
Partnership	The salesperson and customer work together to effect customer savings. The commercial buyer works closely with the supplier to ensure that the deal suits both parties. This should encourage repeat business.

Broadly speaking, the greater the number of customers and the smaller the profit per unit sold, the greater the likelihood that the type of marketing will be **basic**. At the other extreme, where a firm has few customers, but where profits are high, the **partnership** approach is most likely.

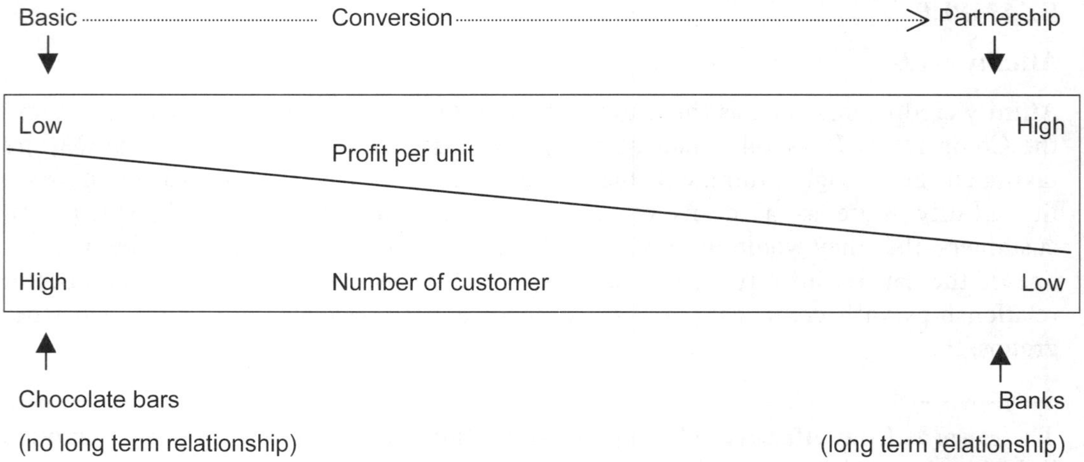

Some firms are trying to **convert** a basic approach into relationship marketing. Many car dealerships, for example, seek to generate additional profits by servicing the cars they sell, and by keeping in touch with their customers so that they can earn repeat business.

7.3 Consumer imagery

An 'image' is an established and enduring perception of something or someone. We all have or hold images of people and things that we have experienced or imagined. For marketers, the images most relevant to consumer behaviour are:

(a) the self-image of the consumer; and

(b) the image consumers have of products and brands, retail and manufacturing organisations.

Self-image

Each individual has a self-image of being a certain type of person, with certain qualities and circumstances: this is his self-image. It is partly developed by reflection from other people, through the interpersonal contacts made in life: the way others respond.

NOTES

In fact, the self-image is not a single 'snap shot' of what the individual is like, but consists of:

(a) *actual self-concept*: how the individual perceives himself - what he is

(b) *ideal self-concept*: how the individual would like to perceive himself - what he wishes to be, and

(c) *expected self-concept*: how the individual expects to perceive himself in future - what he aspires to be.

Self-image affects **product and brand choice**

(a) Products have a symbolic value for consumers: they 'say' something which may or may not be consistent with an individual's actual or aspirational self-image

(b) Consumers need to support or enhance their self images, and can do this by buying products that 'fit' the desired image, and avoiding those that do not

(c) Consumers may also identify with the image of a marketing campaign or retail outlet

(d) Consumers want to achieve their expected self-concept. Apart from a thriving 'personal image consultancy' industry (advice on wardrobe, presentation etc), there is a general vogue for aspirational products, such as mobile phones, Porsches, or membership of a health club.

Activity 11 **(10 minutes)**

(a) Are you a 'boutique' person or a Marks & Spencer person? Does this image hold true across all product ranges (does M&S food have a different image to M&S clothes, say)?

(b) What kind of shop-window mannequins do you identify with (or not)?

(c) What kind of car do you drive? What kind of car would you like to drive? What is the most desirable kind of car you can really see yourself driving?

7.4 Product image

The creation of an image of a product or brand in the market's perception is known as *product positioning*. It is a very important marketing technique. Whatever the actual physical attributes of a product, it is important that consumers perceive that product to possess the attributes that will fulfil their particular needs better than any competing product.

The image presented by a product or brand may:

(a) make the product/brand distinctive in the consumer's mind (differentiate it from its competitors)

(b) make the product/brand fit a distinctive market niche or segment.

> 'Positioning strategy ... conveys the concept, or meaning, of the product (how it fulfils a consumer need) rather than the product idea (the physical properties of the product itself). Different consumer meanings can be assigned to the same product. Thus, it can be 'positioned' differently to different audiences, or it can be 'repositioned' to the same audience, without being physically changed.'
>
> (Schiffman and Kanuk, *Consumer Behaviour*)

BPP PUBLISHING

One technique used by marketers to determine how their products are perceived by consumers, in relation to competing products, is *perceptual mapping*. A grid or cruciform chart is drawn up, indicating key features or benefits. Consumer respondents' perceptions of the products, with reference to those features, are then plotted.

The perceptual map can then be used to identify:

(a) Areas where consumers do not feel their needs are being met

(b) Competing brands are perceived to be similar to your brand - which may therefore need to be differentiated more clearly; and

(c) The strengths and weaknesses of your product in relation to others

The following example of a perceptual map uses toilet tissue as an example. The dotted line indicates where the product would like to be.

Perceptual map for brands of toilet tissue

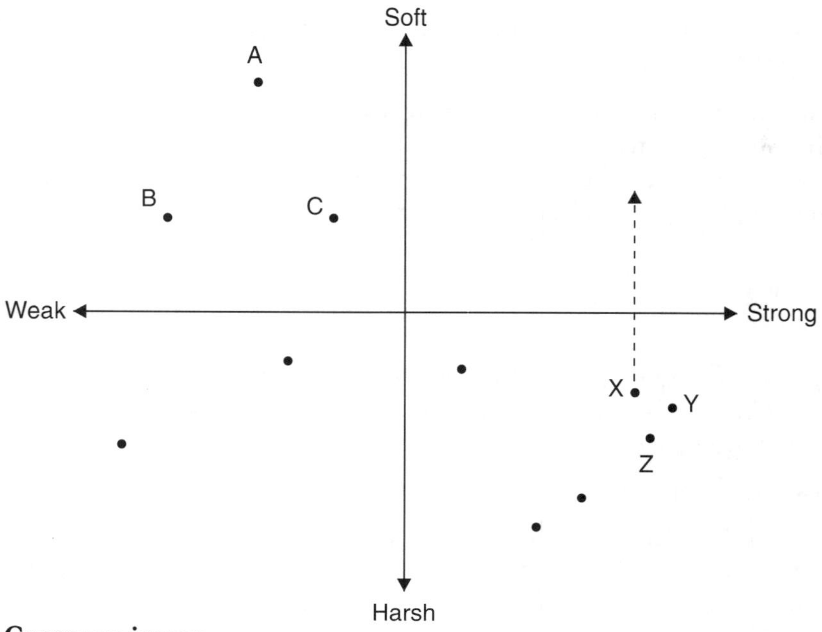

7.5 Company image

Organisations also have images in people's minds.

(a) Retailers have their own image, reinforced by own-brand products and labels, in-store design and marketing 'style'. A consumer's perception of a product may be enhanced by the knowledge of its origin.

(b) Manufacturers and service providers have their own image, distinct from the brand names they produce. Large corporations with a variety of subsidiary companies and brands are increasingly at pains to establish a unifying ('The name behind all these great brands') corporate image: McVitie's and Scott are two recent examples. **Corporate image** may be based on community and environmental responsibility, sponsorship of sporting or artistic events, or sound managerial/financial performance.

EXAMPLE

In the UK, the coprorate image of the Virgin group is very much tied to the corporate image of Richard Branson. The group covers a host of different services from trains to IT.

Organisations have an image as employers, both internally and in the external labour market.

Activity 12 **(30 minutes)**

Select a product and brand that you use frequently and list what you consider to be the brand's determinant attributes. Without disclosing your list, ask a friend of the opposite sex to make a similar list for the same product (the brand may be different). Compare and contrast the identified attributes and report your findings.

Chapter roundup

- Individuals are important in all buying decisions, either for themselves or on behalf of an organisation. Marketers need to understand their motives, psychology and influences, and how these combine to form a motivation mix.
- Models are used to illustrate buyer behaviour as a means of simplifying a complex process.
- Essentially there are two formats for simple buyer behaviour models, black box ones which exclude internal variables and personal variable ones which exclude external variables.
- The key elements of the buying process are problem recognition, information search, evaluation of alternatives, the purchase decision and post-purchase evaluation.
- Diffusion of innovation is the term used to describe the process by which an innovation is spread or disseminated from the source to the consuming public.
- The family is of critical importance to individuals, as a network of relationships, reference group and social unit. The decision making unit operates most often in a family context, with different family members adopting different consumption and hence DMU roles.
- Organisational decision-making is based on the same DMU model but is generally more rational yet inert. The interaction of DMU members is influenced by a great many variables. The AMA model can be used to describe this.
- The DMU is a particularly useful concept in marketing industrial or government goods and services where the customer is a business or other organisation.
- The marketing department of a supplier aiming at corporate clients therefore needs to be aware of:
    - How buying decisions are made by the DMU
    - How the DMU is constructed
    - The identities of the most influential figures in the DMU
- Buyer behaviour is determined by economic, psychological, sociological and cultural considerations.
- The term 'culture' encompasses the sum total of learned beliefs, values, customs, rituals, languages, symbols, artefacts and technology of a society or group.
- Different societies vary greatly in most aspects of culture, but all culture is social, learned, shared, cumulative and adaptive.
- Products can be invested with cultural meaning by marketing efforts; that meaning is transferred to a buyer who uses the product in a cultural context and hence imbues it with further cultural meaning. This is called transfer of cultural meaning.
- Micro-cultures within a culture are usually structured on the lines of class, nationality, ethnicity, geography, religion, age and gender.
- Marketing cross-culturally has many advantages for marketers but brings with it a number of new challenges. Two approaches can be used: localised markets (marketing a product so that it fits into the existing culture) or global marketing (capitalising on the fact that culture changes and develops, so a 'foreign' product can gain acceptance into different cultures in the same form worldwide).

Quick quiz

1. What is a consumer?
2. Why are models used to describe buyer behaviour?
3. Name three criteria that should be applied when evaluating models.
4. What is the basic underlying assumption of black box models?
5. Why are black box models useful?
6. What do personal variable models focus on?
7. What are the four influencing variables in the Engel, Blackwell and Miniard model?
8. List four product characteristics that influence diffusion.
9. What are the five adopter categories?
10. Name four roles in any DMU.
11. Decisions which are reached by both spouses are known as?
12. List four differences between personal and organisational buying decision processes.
13. What are the three key psychological influences on buyer behaviour?
14. What is meant by the tem cognitive dissonance?
15. Which agencies could be said to be instrumental in the socialisation of individuals?
16. What are status symbols?
17. What are the underlying characteristics of culture?
18. What is a micro-culture?
19. What is relationship marketing?
20. What are the five different levels of customer relationship?
21. What does self-image consist of?

Answers to quick quiz

1. A consumer is the end user of a product or service who may or may not be the customer. (See paragraph 1)
2. Models can help researchers to develop theories and they can describe and explain behaviour and so aid prediction. (para 2.1)
3. Validity, factual accuracy and rationality.(para 2.3)
4. That observable behaviour is the only valid object of study. (para 3.1)
5. They include observable, quantifiable variables; they concentrate on a manageable number of relevant input variables, and they help identify stimulus variables. (para 3.1)
6. They focus on internal processes such as beliefs, intentions, motives and perceptions. (para 3.2)
7. Stimulus inputs, information processing, decision process and variables influencing the decision process. (para 4.2)
8. Relative advantage, compatibility, complexity and trialability. (para 4.5)

9 Innovator, early adopter, early majority, late majority and laggard. (para 4.6)

10 Initiator, gatekeeper, decider, buyer. (para 5)

11 Syncratic. (para 5.2)

12 Organisations need to meet wider objectives, they usually have a greater number of people involved, the decision process may take longer and they are more likely to buy a complex total offering. (para 5.4)

13 Attitudes, loyalty and personality. (para 6.2)

14 Cognitive dissonance is the discomfort experienced by an individual when they receive new information which appears to contradict a held belief or attitude. (para 6.5)

15 Family, school, peer groups and the mass media. (para 6.6)

16 Status symbols are products that are purchased and displayed to signal membership of a desirable social class. (para 6.14)

17 Social, learned, shared, cumulative and adaptive. (para 6.15)

18 A micro-culture is a distinct and identifiable cultural group within society as a whole: it will have certain beliefs, values, customs and rituals that set it apart – while still sharing the dominant beliefs, values, customs and rituals of the whole society. (para 6.16)

19 Relationship marketing is the process by which information about the customer is consistently applied by the company when developing and delivering products and services. (para 7.2)

20 Basic, reactive, accountable, proactive and partnership. (7.2)

21 Actual self-concept, ideal self-concept and expected self-concept. (para 7.3)

Answers to activities

1 Examples include:

Medical supplies
Office stationery
Restaurant and catering supplies

2 The result of, or answer to, this activity will depend on the item you have chosen.

3 The customers are the employer organistions which buy the dental benefits programmes for the employees, and indirectly the employees themselves, the users of the dental services.

4 The result of, or answer to, this activity will depend on the item you have chosen.

5 There is no specific answer to this activity.

6 Groceries: may need to spend less money
will need to buy baby food
may be the subject of pressure from older children
likely to buy less exotic, overseas and sophisticated foods.

Cars: more influenced by issues of safety
likely to buy a bigger car
less likely to buy a sports car
influenced by amount of space for luggage, equipment etc

Holidays:	will want childcare facilities (cots early supper etc) will want children's entertainment will want a safe environment (beach, swimming pool) may have to travel in the peak holiday periods less likely to buy long haul or luxury holidays
Furniture:	likely to spend less will want durable furniture, unlikely to suffer damage will need children's furniture (bunk beds etc) furniture purchases will be lower on the list of priorities once initial baby/child furniture has been bought
Domestic appliances:	will want durability will expect reliability may expect guarantees of prompt repair

7 The result of, or answer to, this activity will depend on the item you have chosen.

8 The answer to this activity will depend on your own social culture

9 The result of, or answer to, this activity will depend on the item you have chosen.

10 Cigarettes have a fairly inealstic demand. Purchases of cigarettes do not form a significant part of most people's budget; people who smoke will tend to pay for an increase rather than face the prospect of giving up smoking.

11 The result of, or answer to, this activity will depend on the item you have chosen.

12 The result of, or answer to, this activity will depend on the item you have chosen.

Chapter 2 :
MARKET RESEARCH

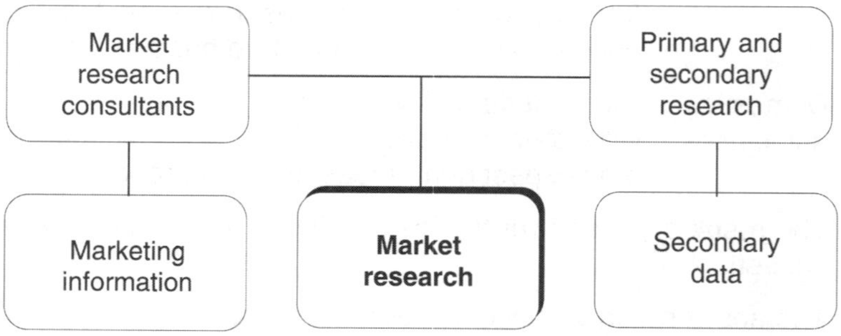

Introduction

Having covered some of the key issues underlying buyer behaviour, we now move on to focus on the techniques firms use to understand how customers behave. The chapter begins by discussing the components of an effective marketing information system. It goes on to discuss what marketing information an organisation might need and suggests how that information might be obtained.

The second section compares and contrasts primary and secondary research and offers some advantages and disadvantages of each type of data. The third section suggests sources of secondary data and offers a set of criteria which can be used when evaluating secondary findings.

The chapter concludes with an overview of market research consultants. This includes how they can selected and the relative advantages and disadvantages of outsourcing research.

Your objectives

In this chapter you will learn about the following:

(a) an overview of the marketing information system

(b) the scope of different types of research

(c) the range of different types of data

(d) the importance of secondary data

(e) the role of market research consultants

NOTES

1 MARKETING INFORMATION

The marketing environment must be constantly analysed. The information produced from such an analysis is a key input to all aspects of strategy formulation.

1.1 The marketing information system

Definition

> The collection, organisation and analysis of marketing information is the responsibility of a **marketing information system** (MkIS) in itself is part of the hierarchy of information systems that exist within organisations. The information collected, organised and analysed by an MkIS will typically include the following.
>
> - Details on consumers and markets
> - Sales - past, current and forecast
> - Production and marketing costs
> - Data on the operating environment: competitors, suppliers, distributors and so on

Typically, an MkIS will have four interlinked components.

(a) **The internal database.** This includes information on costs, production schedules, orders, sales and some types of financial information relating to customers (such as credit ratings). Financial analysis and tools would provide much of this information.

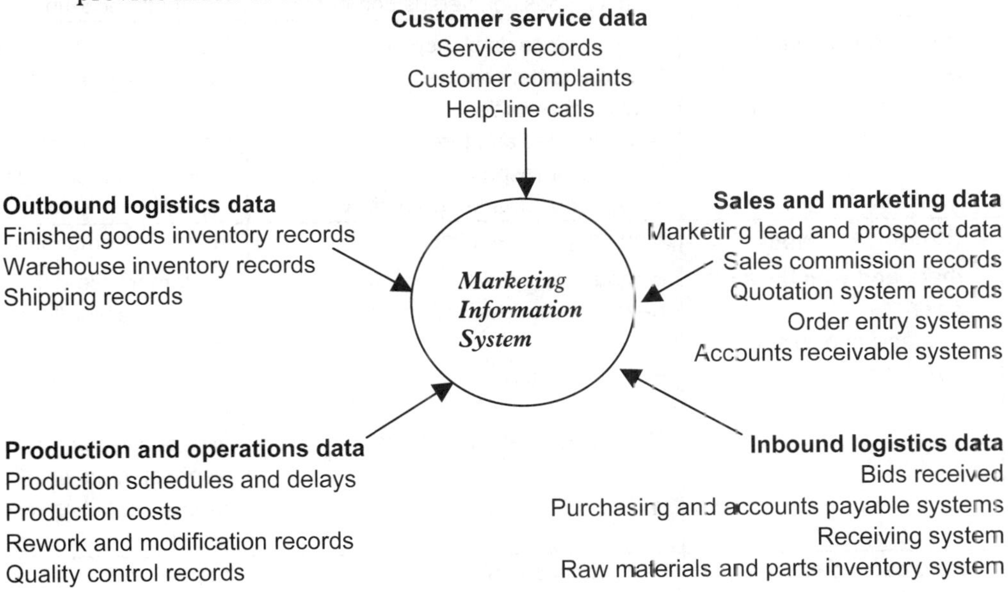

Source: Marshall, Marketing Information Systems

(b) **The external database**. This includes all types of information collected from external sources, commonly described as **marketing intelligence**. This database may take the form of press cuttings and so forth, but can also incorporate subscriptions to external sources of competitive data.

NOTES

(c) **The market research system.** Generally such a system involves the process of information search undertaken on an ad hoc basis to provide answers to specific questions.

(d) **The decision support system.** A DSS is a set of analytical techniques that enable marketing managers to make full use of the information provided by the other three sources. This analysis may range from simple financial ratios and projections of sales patterns to more complex statistical models, spreadsheets and other exercises in extrapolation.

The marketing information needs of the organisation can be assessed by examining the marketing information needed to answer each of the **four key strategic questions** which organisations have to ask themselves.

(a) Where are we **now**?
(b) Where do we **want** to be?
(c) How might we **get there**?
(d) How can we **ensure** we get there?

The following table repeats these four questions, shows what marketing information is needed to answer each question, and suggests how the information may be obtained.

Stage	*Information needed*	*Sources of information: forms of marketing research*
1 **Where are we now?** Strategic, financial and Marketing analysis	Current sales by product/ market Market share by product/market Competitor shares by product/ market Corporate image versus competitors' Company strengths and weaknesses Financial position versus competitors'	Internal accounting Market analysis/surveys Competitor intelligence Customer surveys Internal/external analyses Company accounts
2 **Where do we want to be?** Strategic direction and Strategy formulation	Market forecasts by segment Environmental changes Growth capabilities Opportunities and threats Competitor response New product/market potentials	Industry forecasts/surveys PEST analysis PIMS Competitor research Product/market research
3 **How might we get there and which way is best?** Strategic choice and Evaluation	Marketing mix evaluation Buying behaviour New product development Risk evaluation Alternative strategic options	Internal/external audits Customer research Concept testing/test marketing Feasibility studies/CVP analysis NPV analyses/competitor response modelling/focus groups/marketing mix research
4 **How can we ensure arrival?** Strategic implementation And control	Performance evaluation	Internal accounting/external auditing

This information-seeking process can be best expressed as a flow diagram.

Step 1 → Internal →

1.1	The organisation's marketing information system (MkIS)
1.2	Official company records
1.3	Employees

↓

Step 2 →External (published)→

2.1	Government statistics
2.2	Trade magazines
2.3	Other magazines and newspapers
2.4	Published reports
2.5	Conference papers
2.6	Research registers
2.7	Books

↓

Step 3 →External (surveys) →

3.1	Shared cost or syndicated surveys
3.2	Omnibus surveys
3.3	Interfirm comparison
3.4	Industry surveys

↓

Step 4 → Own survey →

4.1	Use Market Research Agency
4.2	Conduct own survey

1.2 Sources of research data

Primary research involves the marketing researcher in collecting data for a specific problem which has to be solved or decision which has to be made. Primary data may come from surveys, questionnaires, experiments etc.

Secondary research is based on data which for the most part has been collected for some other purpose. Examples include environmental scanning, published statistics and bought-in reports.

1.3 Market research organisation categories

The above categories of marketing research are those used generally in textbooks. In the marketing research industry different categories of research techniques are used.

1.4 Qualitative and quantitative research

- **Qualitative research** is geared towards gathering qualitative information about, for instance, attitudes and motivation, often in the form of pictures and words and using techniques such as discussion groups.

NOTES

Definition

> **Qualitative research** – research data not subject to quantification or quantitative analysis.

- **Quantitative research** is involved with data as numbers, often using questionnaires and surveys.

Definition

> **Quantitative research** – studies that use mathematical analysis.

1.5 Ad hoc and continuous research

Ad hoc research, as the name suggests, is a 'one-off' which comes into being with an initial brief and ends with a report. It is not designed, for instance, to monitor change but rather to find answers to specific problems, often using qualitative research methods. This should be contrasted with *continuous* research which has no identifiable beginning or end but keeps the data constantly 'topped up', so that changes in the environment can be identified. Continuous research often requires a sophisticated management or marketing information system, and frequently involves panels.

1.6 Customised and syndicated research

Customised research is also to some degree 'one off' research, since it comes into being thanks to a commission by a single organisation. *Syndicated* or 'off the peg' research is material which has been put together by one organisation (often a specialist marketing research organisation) and then sold to a number of clients to whom it is more or less equally relevant. Continuous research is often syndicated, mainly so as to spread the considerable cost of initiating and constantly updating the information.

1.7 Contract and consultancy research

Often marketing organisations will ask a research organisation simply to do one part of the marketing research process - such as collecting data which the commissioning organisation then analyses. This is known as *contract* research. This can be contrasted with the increasingly popular *consultancy* research, where the marketing research organisation may be involved in every stage of the process.

1.8 Consumer and business research

This distinguished the type of research on the basis of who the end-user of the product concerned will be. Hence *consumer* research concentrates on individuals and households, while *business* research looks at customers who are organisations.

DISCUSSION

The role of marketing is to create exchanges. What role might marketing research play in the facilitation of the exchange process?

NOTES

2 PRIMARY AND SECONDARY RESEARCH

Here in brief are the types of data.

2.1 Sources of research data

	Secondary data	Primary data
What it is	Data neither collected directly by the user nor specifically for the user, often under conditions unknown to the user – in other words, data collected not by YOU but by someone else for their own purposes or for general use	Data that is collected specifically by or for the user, at source.
Quantitative, 'factual' or 'objective' example	**Government reports** – in the UK a good example is Social Trends, which contains government statistics about British society, employment in different industries, attitudes and so on.	A survey you conduct with a questionnaire you have designed, with regard to a sample. You aim to get a statistically significant result. An experiment
	A company's **published financial statements** summarise and interpret company transactions data for the benefit of **shareholders**, not the needs of the Research and Analysis project.	
Qualitative example	An article or a book about theories of motivation.	A focus group you have conducted to talk about motivation
Advantages	• Cheap • Widely available • Suggests further primary research	• Clear target • Controlled • Up-to-date
Disadvantages	• Lack of focus	• Expensive • Time consuming

3 SECONDARY DATA, INCLUDING THE INTERNET

3.1 Internal sources of secondary data

Most employers probably have large amounts of information, not designed for your research, but useful to you. Monthly management accounts are only part of what is available for your research. And remember, the accounts department is rarely the **driver** of a business.

Accounts department

- Procedures manual
- Management accounts - balance sheets
- Financial data
- Accounting policies
- Tax details
- Working capital

Sales and marketing department

- Sales reports by region
- Sales by customer
- Sales by product
- Competitor intelligence
- Market prospects and reports
- Customer complaints
- Marketing research reports
- Brand strategy and values
- Distribution chains

Production and operations

- Operations data
- Efficiency and capacity detail
- Process flow charts
- Detailed product costings
- Input prices
- Supply chain

Human resources

- Number of employees
- Recruitment procedures
- Training programmes
- Staff turnover details
- Details of pay

In many instances internal data is gathered in a relatively unorganised manner and people in the organisation may have little knowledge of what data is actually available. The growth of marketing information systems alongside the trend towards the computerisation of all records in a business can do much to simplify the organisation and accessibility of internal data.

3.2 External secondary data

It is hard to give detailed rules about where you should look, except that you should search for **relevant** data, and try to make use of the Internet.

Books

Books tend to date quickly but can provide a useful tool.

Journals and articles

Academic journals, such as the **Harvard Business Review**. Again, rather than list them here, you may be able to find a list from your own college library of what is published - perhaps an article may be obtained or copied for you.

Other business or current affairs journals and newspapers, such as the **Economist**, **Euromonitor**, **Asian Wall Street Journal** etc, may have surveys relevant to different business areas.

Trade journals are also useful - most countries have journals produced by relevant trade bodies, detailing developments in the industry. You can use the Internet to access the websites of **trade associations**. Increasingly, businesses in an industry are setting up electronic markets

The **Internet** is an excellent source of secondary data if used with care.

(a) For example, you can use a **search engine** which will bring up websites of interest. Some websites will allow you to download articles. Some of these websites - the **Economist Intelligence Unit** is one - offer articles for download. Another is www.ft.com. Many of these will be in PDF (portable document file) format. You will need to download **Adobe Acrobat Reader** for this - fortunately Acrobat Reader is **free** and it is possible that the site will have a link to Adobe to enable you to download the software yourself.

(b) Your internet service provider may also refer you to magazines and on-line newspapers.

Government ministries and agencies

Government agencies are good sources of economic and other statistical information. Most countries have an agency that provides national statistics. This varies significantly from country to country in terms of what is produced and the format, but you should be able to find:

(a) Economic data (eg UK Annual Abstract of Statistics)
(b) Social data (eg on population size and structure)
(c) Market data (eg export promotion

Regulatory bodies and industry associations

There are many quasi-government and other public sector bodies which can provide data on particular industry sector.

3.3 Using secondary data

Secondary data is used in many business situations, not just in academic research.

Backdrop to primary research

Secondary data may also be used to set the **parameters** for primary research. In an **unfamiliar field**, it is natural that the researcher will carry out some **basic research** in the area, using journals, existing reports, the press and any contacts with relevant knowledge.

Substitute for primary research

The (often substantial) **cost** of primary research **might be avoided** should existing secondary data be sufficient. Given the low response rate available for questionnaires, secondary research might do the job just as well. There are some situations however, in which secondary data is bound to be **insufficient**.

Some types of information can **only be acquired through secondary data**, in particular **trends** over time. The **historical data** published on, say, trends in the behaviour of an industry over time, cannot realistically be replaced by a one-off study.

3.4 Syndicated services

If the expense of conducting their own surveys is too great, companies and organisations can obtain general surveys that they can buy into on a shared basis, for example the Nielsen Retail Audit. A particular form of shared cost research is the omnibus survey, a variety of which are advertised in the Market Research Society Newsletters and range from general weekly surveys done by telephone (such as phonebus) to special sector surveys (for example, Omnicar - motoring, Carrick James - children and youth, small businesses and so on).

The advantage is that for a few hundred as opposed to a few thousand pounds, a company can ask a few questions of a reasonably representative sample and have a report sent within two or three weeks.

Examples are: Nielsen, AGB, Omnimes.

(a) Secondary data, while not necessarily fulfilling your information needs, can be of great use by:

   (i) **Setting the parameters**, defining a hypothesis, highlighting variables, in other words, helping to focus on the central problem

   (ii) **Providing guidance**, by showing past methods of research and so on, for primary data collection

   (iii) **Helping to assimilate the primary research** with past research, highlighting trends and the like

3.5 Issues to bear in mind in using secondary data

Topic	Comment
Relevance	The data may not be relevant to the research objectives in terms of the data content itself, classifications used or units of measurement.
Cost	Although secondary data is usually cheaper than primary data, some specialist reports can cost large amounts of money.
Availability	Secondary data may not exist in the specific product or market area.
Bias	The secondary data may be biased, depending on who originally carried it out and for what purpose. Attempts should be made to obtain the most original source of the data, to assess it for such bias.
Statistical accuracy	Was the sample representative? Was the questionnaire or other measurement instrument(s) properly constructed? Were possible biases in response or in non-response dealt with and accounted for? Was the data properly analysed using appropriate statistical techniques? Was a sufficiently large sample used? Does the report include the raw data? In addition, was any raw data omitted from the final report, and why?
Sufficiency	Even after fulfilling all the above criteria, the secondary data may be insufficient and primary research would therefore be necessary.

Activity 1 **(30 minutes)**

Look for secondary research based on the telecommunications industry over the past 12 months. Use the above criteria to evaluate your findings.

EXAMPLE

'Teenagers Europe is the first multi-country, single-source survey of teenage product use, media consumption and attitudes. Questionnaires were completed by 11- to 19- year-old groups in Britain, France, Germany and Italy. They covered topics ranging from TV viewing to fast-food chains, from sportswear purchasing to views on key social and political issues.

The survey yields a mass of information which is comparable across all four countries, some of which confirms existing hypotheses and some of which surprises.

In terms of market size, the survey base represents a teenage (11 to 19) population of 27 million (64 per cent of the teenage population of the EU). This group has a total disposable income of about £24.8 billion.

The average weekly income differs significantly from country to country. British teenagers, for example, enjoy an income more than twice that of their French counterparts.

But while income levels differ, patterns of expenditure show marked similarity. Clothes are the top priority for teenagers in all countries with the exception of Britain, where most is spent on going out. Music is important in terms of spending and it is worth noting that 60 per cent of teenagers agree with the statement that they 'couldn't live without music'.

Personal appearance is equally important to teenagers in all four countries – nearly half agree that they like keeping up with the latest fashions, and some two-thirds feel that they take a lot of care with the way they look. Shopping habits confirm this. About a fifth of Italian and British teenagers go shopping for clothes at least 26 times a year. Germans are less keen: 40 per cent go clothes shopping less than six times a year, and they are also more likely to agree that 'shopping for clothes is boring'.

Teenagers Europe shows that 'pester power' varies markedly across the four countries. The toiletries market is a good example. It is not the kind of product that teenagers would necessarily expect to buy for themselves. But they do have views on the brands they prefer. Just under half of Britain's teenagers use spot cream, a slightly higher proportion than in the other three countries. Of these, three-quarters decide what brand to use themselves, in Britain and Germany while just over half the teenagers in France and Italy make that decision, with a third leaving it entirely to their parents. Similar patterns can be seen across other markets.

The strategic value of the survey's information on product and brand use is greatly enhanced by the media consumption data. Some of the most revealing statistics in this area relate to TV viewing and computer use. British teenagers watch TV for more than four hours every day – more than any other country surveyed.

This figure is probably helped by the fact that three-quarters of British teenage TV viewers have a set in their bedroom, well ahead of Germany and Italy, and more than twice the proportion measured in France.

Computer use is also more widespread in Britain – nine out of ten teenagers use one, compared with less than 60 per cent of German teenagers. A sixth of the British sample use them to access the Internet – a market currently growing faster in Britain than elsewhere in Europe. Perhaps reassuringly, about half of the teenagers across the four countries agree that they 'really enjoy reading books'. Given the extensive consumption of broadcast media and the relative consistency of expenditure patterns across the four countries, does the study reveal evidence of pan-European branding at work?

There are some impressive examples: over 70 per cent of all teenagers drink Coke; and more than six in ten have visited McDonald's in the past three months. But there are some surprises too: ten per cent of respondents claim to use Clearasil spot treatments – a market of nearly 3 million loyal users across the four countries surveyed. Impulse deodorant shows strongly, as does Sensodyne toothpaste, despite not being the top brand in the UK.

The research also opens up a further dimension for planners, with the inclusion of 160 attitude statements. Six clusters of teenagers have been identified and it may yet prove possible to characterise the elusive 'Euro-teenage' – and to reach that audience through his or her favourite media.' *Marketing Week*, 11 December 1997

DISCUSSION

Market research has traditionally been associated with manufacturers of consumer goods. Today, we are experiencing an increasing number of organisations both profit making and non-profit, using market resarch. Why?

NOTES

4 MARKET RESEARCH CONSULTANTS

Market research has been a growing source of organisation expenditure in recent years. Very few organisations can shoulder the cost of a large full-time staff of marketing research workers, especially a 'field force' of researchers spread around the country. In addition to market research agencies, there are market research departments in many of the large UK advertising agencies.

Definition

> **Field service firms** – companies that only collect survey data for corporate clients or research firms.

4.1 Choosing and using consultants

Choosing the right agency or consultant to work with is a key element in a successful working relationship. The external expert must become a trusted part of the team.

It is equally important that the market researcher has the specialist knowledge and research service capabilities needed by the organisation. In the UK you would expect a research organisation to be associated to the professional body, the Market Research Society, and for those working on the account to have relevant qualifications.

It helps if the agency has some knowledge of the market or business in which the company operates. Therefore, it is worthwhile developing a **long-standing relationship** with the research organisation. As the understanding of the company's business and the marketplace develops over time, there is a real dividend from the two operations working together.

4.2 Steps in choosing a research firm

1. Check sources for finding names of research companies
2. Compile a list of firms and decide on two or three that appear to be the most promising
3. Contact the research firm in writing, giving as full a description as possible of the problem
4. Arrange an interview with the research firm, preferably in its office
5. Find out more about the research supplier and its previous clients
6. Explore how the research firm prefers to work with clients
7. Ask for a written proposal
8. Come to a clear understanding that further discussions may change the proposal in some ways
9. Agree about who will be the prime contacts between client and researcher
10. Make it clear to a firm submitting a proposal that proposals from other firms are also being considered when this is the case

In selecting an outside agency, account should be taken of the degree to which an in-depth knowledge of the employing company and its field is required and the agency's skill in the type of study to be undertaken. An outside agency often needs some weeks of training or instruction about the company and its marketing problems before it can understand what the client requires.

4.3 Types of consultants

Outside agencies offering research may be categorised according to their type and location.

(a) **Local firms offering specialist types of assistance**

These firms may specialise in interviewing, mall intercepts, telephone research etc. They may take on special local assignments for large, nationwide research companies.

(b) **National research firms**

Agencies of this kind may be able to do almost all forms of market research. The companies often offer consulting in marketing and even general management. They also may offer computer-based information for use in databases, marketing strategy decisions and the like.

(c) **Consultants in various specialities**

These firms may consult and advise about packaging, advertising and personnel problems. They also may offer to do some research relating to their specialities. These firms may have a major field of interest such as engineering. The research offered by consultants can include necessary external studies, both marketing and technical.

4.4 External agencies versus in-house programmes

There are a number of advantages and disadvantages to each alternative.

(a) Using an external agency

(i) Advantages

(1) External agencies **specialising** in research will have the necessary expertise in marketing research techniques. This should allow them to develop a cost-effective research programme to a **tighter timescale**.

(2) Skills in **monitoring and interpreting data** will allow the programme to be reviewed and modified as required.

(3) There will be **minimal disruption** to the normal working of the marketing department which might result from releasing internal staff from existing duties.

(4) An external agency can provide an **objective input** without the bias which often results from a dependence on internal resources.

(5) **Costs** can be determined from the outset, thereby allowing better **budgetary control**.

(6) Such an approach might be advantageous when conducting **confidential research** into sensitive area, there being less risk of information being 'leaked' to competitors.

(ii) Disadvantage

Agency knowledge of the industry will be limited. This would be a serious drawback if the agency requires a disproportionate amount of time to familiarise itself with the sector.

(b) In-house programme

(i) Advantages

(1) **Costs can be absorbed** into existing departmental overheads.

(2) It offers an opportunity to **broaden the experience** and skill levels of existing staff.

(3) It might be useful in promoting a **team spirit** and encouraging a 'results-oriented' approach.

(ii) Disadvantages

(1) There is a danger of **overstretching current resources** and adversely affecting other projects.

(2) There is a risk of developing an **inappropriate programme**, yielding insufficient or poor quality data with inadequate analysis and control.

(3) If additional **training or recruitment** is required this could prove expensive and time consuming.

(4) **Bias** could result from using staff with pre-conceived views.

(5) **Company politics** may influence the results.

(6) Considerable **computing resources** with appropriate software packages would be required to analyse the data.

(7) There may be a lack of **appropriate facilities**. For example, focus group research would normally be conducted off premises during an evening or weekend.

In view of the shortcomings of a purely in-house or external agency approach, a **combination** of the two might be more appropriate. For example, it might be deemed preferable to design the programme in-house but contract out certain aspects.

DISCUSSION

Why is market research important to marketing exeuctives? Try to think of several reasons.

NOTES

Chapter roundup

- Market research can take some of the risk out of marketing decision-making by providing information that can contribute to sound marketing decision making.
- This may be achieved in all elements of the marketing mix and, through involvement in problem formulation and solution-finding, market research becomes an integral part of the process of formulating marketing strategy.
- The collection, organisation and analysis of marketing information is the responsibility of a marketing information system.
- Market research can perform a variety of studies and makes use of both primary and secondary data sources.
- The growth of marketing information systems alongside the trend towards the computerisation of all records in a business can do much to simplify the organisation and accessibility of internal data.
- Research can be conducted either in-house or by market research companies which specialise in this form of consultancy. The latter offer a wide range of services from off-the-peg studies to tailor-made studies to meet the needs of individual clients.
- In selecting an outside agency account should be taken of the degree to which an in-depth knowledge of the employing company and its field is required and the agency's skill in the type of study to be undertaken.

Quick quiz

1. What categories of data would you expect to find on an effective internal database?
2. In a marketing research context, what does DSS stand for?
3. What are the four key strategic questions which organisations have to ask themselves?
4. What is primary research?
5. What is secondary research?
6. Define qualitative research.
7. How does quantitative research differ from qualitative research?
8. What is ad hoc research?
9. What is syndicated research?
10. List six issues to consider when using secondary data.
11. What do field service firms do?
12. Name two potential advantages of using an external agency.
13. Discuss two possible disadvantages to undertaking research in-house.

Answers to quick quiz

1. Customer service data, sales and marketing data, inbound and outbound logistics data and production and operations data. (See paragraph 1.1)

2 A decision support system. (para 1.1)

3 Where are we now, where do we want to be, how can we get there, how can we ensure arrival? (para 1.1)

4 Primary research involves the market researcher collecting data for a specific problem which has to be solved. (para 1.2)

5 Secondary research is based on data which for the most part has been collected for some other purpose. (para 1.2)

6 Qualitative research is not subject to quantification or quantitative analysis. (para 1.4)

7 Quantitative research involves studies that use mathematical analysis. (para 1.4)

8 Ad hoc research is a one-off which comes into being with an initial brief and ends with a report. (para 1.5)

9 Syndicated research is assembled by one organisation and then sold to a number of clients. (para 1.6)

10 Relevance, cost, availability, bias, statistical accuracy and sufficiency. (para 3.5)

11 Field service firms only collect survey data for corporate clients or research firms. (para 4)

12 External agencies may have the expertise which is not available in-house and they can provide an objective input without the bias which can result internally. (para 4.4)

13 There is a danger of overstretching current resources and thus adversely affecting other projects and there may be lack of appropriate facilities. (para 4.4)

Answer to activity

1 The result of, or answer to, this activity will depend on the item you have chosen.

Chapter 3 :
THE PROCESSES AND FORMS OF MARKET RESEARCH

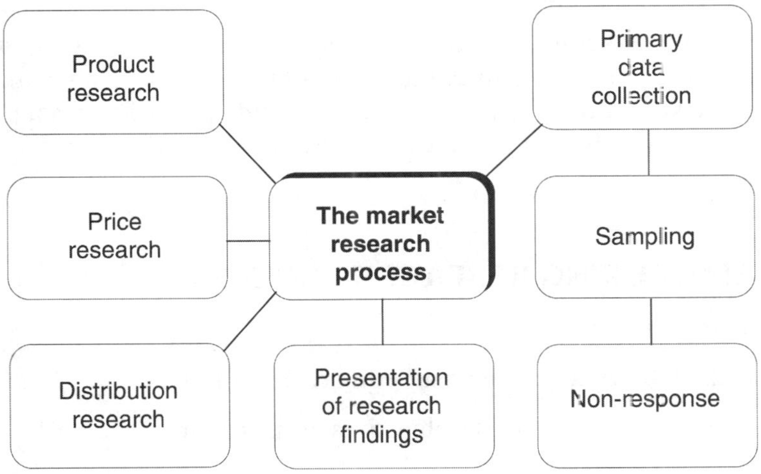

Introduction

This chapter is concerned with the process and main types of market research. It begins by defining the concept of market research and establishing the way in which the results of effective market research can be used as an input to decision making.

The actual stages in the market research process are then described and this is followed by a discussion of the role of the research brief. Primary data collection is defined and the range of primary techniques available to marketers is evaluated. The importance of effective sampling is then explained along with an in-depth discussion of sampling theory which includes the sampling frame, types of sampling and the calculation of sample sizes.

Non-response results from the fact that individuals chosen for the sample who actually respond are systematically different from those who are chosen and do not respond. Methods to reduce this phenomenon are discussed. The challenges of the effective presentation of research findings are noted and the chapter concludes with a discussion of product, price and finally distribution research.

Your objectives

In this chapter you will learn about the following:

(a) an overview of the market research process

(b) the principles of primary data collection

(c) the importance of sampling and non-response

(d) the presentation of research findings

(e) the factors involved in product, price and distribution research

1 INTRODUCTION

Alternative definitions of marketing research you may already be familiar with include the following.

(a) 'The objective gathering, recording and analysing of all facts about problems relating to the transfer and sales of goods and services from producer to consumer or user.' (*Chartered Institute of Marketing*)

(b) 'Systematic problem analysis, model-building and fact-finding for the purposes of improved decision making and control in the marketing of goods and services.' (*Kotler*)

Bear in mind that marketing research, however well organised, is no substitute for decision making. It can help to reduce the risks in business decision making, but it will not make the decision. Professional marketing depends partially on sound judgement and reliable information, but it also needs flair and creativity, the ability to see the wood from the trees.

2 THE MARKETING RESEARCH PROCESS

2.1 Webb's process

Webb suggests the following ten-step marketing research process.

Set the objectives of the research

↓

Define the research problem

↓

Assess the value of the research

↓

Construct the research proposal

↓

Specify data collection method(s)

↓

Specify technique(s) of measurement

↓

Select the sample

↓

Data collection

↓

Analysis of results

↓

Presentation of final report

***Step 1.* Set the objectives of the research**

Webb suggests that 'marketing research should reduce the need for a company to have to react, by making the organisation proactive, ie by sensitising management to oncoming threats and opportunities in a timely way, such that steps can be taken to avoid those threats or to take maximum advantage of the opportunities'.

> **Activity 1** **(15 minutes)**
>
> Your company manufactures cruelty-free beauty products (bubble bath, talcum powder and so on) for a number of supermarket chains. You have been given responsibility for finding out about the market for a new line of cruelty-free cosmetics (lipsticks, eyeshadow and so on).
>
> List the likely research objectives.

Step 2. **Define the research problem**

This vital step in the process establishes the area of research and the type(s) of data required. An accurate assessment of the environment in which the problem/opportunity exists must be made. This may necessitate building a model of the situation so as to allow researchers to put forward possible ways in which the research question may be answered.

Webb suggests the following summary of step 2.

Overall research objective

↓ ← Exploratory research

Definition of the research problem

External expert advice → ↓ ← Exploratory research

Development of the hypothesis

↓

Research proposal

Step 3. **Assess the value of the research**

This step involves carrying out a **cost/benefit exercise** on the desired information. The cost of a research project should always be less than the value of the information provided.

Step 4. **Construct the research proposal**

If the results of marketing research are to prove useful they must provide 'a true, life-like representation of the situation and not a distorted cartoon-like image' (Webb). Both client and researcher must agree on the exact constituents of the research proposal.

The category of research (exploratory, descriptive or causal) must be decided upon.

(a) **Exploratory research** is the least formal and most flexible, looking at the variables which impact on a situation.

(b) **Descriptive research** describes the variables.

(c) **Causal research** (the most formal and inflexible) looks at the relationships between the variables.

***Step 5.* Specify data collection methods**

Data can be collected from either primary or secondary data sources. Secondary data, which we looked at in detail in Chapter 2, is 'data neither collected directly by the user nor specifically for the user, often under conditions that are not well known to the user' (American Marketing Association). Primary data is information collected specifically for the study under consideration.

***Step 6.* Specify the techniques of measurement**

Measurement is the process of turning the factors under investigation into quantitative data. The scale will depend on both the data collection methods being used and the type of data required.

***Step 7.* Select the sample**

Time and money will preclude the researcher from conducting a census of each member of the population in which he/she has an interest unless the population is very small. The researcher must therefore examine a sample.

***Step 8.* Data collection**

This is when the researcher actually goes out and gets the data.

***Step 9.* Analysis of results**

The data collected in Step 8 will not answer the research problem defined in Step 2. The data will have to be processed into information. Note that certain types or levels of analysis are only possible if the data has been collected in a certain way and has been measured using certain instruments and scales of measurement. The researcher, prior to steps 6, 7 and 8 should therefore have decided upon the way in which the data should be analysed.

***Step 10.* Presentation of final report**

We will be looking at this aspect of the marketing research process in Section 6.

2.2 The research brief

The key to good research information, whether collected by an in house section or an external agency lies in the quality of the research brief. You need to be familiar with the content of a brief as you may be called upon to produce one in the examination.

The structure of a research brief will normally cover the following.

(a) **Background**. This covers relevant information about the company product, market place and the factors which have led to the current need for market information.

(b) **The problem**. This may be undertaken in conjunction with the researcher, but defining the problem carefully and agreeing objectives for the research is an essential first step in the research process and is central to the brief.

Too broad a definition leaves the researcher looking for 'everything and anything' whilst too narrow a view can blinker the researcher and limit the potential value of any research.

For example, the **objectives** of a research study into students' choices of text books might be as follows.

(a) Identify the main factors post-graduate students consider when selecting a text book.

(b) Assess the importance of the tutor as influencer in the decision-making process.

(c) Assess the importance of availability in the final selection of a text.

The brief should also contain any **constraining factors** relevant to the process. These can involve time scale, budget or the degree of secrecy necessary.

3 PRIMARY DATA COLLECTION

Definition

> **Primary data** is data collected by or specifically for the user (as opposed to secondary data).

3.1 Off the peg research

Off the peg research may consist of syndicated research or omnibus research.

(a) **Syndicated research** is collected by a research organisation on behalf of a number of organisations requiring the research. Syndicated research is usually too expensive for any individual organisation to collect. The research data is sold on to all the firms who have a use for it and hence the cost of data generation and collection is shared.

(b) **Omnibus research** is where regular surveys of defined populations are undertaken. The research agency doing the work may make the service available as an 'omnibus' for other organisations to climb aboard. Each organisation climbing aboard the omnibus may be allowed to ask a few specific questions.

3.2 Made to measure research

'**Made to measure' research** is the most **expensive** type of research to undertake. The organisation requiring information decides what it is that it exactly wants to know. The organisation then has two choices.

(a) To carry out the research itself
(b) To buy in the services of a research agency

Although it is the most expensive type of research to undertake, it is also the most useful type of research since it is '**customised**'.

3.3 Field research methods

Research in the field is concerned with the generation and collection of original research data.

Field research is the collection of primary data. Such collection methods can be divided into three types.

NOTES

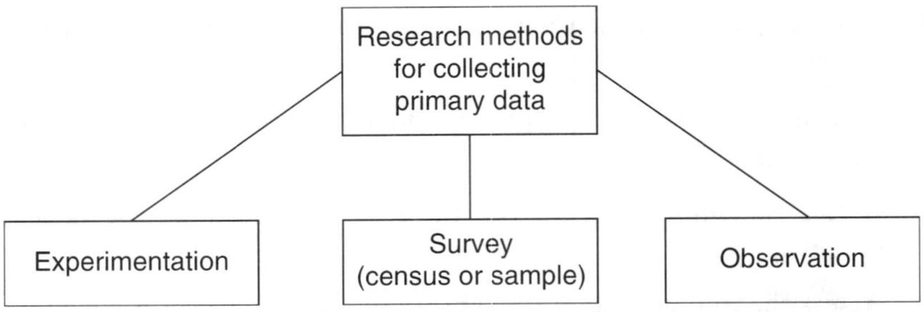

The most well known of these is probably the **market survey**, with the stereotyped image of a lady with a clipboard. Each of the techniques has its particular strengths and the choice of approach is determined by the nature of the problem and the business.

3.4 Experimentation

In a **controlled experiment**, a controlled research environment is established and selected stimuli are then introduced. To the extent that 'outside' factors can be eliminated from the environment the observed effects can be measured and related to each stimulus. Controlled experiments have been used to find the best advertising campaign, the best price level, the best incentive scheme, the best sales training method and so on.

When experiments are conducted in more realistic market settings, results are less reliable because of the researcher's inability to control outside factors. Nevertheless, the local market reaction to a new product, for example, is often a prerequisite to a national launch. This is known as a **test market**.

DISCUSSION

Competitive action is one of the great risks and uncertainties of the traditional test market. Once a major competitor recognises what is happening it may decide to make an effort to kill the test by spending heavy marketing funds on advertising and coupons to distort the test results.

3.5 Survey (census or sample)

The **survey** approach involves asking questions of the target market or population. In marketing research for consumer goods, it will be impossible to obtain data from every consumer in the market. To obtain data, it is therefore usually necessary to obtain a **sample** to provide an estimate of the characteristics of the entire 'population'. The accuracy of the sample will depend on the following.

(a) **How** the sample is taken
(b) The amount of **variability** in the population
(c) The **size** of the sample

The larger the sample, the greater the likelihood that the sample will provide an accurate reflection of the population as a whole. Questions can be limited and highly structured, in the form of questionnaires delivered by post, telephone or in person.

On the other hand, questions can be asked in great depth of a relatively small sample. This is **qualitative or motivational research** and provides information on behaviour and attitudes.

3.6 Observation

Observation involves the personal or mechanical (eg video) monitoring of selected activities. It records actions as they occur and thus there is no lack of accuracy caused by a respondent's faulty recollection of their past actions or inadequate estimate of future ones.

Three conditions must usually exist if the observation method is to be effectively carried out:

1. The event must be observable: attitudes, motives and other mental activities are difficult to record
2. The event must occur frequently or be predictable
3. The event must be completed over a short period of time

Observation is often used in shopping studies, especially in retail outlets, when the customer is looking at the shelves and deciding what to buy. Observations of the in-store environment can include distribution, shelf price, shelf facings, shelf location, display activity, presence of point-of-purchase material.

Observation within both households and stores typically requires the setting up of a panel, making it subject to sampling difficulties and maintaining participation. Another problem is the quality of the data obtained.

4 SAMPLING

Conducting a survey by sampling is one of the most important subjects in marketing research. In most practical situations a population will be too large to carry out a complete survey and only a sample will be examined. The results from the sample are used to estimate the perceptions of the whole population.

Definition

> **Sampling** involves taking a limited number of a large population so that by studying the part something may be learnt about the whole. The population is all those people who have the characteristics in which the researcher is interested.

Occasionally a population is small enough that all of it can be examined: for example, the examination results of one class of students. When all of the population is examined, the survey is called a **census**. This type of survey is quite rare, however.

4.1 Why use sampling?

You may think that using a sample is very much a compromise, but you should consider the following points.

(a) In practice, a 100% survey (a census) never achieves the completeness required.

(b) It can be shown mathematically that once a certain sample size has been reached, very little extra accuracy is gained by examining more items.

(c) It is possible to ask more questions with a sample.

(d) The higher cost of a census may exceed the value of results.

NOTES

Activity 2 **(5 minutes)**

What do you see as the advantages of sampling over complete coverage?

4.2 Selecting a representative sample

We need to be sure of the following.

(a) Our sample is not **unrepresentative or biased**. If the characteristics of the sample are different from those of the population, then the inferences we draw about the population from studying the sample will be unreliable.

(b) The **cost and time** involved in selecting the sample produces the required benefits of **usefulness and accuracy**.

4.3 Biased samples, or sources of sampling error

Bias, or **sampling error**, can occur for the following reasons.

(a) Poorly defined or communicated **research objectives** leading to the wrong information being obtained

(b) **Measurement** errors, because the question posed by the researcher to elicit certain information produces different information entirely

(c) **Badly-defined population** (For instance, the population for a survey concerning purchase of soccer strips should not be 'young males 10-18' but should include young females, plus parents and grandparents, who actually pay)

(d) Inaccurate **sampling frame** (See below)

(e) **Unrepresentative random sample**, usually because the sample size is too small (This is also discussed below)

(f) **Selection error** where non-random sampling is used (If a researcher has a quota of, say, 40 people to interview, and she positions herself outside a sports club at 5pm, she is likely to get 40 people of similar age and interest who are not representative of the population as a whole)

(g) Errors caused by **non-response** (See Section 5 below)

(h) **Mistaken responses**, particularly in answer to badly-worded questions or because the respondent is embarrassed

(i) **Data processing** or input errors

(j) **Collection errors** caused by the interviewers' preconceptions and prejudices when recording qualitative data

(k) **Data analysis** errors, were errors are introduced when data is subjected to further statistical analysis

4.4 Sampling frames

Definition

A **sampling frame** is the list, index, map or any other population record from which the sample can be selected.

Every factor of the survey design is influenced by the sampling frame - the population coverage, the stratifications that are used, the method of sample selection and so on.

(a) Does it adequately cover the population to be surveyed?

(b) Is it complete? Are all members of the population on it? Is it accurate and as up-to-date as possible?

(c) No items should appear more than once.

(d) Is it arranged in a convenient way for sampling? is it readily accessible?

No frame is likely to completely satisfy all the above criteria.

Types of sampling frame

These can be broadly classified as follows.

(a) **Lists of individuals**. Such lists, either of the whole population or of the groups within it can be used. Examples include the electoral register, the lists of members of professional bodies and lists of company employees.

(b) **Complete census returns**. Unfortunately the manner in which the data is collected and processed tends to prevent its use as a frame.

(c) **Returns from an earlier survey**. How useful previous surveys are depends on the questions asked in the original survey and if the data is up to date.

(d) **Lists of dwellings**. Council tax lists are useful as a frame for obtaining samples of dwellings.

(e) **Large scale maps**. Ordnance Survey maps have a grid system which enables areas to be broken down into suitably sized blocks. Sometimes a problem is the availability of up-to-date large scale maps, there having been much town and city re-development in recent years.

The two frames most generally available are council tax or valuation lists and electoral registers. These can be stratified along ACORN geodemographic lines to assist accurate stratified random sampling. An obvious sampling frame is the self-accumulated list: a list already in the hands of the marketing firm. It may include names and addresses of those who have made purchases, had deliveries made, used credit cards or registered at trade shows.

DISCUSSION

What are the problems associated with using a telephone directory for a certain area as a sampling frame of the people who live in that area?

Activity 3 **(15 minutes)**

Locate any recent newspaper or magazine in which survey results are reported. Try to ascertain whether this survey was based on a census, a random sample or a non-random sample.

4.5 Sampling theory

Instead of looking at distributions occurring as a result of considering a whole 'population' of items, we can now construct probability distributions, known as

sampling distributions, for samples rather than whole populations. And when we start taking fairly large random samples from a population and measuring the mean of those samples, we find an uncanny relationship with the normal distribution.

A sampling distribution of the mean has the following important properties.

(a) It is very close to being **normally distributed**. The larger the sample the more closely will the sampling distribution approximate to a normal distribution.

(b) The mean of the sampling distribution is the same as the population mean, μ.

(c) The sampling distribution has a standard deviation which is called the standard error (se) of the mean.

From our knowledge of the properties of a normal distribution, together with the rule that sample means are normally distributed around the true population mean, with a standard deviation equal to the standard error, we can predict the following.

(a) 68% of all sample means will be within 1 standard error of the population mean.

(b) 95% of all sample means will be within 1.96 standard errors of the population mean.

4.6 Deciding on a sample size

What this means is that if you take a reasonably large sample of representative items and find out something about them you can be confident up to a certain level that something that is true of the sample is true of the *whole* population of items.

Suppose, for example, you measured the height of 100 mature labradors and found that the average was, say, 30cm with a standard deviation of 2cm. You could then be 95% certain that the average height of all mature labradors in your market was in the range of $30 \pm (1.96 \times 2) = 26.08$cm to 33.92cm.

In practice you will probably be keen to leave the figurework to marketing research specialists or company statisticians. The important thing is that you understand enough of the jargon to appreciate the scientific basis of such an analysis rather than being blinded by it.

4.7 Practical points regarding sample sizes

Although it is possible to calculate an ideal sample size from a statistical point of view, administrative and practical factors have to be taken into account. These factors are summarised below.

(a) The amount of **money and time** available
(b) The **aims** of the survey
(c) The **degree of precision** required
(d) The number of **sub-samples** required

A sample therefore only need be **large enough to be reasonably representative** of the population.

The aim of sampling is to get accurate and usable data at a reasonable cost within a reasonable timescale. The two main sampling methods are random (probability) sampling and quota (non-probability) sampling.

4.8 Random sampling

Definition

> A **simple random sample** is a sample selected in such a way that every item of the population has an equal and known chance of being selected.

Random samples are not perfect because they may be highly unrepresentative. It is important to appreciate that random selection does not guarantee that the sample will be free from bias - only that the method of selection is free from bias.

Random selection methods are, however, an essential part of the protection against selection error. 'Random' is not equivalent to 'haphazard'; random sampling is a careful, systematic procedure which generates data which is statistically valid and suitable for further statistical analysis.

4.9 Stratified random sampling

In theory, **stratification** uses knowledge of the population to increase the representativeness and precision of the sample. For example, a random sample of Europeans could result in the sample all being Germans. We would therefore select from each country in proportion to its population. Populations can be stratified in many ways such as by sex, age groups, regions and so on.

4.10 Multi-stage random sampling

To reduce the distance a researcher would have to travel which would probably result from simple random sampling, **multi-stage sampling** can be used. The procedure is simple. The country is divided into areas, say counties, and three or four of these are selected at random. These large areas are divided and sub-divided until a sample of small areas is obtained and number of householders can be selected at random in each small area.

Area sampling is basically a form of random sampling in which maps are used in place of lists. This is common in the USA where cities are often laid out in regular patterns and roads dividing blocks make convenient area boundaries. An alternative is to place a grid over a map, number the squares and take a random sample of them.

4.11 Quota sampling

Definition

> **Quota sampling** is used to avoid the time and expense necessary to search for individuals chosen by a random sample. This method of sampling differs fundamentally from random methods in that once the general breakdown is decided (such as how many men and women, how many people in each age group and social class are to be included) the interviewers are left to select the persons to fit this framework.

Opinion on the validity of quota sampling is divided. Statisticians tend to criticise the method for its theoretical weakness, but market and opinion researchers defend it for its cheapness and administrative convenience.

NOTES

The quotas given to the interviewers need to be arranged in such a way that for the whole country and maybe even for each region, the sexes, age groups, and social classes are represented in the correct proportions on the basis of available data. **Age** and **sex** present few problems but **social class** has always been one of the most dubious areas of marketing research investigation. 'Class' is a highly personal and subjective phenomenon, to the extent that some people are 'class conscious' or class aware and have a sense of belonging to a particular group. JICNAR's social grade definitions (A-E) has been the system most frequently used to classify people into social classes for marketing purposes.

DISCUSSION

The major problem with the quota method of sampling is that interviewers are allowed discretion in choosing the individual respondents within the quota categories.

% of population	**JICNAR** Social Grade	Social Status	**Characteristics** of occupation (of head of household)
3	A	Upper middle class	Higher managerial/professional eg lawyers, directors
13	B	Middle class	Intermediate managerial/administrative/ professional eg teachers, managers, computer operators, sales managers
23	C_1	Lower middle class	Supervisory, clerical, junior managerial/ administrative/professional eg foremen, shop assistants
32	C_2	Skilled working class	Skilled manual labour eg electricians, mechanics
19	D	Working class	Semi-skilled manual labour eg machine operators
			Unskilled manual labour eg cleaning, waiting tables, assembly
10	E	Lowest level of subsistence	State pensioners, widows (no other earner), casual workers

DISCUSSION

Statistical laws have established that no matter how large the population being studied, the size of the sample is the main factor that determines the expected range of error in a probability sample.

4.12 Sample sizes

We saw above that the size of a sample is critical to whether or not the results of that sample can be taken to be valid for the population as a whole. It is common sense that a sample of, say, 3 people is not going to be representative of a total population of 100,000

BPP PUBLISHING

NOTES

people. To understand how a valid sample size can be decided on, researchers use **statistical techniques** involved in sampling theory, such as the normal distribution.

4.13 The normal distribution

In your earlier studies you will have seen frequency and probability distributions and the most common example, the **normal distribution,** which is often applied to continuous variables.

(a) A frequency distribution shows how many times each particular value occurs in a set of items.

(b) A probability distribution simply replaces actual numbers (frequencies) with proportions of the total.

For example the marks out of ten awarded to a sample of 50 students might be as follows.

Marks out of 10	*Number of students (frequency distribution)*	*Proportion or probability (probability distribution)*	
0	0	0/50 =	0.00
1	0	0/50 =	0.00
2	1	1/50 =	0.02
3	2	2/50 =	0.04
4	4	4/50 =	0.08
5	10	10/50 =	0.20
6	15	15/50 =	0.30
7	10	10/50 =	0.20
8	6	6/50 =	0.12
9	2	2/50 =	0.04
10	0	0/50 =	0.00
	50		1.00

Examples of **continuous variables** include the following.

(a) The heights of people. The height of a person need not be an exact number of centimetres, but can be anything within a range of possible figures.

(b) The temperature of a room. It need not be an exact number or degrees, but can fall anywhere within a range of possible values.

The normal distribution can also apply to discrete variables which can take many possible values. For example, the volume of sales, in units, of a product might be any whole number in the range 100 – 5,000 units. There are so many possibilities within this range that the variable is, for all practical purposes, continuous.

Whether for continuous or discrete variables, the normal distribution can be drawn as a bell-shaped curve. Compare the curve below with the probability distribution column in paragraph 4.13 above.

NOTES

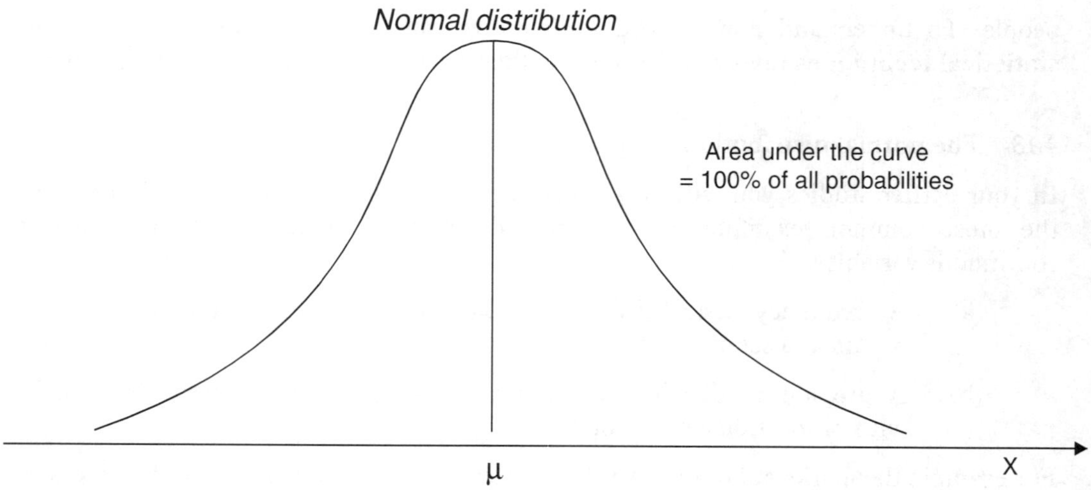

The normal curve is symmetrical. The left hand side of the area under the curve to the left of μ is the mirror image of the right hand side.

- μ (the lower case Greek letter, mu) is the average of the distribution of the population as a whole
- $\bar{x}$ is the mean or average of the distribution of a sample

Because it is a probability distribution, the area under the curve totals exactly 100%.

4.14 The standard deviation

For any normal distribution, the dispersion around the mean of the frequency of occurrences can be measured exactly in terms of the **standard deviation**. This is the most important measure of spread in statistics, measuring the spread about the mean. It is denoted by σ or s.

(a) σ (the lower case Greek letter, sigma) is used for the standard deviation of a **population** of values (all cola-consuming households, say).

(b) The symbol s is used for the standard deviation of a **sample** of values (cola-consuming households in Swindon, say).

As the entire frequency curve represents all the possible outcomes and their frequencies of occurrence and the normal curve is symmetrical, 50% of occurrences must have a value greater than the mean value, and 50% of occurrences must have a value less than the mean value.

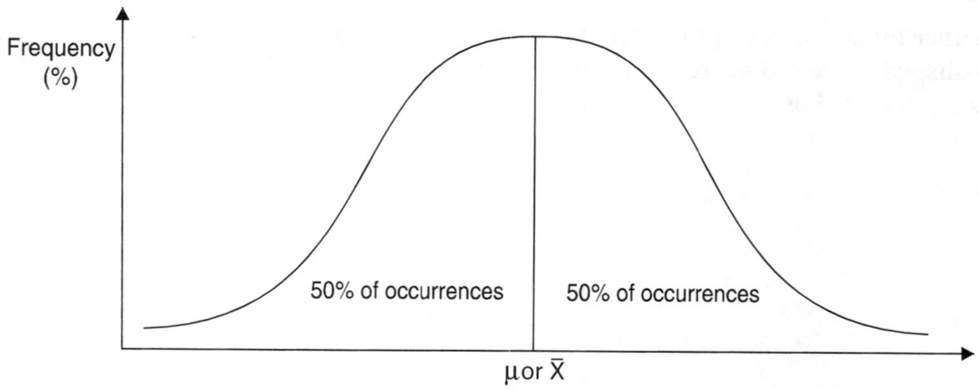

It is known that 68% of frequencies have a value within one standard deviation either side of the mean.

Thus if a normal distribution has a mean of 80 and a standard deviation of 3, 68% of the total frequencies would occur within the range ± one standard deviation from the mean, that is, within the range 77 – 83.

Since the curve is symmetrical, 34% of the values must fall in the range 77 – 80 and 34% in the range 80 – 83.

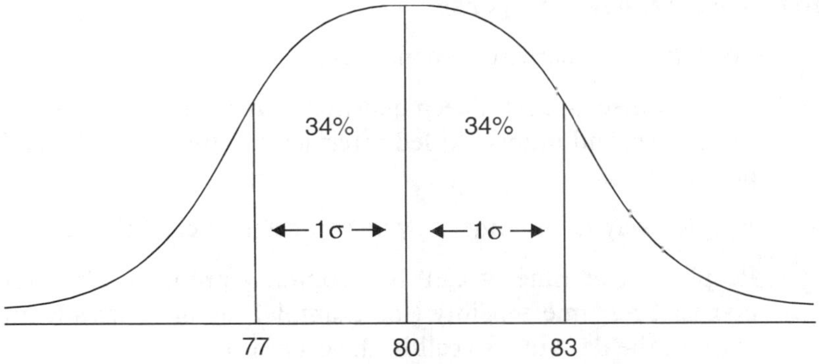

It is known that 95% of the frequencies in a normal distribution occur in the range ± 1.96 standard deviations from the mean.

In our example, when $\mu = 80$, and $\sigma = 3$, 95% of the frequencies in the distribution would occur in the range

$$80 \pm 1.96 \times 3$$
$$= 80 \pm 5.88 \text{ (the range 74.12 to 85.88)}$$

5 NON-RESPONSE

Non-response (of a sample member) cannot be avoided. It can, however, (apart from in mail surveys) be kept at a reasonable level. Experience has shown that the non-response part of a survey often differs considerably from the rest. The types of non-response are as follows.

(a) **Units outside the population**. Where the field investigation shows that units no longer exist (eg demolished houses), these units should be considered as outside the population and should be subtracted from the sample size before calculating the non-response rate.

(b) **Unsuitable for interview**. This is where people who should be interviewed are incapable of supplying responses perhaps through such factors as language barriers or physical infirmity.

(c) **Movers**. People who have changed address since the list was drawn up cannot be interviewed.

(d) **Refusals**. Some people refuse to co-operate.

(e) **Away from home**. People might be away from home for longer than the field work period and call-back might not be possible.

(f) **Out at time of call.**

An article in the *Financial Times* highlighted the effect of social change on the level of non-response. Rising crime means that householders may be afraid to answer the door to strangers and, with women increasingly looking for regular employment, it is becoming more and more difficult to find the standard type of person who used to be the backbone of fieldwork.

Another problem pointed out in the article is that of 'data fatigue', as the public becomes tired of filling in questionnaires and more cynical about the real motives of 'market researchers' because of 'sugging' (selling under the guise of research) and 'frugging' (fundraising under the guise of research).

5.1 How to deal with non-response

The interviewer can try to increase response rate.

(a) To minimise 'refusals', keep questionnaires as brief as possible, use financial incentives, and highly skilled interviewers. Refusal rates tend to be low (3-5 per cent).

(b) People 'away from home' may be contacted later, if this is possible.

(c) People 'out at time of call' is a common problem. The researcher should plan calling time sensibly (for example, as most breadwinners are out at work in the day-time so call in the evening).

6 THE PRESENTATION OF RESEARCH FINDINGS

Once the research process has been completed, the researcher will usually present the findings in a face-to-face session, giving managers the opportunity to ask questions about the results. It takes time and skill to convert the findings into a well-structured oral presentation.

It is very likely that the research must be organised in report form as well. It is always a mistake simply to prepare the oral presentation from the already written report, since the conventions of report writing are quite different from the criteria that govern effective presentations.

The basic requirement is for a report and presentation that can be believed and trusted by everyone who will be affected by the research. The solution to a particular research problem should produce greater efficiency, lower costs and more benefits for the organisation. The presenter of the research results has to convince the audience that the research findings can be acted on for their own benefit. A written report needs to be put together so that interest and belief develop throughout its reading, and the recommended action appears as a natural outcome.

It may be beneficial to delete less important questions in order to emphasise the basic problem. Constant attention to the basic problem and its recommendations will make the study and its presentation more useable and interesting in the minds of the listeners and/or the readers of the final presentation. Presenters have the best chance of success if they have planned their research well and meet the expectations of their listeners.

EXAMPLE

Many growers and retailers, had been misled by surveys suggesting that 70 per cent of consumers would purchase organic vegetables and fruit. In the event only 11 per cent are doing so, the remainder have demonstrated by their actions that *behaviour* and *attitudes* are not necessarily synonymous. Perhaps they had not seriously considered the possibility that organic produce would cost more or that it would look less attractive; quite possibly they gave 'ethically correct' responses when completing a questionnaire, but had no real intention of acting differently.

NOTES

7 PRODUCT RESEARCH

Definition

Product research is concerned with the product itself, whether new, improved or already on the market, and customer reactions to it.

This aspect of marketing research attempts to make product **research and development** customer orientated.

New product ideas may come from anywhere - from research and development personnel, marketing and sales personnel, competitors, customers, outside scientific or technological discoveries, individual employees or executives and so on. Research and development is carried out by company scientists, engineers or designers; much wasted effort can be saved for them, however, if new ideas are first tested in the market, in other words if product research is carried out.

7.1 The process of product research

New ideas are first screened by a range of specialists (market researchers, designers, research and development staff and so on) and are rejected if they have any of the following characteristics.

(a) They have a low profit potential or insufficient market potential.
(b) They have a high cost and involve high risk.
(c) They do not conform to company objectives.
(d) They cannot be produced and distributed with the available resources.

Ideas which survive the screening process should be product tested and possibly test marketed. Product research also includes the need to keep the product range of a company's goods under review for the following reasons.

(a) **Variety reduction** may be desirable to reduce production costs, or when there are insufficient sales of certain items in the product range to justify continued production. In practice, there is often strong resistance, both from within a company and from customers, to the elimination of products from the market.

(b) **Product diversification** increases a product range by introducing new items, and a wide range of products can often improve a company's market image.

(c) **Segmentation** is a policy which aims at securing a new class of customers for an existing range of products, perhaps by making some adjustments to the products to appeal to the new segments.

Product research also involves finding **new uses for existing products**, and this could be considered a means of extending a product range. The uses for plastics and nylon, for example, have been extended rapidly in the past as a result of effective research.

7.2 The product life cycle

The profitability and sales of a product can be expected to change over time. The **product life cycle** (PLC) is an attempt to recognise distinct stages in a product's sales history.

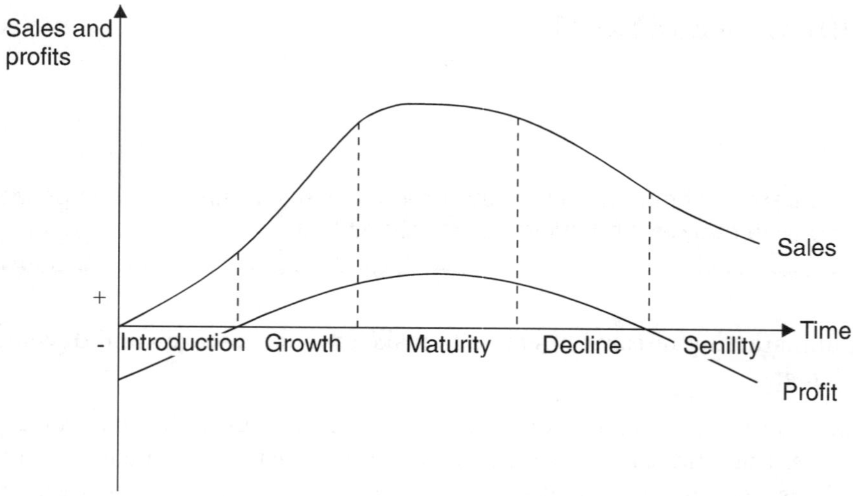

Information about the stage a product has reached in its life cycle may be an important indication of how long its market will continue and how soon new product developments must be introduced to replace it.

(a) There ought to be a **regular review** of existing products, as a part of marketing management responsibilities.

(b) Information should be obtained about the likely future of each product and sources of such information might be as follows.

   (i) An analysis of past sales and profit trends
   (ii) The history of other products
   (iii) Market research
   (iv) If possible, an analysis of competitors

   The future of each product should be estimated in terms of both sales revenue and profits.

Once the assessments have been made, decisions must be taken about what to do with each product.

Activity 4 **(20 minutes)**

Locate a marketing/design publication that describes how any new product was developed. Summarise and evaluate the product research conducted prior to the launch of this product.

8 PRICE RESEARCH

Price sensitivity will vary amongst purchasers. Those who can pass on the cost of purchases will be least sensitive and will respond more to other elements of the marketing mix.

(a) Provided that it fits the corporate budget, the business traveller will be more concerned about the level of service and quality of food when looking for an hotel than price. In contrast, a family on holiday are likely to be very price sensitive when choosing an overnight stay.

(b) In industrial marketing the purchasing manager is likely to be more price sensitive than the engineer who might be the actual user of new equipment that is being sourced. The engineer and purchasing manager are using different criteria in making the choice. The engineer places product characteristics as first priority, the purchasing manager is more price oriented.

8.1 Finding out about price sensitivity

Research on price sensitivity of customers has demonstrated the following.

(a) Customers have a concept of a '**just price**' - a feel for what is about the right price to pay for a commodity.

(b) Unless a regular purchase is involved, customers search for price information before buying, becoming price aware when wanting to buy but forgetting soon afterwards.

(c) Customers will buy at what they consider to be a bargain price without full regard for need and actual price.

EXAMPLE

Bell Telephones in the US were concerned about the lack of sales of extension telephones. When, as part of a market research survey, customers were asked to name the actual price of an extension telephone, most overestimated it. By keeping the existing price but running an advertising campaign featuring it, Bell were able to increase sales as customers became aware of the lower than anticipated price.

8.2 Factors affecting pricing decisions

(a) **Intermediaries' objectives**

If an organisation distributes products or services to the market through independent intermediaries, the objectives of these intermediaries have an effect on the pricing decision. Thus conflict over price can arise between suppliers and intermediaries which may be difficult to resolve.

(b) **Competitors' actions and reactions**

An organisation, in setting prices, sends out signals to **rivals**. These rivals are likely to react in some way. In some industries (such as petrol retailing) pricing moves in unison; in others, price changes by one supplier may initiate a price war, with each supplier undercutting the others.

(c) **Suppliers**

If an organisation's **suppliers** notice that the prices for an organisation's products are rising, they may seek a rise in the price for their supplies to the organisation.

(d) **Inflation**

In periods of inflation the organisation's prices may need to change in order to reflect increases in the prices of supplies, labour, rent and so on. Such changes may be needed to keep relative (real) prices unchanged (this is the process of prices being adjusted for the rate of inflation).

(e) **Quality connotations**

In the absence of other information, customers tend to judge quality by price. Thus a price change may send signals to customers concerning the quality of the product. A rise may be taken to indicate improvements, a reduction may signal reduced quality.

(f) **New product pricing**

Most pricing decisions for existing products relate to price changes. Such changes have a reference point from which to move (the existing price). But when a new product is introduced for the first time there may be no such reference points; pricing decisions are most difficult to make in such circumstances. It may be possible to seek alternative reference points, such as the price in another market where the new product has already been launched, or the price set by a competitor.

(g) **Income effects**

In times of rising incomes, price may become a less important marketing variable than, for instance, product quality or convenience of access. When income levels are falling and/or unemployment levels rising, price will become a much more important marketing variable.

EXAMPLE

In the recession of the early 1990s, the major grocery multiples such as Tesco, Sainsbury, Safeway and Waitrose, who steadily moved up-market in the 1980s with great success leaving the 'pile it high, sell it cheap' philosophy behind, suddenly found bargain stores such as Foodgiant, Aldi, Kwik Save and Netto a more serious threat. They responded by cutting prices on 'staples' (such as baked beans) to draw consumers into their stores. This was backed up by continued product development, customer service pledges and loyalty cards.

---

9 DISTRIBUTION RESEARCH

Place as an element in the marketing mix is largely concerned with the selection of distribution channels and with the physical distribution of goods.

In selecting an **appropriate marketing channel** for a product, a firm has the following options.

(a) **Selling direct to the customer**. Consumer goods can be sold direct with mail order catalogues, telephone selling, door-to-door selling of consumer goods, or selling 'off the page' with magazine advertisements. Industrial goods are commonly sold direct by sales representatives, visiting industrial buyers.

(b) **Selling through agents or recognised distributors**, who specialise in the firm's products. For example, a chain of garden centres might act as specialist stockists and distributors for the products of just one garden shed manufacturer.

(c) **Selling through wholesalers** or to retailers who stock and sell the goods and brands of several rival manufacturers.

Some organisations might use channels of distribution for their goods which are unprofitable to use, and which should either be abandoned in favour of more profitable channels, or made profitable by giving some attention to cutting costs or increasing minimum order sizes.

NOTES

As well as **cost and profitability analyses**, distribution research can embrace the following.

(a) To what extent is the distribution channel **actually working**? In other words, how effective is the distributor at delivering products to customers?

(b) To what extent is the distributor favouring its own brand or competitors' products over your own, in terms of shelf space and positioning and in-store promotions.

This latter point is important as own-brand products are becoming increasingly competitive with branded goods. Supermarket chains promote their own brand extensively.

Normal **market research techniques** can be used to assess the effectiveness of distribution channels. Questions in market research questionnaires can ask how easy it is for customers to obtain products and information, and where they are obtained. An example might be a newspaper readership questionnaire, which will ask where the customer acquires the newspaper (eg delivered at home, or bought on way to work).

Chapter roundup

- Market research can be defined as the objective gathering, recording and analysing of all facts about problems relating to the transfer and sales of goods and services from producer to consumer or user.
- Market research plays an important role in helping to solve problems and improve decision-making by producing information that helps to allay uncertainty.
- Like all project work, market research can be quite complex and requires considerable planning, scheduling and control.
- Primary data is data collected by or specifically for the user
- It has been consistently demonstrated that a relatively small but carefully selected sample can quite accurately reflect the characteristics of the population from which it is drawn.
- Factors such as time, money, objectives and degree of precision required all affect sample sizes.
- A good knowledge and understanding of the audience are essential for good reporting. The presenter of a report should know in advance who will receive copies of the written report or who will attend an oral presentation.

Quick quiz

1 What are the first four stages of Webb's marketing research process?

2 What should SMART objectives be?

3 What two issues does a research brief usually cover?

4 What is an omnibus survey?

5 What is meant by the term field research?

6 Define sampling.

BPP PUBLISHING

7 Suggest two reasons as to why a sampling error can arise.

8 What is a sampling frame?

9 What is a simple random sample?

10 Name three types of non-response.

11 What new product characteristics might cause it to be rejected at the screening stage?

12 What are the five stages in the product life cycle?

13 Name three factors that affect pricing decisions.

14 What are the three key distribution options?

Answers to quick quiz

1 Set objectives, define the research problem, assess the value of the research and construct the research proposal. (See paragraph 2.1)

2 Specific, measurable, actionable, reasonable and timescaled. (para 2.1)

3 Background and the problem. (para 2.2)

4 Omnibus research occurs where regular surveys of defined populations are undertaken. (para 3.1)

5 Research in the field is concerned with the generation and collection of original research data. (para 3.3)

6 Sampling involves taking a limited number of a large population so that by studying the part something may be learnt about the whole. (para 4)

7 Poorly defined research objectives can lead to the wrong information being obtained and an unrepresentative random sample may be selected. (para 4.3)

8 A sampling frame is the list, index, map or any other population record from which the sample can be selected. (para 4.4)

9 A simple random sample is a sample selected in such a way that every item of the population has an equal and known chance of being selected. (para 4.8)

10 Those who are unsuitable for interview, those who have changed addresses and those who refuse to co-operate. (para 5)

11 Low profit potential, insufficient market potential, high cost and so high risk, do not conform to company objectives, cannot be produced and distributed with the available resources. (para 7.1)

12 Introduction, growth, maturity, decline, senility. (para 7.2)

13 Intermediaries' objectives, competitors' actions and reactions, and suppliers. (para 8.2)

14 Direct selling to the customer, eg direct mail; selling through agents or distributors; selling through wholesalers or retailers. (para 9)

NOTES

Answers to activities

1 Research objectives need to be SMART.

Research objectives	Discover re Activity:
Specific	Size of market for *cruelty-free* cosmetics not cosmetics in general
Measurable	Respective market share in percentage terms of leading players
Actionable	Price range within which consumers will buy
Reasonable	A defined number of preferred colours
Timescaled	Information within 3 months so product can be marketed for Christmas

2 It saves time
It can focus on key items
It is cheaper
It can be regarded as mathematically accurate if done properly

3 The result of, or answer to, this activity will depend on the item you have chosen.

4 The result of, or answer to, this activity will depend on the item you have chosen.

Chapter 4 :
MARKET RESEARCH TECHNIQUES

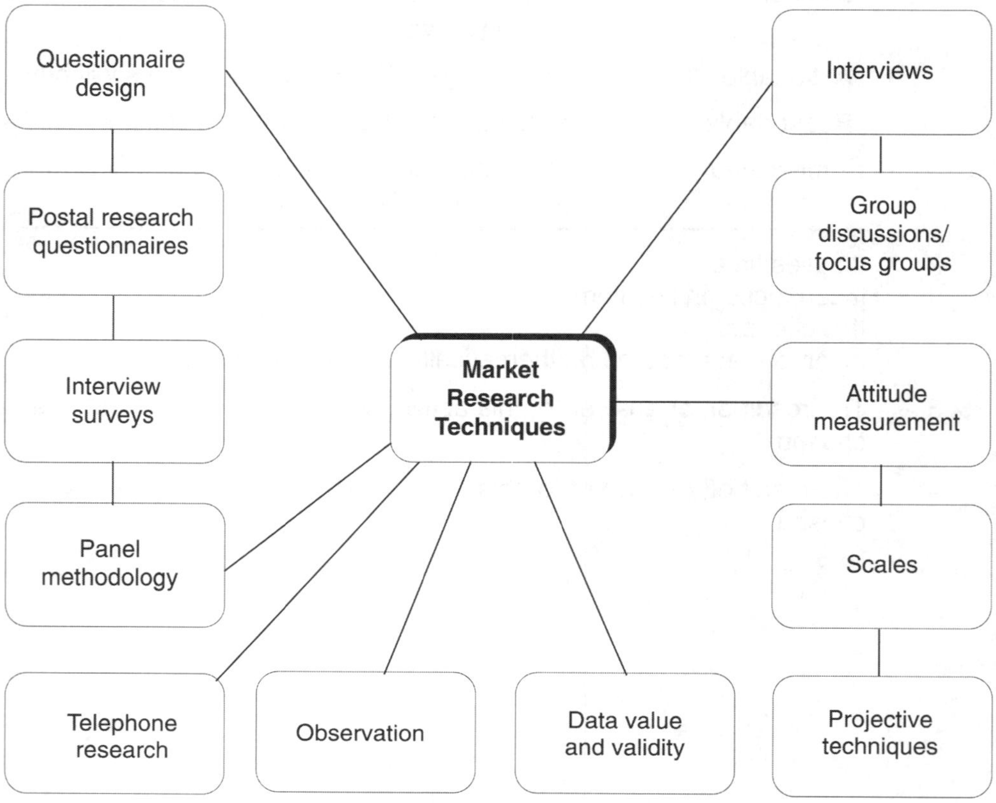

Introduction

This chapter concentrates on the tools that can be used to capture market research information. Each tool has its own advantages and disadvantages and as such there is no perfect research tool, but the same tool may be used in widely different settings and for different purposes.

The first tool to be evaluated is interviewing, and this includes fully structured, semi-structured, unstructured and finally depth interviews. This is followed by group discussions and focus groups where the emphasis is on group dynamics and the skill of the moderator.

The challenges of effective attitude measurement and the measurement scales that can assist in this task are evaluated next. Project techniques are then discussed with a range of tools such as word-association, sentence and story completion, cartoon tests and third person techniques being illustrated.

Questionnaire design, along with postal and interview surveys are next. A discussion of the application of technology in managing data capture is noted in the section on scanning with reference to panel methodology. The advantages and disadvantages of panel research are then illustrated and observation techniques are discussed.

The chapter concludes with a section on data value and validity.

NOTES

Your objectives

In this chapter you will learn about the following:

(a) the role of interviews and group discussions

(b) the importance of attitude measurement techniques such as self-reporting scales and projective techniques

(c) the principles of effective questionnaire design

(d) an overview of postal research questionnaires and interview surveys

(e) the scope of panel methodology, telephone research and observation

(f) the challenges of establishing data value and validity

1 INTRODUCTION

Having looked at some of the underlying methodological issues concerned with the design and execution of a marketing research project, we are now going to explore the range of data capture techniques or research tools which may be used.

Often the same instrument may be used in widely different settings and for different purposes. Questionnaires, for instance, are used not only in survey research, but also in some forms of qualitative research, continuous research and in a wide range of experimental scenarios.

As we shall see, the relationship between researcher and respondent may be direct (as in face-to-face interviews or telephone contacts) or indirect and even remote (as in postal questionnaires or in-home scanning).

Each method of data capture has its own characteristics and advantages or disadvantages. By the time you have read and absorbed this chapter you should be in a much better position to make informed judgements about matching data-gathering techniques to research objectives.

2 INTERVIEWS

Interviews may be either face-to-face or at-a-distance, (via a postal questionnaire or over the telephone). The main advantage personal contact methods have over other methods is that they normally achieve a **high response rate** and that the likely level of error being introduced into the research results is low.

Definition

> An **interview** has been defined as a conversation directed to a definite purpose other than satisfaction in the conversation itself.

2.1 Fully structured interviews

A fully structured interview is controlled through the use of a **structured questionnaire**. The responses to a fully structured interview have been pre-determined by the research design. All respondents are given exactly the same questions and are able to exercise exactly the same responses.

This type of research is most useful in providing the researcher with **quantitative data** such as 'so many people said this, or think that or do this'. Fully structured questions should be easy to ask and easy for respondents to answer.

The major limitation of fully structured questionnaires is in their **structure**. For example, if the researcher wanted to know which factors appeared to be most important in making choices about holiday destinations, a fully structured questionnaire may provide the respondent with five choices which the researcher feels are important. However, if the respondent identified other factors felt to be important, they would be overlooked.

2.2 Semi-structured interviews

Semi-structured interviews consist of both **closed questions** and **'open ended' questions** which offer respondents a free choice. For example, 'Which factors do you consider most important when making a choice of holiday destination?' provides the respondent with an open question to which they may respond freely.

The interviewer may decide to use **probing questions** such as: 'What other factors are there?' Probing questions may trigger further responses and the interviewer may be more confident about the data provided.

2.3 Unstructured interviews

Interviewers may have a checklist of topics to cover in questioning, but they are free to word such questions as they wish. Unstructured interviews are a very useful way of capturing data which is **qualitative** in nature.

2.4 Depth interviews

Motivational research often uses the method of **depth interviews**. Motives and explanations of behaviour often lie well below the surface. It is a time-consuming and expensive method of data collection. Taped interviews and analysis of transcripts is often the way in which the depth interview and subsequent data analysis are conducted.

The strengths of depth interviews include the following.

(a) **Longitudinal information** (such as information on decision-making processes) can be gathered from one respondent at a time, thereby aiding clarity of interpretation and analysis.

(b) **Personal** material can be more easily accessed and discussed.

There are, however, disadvantages to depth interviews.

(a) They are **time-consuming** to conduct and to analyse. If each interview lasts between one and two hours, a maximum of three or four per day is often all that is possible.

(b) They are more **costly** than group discussions.

3 GROUP DISCUSSIONS/FOCUS GROUPS

Definition

> A **focus group** is a group discussion carried out for research purposes.

Group discussions are useful in providing the researcher with qualitative data. Qualitative data can often provide greater insight than quantitative data.

Group discussions usually consist of 8 to 10 respondents and an interviewer taking the role of **group moderator**. The group moderator introduces topics for discussion and intervenes as necessary to encourage respondents or to direct discussions if they threaten to wander too far off the point.

Group discussions may be recorded for later analysis and interpretation. Group discussion is very dependent on the skill of the group moderator. It is inexpensive to conduct, it can be done quickly and it can provide useful, timely, qualitative data. It is often used at the early stage of research to get a feel for the subject matter under discussion and to create possibilities for more structured research.

According to Raymond Kent (*Marketing Research in Action*), the key advantages of group discussions include the following.

(a) The **group environment** with 'everybody in the same boat' can be less intimidating than other techniques of research which rely on one-to-one contact (such as depth interviews).

(b) What respondents say in a group often **sparks off** experiences or ideas on the part of others.

(c) **Differences** between consumers are highlighted, making it possible to understand a range of attitudes in a short space of time.

(d) It is **easier to observe** groups and there is more to observe.

(e) **Social and cultural** influences are highlighted.

(f) Groups are **cheaper and faster** than depth interviews.

The principal disadvantages of groups are as follows.

(a) Group processes may **inhibit** some people from making a full contribution and may encourage others to become exhibitionistic.

(b) Group processes may **stall** to the point where they cannot be retrieved by the moderator.

(c) Some groups may take on a **life of their own**, so that what is said has validity only in the short-lived context of the group.

DISCUSSION

Conduct a focus group in your class on entertainment facilities in your area. What are the key problems with conducting such a focus group?

---

4 ATTITUDE MEASUREMENT AND SELF-REPORTING SCALES

4.1 Definition

> An **attitude** is a predisposition to act in a particular way. A knowledge of attitudes may therefore enable **predictions** about likely behaviour patterns. A significant proportion of marketing research is aimed at finding out about consumer attitudes.

The measurement of behavioural factors such as attitudes and motivation has been attempted by researchers using a variety of techniques. None is fully satisfactory, the ones that are the most reliable and valid from a technical perspective are generally the most difficult and expensive.

There are several types of scaling techniques that can be used to measure attitudes. The following section illustrates a few of these.

4.2 Self-reporting scales

A scale is a set of symbols or numbers so constructed that the symbols or numbers can be assigned by a rule to the individuals (or their behaviours or attitudes) to whom the scale is applied.

A variety of measurement scales exist. However, the three key ones are the semantic differential, the staple and the Likert.

4.3 Semantic differential scale

The scaling technique was developed by Osgood, Suci and Tannerbaum in the late 1980s. The scale consists of a number of bipolar adjectival phrases and statements that could be used to describe the objectives being evaluated. Each bipolar adjective rating scale consists of seven categories, with neither numerical labels nor category descriptions other than for the anchor categories.

To remove any position bias, favourable and unfavourable objectives are randomly distributed to the left and right anchor positions. The respondent is asked to mark one of the seven categories that best describes their views about the object along the continuum implied by the bipolar object pair. An overall attitude score is calculated by summing the responses on each adjective pair. Before calculating the overall score, the response categories must be coded. Usually the categories are assigned values from 1 to 7, where 1 is assigned to the unfavourable adjectival phrase and 7 is assigned to the favourable adjectival phrase.

EXAMPLE

We would like to know what you think about our coffee shop. Below are a number of statements that could be used to describe what we offer. For each pair of adjectival phrases we would like you to mark the category that best describes your feelings about us.

Traditional	_ : _ : _ : _ : _ : _ :	Modern
Expensive	_ : _ : _ : _ : _ : _ :	Cheap
Friendly service	_ : _ : _ : _ : _ : _ :	Unfriendly service
Convenient opening hours	_ : _ : _ : _ : _ : _ :	Inconvenient opening hours
Slow service	_ : _ : _ : _ : _ : _ :	Fast service
Attractive atmosphere	_ : _ : _ : _ : _ : _ :	Unattractive atmosphere
Wide range of food and drink	_ : _ : _ : _ : _ : _ :	Limited range of food and drink

---

4.4 Staple scale

A staple scale differs from the semantic differential because it uses just one term and asks the respondent to describe how well that term describes the subject. Circling +5 means that the respondent agrees very strongly that the term is an appropriate description, while circling –5 indicates the reverse. The scores for each respondent can be summed and compared with the total scores of other respondents.

EXAMPLE

Select a plus number for words that you think describe our coffee shop accurately. The more accurate you think the description is, the larger should be the plus number selected. Conversely, select a minus number for words which do not describe the coffee shop. The less accurate you believe the description to be, the larger should be the minus number you select.

Our coffee shop

+5	+5
+4	+4
+3	+3
+2	+2
+1	+1
Friendly	Unfriendly
–1	–1
–2	–2
–3	–3
–4	–4
–5	–5

4.5 Likert attitude scales

In the Likert method a series of statements is provided and respondents are required to rate each statement on the basis of the strength of their personal feelings toward it. The numbers assigned to the responses are numerical values associated with each possible answer. When analysing the results, the signs of these numbers are reversed when a statement is unfavourable.

EXAMPLE

'Gillette is the best a man can get'

Strongly agree	Disagree	Don't know	Agree	Strongly agree
–2 ☐	–1 ☐	0 ☐	+1 ☐	+2 ☐

4.6 Guidelines for using self reporting techniques

When administering these techniques, respondents are provided with a number of alternative choices – words, statements, numbers – and required to select the one that most closely describes their attitude toward the subject. When applying these techniques, the researcher must decide how many choices to include as well as their wording.

There is disagreement on the ideal number of choices that should be offered to respondents – four to eight choices appears to be preferred, with five the number used most often. There is also a lack of consensus on whether there should be an even or odd number of choices. An even number of choices compels the respondent to declare a position, whereas an odd number usually provides a middle position for those in situations where the respondent cannot identify their feelings. The drawback to offering a neutral position is that this choice attracts many respondents who do not have strong feelings on the issue, and hence it does not allow the researcher to distinguish between answers.

5 PROJECTIVE TECHNIQUES

The objective of any projective test is to delve below the surface responses in order to obtain true feelings, meanings or motivations. The rationale behind projective tests comes from the knowledge that people are often reluctant to, or cannot, reveal their deepest feelings. In other instances they are unaware of those feelings because of psychological defence mechanisms.

The most commonly applied projective tests used in market research are word-association tests, sentence and story completion, cartoon tests and third person techniques.

5.1 Word-association

A respondent is given a series of single words and then asked to match each with one of their own. The goal is to elicit quick, unrestrained answers: it can be used to select brand names, advertising campaign themes and slogans. For example, a cosmetic manufacturer might ask consumers to respond to the following potential names for a new perfume: infinity, encounter, flame, precious.

5.2 Sentence and story completion

Sentence completion follows the same kind of pattern, eg

The people who shop at Asda are ....

Asda should really ....

Story completion is a longer version of sentence completion in which participants are presented with incomplete scenarios and are asked to complete the story. For example,

Mrs X has just moved into the area. Her new neighbour Mrs Y goes to her home to welcome her. Mrs X does not know the area and asks Mrs Y for some advice on where to do her shopping. The nearest supermarket is Asda but she has heard some things about it. What is Mrs Y's reply?

5.3 Cartoon tests

These create a highly projective mechanism by means of cartoon figures or strips, similar to those in comic books. They can be used to measure the strength of an attitude towards a particular product or brand.

NOTES

5.4 Third person techniques

Rather than asking a respondent directly what they think, it is phrased as 'your friend' or 'some people' or some other third party. Rather than ask a parent why they do not provide a nutritionally balanced breakfast, a researcher would ask, 'Why don't some parents provide their children with nutritionally balanced breakfasts?' The third-person technique is often used to avoid issues that might be embarrassing or evoke hostility if answered directly by a respondent.

DISCUSSION

Why do you think projective techniques are so called?

---

6 QUESTIONNAIRE DESIGN

The first step in any type of survey is the outlining of the information to be obtained. The researcher has then to develop a set of questions which can be answered correctly by the respondents.

(a) All the factors which seem to have some bearing on the problem must be set out.

(b) These factors must be discussed with people likely to have some special knowledge of the problem.

Once the list of factors is verified, questions can be drawn up and the questionnaire designed. Each question should be tested against the following criteria.

(a) What is the interviewer trying to find out by asking this question?

(b) Will all the target respondents understand the question?

(c) Will all the target respondents known how to answer?

(d) Have clear unequivocal instructions been given on the format of the answer?

(e) Having got answers to the question, can they be analysed meaningfully?

The initial draft of the questionnaire should be discussed with colleagues prior to being tested in a pilot survey.

The table **on the following page** gives examples of the types of question that can be asked.

In practice both survey design and questionnaire design are fraught with difficulties and marketing managers are well advised to seek the help of experts - preferably experienced members of the Market Research Society.

NOTES

Name	*Description*	*Example*
	CLOSED-END QUESTIONS	
Dichotomous	A question with two possible answers.	'In arranging this trip, did you personally phone British Airways?' Yes ☐ No ☐
Multiple choice	A question with three or more answers.	'With whom are you travelling on this flight?' No one ☐ Spouse ☐ Spouse and children ☐ Children only ☐ Business associates/ friends/relatives ☐ An organised tour group ☐
Likert scale	A statement with which the respondent shows the amount of agreement/	'Small airlines generally give better service Strongly disagree 1 ☐ Disagree 2 ☐ Neither agree nor disagree 3 ☐ Agree 4 ☐ Strongly agree 5 ☐
Semantic differential	A scale connecting two bipolar words, where the respondent selects the point	*British Airways* Large — — — — — — — Small Experienced — — — — — — — Inexperienced
Importance scale	A scale that rates the importance of some attribute.	Extremely important 1 ☐ Very important 2 ☐ Somewhat important 3 ☐ Not very important 4 ☐ Not at all important 5 ☐
Rating scale	A scale that rates some attribute from 'poor' to 'excellent'.	Excellent Very good Good Fair Poor
Intention-to-buy scale	A scale that describes the respondent's intention to buy or use.	'If an inflight telephone was available on a long flight, I would' Definitely use 1 ☐ Probably use 2 ☐ Not sure 3 ☐ Probably not use 4 ☐ Definitely not use 5 ☐
	OPEN-END QUESTIONS	
Completely unstructured	A question that respondents can answer in an almost unlimited number of ways.	'What is your opinion of British Airways?'
Word association	Words are presented, one at a time, and respondents mention the first word that	'What is the first word that comes to mind when you hear the following' Airline __________ British __________ Travel __________
Sentence completion	An incomplete sentence is presented and respondents complete the	'When I choose an airline, the most important consideration in my decision is __________ '
Story completion	An incomplete story is presented, and respondents are asked to complete it.	'I flew B.A. a few days ago. I noticed that the exterior and interior of the plane had bright colours. This aroused in me the following thoughts and feelings.' Now complete the story.
Picture completion	A picture of two characters is presented, with one making a statement. Respondents are asked to identify with the other and fill in the empty balloon.	
Thematic Apperception Test (TAT)	A picture is presented and respondents are asked to make up a story about what they think is happening or may happen in the picture.	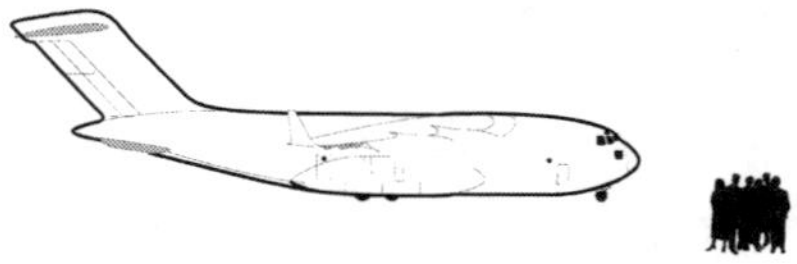

BPP PUBLISHING

7 POSTAL RESEARCH QUESTIONNAIRES

7.1 Definition

> The **questionnaire** is the primary tool of marketing research, a device for delivering questions to respondents and recording their answers.

Questionnaires are sent to respondents for self-completion. The major limitation of postal research is the low response rate. Anything higher than 10% is considered reasonably good.

Pre-coding the questionnaire makes analysis of the data more straightforward. Tick box questionnaires are easy for respondents and stand more chance of providing the researcher with a higher response.

> **Activity 1** **(10 minutes)**
>
> What do you see as the advantages and disadvantages of postal questionnaires as a way of collecting research data when compared with personal interviews?

7.2 Advantages and limitations of postal surveys

Advantages:

- low cost per response
- no interviewer bias
- questionnaire length

Limitations:

- questionnaire scope
- respondent interaction
- sampling problems
- response rate problems
- lack of control over respondents
- wrong respondents and so wrong information

DISCUSSION

What do you consider to be the most appropriate applications for postal surveys?

---

8 INTERVIEW SURVEYS

Most survey work in the UK is conducted through **face-to-face interviews**, usually by employees of a market research company.

8.1 Advantages of interview surveys

Their prevalence as a data collection method and the quality of the data collected are probably due to their obvious advantages.

(a) The interviewer can check the respondent is suitable before beginning the interview.

(b) The use of an interviewer ensures that *all* questions are answered in the correct order.

(c) The interviewer can check that the respondent has understood the questions and can encourage respondents to answer as fully as possible.

(d) Response rates are generally higher than with other forms of questionnaire administration.

(e) Where quotas are applied (such as 20 women under 30), the interviewer can ensure that the target number of interviews is achieved.

(f) Interviewers can attempt to persuade respondents to take part in the survey.

8.2 Types of interview survey

Interview surveys can be classified according to where they are carried out.

(a) **Store/Mall intercept surveys** are carried out in busy town centres, especially shopping centres/malls. The interviewer tends to stand in one position and approaches potential respondents as soon as the previous interview is completed, thereby eliminating time between interviews. The interviews need to be brief, however, as respondents are unlikely to want to stop for more than ten minutes.

(b) **In-house (or more accurately door-step) interviews** are part of those surveys where respondent recruitment is door to door. Interviewers may be given a list of names and addressees, or they may be limited to certain areas. Moreover, they may be given additional information such as call at every fourth house. In contrast to mall intercept interviews, in-house interviews may be prearranged by telephone. Such interview methods can be time consuming but longer interviews than in mall intercept surveys are possible (although likely to be interrupted).

(c) **Hall tests** refer to interviews carried out in a pre-booked location. Recruitment is usually from a nearby street and respondents are often given refreshments. Materials, videos and displays can be used.

(d) **In-store surveys** may take place in a shop or just outside. Permission will of course be needed from the shop. Recruitment could be on the basis of people leaving or entering the store. A study of shopping intentions would require recruitment from the latter.

(e) **Business interviews** will normally take place at the interviewee's place of business but will need to be arranged in advance.

8.3 Choice of respondent

In-house interviewees can be selected using random sampling techniques from the electoral register. Interviewees for most other surveys will need to be selected using quota sampling or random location sampling. Geodemographic analysis can be applied.

8.4 Disadvantages of interview surveys

These surveys can be expensive and it is possible that interviewers interfere with objectivity by unwittingly introducing bias or by creating a particular mood when conducting the interview. For example, if the interviewer takes too light hearted an approach it may mean that the respondent treats the survey in a light-hearted way and data collected is not meaningful as a result.

DISCUSSION

When training interviewers to undertake a specific personal interview survey, what kind of training is necessary?

---

9 PANEL METHODOLOGY

Consumer panel data can be gathered at the point-of-sale using bar-coding and related electronic systems, or in the home by means of home audits, diaries, and more recently, electronic scanners used in panel households.

9.1 Home audits

Home audits involve research staff visiting panel members' homes and, with their permission, physically checking household stocks of specific products surveyed by the panel. Used packaging is saved by the panel member and stored in a special container, so that these can also be checked ('dustbin check'). In addition, respondents usually answer a brief questionnaire.

9.2 Diaries

Most panels use some form of diary, which members complete with details of purchases of a range of food and other frequently purchased products. Some research organisations operate a weekly system of reporting, which is considered to result in more reliable data than if the time interval is extended, but costs are obviously a factor.

9.3 Electronic scanners

The AGB Superpanel in the UK comprises 10,000 households (33,000 individuals) who are equipped with electronic scanners, similar to those used at supermarket check-out desks, which record price, place of purchase and selected brand. This enables rapid trend analysis to be supplied to AGB's clients.

In June 1989, Nielsen launched the Homescan panel, which was the first panel in Europe to use in-home scanning. This consumer panel, based on 7,100 homes, derived from the Nielsen establishment survey of 80,000 households in the UK and was designed to reflect accurately household purchases of all grocery items, from fresh and pre-packed foodstuffs to household products, petfoods, toiletries, confectionery and alcohol.

Each household is provided with a small, hand-held bar-code scanner and after each shopping trip purchased items are recorded; data captured include the date, items bought, any promotional offers applicable, price, quantity and store used. On completion the information is downloaded via a modem to Nielsen's host computer.

Electronic data capture and transfer allow daily collection of purchasing data, so Nielsen clients can be provided with up-to-the-minute information and consumers' responses to marketing initiatives. Core data can vary but standard analyses include: % of households purchasing, % of expenditure, average number of visits per buyer, average spend per buyer, average spend per visit, brand comparisons, level of trial of new products, brand loyalty and demographic analyses.

Activity 2 **(10 minutes)**

A marketing research company proposes to investigate food purchasing patterns among a sample of consumers. It intends using diaries as the research instrument. Which areas of food purchasing may the diaries fail to uncover?

10 TELEPHONE RESEARCH

Telephone research is a relatively fast and low cost means of gathering data. It is most useful when only a small amount of information is required. It has been particularly useful in industrial research, although the technique has been widely used for consumer research with the growth in home telecommunications.

10.1 Disadvantages

There are a number of disadvantages to using the telephone in research, however.

(a) A **biased sample** may result from the fact that a proportion of people do not have telephones, many of those who do are ex-directory and the telephone numbers listed may be outdated.

(b) The **refusal rate** is much higher than with face-to-face interviews.

(c) The interview must be **short**.

(d) There is no way to provide visual aids.

10.2 Advantages

Advantages associated with telephone research include:

(a) a wide geographical area can be covered with no travel costs
(b) there is a compulsion to answer the phone
(c) efficient call backs can be made
(d) relatively high response rate
(e) question modification possible

CATI (computer assisted telephone interviewing) has been used successfully by insurance services and banks as well as consumer research organisations. The telephone interviewer calls up a questionnaire on screen and reads questions to the respondent. Answers are then recorded instantly on computer.

Activity 3 **(15 minutes)**

Identify two marketing research projects for which a telephone questionnaire rather than a mail questionnaire or personal interview would be more appropriate.

11 OBSERVATION

Observation has already been discussed in some detail in Section 3 of Chapter 3.

Interviews and questionnaires depend on respondents answering questions on behaviour and attitudes truthfully. Sometimes it is necessary to **observe behaviour**, not only because respondents are unwilling to answer questions but because such questions are unable to provide the researcher with answers.

The major categories of observations are as follows.

(a) **Home audit**. Also termed indirect observation, this involves the investigation of the respondent's home, office or premises so as to determine the extent of ownership of certain products/brands. (Note that the home audit and diary panels are termed **consumer panel** research.)

(b) **Direct observation**. This involves the direct observation of the behaviour of the respondent by the researcher.

(c) **Recording devices**. Such devices record micro behaviour in laboratory settings and macro behaviour in natural settings.

  (i) Laboratory settings

    (1) **Psychogalvanometers** measure a subject's response to, say, an advertisement by measuring the perspiration rate.

    (2) **Eye cameras** are used to assess those parts of, for example, an advertisement which attract most attention and those parts which are neglected.

    (3) **Pupilometric cameras** are used in assessing the visual stimulation derived from an image.

  (ii) In **natural settings** video and movie cameras are used to record behaviour.

The use of observation as a data collection method has been stimulated by advances in electronics. EPOS systems allow firms to observe stock on hand, inflows, outflows and the speed at which stock items are moving through the store.

12 APPROACHES TO THE ASSESSMENT OF THE VALUE AND VALIDITY OF DATA

Some approaches to this assessment are outlined below.

(a) **Common sense**. Clearly data which is dated, which emanates from dubious sources or which is based on unrepresentative samples should be treated with extreme caution, if not totally disregarded.

(b) **Statistical approaches**. There are a variety of sampling methods for survey data as already described, which are appropriate to different situations. All of them involve some degree of risk (some probability of error). The degree of risk of statistical error can, however, be computed as we have seen.

(c) **Expert judgement**. 'There are lies, damned lies and statistics.' The same data can be interpreted differently by different people - you have only to look at differences between economists or between politicians of different parties on the latest figures to see ample evidence of this. The following array - 98.7,

98.6, 98.6, 98.4, 98.1, 98.1- might be regarded by a statistician as a declining trend but to a marketing manager the figures may represent a very steady state, especially if they were percentages of actual sales against budgeted sales for the last six years. In using this approach, therefore, the marketing manager might be wise to consult more than one expert before making a decision.

(d) **The intuitive approach**. Some people have a better feel for figures than others and seem able to judge the value and validity of data intuitively. For example, it is said that Rank Xerox ignored survey findings that there was no market for a dry copier and in doing so went on to become a world leader in this field. This approach, whilst perhaps successful for a chosen few, is not, however, recommended.

(e) **The questioning approach**. Always question the origin and the basis of the data. Ask for further information. An actual spend of 180% of budget is not important if the amount concerned is only £10. A much smaller variance on a much large amount could, however, be quite serious. Recognise that human errors occur when manipulating data, that bias can occur in questionnaire design: ask to see the questionnaire, check the figures.

12.1 The limitations of market research

You should be aware that research cannot supply marketers with perfect and comprehensive answers to all the questions. This may be because the research itself is badly designed (the sample populations inappropriate, the questions misleading and so on) but it can also happen because systematic research, by definition, can only ask the questions which exist in marketers' mind and elicit responses within the framework of respondents' imaginations.

As Nishikawa claims in his 1989 article for the *Journal of Long Range Planning*, the most important point in building marketing strategy is not logical analysis or investigative excellence, but creative action. Only proactive creativity, generating products and services *in anticipation of* customer needs and expectations, can create marketing advantage; organisations which are customer driven (as opposed to being customer focused) are invariably *reactive*. Responding to declared customer needs is acting too late for successful marketing: in order to forecast the future, organisations require creativity rather than responsiveness, challenge rather than passivity.

Nishikawa claims that marketing research linked to new products and services is especially defective, because of certain features in customer psychology.

(a) **Indifference**. Customers often provide negative responses to ideas for new products/services simply because they are indifferent to something they have not thought about or tried before.

(b) **Absence of responsibility**. People will say more or less anything when responding to research surveys, often out of a desire to please the researcher.

(c) **Conservative attitudes**. Most customers choose conventional and familiar products/services. To put it another way, only about three per cent of customers are Early Adopters.

(d) **Vanity**. Customers will try to put on a good appearance about their motives and will seldom want to admit that cheapness (for example) was the major reason for a purchase decision.

(e) **Insufficient information**. Researchers often approach customers with information and ideas seen from the seller's rather than from the customer's point of view.

One of Nishikawa's key points is that customers are most sincere when **spending rather than talking**.

EXAMPLE

Many growers and retailers, had been misled by surveys suggesting that 70 per cent of consumers would purchase organic vegetables and fruit. In the event only 11 per cent are doing so, the remainder have demonstrated by their actions that *behaviour* and *attitudes* are not necessarily synonymous. Perhaps they had not seriously considered the possibility that organic produce would cost more or that it would look less attractive; quite possibly they gave 'ethically correct' responses when completing a questionnaire, but had no real intention of acting differently.

Chapter roundup

- Interviewing is a core function of market research and types of interview range from formal, unstructured interviews to informal discussions.
- Research directors should pay special attention to the training and monitoring of interviewers in order to keep bias to a minimum.
- Group discussions are often used at the exploratory phase of marketing research to help define the problem.
- Attitude research uses various scaling techniques and because some of these scales are versatile and relatively easy to use, care is needed to ensure that the resultant information is valid and reliable.
- The basic premise of projective techniques is that the best way to obtain the true feelings and attitudes of people is to enable them to present data indirectly about themselves by speaking through others.
- Questionnaires are a vital element of the total market research design but they demand experience and skill in their composition.
- Pilot testing of questionnaires is imperative and this should be undertaken with a representative sample.
- Most survey work in the UK is conducted through face-to-face interviews, usually by employees of a market research organisation.
- Panel or longitudinal research provides data which enable trends to be identified; panels can consist of individuals, households or organisations.
- Telephone research is low cost and fast but has the disadvantage of not being able to explore issues further as with face-to-face interviews, and true feelings about an issue can be disguised.
- Observation techniques may be employed to provide answers to some research problems. For example, observation panels are convened and measured using electronic metering devices to observe TV viewing patterns.

NOTES

Quick Quiz

1 What are the four main types of interview?

2 What are the two disadvantages of depth interviews?

3 How many respondents usually make up a focus group?

4 List three advantages of using focus groups.

5 What does a semantic differential scale consist of?

6 How does a staple scale differ from a semantic differential?

7 How would you describe a Likert scale?

8 Give two examples of situations where word association could be used?

9 Where might the third person technique be employed?

10 Name three advantages of postal surveys.

11 What are the five location types of interview survey?

12 What is the AGB Superpanel?

13 List three disadvantages of using telephone research.

14 What are the three main categories of observation?

Answers to quick quiz

1 Fully structured, semi-structured, unstructured and depth. (See paragraph 2)

2 They are time consuming to conduct and analyse, and so are more expensive. (para 2.4)

3 Eight to ten respondents and a moderator. (para 3)

4 The group environment can be less intimidating than a one-to-one interview, group dynamics can encourage participation, differences between respondents can be highlighted. (para 3)

5 The scale consists of a number of bipolar adjectival phrases and statements, each of which has seven categories. (para 4.3)

6 It uses just one term and asks the respondent to describe how well that term describes a subject on a scale of +5 (very well) to –5 (very poorly). (para 4.4)

7 In the Likert method a series of statements is provided and respondents are required to rate each statement on the basis of the strength of their personal feelings toward it. –2 infers strong disagreement and +2 strong agreement. (para 4.5)

8 Selecting brand names and developing advertising campaign themes and slogans. (para 5.1)

9 When dealing with subjects which may be embarrassing, eg personal hygiene, or those that might evoke hostility if answered directly by the respondent. (para 5.4)

10 Low cost per response, no interview bias and the questionnaire length. (para 7.2)

11 Mall intercept, in-house (ie door-step), hall tests, in-store and business. (para 8.2)

NOTES

12 It comprises 10,000 households who are equipped with electronic scanners to record their purchases. (para 9.3)

13 High refusal rate, incomplete sampling frame and no opportunity to provide visual aids. (para 10.1)

14 Home audit, direct observation and the use of recording devices. (para 11)

Answers to activities

1 *Advantages*
People may be more forthcoming if not dealing with an individual.
Can be used to ask sensitive or potentially embarrassing questions.
Less time-consuming for interviewers
Standard form of question assists continuity
Cost per person is less: can ask more people

Disadvantages
Recipients may throw them away.
Questions cannot be tailored to the recipient.
May be difficult to understand responses without the scope for further questioning.

2 Spontaneous, impulse purchases eg chocolate, sweets.
Purchased by people who are meant to be on a diet (secret purchases).
Goods not purchased as part of the 'weekly shop' eg milk delivered to the door.
'Top up' purchases during the week eg fresh vegetables
Takeaway meals.

3 Two market research projects for which a telephone questionnaire rather than a main questionnaire or personal interview would be more appropriate:

1. Where the impact of a TV advertising campaign was being assessed. Phone calls could be made immediately after the advertisments had run to determine who had seen it and what the impact had been.

2. Telephone questionnaires are particularly useful when time is short and the study requires a broad geographic sample. This could be useful in the prototype phase of a new product or service development.

BPP PUBLISHING

Chapter 5 : CUSTOMER SATISFACTION

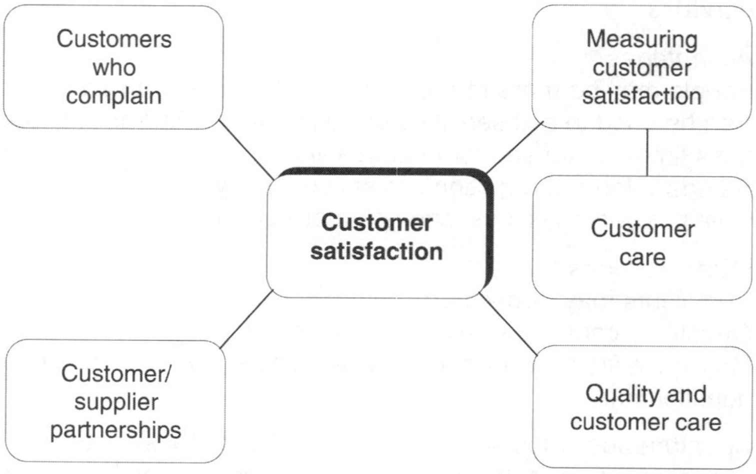

This chapter covers material relevant to both Unit 17 Marketing Intelligence and Unit 20 Sales Planning and Operations.

Introduction

This chapter is concerned with the role of customer satisfaction assurance within a marketing led organisation. It begins with an evaluation of the components of customer satisfaction and the ways in which it can be obtained and so measured. Customer care systems and procedures are then discussed using examples to illustrate how organisational structure can impact on customer care management.

The relationship between quality and customer care is then explored in terms of the absolutes of quality management and the basic elements of improvement. The penultimate section is concerned with the process and management of customer complaints and their role in overall quality improvement.

The final section deals with customer/supplier relationships which have obvious implications for customer satisfaction.

Your objectives

In this chapter you will learn about the following:

(a) the principles of measuring customer satisfaction

(b) the role of effective customer care

(c) the relationship between total quality and customer care

(d) the importance of customers who complain

(e) developments in customer/supplier partnerships

1 MEASURING CUSTOMER SATISFACTION

1.1 Fundamentals of customer satisfaction

(a) **Product/service variables**. The design of the product or service is designed to give customers benefit. Good design maximises those benefits.

(b) **Sales and promotion-related variables**. Three key variables affect customer satisfaction in this area.

 (i) **Messages** which help to shape customers' ideas about the product's benefits before they have experienced it in use.

 (ii) **Attitudes** of everyone in the organisation who comes into contact with customers: salespeople, service staff, telephone operators, and so forth.

 (iii) The use of **intermediaries** to sell on behalf of the organisation: similar selection, training and performance criteria should be applied to intermediaries as are applied to an organisation's own staff.

(c) **After-sales variables**. There are two aspects of after-sales which are especially significant for organisations.

 (i) **Support services**. Covering traditional after-sales activities like warranties, parts and service, and user training.

 (ii) **Feedback and restitution**. The way the organisation handles complaints and the level of priority attached by management to such activities.

(d) **Culture-related variables**. The crucial question here is whether the corporate culture is built around maximising customer satisfaction, or whether management merely pays lip service to it. Would it be acceptable for an employee to postpone a meeting with the managing director in order to meet a customer, for example?

EXAMPLE

'Rude and unhelpful staff are the biggest single hurdle to developing customer loyalty, according to an Air Miles UK survey exclusive to *Marketing Week*.

The survey found that 54 per cent of the 1,000 people interviewed were most likely to become disloyal because of rude and unhelpful staff.

Young people in the 18-to-24 age bracket are the group most affected by rude staff – 60 per cent cited it as a reason for "disloyalty" to a retailer or service provider.

Judith Thorne, Air Miles UK marketing director, says: "This shows that customer service and the way companies interact with customers is an integral part of building customer loyalty."

According to Thorne, advertising which over-hypes the offer can seriously damage loyalty.

She says: "Advertising is fantastic for putting a thought into the consumer's mind, but people will be very disappointed if the promise isn't delivered."

One in five of the survey's respondents said poor value for money would challenge their loyalty and one in ten would turn their backs on suppliers who "do not seem to listen".

Complaints are most likely to come from extremely loyal customers while those claiming to "feel no loyalty" will simply switch retailer without explaining why.

Combining fair prices with good service is the surest way to win loyalty, say 54 per cent of respondents.' *Marketing Week*, 5 March 1998

1.2 Measuring customer satisfaction

Measuring whether customers have got what they wanted can be extremely problematic for a number of reasons.

(a) **Weak anecdotal evidence**, often based on single incidents, is given too much weight, especially if such evidence reinforces what people in an organisation want to hear (wishful thinking).

(b) **Single-incident disasters** may be used by one part of the organisation to attack another, rather than as an opportunity for improving performance.

(c) The views of those customers who complain, which may be **a typical**, are not counter-balanced by the views of those who do not.

(d) Many badly-served customers will not complain, but will simply take their business elsewhere if they can.

EXAMPLE

In 1986, the Ford Motor Company found that customers satisfied with their cars told (on average) eight other people, dissatisfied customers told 22 (who in turn told 22 more, with the story becoming more elaborate and embellished with each repetition).

(e) The opinions of small numbers of **highly articulate** customers, especially if of high status and personally known to top management, or expressed through the public media, will be given excessive emphasis.

(f) **Preconceptions** within the organisation about its customer-service standing and performance may be out-of-date or mistaken, especially if insufficient attention is paid to what the competition is doing.

Definition

> **Customer satisfaction** – the overall attitude a person has about a product after it has been purchased.

1.3 Customer segmentation

So far we have treated customers as if they were all alike, all wanting much the same things, all applying similar criteria when judging the product, the service, or the organisation as a whole. In practice, this is bound to be misleading, especially for organisations with a large customer base, a wide range of products, a global market, and several discrete product/brand names. Customer A may want reliability of delivery on an hourly basis; Customer B may want an unusual range of financial options; Customer C may want the highest possible standards of after-sales support; Customer D is only interested in one product; and so on.

Research shows that there are differences in customers' expectations which can be exploited by offering levels of service which match the needs of particular sectors, possibly withdrawing from some or increasing prices/charges to an economically-justified level.

1.4 Obtaining customer intelligence

Customer research survey method

One way in which customer intelligence can be gathered is via a customer (or consumer) **survey** using a questionnaire. The key steps in planning and implementing such a survey are:

Step 1. **Carry out analysis** of the organisation's customers, to decide whether they already fall into categories with differing service expectations.

Step 2. Decide whether to cover all customers or a **sample**. If the organisation only has a small group of customers, semi-structured interviews may be preferable to written questionnaires.

Step 3. **Pilot-test the questionnaire** to ensure that the questions make sense and that all potential customer concerns are being covered.

Step 4. Decide whether to conduct the survey **in person, by telephone** or via the **post**. Postal distribution may be unavoidable, though it will drastically reduce the response rate and may introduce bias into the sample (unless incentives are offered).

Step 5. If the survey has been well designed and administered, **analyse the results** to reveal gaps in customer-service performance.

Other methods of obtaining customer intelligence via surveys include diary panels, interviews (often known as mall intercept surveys), instore surveys and hall tests. These are all discussed in Chapter 4.

1.5 The complaints system as a research tool

It is surprising how few organisations positively encourage **complaints**, despite the fact that complaints are an essential form of feedback if properly organised. Complaints represent only a small proportion of dissatisfied customers, however: organisations never know the precise number of customers who do not complain but who simply take their business elsewhere. The number of such customers must, of course, be reduced.

Activity 1 **(10 minutes)**

In what ways could you obtain complaints feedback?

We will be considering the impact of quality in more detail in the next section, but what is important to emphasise here is that quality has to be defined from the customer's perspective. Quality does not mean best, or even 'fit for the purpose', but means it **satisfies the needs of the customers**.

Marketers have to avoid falling into the trap of raising a customer's expectations through glamorous promotion and fancy packaging, because if the product fails to meet these expectations, a disappointed and dissatisfied customer may choose alternative suppliers.

Losing customers is bad news for any business; not only are **today's sales lost,** but **future potential earnings** are also sacrificed.

(a) A woman in her mid 20's spends an estimated £100 a year on cosmetics. Dissatisfied by her current brand she switches to a competitor. She remains loyal for over 20 years to the new product. Cash revenue from the lost client is worth £2,000 before the time value of money is taken into account.

(b) The car manufacturer who estimates an average driver will buy seven cars in his or her lifetime is looking at perhaps £140,000 in lost custom if the salesperson fails to provide the service or approach needed to convert the buyer into a driver loyal to the brand.

But besides the lost value from that customer, bad service or products will generate bad word of mouth publicity. This can be very persuasive and can cost the company even more in lost customers or potential customers.

Activity 2

Over the next two weeks keep listening for word of mouth publicity about products or services. Keep a note of the relative proportions of good and bad messages. How much credibility do they have? Do they influence your behaviour?

You will find they come up in many forms.

- Have you tried that new restaurant?
- Did you see the latest film?
- What is the service like?

Try actively eliciting comments by asking for advice on a new car purchase or holiday destination.

DISCUSSION

The customer is always right. Do you agree?

2 CUSTOMER CARE

Inevitably things will go wrong from time to time. Most customers, however, are less concerned with the mishap than how the issue is rectified. This is where **customer care** is relevant. Customer care has been very much in the forefront of management thinking in both the public sector (with the Citizens' Charter etc) and private sector over recent years. Whilst it is easy to scoff, the Citizens' Charter, Patients' Charter, Rail Users' Charter and so on have all tried to specify the level of service users are entitled to expect and compensation if this is not delivered. This start at quantification is an excellent beginning. From these benchmarks improvements can be developed, implemented and monitored.

In *Perfect Customer Care*, Dr Ted Johns argues that 'The majority of customer complaints will not directly relate to the quality of the service/product, but to the peripheral issues. Quality in the eyes of the customer is always supposedly much more than the quality of the product or basic service offered'.

Activity 3 **(10 minutes)**

Assume that you have ordered two fencing panels from a local DIY store. For a small extra charge, the panels will be delivered (as they are too big to fit into your car). On the appointed day, a delivery is made - but only one of the panels you purchased, not two. You phone up; delivery is promised the following day, but fails to arrive. You phone up again and speak to a senior manager, who apologises for his staff. Delivery is made, and you are given a third extra panel to compensate for the inconvenience. The fencing panels themselves are fine. What customer care lessons can you learn from this example?

Most complaints are apparently peripheral to the actual product/service offered, and relate to telephone courtesy, delivery, availability of product, user instructions and so forth. **Customer care programmes** are devoted to maximising the benefits a customer receives within the operating constraints of the business. This means, effectively, that the operations staff who deliver service should do so with a **marketing philosophy** in mind.

In other words, the service should be designed as far as possible with the customer in mind, rather than the procedural conveniences of the company. Although the old adage 'you can't please all of the people all of the time' may still be true, it is still important to put in place systems, procedures and practices to minimise customer dissatisfaction.

For organisations, one of the key components of service excellence is **process alignment**, ie making sure that the organisation serves the customer rather than the other way round. In the words of Arthur Andersen (the global management consultants), it is 'deliberately designing and modifying business processes so that **every activity is geared to meeting the customer's wants**'.

Chris Daffy in his book, *Once a Customer, Always a Customer*, argues that an organisation structure that is totally customer-focused would have just two layers.

The Customer-Focused Company

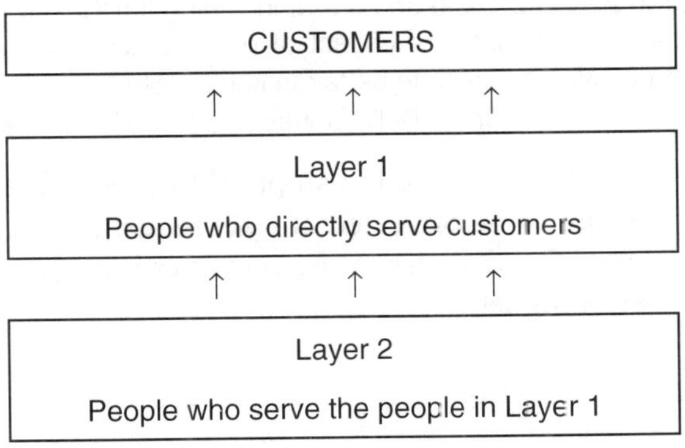

DISCUSSION

Certainly the organisations which are **most effective** at dealing with customers are typically those which have **radically changed their structures** in order to make them **less hierarchical**.

EXAMPLE

(a) **The Automobile Association**

The AA has gone through a major delayering exercise, cutting the number of levels between its front-line employees (the patrolmen) and the Chief Executive from 12 to 5, and delegating much more responsibility at lower levels.

(b) **Cigna Services UK (health insurance)**

Cigna now operates almost totally on the basis of multi-functional teams. The customer is assigned to a team and that team, rather than separate functional groups within the organisation, deals with very aspect of that customer's business with Cigna.

(c) **Hamilton Acorn (paintbrush manufacturer)**

Acorn's customer services department now draws together in a single unit a number of functions that had previously been done separately: warehousing and distribution, customer queries, data input, sales administration and export. The company has also reorganised the factory floor into cells or small teams, each with its own supervisor, and each responsible for a product form start to finish. This manufacturing re-organisation was vital if the improvements demanded by customers were actually going to happen: as the company's Operations Director has said, 'You can't just put a sign up and say, 'Hooray, now we've got a customer services department, now we're going to be great', because they can't do a damned thing unless they've got the back-up from the manufacturing side all the way through.'

2.1 Get it right, first time

One of the basic principles of TQM is that the **cost of preventing mistakes is less than the cost of correcting them** once they occur. The aim should therefore be to **get things right first time**.

> 'Every mistake, every delay and misunderstanding, directly costs a company money through wasted time and effort, including time taken in pacifying customers. Whilst this cost is important, the impact of poor customer service in terms of lost potential for future sales has also to be taken into account.'
>
> (Robin Bellis-Jones and Max Hand, *Management Accounting,* May 1989)

For instance, a 1:3:8 ratio is used in shipbuilding. A defect corrected when it occurs only costs 1 unit; if it has to be corrected at a subsequent inspection it costs 3 units; but if it has to be corrected after delivery to the customer it costs 8 units. Arguably the figure of 8 units could be even higher.

EXAMPLE

Birmingham Midshires Building Society

Until recently, a major source of complaint from the customers of the Birmingham Midshires Building Society concerned delays and errors. In response, the Society has adopted a 'right first time' philosophy throughout the organisation. They recognise, in the words of their director of customer services, Jon Gresham, that 'Re-work is costly, complaints are costly, and to recover properly from complaints about errors is a drain on business resources. Therefore we need to make sure that we've got the right measures and mechanisms in place to start providing a timely, high quality service'.

TNT Express (deliveries and distribution)

According to Alan Jones, Managing Director of TNT Express UK Limited: 'Some people believe that quality actually adds to cost. We do not agree. Our experience in the recession (of the early 1990s) reinforced our view that quality reduces costs. A get-it-right-first-time approach is reducing the often significant cost of correcting mistakes in our business.'

2.2 The Ted Johns blueprint for customer service excellence: the 12 pillars of performance

Ted Johns, A marketing expert, has created the following framework for:

(a) Specifying the desirable mix of internal, external and strategic components needed by an organisation which majors on service as a source of competitive advantage,

(b) Evaluating the actions needed by organisations if they seek to establish themselves as 'contenders' or 'world class' players.

The framework involves three major dimensions: your **strategy**, your **people** and your **customers**. Each in turn has four sub-dimensions. None of the 12 factors is optional, and none is more important than the others (though without the **strategy** impetus, it is very unlikely that anything significant will happen).

Dimension 1: Your strategy

Commitment	Customer service is a key **corporate scorecard indicator**. (Xerox seeks customer delight, satisfaction and retention as key parameters for progress, arguing that profitability will follow from the achievement of these measures.) • **A clear and shared vision** from the top, rooted in the customer. • Sustained top-management **commitment** to change • Visible **role-modelling** by senior managers • Employee **involvement and engagement** • Motivation via **customer-linked rewards and recognition** systems • **Training** • Bold goals for **performance improvement** • **Benchmarking**. Xerox is always prepared to **learn from other organisations**.
Credibility	Your customers must have good grounds for believing your promises. Even when an organisation is trusted by its customers, it must continue to work hard to ensure that its reputation remains intact.
Classification	You segment your customers, periodically review your segmentation profiles and vary your product/service offer across segment boundaries.
Concentration	You focus your marketing efforts on your most profitable customers. Many companies disseminate their marketing efforts without any regard to **customer profitability potential, segment profitability potential**, or even **product/service profitability potential**.

Dimension 2: Your people

Capability	All your people, whether in the front line or not, are recruited and trained against a customer service competency blueprint. Many of the most successful Japanese companies pay much attention, when recruiting people, to possession of the right attitudes (ie customer focus, flexibility, enthusiasm for change, teamworking readiness).
Continuity	You have retention, reward and recognition strategies which encourage your people to remain. The Reichheld service/profit cycle shows the enormous benefits which are likely to accrue from employee retention.
Courtesy	Your people are polite, considerate, tolerant and friendly when dealing with customers.
Creativity	Your people produce ideas for service innovations and improvements. After all, employees at the front line are often the first to notice that customers are asking for different things and are beginning to complain about elements in the product/service package.

Dimension 3: Your customers

Consistency	**Customers like to know what to expect** from have called organisational routines, ie various predictable ways of operating that ultimately help to create customer confidence through familiarity and experience. This does not mean, however, that customer expectations remain static: they are constantly rising.
Communication	Your customers understand what you say to them; equally, you actively promote opportunities for **two-way** dialogue.
Comfort	Your customers feel comfortable with everything which collectively comprises the **company reputation**. Recent surveys on **electronic commerce** have strongly endorsed the argument that customers are much more willing to enter into transactions if they feel they are dealing with a **reputable brand** or organisation.
Contact	You offer customer service at times to suit your customers. Increasingly, customers expect service to be available 24 hours a day, seven days a week. They also expect the person on the other end of the telephone to be able to give them information and solutions.

EXAMPLE

Here are examples of organisations which are trying to create and/or change their culture to promote a service-oriented mentality.

Egg

1. Egg, launched in 1998, is the Prudential's bid to build a next-generation financial services company, with customer-centred values at its core. The company is at pains to demonstrate that it is not a 'me-too' organisation, exactly like all the others in its sector: on the contrary, it is a bold attempt to build a truly values-led company.

2. Egg uses several mechanisms to ensure that its people are 'on board', ie, that they understand what the culture of the organisation is about.

   - Considerable effort has been expended to create, define and disseminate a common language, so that people at Egg can fully understand one another when they communicate.
   - The company deliberately recruits like-minded people who share the aspirational values of Egg.
   - An initial one-week residential training and development programme, called touch, introduces new employees to the core values and the common language; it also aims to enhance their self-esteem and begin to equip them with the skills necessary to succeed.
   - Further training is plentiful, especially around the ideal of 'dancing' with customers (ie, behaving towards customers in ways which coincide with customer expectations, rather than simply working within predetermined 'scripts').
   - All managers and executives consistently 'walk the talk' so that it is apparent that they too live and breathe the Egg values.
   - There is a Values Ignition Group of around 100 people, who meet once a month in order to share ideas about the Egg values can be constantly energised. The intention is that the Group can be disbanded once the 'way of being' at Egg has become totally values-led to the point where it does not need to be promoted explicitly any more.
   - The Egg Intranet site allows employees to learn about the values and the behaviours which support or violate them, and permits individuals some direct access to directors.
   - Adherence to the Egg values is incorporated into the company's performance appraisal processes.

---

3 QUALITY AND CUSTOMER CARE

For marketing service managers, the 'quality control' and 'engineering' of the interactions which take place between customers is a key strategic issue. Customers are often, in the course of service delivery, interacting with other customers to gather information, and form views about the nature and quality of the service of which they are contemplating purchase. Minimising exposure to negative feedback, and promoting the dissemination of positive images and messages about the value of the service, and the quality of customer responses to it, are important objectives here.

Activity 4 **(10 minutes)**

All levels of staff must be involved in customer service. To achieve this end, it is vital for senior management consciously to promulgate values of customer service constantly, in order to create and build a culture of customer service within the company. How do you think that this might be achieved?

Crosby describes his system in two sets of principles, the **absolutes of quality management** and the **basic elements of improvement**.

3.1 Absolutes of quality management.

(a) Quality means conformance to requirements, not elegance.

Crosby insists that quality is a series of requirements which must be clearly stated. It can then be communicated and measured to see if it has been achieved. These measurements will establish the presence or absence of quality.

(b) There is no such thing as a 'quality' problem.

Problems arise in specific departments and must be identified by those departments. Quality, as well as a problem, is created in a specific department and is not the province of a specific 'quality' department within the organisation.

(c) There is no such thing as the economics of quality; it is always cheaper to do the job right first time.

(d) The only performance measurement is the cost of quality.

The cost of quality is the expense of nonconformance. While most companies spend almost 20% of their revenue on quality costs, a well run quality management programme can reduce this to less than 3%.

(e) The only performance standard is zero defects.

Zero defects is a performance standard, with the theme 'do it right the first time'. This means concentrating on the prevention of defects rather than finding and fixing them.

This is, Crosby argues, a matter of concentrating, of applying the same standards we have in our private life to the way in which we approach the workplace. He asserts:

> 'Most human error is caused by lack of attention rather than lack of knowledge. Lack of attention is created when we assume that error is inevitable. If we consider this condition carefully and pledge ourselves to make a constant effort to do our jobs right the first time, we will take a giant leap towards eliminating the waste of rework, scrap and repair that increases cost and reduces individual opportunity.'
>
> (Philip Crosby, *Quality is Free,* 1979)

This is quite clearly different from the ideas of Juran and Deming, neither of whom would have placed this emphasis on the responsibility of the **line worker** when the majority of imperfections in the system of production are due to **poorly designed equipment** and systems which are beyond the control of the individual.

3.2 Basic elements of improvement

(a) **Determination,** or the commitment of management to this process.

(b) **Education,** which involves transmitting the absolutes to the members of the organisation.

(c) **Implementation,** which should clearly specify the process whereby quality is to be established within the organisation.

This has proved a popular approach because it emphasises behaviour processes within organisations rather than simply the use of statistical techniques. It can be fitted alongside existing corporate strategies with minimal disruption and tailored to the enterprise involved to accommodate all kinds of idiosyncrasies.

The power of quality claims is most evident when they are not fulfilled, as when a company's product fails. Here, consumers' expectations are not realised and dissatisfaction results. In these situations marketers immediately take steps to reassure customers.

DISCUSSION

When the company confronts the problem effectively, consumers often are willing to forgive and forget, as was the case with Perrier, when traces of benzene were found in the water.

When a company appears to be acting slowly or attempting a cover-up, consumer resentment is likely to grow, as occurred during Union Carbide's disaster in Bhopal, India and with Exxon following the massive oil spill in Alaska caused by the tanker, the Exxon Valdez.

3.3 Total quality and total customer orientation

A **customer orientation,** seeking to satisfy the customer, is pursued in marketing by recognising that customers buy 'the sizzle, not the steak' - products are bought for the benefits they deliver; how customers can use the product to accomplish the things they want to do.

Feigenbaum (1983) identifies Total Quality Management (TQM) directly with the customer.

Definition

> **Total quality management** is defined as:
>
> '... the total composite product and service characteristics of marketing, engineering, manufacture and maintenance, through which the product and service in use will meet the expectations by the customer.'

What constitutes a 'quality product or service' must, it seems, be related to what the customer wants. Indeed, quality would have no commercial value otherwise. The customer must be the final arbiter of the quality which a product possesses.

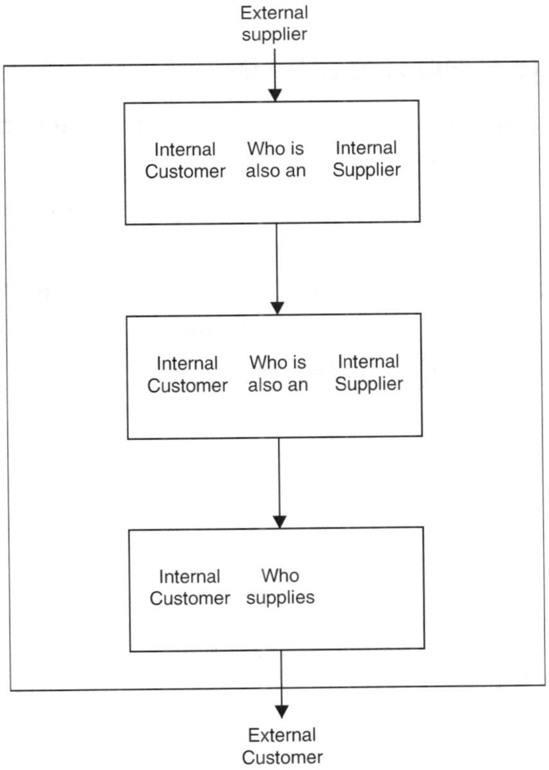

John Oakland argues that **meeting customer requirements** is the main focus in a **search for quality**. While these requirements would typically include aspects such as availability, delivery, reliability, maintainability and cost effectiveness, in fact the first priority is to establish what customer requirements **actually are**.

(a) If the customer is **outside the organisation**, then the supplier must seek to set up a marketing activity to gather this information, and to relate the output of their organisation to the needs of the customer.

(b) **Internal customers** for services are equally important, but seldom are their requirements investigated. The quality implementation process requires that all the supplier/customer relationships within the **quality chain** should be treated as marketing exercises, and that each customer should be carefully consulted as to their precise requirements from the product or service with which they are to be provided. Each link in the chain should prompt the following questions.

Of customers

- Who are my immediate customers?
- What are their true requirements?
- How do or can I find out what the requirements are?
- How can I measure my ability to meet the requirements?
- Do I have the necessary capability to meet the requirements? (If not, then what must change to improve the capability?)
- Do I continually meet the requirements? (If not, then what prevents this from happening, when the capability exists?)
- How do I monitor changes in the requirements?

Of suppliers

- Who are my immediate suppliers?
- What are my true requirements?
- How do I communicate my requirements?
- Do my suppliers have the capability to measure and meet the requirements?
- How do I inform them of changes in the requirements?

4 CUSTOMERS WHO COMPLAIN

If a person is unhappy with a product or service then essentially they have three courses of action open to them:

1	Voice response	- a verbal complaint to the retailer in person or to the manufacturer by phone
2	Private response	- negative word of mouth and/or boycott the retailer or manufacturer
3	Third party response	- take legal action, write to an MP/newspaper, register a complaint with the local authority

A number of factors influence which route is taken. The consumer may in general be assertive or passive.

DISCUSSION

Action is more likely to be taken for expensive products such as household durables, cars and clothing than for inexpensive products.

Also, if the consumer does not believe that the store will respond positively to a complaint, the person will be more likely to switch brands than fight. Marketers should encourage consumers to complain to them as people are more likely to spread the word about unresolved negative experiences to their friends than they are to boast about positive occurrences.

The propensity of customers to complain has changed radically over the past few years. Not only are customers much **more willing to make a noise** about their grievances, but they will also **tolerate much less** by way of restitution and delays - and, moreover, they will (as organisations see it) **fight dirty** more quickly, using threats of disclosure to television programmes and/or litigation in order to achieve their objectives.

(a) Technically, one has to argue that if customers are more prepared to tell you about their dissatisfaction, then this means that the organisation will secure **more reliable, representative and comprehensive customer feedback** than it ever did when it relied on a situation where only 1 in 10 of the customers who were dissatisfied bothered to tell you about it. The remaining nine either quietly took their business elsewhere, or bided their time until the moment when they could do so.

(b) Of course, **not all companies see the complaint process as an opportunity**.

  (i) Some still have **no proper complaint-handling mechanism** at all, which means that customers have some initial communication barriers to overcome; it may also mean that the **treatment of complaining customers is erratic**, with some receiving generous restitution whilst others are simply told to push off.

  (ii) Some organisations **don't keep records of the complaints received** - indeed, they may have **no clear definition** of the term 'complaint' so that, for example, someone telephoning to ask for a copy of assembly instructions accidentally omitted from a flatpack furniture product may find that their call has been classified as 'information request' rather than 'complaint', especially if there is corporate pressure to minimise the number of 'complaint' items.

  (iii) Yet more organisations, receiving complaints, will respond **defensively** and seek to imply, if they can, that there is **something wrong with the complainant,** eg they washed the product by hand when the instructions clearly said that it should only be dry-cleaned.

  (iv) Several will hope, apparently, that if they simply **ignore** complaints then most of them will go away: thus correspondence does not stimulate replies, telephone calls are not returned and customer service managers are mysteriously unavailable.

In fact complaints are part of the marketing process.

(a) If you actively **encourage** your customers to complain, you demonstrate **faith in your product/service** offer.

(b) **Analysing the nature of each complaint**, as well, will show where design, manufacturing, delivery and functionality resources need to be concentrated.

(c) If complaints are handled efficiently, expeditiously and sympathetically, then potentially defecting customers can be tied to you even more closely than before: they will rather **tell others about the wonderful way in which**

you handled their complaint than tell them about what was wrong in the first place.

When customers walk into a shop, or phone the customer complaints line, they want the company's employees to **own the problem**. They do not want to be **passed around** and they do not want to be told about the **organisation's difficulties** ('we're very short-staffed at the moment' or 'the computer's down' or 'she's at lunch').

Ownership of the problem needs to be reinforced by the ability to give an **immediate response**.

(a) **Front-line staff** must be **empowered** to deal with complaints quickly: for most customers, time is of the essence, and if they are kept waiting, or transferred through several departments, then the original complaint rapidly escalates into rage.

(b) **Managers** find empowerment very difficult: they **worry excessively** about what customer-facing people will do if **left to their own devices**. What seems to happen, in effect, is that organisations devote all their energies to designing **procedures** which will prevent recovery and restitution systems from being **abused**, by either customers or employees: they forget that 99 per cent of all complaints are genuine, and 99 per cent of all employees are trying to do their best.

The ability to **empathise** is a key component in the effective handling of customer complaints, yet, typically, organisations are **reluctant to look at 'problems' from the customer's perspective**. If they did then much more attention would be given to creating procedures which lean over backwards to ensure that the complaining customer is mollified.

EXAMPLE

A regular airline customer wrote to the company, complaining that its in-flight golf magazine catered only for Americans. His recommended solution was for the airline to supply equivalent golf magazines for British passengers. The airline wrote back to say that this was not practicable, but that as he was a regular flyer then they had arranged for him to have a year's subscription to the British magazine he'd mentioned. The subscription cost the airline around $30, but every time the magazine landed on the customer's doormat it would remind him positively of the company.

Training staff on how to deal with customers, then **letting them get on with it**, are two fundamental elements in the complaints management process.

Why should a business embrace **customer service** as a source of competitive advantage? The simple answer is that **if you don't, someone else will** - and, all other things (price, availability or whatever) being equal in the eyes of the consumer, better service or customer care will lead the consumer to choose your competitor's product.

5 CUSTOMER/SUPPLIER PARTNERSHIPS AND AGREEMENTS

5.1 Relationships with suppliers

Increasingly, companies are looking to develop **long term relationships with suppliers** they can trust and with whom they can tackle problems and develop opportunities. This symbiotic approach, advocated by those pursuing a total quality approach to management, is the basis of relationship marketing. While relationship marketing is concerned with customers, long-term business relationships can be built up with **favoured suppliers**. There are several factors behind this trend.

(a) Some firms have relationships with favoured suppliers rather than a free-for-all of suppliers competing for business on the basis of price.

(b) Just-in-time production methods, whereby supplies are delivered often and in small quantities, require a relationship of trust between supplier and customer.

(c) Relationships with favoured suppliers are encouraged by the total quality movement.

Supplier relationships can be built up in a number of ways, for example:

(a) Staff secondments.
(b) Joint research and development projects.

The end result of the relationship approach from the company's point of view is a **reduction in vulnerability to changing customer and supplier demands**: the bargaining powers of customers and suppliers are effectively managed in a marketing network.

5.2 Partnership sourcing and partnership marketing

Partnership sourcing and **partnership marketing** are other concepts which you may be asked to compare. The emphasis is on working together with all members of a value chain (suppliers, wholesalers, retailers and so on) to make sure that customer's needs are met profitably.

Definition

> From the perspective of a manufacturer, **partnership sourcing** implies a company seeking co-operation as it works back through the value chain. By contrast, **partnership marketing** implies co-operation as it works forwards through its value chain.

Essential features of partnership sourcing

- Joint involvement in new product development
- Joint solution of distribution problems
- Emphasis on long-term price stability
- Quality standards which are consistent and to an agreed level

Implications of partnership marketing

- Joint **promotional activity** shared by a manufacturer and its wholesalers and retailers

- Joint **research** to assess customers needs

- Joint **monitoring** of quality standards

- Joint **new product development** which is focused on meeting customers' identified needs

Another type of arrangement is the **co-maker agreement**. The examples below illustrate them at work, and show the benefits to be gained.

EXAMPLE

From Mustang Industrial Corp web site:

Co-maker relationships: The 'co-maker' relationships between our customers/suppliers and us are well established. Before our customers develop their new products, their designers will ask for our comments from the view points of a tool maker. With this kind of communication, the designers can avoid many mistakes and impractical designs.

Before we start to make products for our customers, we keep feeding back our professional suggestions, such as how to improve the design for increasing productivity and quality for the customer's benefit. Furthermore, we believe that 'our suppliers and us are on the same boat.'

Our quality control section staff are willing to help our suppliers to improve their quality and management in order that we can help each other.

From Magneti Marelli web site:

Magneti Marelli is a leading international company in automotive systems and components with a high electronics content.

The basic product and process know-how within a company is no longer the key factor in achieving an effective and efficient product development process. Rather, the number and complexity of technologies in today's products require a wide range of technological capabilities and competencies and huge investments in human, technological and financial resources. These investments are both too large and too risky to be undertaken by a single company.

Rather, companies prefer to establish a network of relationships that allows them to share costs, benefits an risks when a new product must be designed and launched. Know-how and knowledge is provided by people who contribute to product development either as single individuals or as a team. The way these teams and individuals are organised to carry out product development is critical to business growth.

Given these various changes, all companies in the car industry are continuously seeking new ways to address competitive pressures. Recognising the need to shorten development cycles, improve quality and increase productivity has historically led these companies to collaborative relationships - relationships that can be facilitated and supported by the implementation of information and communication technologies.

This increasing collaboration has in turn changed the industry's competitive structure, so that the competition is increasingly between groups of companies rather than between individual companies. These groups of companies, organised as networks, are composed of both competitors and suppliers.

The agreements linking network members may take various forms - partnerships, joint ventures, co-maker relationships and so on. Within a network, various inter-organisational projects are established to strengthen and leverage trust and openness relationships.

Against this background, at the end of the 80s Magneti Marelli changed it mission and organisation from product supplier to strategic partner capable of providing complete high-tech solutions. Recognising the importance of collaborative relationships, the company has formed and participated in several networks and network related projects.

Chapter roundup

- Customer satisfaction is the overall attitude a person has about a product or service after it has been purchased.
- Measuring customer satisfaction can be extremely problematic for a variety of reasons including inaccurate customer preconceptions, single incident disasters and weak anecdotal evidence.
- One way in which customer intelligence can be gathered is via a customer survey.
- Complaints are an essential form of feedback when properly organised.
- Customer care has been very much in the forefront of management thinking in both the public sectors (eg the Citizens' and Patients' Charters) and private sector (eg Rail Users' Charter) over recent years.
- The twelve pillars of performance framework have three major dimensions, strategy, people (ie employees) and customers.
- The power of quality claims is most evident when they are not fulfilled, as when a company's product or service fails.
- Total quality management is defined as the total composite product and service characteristics of marketing, engineering, manufacture and maintenance, through which the product or service in use will meet the expectations of the customer.
- Complaints are an essential part of the marketing process and a key component in the effective handling of customer complaints is the ability to empathise.
- Partnership sourcing implies a company seeking co-operation as it works back through the value chain.
- Partnership marketing implies co-operation as it works forward through its value chain.

Quick quiz

1. What are the four fundamentals of customer satisfaction?
2. What are the key problems in measuring customer satisfaction?
3. List five methods of gathering customer intelligence.
4. What does the term process alignment mean in the context of effective customer care?
5. What are the customer dimensions of the twelve pillars of performance?
6. What are the basic elements of quality improvement?
7. What three course of action does a dissatisfied customer have?
8. List three factors behind the trend in developing customer/supplier relationships.
9. Name four essential features of partnership sourcing.

Answers to quick quiz

1 Product/service variables, sales and promotion-related variables, after sales variables and culture-related variables. (See paragraph 1.1)

2 Weak, anecdotal evidence; single incident disasters; lack of counterbalance with positive comments; many simply go elsewhere. (para 1.2)

3 Survey, diary panels, interviews, in-store surveys and hall tests. (para 1.4)

4 It means making sure that the organisation serves the customer rather than the other way round. (para 2)

5 Consistency, communication, comfort and contact. (para 2.2)

6 Management commitment, organisational education and implementation. (para 3.2)

7 Voice response, private response and third party response. (para 4)

8 The move towards favoured suppliers, just in time production methods and the fact that relationships with favoured suppliers are encouraged by the total quality movement. (para 5.1)

9 Joint involvement in new product development, joint solution of distribution problems, emphasis on long-term price stability and quality standards which are consistent and to an agreed level. (para 5.2)

Answers to activities

1 Provide a telephone complaints number (preferably freephone).
Positively request that complaints are sent in.
Advertise an incentive eg a free prize draw as for this book.
Provide a named person to whom complaints should be addressed.

2 The result of, or answer to, this activity will depend on the item you have chosen.

3 Check orders before despatch.

Follow up re-deliveries which have been booked.

Offer some form of compensation: an extra panel may be useless to the customer.

Apologies help.

Poor service detracts from a good product.

4 Senior management are seen to participate in customer service.

Staff training.

Monitoring (eg incoming calls).

Constantly stress the importance of customer service.

Stress the importance from the recruitment stage onwards.

Respond quickly and effectively to customer complaints.

PART B: UNIT 19

MARKETING PLANNING

Chapter 6 :

MARKETING PLANNING AND MARKETING VISION

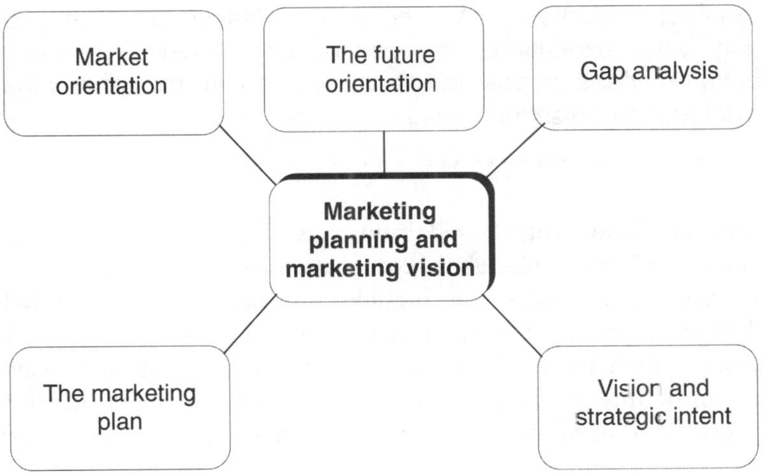

Introduction

This chapter covers market orientation and discusses how organisations can plan for the future using marketing analysis and strategy.

Your objectives

In this chapter you will learn about the following:

(a) What market orientation and a market led organisation are

(b) The role of marketing in market led organisations

(c) How organisations can plan for the future

(d) The importance of developing effective marketing plans

(e) The interrelationships between the marketing and other functional plans

(f) How to produce marketing plans

1 MARKET ORIENTATION

A 'market' is a group of customers. 'Marketing' is a process or activity. Here are some definitions of marketing.

Definition

(a) **Marketing** 'the management process responsible for identifying and satisfying customers' needs profitably.' (CIM)

(b) The American Marketing Association's definition is: 'The process of planning and executing the conception, pricing, promotion, and distribution of ideas, goods and services to create exchanges that satisfy individual and organisational goals.'

Many industries are 'knowledge'-based industries. The ability to tap knowledge and create ideas might be instrumental in corporate success, as might be the ability to communicate these ideas. Ideas can include information that will help customers determine whether the product will, in fact, be able to satisfy their needs. Marketing therefore encompasses many of the qualities that businesses need to have in order to survive. Ideas can be intellectual property, such as software and so forth, which can be sold as products. Marketing is not limited to fmcg (fast moving consumer goods) products.

'Marketing' can also refer to a department within an organisation, with its own professional staff with specialist expertise, and 'potential' interests in terms of other business functions.

DISCUSSION

If you have a good product or service you don't need marketing.

1.1 Marketing-led and market-led orientation

Given that marketing is a process, an organisational function, and an academic discipline, it is worth going back to first principles. A **market** is a customer or group of customers.

Definition

Market orientation is 'an organisational culture where beating the competition through the creation of superior customer value is the paramount objective throughout the business'. (Piercy)

A **marketing-led organisation is led by the marketing department.** Marketing orientation might just refer to increased power for marketing personnel. The customer, however, is not necessarily at the heart of **everyone's** thinking.

In a company with a market orientation, the aim of providing superior customer value dominates **all** thinking.

- What the business is
- Which markets to service
- Investments and acquisitions
- Which people to employ and how to promote them

In **market-led** organisations, the marketing department is **not** in a world of its own. Customer value is designed and created by **multi-function** product teams supporting **all the business functions.**

Activity **(10 minutes)**

Think of a company which is market led. What characteristics does it have? How is it set apart from the competition?

1.2 Market-led strategic change

Market-led strategic change rests on the following assumptions (Piercy, 1997).

Assumptions
All organisations must follow the dictates of the market to survive.
Organisational effectiveness can be pursued by being market-led, focusing on the customer.
Barriers to being market-led come, not from ignorance of customer characteristics, but from the way organisations are run.
Becoming market-led often needs an upheaval.
A deep seated strategic change is not just hiring a marketing executive.

In short the pursuit of **customer satisfaction** is at the heart of the market-led company. Piercy (1997) makes a distinction between **marketing** and **going to market**. Markets are more important than marketing, per se, and markets and customers are important for everyone in a company (not just the marketing department). '**Going to market** is a process owned by everyone in the organisation ... the context for marketing should be the **process** of going to market, not the marketing department.'

The process of going to market needs to be **managed**. Piercy highlights the key elements of this.

(a) Strategies are based on customers and markets.

(b) Internal programmes and external actions are driven by such strategies.

(c) The company must 'get its act together' in order to deliver its strategy into the market. This involves more than the marketing department.

(d) Cross-functional teams cross organisational boundaries to get the job done.

(e) New types of relationships are created.

(f) New ways of doing business are supported by a new information technology infrastructure.

EXAMPLE

Over the last few years ICI (Imperial Chemical Industries) has taken a long hard look at its past and its future. It was felt to be a dated organisation dealing with low profit

NOTES

commodity chemicals. It has been reorganised into a new divisional structure including paints and 'fragrance and flavours' with a substantial increase in profitability.

(Pitcher G Marketing Week, 9 November 2000)

1.3 Challenges for the market-led organisation

Four broad issues arise for the market-led organisation (Piercy 1997).

Issue	Comment
'New' customers	• Rising expectations: customers exposed to world class service will expect it everywhere • Sophistication: customers can see through marketing-speak, and want transparency • Increased cynicism about marketing
New competitors	• From overseas • Reinventing the business (eg Direct Line Insurance)
New type of organisation	• Outsourcing arrangements • Collaboration arrangements • Alliances (eg airlines) • Stakeholder influences
New ways of doing business	• Customer-specific marketing • Databases are used to develop profiles of individual customers to entice them into a **relationship** • Internet marketing: buyers and sellers can conduct a dialogue as the internet is interactive • Customer co-operatives: internet newsgroups and chatrooms enable customers to get together perhaps to negotiate discounts or to share experience of a brand

DISCUSSION

The Internet will take over as the main marketing medium.

EXAMPLE

Sony is the worldwide leader in the games console market. However it has been under strong competition from Sega's launch of the Dreamcast console. In 2000 Sony launched the new Playstation 2 with limited availability. Whether or not the shortgage will make Playstation 2 be more in demand or whether people will switch to Dreamcast remains to be seen.

BPP PUBLISHING

1.4 Role of 'marketing' in market-led firms

What might be the role of marketing and marketing management in this particular context? argues that the role of 'marketing' has changed significantly but has also become much more important to the activities of many firms. The changes Piercy notes are these.

(a) **From staff to line**. Marketing thinking and action are better integrated into the day to day decisions of managers running important parts of the business. In other words, instead of a separate, 'staff' marketing department going its own sweet way and putting a promotional gloss on what the organisation does, marketing is more involved in line decisions, such as segment or product management.

(b) **From specialist to strategic**. 'Marketing in the organisation has evolved beyond its traditional specialist focus. Tasks once exclusively associated with marketing, such as market and competitive assessment or end-user communication, are now only a part of a far more integrated marketing process that may include other functions such as upstream product development or downstream management of distribution.'

(c) **From isolated to widespread**. Marketing has become more diffused within the organisation, and is no longer the concern of the few. In short, Kashani argues, the market orientation is spreading.

1.5 The view from 2005

It is worth having a look at how certain trends might affect how things will appear in a few years times. Introducing the Financial Times *Mastering Marketing* series, **Kotler** made the following predictions.

Trend	Comment
Disintermediation	All products can be bought from the internet, meaning that there is less need for intermediaries
Retailers	Simple shopping is out, as people can buy supplies over the internet. Shops become entertainment venues (eg bookshops with coffee shops)
Mass customisation	Customers can order bespoke products but these can be produced with the efficiency of mass production
Data mining	Firms get more information about customers and use it for cross selling
Management information	Real information about customer profitability can be obtained
Long-term supplies	Customers will be offered 'life-time' supplies
Outsourcing	This will be the norm
Franchising	Most field sales people will become franchisees
End of mass TV	TV advertising takes on the characteristics of magazine advertising, with a proliferation of TV and internet channels
Sustainable competitive advantages	Benchmarking, reverse engineering and technological leapfrogging

EXAMPLE

The Inland Revenue has recently appointed its first ever marketing director (Marketing Week, 23 November 2000). Many organisations who have previously either not felt they needed marketing or which thought it was a waste of money have developed marketing departments.

2 THE FUTURE ORIENTATION

'Some management teams were simply more foresightful than others. Some were capable of imagining products, services and entire industries that did not exist and then giving them birth. These managers seemed to spend less time worrying about how to position the firm in existing competitive space and more time creating fundamentally new competitive space.' (Hamel and Prahalad, 1994)

According to this view, there are two 'approaches' to the future.

- The future will be incrementally similar to the present.
- The future will be radically different.

Hamel and Prahalad suggest that:

- The future is not just something that 'happens' to organisations
- Organisations can 'create' the future

In practice, there is truth in both perspectives.

(a) Some trends are likely to continue indefinitely. In the physical environment, global warming will continue for the long term. In terms of demography, other than wars or famine, it is relatively easy to predict population trends. Forecasting techniques cover this.

(b) Other developments are harder to determine.

  (i) In 1900, a long-term investor would have invested in railway shares.

  (ii) In 1947, it was assumed that demand for computers would be no more than five worldwide.

  (iii) Even now, nobody really knows which inventions or innovations will succeed.

Activity 2 **(10 minutes)**

Think back to five years ago. What events that have had an impact on business organisations have occurred? Which could have been foreseen?

Hamel and Prahalad suggest, however, that **some companies are more 'prepared' to shape the future** than others, and that this **future-orientated stance is somehow embodied in the corporate culture**. Hamel and Prahalad offer a 'diagnostic' to indicate how future-orientated a company is.

Diagnostic statement	Protect the past	Create the future
Senior management's viewpoint about the future is …	Conventional, reactive	Distinctive, far-sighted
Senior management spend most of their time on …	Re-engineering current processes	Regenerating core strategies
Within the industry, the company ...	Follows the rules	Makes the rules
The company is better at …	Operational efficiency	Building new businesses
To what extent does the company pursue competitive advantage by …	Catching up with competitors?	Creating new sources of competitive advantage?
How is the company's agenda for change actually set?	By competitors	By a vision of the future
Are managers	Engineers of the present?	Architects of the future?
Are employees	Anxious?	Hopeful?

Activity 3 **(30 minutes)**

Undertake this diagnostic test for your own company. Carry it out alone and then get another member of staff to do it - from another department, say.

EXAMPLE

The Millennium Dome has been under widespread criticism due to the government and its management's lack of planning. Visitor numbers were forecast far too highly and criticisms were made of the government's involvement in the management of a visitor attraction.

3 GAP ANALYSIS

Strategic planners must think about the extent to which new strategies are needed to enable the organisation to achieve its **objectives**. One technique whereby this can be done is **gap analysis**. Gap analysis is based on establishing:

(a) What are the **organisation's targets for achievement** over the planning period?

(b) What would the organisation be expected to achieve if it **did not** develop any new strategies, but **simply carried on in the current way** with the same products and selling to the same markets?

There will be a difference between the targets in (a) and expected achievements in (b). New strategies will then have to be developed which **will close this gap**, so that the organisation can expect to achieve its targets over the planning period.

NOTES

Definition

Gap analysis is 'the comparison of an entity's ultimate objective with the sum of projections and already planned projects, identifying how the consequent gap might be filled'.

A forecast or projection based on existing performance: F_0 forecasts

The **F_0 forecast** is a forecast of the company's future results assuming that it **does nothing new**. The company is expected to continue to operate as at present without any changes in its products, markets, organisation, assets, human resources, research spending, financial structure, purchasing and so forth. Preparation of an F_0 forecast entails the following.

- The analysis of revenues, costs and volumes
- Projections into the future based on past trends
- Other factors affecting profits and return (eg in the environment, strikes, competitors)
- Finalising the forecast

The purpose of the F_0 forecast and gap analysis is to determine the **size of the task** facing the company if it wishes to achieve its target profits.

Forecasts can never be completely accurate. If possible, the error should be quantified in either of the following two ways.

(a) **Estimating likely variations**. For example 'in 2001 the forecast profit is £5 million with possible variations of plus or minus £2 million'.

(b) **Providing a probability distribution for profits**. For example 'in 2005 there is a 20% chance that profits will exceed £7 million, a 50% chance that they will exceed £5 million and an 80% chance that they will exceed £2½ million. Minimum profits in 2005 will be £2 million.'

The profit gap

The **profit gap** is the difference between the target profits (according to the overall corporate objectives of the company) and the profits on the F_0 forecast. Other forms of gap analysis (eg for sales revenue) can be developed.

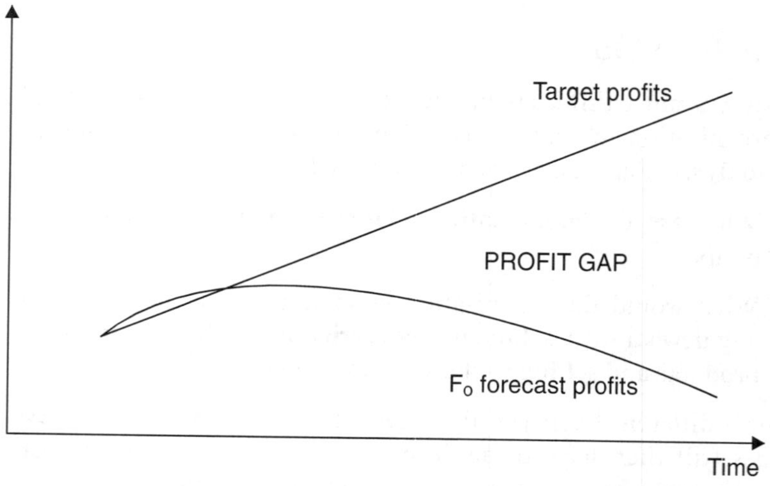

BPP PUBLISHING

NOTES

It is now that the company must decide what the **options are for bridging the gap**. This gap represents the extra task facing the company, in addition to just continuing the existing business. It indicates how much extra profit **has to be** generated by the decisions and the commitments to be made over the next few years. In deciding the size of the gap that must be closed, allowance must be made for errors in the forecast.

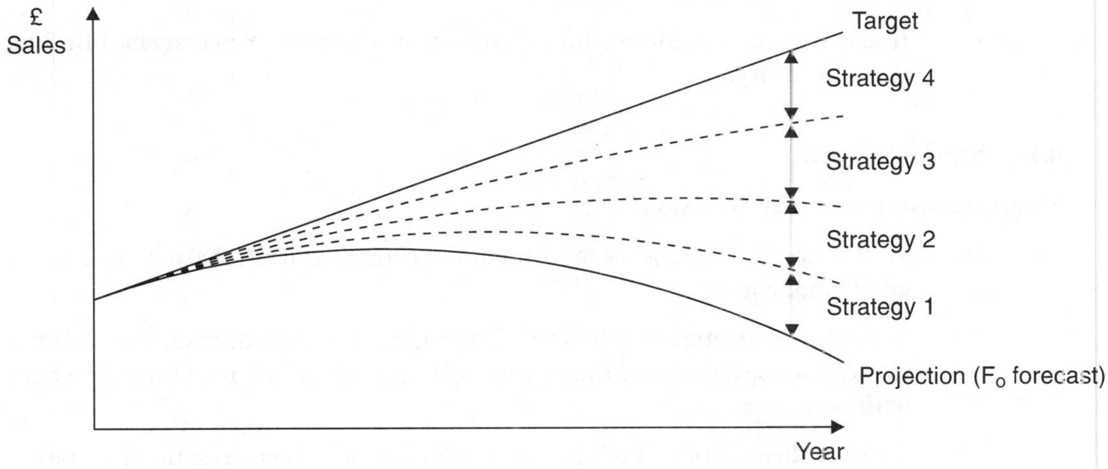

EXAMPLE

Pilkington Glass recently undertook a thorough review and restructuring of its market positioning strategies. Long term plans outlined where they wanted to be in the market place and strategies were designed to get there. These strategies included increased control over distribution and improving margins. Operational plans would then have been developed from these.

(Lorenz A. 'Pilkington Picks up the Pieces', Management Today, March 1996)

---

4 VISION AND STRATEGIC INTENT

A strategic thinker should have a **vision** of:

- What the business is now
- What it could be in an ideal world
- What the ideal world would be like

A vision gives a general sense of direction to the company, even if there is not too much attention to detail. A vision, it is hoped, enables **flexibility** to exist in the context of a guiding idea. 'Like the North Star, a manager's vision is not a goal. Rather, it is the orientation point that guides the company in a specific direction. A vision should be clear.

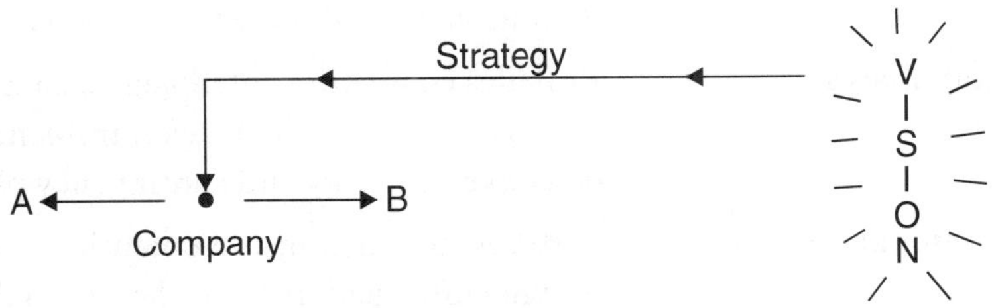

BPP PUBLISHING

A company with two choices would move to 'B' rather than 'A'. The strategy draws on the vision. A vision might provide the 'boundaries' for the firm's direction.

Problems with vision

- It ignores real, practical problems.
- It can degenerate into wishful thinking on the part of managers, blinding them to reality.

4.1 Strategic intent

Strategic intent is similar to vision.

(a) 'A **dream** that energises a company' (Hamel and Prahalad). It has an **emotional** core.

(b) It implies a '**stretch**' for the organisation, even if current resources will not satisfy the aspirations of the vision. It is more than just matching resources with objectives.

(c) Sense of **direction**. It is a long-term ambition, which enables the integration of complex skills within the firm.

(d) Sense of **discovery**: strategic intent offers a new destination for employees to work towards.

(e) It gives **coherence** to strategic plans.

'Strategic intent' aims to enthuse employees with the company's business goals, as if they are fighting a war. (**Values** in the long term are possibly more motivating.)

5 THE MARKETING PLAN

Marketing plans are formulated to show how marketing can contribute to the corporate plan.

Marketing makes a particularly important input to the corporate planning decisions. Information inputs from marketing to the **corporate** planning decisions perform a double duty in that they also provide the bases for deciding marketing objectives and strategies. **Marketing research** is vital to **all stages** of the marketing plan hence the need for an effective marketing information system.

Aspect	Comment
The environmental audit	Reviews the organisation's position in relation to changes in the external environment (social/cultural, legal, economic, political and technological) and provides information which directly affects the setting of corporate objectives. The market place is, by definition, part of the 'environment'.
Competitor analysis	Provides competitor intelligence, competitor response models and so on which again influence corporate objectives, strategy and contingency planning.
The customer audit	Assesses the existing and potential customer bases to provide information as to whether to develop new markets.

Aspect	Comment
Product portfolio analysis	Provides input for decisions as to whether to drop particular products and/or add new ones.
The sales forecast	Provides the basis for all other functional activities as well as marketing.

Activity 4 **(30 minutes)**

Consider the company you work for, or your college. Your brief is to undertake an environmental audit and competitor analysis for the industry, or college sector.

The **marketing plan** uniquely is concerned with **products** and **markets**.

(a) These are typically stated in terms of market share, sales volume, levels of distribution and probability.

(b) Decisions might be taken as to the type of products sold to particular customer groups.

DISCUSSION

Many marketing research methods are needed for successful marketing planning information.

5.1 Marketing plans and other functional plans

Objectives of other departments

(a) The marketing manager's plans are often frustrated by other people in the organisation. These 'blockers' can be people in the marketing department but are more likely to be people in other departments.

(b) The less an organisation is truly market orientated, the more likely it is that marketing plans are ineffective. Each functional area has its own particular concerns and constraints and, at strategic level, marketers have to take these into account if they want to achieve anything.

What other departments do

Department	Activity
Production	Purchasing, acquiring resources and forming them into products/services the firm can offer.
Human resources	Obtaining the right number of people at the right level of skills. This is vital in **service industries** for successful marketing plans – people are integral to the service marketing mix.

Department	Activity
Finance	The need to remain profitable, raising and distributing money and maintaining a healthy cash flow.
Research and development	May be independent of either production or marketing.
IT	In firms where **information** is a key resource, there might be separate plans and strategies for information technology. Financial services firms such as banks pay particular attention to IT. **Database marketing** depends on effective use of IT.

All these functional plans exist in the wide framework of the corporate plan. In practice all these plans are interrelated.

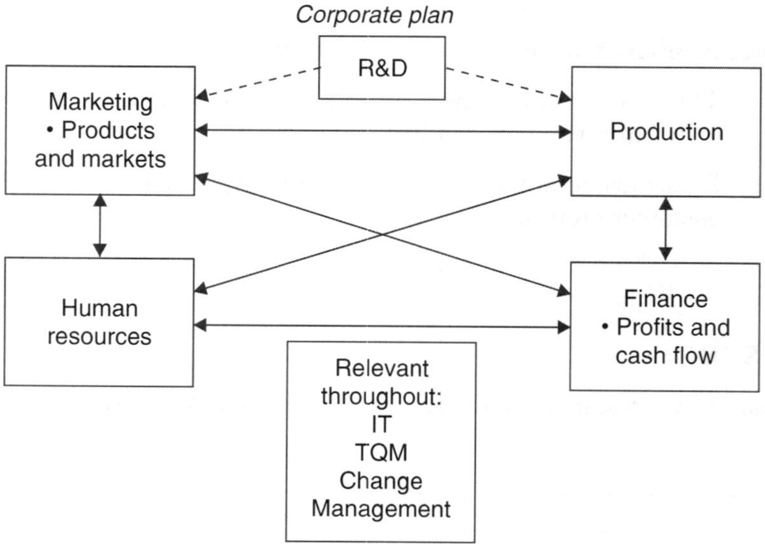

5.2 Activities crossing functional boundaries

Certain activities cannot be really packaged into 'functional plans' even in principle.

(a) Total quality management (TQM) is relevant to the whole organisation.

(i) **Marketing**: quality means satisfying customer needs.

(ii) **Production**: TQM employs a very specific set of production techniques to reduce variation in the physical process of manufacture and to enhance quality.

(iii) **R&D**: TQM requires precise attention to the design of both products and processes.

(iv) **Human resources**: TQM requires a change in the way people work, so that continuous improvement can be made to manufacturing processes.

(v) **Finance**: TQM supporters believe that the cost of preventing mistakes is less than the cost of rectifying them.

(b) **Change management** programmes affect every function within the organisation. Examples include change to the organisation structure and radical new approaches to business such as **business process re-engineering.**

(c) **Research and development.** This requires input from marketing and production.

Inter-relationships between functional plans

At strategic level, marketing cannot be managed in a vacuum. Marketing directors and managers cannot take strategic decisions on their own without reference to the managing director and the directors of other functions - ie corporate management as a team.

5.3 The marketing plan in outline

On the next page we present a **concise** framework for the marketing plan.

5.4 Strategic and tactical decisions in marketing

It is also worthwhile, certainly for exam purposes, deciding the difference between a **strategic marketing plan** and a **tactical marketing plan.**

(a) **Strategic marketing plan**

  (i) Three to five or more years long.

  (ii) Defines scope of product and market activities.

  (iii) Aims to match the activities of the firm to its distinctive competences.

(b) Tactical marketing plan

  (i) One year time horizon.
  (ii) Generally based on existing products and markets.
  (iii) Concerned with marketing mix issues.

NOTES

A CONCISE FRAMEWORK FOR A MARKETING PLAN

1. *ANALYSIS OF CURRENT SITUATION* (Using Marketing Research)

1.1 THE MARKET

	00	01	02	03	04	05	06	07	08	09	10
Mkt size (units)											
Mkt share (units)											
Mkt size (cash)											
Mkt share (cash)											

Mkt trends/forecasts
Company strengths/weaknesses and key features of marketing mixes
Brand strengths/weaknesses and key features of marketing mixes
Competitor strengths/weaknesses and key features of marketing mixes
Customer profiles, buying behaviours, needs
Company sales forecasts

1.2 DISTRIBUTION

Available channels
Sales by outlet
Competitors' distribution methods

1.3 ENVIRONMENTAL FACTORS

2. *BUSINESS MISSION/OBJECTIVES*

What business are we in?
What business would we like to be in 5-10 years hence?
Corporate objectives - profitability, growth, risk reduction.
Marketing objectives - market share, sales.

3. *STRATEGIES* - ANSOFF

	Existing Products	New Products
Existing Markets	Market Penetration	Product Development
New Markets	Market Development	Diversification

SEGMENTATION

- Bases
- Characteristics and measurement
- Strategy

4. *TACTICS/OPERATION PLAN* - MKG MIX PROPOSALS

4.1 PRODUCT DECISIONS

- Objectives
- Branding
- Packaging
- Pre/After sales service

4.2 PRICING DECISIONS

- Objectives
- Strategy - penetration v. skimming
- Discounts

4.3 DISTRIBUTION DECISIONS

- Objectives
- Channels
- Intensive/selective/exclusive distribution

4.4 PROMOTION DECISIONS

- Objectives - roles
- Salesforce size/organisation/motivation
- Sales promotion/PR, merchandising
- Advertising expenditure
- Media - target audiences
- Copy/creative platforms
- Agencies

5. *BUDGETS*

Sales forecasts, Sales budgets
Periods - 1-5 years
Costs - selling, marketing, advertising etc

6. *CONTROL*

To monitor progress

Although you will be familiar with the marketing content, it is important that you are able to produce realistic and credible marketing **plans**. The steps involved in developing a marketing plan are the same as those already examined in depth for the corporate level.

Step 1. Analysis
Step 2. Objective
Step 3. Strategy
Step 4 . Tactics
Step 5 . Control

Activity 5 **(1 hour)**

For your own company or college undertake section 2 of the marketing plan – business mission and objectives.

EXAMPLE

Companies' mission statements are often available on their web pages. They vary in terms of length, detail and appraoch. Gillette's mission is To achieve or enhance clear leadership worldwide in the existing and new core consumer products in which we choose to compete'.

Dell's mission is to be 'the most successful computer company in the world at delivering the best customer experience in the markets we serve'.

5.5 Content of marketing plan

Kotler identifies the formulation of **marketing plans** as follows.

Section	Content
The executive summary	This is the finalised planning document with a summary of the main goals and recommendations in the plan.
Situation analysis	This consists of the SWOT analysis and forecasts.
Objectives and goals	What the organisation is hoping to achieve, or needs to achieve, perhaps in terms of market share or 'bottom line' profits and returns.
Marketing strategy	This considers the selection of target markets, the marketing mix and marketing expenditure levels.
Action programme	This sets out how these various strategies are going to be achieved.
Budgets	These are developed from the action programme.
Controls	These will be set up to monitor the progress of the plan and the budget.

DISCUSSION

'Control' is the most neglected aspect of the marketing planning process.

5.6 Formulating marketing strategy

A **marketing strategy** is a plan to achieve the organisation's objectives by specifying.

(a) What resources should be allocated to marketing.

(b) How those resources should be used to take advantage of opportunities which are expected to arise in the future.

In the context of applying the **marketing concept,** a marketing strategy would:

(a) **Identify target markets** and customer needs in those markets

(b) Plan products which will **satisfy the needs** of those markets

(c) **Organise marketing resources,** so as to match products with customers in the most efficient and effective way possible.

The strategic concepts of **segmentation** and **product positioning** should be at the heart of modern marketing planning.

Analyse and describe market segments

↓

Test segments for (commercial) validity

↓

Choose a competitive segmentation strategy

↓

Develop a market positioning/product positioning strategy

EXAMPLE

According to McDonald (1995) the most frequently cited problems arising from a lack of marketing planning are:

1 Lost opportunities for profit

2 Meaningless numbers in long range plans

3 Unrealistic objectives

4 Lack of actionable market information

5 Interfunctional strife

6 Management frustration

7 Proliferation of products and markets

8 Wasted promotional expenditure

9 Pricing confusion

10 Growing vulnerability to environmental change

11 Loss of control over the business

5.7 The marketing action plan: marketing mix proposals

The link between the formulation and the implementation of marketing strategy is the **marketing action plan,** which identifies how the mix will be deployed. The mix represents the **controlled** use of a firm's resources allocated to the marketing budget.

(a) The marketing mix may be simplified into the four Ps plus three Ps for service.

(i) **Product:** quality, features, fashion, packaging and branding, after sales service, guarantees, durability etc.

(ii) **Price:** the level of price, credit terms, discounts guarantees.

(iii) **Place:** factors here include the location of sales outlets and the number and type of sales outlets (shops, supermarkets etc), the location of service departments, stock levels and transportation and delivery services.

(iv) **Promotion** advertising, sales promotion, selling, PR.

(v) **People**: courtesy, competence of the people delivering the service.

(vi) **Processes**: how the service is delivered.

(vii) **Physical evidence**: the environment of the service encounter.

(b) **Different marketing mixes** will appeal to different **market segments** in any particular market.

(c) The marketing mix for a product must be **planned** in advance. It should also be **reviewed** in the light of experience and, if product sales have not been as good as expected, managers might take **control action** by should be given to changing the mix, for example, lowering product quality, reducing price and spending more on advertising.

Activity 6 **(1 hour)**

Following on from your environmental and competitor audit (activity 4) in your chosen industry or college, investigate what the main market leaders' approach to segmentation and marketing mix are.

NOTES

Chapter roundup

- Marketing as a business orientation is being customer focused on customer needs. It is also a business function often with a department in an organisation.
- Key elements to manage market led strategic change are:
  - Strategies are based on customers and markets
  - Internal programmes and external actions are driven by such strategies
  - The company must 'get its act together' in order to deliver its strategy. This involves more than the marketing department
  - Cross functional teams cross organisational boundaries to get the job done
  - New type of relationships are created
  - New ways of doing business are supported by a new information technology infrastructure
- Challenges to the future centre around:
  - 'New' customers
  - New competitors
  - New types of organisation
  - New ways of doing business
- The future can be more prepared for by using the diagnostic test in section 2.
- Gap analysis shows any differences in an organisation's targets and expectations of achievement if the current strategy was pursued.
- Strategies can then be developed to 'fill' the gap.
- A vision gives general strategic direction to an organisation.
- Marketing plans are designed to contribute to the corporate plan.
- Marketing plans will include information on the following.
  - an environmental audit
  - competitor analysis
  - a customer audit
  - product portfolio analysis
  - sales forecasts
- Other departments in an organisation will have plans that should be interrelated with each other.
- A marketing plan will consist of:
  - (i) Analysis of current situation (market, distribution and environment)
  - (ii) Business mission/objective
  - (iii) Strategies
  - (iv) Tactics (operational plan)
  - (v) Budgets
  - (vi) Control
- Strategies should take account of market segmentation and product positioning.
- The operational plan should cover all aspects of the marketing mix.
- The marketing mix can be extended for services to cover product, price, place, promotion, people, processes, physical evidence.

BPP PUBLISHING

Quick quiz

1 What is meant by market orientation?

2 What are the four main challenges according to Piercy for the market led organisation?

3 How can a company determine how 'future orientated' it is?

4 What is 'gap analysis'?

5 Why should organisations develop marketing plans?

6 What type of information does a company need to develop a marketing plan?

7 Give an example of a business activity that crosses functional boundaries.

8 Outline the steps in developing a marketing plan.

9 What is the extended marketing mix (7 Ps)?

Answers to quick quiz

1 The organisational culture where creating superior customer value is the main business objective. (See paragraph 1)

2 New customers, new competitors, new types of organisations, new ways of doing business. (para 1.3)

3 A company could undertake Hamel and Prahalad's diagnostic test in section 2. (para 2)

4 A comparison of an organisation's ultimate objective with the sum of projections and already planned projects, identifying how a gap could be filled. (para 3)

5 To contribute to the organisation's corporate planning process to enable the organisation to plan strategies for the future. (para 5)

6 Information on the environment, on competitors, on customers, on sales and products. (para 5)

7 Could be TQM, change management programmes or research and development. (para 5.2)

8 Analysis
Objectives
Strategies
Tactics
Control (para 5.4)

9 Product, Price, Place, Promotion, People, Processes, Physical evidence. (para 5.7)

Answers to activities

1 The answer to this will depend on the company you have chosen.

2 The rapid advance of e-commerce: probably the speed of the advance could not be foreseen.

Greater customer willingness to complain; could not be foreseen.

Economic peaks and troughs: should be foreseeable.

NOTES

New financial services legislation: not foreseeable five years ago.

Changes of government: probably foreseeable.

3 The answer to this will depend on the company you have chosen.

4 The answer to this will depend on the company you have chosen.

5 The answer to this will depend on the company you have chosen.

6 The answer to this will depend on the company you have chosen.

Chapter 7 :
ORGANISATIONAL CAPABILITY

Introduction

A look at the internal environment of an organisation is a way of identifying strengths and weaknesses. It therefore covers all aspects of the organisation. This is because the other functions of the organisation effectively act as constraints over what marketing personnel can achieve.

A company needs to evaluate its ability to compete and satisfy customer needs. The firm's resources, once identified, must be harnessed to a market orientation to ensure that those resources are directed at satisfying those needs.

There are a number of approaches to be taken with regard to corporate capability. In this chapter we conduct an overview of resources in the context of organisational effectiveness. The key issues are what resources the organisation has and how they are deployed.

Your objectives

In this chapter you will learn about the following:

(a) How resources and limiting factors can affect business operations

(b) The importance of the marketing audit process

(c) The difference between marketing efficiency and effectiveness

(d) How the PLC concept can be used for marketing planning

(e) How BCG and value chain analysis can be used for strategic planning

1 RESOURCES AND LIMITING FACTORS

An analysis of corporate/marketing resources covers:

- What the organisation currently has or owns
- What the organisation has access to, even if it currently does not own the resources
- How effectively it **deploys** its resources

1.1 Resource audit

A **resource audit** is a review of the organisation resources which can be grouped into these categories (Hooley, Saunders and Piercy).

Resource	Comment
Technical resources	• Technical ability. • Processes for NPD. • Ability to convert new technology into new marketing products.
Financial standing	• Firms with a good financial standing find it easier to raise money.
Managerial skills	Managerial roles and functions were covered in Chapter 2. An effective management is a key organisation resource in planning activities, controlling the organisation and motivating staff.
Organisation	Organisation structure can be a resource for marketers, for example product divisionalisation or brand management control at brand level. The organisation structure should facilitate communication and decision-making.
Information systems	The strategic role of information systems is covered at various times throughout this Study Text.

Resources are of no value unless they are organised into systems, and so a resource audit should go on to consider how well or how badly resources have been utilised, and whether the organisation's systems are **effective** and **efficient** in meeting customer needs profitably.

Activity 1 **(30 minutes)**

Review the above resource audit using the example of either your company or your college.

1.2 Limiting factors

Every organisation operates under resource **constraints.**

Definition

A **limiting factor** or **key factor** is 'a factor which at any time or over a period may limit the activity of an entity, often one where there is shortage or difficulty of supply'.

Examples

- A shortage of production capacity
- A limited number of key personnel, such as salespeople with technical knowledge
- A restricted distribution network
- Too few managers with knowledge about finance, or overseas markets
- Inadequate research design resources to develop new products or services
- A poor system of strategic intelligence
- Lack of money
- A lack of staff who are adequately trained

Once the limiting factor has been identified, the planners should:

- **Short term**, make best use of the resources available
- **Long term**, reduce the limitation

1.3 Resource use

Resource use is concerned with the **efficiency** with which resources are used, and the **effectiveness** of their use in achieving the planning objectives of the business.

Distinctive competences

A strategic approach involves identifying a firm's **competences**. Members of organisations develop judgements about what they think the company can do well - its core competence. These competences may derive from:

- **Experience** in making and marketing a product or service
- The talents and potential of individuals in the organisation
- The **quality of co-ordination**/distribution

Definition

> The **distinctive competence** of an organisation is what it does well, or better, than its rivals.

Tests for identifying a core competence

(a) It provides potential **access to a wide variety of markets**. GPS of France developed a 'core competence' in 'one-hour' processing, enabling it to process films and build reading glasses in one hour.

(b) It **contributes significantly to the value enjoyed** by the customer. For example, in GPS in (a) above, the waiting time restriction was very important.

(c) It should be **hard for a competitor to copy**, if it is technically complex, involves specialised processes, involves complex interrelationships between different people in the organisation or is hard to define.

In many cases, a company might choose to **combine competences**.

Bear in mind that relying on a competence is no substitute for a strategy. However, distinctive competences are an important support for competitive positioning.

FOR DISCUSSION

Skoda have been successful in changing its image over the past few years. What do you consider its core competencies?

EXAMPLE

The most common organisational structure is the family business. Many large organisations are still family firms (Wal-Mart, Gucci, Hyundai). However the need to raise money, to embrace new technology and to develop internationally is forcing some to make more use of professional managers.

(Economist, 2 December 2000)

2 MARKETING AUDITS AND MARKETING EFFECTIVENESS

2.1 Marketing audits

Definition

> 'A **marketing audit** is a comprehensive, systematic, independent and periodic examination of a company's - or business unit's - marketing environment, objectives, strategies and activities with a view to determining problem areas and opportunities and recommending a plan of action to improve the company's marketing performance.' (Kotler, Gregor and Rodgers, 1977)

A marketing audit does not exist in the compulsory formal sense that an external financial audit does. For proper strategic control, however, a marketing audit should have the following features.

(a) **Regular**. It should be conducted **regularly**, for example once a year.

(b) **Comprehensive**. It should take a **comprehensive** look at every product, market, distribution channel, ingredient in the marketing mix etc. It should not be restricted to areas of apparent ineffectiveness (for example an unprofitable product, a troublesome distribution channel, low efficiency on direct selling etc).

(c) **Systematic**. It should be carried out according to a set of predetermined, specified procedures.

(d) **Independence**. A consultant might be appointed, or someone else within the organisation.

DISCUSSION

An outside independent consultant is the best person to undertake a marketing audit.

2.2 The audit procedure

A marketing audit should consider the following areas, according to Kotler.

- The market environment, macro and micro
- Marketing strategies
- Marketing systems
- Marketing organisation
- Marketing function

The marketing environment

(a) **Micro.** What are the organisation's major markets, and what is the segmentation of these markets? What are the future prospects of each market segment?

   (i) Who are the customers, what is known about customer needs, intentions and behaviour?

   (ii) Who are the competitors, and what is their standing in the market?

(b) **Macro.** Have there been any significant developments in the broader environment (for example economic, or political changes, population or social changes etc)?

> **Activity 2** **(30 minutes)**
>
> Choose a magazine you are familiar with. Undertake a short analysis of the micro and macro factors of its marketing environment.

Marketing strategy audit

(a) What are the organisation's marketing objectives and how do they relate to overall objectives? Are they reasonable?

(b) Are enough (or too many) resources being committed to marketing to enable the objectives to be achieved? Is the division of costs between products, areas etc satisfactory?

Marketing systems. What are the procedures for formulating marketing plans and management control of these plans? Are they satisfactory?

Marketing organisation. Does the organisation have the structural capability to implement the plan?

Marketing functions. A review of the effectiveness of each element of the mix (eg advertising and sales promotion activities) should be carried out.

(a) A review of sales and price levels should be made (for example supply and demand, customer attitudes, the use of temporary price reductions etc).

(b) A review of the state of each individual product (ie its market 'health') and of the product mix as a whole should be made.

(c) A critical analysis of the distribution system should be made, with a view to finding improvements.

Marketing productivity. How profitable and cost-effective is the marketing programme?

Advantages of a marketing audit

- It should reduce the need for crisis management
- It should identify information needs
- A formal process forces people to think

2.3 Efficiency and effectiveness of marketing

Definitions

(a) **Efficiency**: gaining maximum output for a minimum input and is normally used relatively (ie in comparison to a standard or norm, to competitors, to industry norms, or the PIMS database).

(b) **Effectiveness**: doing the right things rather than doing things right. A firm can be incredibly efficient in producing widgets at the lowest cost but if no one will buy them it is all to no effect and it will soon be out of business.

A company that is both efficient and effective will prosper. A company that is inefficient but effective will survive, at least in the short term. A company that is both inefficient and ineffective will die quickly. Let us put this on a grid.

		Effectiveness	
		High	*Low*
Efficiency	*High*	THRIVE	DIE SLOWLY
	Low	SURVIVE	DIE QUICKLY

Source: Wilson, Gilligan, Pearson

DISCUSSION

Effectiveness is more important than efficiency.

EXAMPLE

In *Marketing Week*, David Benadly described some of the long-term problems facing the Co-op.

'The Co-operative Bank has shown that it can be done. Tesco demonstrates that supermarkets can do it. But whether the 500-strong Co-operative Retail Society grocery chain can carry it off is by no means assured. "It" is nothing less than staging the complete relaunch of a flagging brand, turning round consumer perceptions and giving a real point of difference to rivals.

But speculation about a possible £500m bid for the non-food parts of the Co-operative Wholesale Society and CRS has drawn attention to the group and could put more pressure on the chief executive to turn things round quickly.

The problems of CRS, a rag-tag portfolio of 500 stores under three different facias - Leo's, Pioneer and Stop & Shop - are profound and difficult. Its market share in the grocery trade has fallen from nearly nine per cent in the late Eighties, to less than six per cent today.

The stores are now being rebranded under two names - the larger stores as Co-operative Pioneer and the convenience stores as Co-operative Local. The variation in store sizes and poor location of some stores means different stores offer different ranges, opening hours and standards of service.

Many CRS customers are older and less affluent than those of Sainsbury's and Tesco, so another objective is to make the stores appeal to a broader, more representative, group of customers.

The problems at CRS have been accentuated by the technical advances made by the other multiples in stock replenishment, electronic point of sale, loyalty and customer service. It is not so much what CRS has been doing wrong, but what the competition has been doing right.

Yet CRS, and the Co-operative movement in general, have some important saving graces. 'The Co-op is one of the best known brands in the UK. It has got latent heritage and there are a lot of things people think are good about the brand - but it has become tarnished in recent years."

But perhaps the most appropriate parallel for what the CRS is trying to do is a similar task carried out by Tesco in the Eighties. The chain also had a downmarket image and its name was synonymous with a 'pile it high, sell it cheap', philosophy.

CRS needs more efficient organisation, and is implementing a new management structure and redefining lines of responsibility and reporting. There is also work to do on product ranges, which are seen as too diffuse. Ranges are decided locally rather than nationally.

While this means local tastes can be targeted accurately, it can lead to confusion in relations with suppliers and in the negotiation of discounts. Part of the new attitude to merchandise and the supply chain at CRS is the introduction of the own-label Co-operative brand.

The strength of the new own-label will go a long way to defining the level of quality of the relaunched CRS.'

2.4 The importance of marketing effectiveness

Although it is obviously true that marketing effectiveness is a vital component of organisational effectiveness, it is not always easy to measure precisely, especially as marketing 'assets' are hard to measure and value.

The marketing excellence framework

In *Manufacturing: the Marketing Solution*, the Chartered Institute of Marketing (CIM) has developed a framework for evaluating companies' marketing operations. A sample of 44 companies from the UK's manufacturing sector was taken, and each company's marketing activities were assessed and scored on a marketing excellence framework. Then, the marketing excellence score was compared with financial results.

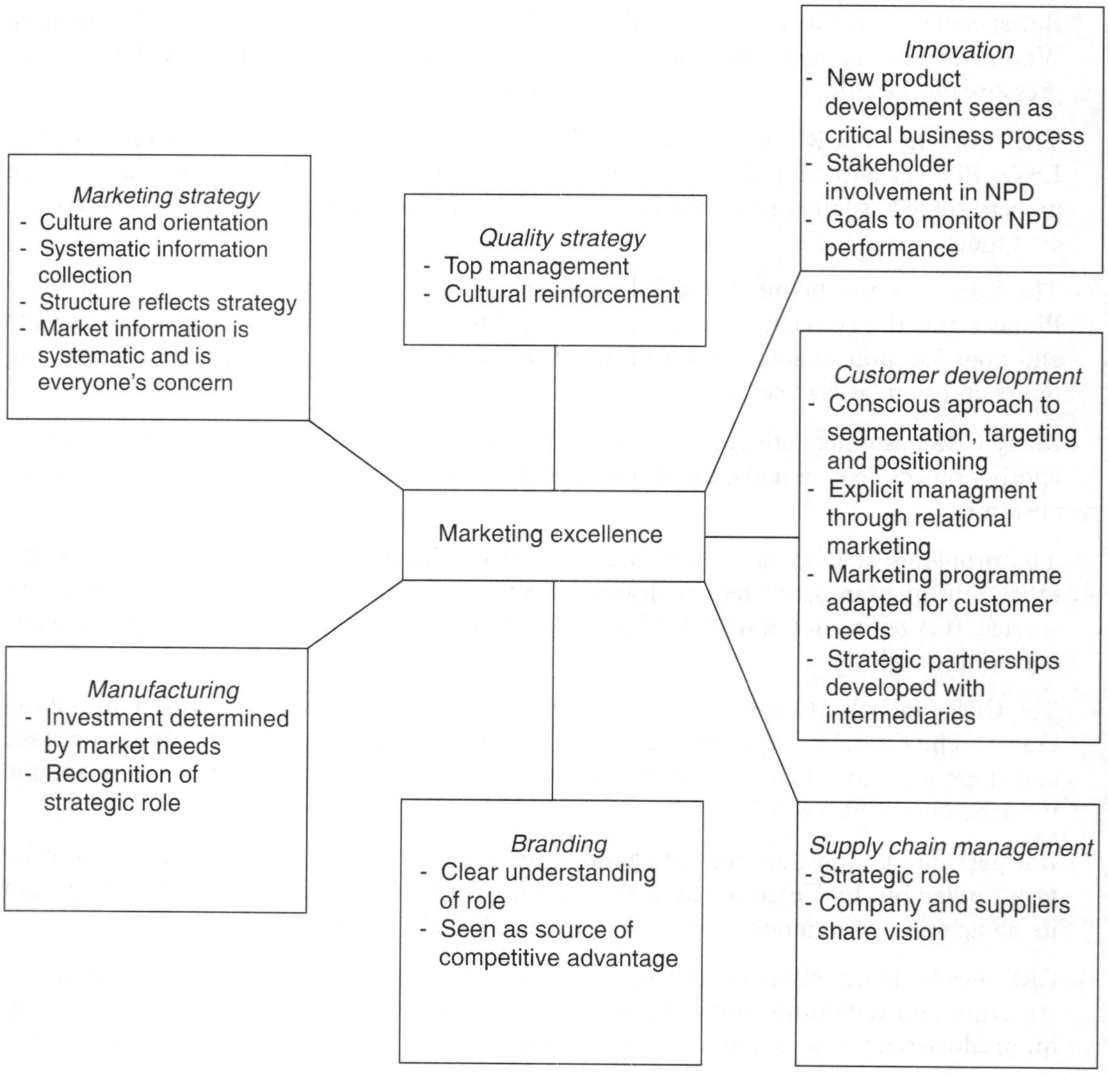

Measuring marketing capability

Kotler has developed the thinking on marketing effectiveness into a general purpose rating tool based upon the following fifteen questions, as adapted in the table below.

Marketing effectiveness rating

Customer philosophy
1 To what extent does management recognise the need to organise the company to satisfy specific market demands?
2 To what extent is the marketing programme tailored to the needs of different market segments?
3 Does management adopt a systems approach to planning, with recognition being given to the interrelationships between the environment, suppliers, channels, customers and competitors?
Marketing organisation
4 To what extent does senior management attempt to control and integrate the major marketing functions?
5 What sort of relationship exists between marketing management and the management of the R&D, finance, production and manufacturing functions?
6 How well organised is the new product development process?
Marketing information
7 How frequently does the company conduct market research studies of customers, channels and competitors?
8 To what extent is management aware of the sales potential and profitability of different market segments, customers, territories, products and order sizes?
9 What effort is made to measure the cost-effectiveness of different levels and types of marketing expenditure?
The strategic perspective
10 How formalised is the marketing planning process?
11 What is the quality of the thinking that underlies the current marketing strategy?
12 To what extent does management engage in contingency thinking and planning?
Operational efficiency
13 How well is senior management thinking on marketing communicated and implemented down the line?
14 Does marketing management do an effective job with the resources available?
15 Does management respond quickly and effectively to unexpected developments in the market-place?

Each question can be answered on three levels.

(a) Question 1 could have answers:

1.1 To no extent
1.2 To some extent
1.3 To a very high extent

(b) Question 5 could have answers:

> 5.1 Extremely poor, antagonism exists, marketing regarded as being too demanding
>
> 5.2 Normally satisfactory although there is an underlying attitude that each department is basically self-serving
>
> 5.3 Extremely good with all departments working together to serve the customer

(c) Each of these three levels is then allocated a score of 0, 1, or 2:

Poor = 0
Satisfactory = 1
Excellent = 2

(d) Each manager works his way through the fifteen questions in order to arrive at a score. The scores are then aggregated and averaged. The overall measure of marketing effectiveness can then be assessed against the following scale.

0 - 5	=	None	Firm's survival in doubt
6 - 10	=	Poor	
11 - 15	=	Fair	Opportunity to improve
16 - 20	=	Good	
21 - 25	=	Very good	
26 - 30	=	Superior	Beware complacency

3 THE PRODUCT LIFE CYCLE

Many firms make a number of different products or services. Each product or service has its own financial, marketing and risk characteristics. The combination of products or services influences the attractiveness and profitability of the firm.

EXAMPLE

Glaxo for many years produced Zantac an anti-ulcer drug. Patents expire after a defined period.

Glaxo anticipated this development and invested in new drugs to provide income when returns from Zantac fall. An alternative would be to build the brand.

The profitability and sales of a product can be expected to change over time. The **product life cycle (PLC)** is an attempt to recognise distinct stages in a product's sales history. Marketing managers distinguish between product class, form and brand.

NOTES

Definitions

(a) **Product class:** this is a broad category of product, such as cars, washing machines, newspapers, also referred to as the generic product.

(b) **Product form:** within a product class there are different forms that the product can take, for example five-door hatchback cars or two-seater sports cars, twin tub or front-loading automatic washing machines, national daily newspapers or weekly local papers etc.

(c) **Brand:** the particular type of the product form (for example Ford Escort, Vauxhall Astra; Financial Times, Daily Mail, Sun etc).

3.1 Stages

The product life cycle applies in differing degrees to each of the three cases. A product-class (eg cars) may have a long maturity stage, and a particular make or brand **might** have an erratic life cycle (eg Rolls Royce) or not. Product forms however tend to conform to the 'classic' life cycle pattern, commonly described by a curve as follows.

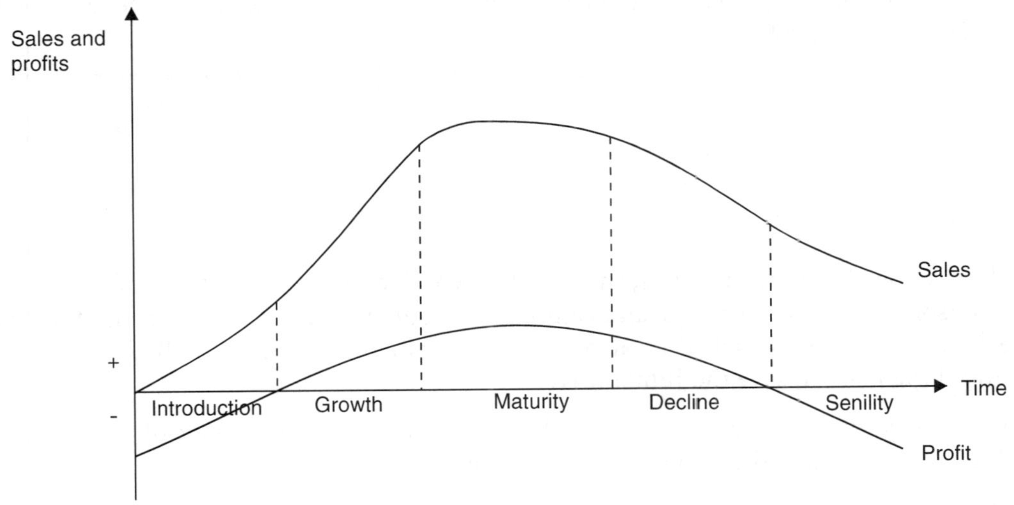

Introduction

(i) A new product takes time to find acceptance by would-be purchasers and there is a slow growth in sales. Unit costs are high because of low output and expensive sales promotion.

(ii) There may be early teething troubles with production technology.

(iii) The product for the time being is a loss-maker.

Growth

(i) If the new product gains market acceptance, sales will eventually rise more sharply and the product will start to make profits.

(ii) Competitors are attracted. As sales and production rise, unit costs fall.

Maturity

(i) The rate of sales growth slows down and the product reaches a period of maturity which is probably the longest period of a successful product's life.

(ii) Most products on the market will be at the mature stage of their life.

(iii) Profits are good.

Decline

(i) Some products reach a stage of decline, which may be slow or fast.

(ii) Eventually, sales will begin to decline so that there is over-capacity of production in the industry.

(iii) Severe competition occurs, profits fall and some producers leave the market.

(iv) The remaining producers seek means of prolonging the product life by modifying it and searching for new market segments.

(v) Many producers are reluctant to leave the market, although some inevitably do because of falling profits.

Activity 3 **(5 minutes)**

What would the PLC curve look like for a 'fad' product such as the Big Billy Bass singing fish?

EXAMPLE

Airbus is now, by some measures, the world's second largest manufacturer of aircraft - it is a consortium of four partners, and commands about 30% of the airliner market outside the EU. Airbus has launched a range of aircraft which compete with Boeing in every sector of the market, save the Jumbo 747.

Airbus is expected to be very profitable. 'It has a relatively modern range of aircraft in an industry with product life cycles of 25 years or more.'

Airbus is seeking to compete with the Boeing 747 perhaps by finding new partners in Asia to build a new 'super-jumbo'. The 'carrot' Airbus offers to potential partners is that it will be able to introduce new technology.

DISCUSSION

PLC analysis can be a self fulfilling prophecy where products are axed before their time.

3.2 The PLC and marketing planning

It is essential that firms plan their portfolio of products to ensure that new products are generating positive cash flow before existing 'earners' enter the decline stage.

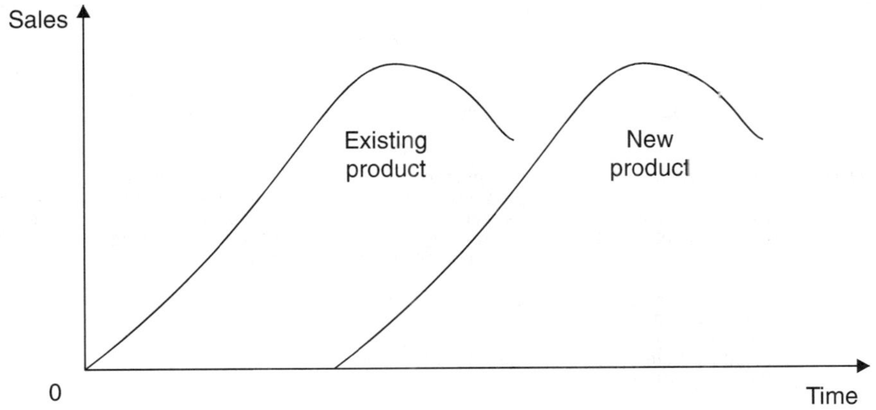

In the situation above the company is likely to experience cash flow problems.

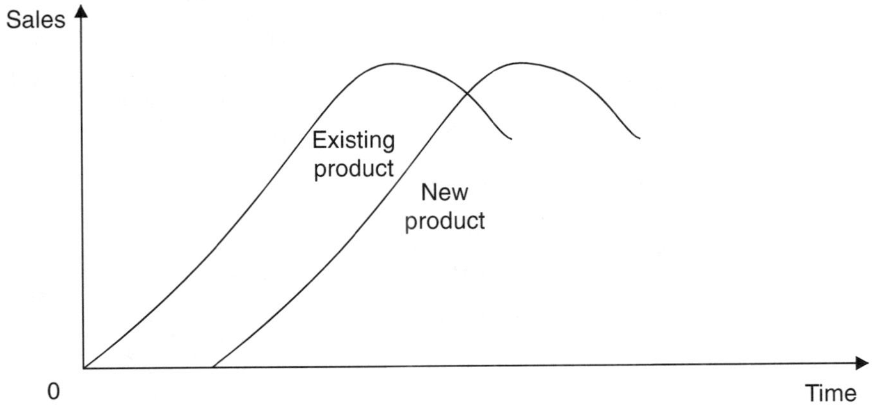

By considering the product life cycle of the existing product when planning the timing for launch of a new product cash flow problems can be avoided.

It is perhaps easy enough to accept that products have a life cycle, but it is not so easy to sort out how far through its life a product is, and what its expected future life might be.

(a) There ought to be a **regular review** of existing products, as a part of marketing management responsibilities.

(b) **Sources of PLC predictions**

- An analysis of past sales and profit trends
- The history of other products
- Market research
- If possible, an analysis of competitors
- A review of technological developments

(c) The future of each product should be estimated in terms of both sales revenue and profits.

Decisions for each product

- **Continue selling,** with no foreseeable intention yet of stopping production
- **Prolong the product's life,** perhaps by adjusting the mix or finding new customers
- **Stop producing** the product

The possible implications of each stage are shown in following table.

	Phase			
	Introduction	*Growth*	*Maturity*	*Decline*
1 *Products*	Initially, poor quality. Product design and development are a key to success. No standard product and frequent design changes (eg microcomputers in the early 1980s).	Competitors' products have marked quality differences and technical differences. Quality improves. Product reliability may be important.	Products become more standardised and differences between competing products less distinct.	Products even less differentiated. Quality becomes more variable.
2 *Customers*	Initial customers willing to pay high prices. Customers need to be convinced about buying.	Customers increase in number.	Mass market. Market saturation. Repeat-buying of products becomes significant. Brand image also important.	Customers are `sophisticated' buyers of a product they understand well.
3 *Promotion*	High advertising and sales promotion costs.	High advertising costs still, but as a % of sales, costs are falling.	Markets become segmented. Segmentation and extending the maturity phase of the life cycle can be key strategies.	Less money spent on advertising and sales promotion.
4 *Competition*	Few or no competitors.	More competitors enter the market. Barriers to entry can be important.	Competition at its keenest: on prices, branding, servicing customers, packaging etc.	Competitors gradually exit from the market. Exit barriers can be important.
5 *Prices and costs*	High prices but losses due to high fixed costs.	High prices. High contribution margins, and increasing profit margins. High P/E ratios for quoted companies in the growth market.	Falling prices but good profit margins due to high sales volume. Higher prices in some market segments.	Still low prices but falling profits as sales volume falls, since total contribution falls towards the level of fixed costs. Some increase in prices may occur in late decline stage.
6 *Manufacturing*	Over-capacity. High production costs.	Under-capacity. Move towards mass production and less reliance on skilled labour.	Optimum capacity. Low labour skills.	Over-capacity because mass production techniques are still used.
7 *Distribution*	Few distribution channels.	Distribution channels flourish and getting adequate distribution channels is a key to marketing success.	Distribution channels fully developed, but less successful channels might be cut.	Distribution channels dwindling.

3.3 The product life cycle and the marketing orientation

Does the PLC promote a 'product orientated' focus when in fact a 'market orientated' focus is necessary? Ansoff follows Levitt's thinking in extending the PLC concept to encompass the **demand/technology life cycle** (DLC), and the technology life cycle (TLC). The diagram below illustrates how a **demand life cycle** is made up of a number of **technology life cycles** which in turn are composed of PLCs.

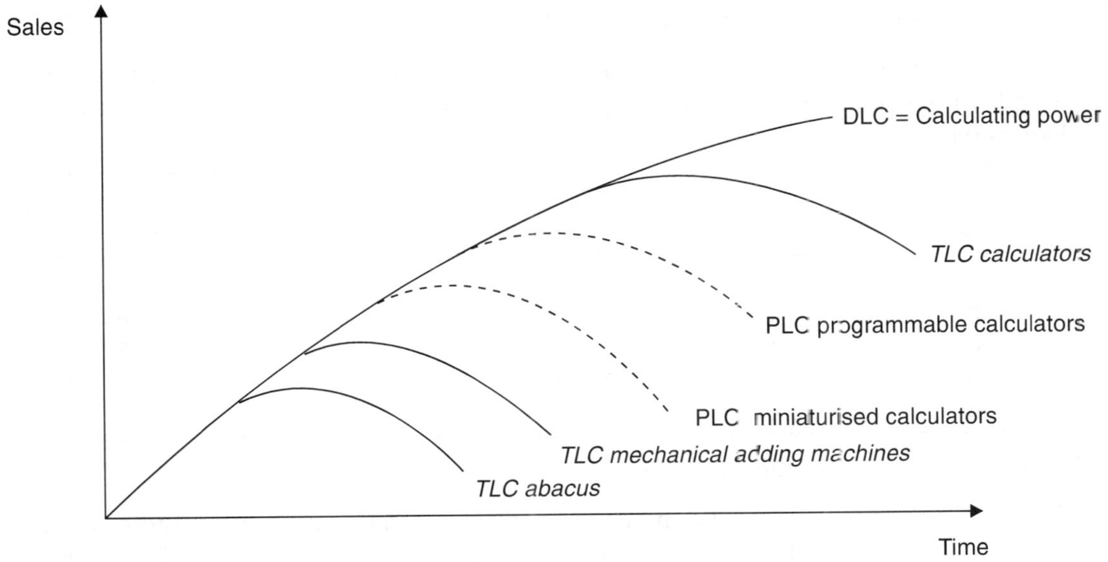

For example, 'calculating power' represents a human demand that is probably in the growth stage of the DLC. This has been composed of a number of TLCs - finger counting, abacuses, slide rules, adding machines, calculators, computers. Each new technology usually satisfies the **generic need** in a **superior way**.

The TLC indicates that for many products, death will eventually transpire through **technology** and **competitive innovation**.

> **Activity 4** **(10 minutes)**
>
> You are a marketing manager for a company manufacturing 'All Bright' toothpaste. Recently sales have been falling for the product, which has been established for a number of years. What type of marketing strategies could you consider to improve sales?

4 PORTFOLIO ANALYSIS

Portfolio planning analyses the current position of an organisation's products on SBUs in their markets, and the state of growth or decline in each of those markets. Several matrices have been developed over the years to analyse market share, market growth and market position.

Definition

> **Portfolio:** A collection of products/SBUs reporting to one entity. Each product SBU can be separately identified for decision-making and performance measurement.

4.1 Market share, market growth and cash generation: the Boston classification

The **Boston Consulting Group** (BCG) developed a matrix, based on empirical research, which classifies a company's products in terms of potential cash generation and cash expenditure requirements. This is related to **market share relative to competitors.**

You should also note that BCG analysis can be applied to:

- Individual products
- Whole strategic business units (SBUs)

To illustrate how to evaluate a portfolio a simulated company example will be provided. An industrial equipment company has five products with the following sales and market characteristics.

Product	*Sales £m*	*£m sales Top 3 firms*	*Market growth rate %*	*Relative share*
A	0.5	0.7 0.7 0.5*	15%	0.71
B	1.6	1.6 1.6* 1.0	18%	1.0
C	1.8	1.8* 1.2 1.0	7%	1.5
D	3.2	3.2* 0.8 0.7	4%	4.0
E	0.5	2.5 1.8 1.7	4%	0.2

* Company sales within the market

This information can then be plotted on to a matrix. The circles indicate the contribution the product makes to overall turnover. The centre of circles indicates their position on the matrix:

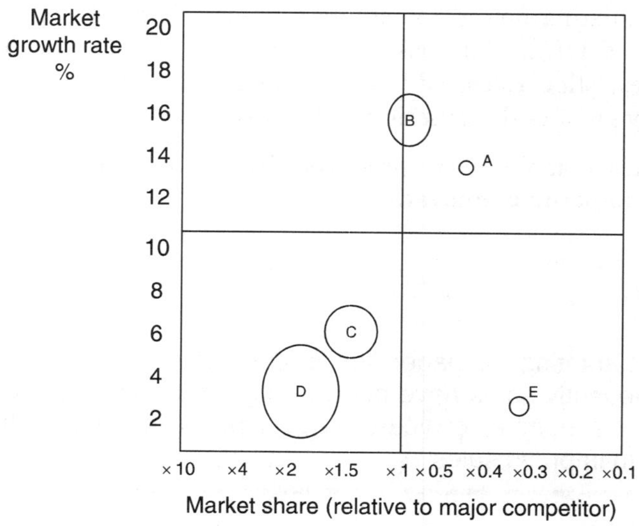

This growth/share matrix for the classification of products into cash cows, cash dogs, stars and question marks is known as the **Boston classification** (or the **Boston Matrix**).

(a) **Stars** are products with a high share of a high growth market. In the short term, these require capital expenditure in excess of the cash they generate, in order to maintain their market position, but promise high returns in the future.

(b) In due course, stars will become **cash cows**, with a high share of a low-growth market. Cash cows need very little capital expenditure and generate high levels of cash income. Cash cows generate high cash returns, which can be used to finance the stars.

(c) **Question marks** are products in a high-growth market, but where they have a low market share. Do the products justify considerable capital expenditure in the hope of increasing their market share, or should they be allowed to 'die' quietly as they are squeezed out of the expanding market by rival products? Because considerable expenditure would be needed to turn a question mark into a star by building up market share, question marks will usually be poor cash generators and show a negative cash flow.

(d) **Dogs** are products with a low share of a low growth market. They may be ex-cash cows that have now fallen on hard times. Dogs should be allowed to die, or should be killed off. Although they will show only a modest net cash outflow, or even a modest net cash inflow, they are 'cash traps' which tie up funds and provide a poor return on investment, and not enough to achieve the organisation's target rate of return.

There are also **infants** (ie products in an early stage of development), **warhorses** (ie products that have been cash cows in the past, and are still making good sales and earning good profits even now) and even **cash dogs,** which are dogs still generating cash.

The evaluation and resulting strategic considerations for the company in the diagram above are these.

(a) There are two cash cows, thus the company should be in a cash-positive state.

(b) New products will be required to follow on from A.

(c) A is doing well (15%) but needs to gain market share to move from position 3 in the market - continued funding is essential. Similar for B.

(d) C is a market leader in a maturing market - strategy of consolidation is required.

(e) D is the major product which dominates its market; cash funds should be generated from this product.

(f) E is very small. Is it profitable? Funding to maintain the position or selling off are appropriate strategies.

Activity 5 **(10 minutes)**

The marketing manager of Juicy Drinks Ltd has invited you in for a chat. Juicy Drinks Ltd provides fruit juices to a number of supermarket chains, which sell them under their own label. 'We've got a large number of products, of course. Our freshly squeezed orange juice is doing fine - it sells in huge quantities. Although margins are low, we have sufficient economies of scale to do very nicely in this market. We've got advanced production and bottling equipment and long-term contracts with some major growers. No problems there. We also sell freshly squeezed pomegranate juice: customers loved it in the tests, but producing the stuff at the right price is a major hassle: all the seeds get in the way. We hope it will be a winner, once we get the production right and start converting customers to it. After all the market for exotic fruit juices generally is expanding fast.'

What sort of products, according to the Boston classification, are described here?

The **product life cycle** concept can be added to a market share/market growth classification of products, as follows.

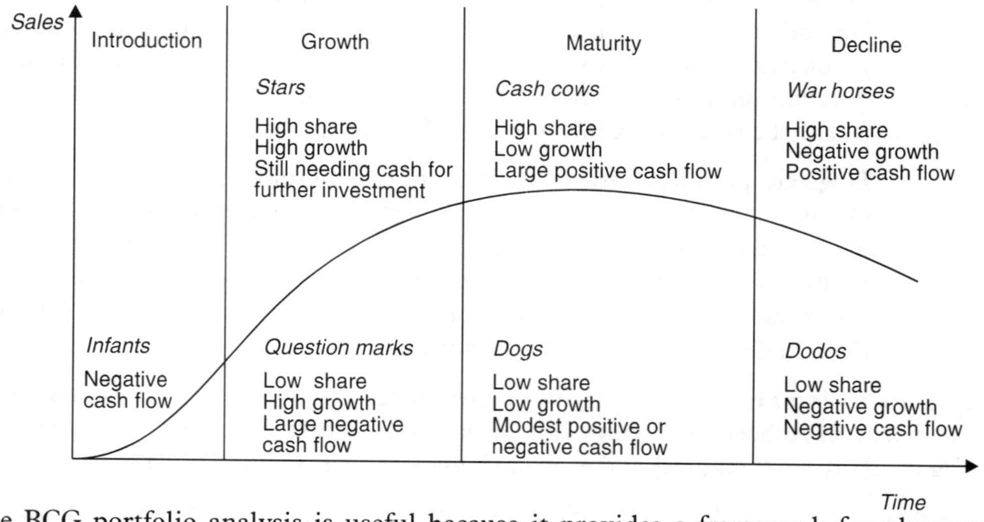

The BCG portfolio analysis is useful because it provides a framework for planners to consider and forecast potential market growth and to evaluate the competitive dimension through an evaluation of market share and the likely changes in cash flow.

4.2 Competitiveness of products

As a result of some of these weaknesses in the BCG model variations have evolved. Johnson and Scholes cite **General Electric's Business Screen** which compares market attractiveness with business strength.

(a) Determinants of industry/market attractiveness

- Market factors (eg size, growth)
- Competitors
- Investment factors
- Technological change
- Other PEST factors

(b) Determinants of business strength

- Product quality
- Distribution
- Brand reputation
- Production capacity
- Management skill

(c) These factors can then be scored and weighted. For example, a market with a low size and intense competition based on price might receive a lower weighting than a market with high growth and limited competition. The GE matrix is based on Return on Capital Employed.

(d) Business strengths and market attractiveness are thus plotted on a grid, and a strategy appropriate to each can be considered.

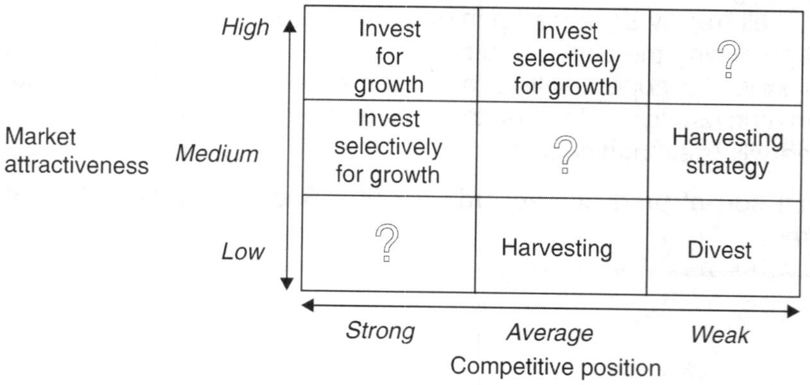

Each 'cell' requires a different management approach.

(a) Each SBU can be plotted in one of the cells and the appropriate management approach adopted.

(b) It is possible that SBUs might move around the matrix. Changes in PEST factors may change an industry/market's attractiveness.

(c) The matrix ignores the possibility of **knowledge generation** and **competence** sharing between SBUs. Applications in one SBU may be of value elsewhere.

The advantages and disadvantages of portfolio planning

Portfolio planning provides an excellent framework for analysis, and a starting point for developing a product-market mix strategy.

EXAMPLE

Adidas recently overtook Nike in both turnover and customer perceptions (Brassington and Pettit 2000). However it has announced the launch of a new fashion label and some analysts have questioned the move away from its core business.

(Day, Marketing Week, 12 August 1999)

Drawbacks

(a) Portfolio models are simple: they do not reflect the uncertainties of decision-making.

(b) BCG analysis, in particular, does not really take risk into account.

(c) They ignore opportunities for creative segmentation or identifying new niches.

(d) They assume a market is 'given' rather than something that can be created and nurtured. After all, industries may be 'unattractive' because customer needs have not been analysed sufficiently.

(e) A lot of complicated analysis is needed to come up with relevant data. How do you decide whether an industry is attractive or not?

DISCUSSION

What type of data is needed for adequate analysis for portfolio planning?

---

5 THE VALUE CHAIN

The **value chain** model of corporate activities, developed by Michael Porter, offers a bird's eye view of the firm and what it does. Competitive advantage, says Porter, arises out of the way in which firms organise and perform **activities.** (In other words, this describes **how** an organisation uses its inputs and transforms them into the outputs that customers pay for.)

Definition

> **Activities** are the means by which a firm creates value in its products. (They are sometimes referred to as **value activities.)**

Activities incur costs, and, in combination with other activities, provide a product or service which earns revenue. 'Firms create value for their buyers by performing these activities.'

Let us explain this point by using the example of a **restaurant**. A restaurant's activities can be divided into buying food, cooking it, and serving it (to customers). There is no reason, in theory, why the customers should not do all these things themselves, at home. The customer however, is not only prepared to **pay for someone else** to do all this but also **pays more than the cost of** the resources (food, wages etc). The ultimate value a firm creates is measured by the amount customers are willing to pay for its products or services above the cost of carrying out value activities. A firm is profitable if the realised value to customers exceeds the collective cost of performing the activities.

(a) Customers '**purchase**' **value,** which they measure by comparing a firm's products and services with similar offerings by competitors.

(b) The business '**creates**' **value** by carrying out its activities either more efficiently than other businesses, or combine them in such a way as to provide a unique product or service.

Porter (in *Competitive Advantage*) grouped the various activities of an organisation into a **value chain.** Here is a diagram.

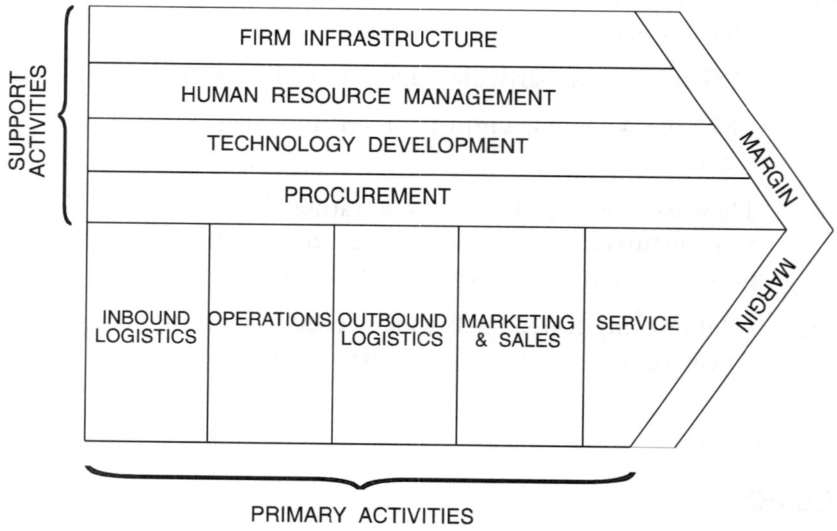

The **margin** is the excess the customer is prepared to **pay** over the **cost** to the firm of obtaining resource inputs and providing value activities.

Primary activities are directly related to production, sales, marketing, delivery and service.

Activity	Comment
Inbound logistics	Receiving, handling and storing inputs to the production system (ie warehousing, transport, stock control etc).
Operations	Convert resource inputs into a final product. Resource inputs are not only materials. 'People' are a 'resource' especially in service industries.
Outbound logistics	Storing the product and its distribution to customers: packaging, warehousing, testing etc.
Marketing and sales	Informing customers about the product, persuading them to buy it, and enabling them to do so: advertising, promotion etc.
After sales service	Installing products, repairing them, upgrading them, providing spare parts and so forth.

Support activities provide purchased inputs, human resources, technology and infrastructural functions to support the primary activities.

Activity	Comment
Procurement	Acquire the resource inputs to the primary activities (eg purchase of materials, subcomponents equipment).
Technology development	Product design, improving processes and/or resource utilisation.
Human resource management	Recruiting, training, developing and rewarding people.
Management planning	Planning, finance, quality control: Porter believes they are crucially important to an organisation's strategic capability in all primary activities.

Linkages connect the activities of the value chain.

(a) **Activities in the value chain affect one another**. For example, more costly product design or better quality production might reduce the need for after-sales service.

(b) **Linkages require co-ordination**. For example, just-in-time requires smooth functioning of operations, outbound logistics and service activities such as installation.

EXAMPLE

Tesco has an Internet Superstore. IT can be combined with home delivery. The customer goes to the Tesco website and builds up a 'shopping list' by selecting items from a product database, and then selects a time and date for delivery.

Amazon is the world's most successful Internet bookstore. It is based near America's main book wholesalers. It does not have a warehouse of its own.

Value system

Activities that add value do not stop at the organisation's **boundaries**. For example, when a restaurant serves a meal, the quality of the ingredients - although they are chosen by the cook - is determined by the grower. The grower has added value, and the grower's success in growing produce of good quality is as important to the customer's ultimate satisfaction as the skills of the chef. A firm's value chain is connected to what Porter calls a **value system**.

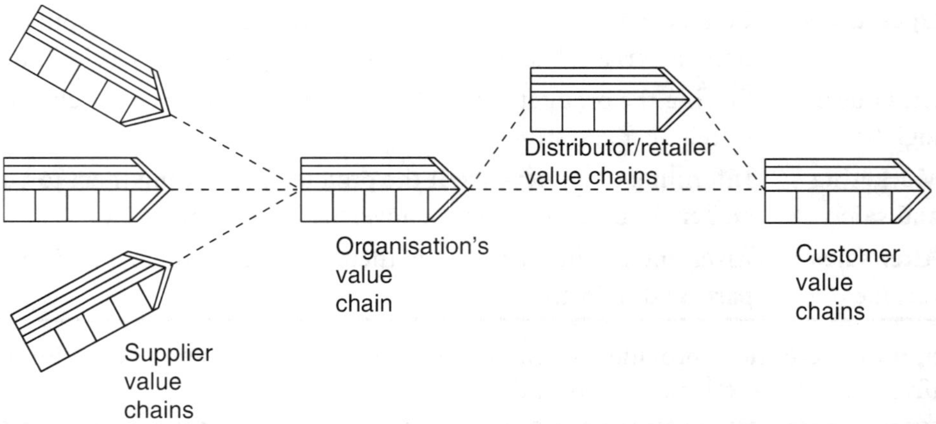

Using the value chain. A firm can secure competitive advantage by:

- Inventing new or better ways to do activities
- Combining activities in new or better ways
- Managing the linkages in its own value chain
- Managing the linkages in the value system

Activity 6 **(10 minutes)**

Sana Sounds is a small record company. Representatives from Sana Sounds scour music clubs for new bands to promote. Once a band has signed a contract (with Sana Sounds) it makes a recording. The recording process is subcontracted to one of a number of recording studio firms which Sana Sounds uses regularly. (At the moment Sana Sounds is not large enough to invest in its own equipment and studios.) Sana Sounds also subcontracts the production of records and CDs to a number of manufacturing companies. Sana Sounds then distributes the disks to selected stores, and engages in any promotional activities required.

What would you say were the activities in Sana Sounds' value chain?

NOTES

The examples below are based on two supermarket chains, one concentrating on low prices, the other differentiated on quality and service. See if you can tell which is which.

(a)

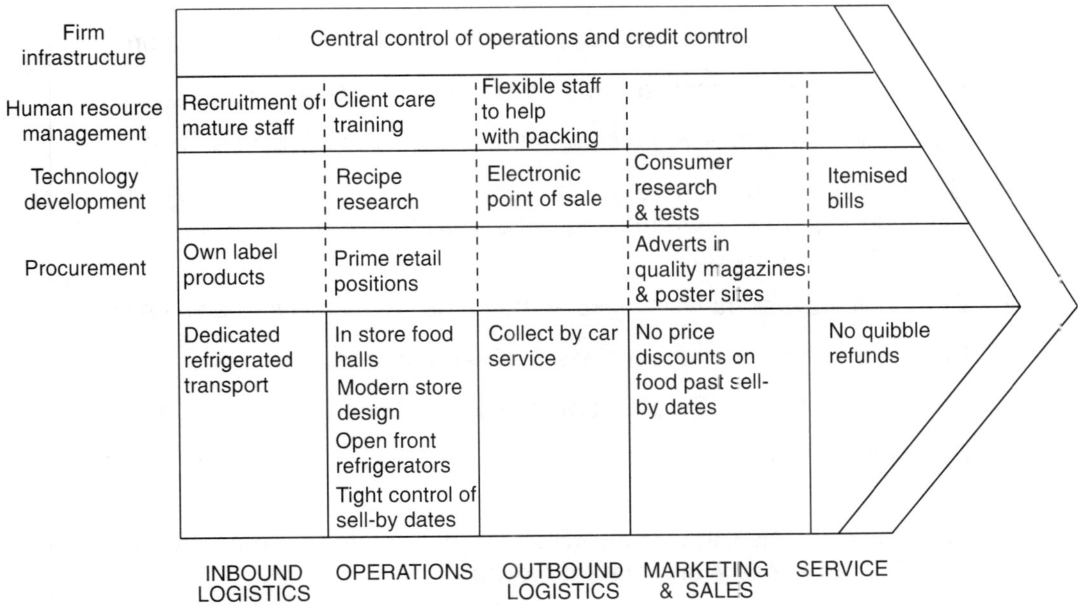

(b)

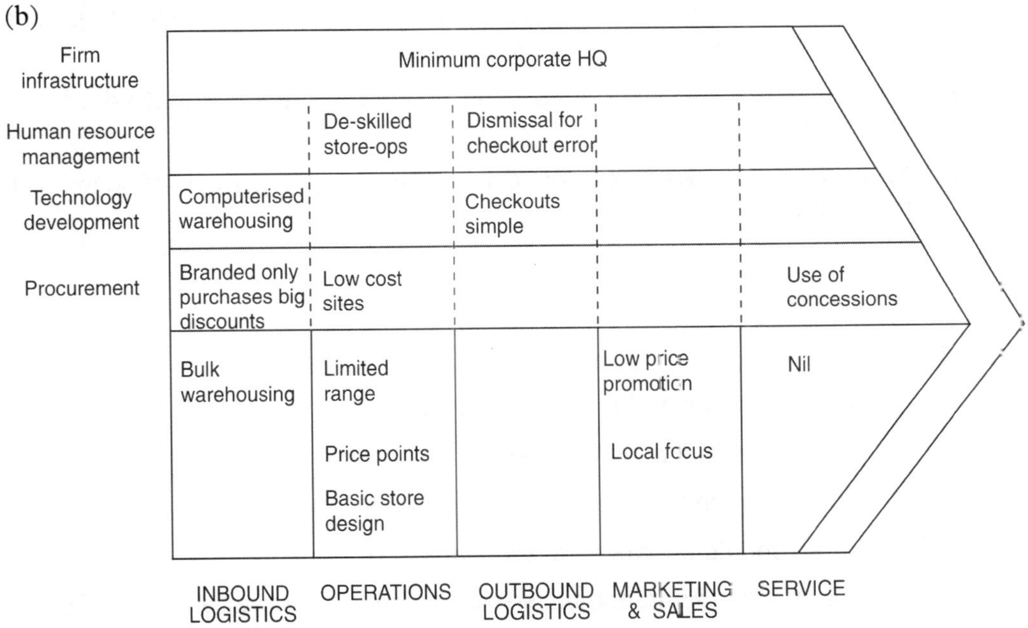

The two supermarkets represented are based on the following.

(a) The value chain in (a) above is based on Marks & Spencer foods, which seeks to differentiate on quality and service. Hence the 'no quibble' refunds, the use of prime retail sites, and customer care training.

(b) The value chain in (b) above is similar to that of Lidl, a 'discount' supermarket chain which sells on price, pursuing a cost leadership, or perhaps more accurately, a cost-focus strategy. This can be seen in the limited product range and its low-cost sites.

BPP PUBLISHING

Chapter roundup

- An organisation's resources can be audited. These will include technical, financial, managerial, organisational and information resources.
- Organisation's activities can run into difficulties due to limiting factors.
- Distinctive competencies are what organisations do well.
- Marketing audits review the company's overall marketing operation.
- Companies should strive to be both efficient and effective in their marketing operations. Marketing effectiveness can be measured using the table developed by Kotler.
- Product life cycle analysis looks at the stages in a product's sales history.
- PLCs vary between product class, form and brands.
- Each stage of the PLC has characteristics and strategic implications.
- Portfolio analysis looks at the products or SBUs an organisation has and their markets.
- The Boston Consulting Group (BCG) matrix relates a company's product or SBU market share and market growth.
- Products or SBUs can then be put into categories of stars, dogs, cash cows or question marks.
- General Electric's Business Screen compares market attractiveness and business strength.
- The value chain was developed by Porter to give an overall view of the firm and what it does.

Quick quiz

1 What are 'limiting factors' to an organisation's strategy?

2 Where might a company derive distinctive competences from?

3 How often should a company undertake a marketing audit?

4 What should a marketing audit look into?

5 What is the difference between marketing effectiveness and efficiency?

6 Why might the PLC be different for a product category and a brand?

7 If the rate of sales growth has slowed but profits are still made what stage of the PLC is the product in?

8 BCG analysis can only be used on products. True or false?

9 What 'primary activities' are included in value chain analysis?

Answers to quick quiz

1 Factors that limit the organisation's activities such as shortage of money. (See paragraph 1.2)

2 Production, marketing, human resources, integration/coordination or distribution. (para 1.3)

NOTES

3 About once a year. (para 2.1)

4 The marketing environment (micro and macro)
Marketing strategy
Marketing systems (para 2.2)

5 Efficiency – maximum output for minimum input
Effectiveness – making sure the organisation is doing the right things (para 2.3)

6 Brands will usually have a shorter PLC than the product category, eg coffee (the category) will have a longer PLC than Gold Blend (a brand). (para 2.3)

7 Maturity. (para 3.1)

8 False – can be for strategic business units. (para 4.1)

9 Inbound logistics, operations, outbound logistics, marketing and sales and service. (para 5)

Answers to activities

1 The answer will depend on the precise circumstances of your company or college.

2 The answer will depend on the magazine you have chosen.

3

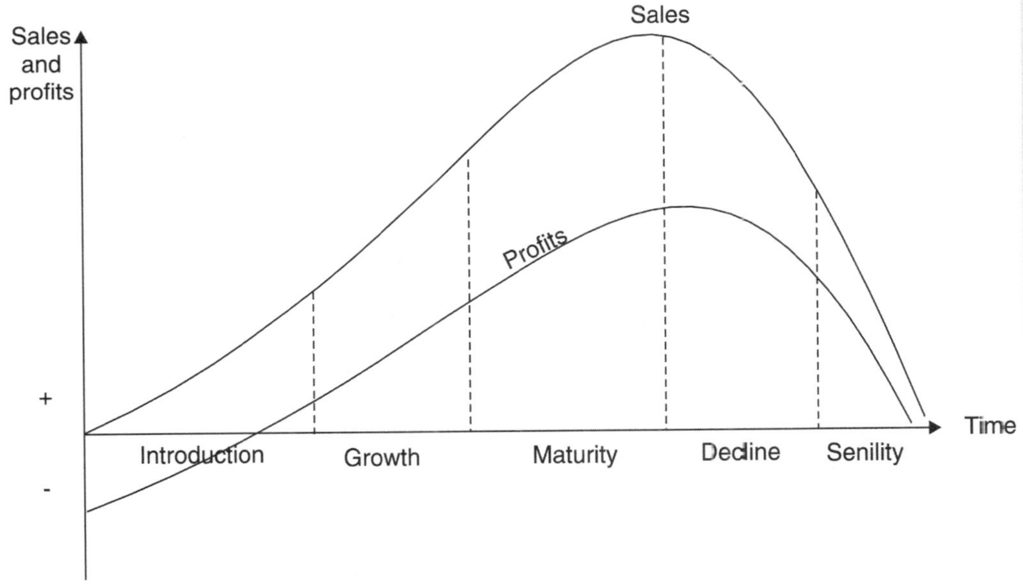

4 New packaging and a relaunch
Link product with dental research
Aim at a specific sector eg children, housewives, the elderly
Free toothbrush attached
Money off coupons
'Buy one get one free'

5 Freshly squeezed orange juice: cash cow
Pomegranate juice: probably a question mark; might become a star

6 *Primary activities*

- Inbound physical distribution. Sana Sounds do not manufacture 'products' as such, but the acquisition of bands can be placed in

BPP PUBLISHING

this section. Inventory and warehousing of manufactured CDs will also be included here.

- Outbound physical distribution – the delivery of manufactured CDs to outlets.
- The marketing of the bands.
- Service to both 'customers' – ie bands and retail outlets.

Support activities

The rise of technology in terms of general IT facilities and in procurement aspects ie which recording studios to use.

Human resource management issues will be vital, to keep the bands from taking their business elsewhere.

Firm's infrastructure will consist of general management of the business, planning and finance.

Chapter 8 :

EXTERNAL ENVIRONMENTAL ANALYSIS

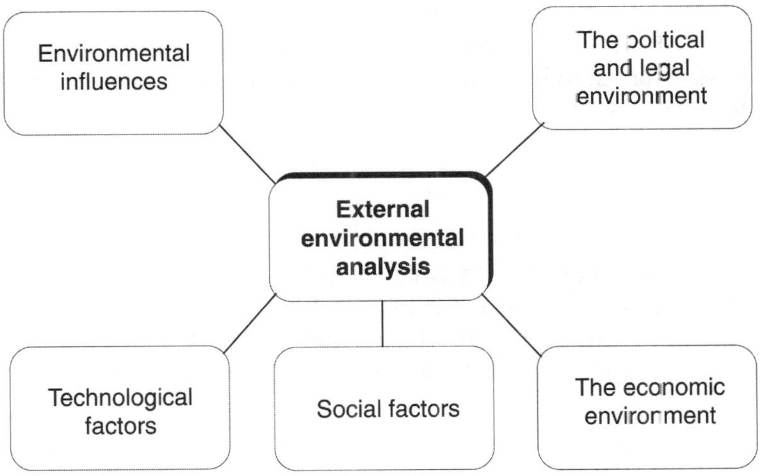

Introduction

Business plans cannot be produced in a vacuum. They must be developed within the context of the wider environment in which the organisation is operating. They need to take into account the opportunities and threats which are emerging as these external factors change. These are the issues this chapter will be covering.

A key issue to keep in mind is **environmental change**. Some organisations face more complex and changing environments than others; the fashion industry is in a 'fast-moving' environment, but this speed of environmental change does not exist for all industries.

Your objectives

In this chapter you will learn about the following:

(a) The factors that make up the external environment

(b) Aspects of the political and legal influences

(c) The importance of economic factors

(d) The importance and diversity of social aspects

(e) The impact technology has on business enterprises

1 ENVIRONMENTAL INFLUENCES

As we have seen earlier, planning is a central part of the management task wherever you are working in the organisation and the first stage should always be to clarify the current position.

(a) **Controllable.** Different managers need to review different aspects of the business. The factors which can be controlled by the **marketing** manager can be primarily represented by the 7P's of the marketing mix.

(b) **Not controllable.** Issues of production capacity and sources of supply are of interest and of indirect importance to the marketing manager, but outside the area of direct control. That said, marketing mix decisions and marketing activities do have a significant impact on these other departments.

Activity 1 **(30 minutes)**

Choose a business/market with which you are familiar. How has it changed over the last five years? Produce a list of all the external factors (things which the organisation cannot control) which have had a significant impact on the organisation in that time. Refine your list as you work through the rest of this chapter.

Definition

The **environment** of an organisation is everything outside its boundaries. All the factors affect the organisation's performance, but the organisation cannot control them.

DISCUSSION

There is no real point in assessing the external environment when an organisation cannot do anything about it.

Organisations have a variety of relationships with the environment.

NOTES

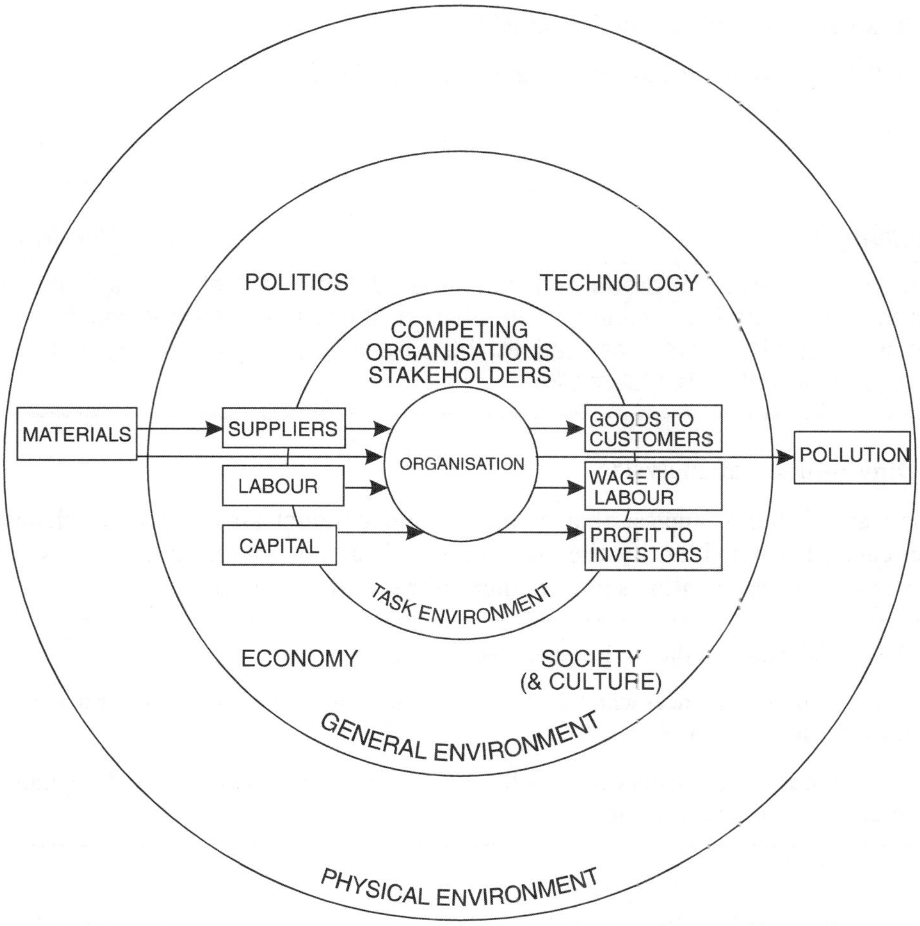

1.1 Classifying the environment

(a) The **micro environment** is of immediate concern, and is uniquely configured for each organisation: no organisation has a network of suppliers, customers, competitors or stakeholders identical to another's.

(b) The **macro environment** relates to factors in the environment affecting all organisations.

- Political-legal factors
- Economic factors
- Social and cultural factors
- Technological factors

(PEST)

EXAMPLE

For many years, Monsanto has been developing genetically modified foods, and these new substances have been marketed very successfully in the USA, with no public disquiet. In the UK and the EU generally, a combination of factors has led to public concern.

(a) Suspicion of industrial food production processes, especially after the BSE crisis
(b) Concern about ecology
(c) Trends towards 'organic' food
(d) The relative success of the UK's biotechnology industry

NOTES

(e) Trade friction between the UK and US

Many UK food producers have decided not to use GM foods.

Activity 2 **(30 minutes)**

Choose an industrial product, a consumer durable, a fast moving consumer good and a service business. For each of them identify **how** you think the environmental factors identified in the following paragraphs might affect a business operating in that market.

1.2 Environmental analysis

Johnson and Scholes suggest that a firm should conduct an **audit of environmental influences.** This will identify the environmental factors which have had a significant influence on the organisation's development or performance in the past.

1. Assess the nature of the environment (eg is it changing?)
2. Identify those influences which have affected the organisation in the past or which are likely to do so in future
3. A structural analysis will be prepared, identifying the 'key forces at work in the immediate or competitive environment'.

↓

These steps should identify important developments. Then the following questions should be asked.

↓

4. What is the organisation's position in relation to other organisations?
5. What threats and/or opportunities are posed by the environment?

Strategic decisions are made in partial ignorance, as we have seen, because the environment is uncertain. Uncertainty relates to the **complexity and dynamism** of the environment.

(a) **Complexity** arises from:

(i) The **variety of influences** faced by the organisation. The more open an organisation is, the greater the variety of influences. The greater the number of markets the organisation operates in, the greater the number of influences to which it is subject.

(ii) The amount of **knowledge** necessary. All businesses need to have knowledge of the tax system, for example, but only pharmaceuticals businesses need to know about mandatory testing procedures for new drugs.

(iii) The **interconnectedness** of environmental influences. Importing and exporting companies are sensitive to exchange rates, which themselves are sensitive to interest rates. Interest rates then influence a company's borrowing costs.

(b) **Dynamism**. Stable environments are unchanging. Dynamic environments are in a state of change. The computer market is a dynamic market because of the rate of technological change.

It is not always easy to detect which environmental factors will be relevant in future.

DISCUSSION

Information needs for assessing environmental factors are diverse and complex.

Activity 3 **(5 minutes)**

How do you consider that the Johnson and Scholes model can be applied to the scare about genetically modified foods?

2 THE POLITICAL AND LEGAL ENVIRONMENT

We will outline in **general** terms some key issues to keep in mind. Laws come from common law, parliamentary legislation and government regulations derived from it, and obligations under EU membership and other treaties.

2.1 Legal factors affecting all companies

Factor	Example
General legal framework: contract, tort, agency	Basic ways of doing business; negligence proceedings
Criminal law	Theft (eg of documents in Lanica's failed bid for the Co-op); insider dealing; bribery; deception
Company law	Directors and their duties; reporting requirements; takeover proceedings; shareholders rights; insolvency
Employment law	Trade Union recognition; Social Chapter provisions; possible minimum wage; unfair dismissal; redundancy; maternity; Equal Opportunities
Health and Safety	Fire precautions; safety procedures
Data protection	Use of information about employees and customers
Marketing and sales	Laws to protect consumers (eg refunds and replacement, 'cooling off' period after credit agreements); what is or isn't allowed in advertising
Environment	Pollution control; waste disposal
Tax law	Corporation tax payment; Collection of income tax (PAYE) and National Insurance contributions; VAT

Some legal and regulatory factors affect **particular industries**, if the public interest is served. For example, electricity, gas, telecommunications, water and rail transport are subject to **regulators** (Offer, Ofgas, Oftel, Ofwat, Ofrail) who have influence over:

- Competition and market access
- Pricing policy (can restrict price increase)

This is because either:

- The industries are, effectively, monopolies, and/or
- Large sums of public money are involved (eg in subsidies to rail companies).

EXAMPLE

Gas deregulation

Government policy. Gas used to be a state monopoly. The industry was privatised as one company, British Gas. Slowly, the UK gas market has been opened to competition: now about 20 suppliers compete with British Gas.

Regulators. Ofgas regulates the gas industry. Ofgas has introduced a Code of Conduct requiring gas suppliers to train sales agents, allow for a cooling off period and so on.

Contracts. British Gas is vulnerable to competitors because of its prices. When it was privatised, it inherited 'take or pay contracts' requiring it to buy gas at a specific price from gas producers. Since that time, gas prices have fallen, and competitors have been able to benefit from this.

New markets. Government policy has also deregulated the electricity market, so that companies such as British Gas can now sell electricity.

2.2 Anticipating changes in the law

- The governing party's election **manifesto** is a guide to its political priorities, even if these are not implemented immediately.
- The government often publishes advance information about its plans (**green paper** or **white paper**) for consultation purposes.
- The **EU's single market programme** indicates future changes in the law.

The general political environment will have implications for business because of the attitudes to business and support for business and/or trade unions and related legislation.

EXAMPLE

There are many examples of products in the UK that have caused a furore when they are not recognised by the EU. Examples such as chocolate and ice cream have different regulations in terms of content and labelling in various EU countries.

NOTES

DISCUSSION

The political and legal environment is influenced by sociocultural factors.

3 THE ECONOMIC ENVIRONMENT

The economic environment is an important influence at local and national level.

3.1 Influence of the economic environment

Factor	Impact
Overall growth or fall in Gross Domestic Product	Increased/decreased demand for goods (eg dishwashers) and services (holidays).
Local economic trends	Type of industry in the area. Office/factory rents. Labour rates House prices.
National economic trends:	
• Inflation	Low in most countries; distorts business decisions; wage inflation compensates for price inflation
• Interest rates	How much it costs to borrow money affects **cash flow**. Some businesses carry a high level of debt. How much customers can afford to spend is also affected as rises in interest rates affect people's mortgage payments.
• Tax levels	Corporation tax affects how much firms can invest or return to shareholders. Income tax and VAT affect how much consumers have to spend, hence demand.
• Government spending	Suppliers to the government (eg construction firms) are affected by spending.
• The business cycle	Economic activity is always punctuated by periods of growth followed by decline, simply because of the nature of trade. The UK economy has been characterised by periods of 'boom' and 'bust'. Government policy can cause, exacerbate or mitigate such trends, but cannot abolish the business cycle. (Industries which prosper when others are declining are called **counter-cyclical** industries.)

The **forecast state of the economy** will influence the planning process for organisations which operate within it. In times of boom and increased demand and consumption, the overall planning problem will be to **identify** the demand. Conversely, in times of recession, the emphasis will be on cost-effectiveness, continuing profitability, survival and competition.

BPP PUBLISHING

3.2 Impact of international factors

Factor	Impact
Exchange rates	Cost of imports, selling prices and value of exports; cost of hedging against fluctuations
Characteristics of overseas markets. Different rates of economic growth and prosperity, tax etc.	Desirable overseas markets (demand) or sources of supply.
Capital, flows and trade	Investment opportunities, free trade, cost of exporting

DISCUSSION

Information on foreign markets is notoriously difficult to gather and assess.

EXAMPLE

Growth in trade has affected the **logistics industry (transport, warehouse, etc)** (worth US $130bn of which £31.6bn is outsourced). Total logistics expenditure in the EU is likely to rise from £130bn in 1996 to $155bn in 2001.

The major problem is congestion. The EU is planning ECU 350bn on trans-European networks (road, rail and air links) with possible extensions into Eastern Europe. Despite the single market, goods are still being held up at national borders.

3.3 The single European currency

Most countries in the EU now account in euros. Interest rates are set by the European Central Bank whose goal is price transparency. Notes and coins will be introduced in 2002. Implications are:

(a) **Price transparency**: it will be obvious that prices differ in various markets. Cars are known to be priced higher in the UK than elsewhere. Markets may become harder to segment.

(b) **Interest rates** will be set for the whole of Europe, not by country.

4 SOCIAL FACTORS

These were covered comprehensively in Chapter 1 (Unit 17) on Buyer Behaviour.

4.1 Different social factors

Factor	Comment
Growth	The rate of growth or decline in a national population and in regional populations.
Age	Changes in the age distribution of the population. In the UK, there will be an increasing proportion of the national population over retirement age. In developing countries there are very large numbers of young people. • Elderly people have unique needs • As a segment they will become increasingly powerful.
Geography	The concentration of population into certain geographical areas.
Ethnicity	In the UK, about 5% come from ethnic minorities, although most of these live in London and the South East.
Household and family structure	A household is the basic social unit and its size might be determined by the number of children, whether elderly parents live at home etc. In the UK, there has been an **increase in single-person households** and lone parent families. Obviously, this impacts on the relevance of models such as the **family life cycle**
Social structure	The population of a society can be broken down into a number of subgroups, with different attitudes and access to economic resources. Social class, however, is hard to measure (as people's subjective perceptions vary). • Social classification systems are changing. The old systems based on the registrar-general grades (I, II, III etc) are to be replaced, from the 2000 census. The new grading covers occupations more closely: 1 Higher managerial and professional; 2 Lower managerial and professional; 3 Intermediate; 4 Small employers and own account workers; 5 Lower supervisory craft and related occupations; 6 Semi-routine occupations; 7 Routine occupations • Social status generally passes from generation to generation, despite evidence of social mobility in individual cases.
Employment	Many people believe that there is a move to a casual flexible workforce; factories will have a group of **core employees,** supplemented by a group of **peripheral employees,** on part-time or temporary contracts, working as and when required. Some research indicates a 'two-tier' society split between '**work-rich**' (with two wage-earners) and '**work-poor**' households. However **most employees are in permanent, full-time employment.**
Wealth	Rising standards of living lead to increased demand for certain types of consumer good. This is why developing countries are attractive as markets.

Activity 4 **(20 minutes)**

Club Fun is a UK company which sells packaged holidays. Founded in the 1960s, it offers a standard 'cheap and cheerful' package to resorts in Spain and, more recently, to some of the Greek islands. It was particularly successful at providing holidays for the 18-30 age group. What do you think the implications are for Club Fun of the following developments?

(a) A fall in the number of school leavers.

(b) The fact that young people are more likely now than in the 1960s to go into higher education.

(c) Holiday programmes on TV which feature a much greater variety of locations.

(d) Greater disposable income among the 18-30 age group.

4.2 Business ethics

The conduct of an organisation, its management and employees will be measured against **ethical standards** by the customers, suppliers and other members of the public with whom they deal.

Types of ethical problems a manager may meet with in practice

(a) **Production practices**. Attempts to increase profitability by cutting costs may lead to dangerous working conditions, inadequate safety standards in products or reprehensible practices (eg child labour). This is a problem for firms which outsource production to low-cost factories overseas.

(b) **Gifts**. There is a fine line to be drawn between gifts, accepted as part of a way of doing business, and bribes.

(c) **Social responsibility**: companies are being held to account for pollution and human rights issues.

(d) **Competitive behaviour**. There is a distinction between competing aggressively and competing unethically and illegally.

DISCUSSION

If a business practice is operating overseas it should only concern itself with local business practices not what it would do in its home country.

---

5 TECHNOLOGICAL FACTORS

Technology refers to:

(a) Apparatus or equipment: eg a TV camera.

(b) Technique: eg how to use the TV camera to best effect, perhaps in conjunction with other equipment such as lights.

(c) Organisation: eg the grouping of camera-operators into teams, to work on a particular project.

Technology contributes to overall economic growth. Technology can increase total output, by enabling gains in productivity (more output per units of input), reduced costs (eg transportation technology, preservatives) and new types of product.

5.1 Effects of technological change on organisations

(a) The type of products or services that are made and sold.
(b) The way in which products are made (eg robots, new raw materials).
(c) The way in which services are provided.

EXAMPLE

Mail order/Internet

(a) Companies selling easily transportable goods - for instance, books and CDs - can offer much greater consumer choice and are enjoying considerable success.

(b) The financial sector is rapidly going electronic - call centres are now essential to stay in business, PC banking is now being sold, and the Internet and interactive TV are starting to feature in business plans.

(c) **The way in which markets are identified.** Database systems make it much easier to analyse the market place. We explore database marketing in brief below.

(d) **The way in which firms are managed.** IT encourages 'delayering' of organisational hierarchies, homeworking, and better communication.

(e) **The means and extent of communications with external clients, via Website, e-mail etc).**

EXAMPLE

The **Internet** has implications for the structure and strategies of some industries and their marketing mixes. Take telecommunications. The telephone tariff system is 'fundamentally a fixed cost system, but we pay for it on the basis of a variable - mainly voice minutes. What is more, where the charges are levied bears no relation to where the costs occur'.

The Internet threatens to undermine this. Access to the Internet is normally charged at **local** call rates. It will soon be possible to hold conversations over the Internet, which 'will undermine the "price per distance" business model' which allows telephone companies to charge more for long distance calls.

The impact of **recent** technological change also has potentially important social consequences, which in turn have an impact on business.

(a) **Homeworking.** Whereas people were once collected together to work in factories, home working will become more important.

(b) **Intellective skills.** Certain sorts of skill, related to interpretation of data and information processes, are likely to become more valued than manual or physical skills.

(c) **Services.** Technology increases manufacturing productivity, releasing human resources for service jobs. These jobs require **greater interpersonal skills** (eg in dealing with customers).

EXAMPLE

TNT

TNT's website features 'Web-tracker' enabling users to see how their consignments are being transported. The Internet is being exploited to enhance a particular service.

Chapter roundup

- The environment in which an organisation operates is made up of non-controllable factors.
- The environment can be subdivided into micro (specific to the organisation) and macro (affecting all organisations within the industry).
- Johnson and Scholes have developed a framework for auditing environmental influence.
- The political and legal environment will include all aspects of law (criminal and commercial law) and European and other agreements.
- The economic environment includes local, national and international trends.
- Social factors include demographic social and cultural aspects. Business ethics can also be considered within social factors.
- Technological factors can be thought of in terms of equipment, techniques or organisation.

Quick Quiz

1. What are the main categories of external influences which affect the organisation?
2. What is the source of environmental complexity?
3. How does the legal framework potentially affect an organisation?
4. Give two examples of national economic trends which companies need to monitor.
5. Give two examples of international economic factors which companies operating overseas (or wishing to) should monitor.
6. How has the changing age structure affected business plans?
7. What ethical problems might a business organisation face, especially when expanding abroad?
8. In what three ways does technological change affect business?

Answers to quick quiz

1. Political, Economic, Social, Technological. (See para 1)
2. Variety of influences, amount of knowledge needed, interconnections of influences. (para 1.2)
3. In many ways – the general legal framework, health and safety, environmental and marketing legislation. Also treaties and EU regulations. (para 2.1)
4. Can include inflation, taxes, interest rates, government spending, the business cycle. (para 3.1)
5. Can include exchange rates, economic characteristics, growth, tax, wealth, capital aspects, interest rates. (para 3.2)
6. The profile of customers or potential customers may change. Segments may become more/less attractive as might certain products/services. (para 4.1)
7. Can be examples of production practices, gifts, social responsibility and competitive behaviour. (para 4.2)
8. (a) Type of products/services that are made/sold.
   (b) Way in which products are made.
   (c) Way in which services are provided. (para 5.1)

Answers to activities

1. The answer will depend on the business or market which you have chosen.
2. The answer will depend on the products chosen.
3. Johnson and Scholes' approach to change will indicate that the pressure from consumers, consumer groups and the media means that GM producers and users will have to take notice of the cultural change that has damaged the image of GM food.

   Decisions would have to be made over whether to use GM products or produce them at all, or whether the customer could/should be 'educated' to use them.

   According to the Johnson and Scholes model this might include the training and management style of staff to allow for strategic change. It may be that the organisation's culture will have to change because of the challenge of the GM food issue.
4. (a) Fewer potential customers
   Fewer potential staff, as they are presumably recruited from the same age group.

   (b) Less disposable income among the target age group
   Greater expectations among the target group.
   Greater desire for long haul, backpacking travel.

   (c) Greater choice.
   Greater expectations from holidays
   Club Fun's locations perceived as cheap, boring or mundane.

   (d) A greater number of potential customers, but also the risks that they will travel further afield, be prepared to spend more and avoid 'cheap and cheerful' holidays.

   Company may have to improve the quality of the product.

Chapter 9 :
COMPETITOR ANALYSIS

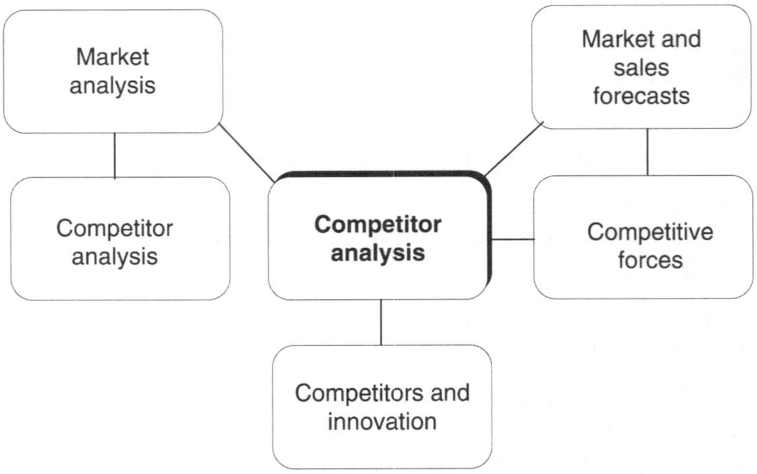

Introduction

The chapter begin by considering the components and importance of market and sales forecasts, along with a discussion concerned with estimating market demand.

The second section reviews the competitive forces which can impact on industries and need to be analysed if we are to understand the nature of competition. Porter's Five Forces model is illustrated and explained. The following section notes the challenges of undertaking a market analysis as a range and variety of inputs can be included.

The penultimate section identifies the key aspects of competitor analysis. This includes who they are, their goals, their strategies, their strengths and weaknesses and how they are likely to respond.

The final section considers the importance of innovation in competition and as well as illustrating how value can be created through innovation, it lists the characteristics of innovators.

Your objectives

In this chapter you will learn about the following:

(a) the importance of market and sales forecasts

(b) the scope of competitive forces

(c) the principles of market and competitor analysis

(d) competitors and innovation

Note

Strictly speaking, the content of this chapter is included in Unit 17, Marketing Intelligence. However it is also of relevance in the consideration of Marketing Planning, and so is included here.

NOTES

1 MARKET FORECASTS AND SALES FORECASTS

Market forecasts and sales forecasts complement each other. The market forecast should be carried out first of all and should cover a longer period of time.

Definition

> **Market forecast.** This is a forecast for the market as a whole. It is mainly involved in the assessment of environmental factors, outside the organisation's control, which will affect the demand for its products/services.

(a) Components of a market forecast

  (i) The **economic review** (national economy, government policy, covering forecasts on investment, population, gross national product, etc).

  (ii) **Specific market research** (to obtain data about specific markets and forecasts concerning total market demand).

  (iii) Evaluation of **total market demand** for the firm's and similar products, for example profitability, market potential etc.

(b) **Sales forecasts** are estimates of sales (in volume, value and profit terms) of a product in a future period at a given marketing mix.

1.1 Research into potential sales

Definition

> **Sales potential** is an estimate of the part of the market which is within the possible reach of a product.

Factors governing sales potential

- The price of the product
- The amount of money spent on sales promotion
- How essential the product is to consumers
- Whether it is a durable commodity whose purchase is postponable
- The overall size of the possible market
- Competition

Whether sales potential is worth exploiting will depend on the cost which must be incurred to realise the potential.

Example

Market research has led a company to the opinion that the sales potential of product X is as follows.

	Sales value	*Contribution earned before selling costs deducted*	*Cost of selling*
either	£100,000	£40,000	£10,000
or	£110,000	£44,000	£15,000

BPP PUBLISHING

In this example, it would not be worth spending an extra £5,000 on selling in order to realise an extra sales potential of £10,000, because the net effect would be a loss of £(5,000 – 4,000) = £1,000.

1.2 Estimating market demand

Estimating market demand is not necessarily as straightforward as you might at first think. Imagine you are the marketing manager of a company producing sports footwear. What is your market demand? Is it the volume of shoes purchased in the UK, or Europe, or the whole world? Should you be considering tennis shoes as well as running shoes? Shoes for children or only adults? And should you be forecasting demand for next year or over the next five years? The permutations seem endless. Kotler identifies 90 possible combinations of market demand definitions based on product level, geographic area and time horizon.

A demand function is simply an expression which shows how sales demand for a product is dependent on several factors. These demand variables can be grouped into two broad categories.

(a) **Controllable variables or strategic variables.** These are factors over which the firm's management should have some degree of control, and which they can change if they wish. Controllable variables are essentially the marketing mix.

(b) **Uncontrollable variables.** These are factors over which the firm's management has no control.

   (i) **Consumer variables** depend on decisions by consumers, or the circumstances of consumers (for example their wealth).

   (ii) **Competitor variables** depend on decisions and actions by other firms, particularly competitors.

   (iii) **Other variables.** These include decisions by other organisations (for example the government) or factors which are outside the control of anyone (for example weather conditions, or the total size of the population).

A demand function can be set out as follows.

$$Q_a = f(P_a, A_a, D_a, O_a; \quad I_c, T_c, E_c; \quad P_b, A_b, D_b, O_b; \quad G, N, W \ldots)$$

P_a, A_a, D_a, O_a	I_c, T_c, E_c	P_b, A_b, D_b, O_b	$G, N, W \ldots$
Strategic variables	Consumer variables	Competitor variables	Other variables
Controllable variables	Uncontrollable variables		

where

Q_a is quantity demanded of a product A per period
P_a is price of product A
A_a is advertising and sales promotion for product A
D_a is the design or quality of product A
O_a is the number of retail outlets or other outlets for distribution of product A

I_c is incomes of consumers/customers
T_c is the tastes and preferences of consumers

E_c is the expectation of consumers about future prices etc

P_b is the prices of related goods (substitutes, complements)
A_b is advertising/promotion for related goods
D_b is design and quality of related goods
O_b is the number of outlets for distribution of related goods

G is government policy
N is the number of people in the economy/potential market
W represents the weather conditions

The demand function set out above is little more than common sense. But what firms should want to estimate or forecast is what future demand is likely to be. To do this, **an attempt should be made to quantify the relationship between demand for a product and the significant demand variables.** For example a demand function might be measurable as

$$Q_a = 3{,}000 - 0.032\ P_a + 240\ A_a + 0.05\ O_a + 0.35\ P_b - 320\ A_b - 0.02\ O_b + 36\ I_b$$

There are two problems with measuring a demand function in this way.

(a) **Measurement.** There is the problem of deciding how to measure variables, especially qualitative variables such as product design, and consumer tastes.

(b) **Valuation.** Then there is the mathematical problem of putting values to the 'constants' or coefficients for each variable. This might be done using **regression analysis.**

Follow a few simple guidelines in choosing forecasting methods:

1 Use the simple methods you understand rather than complex methods that few people do

2 Simple methods are often as good as complicated ones

3 Use different methods and combine them

4 Expensive does not necessarily mean good

5 Before making decisions based on forecasts, be aware of the way they are produced, as well as the limitations and risks involved

DISCUSSION

If the environment is uncertain, flexibility, not forecasting, is the key!

2 INDUSTRY ANALYSIS: THE COMPETITIVE FORCES

In discussing competition Porter (*Competitive Strategy*) distinguishes between factors which characterise the nature of competition:

(a) **In one industry compared with another** (eg in the chemicals industry compared with the clothing retail industry) and make one industry as a whole potentially more profitable than another (ie yielding a bigger return on investment).

(b) **Within a particular industry.** These relate to the competitive strategies that individual firms might select.

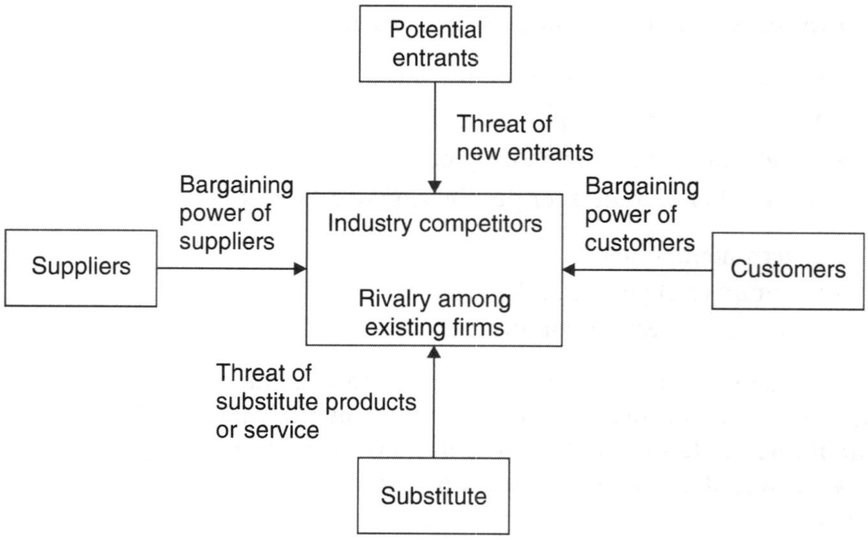

Source: adapted from Porter *(Competitive Strategy)*

2.1 The threat of new entrants (and barriers to entry to keep them out)

A new entrant into an industry will bring extra capacity and more competition. The strength of this threat is likely to vary from industry to industry, depending on:

(a) The strength of the **barriers to entry**. Barriers to entry discourage new entrants.

(b) The likely **response of existing competitors** to the new entrant.

The diagram on the next page outlines the driving force and critical success factors of competition.

NOTES

COMPETITION – THE DRIVING FORCES AND CRITICAL SUCCESS FACTORS

(Adapted from: Institute of Personnel and Development, 'People Make the Difference, 1995)

The driving forces

- Customers demand products and services increasingly customised to their needs
- Customer satisfaction standards are increasingly established by global competition
- Reductions in international trade barriers
- Industrialisation of Pacific rim countries
- Slow growth in the mature economies
- New overseas competitors in mature production and service sectors
- Technology is rapidly changing and easily transferable
- Public sector financial constraints, political pressures for higher value for money and privatisation or market testing
- Communities are becoming more concerned about the effects of economic development on the environment and social well being

How organisations are responding

- Highly differentiated goods and services
- Customer-led organisations; relationships
- 'Step' change and continuous improvement of products, processes and services
- Quicker response times
- Lower costs and sustainable profits
- Flexibility from people and technology
- Investing in and developing the core competences of people

How this is affecting the way people are organised and managed

- Decentralisation and development of decision-making
- Slimmer and flatter management structures
- Total quality and 'lean organisation' initiatives
- Fewer specialists directly employed
- Developing a flexible workforce
- More project based and cross functional initiatives and team working
- Empowered rather than command structures
- Partnership approach to supplier links

What this means for employees

- Customer-orientation to meet the needs of both internal and external customers
- Greater self-management and responsibility for individuals and teams
- Contributing to the continuous improvement of processes, products and services
- Commitment to personal training, development and adaptability

What this means for managers

- Facilitating, co-ordinating roles
- Greater interpersonal, team leadership and motivational skills
- Integrated management and communication systems
- Openness, fairness and a partnership in employment relations
- Managing constructively the interests of groups of employees and their collective and individual representation
- Ensuring part-time and temporary employees and those contracted to supply services are fully integrated

2.2 The threat from substitute products

A **substitute product** is a good/service produced by **another industry** which satisfies the **same customer needs**. Substitutes put a lid on what firms in an industry can charge.

EXAMPLE

The Channel Tunnel

Passengers have several ways of getting from London to Paris, and the pricing policies of the various industries transporting them there reflects this.

(a) 'Le Shuttle' carries cars in the Channel Tunnel. Its main competitors are the ferry companies, offering a substitute service. Therefore, you will find that Le Shuttle sets its prices with reference to ferry company prices, and vice versa.

(b) Eurostar is the rail service from London to Paris/Brussels. Its main competitors are not the ferry companies but the airlines. Prices on the London-Paris air routes fell with the commencement of Eurostar services, and some airlines have curtailed the number of flights they offer.

2.3 The bargaining power of customers

Customers want better quality products and services at a lower price. Satisfying this want might force down the profitability of suppliers in the industry. Customer strength depends upon the following.

(a) How much the **customer buys**.

(b) How **critical** the product is to the customer's own business.

(c) **Switching costs (ie the cost of switching supplier).**

(d) Whether the products are **standard items** (hence easily copied) or **specialised.**

(e) The **customer's own profitability:** a customer who makes low profits will be forced to insist on low prices from suppliers.

(f) The customer's **ability to bypass** the supplier or **take over** the supplier.

(g) The **skills** of the customer's **purchasing staff**, or the price-awareness of consumers.

(h) When **product quality** is important to the customer, the customer is less likely to be price-sensitive, and so the industry might be more profitable as a consequence.

EXAMPLE

Although the Ministry of Defence may wish to keep control over defence spending, it is likely as a **customer** to be more concerned that the products it purchases perform satisfactorily than with getting the lowest price possible for everything it buys.

2.4 The bargaining power of suppliers

Suppliers can exert pressure for higher prices, depending upon the following factors.

(a) Whether there are just **one or two dominant suppliers** to the industry, able to charge monopoly or oligopoly prices.

(b) The threat of **new entrants** or substitute products to the **supplier's industry**.

(c) Whether the suppliers have **other customers** outside the industry, and do not rely on the industry for the majority of their sales.

(d) The **importance of the supplier's product** to the customer's business.

(e) Whether the supplier has a **differentiated product** which buyers need to obtain.

(f) Whether **switching costs** for customers would be high.

EXAMPLE

Food products in the UK are largely sold through supermarket chains, and it can be difficult for a new producer to get supermarket organisations to agree to stock its product. As retailers become more powerful, they are placing more and more demands on food producers: failure to comply can mean exclusion from the channel of distribution. Supplier bargaining power is low. Sophisticated marketing firms try to get round this by using advertising, for example, to stimulate customer demand by implementing 'pull strategies'.

Other suppliers try to restrict distribution outlets to maintain high prices, particularly in the case of perfumes and cosmetics, by banning sales of these items in 'undesirable' outlets.

2.5 The rivalry amongst current competitors in the industry

The **intensity of competitive rivalry** within an industry will affect the profitability of the industry as a whole. Competitive actions might take the form of price competition, advertising battles, sales promotion campaigns, introducing new products for the market, improving after sales service or providing guarantees or warranties.

Activity 1 **(10 minutes)**

Coca-Cola and Pepsi compete on the basis of massive advertising spend on image and packaging to position against each other. They will respond to each other's advertising and promotion with anything except one thing – price. Coca-Cola and Pepsi have experienced price wars and they do not like them. This made the big brands highly vulnerable to attack by cheaper substitutes – Sainsbury own label and Virgin Cola have taken significant market share in the UK market driven mainly by lower prices. Can you think of any other similar examples?

3 MARKET ANALYSIS

Definition

A **market** is a group of actual and potential customers, who can make purchase decisions.

Businesses also talk about the market 'for' a product (eg the 'confectionery market') as well as other classifications such as 'the youth market'.

Many firms compete in several markets, if they are diversified or if they have a distinctive competence or brand which can be exploited.

EXAMPLE

Conventional financial services providers were wrong-footed by Virgin's entry into the market with simplified products and direct marketing techniques, and seem unable to respond to the entry of diverse firms like supermarkets into financial services.

A **market analysis** will be made up of a range of factors. Here is a checklist. (adapted from Dibb and Simkin, 1996).

Statistical data	**2001**	**2002**	**2003 (forecast)**
Company/SBU data			
Market name			
Unit sales			
£ sales			
Profitability			
Market data			
Market size			
Market share			
No. of main customers			
No. of dealers/distributors			
Concentration ratio			
Qualitative data			
Environmental factors			
Critical success factors			
Growing/stable/declining			
Key competitors and their strategies			
Future competitors			
Segmentation opportunities			
Ease of entry			

We can expand upon some elements of the above checklist.

(a) **Market size**. This refers to both actual and potential (forecast) size. A company cannot know whether its market share objectives are feasible unless it knows the market's overall size. Forecasting areas of growth and decline is also important.

(b) **Customers**. The analysis needs to identify who the customers are, what they need, and their buying behaviour (where, when and how they purchase products or services). This will help to point out opportunities.

(c) **Distributors**. The company will need to evaluate its current arrangements for getting goods or services to the customer. Changes in distribution channels can open up new fields of opportunity (eg the Internet).

Often these factors overlap and PEST factors will affect many areas. For example at the present time the UK government is considering how best to free the country's postal systems from monopoly. Parliamentary bills will eventually need to be passed. Here the major driving force could be said to be political, triggered by economic necessity, facilitated by law. The markets will cease to be a monopoly. They might fragment into public and private sectors.

4 COMPETITOR ANALYSIS

Many firms identify key competitors and plan their strategies with competitors in mind.

4.1 Key questions for competitor analysis

- Who are they?
- What are their goals?
- What strategies are they pursuing?
- What are their strengths and weaknesses?
- How are they likely to respond?

The complexity facing the modern business is that its main competitor, customer and collaborator may be the same company. For example, Kodak and Fuji are intense rivals in the photographic film business, yet in 1996 they collaborated to bring the Advanced Photographic System (APS) to market while at the same time fighting in the Japanese courts over market protection issues.

Similarly the Efficient Consumer Response programme involves groups of competing manufacturers working together with retailers to streamline supply chains – an alliance of competitors, customers and collaborators. The complexity and ambiguity faced by executives in many modern markets underline yet further the imperative of identifying and understanding competitors.

4.2 Who are our competitors?

Identifying current competitors is easy. Identifying **potential** competitors is harder as potential competitors might be:

- Smaller companies attacking the market segment
- Companies operating in other markets wishing to expand
- Companies wishing to diversify

Finally a firm can **define** who its competitors actually are. Coca-Cola, for example, competes against:

- Pepsi in the Cola market
- All other soft drinks
- Tea and coffee
- Tap water: Coca-Cola's chief executive has declared that 'the main competitor is tap water: any other share definition is too narrow'

EXAMPLE

South Western Airlines is one of the most profitable in the US, partly because it defined its competition carefully.

Most airlines in the US have a 'hub' airport and 'spokes' from it. They compete with each other heavily on matters such as air miles, price and so on.

South Western does not use this arrangement and instead it flies 'point to point' over short distances. It has defined its competitor as the motor car - a substitute product - and has designed its marketing mix so as to minimise the time the customer takes travelling. This has meant flying from smaller, less congested airports, speeded-up check-in times and so on.

4.3 What are competitors' goals?

Next, you need to discern what the competitors' goals and objectives are.

(a) Relevant goals and objectives

- (i) Goals and objectives of the **parent company**, if the competitor is part of a larger group.
- (ii) The competitors' assessment of risk; a higher risk will require a higher return from a market.
- (iii) The personal goals of key managers. For example, a new chief executive may be brought in to 'turn the company round'. The new chief executive may have made a **public commitment** to one set of goals and may have invested a lot of prestige in achieving these goals.
- (iv) A company facing cash flow problems may do anything to maximise cash inflow.
- (v) The competitors' history, position and the underlying assumptions of their management. For example, some firms consider themselves to be 'market leaders'.
- (vi) **How dependent** the competitor is on the current business? A competitor with one main business will fight much harder to defend it than a competitor exposed to several sectors.

(b) Types of goals

- Profit
- Market share
- Cash flow
- Technological leadership
- Service leadership

Suffice it to say that competitors' goals can be taken into account. Different competitors put different weights on certain goals, particularly with regard to time horizons. Some might sacrifice profit, in the short term, for market share.

4.4 Current competitor strategies

Assessing current competitor strategies is relatively simple, as competitors send out signals to the same customer base. A company's closest competitor is one competing in the same target market.

4.5 Strategic group analysis: a constraint on competitive choice

Strategic group analysis tries to show how firms are positioned in a particular market or segment. Porter identifies a number of dimensions in which firms can differ.

- **Specialisation.** (Limited number of segments? Does it have a narrow product range?)
- **Brand.** Does the firm promote a brand or compete on price?
- **Distribution.** What channels are used? **Push** or **pull** approach to distribution?
- **Quality**
- Technological **leader** or follower?
- Degree of vertical **integration**
- **Cost structure**
- **Add-on services**
- **Price policy**
- **Indebtedness**
- Degree of **control** by holding company
- **Government involvement**

Any firm can be defined according to these dimensions. Firms with **low relative prices** are usually **able to control costs,** but **do not have superior product quality.**

Definition

> In any industry, especially with a large number of firms, some will pursue similar strategies in which case they can be considered a **strategic group**.

For any two of the attributes in 4.4 above it should be possible to map how firms relate to each other. The number of dimensions of course is very large, so a strategic group is best identified by taking the two most significant dimensions in the industry.

Mobility barriers constrain organisational endeavours and function as barriers to entry. **Mobility barriers** make it hard for a firm in one strategic group to develop or migrate to another.

(a) **Market factors**

   (i) Some supermarket chains (eg **Morrisons**) have a low presence in the South-East of England, where there is substantial competition.

   (ii) The brand name may be a mobility barrier, if it is unknown in the particular segment.

   (iii) The product line may not be extensive enough.

   (iv) Other factors include user technologies and selling systems.

(b) **Industry characteristics.** To move into a mass volume end of the market might require economies of scale and large production facilities. To move to the quality end might require greater investment in research and development.

(c) The organisation may lack the **distinctive skills** and competences in the new market area.

(d) **Legal barriers** might exist.

Porter cites the US chainsaw industry as an example.

Illustrative map of the U.S. chain saw industry

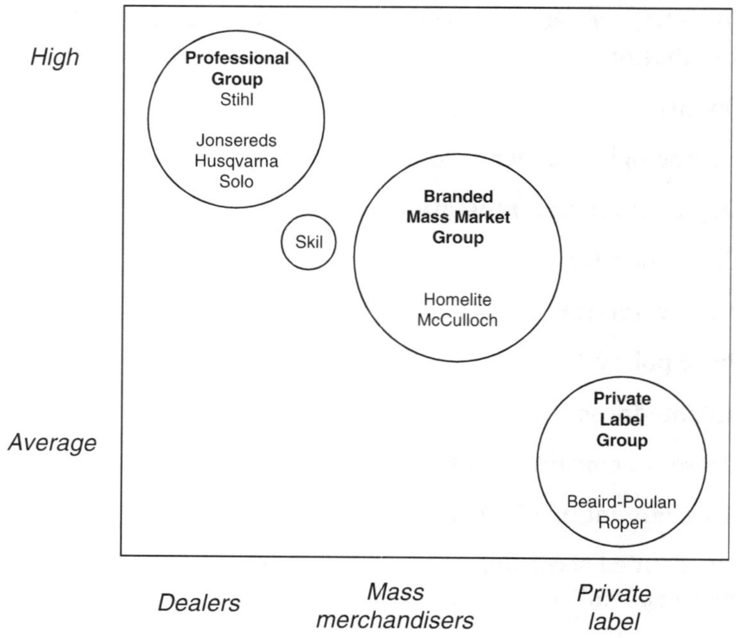

4.6 Competitors' strengths and weaknesses

SWOT analysis is covered in a later chapter, but it is relatively easy to assess a competitor's **strengths** and **weaknesses**. Here are some examples.

- Brand strengths, customer loyalty
- Market share
- Quality of management team
- Resources, financial and otherwise
- Intellectual property
- Distribution network
- Relative cost structure
- Distinctive competence

In marketing, Kotler suggests the following table for consideration for **marketing strengths and weaknesses.**

- Customer awareness
- Product quality
- Product availability
- Technical assistance
- Sales staff
- Market share
- 'Mind' share (% of customers who had heard about the company)
- Share of benefit

4.7 Analysing competitors' costs

Clearly the strategic response of competitors can vary significantly on the cost profile of the competitor. **Relative costs** are more important than absolute costs: Ward believes that it took Western firms too long to understand that Japanese firms had **sustainable cost advantages,** and hence were able to compete on price on a sustained basis.

Furthermore, even if the competitor is not competing on price, despite having a lower cost base, the competitor is:

NOTES

- Under no pressure to raise prices, thus limiting the firm's ability to raise its own
- More profitable, and hence can invest more

4.8 Competitor reaction and response

Kotler identifies the following types of competitor response.

Predictable	Unpredictable
(i) **Laid-back**: competitor does not respond (ii) **Selective**: competitor only responds to certain types of attack (iii) **Tiger**: competitor reacts to any attack	Unstochastic: **impossible to predict** how **competitor will** react

DISCUSSION

Why might a competitor be 'laid-back'?

Activity 2 **(5 minutes)**

Jot down a list of items of information that might be obtained from an analysis of competitors.

4.9 'Good' competitors

Monopolies are hard to come by, but some competitors are definitely easier to deal with than others. A 'good' competitor:

- Deters new entrants (assuming you are not a new entrant)
- Shares similar assumptions about the industry
- Prefers differentiation and focus to competing on price

	Balance	Strength	Weakness
Competitive maturity	• understand the rules • realistic assumptions • support industry structure	• credible/viable • know the industry costs	• clear weaknesses • limited strategic concept
Reconcilable goals	• moderate strategic stake • accept current profitability • desire cash generation	• comparable ROI targets	• short time horizons • risk averse

EXAMPLE

Among the British clearing banks in the late 1980s both Midland and Lloyds introduced interest-bearing current accounts. This gave them a short-term competitive edge, but once the market leaders followed, the result was everyone losing money on this major part of their business. Once locked in, it was difficult for any of the banks to extricate themselves from this self-defeating position.

5 COMPETITORS AND INNOVATION

5.1 Hamel's company types

Gary Hamel ('*Strategy as Revolution*', Harvard Business Review, July/August 1996) is one of the principal advocates of the view that organisations cannot succeed if they simply imitate what has gone before. In essence, he defines three principal types of company.

Company type	Comment
Rule makers	Dominate their respective marketplaces and who (try to) set the competitive conditions under which they and others will operate. The rule makers in today's environment include Microsoft, Hertz, General Electric and McDonalds.
Rule takers	The companies who, in effect, imitate the rule makers, who accept the competitive framework which has been established by the dominant players, and who try to beat the rule makers at their own game. Rule takers include Avis and Burger King.
Rule breakers	Organisations which refuse to accept the implicit assumptions made by existing competitors, and which therefore seek to establish a new paradigm. Companies in the rule breaker category include Amazon.com. Eventually, if a rule breaker becomes highly successful, it dominates its market place and can fall into the trap of turning into a rule maker.

5.2 Kotler's five dimensions of strategy

A similar framework is offered in another Harvard Business Review article by Kotler.

Creating Value Through Innovation		
Five dimensions of strategy	**Conventional logic**	**Value innovation logic**
• Industry assumptions	Industry's conditions are given.	Industry's conditions can be shaped.
• Strategic focus	Competitive advantages to beat the competition.	Competition not the benchmark. A company should pursue a quantum leap in value to dominate the market.
• Customers	Further segmentation and customisation, focussing on the differences in what customers value.	A value innovator targets the mass of buyers and willingly lets some existing customers go. It focuses on the key commonalities in what customers value.
• Assets and capabilities	A company should leverage its existing capabilities.	A company must not be constrained by what it already has. It must ask, 'What would we do if we were starting a new?'
• Product and service offerings	An industry's traditional boundaries determine the products and services a company offers. The goal is to maximise the value of those offerings.	A value innovator thinks in terms of the total solution customers seek, even if that takes the company beyond its industry's traditional offerings.

5.3 Characteristics of innovators

It is of crucial importance to the marketer of an innovation to know who the innovators/early triers are, and how they can be reached and influenced. 'Consumer innovators' is a term for the relatively small group who are the earliest purchasers of a new product or service (whether this is defined as the first 2.5% of adopters of a particular new product, or the people who purchase a number of new products and are therefore inferred to be 'innovative'.)

Characteristics which distinguish innovators from later adopters and non-adopters.

(a) **Interest in the relevant product category**. People who show an interest in fashion or technological inventions, say, are more likely to be the ones who will try out a new 'look' or device. Innovators can be identified and targeted by their tendency to seek information on the areas of their interest from special-interest mass-media sources - publications, conferences and exhibitions. Attitude surveys and lifestyle analysis may also pinpoint people with particular interests.

(b) **Opinion leadership**. We noted earlier that opinion-leaders tend to be innovators, and are therefore gatekeepers of new product information: if the opinion leaders get interested and have positive experience of the innovation, they will tell and influence others. By identifying opinion leaders, marketers can target motivational communication at innovative individuals.

(c) **Personality traits**

(i) Attitude flexibility, or open-mindedness.

(ii) Independence of judgement.

(iii) Variety-seeking, and the ability to deal with complex or ambiguous stimuli.

(iv) High tolerance for risk, low perception of risk, 'venturesomeness'. Innovators tend to be willing to risk a poor choice in order to increase their exposure to new ideas and experience.

Non-innovators seem to possess the opposite characteristics. Separate promotional approaches might therefore be required. Innovators respond to informative messages appealing to their interest, open-mindedness and willingness to make independent evaluations. Non-innovators respond to reference group influence, and the use of trusted/well known spokespersons, to reduce perceived risk and give their evaluation the support of others' opinions.

(d) **Consumption habits**. Innovators are less brand loyal, willing to switch to other brands for variety and respond more to promotional 'deals'. They also consume heavily (in volume) in the product areas in which they are the innovators.

(e) **Media selection**. Innovators expose themselves to more magazines and journals - especially those related to their particular interests. Targeting innovators can thus be efficiently achieved through advertising/editorials in special interest publications.

(f) **Social profile**. Innovators are more socially involved and accepted than non-innovators, meaning that they are more likely to belong to social groups and organisations. They therefore also function well as opinion leaders.

(g) **Demographic factors**. Innovators tend to be younger than non-innovators, although this depends to an extent on the nature of the product. They tend to have higher status in terms of education, occupation (three quarters have professional or technical jobs) and income. Innovators may thus be targeted through the use of geo-demographic techniques.

Chapter roundup

- Companies that have not mastered forecasting are likely to build positions that defend against yesterday's competitors or appeal to yesterday's customers.
- Competition between firms to serve customers is the very essence of modern, market-led economies.
- Systematic analysis of the business environment typically commences at the macro level, highlighting aspects of the broader environment that may impinge on the specific markets the firm operates in.
- Many firms such as Virgin compete in several markets and as such are diversified.
- Without a knowledge of competitors' strengths and their likely actions, it is impossible to formulate the central component of marketing strategy – finding a group of customers for whom one has a competitive advantage over the competition.
- It must also be true that, since competitive advantage is a relative concept, a company that has poor understanding of its competitors can have no real understanding of itself.
- The identification of strategic groups is fundamental to industry analysis since, just as industries can rise or fall despite the state of the overall business environment, so strategic groups with the distinctive competencies of their members can defy the general fluctuations within an industry.
- When a company chooses to enter a market, it also chooses its competitors. Therefore, in the selection of new opportunities it is important to realise that not all competitors are equally attractive.
- The more a firm innovates, the greater the experience accumulated; the greater the experience gained, the better the firm gets at innovation; the better the firm becomes at this activity, the greater its chances of competitive survival. A cycle of innovation is thus established.

Quick quiz

1 What is involved in a market forecast?

2 List three factors that govern sales potential.

3 What are Porter's Five Forces?

4 Name three factors which can encourage suppliers to exert pressure for higher prices.

5 What are the five key questions when undertaking a competitive analysis?

6 What types of goals might an organisation establish?

7 What is a strategic group?

8 What are the four main types of competitor response?

9 What three types of company has Hamel defined?

10 What are Kotler's five dimensions of strategy?

11 List four factors that distinguish innovators from later or non-adopters.

Answers to quick quiz

1. An assessment of environmental factors, outside the organisation's control, which will affect the demand for its products and services. (See paragraph 1)
2. The price of the product, sales promotion expenditure, competition. (para 1.1)
3. The threat of new entrants and substitute products/services, the bargaining power of suppliers and customers and the rivalry among existing firms. (para 2)
4. The importance of the supplier's product to the customer's business, whether the supplier has a differentiated product which buyers need to obtain, whether switching costs for customers would be high. (para 2.4)
5. Who are they, what are their goals, what strategies are they pursuing, what are their strengths and weaknesses and what are their response patterns? (para 4.1)
6. Goals could be concerned with profit, market share, cash flow and technological or service leadership. (para 4.3)
7. A strategic group is composed of firms within an industry following similar strategies aimed at similar customers or customer groups. (para 4.5)
8. Laid-back, selective, tiger and stochastic. (para 4.7)
9. Rule makers, takers and breakers. (para 5.1)
10. Industry assumptions, strategic focus, customers, assets and capabilities, product and service offerings. (para 5.2)
11. Interest in the relevant product category, they tend to be opinion leaders, their consumption habits and their media selection. (para 5.3)

Answers to activities

1 Petrol: supermarkets have entered the market.
Financial services/banking.
Books and CDs (threat from e-retailers)
Cars. Impact of cheaper imported cars has been to drive down the price.
Medicines: some chemists now sell at below the RRP.

2
- Their current and future objective – this will give clues as to the direction it will take and the aggressiveness with which it will pursue that direction.
- Their current strategies – can help to identify threats and opportunities arising from competitor actions.
- Their resources – asset and capability profile will indicate how they will move in the future and how they may react to threats.
- Predict their future strategies – a combination of the above findings should help to indicate what they are most likely to do in the future.

Chapter 10 : NEW PRODUCTS

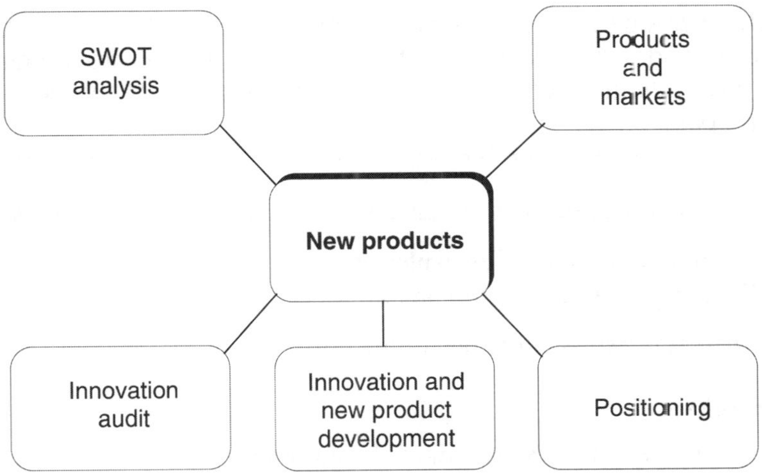

Introduction

This chapter will look at new product development and innovation. First however organisations must look at their external and internal environment, their products and markets and associated positioning.

Your objectives

In this chapter you will learn about the following:

(a) How to undertake a SWOT analysis

(b) The importance of product-market analysis

(c) Product-market strategies

(d) The steps involved in a systematic new product development (NPD) process

(e) The importance of innovation to an organisation

1 SWOT ANALYSIS

The purpose of **corporate appraisal** (SWOT analysis) is to **combine** the assessment of the environment and the analysis of the organisation's internal resources and capabilities.

Definition

> **Corporate appraisal:** 'a critical assessment of the strengths and weaknesses, opportunities and threats in relation to the internal and environmental factors affecting the entity in order to establish its condition prior to the preparation of a long-term plan.'

A **strengths and weaknesses** analysis expresses which areas of the business have:

- Strengths that should be exploited
- Weaknesses which should be improved

It therefore covers the results of the position audit.

1.1 Opportunities

- What opportunities exist in the business environment?
- Their inherent profit-making potential
- The organisation's ability to exploit the worthwhile opportunities

1.2 Threats

- What threats might arise?
- How will competitors be affected?
- How will the company be affected?

The opportunities and threats might arise from PEST and competitive factors.

1.3 Bringing the SWOT elements together

The internal and external appraisals will be brought together, and perhaps shown in a cruciform chart.

EXAMPLE

Strengths	**Weaknesses**
£10 million of capital available	Heavy reliance on a small number of customers
Production expertise and appropriate marketing skills	Limited product range, with no new products and expected market decline. Small marketing organisation.
Threats	**Opportunities**
A major competitor has already entered the new market	Government tax incentives for new investment
	Growing demand in a new market, although customers so far relatively small in number

The company is in imminent danger of losing its existing markets and must diversify its products and/or markets. The new market opportunity exists to be exploited, and since the number of customers is currently small, the relatively small size of the existing marketing force would not be an immediate hindrance. A strategic plan could be developed to buy new equipment and use existing production and marketing to enter the new market, with a view to rapid expansion. Careful planning of manpower, equipment, facilities, research and development would be required and there would be an objective to meet the threat of competition so as to obtain a substantial share of a growing market. The cost of entry at this early stage of market development should not be unacceptably high.

The SWOT technique can also be used for specific areas of strategy such as IT and marketing.

Effective SWOT analysis does not simply require a categorisation of information, it also requires some **evaluation of the relative importance** of the various factors under consideration.

(a) These features are only of relevance if they are **perceived to exist by the customers.** Listing corporate features that internal personnel regard as strengths/weaknesses is of little relevance if customers do not perceive them as such.

(b) In the same vein, threats and opportunities are conditions presented by the external environment and they should be independent of the firm.

The SWOT can now be used to guide strategy formulation. The two major options are **matching** and **conversion**.

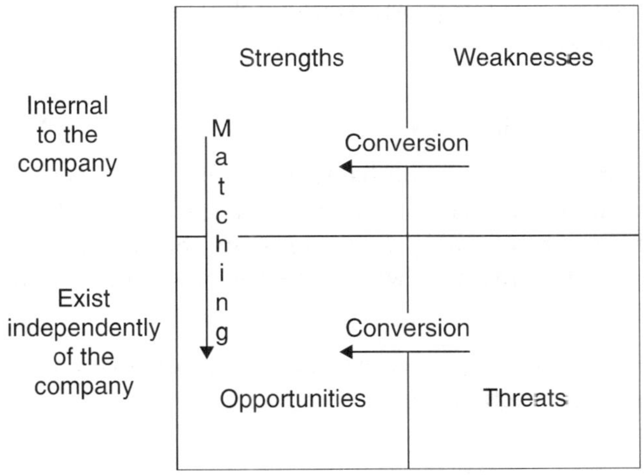

(a) Matching

This entails finding, where possible, a match between the strengths of the organisation and the opportunities presented by the market. Strengths which do not match any available opportunity are of limited use while opportunities which do not have any matching strengths are of little immediate value.

(b) Conversion

This requires the development of strategies which will convert weaknesses into strengths in order to take advantage of some particular opportunity, or converting threats into opportunities which can then be matched by existing strengths.

Activity 1 **(20 minutes)**

Hall Faull Downes Ltd has been in business for 25 years, during which time profits have risen by an average of 3% per annum, although there have been peaks and troughs in profitability due to the ups and downs of trade in the customers' industry. The increase in profits until five years ago was the result of increasing sales in a buoyant market, but more recently, the total market has become somewhat smaller and Hall Faull Downes has only increased sales and profits as a result of improving its market share.

The company produces components for manufacturers in the engineering industry.

In recent years, the company has developed many new products and currently has 40 items in its range compared to 24 only five years ago. Over the same five-year period, the number of customers has fallen from 20 to nine, two of whom together account for 60% of the company's sales.

Give your appraisal of the company's future, and suggest what it is probably doing wrong.

1.4 The marketing SWOT

Having looked at corporate level SWOT analysis we should now turn our attention to the marketing level. It is important to remember that the concept and approach remains the same, it is only the factors which we are considering which vary. Corporate SWOTs are concerned with everything. Marketing SWOTs concentrate more specifically on **markets** and the mix.

1.5 Strengths and weaknesses

The marketing department is probably the most important source of 'bottom up' information, opinions and views which influence the development of the corporate strategy. But the marketing audit also represents the starting point for developing the **marketing** plan, answering the 'where are we now' question in terms of marketing controllables.

A **marketing audit** as we have seen earlier, should involve a thorough 'taking stock' of the complete marketing activity.

Activity 2 **(10 minutes)**

Jot down some of the elements of the marketing audit which you might consider useful inputs to the marketing SWOT.

A prime objective as far as the marketing manager is concerned of this internal marketing analysis is to be able to log the company's current market position on a **positioning map**.

NOTES

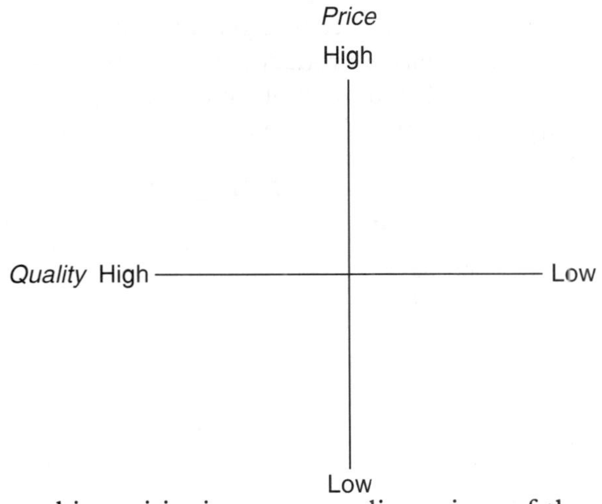

The variables used on this positioning map are dimensions of the marketing mix. You may need several such maps to consider the real position of a complex product, but the variables you should focus on are those recognised as having the greatest influence on purchasing decisions.

Activity 3 **(10 minutes)**

Use the positioning maps above and below to log the positions of your company or college and its key competitors.

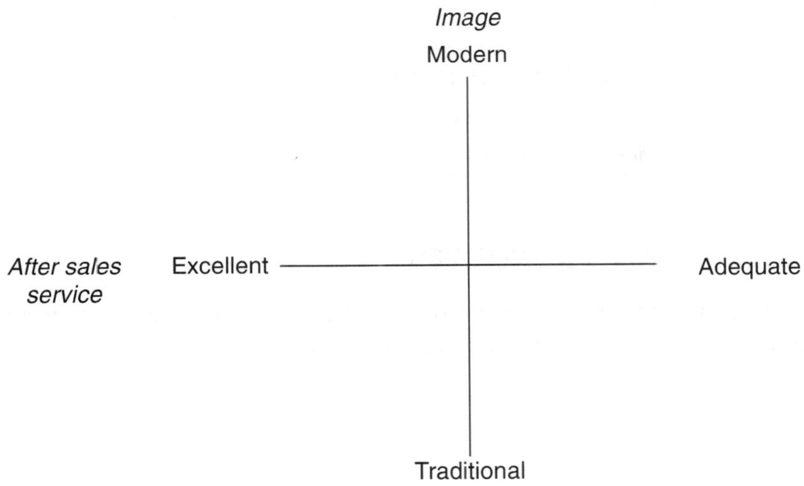

1.6 Opportunities and threats

The external aspects of the marketing SWOT are the product/market opportunities and threats which evolve from changes in the macro environment identified at the corporate level. For example a demographic shift increasing the proportion of older customers for overseas holidays may have been identified in the environmental analysis of a package holiday company. At **marketing** level this translates into a number of possibilities.

(a) An opportunity to sell existing holidays to this new target market.

(b) An opportunity to develop new products specifically developed to meet the needs of this emerging segment.

(c) The possible option of switching resources away from segments which are showing less growth potential.

At marketing level, opportunities can be considered and communicated using the **Ansoff matrix** which provides the alternative product/market options available to a company. (*Note*. Although not specifically shown by implication the threats at this level are factors which reduce the viability or potential of any of the product/market possibilities.)

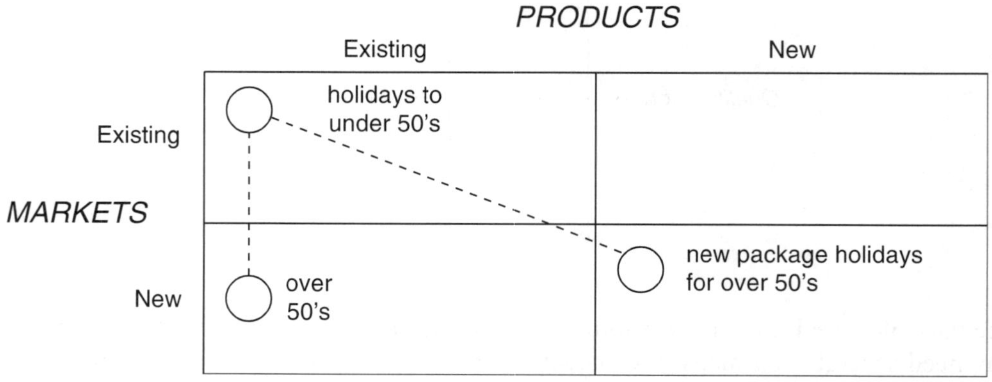

To summarise the marketing SWOT:

Strengths	*Weaknesses*
These are **internal** factors controllable by marketing managers; they are the 7P's	
Opportunities	*Threats*
These are **external** uncontrollable factors related to an appraisal of changing product/market position	

2 PRODUCTS AND MARKETS

Ansoff drew up a **growth vector matrix**, describing a combination of a firm's activities in current and new markets, with existing and new products.

Definition

Product-market mix is a short-hand term for the products/services a firm sells (or a service which a public sector organisation provides) and the markets it sells them to.

Ansoff's product-market growth matrix

	Existing products	*New products*
Existing markets	*Market penetration strategy* 1 More purchasing and usage from existing customers 2 Gain customers from competitors 3 Convert non-users into users (where both are in same market segment)	*Product development strategy* 1 Product modification via new features 2 Different quality levels 3 'New' product
New markets	*Market development strategy* 1 New market segments 2 New distribution channels 3 New geographic areas eg exports	*Diversification strategy* 1 Organic growth 2 Joint ventures 3 Mergers 4 Acquisition/take-over

2.1 Current products and current markets: market penetration

Market penetration. The firm seeks to:

(a) **Maintain or to increase its share** of current markets with current products, eg through competitive pricing, advertising, sales promotion

(b) Secure dominance of growth markets

(c) Restructure a mature market by driving out competitors

(d) Increase usage by existing customers (eg airmiles, loyalty cards)

EXAMPLE

Good examples of strategies for market penetration are air miles and 'frequent flier' services. A decision to fly with an airline gives the customer air miles, which can be redeemed on later flights, and which will encourage the customer to fly again.

2.2 Present products and new markets: market development

Market development is when the firm seeks new markets for its **current** products or services. It is appropriate when its products are strengths which can be matched by opportunities in new markets. Ways of developing markets include:

(a) **New geographical areas** and export markets (eg a radio station building a new transmitter to reach a new audience).

(b) **Different package sizes** for food and other domestic items so that both those who buy in bulk and those who buy in small quantities are catered for.

(c) **New distribution channels** to attract new customers (eg organic food sold in supermarkets not just specialist shops).

(d) **Differential pricing policies** to attract different types of customer and create **new market segments**. For example, travel companies have developed a market for cheap long-stay winter breaks in warmer countries for retired couples.

2.3 New products and present markets: product development

Product development is the launch of new products to existing markets.

(a) Advantages

- Product development forces competitors to innovate
- Newcomers to the market might be discouraged

(b) The **drawbacks** include the expense and the risk.

2.4 New products: new markets (diversification)

Diversification occurs when a company decides to make **new products for new markets.** It should have a clear idea about what it expects to gain from diversification. There are two types of diversification, related and unrelated diversification.

(a) **Growth.** New products and new markets should be selected which offer prospects for growth which the existing product-market mix does not.

(b) **Investing surplus** funds not required for other expansion needs: but the funds could be returned to shareholders.

(c) The firm's strengths match the opportunity if:

(i) Outstanding new products have been developed by the firm's research and development department

(ii) The profit opportunities from diversification are high.

DISCUSSION

In the late 1980s many building societies found difficulties when they diversified into estate agency businesses.

2.5 Related diversification

Definition

> **Related diversification** is 'development beyond the present product market, but still within the broad confines of the industry ... [it] ... therefore builds on the assets or activities which the firm has developed' (Johnson and Scholes). It takes the form of vertical or horizontal integration'.

NOTES

Horizontal integration refers to 'development into activities which are competitive with or directly **complementary** to a company's present activities. Sony, for example, started to compete in computer games.

Vertical integration occurs when a company becomes its own:

(a) **Supplier** of raw materials, components or services (**backward vertical integration**). For example, backward integration would occur where a milk producer acquires its own dairy farms rather than buying raw milk from independent farmers

(b) **Distributor** or sales agent (**forward vertical integration**), for example where a manufacturer of synthetic yarn begins to produce shirts from the yarn instead of selling it to other shirt manufacturers.

2.6 Advantages of vertical integration

(a) A **secure supply of components** or raw materials with more control. Supplier bargaining power is reduced.

(b) **Strengthen the relationships** and contacts of the manufacturer with the 'final consumer' of the product.

(c) Win a share of the **higher profits**

(d) Pursue a **differentiation strategy** more effectively

(e) Raise **barriers to entry**

2.7 Disadvantages of vertical integration

(a) **Overconcentration.** A company places 'more eggs in the same end-market basket' (Ansoff). Such a policy is fairly inflexible, more sensitive to instabilities and increases the firm's dependence on a particular aspect of economic demand.

(b) The firm **fails to benefit from any economies of scale or technical advances** in the industry into which it has diversified. This is why, in the publishing industry, most printing is subcontracted to specialist printing firms, who can work machinery to capacity by doing work for many firms.

EXAMPLE

(a) Horizontal integration. Since water and electricity distribution were privatised in the UK, there have been a number of changes. Regional water companies have purchased regional electricity distribution firms. For example, Norweb has been bought by North West Water. Although the businesses are very different, they have a very similar customer base, and cost savings can be achieved by shared billing, accounts management etc.

(b) Vertical integration. Before privatisation, the UK electricity industry was a state-owned monopoly, vertically integrated from power generation to distribution. Privatisation effectively split up these two businesses, to introduce competition in power generation, so that the regional distribution companies could buy from a number of suppliers. However, the power distribution companies sought to buy a regional distribution company, giving them a captive market: National Power was set to buy Southern Electric, but the bid was blocked by the government on the grounds that it would inhibit competition

---

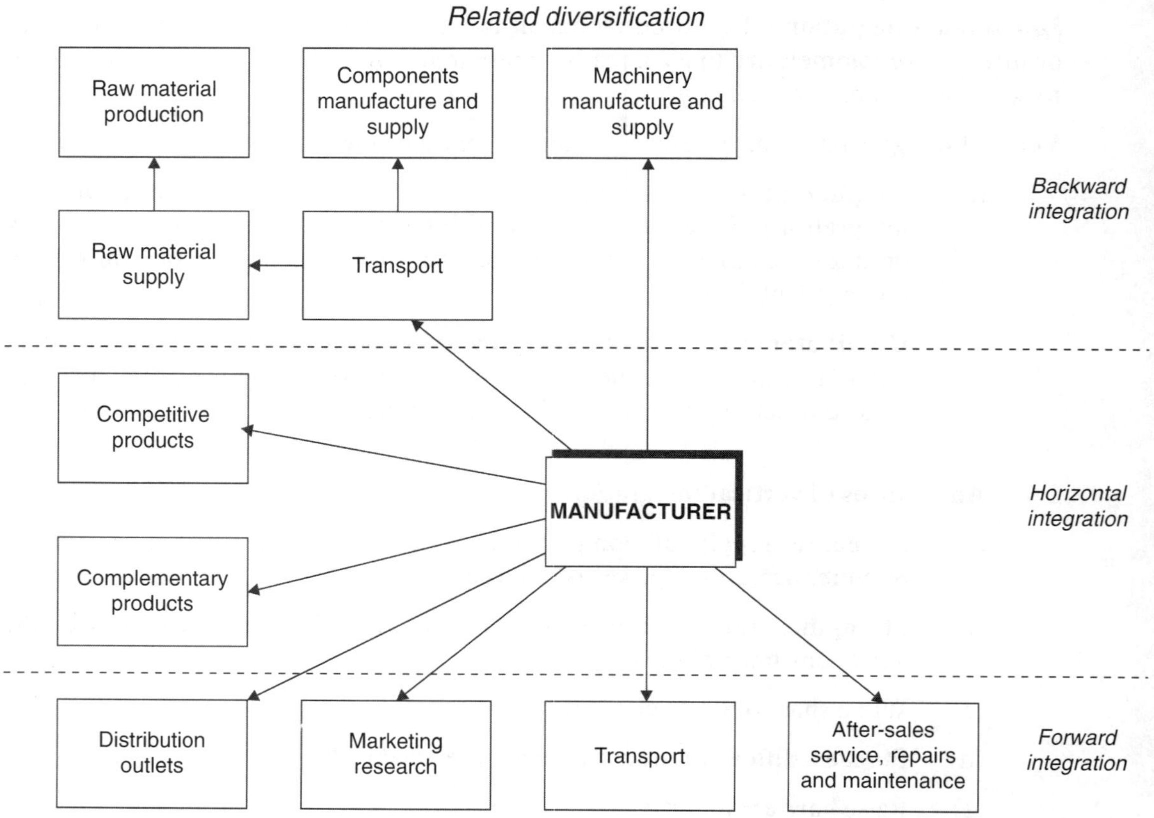

Source: Johnson and Scholes

2.8 Unrelated diversification

Definition

Unrelated or conglomerate diversification 'is development beyond the present industry into products/ markets which, at face value, may bear no close relation to the present product/market.'

Conglomerate diversification is now very unfashionable. However, it has been a key strategy for companies in Asia, particularly South Korea.

2.9 Advantages of conglomerate diversification

(a) **Risk-spreading.** Entering new products into new markets offers protection against the failure of current products and markets.

(b) **High profit opportunities**. An improvement of the **overall profitability and flexibility** of the firm through acquisition in industries which have better economic characteristics than those of the acquiring firms.

(c) **Escape** from the present business. For example, Reed International moved away from paper production and into publishing.

(d) **Better access to capital** markets.

(e) **No other way to grow.** Expansion along existing lines might create a monopoly and lead to government investigations and control. Diversifications offer the chance of growth without creating a monopoly.

(f) **Use surplus cash.**

(g) **Exploit under-utilised resources.**

(h) **Obtain cash**, or other financial advantages (such as accumulated tax losses).

(i) **Use a company's image and reputation** in one market to develop into another where corporate image and reputation could be vital ingredients for success.

2.10 Disadvantages of conglomerate diversification

(a) The **dilution of shareholders' earnings** if diversification is into growth industries with high P/E ratios.

(b) **Lack of a common identity and purpose** in a conglomerate organisation. A conglomerate will only be successful if it has a high quality of management and financial ability at central headquarters, where the diverse operations are brought together.

(c) **Failure in one of the businesses will drag down the rest**, as it will eat up resources. **British Aerospace** was severely damaged by the effect of a downturn in the property market on its property subsidiary, **Arlington Securities**.

(d) **Lack of management experience** in the business area. **Japanese steel companies** have diversified into areas completely unrelated to steel such as personal computers, with limited success.

(e) **No good for shareholders.** Shareholders can spread risk quite easily, simply by buying a diverse portfolio of shares. They do not need management to do it for them.

Activity 4 **(20 minutes)**

A large organisation in road transport operates nationwide in general haulage. This field has become very competitive and with the recent down-turn in trade, has become only marginally profitable. It has been suggested that the strategic structure of the company should be widened to include other aspects of physical distribution so that the maximum synergy would be obtained from that type of diversification.

(a) Name three activities which might fit into the suggested new strategic structure, explaining each one briefly.

(b) Explain how each of these activities could be incorporated into the existing structure.

(c) State the advantages and disadvantages of such diversification.

2.11 Withdrawal

It might be the right decision to cease producing a product and/or to pull out of a market completely. This is a hard decision for managers to take if they have invested time and money or if the decision involves redundancies.

Exit barriers make this difficult.

(a) Cost barriers include redundancy costs, the difficulty of selling assets.

(b) Political barriers include government attitudes. Defence is an example.

(c) Marketing considerations may delay withdrawal. A product might be a 'loss-leader' for others, or might contribute to the company's reputation for its breadth of coverage.

(d) Psychology. Managers hate to admit failure, and there might be a desire to avoid a 'bloodletting'. Furthermore, people might wrongly assume that carrying on is a low risk strategy, especially if they (wrongly) feel bound to carry on, as they have spent money already.

2.12 Reasons for exit

(a) The **company's business** may be in buying firms, selling their assets and improving their performance, and then selling them at a profit.

(b) **Resource limitations** mean that less profitable businesses have to be abandoned. A business might be sold to a competitor, or occasionally to management (as a buy-out).

(c) A company may be forced to quit, because of **insolvency**.

(d) **Change of competitive strategy**. In the microprocessor industry, many American firms have left high-volume DRAM chips to Asian firms so as to concentrate on high value added niche products.

(e) **Decline in attractiveness of the market**

(f) **Funds can earn more elsewhere.**

2.13 Section summary

Product-market strategy can be:

- **Penetration**: same products, same markets
- **Product development**: new products, same markets
- **Market development**: same products, new markets
- **Diversification**: new products, new markets
- **Withdrawal**
- Any **combination** of the above, depending on the product portfolio

3 POSITIONING

Definition

> **Positioning** is the act of designing the company's product and image so that it offers a distinct and valued place in the target customer's mind.

EXAMPLE

Volvo originally positioned itself as a car for safety, whose most touted qualities were 'safety, reliability, and recently, environmental friendliness'. Recent advertising has identified speed and excitement.

Following the collapse of a proposed merger with Renault, the group's strategy 'is to forge Volvo into a niche producer of premium cars. Volvo's product range is moving, and the firm is using the design and marketing processes to ensure that the Volvo image moves in step. The aim is to attract younger 'pre family' and older 'post family' buyers without losing traditional customers'.

3.1 Problems with positioning

How much do people remember about a product or brand?

(a) Many products are, in fact, very similar, and the key issue is to make them distinct in the customer's mind.

(b) People remember 'number 1', so the product should be positioned as 'number 1' in relation to a valued attribute.

(c) Cosmetic changes can have the effect of repositioning the product in the customer's mind. To be effective, however, this psychological positioning has to be reinforced by 'real' positioning.

Given that positioning is psychological as well as real, we can now identify positioning errors.

Mistake	Consequence
Underpositioning	The brand does not have a clear identity in the eyes of the customer.
Overpositioning	Buyers may have too narrow an image of a brand.
Confused positioning	Too many claims might be made for a brand.
Doubtful positioning	The positioning may not be credible in the eyes of the buyer.

DISCUSSION

Marks and Spencer has been recently criticised in terms of poor positioning.

3.2 Positioning strategy checklist

Positioning variable	Comment
• Attributes	Size, for example
• Benefit	What benefits we offer
• Use/application	Ease of use; accessibility
• User	The sort of person the product appeals to
• Product category	Consciously differentiated from competition
• Quality/price	Superior quality/low price

3.3 Perceptual maps

One simple perceptual map that can be used is to plot brands or competing products in terms of two key characteristics such as price and quality.

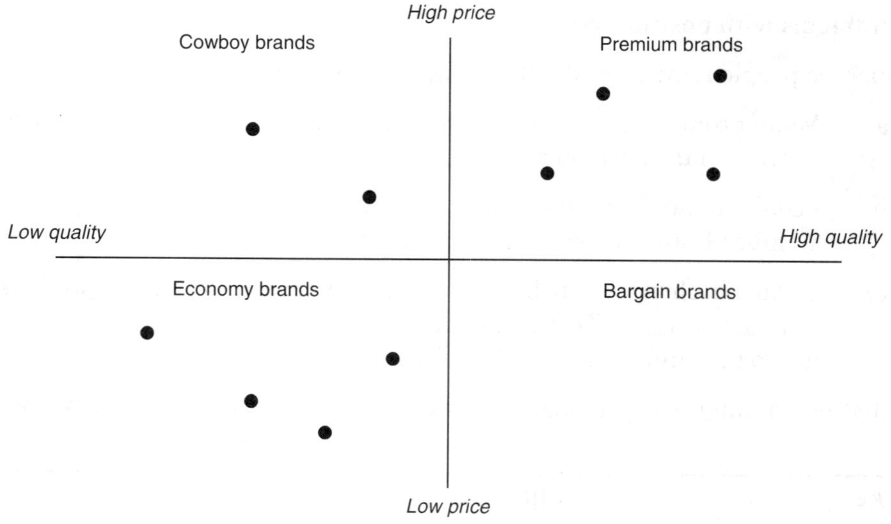

A perceptual map of market positioning can be used to **identify gaps in the market**. This example might suggest that there could be potential in the market for a low-price high-quality 'bargain brand'. A company that carries out such an analysis might decide to conduct further research to find out whether there is scope in the market for a new product which would be targeted at a market position where there are few or no rivals.

3.4 Mapping positions

Kotler identified a 3 × 3 matrix of nine different competitive positioning strategies.

Product quality	*Product price*		
	High price	*Medium price*	*Low price*
High	Premium strategy	Penetration strategy	Superbargain strategy
Medium	Overpricing strategy	Average-quality strategy	Bargain strategy
Low	Hit-and-run strategy	Shoddy goods strategy	Cheap goods strategy

Once selected, the needs of the targeted segment can be identified and the marketing mix strategy developed to provide the benefits package needed to satisfy them. Positioning the product offering then becomes a matter of matching and communicating appropriate benefits.

NOTES

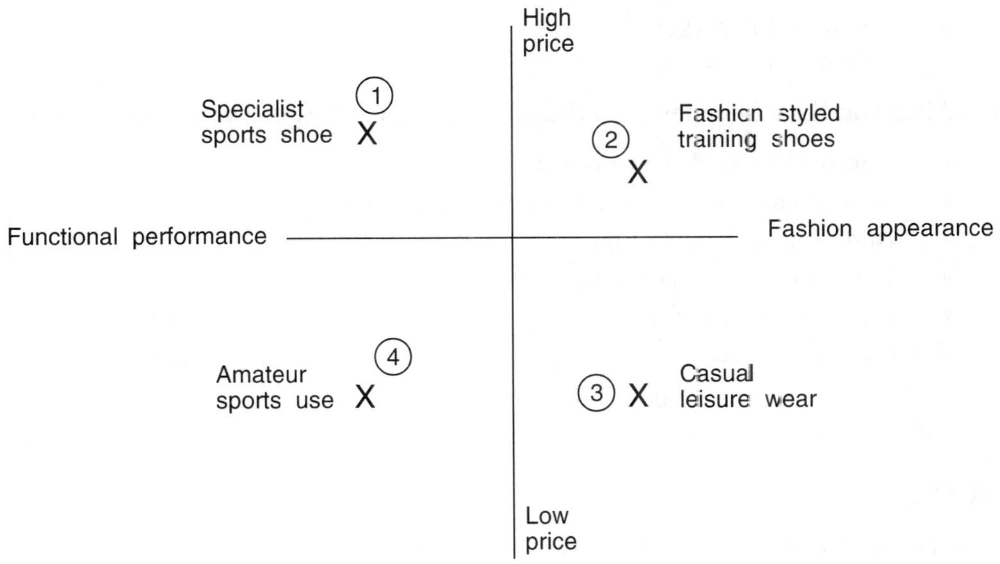

3.5 Steps in positioning

Step 1. Identify differentiating factors in products or services in relation to competitors

Step 2. Select the most important differences

Step 3. Communicate the position to the target market

The value of positioning is that it enables **tactical marketing mix decisions to be made**.

4 INNOVATION AND NEW PRODUCT DEVELOPMENT

4.1 New products

New products feature in a firm's competitive and marketing strategies.

(a) New and innovatory products can **lower entry barriers** to existing industries and markets, if new technology is involved.

(b) The market for any product changes over time and its life. The interests of the company are therefore best met with a **balanced product portfolio**. Managers therefore must plan when to introduce new products, how best to extend the life of mature ones and when to abandon those in decline.

A firm should identify its strategy underlying new product development.

(a) **Leader strategy.** Will the firm gain competitive advantage by operating at the leading edge of new developments? If yes, there are significant implications for the R&D activity and the likely length of product life cycles within the portfolio.

(b) **Follower strategy.** Will the firm be more pro-active, adopt a follower strategy, which involves lower costs and less emphasis on the R&D activity? It sacrifices early rewards of innovation, but avoids its risks. A follower might have to license certain technologies from a leader (as in the case with many consumer electronics companies).

4.2 What are new products?

The term **new product development** encompasses a wide range of different types of activity ranging form the development of completely new products and technologies to repackaging of existing ones. Bear in mind that new products can be:

BPP PUBLISHING

- New to the market
- New to the company

Booz, Allen and Hamilton identified the following categories, in a survey of 700 firms

- New to the world: new market 10%
- New product lines to enable a firm to enter a new sector 20%
- Additions to product line 26%
- Repositionings to new segments 7%
- Improvements/revisions 26%
- Cost reductions 11%

DISCUSSION

There are very few true new products that come into the market.

4.3 The process of NPD in overview

Key factors for NPD success. A systematic NPD process is outlined in the diagram on the following page.

Step 1. **Idea generation** requires the maximum number of new ideas to be generated. This necessitates an active search of the environment and for no suggestion to be rejected out of hand. Sources include employees, scientists, competitors, customers.

Step 2. **Screening** sorts the ideas for compatibility with organisational strategy, resources, distribution channels, competitive advantage etc.

Step 3. **Concept development and testing** is focused on customer needs. Can we find a concept that wraps the idea up into a package that will be adopted by enough consumers? Conceptual **positioning maps** are often used.

Step 4. **Marketing strategy**. The next stage is to draft a marketing plan including short and long-term sales, profit and market share objectives and the structure of the marketing mix.

Step 5. **Business analysis** is focused on determining whether the product will meet the plan's objectives. Sales forecasting is used with estimates firstly on the level and speed of first-time sales and secondly the level of replacement sales. Costs and profits are also estimated.

Step 6. **Product development** involves the physical development of the product in the form of a prototype and a substantial increase in commitment and investment. Tests are then conducted (eg food, for taste and shelf life).

Step 7. **Market testing.** Test marketing is often used to arrive at a more reliable sales forecast and to pre-test marketing plans. Store tests are often used in consumer markets with product use tests and trade shows used more in industrial markets.

Step 8. **Commercialisation.** Often, market testing is omitted and full scale product launch occurs. The questions to ask at this stage are: when to launch? Where to launch? Which groups should be targeted? How should the product be launched?

4.4 Responsibility for NPD

At strategic level, NPD is ultimately the responsibility of the **board**. NPD requires, at different stages, the co-operation of R&D, marketing and production departments.

- The **marketing** department should identify the opportunity.
- The **designers** should, ideally, develop the product so that it satisfies customers' need.
- The **products** should be designed also to be produced in the most cost-effective way.

The ideal management structure for the NPD process involves:

- Clear, realistic planning targets
- A project manager to drive the project, perhaps with a sponsor at Board level

A key relationship is that between marketing personnel and R&D. The **danger** is that **NPD will be 'owned' by R&D**, so technically perfect products are produced which do not meet customer needs profitably.

The relationship of the R&D department with marketing personnel is sometimes problematic.

(a) **Cultural**. The R&D department may have an 'academic' or university atmosphere, as opposed to a commercial one.

(b) **Organisational**. If R&D consumes substantial resources, it would seem quite logical to exploit economies of scale by having it centralised.

(c) **Work.** Marketing work and R&D work differ in many important respects. R&D work is likely to be more open ended than marketing work.

DISCUSSION

Many technological products are too focused on being technically superior rather than customer focused.

4.5 Why R&D should be more closely co-ordinated with marketing

(a) If the firm operates the **marketing concept**, then the 'identification of customer needs' should be a vital input to new product development.

(b) The R&D department might identify possible changes to product specifications so that a **variety of marketing mixes** can be tried out and screened.

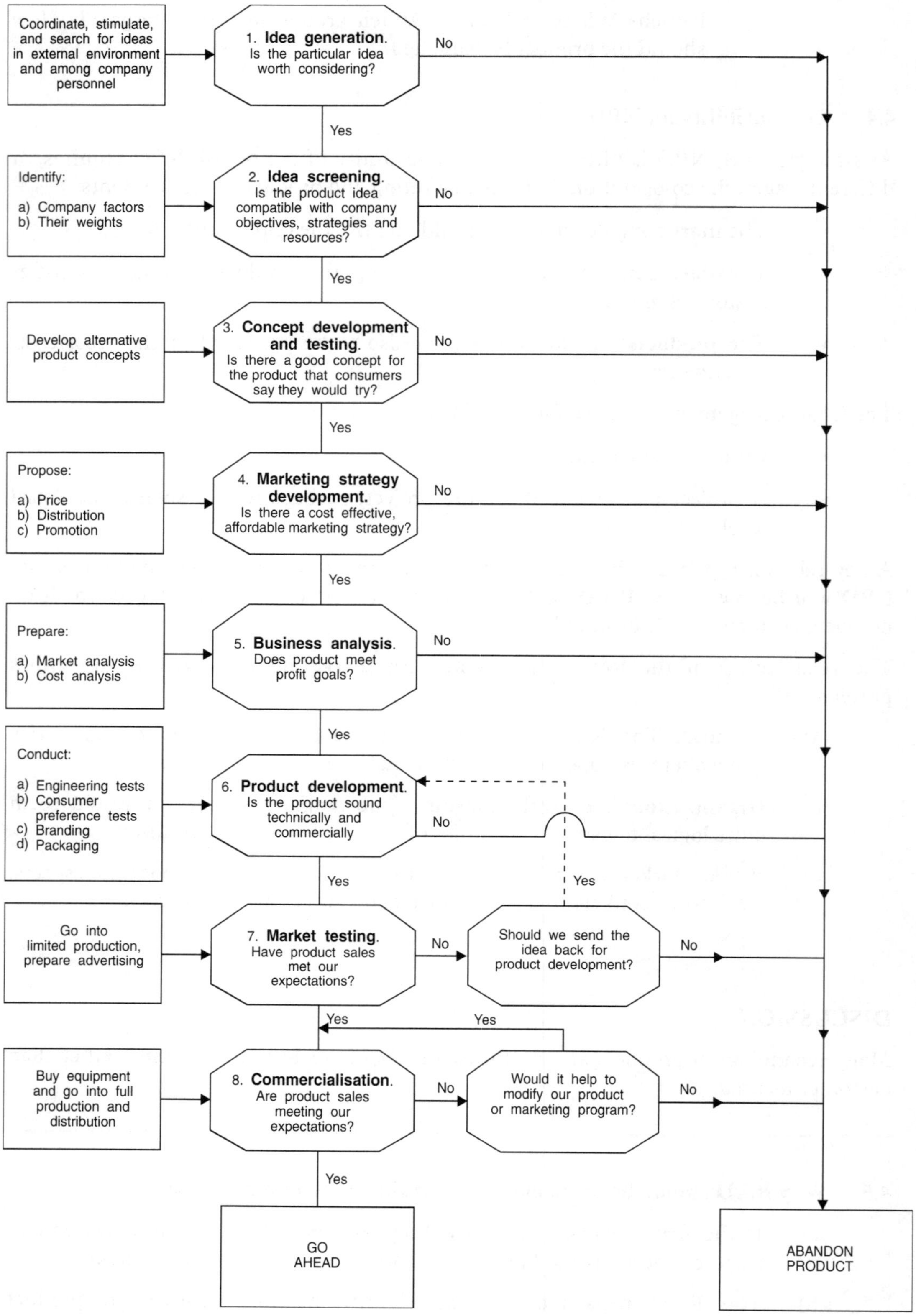
Coordinate, stimulate, and search for ideas in external environment and among company personnel
1. Idea generation. Is the particular idea worth considering?
No
Yes
Identify:
a) Company factors
b) Their weights
2. Idea screening. Is the product idea compatible with company objectives, strategies and resources?
No
Yes
Develop alternative product concepts
3. Concept development and testing. Is there a good concept for the product that consumers say they would try?
No
Yes
Propose:
a) Price
b) Distribution
c) Promotion
4. Marketing strategy development. Is there a cost effective, affordable marketing strategy?
No
Yes
Prepare:
a) Market analysis
b) Cost analysis
5. Business analysis. Does product meet profit goals?
No
Yes
Conduct:
a) Engineering tests
b) Consumer preference tests
c) Branding
d) Packaging
6. Product development. Is the product sound technically and commercially
No
Yes
Go into limited production, prepare advertising
7. Market testing. Have product sales met our expectations?
No
Should we send the idea back for product development?
No
Yes
Yes
Buy equipment and go into full production and distribution
8. Commercialisation. Are product sales meeting our expectations?
No
Would it help to modify our product or marketing program?
No
Yes
GO AHEAD
ABANDON PRODUCT

EXAMPLE

Nestlé once had a central R&D function, with regional development centres. The central R&D function was involved in basic research. 'Much of the lab's work was only tenuously connected with the company's business... When scientists joined the lab, they were told "Just work in this or that area. If you work hard enough, we're sure you'll find something".' The results of this approach were:

- The research laboratory was largely cut off from development centres
- Much research never found commercial application

Nestlé reorganised the business into strategic business units (SBU's). Formal links were established between R&D and the SBUs. This means that research procedures have been changed so that a commercial time horizon was established.

The purpose of **test marketing** is to obtain information about how consumers react to a new product - ie will they buy it, and if so, will they buy it again?

- The total market demand for the product can be made
- The product/service can be amended
- Other aspects of the marketing mix can be changed

A test market involves testing a new consumer product in selected areas which are thought to be '**representative**' of the total market. In the selected areas, the firm will attempt to distribute the product through the same types of sales outlets it plans to use in the full market launch, and also to use the advertising and promotion plans it intends to use in the full market.

4.6 Characteristics of a good test marketing exercise

Size of market	The test market area should be **large enough** to be representative of how the 'full' market might behave, but not so large as to be almost as expensive as a full national market launch
Time	The test period should be sufficiently long to give customers time to become aware of the product, and to monitor not only initial sales demand but also 'repeat buying' habits.
Representative	The test market must be as closely representative of the national market as possible.
Promotional facilities	One of the television regions could be used as a test area.

4.7 Benefits of test marketing

(a) The company **can pre-test a planned marketing mix**. For example, they may be able to identify product faults not identified at the development stage, or they may discover potential distribution problems.

(b) Expensive product failure may be avoided.

(c) **Results** from the test market may enable the company to prepare more accurate **sales forecasts**.

(d) The costs and risks of a full time launch are postponed.

4.8 Disadvantages of test marketing

(a) Unless the test market area is **typical** of the market as a whole, the information obtained about potential demand will be **biased** and misleading.

(b) A lengthy test market will **alert competitors** to what the firm is planning to do, and give them time to prepare their own response to the new product.

(c) Only a **small sample** will be used, which raises statistical problems.

(d) Consumers may be aware of the test and **distort their answers** accordingly.

(e) Estimates for the future cannot reliably be based on results recorded today.

(f) **Competitors** may decide to **sabotage** the test, for example by flooding the area with increased advertising activity.

(g) It is difficult to translate national media plans into local equivalents.

(h) Some goods, for example consumer goods such as household furniture, have lengthy repurchase cycles which would make test marketing far too lengthy to be of any practical forecasting value.

4.9 Other forms of experimentation (different from test marketing).

(a) **Simulated store technique (or laboratory test markets)**. In these tests, a group of shoppers are invited to watch a selection of advertisements for a number of products, including an advertisement for the new product. They are then given some money and invited to spend it in a supermarket or shopping area. Their purchases are recorded and they are asked to explain their purchase decisions (and non-purchase decisions).

(b) **Controlled test marketing.** In these tests, a research firm pays a **panel of stores to carry the new product for a given length of time**. This test helps to provide an assessment of 'in-store' factors.

DISCUSSION

Many product failures could be prevented if adequate market testing was undertaken.

4.10 New product pricing: market penetration and market skimming

There are three elements in the pricing decision for a new product.

- Getting the product accepted
- Maintaining a market share in the face of competition
- Making a profit from the product

When a firm launches a new product on to the market, it must decide on a pricing policy which lies between the two extremes of market penetration and market skimming.

Market penetration pricing is a policy of low prices when the product is first launched in order to gain sufficient penetration into the market. It is therefore a policy of sacrificing short-term profits in the interests of long-term profits.

4.11 In favour of a penetration policy

(a) The firm wishes to **discourage rivals** from entering the market.

(b) The firm wishes **to shorten the initial period of the product's life cycle**, in order to enter the growth and maturity stages as quickly as possible. (This would happen if there is high elasticity of demand for the product.)

(c) A firm might therefore deliberately build excess production capacity and set its prices very low; as demand builds up, the spare capacity will be used up gradually, and unit costs will fall; the firm might even reduce prices further as unit costs fall.

(d) In this way, early year losses will enable the firm to dominate the market and have the lowest costs.

4.12 Market skimming

The aim of market skimming is to gain **high unit profits very early** on in the product's life.

(a) The firm charges **high prices** when a product is **first launched**.

(b) The firm **spends heavily on advertising** and sales promotion to win customers.

(c) As the product moves into the later stages of its **life cycle** (growth, maturity and decline) **progressively lower prices will be charged**. The profitable 'cream' is thus 'skimmed' off in progressive stages until sales can only be sustained at lower prices.

(d) **Conditions suitable for a skimming policy**

  (i) Where the **product is new and different**, so that customers are prepared to pay high prices.

  (ii) **Where demand elasticity is unknown**. It is better to start by charging high prices and then reducing them if the demand for the product turns out to be price elastic than to start by charging low prices and then attempting to raise them substantially when demand turns out to be price inelastic.

  (iii) High initial prices might not be profit-maximising in the long run, but they generate **high initial cash flows**. A firm with liquidity problems may prefer market-skimming for this reason.

  (iv) Skimming may also enable the firm to identify **different market segments** for the product, each prepared to pay progressively lower prices.

(e) The firm may lower its prices in order to attract more price-elastic segments of the market; however, these price reductions will be gradual. Alternately, the entry of competitors into the market may make price reductions inevitable.

EXAMPLE

OnDigital initially charged £200 for a set-top box, but has switched to offering these free of charge to build up demand and also to pre-empt competition from Sky Digital and cable digital firms.

Introductory offers may be used to attract an initial customer interest. Introductory offers are temporary price reductions, after which the price is then raised to its normal 'commercial' rate.

New products can fail in the short-term or in the long-term. The NPD process should improve success rates, but success is never guaranteed.

A successful new product or brand satisfies corporate objectives by:

- Gaining/sustaining market share
- Meeting profit targets
- Generating cash inflows
- Doing (a), (b) and (c) above in the right time.

4.13 Reasons for failure

Reason	Comment
Poor commitment	NPD is a sideline; managers want to do NPD, but are unwilling to risk the resources to develop the competences necessary
Poor thinking	Designers and promoters of NPD within the organisation have their own interests to pursue and downplay potential problems
Poor execution	Many NPD processes involve uncertain outcomes but the product is wanted in an unrealistic timescale
Poor management	The research process for NPD may not be run properly
Poor marketing	The product might fail because of poor marketing research or by poor marketing
Poor analysis	Both the process of NPD and the product can be more time consuming and expensive than anticipated

4.14 Enhancing innovation

The need to speed up innovation is a key issue

> 'Innovation has become the religion of the late 20th century' (Economist, 20 February 1999). Commonly cited spurs to innovation are:
>
> - Shorter product life cycles
> - Increasing prosperity
> - New technology enabling new services

A *Marketing Business* survey of UK marketers (March 1996), offers the following findings.

(a) 71% of respondents 'considered innovation to be more important then marketing existing products and services'.

(b) Whilst 59% of respondents believe strongly that innovation is 'key to British business surviving the millennium', only 31% believe their companies share this view.

(c) When asked to consider what would improve the potential for innovation, 71% said that 'the key to making their own companies more innovation-driven lay in **management initiatives**... The need for a **risk taking culture** and **better communications** were also mentioned.' Two-thirds identified lack of time as a constraint.

NOTES

Drucker lists seven types of 'opportunity' for innovation

- The 'unexpected success': exploit it
- The difference between what did happen and what was supposed to happen: find out why
- Inadequacy in an underlying process: reforms to process
- Changes in industry or market structure
- Demographic changes
- Fashion
- New knowledge and technology

Many businesses only concentrate on new technology (in other words, option (g) in the list above) rather than the other opportunities ((a) to (f))to innovate. Many businesses feel that their future survival is at stake if they do not innovate. Companies are keen to find out a more **predictable way of emerging with winners**. There is no systematic way to encourage innovation but the Economist suggests these steps.

Step 1. **Imagining**: the initial insight about a market opportunity for a particular technology

Step 2. **Incubating**: nurturing the technology to gauge whether it can be commercialised.

Step 3. **Demonstrating**: building prototypes and getting feedback from potential customers

Step 4. **Promoting**: persuading the market to adopt the invitation

Step 5. **Ensuring** the product or process has as **long a life as possible**

Steps 1, 2 and 3 cannot be managed in a conventional way. Firms could:

- Create a culture in which **innovation and learning exist** throughout the organisation
- Designate separate teams, or individuals to come up with ideas.

An innovation culture can be considered in the context of a **learning organisation**.

4.15 Creativity and innovation

Creative ideas can come from anywhere and at any time, but if management wish to foster innovation they should try to provide an organisation structure in which innovative ideas are encouraged to emerge.

(a) **Innovation requires creativity**. Creativity may be encouraged in an individual or group by establishing a climate in which free expression of abilities is allowed. 'Hot water thought sessions' (brainstorming etc) could be used.

(b) Creative ideas must then be **rationally analysed** (in 'cold water thought sessions') to decide whether they provide a viable (commercial etc) proposition.

DISCUSSION

Innovation can be managed.

BPP PUBLISHING

In an article in *Marketing Business* (April 2000), Ty Francis exposes ten myths about innovation. In his view:

(i) Innovation dose not depend on doing extensive **market research**. Creativity is more important than collecting more data.

(ii) Innovation requires **huge creative leaps** into the unknown that change the entire company. As Francis puts it, there is no place in today's business environment for 'steady-as-she-goes incrementalism'.

(iii) Innovation is the responsibility of the **entire enterprise**. Focusing on existing products and customers will achieve nothing. Functional responsibilities need to be disregarded: 'if you do what you've always done you'll get the results you've always had'.

(iv) Innovation is about more than simply **intellectual** endeavour. **Core creative competencies** are needed, and a creative culture needs to be stimulated.

(v) Innovation is not just about **NPD**. Innovation may simply mean a new process or a new component material for an existing product. The biggest returns came from **innovative strategy**.

(vi) Where innovation is concerned, **the future is happening now**. Organisations need to get away from a problem solving orientation, and become more involved in **creating their future** rather than simply planning for it.

(vii) Innovation should not just occur quickly and under duress when a company is **desperate**. Real innovative breakthroughs need proper consideration and thought.

(viii) There is no such thing as a foolproof or faddish **toolkit** for innovation. Commercially viable innovations only come from a **proper knowledge** of the company's abilities and its industry.

(ix) Innovation is not a **mechanistic business process**, but rather a way of working that should colour everything the company does. 'In a very real sense, innovation is better approached as an art form rather than a science.'

(x) Innovation does not live off **existing brands and products**. Companies must move on. Strong brands can actually stifle innovation, and in any case some competitors are always going to be able to copy what you do.

According to Francis: 'Building innovation ... is the only way to achieve significant and sustainable competitive advantage.'

5 INNOVATION AUDIT

The chief object of being innovative is to ensure organisational success in a changing world. It can also have the following advantages.

(a) Improvements in quality of **products** and **service**

(b) A **leaner structure** - layers of management or administration may be done away with

(c) Prompt and imaginative **solutions to problems**

(d) **Less formality** in structure and style, leading to better communication

(e) **Greater confidence** inside and outside the organisation in its ability to cope with change

Innovation and new product development (NPD) is therefore essential for many firms to survive and prosper. It is an increasingly important area.

Definition

> **Innovation audit:** a critical assessment of the firm's innovation record, the internal obstacles to innovation and how performance can be enhanced.

A firm needs to assess how well it is able to deliver the level and type of innovation necessary to continue to meet customer needs and expectations. Drummond and Ensor (1999) identify **four key areas** for the innovation audit.

- The current organisational climate
- Measures of the organisation's current performance with regard to innovation
- Review of policies and practices supporting innovation and facilitating it
- The balance of styles of the management team

5.1 Organisational climate

Barriers to innovation include the following.

(a) Resistance to change

Any new method of management thinking can experience some resistance from established managers. This resistance may be due to concern to protect the status quo, or because managers are ignorant of the new thinking. Integrating marketing communications seems so obvious that it may be overlooked or seen as a superficial approach.

(b) Old planning systems

Old planning systems have sometimes downgraded promotional decisions to the tactical level. Advertising expenditure is decided on the basis of what the company can afford rather than what is strategically required. Promotion is seen as a series of short-term actions rather than as a long-term investment.

(c) Old structures/functional specialists

Complementing traditional planning systems are traditional organisation structures. These structures freeze out new thinking on integrated marketing communications strategy. Individuals have limited specific responsibilities - just for advertising, say, or just for public relations - and this inhibits new thinking on integration.

(d) Centralised control

If the chief executive keeps tight control of the organisation and of its planning and is unconvinced either of the benefits of marketing communication or of integrated marketing communications then the new integrated approach will not happen.

(e) External agencies

External agencies have formerly been organised in specialist areas such as advertising, public relations, sales promotion and marketing research and are not able to offer a complete and integrated service.

(f) Cost consideration

Replacing all old promotional materials with a new integrated set has cost implications.

Methods of overcoming these barriers include those described below.

(a) Top management commitment

The most effective way of overcoming these barriers to change is through the commitment of top management. The chief executive in particular needs to be convinced of the appropriateness of the new thinking and be enthusiastic about its implementation throughout the organisation.

(b) Marketing reorganisation

One way in which the chief executive can take advice is through a reorganisation of the marketing function in the organisation. In particular the company should seriously consider the appointment of an individual with overall responsibility for brining about the adoption of an integrated marketing communications program throughout the organisation.

(c) Training and development

It is one thing to change attitudes. It is another thing to be in a position to know exactly what to do. The integration of a marketing communications programme is not an easy or a short term task. It needs the services of individuals trained in strategic thinking. Such individuals also need to be aware of the appropriateness of a wide range of promotional tools. The individuals chosen to implement any new programme must be enthusiasts capable of overcoming resistance to change.

(d) Communications as a competitive advantage

Those with responsibility for implementing an integrated marketing communications programme must do so with the objective of developing communications as a sustainable, long term competitive advantage.

(e) Producing the results

Nothing succeeds like success. Producing the business results as a consequence of effective marketing communications will boost confidence and gain management converts to the new thinking on an integrated approach.

5.2 Encouraging innovation

To encourage innovation the objective for management should be to create a more outward-looking organisation.

- People should be encouraged to look for new products, markets, processes and designs
- People should seek ways to improve productivity

Thomas Attwood suggests the following steps for creating an innovative culture from one which has previously existed in a cosy, unthreatening world.

- Ensure management and staff know what innovation is and how it happens
- Ensure that senior managers welcome, and are seen to welcome, changes for the better
- Stimulate and motivate management and staff to think and act innovatively
- Understand people in the organisation and their needs
- Recognise and encourage potential 'entrepreneurs'

An innovation strategy calls for a management policy of **giving encouragement** to innovative ideas. This will require the following.

(a) Giving **financial backing** to innovation, by spending on R & D and market research and risking capital on new ideas.

(b) Giving employees the **opportunity** to work in an environment where the exchange of ideas for innovation can take place. Management style and organisation structure can help here.

  (i) Management can actively encourage employees and customers to put forward new ideas.

  (ii) **Development teams** can be set up and an organisation built up on project team-work.

  (iii) **Quality circles** and brainstorming groups can be used to encourage creative thinking about work issues.

(c) Where appropriate, **recruitment policy** should be directed towards appointing employees with the necessary skills for doing innovative work. Employees should be trained and kept up to date.

(d) Certain managers should be **made responsible for obtaining information** from outside the organisation about innovative ideas, and for **communicating** this information throughout the organisation.

(e) **Strategic planning** should result in targets being set for innovation, and successful achievements by employees should if possible be rewarded.

5.3 Measures of performance

This may include measures such as the rate of successful **new product development** and related sales over the past years, or **customer satisfaction ratings**.

Customer satisfaction ratings. An important input to innovation is the degree of customer satisfaction, both from the product itself and service levels.

(a) Customer satisfaction can be measured on a scale (eg from **highly satisfied** to **highly dissatisfied**).

(b) Customers can also be asked to identify which features of a service/product they found most useful.

(c) Firms should **actively measure** customer satisfaction, rather than simply **react to complaints**.

NOTES

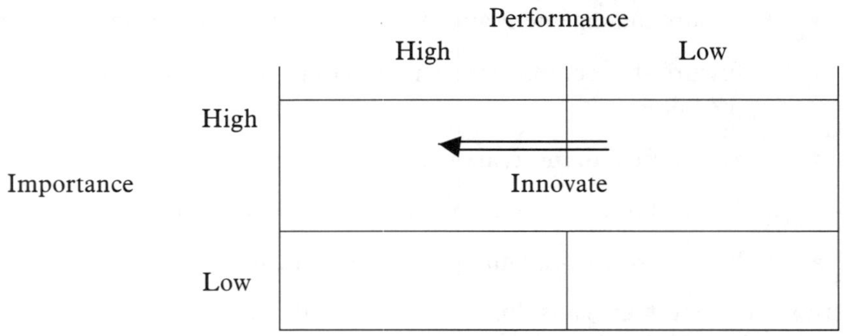

Clearly, a firm should be most concerned about matters of high importance with 'low' performance. Innovation may be necessary to ensure that high performance is achieved on matters of high importance.

5.4 Innovation/value matrix

(a) A similar methodology can apply to innovation and its **value** to the customer. Clearly, the best sort of innovation gives highest customer value for the lowest cost or effort. Businesses can be categorised between those that offer the normal level of innovation and market value, those that offer some improvement on the offerings of competition, and finally those that offer significant innovations and value for the customer.

(b) There is a danger that too many innovations can, in fact, confuse the customer. Recent research has encouraged some companies (such as Procter & Gamble) to reduce the variety of goods on offer.

(c) The innovation process should consider both the **technology** and **customer needs**.

(d) For example, once the limitations of the silicon chip are reached, optical computers might be invented. In some cases, instead of technical developments being used to predict future technologies, future social developments can be predicted, in order to **predict future customer needs**. The likely technologies which will satisfy these needs can then be considered.

5.5 The management team

The management team are key in setting the scene for innovation. The management team is also a critical influence on corporate culture. Belbin drew up a list of the characteristics of an ideal team.

Member	Role
Co-ordinator	Presides and co-ordinates; balanced, disciplined, good at working through others.
Shaper	Highly strung, dominant, extrovert, passionate about the task itself, a spur to action.
Plant	Introverted, but intellectually dominant and imaginative; source of ideas and proposals but with disadvantages of introversion.
Monitor-evaluator	Analytically (rather than creatively) intelligent; dissects ideas, spots flaws; possibly aloof, tactless - but necessary.
Resource-investigator	Popular, sociable, extrovert, relaxed; source of new contacts, but not an originator; needs to be made use of.

BPP PUBLISHING

Member	Role
Implementor	Practical organiser, turning ideas into tasks; scheduling, planning and so on; trustworthy and efficient, but not excited; not a leader, but an administrator.
Team worker	Most concerned with team maintenance - supportive, understanding, diplomatic; popular but uncompetitive - contribution noticed only in absence.
Finisher	Chivvies the team to meet deadlines, attend to details; urgency and follow-through important, though not always popular.

The dynamics of the management team affects how it perceives the work environment.

Definition

> The **recipe**, according to Johnson and Scholes, is an evolving set of beliefs, a way of looking at the world, and a way of interpreting information based on **management's shared experience.**

Although the **environment poses strategic questions,** it is **people who make sense of it** and devise strategies. Whilst the recipe provides cultural coherence it can impede strategic renewal. If the corporate strategy is failing, a company will:

(1) Place tighter **controls** over implementation (eg give tougher performance targets to sales staff); but if **this** fails ...

(2) Develop a new strategy (eg sell in a new market); but if this fails as well ...

(3) Only now will the company abandon the recipe (eg realise that the product is obsolete).

This is significant if it impacts on the management team's attitude to innovation. A management team might be unbalanced if it has too many 'ideas' people and not enough implementers able to bring projects to fruition.

To summarise here are some suggested stages for an innovation audit.

Step 1. **Benchmark with leading competitors**. For example, many motor firms regard the rate and speed of NPD as something they must emulate.

Step 2. **Identify performance indicators** for innovation and compare with previous years (Davidson), such as the **rate of NPD.**

- Number of innovations
- Success rate (more important than quantity)
- Percentage of revenue derived from **innovations** (3M has a target)
- **Incremental** sales resulting from innovation
- Average annual sales per new product/service

Note that if a higher percentage of revenue comes from **innovation** then **incremental** products, it looks as if innovatory products are **cannibalising** existing sales.

NOTES

Step 3. Identify obstacles to innovation which typically reside in the corporate culture of structure.

Step 4. Recommend innovation objectives.

Activity 5 **(30 minutes)**

Bowland Carpets Ltd is a major producer of carpets within the UK. The company was taken over by its present parent company, Universal Carpet Inc, in 1993. Universal Carpet is a giant, vertically integrated carpet manufacturing and retailing business, based within the USA but with interests all over the world.

Bowland Carpets operates within the UK in various market segments, including the high value contract and industrial carpeting area - hotels and office blocks etc - and in the domestic (household) market. Within the latter the choice is reasonably wide ranging from luxury carpets down to the cheaper products. Industrial and contract carpets contribute 25% of Bowland Carpets' total annual turnover which is currently £80 million. During the late 1980s the turnover of the company was growing at 8% per annum, but since 1992 sales have dropped by 5% per annum in real terms.

Bowland Carpets has traditionally been known as a producer of high quality carpets, but at competitive prices. It has a powerful brand name, and it has been able to protect this by producing the cheaper, lower quality products under a secondary brand name. It has also maintained a good relationship with the many carpet distributors throughout the UK, particularly the mainstream retail organisations.

The recent decline in carpet sales, partly recession induced, has worried the US parent company. It has recognised that the increasing concentration within the European carpet manufacturing sector has led to aggressive competition within a low growth industry. It does not believe that overseas sales growth by Bowland Carpets is an attractive proposition as this would compete with other Universal Carpet companies. It does, however, consider that vertical integration into retailing (as already practised within the USA) is a serious option. This would give the UK company increased control over its sales and reduce its exposure to competition. The president of the parent company has asked Jeremy Smiles, managing director of Bowland Carpets, to address this issue and provide guidance to the US board of directors. Funding does not appear to be a major issue at this time as the parent company has large cash reserves on its balance sheet.

Required

(a) To what extent do the distinctive competences of Bowland Carpets conform with the key success factors required for the proposed strategy change?

(b) Suggest and discuss what might be the prime entry barriers prevalent in the carpet retailing sector.

(c) In an external environmental analysis concerning the proposed strategy shift, what are likely to be the key external influences which could impact upon the Bowland Carpets' decision?

NOTES

Chapter roundup

- SWOT analysis is an assessment of a company's strengths and weaknesses (internal to the organisation) and opportunities and threats (external to the organisation).
- A SWOT analysis should also include some evaluation of the relative importance of factors.
- Following a SWOT analysis strategy formulation should try to match company strengths to industry opportunities. Weaknesses should be developed into strengths if at all possible.
- SWOT analysis can be done at corporate or functional levels.
- Ansoff developed a product-market growth matrix and corresponding strategic implications of market penetration, product development, market development and diversification.
- Diversification can be vertical (backwards or forwards) or horizontal, which are complementary or competitively positioned to a company's present activities.
- If there is diversification that has no relation to the company's existing products/markets this is termed as unrelated or conglomerate diversification.
- Positioning is designing a product/service, so it holds a certain image in the consumer's mind.
- The foundation of a positioning strategy is to align what the company can do with what customers want.
- New products can either be new to the market or new to the company.
- There are eight steps to a systematic new product development process.

  1 Idea generation
  2 Screening
  3 Concept development
  4 Marketing strategy
  5 Business analysis
  6 Product development
  7 Market testing
  8 Commercialisation
- The relationship between the research and development department and the marketing department needs to be done.
- A critical assessment of an organisation's record of innovation can be audited. Innovation strategy should encourage innovative ideas.
- Positioning can be 'psychological' and 'real'. Perceptual maps enable users to identify positioning options.
- An innovation audit identifies a firm's record of innovation and how it can be enhanced. It covers the organisation climate and culture, the value to the customer, the management team and the 'recipe'.

NOTES

Quick quiz

1 What is the purpose of SWOT analysis?

2 What does a positioning map look like?

3 What does Ansoff's growth vector matrix show?

4 Give two advantages of vertical integration.

5 What is positioning?

6 What is market penetration pricing?

7 What are the main components of the ideal management team?

Answers to quick quiz

1 To combine the assessment of the environment and the analysis of the organisation's internal resources and capabilities. (See para 1)

2

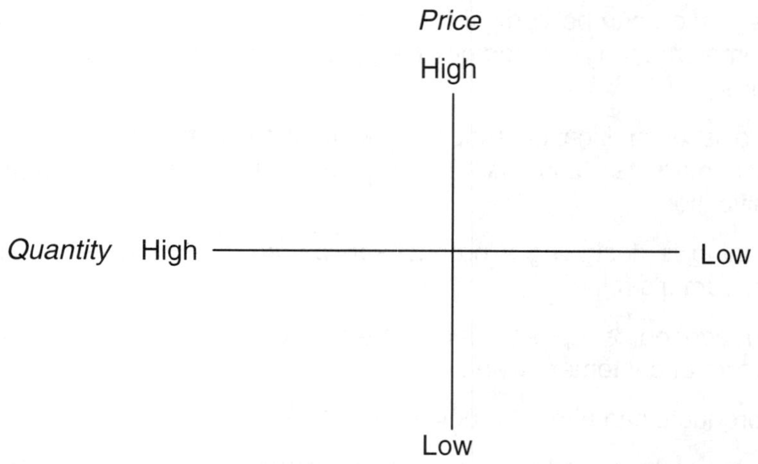

(para 1.5)

3 It describes a combination of a firm's activities in current and new markets, with existing and new products. (para 2)

4 Secure supply of components
Strengthening relationships. (para 2.5)

5 The act of designing the company's product and image so that it offers a distinct, and valued place in the target customer's mind. (para 3.1)

6 A policy of low prices when the product is just launched to gain sufficient penetration in the market. It sacrifices short term profits in the interests of long term products.

7 Co-ordinator
Shaper
Plant
Monitor – evaluator
Resource – investigator
Implementor
Team worker
Finisher (para 5.5)

BPP PUBLISHING

Answers to activities

1 Essentially the company has lost its vision on the market. It seems as if the company has invested much time, effort and money into new product development with a proliferation of new products that do not seem to be profitable.

The company should undertake a full SWOT analysis and then carefully look at the profitability of its customers individually. It may be that the two customers who account for 60% of sales should be developed and concentrated on. New product development should therefore be in line with what these companies require.

2 Strengths/weaknesses

- Reputation
- Added value
- Market knowledge
- Distribution structure
- Promotional activities

Opportunities/threats

- Economic aspects of the particular market
- Any technological changes
- Changes in socio-cultural aspects that might affect the attractiveness of your product
- Environmental awareness
- Legislation covering your product or promotional activities

3 The answer will depend on the nature of your own company or college and its key competitors.

4 Your answer might include:

(a) Acquiring specialist knowledge eg frozen foods

(b) Developing a nationwide courier service

(c) Developing a European haulage service

Each one of these could be put into the existing structure by running, as a division or SBU (Strategic Business Unit) It could either be autonomous or closely integrated with the general haulage business.

Advantages would include increased markets, possible increased profits.

Disadvantages would include additional costs in terms of specialist lorries/vans, additional staff, specialist knowledge required.

5 (a) An organisation's **distinctive competences**, highlighted in its internal analysis, are those features, skills or processes that differentiates an organisation and is performance/products attractively from its competitors and enable it to obtain a special sphere of influence or a strong competitive position. Competences derive from experience, staff skills and the quality of co-ordination.

Key or critical success factors. Organisations need to identify the key success factors, assets and skills needed to compete successfully in a market.

(i) **Strategic necessities** do not necessarily provide an **advantage,** because others have them, but their **absence** will cause a substantial weakness.

(ii) **Strategic strengths** (in which the organisation excels), are superior to those of competitors and provide a base of advantage. The market analysis will also be looking at how these will change in the future and how the assets and skills of competitors can be neutralised by strategies.

Key success factors include good distribution networks, advanced office systems and up-to-date marketing intelligence.

Mismatches between competences and success factors

Most organisations doing a SWOT analysis will find a mismatch somewhere. A company may be successful at establishing a strong position during the early stages of market development, only to lose ground later when the key success factors have changed. With consumer products marketing and distribution skills are dominant during the early phases but operations and manufacturing become more crucial as the product moves into the maturity and decline stage.

Bowland's new strategy. The management at the US parent company of Bowland Carpets have come up with a new strategy in an attempt to solve the problem of the declining carpet sales in the UK, mainly in the domestic market. The contract and industrial carpet segment will not be affected radically as the distribution network generally uses direct sales.

Bowland UK's competences are the ability to:

(i) Offer a wide range of high quality products at **competitive prices**.

(ii) Sustain **powerful brand names**, presence in different market segments.

(iii) Sustain **good relationships** with distributors.

Success factors for retailing

The proposed option of vertical integration into retailing will require a set of key success factors which will include some of these competences. However, there are gaps which are a cause for concern.

The key success factors for vertical integration into retail sales which have been developed in the US will not be totally transferable to the UK and the domestic company has no expertise in this field.

(i) **Distribution.** It is not clear whether the intention is to introduce this strategy as an addition to the current distribution network or instead of it. Both of these options would affect the **relationship with distributors** that has built up over a period and could be very **damaging to sales**. To compensate for this loss, Bowland Carpets would need to have a strong **geographical** presence either in High Street positions or in out-of-town developments. This could be **very costly** in both site selection and development.

(ii) **Expertise** in **retailing** and **distribution**. Staffing and servicing the retail outlets and training the staff in the skills required will be time-consuming and expensive. When customers buy carpets they expect a measuring, fitting and laying service as well as after-sales support. It may be that the UK company can learn from the USA but the culture of marketing household durables is different in both countries.

(iii) The **ability to provide a choice of products and services for the customer**. If there is insufficient choice, Bowland Carpets will have to find competitive manufacturers to fill the gap. This action may defeat the strategy to raise the sales in the **domestic** carpet market.

Conclusion. Bowland's distinctive competences are not appropriate to the key success factors required for retailing.

(b) **Entry barriers prevalent in the carpet retailing sector**

- The number of established carpet retailers in an already mature market
- The variety of 'own brands' available in dominant department stores
- The cost, availability and maintenance of suitable retail sites
- Suitable suppliers and reasonable terms
- The retailing skills which will need to be developed
- Marketing investments (research, staffing)
- The ability to offer a broad product line
- The level and nature of the service offered
- Brand loyalty

(c) An external environmental analysis identifies emerging trends, **opportunities** and **threats** created by the forces outside the organisation.

(i) Firms must avoid major surprises by anticipating major changes in their business circumstances.

(ii) Firms must make daily responses to changes among their customers, suppliers and workforce. Those who discover the longer-term patterns can decide whether they pose a threat or an opportunity and can gain a headstart on their competitors.

Contents of the analysis

(i) The **competitive** environment. Knowledge of the reactions of the other players in the market, both manufacturers and retailers, could be crucial to the success or otherwise of a new entrant's plan. Established businesses can adopt **retaliation strategies** to make it difficult for new companies to enter the market.

(ii) **Economic** factors include the **rate of growth** and the associated increase/decrease in **disposable income**, the **rate of inflation**, the state of the domestic housing market (house moves are often associated with new refurbishments), unemployment, interest rates and the availability of credit, taxation levels and incentives.

(iii) **Political** factors include laws on the safety of the product, town planning, selling practices adopted and the way a firm treats its employees.

(iv) The **social, demographic and cultural** environment analysis would highlight issues such as: the growth or decline in population; changes in ages when people leave home and start their own household; trends in house refurbishments; trends towards car-centred shopping in superstores and out-of-town shopping 'cities'.

(v) The **technological** environment. Consumers expect modern carpets to have properties which keep stains and insects away. The manufacturing environment is undergoing rapid changes with the growth of advanced manufacturing technology. Retail outlets are using point of sale equipment which can be used for stock control and to analyse the customer trends. **Some DIY stores allow customers access to large cutting machines to avoid expensive cutting and laying services.**

Chapter 11 :

IMPLEMENTING THE EXTENDED MARKETING MIX

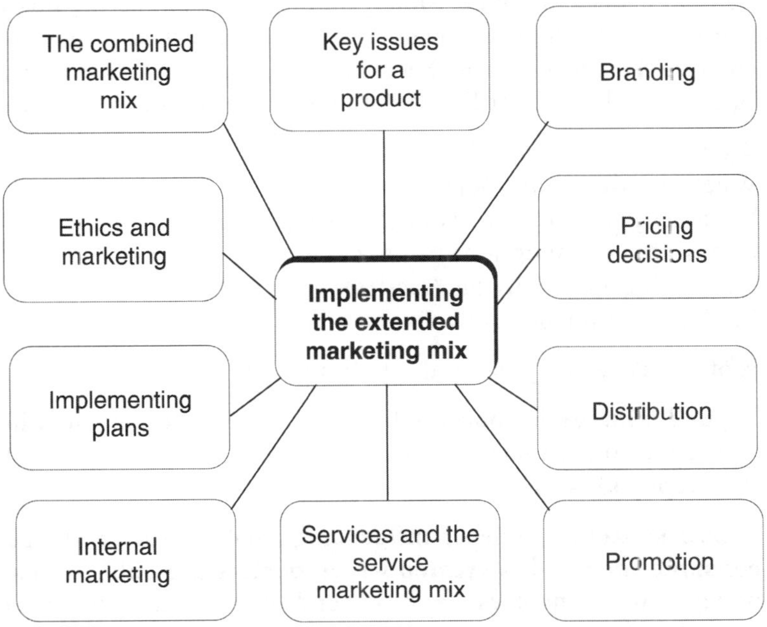

Introduction

This chapter will cover the integration of the elements of the extended marketing mix and associated implementation issues. Ethical considerations are coming to the fore in future orientated organisations and this will also be discussed.

Your objectives

In this chapter you will learn about the following:

(a) The 7Ps and how they are integrated

(b) Specific characteristics of services

(c) How marketing plans are integrated

(d) What is meant by internal marketing

(e) Developments in ethics and marketing

1 THE COMBINED MARKETING MIX

Definition

Kotler defines the mix as follows. '**Marketing mix** is the set of controllable variables and their levels that the firm uses to influence the target market.'

The **marketing plan** is made up of decisions relating to the marketing mix for a product or service. In turn, each of these mix elements would be turned into a plan, at a more tactical level within the organisation. Each of these plans is prepared using the same basic framework that we have identified at both corporate and marketing level.

(a) Where are we now? (audit)
(b) Where are we going? (objectives)
(c) What are the alternative ways of getting there?
(d) Choosing the best option
(e) Developing an action plan (tactics)
(f) Implementation and control

The balance is often between a 'push' and a 'pull' strategy.

(a) A **push strategy** is concerned with moving goods out to wholesalers and retailers who then have the task of selling to customers, **ie getting dealers to accept goods**.

(b) A **pull strategy** is one of influencing final consumer attitudes so that a **consumer demand is created which dealers are obliged to satisfy;** a pull policy usually involves heavy expenditure on advertising, but holds the promise of stimulating a much higher demand.

(c) A proper balance between 'push' and 'pull' is necessary to optimise sales.

Stages in the formulation of a marketing mix

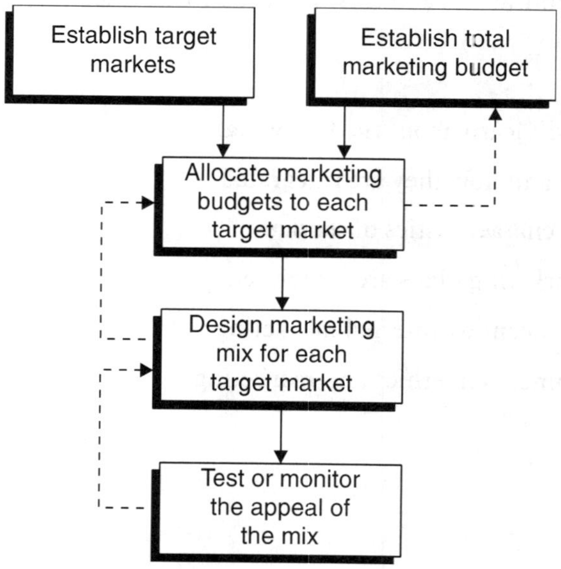

1.1 Design issues for the marketing mix

Issue	Comment
Profit/volume	The sales response function shows how different areas of the mix affect volume sales and **profits.** All other things being equal, the mix design should maximise profits.
Brand value	The mix should, where relevant, support the brand value, if a strong brand is important. Not all firms depend on branding.
Customers and distribution, segmentation	The mix should satisfy customer needs, but note in many cases there are two customers to consider: the end-user and the intermediary or reseller.
Life cycle	The appropriate mix changes over the life cycle of the product. For example a firm might adopt **penetration** or **skimming** prices at launch.
Marketing environment	This affects the optimal mix, but should be taken into account earlier in the planning process.
Seasonality	Clothes retailers are seasonally based, hence 'sales' after Christmas.
Integration	The elements of the marketing mix must support each other. There is no point promising the earth (promotion) if this cannot be delivered.
Push/pull	The mix can pull demand through the distribution chain or push it down.
Competitive strategy	The mix will support the competitive strategy.

EXAMPLE

You might like to contrast the marketing mix of these **holiday firms**. Each has been designed to appeal to a particular market segment.

(a) *British Museum Tours.* These are tours with an archaeological or cultural interest, and are accompanied by a leading academic. The tours are expensive and might include destinations such as Iran and Ethiopia. Hotels are the most comfortable available. Advertising is not high profile, and is often directed to those who are already members of the British Museum Society.

(b) *Explore*. This firm offers escorted holidays to small groups, in a variety of locations, which may involve some trekking and camping. Locations might include isolated villages in northern Thailand. The firm advertises itself on the basis of 'You'll see more'. The firm advertises in newspapers, but also likes to generate repeat business and word of mouth recommendation. Poster or TV advertising is not used.

(c) *Club 18-30.* Targeted at a specific age group, these promise 'fun' or 'activity' holidays in or round beach resorts. A poster advertising campaign in 1994/5 had to be suspended owing to complaints that they were to 'raunchy'. Holidays are fairly cheap.

1.2 Combining the marketing mix in practice

For high-selling products some firms prepare a demand function showing the relationship between price and quantity of demand. This is not always possible.

(a) It may not be possible to establish, scientifically, how the different elements of the mix might interact.

(b) Many smaller businesses do not have the resources to prepare complicated models in this way.

(c) Another problem, especially true of business-to-business markets, is that there might be relatively **few customers**, who might be able to dictate, quite precisely, product specifications and other arrangements. The price may be negotiated after the sort of hard bargaining rarely encountered in consumer markets.

We will now briefly identify some issues regarding each element of the mix. This section is partly revision and partly to get you thinking about key issues of each element of the mix, including the marketing mix for services. In the **UK and most of the developed world, services account for greater economic output than manufacturing**, so we will take a 7P rather than a 4P approach to this issue.

- Product
- Place
- Price
- Promotion
- People
- Processes
- Physical evidence

2 KEY ISSUES FOR A PRODUCT

What is a product?

Definition

A **product** is a 'package of benefits' meeting particular needs. It is anything that can be offered to a market, for attention, acquisition, use or consumption that might satisfy a want or need.

Product decisions were dealt with in the previous chapter in detail.

Aspect	Example
Physical aspect: what the product is	Bank account
Functional aspect: what the product does	Keeps your money safe
Symbolic aspect: what the product means	If you bank with Coutts, you are a member of an exclusive set of people

NOTES

Levels of a product (Kotler)

Level	Comment
Core benefit	A hotel offers rest and sleep away from home
Generic product	Any hotel is a building with rooms to rent
Expected product	Must expect cleanliness and quiet
Augmented product	Additional benefits (eg taxi service)
Potential product	Possible augmentations in the future (for example fax machines for business travellers)

The expected product in one country may be the augmented product in a poor country. Most **competition** in the developed world is based around the **augmented product**.

> **Activity 1** **(10 minutes)**
>
> Compare the levels of a product such as a car to a service such as home insurance.

Strategic issues for product

(a) **Defining the product.** Product/service is key in differentiation strategy, as the product can be manipulated to satisfy the needs of different market segments.

(b) **Selecting the product range**, in terms of **width** (how many segments) and **depth** (variety of options in each segment).

(c) Building a **brand**.

(d) Managing the **product portfolio** with new launches and deletions.

(e) **Quality**: this is 'fitness for use' and can be analysed as quality of design, and quality of conformance (the product has been manufactured without defects).

3 BRANDING

Branding is also dealt with in chapter 13 of this book as part of Unit 18.

Definitions

> - A '**brand**' is a collection of attributes which strongly influence purchase (Davidson)
> - 'A name, term, sign, symbol or design or combination of them, intended to identify the goods or services of one seller or group of sellers and to differentiate them from those of competitors.' (Kotler)

BPP PUBLISHING

Branding and a firm's reputation are linked. The important thing to remember is that a brand is something **customers** value: it exists in the customer's mind. A brand is the link between a company's marketing activities and the customer's perception.

DISCUSSION

Brands are only in the mind of consumers, therefore it is a waste of money to pay premium prices for them.

EXAMPLE

Virgin is a brand that covers airlines, pensions, bank accounts, record stores, coca-cola and, notoriously, railways.

There is clearly little in common with the services on offer. Virgin Trains have a poor reputation, whereas the airline has a good reputation for service. Virgin Train's **aspiration** however is towards providing excellent service, even though the execution has some way to go.

What makes up a brand?

Effective product Distinctive identity Added values	supported by	Visible: Symbol, advertising, presentation (eg packaging) Invisible: assets and competences, strong R&D, supply chain, effective selling, costs

(Sources: Doyle, Davidson)

Benefits of branding

Beneficiary	Benefit of branding
Customers	• Branding makes it easier to choose between competing products, if brands offer different benefits. Brands help consumers cope with information overload • Brands can support 'aspirations' and self image • Branding (eg Nike) can confer membership of reference groups
Marketers	• Enables extra value to be added to the product • Creates an impression in the consumer's mind; encourages re-purchase • Differentiates the product, especially if competing products are similar • Reduces the importance of price • Encourages a 'pull' strategy • Other products/services can exploit the brand image (eg Virgin)

Beneficiary	Benefit of branding
Shareholders	• A brand is an intangible asset; even though it is not on the financial statements, a strong brand promises to generate future cash inflows and profits. This is called **brand equity**. • Brands build market share, which can generate high profits through: o higher volume o higher value (higher prices) o higher control over distributors

Definition

> **Brand equity** is the asset the marketer builds to ensure continuity of satisfaction for the customer and profit for the supplier. The asset consists of consumer attitudes, distribution.

DISCUSSION

It is dangerous to put any monetary value on brands as they can be damaged by poor publicity.

3.1 Brand strategies

Different types of brand strategy

(a) **Company brand**. The company name is the most prominent feature of the branding (eg Mercedes).

(b) **The company brand combined with an individual brand name** (eg Kelloggs - Corn Flakes, Rice Krispies). This option both legitimises (because of the company name) and individualises (the individual product name). It allows **new 'names' to be introduced quickly and relatively cheaply.** Sometimes known as **umbrella branding**, firms might use this approach as a short-term way to save money.

(c) **Range brand**. Firms group types of product under different brands. For example, Sharwoods is a brand owned by **RHM Foods**. Sharwoods offers pickles, poppadums, sauces etc.

(d) **Individual name.** Each product has a unique name. This is the option chosen by Procter and Gamble for example, who even have different brand names within the same product line, eg Bold, Tide. The main advantage of individual product branding is that an unsuccessful brand does not adversely affect the firm's other products, nor the firm's reputation generally.

Choice of brand strategy

(a) Company and/or umbrella brand name

Advantages	Disadvantages
• Cheap (only one marketing effort)	• Not ideal for segmentation
• Easy to launch new products under umbrella brand	• Harder to obtain distinct identity
• Good for internal marketing	• Risk that failure in one area can damage the brand
	• Variable quality

For example, Virgin is a company brand name, supported by advertising, PR and the 'celebrity' status of Richard Branson.

(i) Service industries use 'umbrella' marketing as customer benefits can cross product categories. Marks & Spencer diversified from clothes, to food and to financial services. Tesco and Asda have followed suit.

(ii) Communication media are more diffuse and fragmented.

(iii) One brand is supported by integrated marketing communications.

(iv) Umbrella branding supports **database marketing** across the whole product range.

(v) Distributor/retailer brands are 'umbrella' brands in their own right, so **brand owners** have to follow suit.

(b) Range brands offer some of the advantages of an umbrella brand with more precise targeting.

(c) Individual brand name

Advantage	Disadvantages
• Ideal for precise segmentation	• Expensive
• Crowds out competition by offering more choice	• Risky
• Damage limitation to company's reputation	

Activity 2 **(10 minutes)**

Give some examples from different industries of the above brand strategies.

Brand values

'Added values - the **subjective beliefs of customers** - are at the heart of building **brands**' (Doyle). These added values are largely subjective. In 'blind testing' many consumers cannot tell the difference between different products; however, they will exhibit a preference for a strong brand name when shown it.

Most consumer buying decisions, therefore, do not depend on the functionality of the product.

(a) Products are bought for 'emotional reasons'. For example, most sports trainers are 'fashion' products.

(b) Branding reduces the need to choose.

EXAMPLE

Early in 1993, it was announced that the price of Marlboro cigarettes was to be cut in some of its US markets. Marlboro had been one of the USA's most heavily supported brands, but was losing ground to cheap discounted competitor brands. What do you think might be the significance of this?

The purpose of a brand is, in part, to reduce the consumer's sensitivity to price. It might promise an income stream in future and hence be worth valuing as a fixed asset. However, the price cut of Marlboro cigarettes sends a significant message to many brand-based businesses. US analysts believed that Marlboro was one of the strongest brands ever promoted, recognised world wide and supported by consistently heavy investment. Cutting the price of Marlboro indicated the fact that some brands are never impervious to price competition. The price cut led to a fall in the share price of companies dealing heavily in branded goods, indicating that the value of their main asset, their brand, was less than supposed.

Sources of brand values

Source	Comment
Experience	Customer's actual usage of a brand can give positive or negative associations.
User associations	Brands get an image from the type of people using them; brands might be associated with particular personalities.
Belief	This might be a 'placebo' effect; **belief** in a brand may enhance its effectiveness.
Appearance	Design appeals to people's aesthetic sensibilities.
Manufacturer's name	The company reputation may support the brand.

3.2 Brand identity

Definition

Brand identity: 'the message sent out by the brand through its product form, name, visual signs, advertising. This is not the same as **brand image** which is how the target market perceives the brand.

Three aspects to a brand (Doyle)

Aspect	Comment
Core	Fundamental, unchanging aspect of a brand. (Hooper's Hooch is a fizzy **alcoholic** fruit drink.)
Style	This is the brand's culture, personality, the identity it conveys and so on.
Themes	These are how the brand communicates through physical appearance of the product.

Clearly, the **themes** are more easy to change than the **style**, which is more easy to change than the **core**.

3.3 How to build brands

The process for building the brand is similar to that of building a product (core product, an expected product, an augmented product and a potential product). However, a product is, in some respects, purely functional, whereas a brand offers more.

A step approach to designing brands

Step 1. **Have a 'quality' product** - but remember quality means 'fitness for use' not 'the maximum specification'. Functionality is only a starting point.

Step 2. **Build the basic brand**. These are the marketing mix criteria.

- They should support product performance
- They should differentiate the brand
- They should be consistent with positioning
- The basic brand delivers the core product in an attractive way.

Step 3. **Augmentations** include extra services, guarantees and so on. (Expensive guarantees provide evidence that the firm takes quality seriously.)

Step 4. **Reaching its potential,** so that customers will not easily accept substitutes.

Step 5. Maintain **brand value** by using the marketing mix to persuade customers to re-buy.

Step 6. **Build brand loyalty**. Customers who rebuy and are loyal are valuable because:

- Revenue from them is more predictable
- Existing customers are 'cheaper' than new customers

Step 7. **Know where to stop in developing the brand. (For example, an alcohol-free version of 'alcoholic lemonade' would be pointless.)**

3.4 Implementing the brand strategy

Brands that **reach their potential** have five key characteristics (Doyle).

- A quality product underpinning the brand
- Being first to market, giving early mover advantages
- Unique positioning concept: in other words they are precisely positioned
- Strong communications underpinning the brand
- Time and consistency

3.5 The brand planning process

Brand strategy is one of the steps in the brand planning process just as marketing strategy is one step in the marketing planning process. Arnold (1992) in *The Handbook of Brand Management* offers a five stage brand planning process.

NOTES

Stage	Description
Market analysis	An overview of trends in the macro and micro environment and so includes customer and competitor analysis and the identification of any PEST factors which may affect our brand. For soft drinks, the explosion of competitive activity, particularly by own label, and new product introductions, such as Fruitopia, will be important.
Brand situation analysis	Analysis of the brand's personality and individual attributes. This represents the internal audit and questions such as, 'Is advertising projecting the right image?', 'Is the packaging too aggressive?', 'Does the product need updating?' need asking. This is a fundamental evaluation of the brand's character.
Targeting future positions	This is the core of brand strategy. Any brand strategy could incorporate what has been learnt in steps (i) and (ii) into a view of how the market will evolve and what strategic response is most appropriate. Brand strategy can be considered under three headings. (1) Target markets (2) Brand positions (3) Brand scope
Testing new offers	Once the strategy has been decided the next step is to develop individual elements of the marketing mix and test the brand concept for clarity, credibility and competitiveness with the target market.
Planning and evaluating performance	The setting of the brand budget, establishing the type of support activity needed and measurement of results against objectives. Information on tracking of performance feeds into step (i) of the brand management process.

EXAMPLE

Unilever launched a new low suds detergent brand, Radion, on to a mature and saturated market. In 1980 Lever held 61% of the market by value but by 1988 this had fallen to below 40% with Procter & Gamble and own label taking the majority of the share. In the US the company increased the share of its Surf brand by positioning it as the 'fights dirt and odours' brand. This was not possible in the UK as Surf's brand values were based on the 'Square Deal Surf' proposition. Therefore the company had to introduce a new brand - enter Radion. The first year objective was 35% penetration and 24% repeat purchase. The key strategic questions were these.

(i) How could Radion attract consumers away from long established brands?

(ii) How could Lever ensure that Radion sales were not gained at the expense of its other brands?

The solution in brand strategy terms is outlined below.

(i) Target market

Housewives owning front-loading automatic washing machines, who were attracted to functional cleaning promise and who were responsive to an authoritarian tone in advertising.

(ii) Position

Radion was positioned as a superior alternative to competitor brands based on two functional (tangible) brand values: odour removal and cleaning effectiveness and supported with the emotional (intangible) brand values of modern, vigorous, uncompromising and challenging.

(iii) Brand scope

Radion was launched in same formats as current brands: powders and liquids, biological and non-biological, various pack sizes.

(iv) Promoted differently to other Lever brands

Radion advertising included TV, posters, radio, 'day-glo' orange packaging, all with a modern, vigorous, uncompromising and challenging tone of voice. The advertising proportion was, 'New Radion is as good as any other brand at cleaning and removes lingering odours that they sometimes leave behind' with the strapline of, 'Removes dirt and odours'.

(v) Competitive pricing parity with other premium brands

Radion was launched in October 1989 and by March 1990 Lever's share had increased from 41.7% to 44.8%. This excellent brand strategy, supported by a £8.98m spend, resulted in a 7% market share increase in just six months.

3.6 Specific strategies for brands

Brand stretching

Definition

> '**Brand extension** involves using the same brand name, successfully established in one market or channel, to enter other' (Doyle). It is often termed **brand stretching** when the markets are very different.

EXAMPLES

Brand extension

- **Retailers** such as Dixons and Tesco launching themselves as **Internet Service Providers**
- Penguin Books launching its own 'brand' of compact discs
- Swatch becoming involved in motor vehicles

3.7 Conditions for brand stretching/extension

(a) The **core values** of the brand must be **relevant to the new market.**

(b) The new market area must not affect the core values of the brand by association. Failure in one activity can adversely affect the core brand.

3.8 Advantages of brand extension

Advantage	Comment
Cheap	It is less costly to extend a brand then to establish a new one from scratch.
Customer-perception	Customer expectations of the brand have been built up, so this lower risk for the customer encourages 'trial'.
Less risky	Failure rate of completely new brands.

Disadvantages of brand extension

Disadvantage	Comment
Segments	The brand personality may not carry over successfully to the new segment. The brand values may not be relevant to the new market.
Strength	The brand needs to be strong already.
Perception	The brand still needs a differential advantage over competitors.
Over-dilution	Excessive extensions can dilute the values of the brand.

Activity 3 **(5 minutes)**

What problems are associated with brand extensions outside companies' core businesses, such as supermarkets extending into financial service providers.

3.9 Revitalising brands

At times, the performance of a brand will falter and managers will attempt to rectify the situation by:

- Enhancing sales volume
- Improving profits in other ways

Revitalisation means increasing the sales volume through:

- New markets (eg overseas)
- New segments (eg personal computers are being sold for family, as opposed to business, use)
- Increased usage (encouraging people to eat breakfast cereals as a snack during the day)

Repositioning is more fundamental, in that it is a **competitive strategy** aimed to change position to increase market share.

NOTES

Type of position	Comment
Real	Relates to actual product features and design
Psychological	Change the buyer's beliefs about the brand
Competitive	Alter beliefs about competing brands
Change emphasis	The emphasis in the advertising can change over time

EXAMPLE

Penguin Books vs Mills & Boon

Penguin is one of the oldest brands in UK paperback publishing and over the years has introduced brand extensions (Puffin for children, Pelican for academic) and sub-brands (Penguin Classics, Penguin Modern Classics).

A key issue for publishing is to identify the core of the brand.

(a) The imprint or publisher?

(b) The author? It appears to go without saying that people will buy a book by a recognised author, and that the author is at the heart of the brand.

In contrast, people buy 'Mills & Boon' books - the core of the brand is the publisher not author.

DISCUSSION

Mills and Boon are more susceptible to downturns in the market than Penguin.

3.10 Success criteria for branding

Worldwide research suggests that the beneficial qualities of a brand name are that they should:

(a) Suggest **benefits**, eg Ultrabrite toothpaste, Slimline tonic

(b) Suggest qualities such as **action** or **colour**, (eg Shake 'n Vac)

(c) Be **easy to pronounce**, recognise and remember

(d) be **acceptable in all markets** both linguistically and culturally. For international companies name research can avoid possible faux pas because of cultural and language differences, eg 'Body Mist' when translated into German means 'manure'!

(e) Be distinctive

(f) Be meaningful. When Procter and Gamble wished to launch 'Crest Tartar Control' into South American countries, research found that there was no recognised Spanish translation for dental tartar. The brand name had to be changed.

3.11 Global or local brand?

The key differences between a standardised global brand approach and an approach based upon identifying and exploiting global marketing opportunities are as described below.

(a) The standardised global brand approach requires:

(i) A standardised product offering to market segments which have exactly similar needs across cultures

(ii) A common approach to the marketing mix and one that is as nearly standardised as may be, given language differences

(b) An approach based upon **global marketing opportunities** reflects:

(i) A recognition that the resources of the company may be adapted to fulfil marketing opportunities in different ways taking into account local needs and preferences but on a global basis

(ii) A willingness to sub-optimise the benefits of having a single global brand (eg advertising synergy) in order to optimise the benefits of meeting specific needs more closely

For the international company marketing products which can be branded there are two further policy decisions to be made. These are:

(a) The problem of deciding if and how to protect the company's brands (and associated trademarks)

(b) Whether there should be one global brand or many different national brands for a given product

The most successful examples of worldwide branding occur where the brand has become **synonymous with the generic product**, (eg Sellotape, Anadin).

4 PRICING DECISIONS

4.1 Factors to consider when making pricing decisions

The selling price of a product should exceed its average unit cost in order to make a profit, but cost is only one of the factors to bear in mind when setting a price.

(a) **The organisation's objectives**. Although we generally assume that an organisation's objective is to maximise profit, it could be that increased market share, maximisation of sales revenue, to be known as a supplier of luxury goods or to provide a service to the community is the objective.

(b) **The market in which the organisation operates**. If the organisation is operating under conditions of **perfect competition** (many buyers and many sellers all dealing in an identical product), neither producer nor user has any market power and both must accept the **prevailing market price**. If the organisation is in the position of a **monopolist** (one seller who dominates many buyers), it can use its market power to set a profit-maximising price. Most of British industry can be described as an **oligopoly** (relatively few competitive companies dominate the market). Whilst each large firm has the ability to influence market prices, the **unpredictable reaction** from the other giants makes the price difficult to determine.

(c) **Demand**. Economic theory suggests that the volume of demand for a good in the market is influenced by variables such as the price of the good, price of other goods, size and distribution of household income, tastes and fashion, expectations and obsolescence. The volume of demand for one organisation's goods rather than another's is influenced by three principal factors: **product life cycle**, **quality** and **marketing**.

(i) **Product life cycle**. Most products pass through the phases of introduction, growth, maturity and decline. Different versions of the same product may have different life cycles, and consumers are often aware of this. For example, the prospective buyer of a new car is more likely to purchase a recently introduced Ford than a Vauxhall that has been on the market for several years, even if there is nothing to choose in terms of quality and price.

(ii) **Quality**. One firm's product may be perceived to be better quality than another's. Other things being equal, the better quality good will be more in demand than other versions.

(iii) **Marketing**. The 'four Ps' of the marketing mix (or 7 Ps for services) all influence demand for a firm's goods or services.

(d) **Price elasticity of demand**. The price an organisation charges will be affected by whether demand for an item is **elastic** (a small change in the price produces a large change in the quantity demanded) or **inelastic** (a small change in the price produces only a small change in the quantity demanded).

EXAMPLE

'When your biggest brand launch in three decades succeeds only on its price – especially when you have spent an estimated £20 million on advertising it – something has gone wrong.

This was the situation faced by the UK's biggest tobacco manufacturer Gallaher, which launched its mid-market cigarette brand Sovereign in an effort to claw back share from Imperial's buoyant Lambert & Butler brand.

L&B's share has been growing rapidly at the expense of more glamorous premium brands such as Gallaher's Benson & Hedges and Silk Cut, as smokers switch to cut-price cigarettes (which now account for nearly one-third of the market) in the face of relentless tax hikes and price rises.

Marketing Week

(e) **Costs**. An organisation has to decide whether a price should be based on fully absorbed cost or marginal cost.

The company

Pricing is a key decision as it can very easily affect margins and profits.

	A	*B*
	£	£
Price	10	9.50
Cost	8	8.00
Profit	2	1.50

B is priced at 5% cheaper than A, but is 25% less profitable. In other words, a 5% cut in price leads to a 25% cut in profits. Clearly more of the unit will have to be sold to make up the shortfall.

The problem is that the **cost of producing something is not determined by the price** charged. As firms aim to make profits for shareholders, prices are often set with costs in mind, as a floor. The marketer thus does not have complete freedom to determine prices.

(f) **Competition**. When competitors sell exactly the same product in the same market, price differences are likely to have a significant effect on demand. For example, the price of petrol at filling stations in a local area will be much the same. When organisations sell similar products which are not exactly identical, or where the **geographical location** of the sales point is of some significance, there is more scope for charging different prices.

EXAMPLE

Developing drugs to combat AIDS has been expensive. The prices charged put the treatment way out of reach of sufferers in poorer countries where AIDS is prevalent. Some say that this pricing strategy is unethical. Others say that the money spent researching into drugs for AIDS could be spent on dealing with other life-threatening illnesses in poorer countries. Price does have 'ethical' connotations.

(g) **Inflation**. An organisation should recognise the effects of inflation on its pricing decisions. When its costs are rising, it must try to ensure that its prices are increased to make an adequate profit or to cover its costs (in the case of non-profit-making organisations).

(h) **Legislation**. Certain organisations have their prices controlled by legislation or regulatory bodies.

(i) **Availability of substitutes**. When an organisation is making a pricing decision it must take into account products/services that customers could switch to if they were not happy with the price set.

4.2 Approaches to pricing

Full cost plus pricing

A traditional approach to pricing products is **full cost plus** pricing.

Definition

> **Full cost plus pricing** is a method of determining the sales price by calculating the full cost of the product and adding a percentage mark-up for profit.

A business might have an idea of the **percentage profit margin** it would like to earn and so might decide on an average profit mark-up as a general guideline for pricing decisions. The percentage profit mark-up does not have to be fixed, but can be varied to suit the circumstances. In particular, it can be varied to suit demand conditions in the market.

This approach to pricing fails to recognise that since demand may be determined by price, there will be a **profit-maximising combination** of price and demand.

The **advantage** of full cost plus pricing is that since the size of the profit margin can be varied at management's discretion, a decision based on a price in excess of full cost should ensure that a company working at normal capacity will cover all its fixed costs and make a profit. It is also a simple and quick method.

Marginal cost plus or mark-up pricing

Instead of pricing products or services by adding a profit margin on to **full cost**, a business might add a profit margin on to **marginal cost**. This is sometimes called **mark-up pricing.**

Definition

> **Marginal cost plus pricing/mark up pricing** is a method of determining the sales price by adding a profit margin on to marginal cost.

The **advantages** of a marginal cost plus approach to pricing are as follows.

(a) It can be adjusted to reflect demand conditions.

(b) It draws management attention to **contribution** and the effects of higher or lower sales volumes on profit.

(c) Mark-up pricing is convenient where there is a **readily identifiable basic variable cost**. Retail industries are the most obvious example, and it is quite common for the prices of goods in shops to be fixed by adding a mark-up (20% or 33$^{1}/_{3}$%, say) to the purchase cost. The price must of course be high enough to ensure that a profit is made after covering fixed costs.

Minimum pricing

A **minimum price** is the price that would have to be charged so that the **incremental costs** of producing and selling the item, and the **opportunity costs** of the resources consumed in making and selling the item, are just covered. A minimum price would leave the business no better or worse off than if it did not sell the item.

Two essential points about a minimum price are as follows.

(a) It is based on **relevant costs.**

(b) It is unlikely that a minimum price would be charged because it would not provide the business with any profit. However, the minimum price for an item shows the **absolute minimum below which the price should not be set** and the incremental profit that would be obtained from any price that is charged in excess of the minimum.

Limiting factor pricing

Another approach to pricing might be taken when a business is working at full capacity, and is restricted by a shortage of resources from expanding its output further. By deciding what target profit it would like to earn, it could establish a **mark-up per unit of limiting factor**.

The demand-based approach to pricing

We have now looked at a variety of cost-based approaches to pricing. **Demand-based approaches** are less common and more difficult to set.

(a) Price theory or demand theory is based on the idea that a connection can be made between price, **quantity** demanded and sold, and total **revenue**. The theory of demand cannot be applied in practice, however, unless **realistic estimates of demand at different price** levels can be made.

(b) In practice, businesses might not make estimates of demand at different price levels, but they might still make pricing decisions on the basis of **demand conditions** and **competition** in the market. When competitors sell exactly the same product in the same market, price differences are likely to have a significant effect on demand.

EXAMPLE

This is the case with oil companies and the price of petrol at filling stations: different companies sell the same product and so, within a local area, the prices charged at each station (whether BP, Shell, Esso or Texaco) will be much the same. If they were not, customers would go to the cheapest place.

When companies sell similar products which are not exactly identical, or where the geographical location of the sales point is of some significance, there is more scope for charging different prices. Even so, the prices charges by competitors cannot be ignored altogether. Price differences can be achieved in a number of ways.

(a) Through product quality
(b) Through design differences (Motor cars are an obvious example)
(c) Through geographical location
(d) Through **brand loyalty**.

EXAMPLE

The prices of crossing the English Channel by ferry vary between different ports of departure. Holiday flights from different regional airports may attract varying regional supplements.

An **average price strategy** and a **lowest price strategy** are two forms of price strategy based on what competitors charge.

(a) An **average price strategy** is to set prices which are average for the industry and might be adopted either if the products sold by all firms in the market are roughly the same or if the company does not wish to be an aggressor in the market, for fear of provoking a **price war** or increased competition.

(b) A **lowest price strategy** is to set the lowest prices available. A lowest price strategy might be associated with aggression in the market, in order to attract more customers or with products of a lower quality.

4.3 Pricing and market share

Generally speaking, price cuts to increase market share will be matched by competitors in some way. If a rival firm cuts its prices in the expectation of increasing its market share, a firm has the following options.

(a) **Maintain its existing prices**. This would be done if the expectation is that only a small market share would be lost, so that it is more profitable to keep prices at their existing level.

(b) **Maintain prices but responding with a non-price counter-attach**. This is a more positive response, because the firm will be securing or justifying its current prices with a product change, advertising, or better back-up services, etc.

(c) **Reduce prices**. This should protect the firm's market share so that the main beneficiary from the price reduction will be the consumer.

(d) **Raise prices and respond with a non-price counter-attack**. A price increase would be based on a campaign to emphasise the quality difference between the rival products.

EXAMPLE

During the summer of 1995 Superdrug, the fast-growing discount drugstore company, cut its branded suncare prices by 25%, in a headline-grabbing price offensive. Days after Superdrug acted Boots, Britain's largest chemists chain, announced 30% price cuts. These strategies were repeated during the summer of 1996 in the Baked Bean wars, when the price of own-brand baked beans in large retailers such as Sainsbury and Tesco fell to 9p in a bid to see off the low price strategy of Kwik-Save. Recently the supermarkets indulged in a price war over white bread, which saw loaves priced as low as 9p.

4.4 Pricing strategies

New product pricing strategies

A **new product pricing strategy** will depend on whether the product is the first of its kind on the market, in which case the company will be able to set a price at which it thinks its profits will be maximised, or if it is following a competitor's product onto the market, in which case the pricing strategy will be constrained by what the competitor is doing. There are two alternative strategies.

(a) **Market penetration pricing** is a policy of **low prices** when the product is **first launched** in order to obtain sufficient penetration into the market. A penetration policy may be appropriate in the following circumstances.

  (i) If the firm wishes to **discourage new entrants** into the market

  (ii) If the firm wishes to **shorten the initial period of the product's life cycle** in order to enter the growth and maturity stages as quickly as possible

  (iii) If there are significant **economies of scale** to be achieved from a high volume of output, so that quick penetration into the market is desirable in order to gain unit cost reductions

  (iv) If demand is **highly elastic** and so would respond well to low prices.

(b) In contrast, **market skimming** involves charging **high prices** when a product is first launched and spending heavily on **advertising and sales promotion** to obtain sales. As the product moves into the later stages of its life, progressively lower prices will be charged. The aim of market skimming is to **gain high unit profits early in the product's life**.

Product mix pricing strategies

The strategy for setting a price often has to be changed when the product is part of a **product mix**. The organisation looks for a set of prices that maximise the profit on the total mix. Various pricing strategies exist.

(a) **Product line pricing** involves developing a product line in which each successive item in the line offers more features/higher quality for a higher price. If the price difference between two successive products is small, buyers will usually buy the more advanced/better quality product. If the cost difference is smaller than the price difference, profits are increased, and the profitability of the line as a whole is maximised.

(b) **Optional product pricing** involves selling optional or accessory products along with the main product. For example a car buyer can order electric windows and a sunroof.

(c) **Captive product pricing** involves selling products that must be used along with a main product. The main products (such as razors) are priced low and the related products (such as blades) are priced high. In the case of services this strategy is called **two-part pricing**. The price of the service is broken down into a fixed fee (entry into an amusement park) plus a variable usage rate (fees for food and rides).

(d) **By-product pricing** involves accepting any price for a low value by-product that covers more than the cost of storing and delivering it. The price of the main product can then be reduced to make it more competitive.

(e) **Product bundle pricing** involves combining several products and offering the whole bundle at a reduced price.

EXAMPLE

Hotels sell specially-priced packages which include room, meals and entertainment. Entire holidays, especially in the Caribbean, are now sold on this all-inclusive basis, covering everything from flights to jet ski hire.

4.5 Price adjustment strategies

Basic prices may need to be **adjusted** to account for customer differences and changing situations. There are a number of relevant strategies.

(a) **Discount pricing and allowances**

(i) **Cash discount** is a price reduction for buyers who pay their bills promptly.

(ii) **Quantity discount** is a price reduction for buyers who buy large volumes.

(iii) **Trade discount** (also called a **functional discount**) is a price reduction given to an intermediary for performing certain functions such as storage.

(iv) **Seasonal discount** is a price reduction for buyers who buy products or services out of season, such as cheaper hotel prices in the winter.

(v) **Allowances** include **trade in allowances and promotional allowances**.

Activity 4 **(5 minutes)**

What are the disadvantages of offering price discounts to cash customers in an attempt to increase customer numbers?

(b) **Discriminatory pricing**. Where a company can sell to two or more separate markets, it might be able to charge a different price in each market to maximise its profits. There are several ways in practice by which price discrimination can be exercised.

(i) **Negotiation with individual customers**. For example, customer A might buy a video cassette recorder from Firm X for £600 cash, whereas customer B might buy the same item and negotiate a discount for cash of, say, 10%.

(ii) **On the basis of quantities purchased**. Bulk purchase discounts are a well-established form of price discrimination, offering favourable prices to large customers.

(iii) **By product type**. This involves some form of product differentiation so that customers in one market segment will buy a product basically similar to (but differentiated from) a product sold to another market segment, but at a different price. Examples of price discrimination through product differentiation are to be found in the sale of clothing and cars (customers may pay disproportionately higher amounts for a car with a larger engine capacity or a more comfortable interior).

(iv) **By time**. Examples are services with peak time and off-peak tariffs, such as hotel accommodation in holiday resorts and charges for telephone calls.

(v) **By location**. Higher prices may be charged in some locations than in others so that a firm with several branches in various towns may set different prices in each branch. Branches in remote locations might set higher prices and in poorer areas they might set lower prices.

For price discrimination to be successful, certain **market conditions** must exist.

(i) The producer must enjoy a **dominant position** in the market, perhaps as a monopolist or as the provider of a branded product or quality product which commands a high degree of **customer loyalty**.

(ii) Where price discrimination is exercised on the basis of individual negotiation or by geographical area, there must be no opportunity for rivals to buy the product at the cheaper price and sell it at a competitive higher price to the higher priced market.

EXAMPLE

Many supermarkets and multiple retail stores sell their 'own label' products, often at a lower price than established branded products. The supermarkets or multiple retailers do this by entering into arrangements with manufacturers, to supply their goods under the 'own brand' label. This is a form of price discrimination.

(c) **Psychological pricing** considers the psychology of prices and not simply the economics. The price is used to say something about the product.

(d) **Promotional pricing** involves temporarily pricing products below list price, and sometimes below cost, to increase short-run sales.

(i) **Loss leaders** are used to attract customers in the hope that they will buy other goods at normal mark-up.

(ii) **Special event pricing** might be used in certain seasons.

(iii) **Cash rebates** are offered to consumers who buy the product from dealers within a specified time.

(iv) **Discounts** may be offered.

EXAMPLE

'Everyday low pricing strategies - the policy of scrapping promotions in favour of sharp, permanent price cuts - were pioneered by Procter & Gamble in the US where they helped the company reclaim market share from competing brands and "own label" products.

The latest company to adopt this strategy is Esso which launched its "Pricewatch" initiative offering "normally unbeatable" prices within a distance of three miles. The policy was introduced after research showed that customers valued lower prices above collections and promotions. Asda in the UK tries to differentiate itself from rivals by emphasising its "permanently low prices".

The logic of getting away from promotions is supported by research which shows that promotions are only taken up by people who were already customers.'

Financial Times

(e) **Geographical pricing strategies** cover different freight charging strategies (which depend on the location of customers).

4.6 Discount policy and competitive bidding

The purpose of discounts is to encourage **more sales (or earlier payment)**. The cost of discounts should not exceed the benefits from extra sales or earlier payment, and the size of discounts offered should not be excessive. After all, why offer a 15% discount for a sale if the customer would still buy if he obtained a 10% discount?

Discounts help to make a firm's products more price-competitive, but the size of discount that can be offered must depend on the **variable cost/sales price ratio**. For example, a firm whose variable costs are 25% of the gross sales price will have more flexibility with discount policy than a firm whose variable costs are 80% of the gross sales price, because it has a bigger contribution margin to play with. Stepped discounts, ie bigger discounts rising in steps for bigger sales orders, must also be planned carefully, and the size of the price breaks should be sensible.

Competitive bidding calls for the preparation of cost data for the purpose of submitting a bid to a potential customer, in the hope of securing his order. There will be three factors in the customer's choice of supplier from among the tenders submitted.

(a) The **price** itself

(b) **Performance**, especially if the product is new and largely untested in the open market, reliability, service etc

(c) **Financial matters**, such as inflation (and cost escalation clauses) and foreign exchange rates (for overseas contracts), export credit insurance

Co-operation is needed between the accounting and marketing departments of a bidding company because a balance has to be drawn between putting in a bid which is too low to make an adequate profit, but keeping the bid low enough to stand a good chance of winning the contract. Consideration must be given to the following.

(a) The **contribution to profit** that would be obtained from the contract

(b) The **consequences** for the company if it failed to win the order

(c) The **probability** of winning the order, which might be assessed on the basis of past experience

(d) **Possible non-price product differentiation** in favour of the supplier eg quality of service, reliable delivery times, finance facilities offered

4.7 Other pricing decisions

Promotional prices are short-term price reductions or price offers which are intended to attract an increase in sales volume. (The increase is usually short-term for the duration of the offer, which does not appear to create any substantial new customer loyalty.) Loss leaders and 'money off' coupons are a form of promotional pricing.

A **temporary price cut** may be preferable to a permanent reduction because it can be ended without unduly offending customers and can be reinstated later to give a repeated boost to sales. They may be used as sales promotions to establish new brands.

Short-term pricing. Marketing management should have the responsibility for estimating the relationship between price and demand for their organisation's products.

(a) The sales-revenue maximising price for a product and the profit-maximising price might not be the same.

(b) Simple **CVP analysis** can be used to estimate the breakeven point of sales, and the sales volume needed to achieve a target profit figure. We cover this in the next chapter.

(c) As we have seen in this chapter, many organisations use a **cost-plus approach** to pricing. Accounting figures are needed for cost in order to establish a floor for making a cost-plus pricing decision. The size of the profit margin will be decided by marketing management.

The marketing department's contribution to **short-run pricing decisions** is not only to assess a basic demand curve relationship between price and sales volume, and an assessment of the elasticity of demand for the firm's products, but also to consider how prices might be adjusted to allow for particular product, market or customer characteristics.

(a) **Product analysis pricing** combines the effects of cost-plus pricing and what the market will bear. An attempt is made to add up all the attributes of the product to ascertain the price that the customer will pay. The characteristics will include finish, strength, durability etc, and the pricing model will be built up using a sample of products with known selling prices and values for each of the characteristics. A price for other products can then be decided accordingly. It works well if the decision is fairly routine.

(b) **Quality adjusted pricing** brings in the aspect of product quality into the assessment of price.

4.8 Data for pricing decisions

Organisations need a multitude of data to make pricing decisions.

(a) Cost data

This can be obtained from internal cost and management accounting records and other internal secondary data sources.

(b) Demand data

To be able to estimate demand for products or services at different price levels an organisation may well have to commission pricing research. We will be looking at pricing research in detail in Part D of the Study Text. Such research will need to consider, for example, elasticities of demand and customer perceptions of price and quality.

(c) Competitor data

Information about competitors is vital for pricing decisions. The sources of competitor information are summarised below.

(i) Published data sources (eg published financial statements, press releases)

(ii) Sales force data

(iii) Trade databases

(iv) Industry experts

(v) Trade press

(vi) Distributors

(vii) Suppliers

(viii) Customers

5 DISTRIBUTION

Distribution or place refers to the 'availability' of the product to the customer and involves:

- Logistics (warehouses, lorries)
- The distribution channel, other companies (wholesalers etc)

Logistics is a significant problem for many companies, particularly if they provide 'just-in-time' services. Logistics, however, is something that it increasingly outsourced to specialist delivery firms such as **Eddie Stobart** (a brand in its own right) and specialist warehousing firms.

(a) The Channel Tunnel has changed some of the economics of long-term distribution.

(b) The UK and European governments would wish to encourage more use of rail on ecological grounds.

The **distribution channel** dilemma facing management is that of the trade-off between cost and control. The shorter the distribution channel the more control managers have over the marketing of the products, but the higher their distribution costs. Long distribution channels cut the costs but also reduce the firm's control. The various channels are outlined in the diagram below.

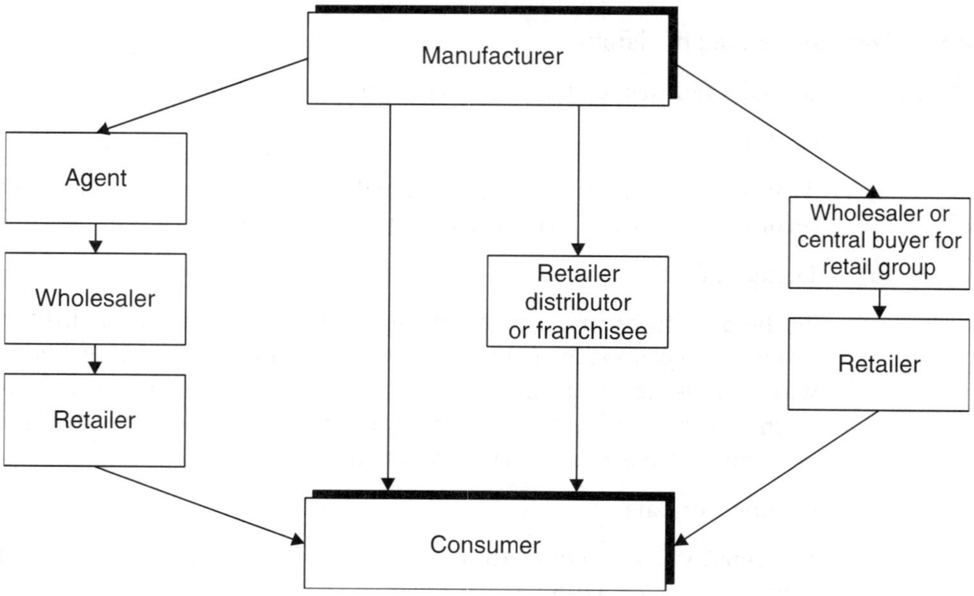

EXAMPLE

Direct Line Insurance revolutionised insurance selling in the UK, by cutting out the network of brokers and selling direct to the public. Originally it concentrated on selling car insurance, but expanded to include other financial services products such as mortgages. For a number of years it raked in the profits, but many of the other insurance companies have followed suit. Book publishers and CD-makers are increasingly using the post.

5.1 Choosing or designing the distribution channel

Key issues relating to the choice of distribution channel

- Number of intermediaries
- Support given to distributors (eg technical advice)
- Control of distribution
- Integration of marketing effort throughout this chain
- Positioning of the product: the distribution should be aligned with this
- Possibility of direct marketing

EXAMPLE

Brand owners of cosmetics firms have tried to set up exclusive distribution outlets with selected retailers, on the understanding that a premium price policy would be maintained, to support the brand values.

Superdrug purchased some cosmetics lines on the grey market and sold them at a low price. The brand owners took Superdrug to court.

Why do firms use intermediaries?

- Geography: customers may live too far away to be reached directly, or may be too dispersed
- Consolidation of small orders into large ones
- Better use of resources elsewhere
- Lack of retailing know-how
- Segmentation, with different segments for each market being reached by different distribution channels

5.2 Current strategic developments in distribution

According to Peter Drucker, in the near future: 'The greatest change will be in distribution channels, not in new methods of production and consumption'. The spurs to change are these.

(a) **Physical distribution costs** are increasing **relative** to other costs (ie as production costs fall). Sometimes these amount to 50% of the price the end-consumer pays.

(b) **Changing consumer lifestyles:** 'one small example is that those in work are time-poorer but money richer ... no wonder there's been a rapid rise in home delivery, from pizzas to wine to potatoes'.

(c) 'Long established discrete **distribution channels are beginning to 'leak'** (eg beer-buyers can go to France and stock up with lower-taxed drinks).

(d) Offering EDI (**electronic data interchange**) enables a firm to cut lead times for orders. This can be a source of differentiation.

(e) **Distribution has a 'branding effect'.** 'Distribution can be a central and, explicit part of a brand's identity, such as First Direct (Midland Bank's telephone banking subsidiary).

(f) **Distribution channels' generation of customer information opens the door to marketing insight and power.** Retailers (through using EPOS) probably know more about customers than manufacturers. Distribution might become 'essentially an information system'.

(g) There has been a move towards a **concentration of retailer power** with large **retailers** tending to gain **power over the manufacturers in the distribution channel**. This shift in the balance of power has two consequences. **Large multiples** are able to **dictate product specifications,** and drive much harder bargains on matters of price and delivery. The large multiples' **own-label brands** are increasingly the major competition against branded goods.

(h) **Just-in-time** is a philosophy which applies to the whole production chain, but it is increasingly relevant to distribution, in satisfying the needs of demanding customers, particularly in business-to-business markets.

   (i) Manufacturers are seeking to reduce their stocks of components and raw materials, to eliminate stock holding costs and wasteful activities.

   (ii) Consequently they expect their suppliers to deliver in very small batches as and when demanded.

Mail order, in which goods are sold by catalogue, over the Internet, delivered by post or directly, is common in some markets. Reasons why include:

- **Retailers do not have to be offered a mark-up**. This is why **book clubs** are able to offer discounts on recommended retail prices.
- **Customers can be reached** who might not normally be able to purchase the product **from a shop.**
- This makes it easier to sell to customers who **cannot do their shopping in normal shopping hours**.
- **No large and expensive display area** in a shop.
- Mail-order facilities can be **combined with an Internet web-site**.

Activity 5 **(10 minutes)**

What social trends do you think might increase home delivery?

5.3 Evaluating current distribution channels

Criteria which may be used to evaluate distribution channels and logistics include:

(a) **effectiveness** in getting products to customers (i.e. sales) and in performing each of the distributive functions that leads to sales;

(b) **efficiency and economy** in terms of the costs of distribution;

(c) **level of service** offered to customers, supporting loyalty and repeat sales;

(d) **degree of control** achieved over the distribution channel, where desired for competitive advantage or integration of marketing effort up to the point of sale;

(e) **degree of co-operation or conflict** with the distributor (channel dynamics).

DISCUSSION

Shopping is now a lesiure activity so the internet will only have limited effect.

5.4 Effectiveness

The measure of effectiveness will depend on specific objectives and criteria appropriate to the processes and channels used. **Sales** made through the distribution channels(s), however, are a key indicator and can be either compared month-on-month or year-on-year to show growth or decline trends or compared for different channels, to show which are more effective than others.

Sales results are, however, only the reflection of underlying factors, relating to the distributors capabilities for undertaking and fulfilling the objectives of distribution tasks.

(a) A retail outlet may or may not give attention to point-of-sale display of the product, since it has a wide product portfolio and limited space.

(b) A retail outlet may or may not distinguish between competing products, or favour the competing brand in its shelf space or promotions.

(c) Intermediary's profit margins may affect the sale price to the consumer, with a depressing effect on sales.

(d) A distributor or transporter may or may not be able to service a widely-dispensed market swiftly and effectively. There may be regional gaps or delays which waste sales potential.

(e) Customers' buying habits and geographical location may favour one type of distribution channel over another. In remote areas, for example, retailers may not be as effective as mail order.

(f) The product may be better suited to one type of distribution channel than another. 'Perishable' products (such as fresh food and newspapers) need to be distributed quickly, or they become worthless.

(g) The supplying/marketing organisation itself may be responsible for insufficient 'pull' promotion motivating consumers to approach the point of sale.

EXAMPLE

The importance of place in marketing was borne out by the success of *Thorntons* in gaining a 13% rise in like for like sales, lifting interim profits by 30%. Roger Paffard newly appointed chief executive has seen his strategy of paying attention to the stores in which the company sells its chocolates pay off handsomely - in refitted stores, like for like sales were up by 22.5% he claimed. Pre-tax profits increased from £7.63m to £9.94m in the 28 weeks to January 11. Christmas sales were up by 25%.

(Adapted from the Financial Times, 3/4/97)

In the early 90s, *Sony* was a nonentity in the video games market. It is now the market leader. (The *Financial Times*, 4/3/97, reported sales by Sony Computer Entertainment of 12 million of its 32-bit Play Station games, compared with Sega's 7m and Nintendo's 4m). As well as canny branding and timely product launch, Sony revolutionised its distribution. Market research in Japan had shown that consumers do not buy video games machines at consumer electronics retailers, but at discount stores and specialist video games stores. The move was unprecedented and triggered protests from retailers of Sony's other products. SCE stood its ground as a separate division which wanted to build its own identity as a video games maker.

5.5 Efficiency

Cost of distribution is one of the key factors in selecting distribution channels. Intermediaries may reduce the costs of selling for the manufacturer by bearing or sharing the costs of stockholding, transportation and display. In addition, manufacturers may receive payment more quickly from intermediaries than by selling direct to the consumer.

Distribution costs should be monitored to ensure that:

- cost savings are being obtained, compared to estimated costs of other channels;
- costs are in line with negotiated and budgeted expenditure;
- the channel is cost-efficient: that is, that no re-organisation of the network or logistics could reduce costs while maintaining the present level of service to the customer.

Kotler, Shaw and Fitzroy suggest measurement of **physical distribution** by means of a total distribution cost:

$$D = T + FW + VW + S$$

where D = total distribution cost
T = total transportation cost
FW = total fixed warehouse cost
VW = total variable warehouse cost
S = total cost of lost sales due to average delivery delay.

An efficient system should minimise D for a given level of service.

EXAMPLE

Safeway has introduced a satellite tracking system in order to improve its distribution system. The company is to employ the system to track the movements of 600 trucks around the country and computers to check on drivers' techniques. It hopes to save at least £1m per year in fuel costs as well as improving the efficiency of its distribution system serving 420 supermarkets. The system could be used to tell, for example, whether a driver was overrevving in third gear, and using more fuel as a consequence; drivers could also be routed around traffic congestion, and stores warned of late deliveries. Safeway expect to recoup the costs (£1.5m installation and £350,000 per year operational) within the first year. Satellite tracking has already cut 10% off the full costs of one of the groups largest distribution depots at Warrington, and the savings could potentially be far greater in delay reduction and reduced labour costs. Streamlining the system is felt to be an essential element in improving service to customers. According to a spokesman: 'By changing the warehouse process, we can add one days life to fresh produce'.

The computer software involved will be integrated with the Safeway bar coding system for products coming into and leaving the depots, allowing managers to track the whereabouts of individual items as they move from depot to store.

(Adapted from the Financial Times, 24/2/97)

5.6 Level of service

Customer service is a key source of competitive benefit, and therefore a key objective of distribution systems. It may include:

(a) the availability of, and charges for, installation, repair and after-sales service;

(b) readiness to take back and quickly re-supply defective goods;

(c) the preparation of orders delivered with correct contents and in good condition;

(d) lead time from placement of an order to delivery;

(e) choice and flexibility in product specifications, size of order accepted and ordering convenience;

(f) the availability of product information and/or demonstration (particularly for technical products);

(g) a customer service orientation in front line staff.

Such factors are part of the offer to the customer, and responsibility for them should be clearly apportioned by negotiation between manufacturers and intermediaries and monitored. If the manufacturer has a service policy of re-supplying faulty goods, the willingness of a retailer (for example) to mediate the return and exchange should be ascertained.

5.7 Degree of control

Manufacturers may wish to control or dominate a distribution channel in order to:

(a) ensure that its policies with regard to pricing, promotion and sales service are carried out, and its marketing message is integrated all the way to the point of sale;

(b) maintain closer contact with consumers and sources of marketing information;

(c) gain competitive advantage by having exclusive distribution through major retailers or distributors (like car dealers).

5.8 Degree of co-operation or conflict

As business relationships, channels are subject to conflicts of interest, culture, priorities and personalities. Attention will need to be given to channel management where negotiations and problem-solving take up an unacceptable amount of managerial time, or result in lost sales (for example, though lack of co-operation on promotions or point-of-sale display).

6 PROMOTION

This is covered in detail in unit 18.

6.1 Categories

Kotler identifies four **categories of promotional activity**

Promotional	Comment
Advertising	Any **paid** form of non-personal presentation and promotion of ideas, goods or services by an identified sponsor.
Sales promotion	Encourage through incentives, over a short-term period, the purchase of the good or service.
Personal selling	The oral presentation of the goods or services, either to make a sale, or to create goodwill to improve the prospects of sales in the future.
Public relations	Unlike advertising, publicity cannot be bought and it might be thought of as unpaid advertising. Although organisations will spend large sums of money on publicity, they do not formally buy space in a newspaper or time on television or radio. Nor do they usually control the content of the publicity message, and so some publicity can be bad rather than good. However, they often try to manage publicity through the use of public relations.

Marketing communications convey information about the product and the company. Recently, the trend is towards **integrated marketing communications**. In other words, the marketing communications should be integrated with the business strategy, the other elements of the marketing mix, and with each other. Few organisations practise an integrated communications approach in any systematic way. The various tools of marketing communications have traditionally been the exclusive preserve of different groups within the organisation.

Promotion is the element of the mix most under control of the marketing department. Piercy suggests that, as far as managers are concerned, there are a number of issues which must be considered strategically for each form of communication.

6.2 Piercy's issues

Issue	Comment
Role	**Each form of communication has a different target**. Media advertising is direct to the end user, whereas personal selling may be preferred for distributors.
Objectives	Each form of communication needs specific objectives: • Advertising: raising awareness, repositioning • Public relations: favourable press exposure • Personal selling: sales targets, client relationships • Sales promotion: sample rates
Process management	This covers relationships with external suppliers, budgeting, recruiting and personnel
Integration	The elements of the mix should be integrated so that all customers get the appropriate message, and the different elements of the mix do not conflict with each other.

6.3 Key strategic developments in promotion

Development	Consequence
Database marketing and data mining	This enables targeting of promotional messages.
Digital TV, many channels	It will be harder to reach a single audience: rather like the trade magazine sector, fragmentation may cut advertising rates.
Internet	Internet advertisements are generally **sought** out by 'surfers' , possibility of interactive marketing, concerns about junk e-mail, concerns about low profitability of Internet firms.
Call centres	Telephone call centres are mushrooming over the country. They provide sales and customer support activity. They tend to be rigid and bureaucratic in style.
Sponsorship	Sports and cultural organisations are seeking sponsors. Like all forms of activity, the sponsor has objectives to fulfil. This can be a difficult relationship. Sponsorship is not intrusive.
Personal advice and loyalty	As service industries develop, there will be greater scope for personal service such as financial services.
Lobbying	Some decisions regarding product standardisation and safety will be taken at EU level. Expertise in this area is necessary.

7 SERVICES AND THE SERVICE MARKETING MIX

7.1 The importance of services

(a) The service sector accounts for most economic activity in the UK accounting for more employment than manufacturing, although many services cannot be exported.

(b) Competition has been introduced to service industries.

(c) Many 'products' contain a service element.

(d) Service can be a differentiating factor in a firm's offer to the market.

(e) Bad service is costly.

EXAMPLE

Bank accounts

A study by the Henley Centre indicated that 17% of a typical company's customers were affected by a range of service problems, such as poor information or inefficiency. 15% of people who switched bank account cited poor service as the reason. An unhappy customer tells up to nine others about bad service received.

7.2 Elements of services

Services differ from physical goods.

Intangibility	A service cannot be seen, touched or displayed until after purchase sometimes not even then (eg life assurance). The service is often difficult for the consumer to understand.
Inseparability	For many services, it is impossible to separate the production and consumption of a service. (For example, a theatrical event is consumed when it is produced.)
Perishability	Services are perishable. They cannot be stored, they must be produced on demand and often can only be produced in the presence of the customer. Transport is a sort of service industry. A bus journey cannot be 'stored'.
Variability	The quality of the service product is typically highly dependent on the quality of the personnel conducting the transaction.

DISCUSSION

Services that are intangible are difficult to 'sell' to customers.

7.3 Products and services combined

Many offers to the market have **both a product and a service element** to them.

- Teaching is almost entirely a service

- A restaurant meal is part product and part service
- A 'house' is almost entirely a product, but it is acquired with the help of service firms

7.4 Dimensions of service quality

(a) **Technical quality** of the service encounter (what is received by the customer). For example, a customer is going to a bank about a pension. The quality of financial advice received can sometimes be evaluated by a customer. The dimension is based on the technical product training of the staff and their knowledge of the bank's services. It can be backed up by a range of sales aids, such as brochures and even computer based product illustrations which feed the customer's specific requirements into an interactive programme when then produces a customised quotation.

(b) **The functional quality** of the service encounter is how the service is provided. The dimension relates to the psychological interaction between the buyer and seller and is typically perceived in a very subjective way. It includes elements such as the following: the attitudes and behaviour of the employees, how they appear, how accessible the service is, the interrelationships between employees and customers.

(c) The **corporate image** dimension of service quality is a result of how consumers perceive the firm. This dimension can be affected by many factors including advertising and past experience with the firm.

7.5 Determinants of service quality

Determinant	Quality
Tangibles	The physical evidence, such as the quality of fixtures and fittings of the company's service area, must be consistent with the desired image.
Reliability	Getting it right first time is very important, not only to ensure repeat business, but, in financial services, as a matter of ethics, if the customer is buying a future benefit.
Responsiveness	The staff's willingness to deal with the customer's queries must be apparent.
Communication	Staff should talk to customers in non-technical language which they can understand.
Credibility	The organisation should be perceived as honest, trustworthy and as acting in the best interests of customers.
Security	This is specially relevant to medical and financial services organisations. The customer needs to feel that the conversations with bank service staff are private and confidential. This factor should influence the design of the service area.
Competence	All the service staff need to appear competent in understanding the product range and interpreting the needs of the customers. In part, this can be achieved through training programmes.
Courtesy	Customers (even rude ones) should perceive service staff as polite, respectful and friendly. This basic requirement is often difficult to achieve in practice, although training programmes can help.

Determinant	Quality
Understanding customers' needs	The use of computer-based customer databases can be very impressive in this context. The service personnel can then call up the customer's records and use these data in the service process, thus personalising the process. Service staff need to meet customer needs rather than try to sell products. This is a subtle but important difference.
Access	Minimising queues, having a fair queuing system and speedy but accurate service are all factors which can avoid customers' irritation building up. A pleasant relaxing environment is a useful design factor in this context.

7.6 Deploying the marketing mix in services

As services differ from manufactured products, this causes potential **marketing problems.**

(a) The degree of **complexity** which characterises, for example, many financial products.

(b) **Inseparability**: the difficulty for consumers to distinguish between the service itself and its delivery system. The delivery system will be inextricably linked with the service itself and will often be considered as a component of that product. In this sense, there will be some aspects of the delivery system which must be seen as components of the core or tangible product while others may usefully be characterised as part of the augmented product.

7.7 Marketing services

(a) Poor service quality in one case (eg lack of punctuality of trains, staff rudeness, a bank's incompetence) is likely to lead to widespread distrust of everything the organisation does.

(b) If the service is intangible and offers a complicated future benefit, or is consumed 'on the spot', then attracting customers means promoting an attractive image and ensuring that the service lives up to its reputation, consistently.

(c) The pricing of services is often complicated, especially if large numbers of people are involved in providing the service.

(d) Human resources management, not just customer care, is a key ingredient in the services marketing mix, as so many services are produced and consumed in a specific social context. The human element cannot always be designed out of a service.

Service marketing involves three additional 'P's: people, processes and physical evidence.

7.8 People

That **employees** are relevant as an element in the marketing mix is particularly evident in service industries. After all, if you have had poor service in a shop or restaurant, you may not be willing to go there again. An American retailing firm estimated that there was an identifiable relationship between low staff turnover and repeat purchases. Managing front-line workers (eg cabin-crew on aircraft), who are the lowest in the organisational hierarchy but whose behaviour has most effect on customers, is an important task for senior management. It involves corporate culture, job design and motivational issues.

- Appearance
- Attitude
- Commitment
- Behaviour
- Professionalism
- Skills
- Numbers
- Discretion

7.9 Processes

Processes involve the ways in which the marketer's task is achieved. Efficient processes can become a **marketing advantage** in their own right. For example, if an airline develops a sophisticated **ticketing system**, it can encourage customers to take connecting flights offered by allied airlines. Efficient processing of purchase orders received from customers can decrease the time it takes to satisfy them. Efficient procedures in the long term save money.

- Procedures
- Policies
- Mechanisation
- Queuing
- Information
- Capacity levels
- Speed/timing
- Accessibility

7.10 Physical evidence

Physical evidence. Again, this is particularly important in service industries, for example where the ambience of a restaurant is important. Logos and uniforms help create a sense of corporate identity.

Environment	Facilities	Tangible evidence
• Furnishings	• Vans/vehicles/ aeroplanes	• Labels
• Colours	• Equipment/tools	• Tickets
• Layout	• Uniforms	• Logos
• Noise levels	• Paperwork	• Packaging
• Smells		
• Ambience		

EXAMPLE

Telecommunications is a service, and an important aspect of physical evidence in telecommunications is the public phone box. BT replaced its old, expensive-to-maintain red phone boxes and introduced nondescript metallic kiosks, in which the phones actually worked. Scrapping the red phone boxes caused outrage.

8 INTERNAL MARKETING

Definition

> **Internal marketing** is the use of marketing approach in the internal environment of organisation, whose employees are seen as 'customers' and have to be persuaded to buy into management ideas.

Internal marketing is particularly important in introducing strategic marketing organisation or in any change. In service industries, the employee is the deliverer of the service (interactive marketing). Kotler identifies a **marketing triangle**, which is adapted below.

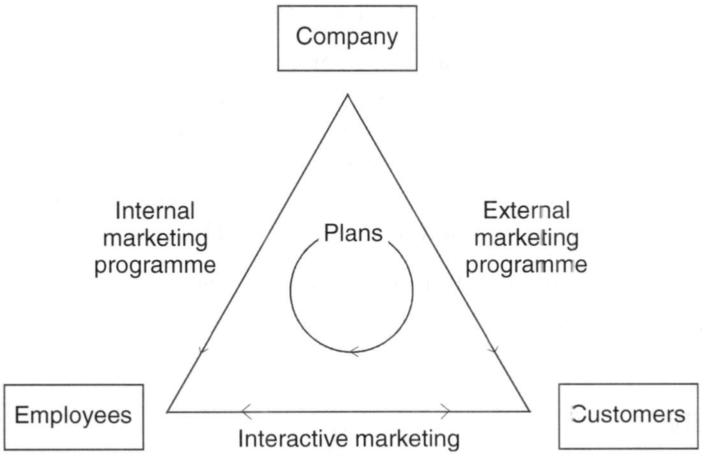

This shows that the external customer and employees need to be marketed to, but that in a marketing-oriented company the natural planning cycle considers the needs of the external customer first.

A similar step approach can be taken to planning internal marketing as in external marketing.

Step 1. Internal marketing objectives and strategy

The internal marketing programme should be designed to achieve the external marketing strategy. Research may be needed to assess the implications of the external marketing programme for the internal customer.

Step 2. Segment the internal market, identifying:

- Influential supporters of the strategy
- Influential opponents of the strategy (how do we win them over?)
- Non involved supporters of the strategy (how do we increase their influence?)
- Non involved opponents

Step 3. Develop an internal marketing mix.

(a) Product: this is the plan or change which management wants to implement.

(b) Price: there will be a price tag. The costs and benefits to staff need to be clearly assessed. As with any product there may need to be negotiation, but managers must be clear what the costs and benefits are. For example a move to a new office block may entail a longer journey to work, but offers improved working conditions. A change in the sales commission package may depress potential earnings in exchange for a higher average salary.

(c) Place: in marketing, place represents when and where the product is available. The timing of the announcement of plans can have a dramatic effect on the way they are received and this needs careful consideration. The distribution of internal marketing is perhaps an issue for human resources management. Appropriate appraisal systems need to be devised, in which customer commitment is seen as core. Some firms employ 360° appraisal techniques whereby customer input is used to measure performance.

(d) Promotion: poor communication is probably the biggest single failure when evaluating internal company problems. The grapevine tends to work quickly and not always very accurately. Communication should be two way and meetings and discussions to take account of staff's views and thoughts at an early stage will help implementation later.

Step 4. Gain commitment: monitor the success of the internal marketing programme

Activity 6 **(5 minutes)**

Some time ago, those who travelled by train were referred to as 'passengers': recently, the word has changed to 'customers'. What do you think the significance of this might be?

9 IMPLEMENTING PLANS

Having determined objectives, appraised strategy and formulated plans, it is time to put the corporate plan into action. Everyone involved should know what is required and when, and should be committed to the successful accomplishment of the plan.

Senior management cannot just leave it to their middle managers to finish off the work by putting the plans into effect.

(a) Senior managers have the **ultimate responsibility** for ensuring that the organisation achieves its objectives. Monitoring actual results is thus an essential ingredient of the control cycle.

(b) Senior management need to remain committed to the wider picture. Middle management almost invariably, when left to themselves, spend their time on short term or pressing issues, rather than dealing with the less immediate problems of the corporate plan.

(c) The performance appraisal of middle and junior management is based on achieving short-term or budgeted tasks and targets.

9.1 Implementation of the corporate or marketing plan

(a) Converting strategic plans into action plans, ie operations plans and budgets.

(b) Allocating responsibilities and giving authority to individual managers to use resources, for example spend sufficient money to allow them to achieve their individual targets.

(c) Establishing checkpoints to monitor activities, such as:

 (i) Have deadlines been met and are future deadlines going to be met?

 (ii) Are any targets in danger of being missed?

(iii) Will the required resources be available to make the products/services?

(iv) Will the products be available in sufficient numbers to achieve the aims of the marketing plan?

(d) **Exerting pressure for control action** where necessary, to ensure that things get done according to the aims of the plan.

(e) **Modifying the plan** in the light of changing circumstances.

There are always **unforeseen** events to deal with, some of them controllable and others uncontrollable and unavoidable.

9.2 External factors

By now you should have a thoroughly realistic idea of external environmental factors which affect marketing, both in PEST/SLEPT terms, and in the actions of competitors, suppliers and customers.

9.3 Internal factors

As problematic are the internal factors. The marketing department is only one of many, and competes with others for resources. Moreover, the marketing department **depends** on other business functions to deliver the marketing mix.

9.4 Frequently encountered implementation problems

Problem	Comment
Weak support from the chief executive and top management	Without this support it is unlikely that other functional managers will take the marketing manager's initiatives very seriously.
Lack of a plan for planning	It is naïve to assume that once a marketing planning system has been designed that it will operate smoothly from day one. The evidence indicates that a period of around three years is required in a large company to overcome resistance to the change that planning inevitably brings. Internal marketing is required.
Lack of line management support	Operational managers are often unwilling to participate fully because of hostility, lack of skills, lack of information, lack of resources and an inadequate organisational structure without a fully integrated marketing function.
Confusion over planning terms	The initiators of the system often use academic planning terminology which line managers see as meaningless jargon.
Numbers in lieu of written objectives and strategies	Prior to a planning system, often all that is used is sales forecasts and financial projections. Making explicit the route to achieving these objectives is a new and difficult skill. It requires managers to express the logic of their objective and in this sense is a creative process requiring qualitative rather than quantitative information.

Problem	Comment
Too much detail, too far ahead	Overplanning is often associated with too much information and ends with piles of paperwork which confuses and demotivates rather than promoting positive participation. Marketing auditing can result in far too many issues demanding management attention. Key issues need to be identified – the wood needs to be drawn from the trees.
Once a year ritual	This is a common barrier to effective implementation, when the task is seen as just another job to do which gets in the way of the really pressing day-to-day activities. Plans which are written and then filed away until next year do not work. Planning needs to be an integral part of the manger's job with progress towards objectives being reviewed and discussed on a regular basis.
Separation of operational planning from strategic planning	Strategic plans need to be built up from sound analysis at grass-roots level, and all managers need to consider not just continuing in the same direction but what longer term changes may be required.
Failure to integrate marketing planning into a total corporate planning system	Unless marketing plans are considered in relation to the plans of finance, production and personnel it becomes impossible to resource accurately the plan's product/market requirements.
Delegation of planning to a planner	When planning is divorced from the reality of operations, and the people who are expected to put the ideas into action are not involved, it is not surprising that resistance and lack of commitment can exist.

10 ETHICS AND MARKETING

10.1 Stakeholder response

Stakeholder analysis identifies the interest groups in an enterprise. Different stakeholders will have their own views as to strategy. As some stakeholders have **negative power,** in other words power to impede or disrupt the decision, their likely response might be considered. An analysis of **stakeholder risk** has two elements.

(a) The risk that any particular strategic option poses to the **interests of the different stakeholders.**

(b) The **risk that stakeholders might respond** in such a way as to make a proposed strategy less attractive.

Stakeholder	Interests at stake	Response risk
Management	Pay, status, power, promotion	Subtle sabotage, procrastination, internal politics
Employees	Pay, security, expertise	Strike action, resignation
Shareholders	Return on investment	Sell shares, leaving the firm vulnerable to take over; refuse to invest more

Stakeholder	Interests at stake	Response risk
Bankers	Loan security; profits	Refusal to continue lending arrangements; call in liquidator
Customers	Product	Switch to another supplier
Suppliers	Business	Will fail to deliver
Government	The public interest; election success; tax	Will regulate or tax

10.2 The strategic value of stakeholders

The firm can make strategic gains from managing stakeholder relationships. This was highlighted by a recent report by the Royal Society of Arts on **Tomorrow's Company.** 'Failure to manage such relationships can carry heavy penalties.' Studies have revealed:

(a) **Correlation between employee retention and customer loyalty** (eg local staff turnover in service firms generally results in more repeat business).

(b) **Continuity and stability** in relationships with employees, customers and suppliers is important in enabling organisations to **respond to certain types of change**.

These 'soft' issues are particularly pertinent for industries where creativity is important and for service businesses. 'Knowledge' based and service industries are likely to be the growth industries of the future.

10.3 The societal marketing concept

Kotler suggested that a **societal marketing concept** should replace the marketing concept as a philosophy for the future.

Definitions

'The **societal marketing concept** is a management orientation that holds that the key task of the organisation is to determine the needs and wants of target markets and to adapt the organisation to delivering the desired satisfactions more effectively and efficiently than its competitors in a way that preserves or enhances the consumers' and society's well-being.'

10.4 Ethics

In general, ethical issues - how companies behave - have become of more importance recently. Many companies are exploiting new found public concern with **ethical behaviour**. The Co-operative Bank developed a whole advertising campaign around avoiding investment in countries with oppressive regimes. For some companies, copying Body Shop and the Co-operative Bank is not really an option (eg tobacco firms, drinks firms).

Activity 7 **(5 minutes)**

Can all organisations be made 'ethical' in some way?

Responses to ethical concerns

- Introducing codes of **conduct** (eg to help and guide employees in difficult situations)
- Inviting outsiders to review ethical performance in some way.

Business ethics aspects can also be found in part 4 of Chapter 8.

EXAMPLE

In 1997 Shell announced that it was to invite environmental and human rights groups to participate in some of its more sensitive projects in the developing world.

This comes after criticism of its activities in Nigeria and the North Sea.

Ultimately, however, 'ethics' comes down to the individual behaviour of managers and employees. Acting ethically is often good business. *Which?* magazine alleged that BT employees had given misleading or inaccurate information about telephone services offered by cable firms. The poor publicity can hardly have helped BT's campaign to win back 'cable' customers.

10.5 Ethical issues and marketing

An August 1996 edition of *Marketing Success* briefly covered some issues of ethics which might be of relevance to marketers, using the 4Ps of the marketing mix as a framework.

(a) Product/service

  (i) Failure to inform customers about risks associated with the use of the product: **dishonesty**. Currently, there are lawsuits in the US in which people are suggesting that the tobacco companies, despite their denials, have known for some time that nicotine is addictive.

  (ii) Using materials of a poorer quality in a bid to cut costs.

  (iii) Does manufacture involve an unacceptable environmental cost?

(b) **Pricing.** In economic terms, price is a matter of supply and demand and, in the pursuit of profit, prices are 'what the market will bear'. Ethics come into the discussion when:

  - Cartels attempt to 'fix' prices by rigging the market
  - Consumers are sometimes charged extras, not officially disclosed

(c) Promotion

  - Advertising: honest, legal, decent and truthful
  - Tastefulness of imagery (eg violence, sexual stereotyping)

(d) **Place.** Ethical concerns regarding relationships with intermediaries can involve the use of power, or delays in payment.

Of course, ethics concerns many non-marketing issues.

- Employees: keeping to terms of the contract and avoiding discrimination
- Suppliers: paying on time.

Some of the 'ethical' issues are backed up by law (eg against price fixing and unfair contracts). The firm also has an ethical duty to its investors not to squander their money.

A wider issue relating to stakeholders is a business's whole stance toward **social responsibility** especially with regard to pollution.

DISCUSSION

Marketers should not concern themselves with ethical issues unless something is actually illegal.

EXAMPLE

The Chartered Institute of Marketing's *Code of Professional Standards* is repeated below.

1 A member shall at all times conduct himself with integrity in such a way as to bring credit to the profession of marketing and The Chartered Institute of Marketing.

2 A member shall not by any unfair or unprofessional practice injure the business, reputation or interest of any other member of the Institute.

3 Members shall, at all times, act honestly in their professional dealings with customers and clients (actual and potential), employers and employees.

4 A member shall not, knowingly or recklessly, disseminate any false or misleading information, either on his own behalf or on behalf of anyone else.

5 A member shall keep abreast of current marketing practice and act competently and diligently and be encouraged to register for the Institute's scheme of Continuing Professional Development.

6 A member shall, at all times, seek to avoid conflict of interest and shall make prior voluntary and full disclosure to all parties concerned of all matters that may rise to any such conflict. Where a conflict arises a member must withdraw prior to the work commencing.

7 A member shall keep business information confidential except: from those persons entitled to receive it, where it breaches this code and where it is illegal to do so.

8 A member shall promote and seek business in a professional and ethical manner.

9 A member shall observe the requirements of all other codes of practice which may from time to time have any relevance to the practice of marketing insofar as such requirements do not conflict with any provisions of this code, or the Institute's Royal Charter and Bye-laws; a list of such codes being obtainable from the Institute's head office.

10 Members shall not hold themselves out as having the Institute's endorsement in connection with an activity unless the Institute's prior written approval has been obtained first.

11 A member shall not use any funds derived from the Institute for any purpose which does not fall within the powers and obligations contained in the Branch or Group handbook, and which does not fully comply with this code.

12 A member shall have due regard for, and comply with, all the relevant laws of the country in which they are operating.

13 A member who knowingly causes or permits any other person or organisation to be in substantial breach of this code or who is a party to such a breach shall himself be guilty of such breach.

14 A member shall observe this Code of Professional Standards as it may be expanded and annotated and published from time to time by the Ethics Committee in the manner provided for below.

Transgressions of morality or ethics will quite rightly invoke the wrath and retaliation of **consumer watchdogs, ombudsmen** and last but by no means least, unfavourable **publicity in the media**. Gratifying needs and wants at the expense of others has become commercially if not politically incorrect. Matters such as smoking, litter, pollution, waste and noise have been issues of public concern.

There is increasing debate on the subject of '**ethical marketing**' and we are reading of the possibility of banks conducting 'environmental accounting' before agreeing to fund companies in industries which might have to conduct punitive environmental cleansing in response to future European legislation. In strategic marketing planning, therefore, ethical issues are of increasing concern.

NOTES

Chapter roundup

- The marketing mix is the operational aspect of the marketing planning process.
- The 7Ps include product, price, place, promotion, people, processes and physical evidence.
- Product analysis can be at various levels: core, generic, expected, augmented, potential.
- Branding is a very important aspect of product and promotional strategy.
- Types of branding strategy are company brands, company and individual brand name, range brand, individual name.
- Brands need to be managed in terms of launch planning, extensions and internationalisation.
- When organisations set prices they should take into account
  - organisation's objectives
  - the market characteristics
  - demand and price elasticity
  - inflation
  - legislation
  - availability of substitutes
- Approaches to pricing include full cost plus pricing, marginal cost plus pricing, minimum pricing, limiting factor pricing and demand based.
- In some sectors, especially business to business discounting, bidding and tendering are common.
- Distribution is often referred to as 'place' in the marketing mix. It involves the logistics of getting products from A to B and the distribution channels such as retailers.
- Internet developments are having a major impact on distribution strategies.
- Promotional activities include advertising, sales promotions, personal selling and public relations. Again the internet is a new development in this area.
- The traditional marketing mix has been extended to the 7Ps (see above) for services. Characteristics of services include intangibility, inseparability, perishability and variability.
- Internal marketing is essentially companies marketing to their own employees.
- Controls need to be in place for implementing marketing plans where critical analysis of the effectiveness of the plan should be made.
- Ethical concerns of marketing are becoming more important to companies and customers.
- Societal marketing strives to preserve or enhance customers' and/or society's well being.
- Ethical issues are important in all aspects of the marketing mix.

Quick quiz

1 What are the 7Ps?

2 What advantages are there to having a company brand name?

3 How can a brand's performance be improved if sales are declining?

NOTES

4 What are the two basic branding decisions when operating internationally?

5 Why do a company's objectives affect pricing decisions?

6 What is the difference between market skimming and market penetration pricing policies?

7 Why do firms use intermediaries?

8 What are the four main promotional activities?

9 What is meant by service variability?

10 What ethical aspects are there to the product/service aspect of the marketing mix?

Answers to quick quiz

1 Product, price, place, promotion, process, physical evidence, people. (See paragraph 1.2)

2 Cheapness, easy to launch new products, good for internal marketing, benefits can cross product categories. (para 3)

3 Revitalising strategies include looking at new markets, new segments, increasing usage. Repositioning is a more fundamental change to brand design and management. (para 3.9)

4 Standard global or local branding. (para 3.11)

5 Objectives may include maximising profits, improving image and increasing market share, all of which will have different implications to price setting. (para 4.1)

6 Market penetration – low prices when launched
Market skimming – high prices when launched. (para 4.3)

7 Geographic factors, consolidation of orders, lack of retailing knowledge, segmentation. (para 5.1)

8 Advertising, sales promotion, personal selling, public relations. (para 6.1)

9 It is dependent on the person delivering the service. (para 7.2)

10 Risks associated with the product, dishonesty, material quality (safety), environmental aspects in production. (para 10.4)

Answers to activities

1 The answer will depend on the products you have chosen.

2

Company brand:	Hotpoint, Hoover
Umbrella branding:	Ford Focus Cadbury's milk chocolate Gordon's gin
Range brand:	Cadbury-Schweppes Suchard Diageo
Individual name:	Fairy liquid Black magic chocolates Gold blend

BPP PUBLISHING

NOTES

3 No longer focusing on their areas of strength
Risk of public confusion
Lack of resources
Failure to estimate demand
Lack of experience and expertise

4 Lower revenues
Customers will expect the discount in future
Customers will believe all rates are negotiable
Customers will henceforth only buy for cash

5 People's working hours: evenings, weekends when shopping is traditionally done

Greater leisure time: desire to spend it on leisure pursuits

Higher disposable incomes

Homeworking: people will not shop on the way home from work, and will have the necessary technology available.

6 Train travellers are now perceived as having an 'active' rather than a 'passive' voice.

Heightened awareness of customer service; travellers are less willing to put up with poor service.

7 Probably not all. Battery chicken farms cannot by definition be ethical.

BPP PUBLISHING

PART C: UNIT 18

ADVERTISING AND PROMOTION

Chapter 12:

THE COMMUNICATIONS ENVIRONMENT

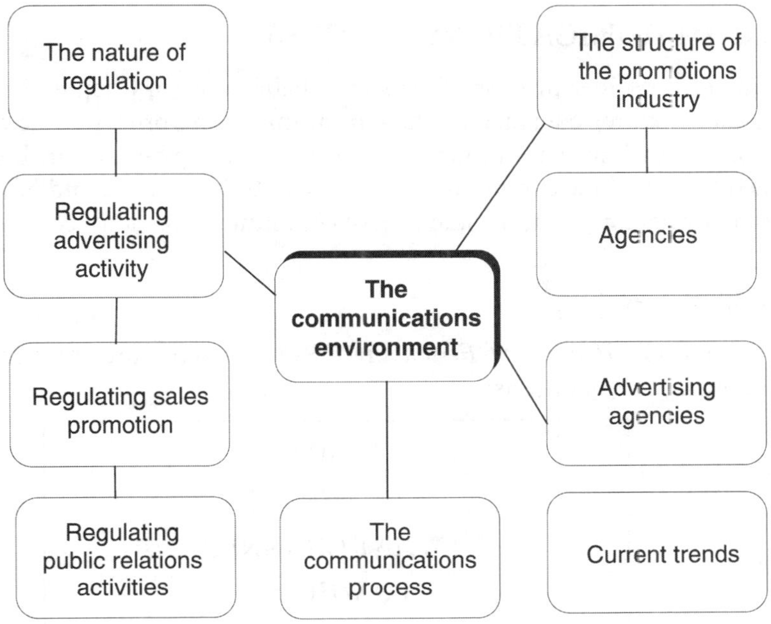

Introduction

This chapter begins our analysis of advertising and promotion. It concludes with Chapter 15 where we consider the promotional strategy process. This chapter begins by discussing the basic process of communication as this is fundamental to the development of an appreciation of how marketing communications function. Communications will be considered from the consumer's perspective and various models will be evaluated.

The structure of the promotions industry is as varied as the range of skills and services which those within the industry can offer. Recent years have seen an increasing degree of specialisation within the field of advertising, although there will inevitably continue to be some degree of overlap between the different agency provisions.

The laws and codes of practice regulating the marketing communications industry are constantly being reviewed. The amount and balance of legal control as opposed to self regulation varies from country to country, and with the growth of the powers of the European Community, there is concern over the standardisation of these controls. Regulation will be discussed with reference to three key aspects of marketing communications – advertising, sales promotion and public relations.

Finally, contemporary marketing communications issues are considered. These include media developments such as media fragmentation, and new media such as the internet.

Your objectives

In this chapter you will learn about the following:

(a) The structure of the promotions industry

(b) How advertising agencies operate

(c) The difference between legislation and regulation

(d) What the current developments are in the communications environment

1 THE COMMUNICATIONS PROCESS

Having looking at the wider process of consumer behaviour (in Chapter 1) a framework needs to be established for considering the **communications** process. The prime aim of marketing communications is to influence consumer's buying behaviour. Because of this marketers need to know how communication works. Models can be, and have been, used to develop frameworks for the understanding of communication activity.

1.1 Lasswell's theory

According to Lasswell, *Power and Personality* (1948), a communication model should answer the following five questions:

WHO?
SAYS WHAT?
IN WHAT CHANNEL?
TO WHOM?
WITH WHAT EFFECT?

DISCUSSION

Oil giants BP and Mobil have entered into a partnership in Europe which involves the rebranding of Mobil service stations and they are engaged in an advertising campaign costing about £18.5m in 1997.

The first phase, featuring two workmen drumming on giant oil drums ran for about four weeks and was simply intended to alert customers to the forthcoming change. A second phase is planned which will run for longer and will spell out new benefits such as greater convenience or improved quality of service, although part of the task is to reassure customers that benefits presently associated with the Mobil brand will not disappear.

Who is saying what in what channel to whom with what effect? (Besides the obvious, think about employees of the two companies as well as customers, and about other channels that might be used.)

1.2 Kotler's model

Kotler, *Marketing Management: Analysis, Planning, Implementation and Control* (1991), has put forward a sender-receiver model of the communication process to provide a framework for answering these questions. This is shown in the diagram below.

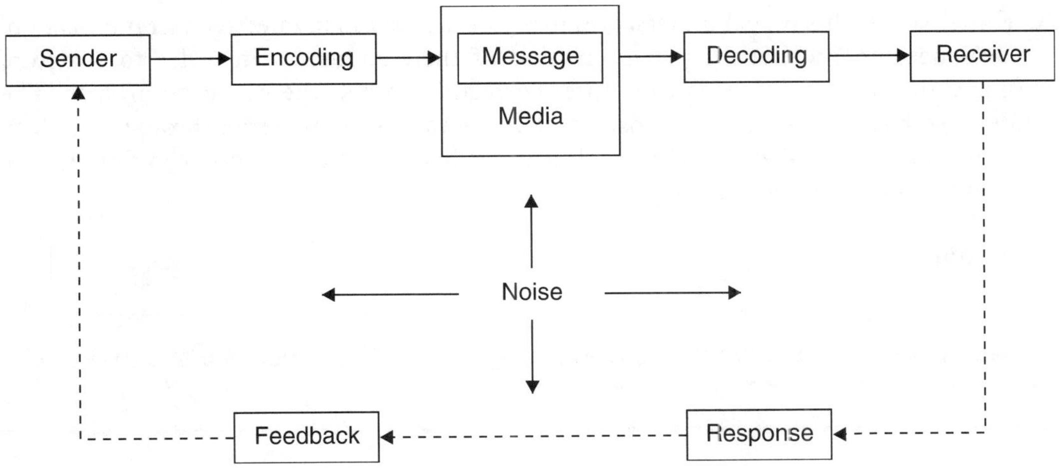

The elements of the model can be classified in the following way.

(a) Parties

  (i) Sender
  (ii) Receiver

(b) Communication tools

  (i) Message
  (ii) Media

(c) Communication functions

  (i) Encoding
  (ii) Decoding
  (iii) Response
  (iv) Feedback

Another element of the process that does not fit into these categories is **noise**, which can be defined as all those factors which prevent the decoding of a message by the receiver in the way intended by the sender. It could perhaps be called a communication **dysfunction**.

1.3 How the model works

The **sender** is the party sending the message to the other party, and may also be referred to as the communicator or the source. The **receiver** is the party who receives the message, and who may also be known as the audience or the destination.

The **coding** process encompasses the means by which a meaning is placed into symbolic form (words, signs, sounds and so on).

The **media** is the communication channel or channels through which the message moves from sender to receiver.

The **decoding** process is carried out by the receiver who converts the symbolic forms transmitted by the sender into a form that makes sense to him. In other words, it is how the receiver interprets the message sent.

When the message has been decoded the receiver will react to it - this is the **response**.

Feedback is the part of the receiver's response that the receiver communicates back to the sender.

NOTES

As Kotler states, this model underscores many of the factors in effective communication. Senders need to understand the motivation of their audiences in order to structure messages that the audience will interpret correctly through the decoding process. The sender also has to ascertain the most effective communication media through which to reach the audience and also establish effective feedback channels in order to find out the receiver's response to the message.

Definition

Noise: distortions created in the encoding or decoding process that can result in inaccurate interpretation of meaning.

Activity 1 **(45 minutes)**

(a) Find some adverts - watch TV for half an hour or flick through a newspaper or a magazine and

(b) Analyse each ad in the above terms. Consider who are the parties involved (*you* may not be the intended receiver), what communication tools are used, what sort of codes are used and how they will be decoded (for example by people in different income brackets or with different tastes), what form feedback will take, and so on.

DISCUSSION

The challenge of marketing communciations is to communciate the right message, in the right way, to the right people, in the right place, at the right time!

1.4 Noise and selectivity

This communication process is not carried out in isolation. There are many senders competing with their messages for the attention of the receiver. As a result there is considerable noise in the environment and an individual may be bombarded by several hundred commercial messages each day. The task of the sender is to get his message to the receiver but, as Kotler states, there are a number of reasons why the target audience may not receive the message.

1.5 Selective attention

A receiver will not notice all the commercial messages that he comes into contact with, so the sender must design the message in such a way so as to win attention in spite of the surrounding noise.

1.6 Selective distortion

In many cases receivers may distort or change the information received if that information does not fit in with their existing attitudes, beliefs and opinions. In other words, people hear what they want to hear. Selective distortion may take a variety of forms:

(a) amplification (where receivers may add things to the message that are not there); or

(b) levelling (where receivers do not notice other things that *are* there).

The task of the sender is to produce a message that is clear, simple and interesting.

1.7 Selective recall and message rehearsal

A receiver will retain in his permanent memory only a small fraction of the messages that reach him. The sender's aim, therefore is to get the message into the receiver's long-term memory, because once in the long-term memory the message can modify the receiver's beliefs and attitudes. However, to reach the long term memory the message has to enter the short-term memory, which has only a limited capacity to process information. Kotler states that the factor influencing the passage of the message from the short- or the long-term memory is the amount and type of **message rehearsal** by the receiver.

In message rehearsal the receiver elaborates on the meaning of the message in a way that brings related thoughts from the long-term memory into his short-term memory.

(a) If the receiver's initial attitude to the object of the message is positive and he rehearses support arguments then the message is likely to be accepted and have high recall.

(b) If the receiver's initial attitude is negative and the person rehearses counter arguments against the object of the message then the message is likely to be rejected, but it will remain in the long-term memory.

2 THE STRUCTURE OF THE PROMOTIONS INDUSTRY

2.1 Industry structure

The structure of the promotions industry is a relatively complex one, with many thousands of companies supplying specialist services. Although some advertisers prefer to buy these services directly themselves, the very complexity of the situation, both in the past and also currently, is the reason for the continuing existence of the advertising agencies.

Simplified structure of the promotions industry

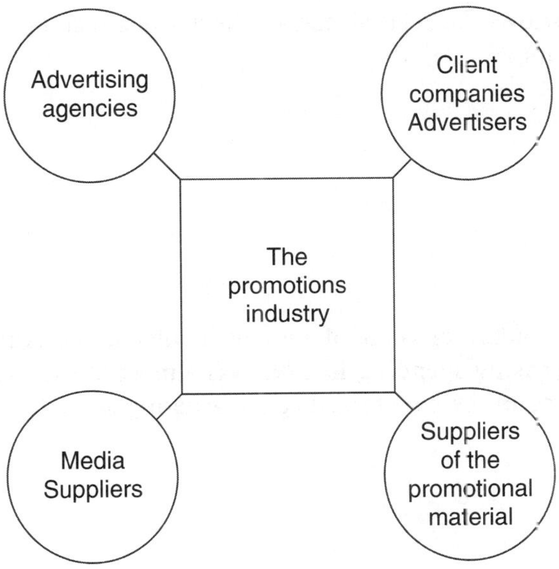

(a) *Agencies*. Although these still tend to be called advertising agencies they do in fact provide a wide range not only of promotional services but also marketing services. The activities of agencies are described in more detail later in this Study Text. The main ones include:

- The planning of campaigns;
- The design of creative components;
- The scheduling and buying of media;
- The buying and integration of other promotional materials;
- The administration and accountancy for the process;
- The implementation of campaigns;
- The monitoring and evaluation of the results.

In effect an agency acts as an additional resource to the client company's own marketing resources.

(b) *Clients*. These are properly known as the 'advertiser' and are really the lynchpin in the whole structure. Their role is a very obvious one which can be summarised as:

- providing the original need for the campaign;
- selecting and briefing the agency;
- discussing and agreeing campaign plans;
- integrating the promotional planning into marketing planning;
- evaluating and controlling the campaign;
- financing the whole process.

(c) *Media suppliers*. The media suppliers consist of the commercial television companies, commercial radio companies, newspapers and magazine owners, poster companies and a whole variety of new media owners. For example, Stoke City Football Club, who feature the brand name of Britannia Building Society on their strips can be regarded as a media supplier.

(d) *Suppliers of the other promotional materials*. A vast range of other specialist suppliers exists, from printers to producers of promotional gifts, from exhibition organisers to organisers of corporate hospitality. These specialist services are provided cost effectively and are bought directly by client companies or managed through advertising agencies.

2.2 Size of promotion sectors

The following table shows the relative size of the various sectors of the UK promotions industry in recent years.

Sector	%
Sales promotion	43.7
Advertising	42.7
Public Relations	3.4
Direct Marketing	4.4
Exhibitions	4.4
Point of purchase	1.4

To give you an idea of the amount of money involved, the Advertising Association reports that UK advertising spending in 1996 was almost £11bn, an increase of 6% over the previous year. Of all of these sectors, direct marketing is the fastest growing.

Advertising expenditure by medium (UK)

	%
Total press	60.6
Television	31.5
Posters (outdoor and transport)	4.0
Radio	3.2
Cinema	0.7
Total	£10,590m

Source: The Advertising Association's Advertising Statistics Yearbook (1997)

3 AGENCIES

3.1 Types of agency

In-house

The advertising function can be handled in a variety of ways. Firstly, if a potential advertiser has sufficient expertise, they may decide to handle advertising in-house.

Full service agency (or one-stop shop)

Alternatively, an advertiser may decide to use a full service agency. This is an agency which provides a complete advertising service encompassing creative work, production, media planning and buying. The full service agency may also provide or sub-contract research services for a client. Some large advertising agencies will provide other communications services, for example direct marketing, public relations or sales promotion. Doubts are frequently raised within the industry about the wisdom and economy of using these. Often their services do not strictly encompass the full range of activities as typically they are part of a larger group of agencies.

Creative hot shops

The 1980's saw some agency personnel breaking away from their full service employers in order to provide specialist creative services to clients. These smaller operators became known as creative shops or sometimes 'hotshops' or 'boutiques'. These agencies specialise in creative ideas and solutions.

Media independents

Clients may choose to combine the services of a creative hot shop alongside media planning and buying services from a media specialist. These media independents specialise in planning and buying media. They buy space and time (eg TV) from media owners, and sell to agencies and advertisers.

A la carte

A client may decide to share out their communication tasks, choosing to cherry pick services *à la carte* from the different providers available. For example, they may decide to use only the creative and account planning services of a full service agency but, although a media department is also available to them from the full service agency, they may choose to use media planning and buying services from a media independent. Likewise, sales promotion, public relations, direct marketing and research services may be commissioned and used on an *ad-hoc* basis as required. Responsibility for controlling

NOTES

and co-ordinating the activities of these service providers rests with the client, usually in the form of the Brand or Marketing Manager.

Definition

> **Virtual agencies:** Term used to describe the selection of specialist individuals from different agencies or from within an agency group to work together as though they were members of the same agency.

4 ADVERTISING AGENCIES

4.1 Selecting an agency

The pages of the trade magazine *Campaign* regularly carry news of client accounts on the move from their incumbent agencies. There are a number of reasons why clients may change agencies. As mentioned above, the client may feel the agency is lacking in new ideas, or that it is overcharging them for services. Alternatively, a new client won by the agency may result in a conflict of interests between new and old clients. Often, a change in personnel on either the client or the agency side can result in an account moving on.

4.2 Search

The process of selecting a new agency is likely to follow a series of fairly well defined stages, the first of which is an initial search for suitable agency candidates. New clients can find out about agencies from a number of sources, such as *Campaign Portfolio* or the Advertising Agency Register (AAR).

When considering agency options it is important to be realistic. A budget of, say, £5 million, will not be of paramount interest to the larger full service agencies who are used to dealing with budgets several times that amount. A medium-sized full service agency would certainly be interested in doing business with a client with this amount to spend, however.

When choosing any agency the task is further complicated by the number of variables which need to be considered in the decision-making process.

4.3 Agency selection criteria

(a)	Services offered	-	planning, creative, research, integrated, international?
(b)	Agency size	-	how many clients, is it part of a group?
(c)	Quality of work	-	Past and present, any creativity or effectiveness awards?
(d)	Relevant experience	-	In market sector and promotional discipline?
(e)	Competing accounts	-	Are there any current or potential clashes or conflicts of interest?
(f)	Cost	-	What is the likely cost and method of remuneration?
(g)	Location	-	Is the agency conveniently located for meetings?
(h)	Reputation	-	Track record, working relationships and success.

BPP PUBLISHING

4.4 Credentials shortlist and brief

Definition

> **Credentials presentation.** An opportunity for agencies to present their organisational details in order to persuade a potential client to short list them.

The agencies selected are usually invited to a credentials presentation and then a shortlist of three or four agencies is determined. Those agencies will then attend a briefing meeting. The brief will usually include company history, marketing communications objectives, target markets, marketing mix strategies, budget and time considerations.

Definition

> **Client brief.** A presentation, usually accompanied by a brief report, outlining relevant background information and the marketing communications task to be undertaken.

4.5 Pitch

The time allowed between the delivery of the brief and the pitch is usually between four and six weeks and the cost can vary significantly depending on the nature of the brief.

Definition

> **Pitch**. Abbreviated from agency sales pitch, the pitch is an opportunity for the agency to sell itself, its creative ideas and its response to a client's brief. This is usually a competitive process.

4.6 Final selection

The **final selection** will involve a judgement about how well the client believes the agency has responded to the brief in terms of the strategic thinking involved the creative work (if presented) and the agency's all round understanding of the client's industry. Courtesy dictates that the client should inform both the successful agency and the unsuccessful ones in a prompt manner.

> **Activity 2** **(10 minutes)**
>
> Make sure you know what the following acronyms mean.
>
> SMART
> PEST
> SLEPT
> fmcg

4.7 Agency remuneration

Historically, agencies have earned their money through commission on media space purchased for their clients. The practice arises from the time when the advertising agent was a media broker who also provided other services. This method of payment also highlights the agency's legal standing. The agency is liable for bills to the media if the client defaults on payment.

Agency commission

The advertising agency earns money from the commission given by the media. This allows the agency to pay media invoices to TV stations, newspapers, magazines and so on, net of commission, but to charge the client the gross cost. Creative and other services are charged to the client at cost plus an equivalent mark up.

15% used to be the standard rate of agency commission. This is now no longer the case. Some large clients, who spend highly on media have argued that they should pay the agency a discounted rate of commission, because of the volume of media throughput that the agency handles. Other clients, themselves under pressure to make advertising money work harder, have argued that 15% is too high, and that the agency should charge a lower rate. Commission rates of 10% or 13% are now not uncommon.

(a) *Agency perspective*

Advantages	Traditional and so comfortable
	It encourages media buyers to get good discounts by taking advantage of bulk buying
	Can result in good profits when the media spend is high
	The agency is paid irrespective of performance
Disadvantages	There is no financial recognition for a successful campaign
	May be difficult to calculate if all costs have been covered

(b) *Client perspective*

Advantages	They are used to it and it is simple
	They know that it can encourage the agency to get good deals
Disadvantages	Fees are not known in advance and thus budgeting is made problematic
	Additional fees may have to be paid to cover production costs
	There is no agency accountability built into the pricing structure
	There is concern that agencies may recommend high cost media for maximum commission

Mark-ups

Agencies will contract work out to third parties, eg print, radio and video production and creative artwork. Agencies will then receive part of their remuneration from an agreed mark-up charged on the cost of purchases from third parties. Mark-up between 10% and 15% would not be unusual but can vary significantly depending on the nature of the work undertaken and the degree of agency involvement.

Fee payment

Some advertisers and their agencies prefer to work on a project-by-project fee system. This ensures the agency earns money, whether or not the work is media based. It is usual for agencies to work on an agreed monthly or quarterly fee, known as a retainer.

Performance related

Performance related schemes are being used increasingly. The agency is judged on the effect its advertising has on client company sales. Different rates of commission then come into force, depending on performance to target, over-achievement or under-achievement. The major drawback to this method of remuneration is that it pre-supposes a direct correlation between advertising effort and sales.

Performance related can be evaluated in a number of different ways. Criteria include increased sales, consumer measures (such as increased awareness or spontaneous recall) and other qualitative measures such as brand elevation.

(a) *Agency perspective*

Advantages	Can compete better on price and can breakdown costs accurately
	Allows for individual performance evaluation
	A successful campaign would generate higher returns
	Might motivate the agency and so improve the client relationship
Disadvantages	External factors may influence results
	It is more difficult to budget income and there is no guarantee that costs will be covered
	The timings of the evaluation and payments are critical, especially to a small agency
	There is the potential to encourage an atmosphere of distrust
	Creativity may be sacrificed for quick results

(b) *Client perspective*

Advantages	Could reduce bias in media spending
	Will favour smaller clients, who may be cost conscious, and so reduces their risks
	Will encourage the agency to be more accountable and so develop a closer relationship
	Poor performance could be rectified
Disadvantages	Potentially confusing and complicated to administer
	Measurement means additional costings
	Concentrates on the short term
	Could result in lots of similar campaigns, as agencies discover what gives fast results
	Uncontrollable elements (eg a poor product) are not taken into account
	Could undermine the relationship between the agency and the media sellers

Performance related effectively isolates advertising from the other marketing activities of the organisation and as such relies on a false divide. The major difficulty for the industry is to come up with a formula that can assess effectiveness of a particular campaign without penalising the agency for factors beyond its control.

DISCUSSION

From a client's perspective, there is a lot to commend performance-related payment by results remuneration.

4.8 Account management

Within the agency, a **variety of personnel** will be involved in handling the client's business. The account executive or account manager is the lynchpin between the numerous agency personnel and their client. Their role is to liaise with client staff and to brief, supervise and co-ordinate the appropriate agency staff at appropriate times.

The account executive and, through him, the agency should be seen as a natural extension of the client's own marketing resources.

Definition

> **Account planners:** agency people responsible for developing a clear understanding of the market situation in which marketing communications will take place. Involves research and knowledge of the market, relevant buying processes and the client's position.

The internal structure of an agency can best be explained by considering how the agency handles a piece of client work.

Step 1. **The client problem**

A client and agency who have been together for some time will have built up a good working relationship. The agency will understand the client's business and will have a good knowledge of the dynamics of the market in which the client operates. Equally, the agency will be aware of the motivations and decision-making processes of end consumers. A new product or service, new situation or changing market conditions may provide the starting point for a new role to be performed by advertising. The client needs to brief the account executive on the task in hand.

Step 2. **The internal briefing**

The account executive will brief the members of the account team who work on the client's business. The account group will usually compromise:

(i) An account planner, responsible for using market research to develop advertising strategy for the client

(ii) A creative team duo of art director and copywriter, responsible for conceiving a creative idea which meets the advertising brief and working that idea up into visual form and written copy

(iii) A media planner/buyer, responsible for recommending an appropriate media strategy and ensuring media is bought cost effectively

NOTES

Step 3. **The client presentation**

Once the account team have worked on the client brief and are happy with their response to it, the account executive will present back to the client. He will show examples of how the final advertising execution will look, using rough visuals or storyboards and will explain the rationale for the ideas presented. Depending on the client's reaction to the team's interpretation of the brief, the team will either be asked to go ahead in developing the work, or will be asked to rework their ideas.

The go-ahead stage may include a decision to test the advertising in research prior to full production of the advert.

Step 4. **Production of advert(s)**

Some simple advertising executions will be carried out almost entirely in-house by the advertising agency. For more complex executions, the agency will buy in specialist functions on behalf of the client. For instance, a production company would work alongside the agency in the filming of a TV commercial.

Whilst production is ongoing, the media department will be involved in the actual commitment of the media budget. Dates, times and positions will be agreed with media owners.

During this stage, there will be continuous liaison between the account executive and the client. The client is likely to attend some of the key production stages such as filming or photography of the commercial.

If time allows, further research may take place to identify the need for any additional changes.

Step 5. **The campaign appears**

The time span between the briefing of the account executive by the client and the campaign appearing can be as little as six or eight weeks for a simple photographic newspaper execution, to twenty weeks plus for an animated TV commercial. Once the campaign has appeared, it is important that it is properly evaluated against the objectives initially set.

The staff comprising the account team who work directly on the client's business in creating a campaign are those the client is most likely to come into contact with, although the main point of contact will of course be the account executive. There are other behind-the-scenes staff with whom the account executive must liaise but who will not have direct client contact.

Activity 3 **(45 minutes)**

Look through the previous three month's issues of industry magazines such as Admap, Campaign, Marketing Week, Revolution etc and identify agency operations, remuneration, pitches and new accounts. Write a short report on some of the more significant changes taking place and opinions expressed by industry commentators.

5 THE NATURE OF REGULATION

5.1 Overview

All organisations have to engage in promotional activity, utilising the various elements of the marketing communications mix - advertising, sales promotion, public relations and personal selling. As with other areas of business activity the organisation's freedom of action is constrained by the legal and regulatory process. In contrast to other areas of operations, the regulation of promotional activity is far more dependent on self regulatory codes of practice, particularly with regard to advertising and sales promotion, because of the piecemeal nature of the statutory provision in these areas.

In the UK no one Act of Parliament provides a comprehensive framework for the regulation of promotional activity. Over 150 Acts of Parliament and Statutory Instruments (quite apart from case law) form the legal framework within which advertising and sales promotion operate. New rules are likely as the use of technology such as the Internet becomes widespread.

Despite the impression that all these statutes might create, the UK tends to favour a broadly voluntary code of practice because of the advantages this has over legal controls. Many of the Acts affect very specific areas of business and are not necessarily applicable to all.

The rules governing the acceptability of communication can be summed up in a phrase that is widely recognised by advertising practitioners and general public alike: communication must be 'legal, decent, honest and truthful.' We will look at each aspect in turn.

5.2 Legality

Advertisements should not contain anything which is in breach of the law or omit anything required by law. For example, adverts should not show discrimination on the grounds of colour, race or ethnic origin (Race Relations Act, 1976) or on the grounds of sex and marital status (Sex Discrimination Act, 1975), or on the grounds of disability (Disability Discrimination Act 1995).

5.3 Decency

The Obscene Publications Acts 1959 and 1964 state that it is an offence to publish an obscene article, 'whether to gain or not.' An article is defined as obscene if 'the effect is likely to deprave or corrupt persons who are likely to see, read or hear the matter embodied in it.' Basically promotions should not contain anything likely to cause widespread offence, fear or distress.

5.4 Honesty and truthful presentation

These last two elements can be combined as the legal provision in this area does not make a clear distinction between the two for practical purposes. The main statute covering this area is the **Trade Descriptions Act 1968**, which prohibits any person, in the course of a trade or business, from applying a false description to goods, or from supplying or offering to supply any goods with a false trade description.

DISCUSSION

The regulatory system cannot ensure that offence is never caused. What regulators attempt to do is avoid offence being serious or widespread.

Definition

> The Act defines a **trade description** as an indication, either direct or indirect, regarding such issues as quantity, size, composition, method of manufacture, fitness for purpose, approval or endorsement by any individual or organisation and the past history of the product. The scope of this legislation applies to all areas of promotion, including packaging, illustrations, advertisements, demonstrations and oral statements.

5.5 Data Protection Acts 1984 and 1998

The **Data Protection Act 1984** was the first piece of legislation to come into force that addressed growing popular fear that information about individuals which was stored on computer files and processed by computer could be **misused**. In particular, it was felt that an individual could easily be harmed by the existence of computerised data which was **inaccurate** or misleading.

The Act attempted to afford some measure of protection to **the individual** regarding data which is processed mechanically, that is by 'equipment operated automatically in response to the instructions given for that purpose'.

(a) **Personal data** is information about a living individual, including expressions of opinion about him or her.

(b) **Data users** are organisations or individuals who control the contents and use of files of personal data.

(c) A **data subject** is an individual who is the subject of personal data.

(d) A **computer bureau** processes personal data for data users, or allows data users to process personal data on its equipment.

The main features of the Data Protection Act were as follows.

(a) With certain exceptions, all data users and all computer must **register** under the Act with the Data Protection Registrar. This currently costs £75 for three years.

(b) Data subjects are awarded certain legal rights, such as the right of access to information held about them.

(c) Data users and computer bureaux must adhere to data protection principles.

(d) The Act establishes certain civil proceedings and a number of criminal offences.

(e) The office of Data Protection Registrar was set up to establish a register of data users and computer bureaux and to consider complaints about the contravention of the principles or the Act's provisions.

The terms of the Data Protection Act 1984 have now been extended by the **Data Protection Act 1998**, which implements the EU Data Protection Directive in the UK. It contains familiar elements from the 1984 legislation, but there are additional requirements imposed by the EU Directive.

It is now possible for a data subject to find out not only what data is being held, but what it is being held for. In the case of inaccurate data, an individual can apply to the courts for correction, blocking, erasure or destruction. The Act specifies the following.

(i) **Express consent** is needed when processing sensitive data such as ethnic origin or criminal convictions. Data subjects will have the right not to have certain decisions made about them which are based solely on automated processing, eg psychometric tests for recruitment decisions.

(ii) The 1998 Act is extended to cover data held in any kind of 'relevant filing system' where 'specific information relating to a particular individual is readily accessible.' This may be taken to include **manual filing methods.**

(iii) The Data Protection Registrar is renamed the **Data Protection Commissioner,** whose powers will be strengthened.

(iv) The transfer of personal data **outside the EU** is restricted.

5.6 Self-regulatory codes of practice

These are the main statutory requirements as far as promotion is concerned. However there is another vehicle that regulates activity in this area which is designed to complement the statutory provision - self-regulatory codes of practice, administered by the communication industry itself. Self-regulatory codes of practice are usually issued by the bodies representing the marketing communications industry in order to establish standards for members to follow. Under the provisions of the Fair Trading Act 1973 the Director General of the Office of Fair Trading (OFT) is obliged to encourage the creation and dissemination of such OFT approved codes. Prime examples are the *British Codes of Advertising and Sales Promotion* which are administered by the Advertising Standards Authority (ASA). The current versions came into effect in February 1995 and was the ninth edition of the Advertising Code and the sixth edition of the Sales Promotion Code.

The principal advantages of self-regulation controls over legal controls are that they are significantly more flexible, easy to administer and can be changed relatively easily and quickly to take account of changing circumstances. Adoption of self-regulatory controls show the promotions industry in a favourable light and can encourage public respect.

6 REGULATING ADVERTISING ACTIVITY

Advertising is, in practice, controlled according to the media used, the nature of the product or service advertised and the nature of the business of the advertiser.

6.1 General

The media used

Because of the different characteristics of the various media from which an advertiser can choose, different levels of regulation as to what constitutes acceptable and unacceptable practice exist. Television is the most heavily regulated medium in terms of constraints being placed on advertisers' freedom of action and the products that can be advertised.

The nature of the products or service advertised

Varying levels of regulation may exist, by virtue of the nature of the product advertised. Those products that are potentially harmful, such as alcohol and cigarettes, have a great level of regulation. However, increased levels of regulation also apply where the target audiences could be more easily manipulated because of their credulity (such as children) or their strong desire for the increased social acceptance that use of the products may bring (such as slimmers).

The nature of the business of the advertiser

Some organisations that provide products and/or services of a sensitive nature may face a greater level of regulation. For example, organisations such as matrimonial and dating agencies are not allowed to advertise on television. This regulation also applies to undertakers.

However, as has been stated, there is no one comprehensive Act of Parliament covering advertising activity and this is why the Codes of Practice are so important. Both the Advertising Standards Authority and the Independent Television Commission, who administer the codes of practice relating to advertising, have used the framework articulated in the statement that all advertising must be 'legal, decent, honest and truthful' as the starting point for their provisions.

6.2 The Advertising Code

The regulatory provisions embodied in the Advertising Code apply to the following forms of advertising:

(a) advertisements in newspapers, magazines and other printed publications;

(b) advertising material such as brochures, circulars, mailings and catalogues;

(c) indoor and outdoor posters and other outdoor advertisements, including aerial advertisements;

(d) cinema and video commercials;

(e) adverts in non-broadcast electronic media such as computer games;

(f) advertisements on viewdata services.

The code imposes two main obligations on the advertiser. The first is that the **primary responsibility** for observance of the code falls upon him, even when delegated, for all practical purpose, to an advertising agency or other intermediary. The second obligation is that of **substantiation**, which means that before offering an advertisement for publication, the advertiser should have available all documentary and other evidence necessary to demonstrate the advertisement's conformity to the code. This information should be made available without delay if requested by the regulatory authorities.

There are also provisions regarding safety (adverts should not encourage unsafe practices, especially drinking and driving), violence and anti-social behaviour.

The code also provides specific rules regarding particular categories of advertisement.

- Alcoholic drinks
- Children
- Motoring
- Environmental claims
- Health and beauty products
- Slimming
- Distance selling
- List and database practice
- Employment and business opportunities
- Financial services and products

There is now a special set of rules for cigarette and tobacco advertising - the Cigarette Code. In essence, no advertisement should incite people to start smoking or encourage them to increase their cigarette consumption. Various way in which this might be done (sex, cult figures, wholesome images) are discouraged.

6.3 Implementing the code

DISCUSSION

The ASA only require one complaint to trigger an investigation.

The Advertising Code is administered by the Advertising Standards Authority (which deals with complaints from members of the public) and its sub-committee, the Committee of Advertising Practice (which deals with complaints from commercially interested parties). Both groups act in response to complaints made in writing about published advertisements.

Complaints received by the ASA are investigated free of charge but they must be in writing and be accompanied by a description or copy of the offending promotion. Complaints fall into one of five broad categories.

1. Promotions which conflict with the Code.
2. Complaints where there is a well-founded case for investigation.
3. Promotions where the promoter needs only to make minor modifications.
4. Complaints where the complainant's interpretation of either the promotion or the Codes does not correspond with the ASA's.
5. Promotions which are outside the scope of the Code.

A number of sanctions exist where an advertisement or promotion is in conflict with the Codes.

1. The media can refuse to accept the advertisement.
2. Adverse publicity may result from the ruling.
3. Trading sanctions may be imposed.
4. Financial and other incentives provided by trade, media or professional organisations may be withdrawn.
5. Legal injunction to prevent further appearance.
6. A mandatory two-year poster pre-vetting.

Definition

> **Pre-vetting:** the process of checking and approving advertisements before they are released.

EXAMPLE

The ferry company 'Sally Lines' used a headline in one of their advertisements, 'Only Sally goes all the way for £40'. On seeing the advertisement, a woman named Sally took offence. She complained directly to the organisation and then the ASA. The ASA agreed that she had been offended but ruled that the advertisement was acceptable as it was unlikely to cause grave or widespread offence.

DISCUSSION

The number of items that receive complaints is only a very tiny percentage of all marketing comunications. Of this, still fewer complaints are upheld.

6.4 ITC Code Of Advertising Standards And Practice

The ITC Code of Advertising Standards and Practice is a statutory code of practice, established under the provisions of the Broadcasting Act 1990 and most recently revised in 1995. It applies to all television services regulated by the ITC: ITV, Channel 4, Channel 5, UK direct broadcast satellite (DBS) services and other satellite services operating out of the UK but not using broadcasting frequencies allocated to the UK, cable and local delivery services and the Welsh Fourth Channel which is regulated by S4C. (Radio is monitored by the Radio Authority (RA).)

6.5 Implementing the ITC Code

Broadcasters licensed by the ITC are expected to investigate all claims made by advertisers carefully before accepting them for broadcast and to make their own initial judgements as to whether the commercials comply with the ITC code. The ITC provides guidance on code interpretation but does not offer a routine pre-vetting service. It concentrates on setting standards, ensuring their maintenance and regular review. When complaints arise the ITC will investigate using a similar procedure to the Advertising Standards Authority. Like the ASA the ITC is empowered to issue directives to broadcasters to remove offending advertising and also has the power to fine broadcasters where breaches of the code have occurred, whether by negligence or wilful disregard of the rules.

Examples of ITC and RA unacceptable product categories:

- breath testing devices which claim to mask the effects of alcohol
- the occult
- betting tips
- betting and gambling (except those granted special permission, eg lotteries)
- all tobacco products
- private investigation agencies
- guns
- pornography

6.6 The Broadcasting Standards Commission

BBC broadcasting used to be governed by the Broadcasting Complaints Commission and the Broadcasting Standards Council. However, the Broadcasting Act 1996 set up a Broadcasting Standards *Commission*. This will not directly affect advertisers, obviously, but it is likely to influence the thinking of bodies such as the ITC.

DISCUSSION

Acceptance of images and messages vary widely across the world. Perfectly acceptable marketing communications in one country would be banned in another.

---

7 REGULATING SALES PROMOTION

7.1 The law

The statutory framework governing sales promotion in the UK is not comprehensive. Like advertising, sales promotion is governed by small sections of a large number of Acts of Parliament, the provisions of which are often somewhat ambiguous.

> The British Codes of Advertising and Sales Promotion include the following legislative controls on this area of marketing activity.
>
> - Consumer Credit Act 1974 (and regulations and orders thereunder)
> - Consumer Protection Act 1987 and the Code of Practice for Traders on Price Indications, published thereunder
> - Consumer Transactions (Restrictions on Statements) Order 1976
> - Control of Misleading Advertisements Regulations 1988
> - Data Protection Act 1984 and 1998
> - Fair Trading Act 1973
> - Financial Services Act 1986 (and regulations and orders, and rules of the Securities and Investments Board, recognised self-regulating organisations and recognised professional bodies made thereunder).
> - Income and Corporation Taxes Act 1988
> - Lotteries and Amusements Act 1976 (and amendments thereto)
> - Mail Order Transactions (Information) Order 1976
> - Misrepresentation Act 1976
> - National Lottery Act 1993 and National Lottery Regulations 1994
> - Sale of Goods Act 1979
> - Supply of Goods and Services Act 1982
> - Trade Descriptions Act 1968
> - Trading Stamps Act 1964
> - Unfair Contract Terms Act 1977
> - Unsolicited Goods and Services (Amendment) Act 1975.

With such a diverse range of statutory provision the law in this area has an 'individual and often unintended effect' (Circus and Painter, 1989). Given these circumstances it is hardly surprising that the regulatory framework imposed from within the industry by voluntary codes of practice is an important restraining influence. The most important codes include:

(a) the British Codes of Advertising and Sales Promotion
(b) the Institute of Sales Promotion Promotional Handling Code of Practice
(c) the Institute of Sales Promotion Competition Rules
(d) the Institute of Purchasing and Supply Rules for Trade Promotions

Given the complexity of the regulatory framework, restraining the freedom of action of a promoter through a variety of means, it is essential that promoters take expert legal advice in the early stages of planning sales promotion activity.

We will now go on to look at the regulatory framework for sales promotion in more detail, considering the influence of the law in this area and the complexities arising from its ambiguity, and then looking at the relevant codes of practice, both self regulatory and statutory, that try to remove this ambiguity in practical terms and thereby act as a true complement to the statutory provision.

7.2 Sales promotion - the regulatory framework

Contract law

With regard to sales promotion, the offer of goods and/or services with incentives by a promoter and the acceptance of that offer by the consumer constitute a contract that is enforceable in law. The basic requirements for the existence of a contract are the **capacity to contract**, the existence of an offer, the acceptance of that offer and consideration.

(a) Both parties to a contract must have the legal *capacity to contract.* In other words they must be fully aware of the formal legal consequences of their actions. This is particularly relevant with regard to young people entering into contracts. The Sales Promotion Code defines a child or young person as someone under 16 years of age and warns that promotions addressed to, or likely to attract, young people should not take advantage of their credulity or lack of experience.

(b) With regard to the **contract obligations** of the promoter, the basic principles of the Sales Promotion Code ensures that the consumer is fully aware of the implications of a specific promotion.

(c) Some general legal principles with regard to the *offer* of contract include the fact that the offer can be made to one person or can be of general applicability. The offer must be communicated before it is capable of being accepted and the terms of the offer must be clear.

(d) As the **acceptance** of an offer of goods with incentives constitutes a legal contract the **terms** of the offer must be clearly stated by the promoter, as stated in the Sales Promotion Code. This is particularly appropriate if any exclusions apply to participation (eg time limits, number of prizes per household) and if any limits on eligibility are imposed by the promoter. If such terms are not clear and easy to understand then any dispute over the contract will most likely go in favour of the consumer.

Acceptance of an offer must be made to the person making the offer and it must be without qualification otherwise it becomes a counter offer. Postal acceptance of an offer is valid from the time of posting and not at the moment of delivery.

The last requirement for a contract to exist is *consideration*. English and Welsh law will not enforce a mere promise. The promise must be supported by something that will benefit one of the parties and cause detriment to the other - known as consideration. This is usually money.

Product liability

In terms of the quality of goods and incentives offered by promoters all products must comply with the implied conditions of sale stated in the **Sale Of Goods Act 1979** - namely, that the goods are of merchantable quality, fit for the purpose(s) for which they are sold, and that they are as described.

The remedy that a consumer can claim in law for any breach of the implied conditions of sales of the Sale of Goods Act is a refund of the purchase price. A seller may offer to exchange the goods, give a credit note or repair the goods, but the consumer is not obliged to accept any of these, nor the seller to give them.

Trade descriptions

The Trade Descriptions Act 1968 applies to sales promotions just as much as advertising, and implicit in the Sales Promotion Code is the requirement upon the promoter to ensure that all information is presented clearly and is not misleading.

Incomplete information or information that is complete but confusing is likely to render a contract unenforceable in law.

Lotteries and amusements

It is in this area that the requirements of statute law create the most problems for promoters, particularly with regard to prize competitions. (Note that separate legislation and regulations apply to the National Lottery.) Section I of the Lotteries and Amusements Act 1976 states that all lotteries which do not constitute gaming (playing games of chance for money) are illegal. The Act provides no definition of a lottery, but this has been largely accomplished by common law, as follows.

> 'A lottery consists of the 'distribution of prizes by chance', that is to say where there is no element of skill whatever on the part of the participant. If there is a degree of skill involved then there is no lottery (Whitbread and Co v Bell (1970))

Therefore a lottery is a distribution of prizes where those prizes are distributed by chance and no element of *skill* should be required, otherwise the promotion will not be a lottery. The emphasis on the absence of skill is shown by the following ruling.

> Any kind of skill or dexterity, whether bodily or mental, in which persons can compete would prevent a scheme from being a lottery if the result depended partly upon such skill or dexterity. (Scott v DPP (1914))'

Such rulings, while clarifying the situation somewhat, still leave much scope for interpretation of the law and it is recommended in the Sales Promotion Code that any promoter intending to implement a competition with prizes seek expert legal advice because of the continuing uncertainty as to what constitutes an appropriate element of genuine skill, which makes the promotion legal.

7.3 Statutory codes of practice

The aim of statutory codes of practice is to facilitate the implementation of particular Acts of Parliament. Of particular relevance to sales promotion is the *Code of Practice for Traders on Price Indication* which deals specifically with pricing and bargain offers. The law in this area was reworked in 1989 with the repeal of Section II of the Trade Descriptions Act 1968 and the Price Marking (Bargain Offers) Orders 1979. These provisions have been replaced by the Consumer Protection Act 1987, Part III which states that a trader will be guilty of an offence:

> 'If, in the course of any business of his, he gives (by any means whatever) to consumers an indication which is misleading as to the price at which any goods, services, accommodation or facilities are available (whether generally or from particular persons).'

It is also an offence to fail to take reasonable steps to correct an indication as to the price of any goods, services, accommodations or facilities given to consumers in the course of a business where the indication has subsequently become misleading.

This legislation has been backed up by the *Code of Practice for Traders on Price Indications*, adherence to which will ensure good trading practices. The code of practice states a variety of general principles relating to price marking and then articulates specific guidelines with regard to the indication of bargain offers that are of particular relevance to promoters.

There are a number of self-regulatory codes of practice relevant to sales promotion, the most important of which is the* Sales Promotion Code, *which remains the most comprehensive framework for the regulation of this area. This section considers its provisions and those of other relevant codes.

7.4 The Sales Promotion Code

The aim and scope of the 1995 Sales Promotion Code is to regulate:

> 'the nature and administration of promotional marketing techniques. These techniques generally involve providing a range of direct or indirect additional benefits, usually on a temporary basis, designed to make goods or services more attractive to purchasers'.

In order to accomplish the aim of the code more specifically, the Code states that all promotions should be, 'legal, decent, honest and truthful', echoing the parallel codes regulating advertising activity. Sales promotions should be prepared with a sense of responsibility to consumers and society, they should be fair, and they should not disappoint unnecessarily.

Many of the provisions are similar to those in the Advertising Code, as described above. Certain others, such as stipulations about participation have also been covered above.

Free offers

If the word 'free' is used in a promotion the code has no objection to making a free offer conditional on the purchase of other items, but regards such a description as inappropriate if there is a cost to the consumer attributable to the offer. The code allows a charge not exceeding current public rates of postage, the actual cost of freight or delivery of the promotional goods, or the cost, including incidental expenses, of any travel involved if the consumer collects the offer.

Promotions with prizes

The code identifies several types of prize promotions - competitions, free draws and instant win offers - and advises that promoters seek expert legal advice in this area before beginning a promotion. However some guidelines are laid down regarding conditions of entry, availability of results, advertising of such promotions and their handling and administration. The code states that instructions for entry should be clearly worded and that supplementary rules should be avoided if at all possible.

7.5 Trade promotions to employees and distributors

Trade incentives and competitions should be designed and implemented so as to take account of the interests of everyone involved and should not compromise the obligation of employees to give honest advice to consumers.

Promoters should secure the prior agreement of employers if they intend to ask for assistance from or offer incentives to any other company's employees.

7.6 Codes of practice relating to trade promotions

Trade promotions are also the subject of regulation by the Institute of Purchasing And Supply (IPS) Ethical Code, The IPS Rules For Trade Promotions and the Incorporated Society of British Advertisers, *Trade Incentives - Good and Bad Practice.*

The IPS *Ethical Code* considers the relationship between promoter and recipient of a trade promotion from the point of view of the recipient.

(a) The code states that business gifts other than items of small intrinsic value should not be accepted and that 'modest hospitality' is allowable.

(b) The ISBA *Trade Incentives - Good And Bad Practice* emphasises the importance of adherence to the relevant statute laws and codes of practice in this area and advises that, in a company using trade incentives, a policy defining the proper use and administration of such incentives should be laid down by the board in writing, making it clear that improper payments will not be sanctioned or condoned in any circumstances. This policy should be broadcast both internally and externally.

7.7 Institute of Sales Promotion regulation

The Institute of Sales Promotion endorse two self-regulatory codes of practice - the ISP *Competition Rules* and the ISP *Promotional Handling Code of Practice.*

ISP Competition Rules

The ISP encourages registration of any promotional competition with themselves. The intention of this is 'to improve on current working practice. In particular, ISP's aim is to secure closer adherence to the Sales Promotion Code, issued by the Committee of Advertising Practice (CAP) Committee, of which the ISP is a member.' Registration of a promotional competition confers the benefit of objective advice from the ISP Secretariat on competition copy, with specific regard to conformity with the Sales Promotion Code. A 'reminder' service is also available from the ISP Secretariat advising promoters, shortly before competitions are due to be judged, of recommended practice regarding the judging and publication of results. The emphasis is to reassure both consumers and promoters that the competition is being conducted in accordance with recognised best industry practice.

DISCUSSION

While it is argued that promotions should avoid shocking in order to gain attention, it is clear that there is an increasing incidence of this happening.

---

8 REGULATING PUBLIC RELATIONS ACTIVITY

8.1 Institute of Public Relations

An important document for the regulation of public relations activity in the UK is the *Code of Professional Conduct* drawn up by the Institute of Public Relations (IPR). The aim of the IPR Code is 'to set down standards, which will, it is hoped, make for good relationships and reputable business dealing by public relations practitioners.' The Code of Professional Conduct is binding on all IPR members.

Complaints about breaches of the code by IPR members can originate from an individual or an organisation. Any complaint is investigated by the Institute's Professional Practices Committee which, if considered appropriate, may refer the complaint to the Disciplinary Committee for further action.

(a) Regarding conduct towards *the public*, the media and other professionals the code states that a PR practitioner should conduct his or her professional activities with proper regard to the public interest, emphasising the importance of responsible behaviour. The code calls for a responsible attitude to all sections of the public, recognising the fact that the public interest is not easy to define as the interests of different public groups may be contradictory.

(b) In relationships with *employers and clients* the code states that the PR practitioner should safeguard the confidences of both present and former employers or clients and should not use these confidences to the disadvantage or prejudice of such employers or clients, or to the financial advantage of the member (unless this information has been released for public use or permission for disclosure has been given). However, the code states that this clause can be overruled by a Court of Law.

8.2 The Public Relations Consultants Association (PRCA)

The Public Relations Consultants Association (PRCA) says that:

> Persuasion in Public Relations is perfectly justified in a democratic society, provided it is handled honestly, openly and professionally. All members of the Public Relations Consultants Association adhere to the Professional Charter in order to ensure that their clients and outside bodies (such as the media) act professionally in all respects.

The PRCA sees it as its objectives (amongst others) to raise and maintain professional and ethical standards in PR consultancy practice, to promote confidence in public relations consultancy and public relations as a whole, and to act as spokesman for consultancy practice and to help members improve their efficiency, understanding, skills, professionalism and ethics. The PRCA publishes a disciplinary code, setting out the procedure that will be followed if a member breaches its professional charter.

FOR DISCUSSION

The complete PRCA charter is set out below. You should skim-read it: there is no need to learn it by heart. It is included to give you the full flavour of self-regulation. Is it strict enough or does it merely encourage self-interest?

PRCA Professional Charter

1 A member firm shall:

1.1 Have a positive duty to observe the highest standards in the practice of public relations. Furthermore a member has the responsibility at all times to deal fairly and honestly with clients, past and present, fellow members and professionals, the public relations profession, other professions, suppliers, intermediaries, the media of communication, employees, and above all else the public.

1.2 Be expected to be aware of, understand and observe this code, any amendment to it and any other codes which shall be incorporated into this code, and to remain up-to-date with the content and recommendations of any guidance or practice papers issued by the PRCA, and shall have a duty to conform to good practice as expressed in such guidance or practice papers.

1.3 Uphold this code and co-operate with fellow members in so doing by enforcing decisions on any matter arising from its application. A member firm that knowingly causes or permits a member of its staff to act in a manner inconsistent with this code is party to such action and shall itself be deemed to be in breach of it. Any member of staff of a member company who acts in a manner inconsistent with this code must be disciplined by the employer.

A member firm shall not:

1.4 Engage in any practice nor be seen to conduct itself in any manner detrimental to the reputation of the Association or the reputation and interests of the public relations profession.

2 *Conduct towards the public, the media and other professionals*

A member firm shall:

2.1 Conduct its professional activities with proper regard to the public interest.

2.2 Have a positive duty at all times to respect the truth and shall not disseminate false or misleading information knowingly or recklessly, and to use proper care to avoid doing so inadvertently.

2.3 Have a duty to ensure that the actual interest of any organisation with which it may be professionally concerned is adequately declared.

2.4 When working in association with other professionals, identify and respect the codes of these professions and shall not knowingly be party to any breach of such codes.

2.5 Cause the names of all its directors, executives and retained consultants who hold public office, are members of either House of Parliament, are members of Local Authorities or of any statutory organisation or body, to be recorded in the relevant section of the PRCA Register.

2.6 Honour confidences received or given in the course of professional activity.

2.7 Neither propose nor undertake any action which would constitute an improper influence on organs of government, or on legislation, or on the media of communication.

2.8 Neither offer nor give, nor cause a client to offer or give, any inducement to persons holding public office or members of any statutory body or organisation who are not directors, executives or retained consultants, with intent to further the interests of the client if such action is inconsistent with the public interest.

3 *Conduct towards clients*

A member firm shall:

3.1 Safeguard the confidences of both present and former clients and shall not disclose or use these confidences, to the disadvantage or prejudice of such clients or to the financial advantage of the member firm, unless the client has released such information for public use, or has given specific permission for its disclosure; except upon the order of a court of law.

3.2 Inform a client of any shareholding or financial interest held by that firm or any member of that firm in any company, firm or person whose services it recommends.

3.3 Be free to accept fees, commissions or other valuable considerations from persons other than a client, only provided such considerations are disclosed to the client.

3.4 Shall list the names of its clients in the Annual Register of the Association.

3.5 Be free to negotiate with a client terms that take into account factors other than hours worked and seniority of staff involved. These special factors, which are also applied by other professional advisers, shall have regard to all the circumstances of the specific situation and in particular to:

(a) The complexity of the issue, case, problem or assignment, and the difficulties associated with its completion.

(b) The professional or specialised skills and the seniority levels of staff engaged, the time spent and the degree of responsibility involved.

(c) The amount of documentation necessary to be perused or prepared, and its importance

(d) The place and circumstances where the assignment is carried out in whole or in part.

(e) The scope, scale and value of the task, and its importance as an issue or project to the client.

A member firm shall not:

3.6 Misuse information regarding its client's business for financial or other gain.

3.7 Use inside information for gain. Nor may a consultancy, its members or staff directly invest in their clients' securities without the prior written permission of the client and of the member's chief executive or chief financial officer or compliance officer.

3.8 Serve a client under terms or conditions which might impair its independence, objectivity or integrity. Represent conflicting or competing interests without the express consent of clients concerned.

3.9 Represent conflicting or competing interests without the express consent of the clients concerned

3.10 Guarantee the achievement of results which are beyond the member's direct capacity to achieve or prevent.

3.11 Invite any employee of a client advised by the member to consider alternative employment; (an advertisement in the press is not considered to be an invitation to any particular person).

4 *Conduct towards colleagues*

A member firm shall:

4.1 Adhere to the highest standards of accuracy and truth, avoiding extravagant claims or unfair comparisons and giving credit for ideas and words borrowed from others.

4.2 Be free to represent its capabilities and services to any potential client, either on its own initiative or at the behest of the client, provided in so doing it does not seek to break any existing contract or detract from the reputation or capabilities of any member consultancy already serving that client. A member firm shall not:

4.3 Injure the professional reputation or practice of another member.

5 *Discriminatory conduct*

A member is required to take all reasonable care that professional duties are conducted without causing offence on the grounds of gender, race, religion, disability or any other form of discrimination or unacceptable reference.

Activity 4 **(60 minutes)**

Identify current examples of marketing communications you suspect might contravene the regulations. Using these as examples, prepare a presentation giving a balanced case for regulatory control while maintaining freedom of speech and information.

Having given a broad overview of the industry and regulatory environment we now cover some technological issues.

9 CURRENT TRENDS: TECHNOLOGICAL DEVELOPMENTS

Developments in telecommunications, electronics and computing are now ushering in a new era and have opened up new opportunities for marketing communications. The term 'new media' has been used to reflect these new opportunities and is associated almost exclusively with such high tech developments as digital and interactive TV, teletext and videotext, the World Wide Web and the internet, CD-ROM, DVD, video and multimedia.

Significantly and increasingly, the technology associated with new media permits:

- interactivity
- more direct and sophisticated communications
- shorter response times

A communications agency has predicted that by 2005, there will be 200 TV channels available in the UK, that the number of poster sites will have increased dramatically and that there will be as many as 350 radio stations. Details of these and other predictions can be found in the following table:

Media and the future

Media	*1985*	*1997*	*2005*
Internet usage	-	3%	60%
Digital TV	-	-	55%
PC	-	20%	45%
Radio stations	49	152	350
Outdoor sites	32,500	72,678	79,000
Consumer magazines	1,763	2,438	3,500
Cable/satellite penetration	-	24%	53%
Number of TV channels	4	16	200+
VCRs	28%	74%	85%
Teletext	12%	52%	80%

9.1 The internet

Definition

The **Internet** is the name given to the technology that allows any computer with a telecommunications link to send and receive information from any other suitably equipped computer. Terms such as 'the net', 'the information superhighway', 'cyberspace', and the 'World Wide Web (www)' are used fairly interchangeably, although technically the 'web' is what makes the 'net' user friendly (rather as Windows did for MS-DOS).

About 40m households in the US have a PC and about half of those also have a modem to connect to the telecommunications network. Either at home or at work, around 10m people (25%) are now connected to the Internet and 9m US households have purchased some form of on-line service.

Access to the Internet has become easier and cheaper: most new PCs now come pre-loaded with the necessary software, cheaper Internet devices are about to hit the market, and developments in telecommunications networks will eventually render modems unnecessary. Wireless application protocol (WAP) ensures that the internet can be reached from mobile phones. The decision to use the **Internet and related digital technologies** for either the whole or as a part of the business operations is a **strategically significant decision**. In reality, the majority of organisations see huge opportunities from use of the Internet and their involvement with it is more incremental than revolutionary. The Internet can be used by organisations for business-to-consumer and/or business-to-business purposes and in the UK some 80% of Internet activity is **business-to-business related** although as more members of the public get on-line and telephone and access costs reduce so this divide should narrow.

9.2 Websites

Most companies of any size now have a 'site' on the Net. A site is a collection of screens providing information in text and graphic form, any of which can be viewed simply by clicking the appropriate button, word or image on the screen. The user generally starts at the site's 'home page', which sets out the contents of the site. For instance, Penguin Books have a home page which includes the following options.

EXAMPLE

The Penguin Home Page

Preview	Read about our brand new titles, including sample extracts
Penguin direct	Order books here
World of Penguin	Search or browse our unique database. It contains over 10,000 Penguin titles
Penguin press	Browse through our whole range of academic titles
Features	The latest news and events from Penguin
For children	A special site dedicated to Puffin books
Penguin history	Find out why we've been world famous since 1935
Competitions and quizzes	Win some great prizes
Penguin search	Search the whole Penguin site by author, title or keyword

If you click on, say, *Penguin direct* you are taken to a page that allows you to fill in your name and address and credit card details and then enter details of the titles you want (perhaps obtained from browsing among the Penguin database or in response to a news feature. You then click on a button to submit your order directly over the telecommunications link to Penguin and receive the books by post a few days later.

9.3 Audience profile

The Internet is reckoned to be currently the fastest growing communications medium in Britain. It is thought that use is growing at between 10% and 15% per month. Recent research has suggested that by the end of 2001 23m people will have access to the internet through work or home. This figure accounts for almost half the UK population. Many net users use it both at work and at home.

It appears that most users are male, aged over 30, and in a white collar occupation, although the number of women and younger people using it is steadily growing.

9.4 Internet Service Providers (ISPs)

Connection (if not available through a user's organisation) is made via an Internet Service Provider (ISP). The user is registered as an Internet subscriber and pays a small monthly fee together with *local* telephone call charges, even if contacting other users on the other side of the world. This model is changing as some ISPs offer free access for a monthly fee.

ISPs such as America Online (AOL) and The Microsoft Network provide their own services, in addition to Internet access and e-mail capability. For instance, AOL also offers a main menu with options such as Life, Travel, Entertainment, Sport, Kids. It is rather like a quality Sunday newspaper, except that the sections are updated at least daily, and it provides much larger information resources (one option in the travel section, for instance, is to find out about train and plane timetables throughout the UK or worldwide).

There are many ISPs offering a combination of cost and performance and change is swift. At present, internet users in the US are only charged by their service providers. There are no telephone costs. This has undoubtedly contributed to the growth in internet usage in the US. Telephone charges have tended to limit the use of the internet in Europe and elsewhere in the world. It is highly likely that this situation will not continue.

9.5 Browsers, search engines and promotion

Most people use the Net through interface programs called **browsers** that make it more user-friendly and accessible. The most popular and best known ones are Internet Explorer and Netscape. Surfing the Net is done using a **search engine** such as Yahoo!, Excite and AltaVista. These guide users to destinations throughout the world: the user simply types in a word or phrase such as 'beer' to find a list of thousands of websites that contain something connected with beer.

Definition

Search engine: Website that maintains an index of other web pages and sites that may be searched using key words. Access to other sites is facilitated by hypertext links – links that may be simply clicked on to move from one site or page to another.

Companies like Yahoo! make money by selling advertising space. For instance if you type in 'beer', an advertisement for Miller Genuine Draft may well appear, as well as your list of beer-related sites.

Activity 5 **(60 minutes)**

Spend an hour surfing the internet. Contrast the websites of different organisations and assess their communications impact – what features work best, how is advertising managed, what about the quality of content and graphics?

Before we look at some of the strategic issues associated with marketing communications and the Internet, it is important to establish what is meant by some key terms, namely, eCommerce and Internet marketing.

NOTES

9.6 Marketing and eCommerce

Definitions

> **eCommerce** (also known as ebusiness) is about transactions involving the **exchange of goods and services, for payment**, using the Internet and related digital facilities.
>
> Internet marketing is about the application of the Internet and related digital facilities to help determine and **satisfy marketing objectives**.

The problem that arises is that many organisations are trying to practise relationship marketing and this concerns a one-to-one dialogue and where transactions between parties are viewed over a long period of time. Although Internet marketing (or cybermarketing) is not concerned with the mechanics associated with payments and security, the boundaries between eCommerce and Internet marketing are becoming blurred. As a result of this these phrases will be used interchangeably.

Definition

> **Cybermarketing**: Term used to describe marketing activities using new media.

The development of an interactive facility requires a major shift away from conventional commercial activities. According to Bickerton, Bickerton and Simon-Holley (1998) this is often achieved in three phases:

Phase 1. **Presentation.** The use of a web site to enable visitors/customers to **access information**, provides an opportunity to stand out from competitors and **enhance corporate image**. It is an opportunity to illustrate the organisation's products and services. This facility is often referred to as *brochureware.*

Phase 2. **Interaction.** This phase is characterised by **two-way communication**. Questions and answers flow between the system and the user. Visitors to the site are able to enquire more deeply than at the presentation stage and **information about the visitor** is logged and stored on a **database** for future reference and for both on and off-line communications.

Phase 3. **Representation.** When this phase is reached the organisation will have replaced parts of its commercial activities with **full on-line transactions**. The organisation's traditional commercial trading methods and channels may still be in place and the new interactive facility provides a complementary and/or alternative method for particular market segments.

> **Activity 6** **(15 minutes)**
>
> Look at the Iceland and Tesco websites – what advantages do they offer the customer who does not want to shop in store? What are the potential disadvantages from the retailer's perspective?

9.7 eCommerce and Web Site Management

Management need to attend to three main decisions concerning their Internet and digital related facilities. These are their **development, maintenance and promotion.** All of these use resources and management need to be clear about the level of support that is appropriate. One of the key concerns is the web site itself. To be successful the web site should

- **Attract Visitors** – with on-line and off -line methods
- **Enable Participation** - interactive content, and suitable facilities to allow for transactions
- **Encourage Return Visits** - design targeted at needs of particular segments, free services and added value facilities
- **Allow for Two-Way Information Sharing** - personalisation reflecting visitor preferences, direct marketing and information retrieval provide visitors with the information they are seeking

Use of the Internet to support stages in the Buying Process

Awareness
Not very effective at generating awareness and needs the support of off-line communications to drive visitors to the site.

Positioning
As a means of presenting features and benefits the Web is very good once a prospective customer has determined a need for a supplier search and is looking to compare offerings.

Lead generation
Once an active search commences leads can be obtained and used to reach prospects in the future.

Purchase decision support
By carrying vast amounts of information at low cost web sites provide good opportunities to impress visitors and build credibility.

Facilitate purchase
Through the provision of basic transaction facilities (credit card payment) sales should not be lost once a decision to buy has been made.

Post purchase support and retention
Through the provision of free customer support and advice, levels of cognitive dissonance in customers can be reduced. Feedback from customers, email updates about product developments and the use of sales promotions to stimulate repeat site visits can improve reputation, enable cross selling and promote favourable word of mouth recommendations.

Adapted from Chaffey, Mayer, Johnston and Ellis-Chadwick, (2000)

9.8 Potential pitfalls of internet marketing

The internet offers exciting prospects for marketers to assist in many aspects of marketing, from communications and research to relationship marketing with customers and other stakeholder groups. Here is a list of potential disadvantages, many of which can be overcome with effective management.

NOTES

(a) Poor targeting – as more websites are developed it becomes more difficult to differentiate. The fact that the user is proactively surfing means that effective search engine registration is vital.

(b) Cost – development and maintenance of the site and any customer database connectivity can be high.

(c) Lack of synergy – websites need to be developed with input from the marketing department to ensure integration.

(d) Medium immaturity – at present the internet is surfed by a large number of early adopters/early majority but until the speed, cost and reliability issues are improved, then the medium is unlikely to be adopted by the mass market.

(e) Security – research indicates that concerns over security and in particular credit card transactions are still a major barrier.

(f) Search difficulties – casual users may find searching for sites frustrating and time consuming.

DISCUSSION

The internet offers tremendous new opportunities to all businesses – this is set to continue.

9.9 Digital TV

The way was cleared for digital TV to go ahead by the Broadcasting Act 1996 which made 'new provision about the broadcasting in digital form of television and sound programme services and the broadcasting in that form on television or radio frequencies of other services'. Digital TV is available via terrestrial networks (OnDigital), satellite and cable.

(a) Transmitting programmes by digital signal rather than by conventional means **dramatically increases the number of services which can be delivered to audiences**: as many as ten digital services will be able to occupy the frequency previously occupied by one conventional 'analogue' service.

(b) Digital broadcasting allows viewers greater choice over how and when they watch, eventually allowing them to interact with programmes and select their own programme content.

(c) At the touch of a button, viewers are able to get supplementary information on the programmes they are watching.

(d) Broadcasters are also able to make use of the improved sound quality available on digital television to offer alternative soundtracks, for example the original language version of foreign films.

The advent of interactive TV is predicted to have an enormous impact, particularly for services such as video-on-demand, home shopping and home banking services.

9.10 Multimedia and home shopping

Multimedia can be defined as the combination of different formats, including text, pictures, animation, narrative, video and music into a single medium. Applications are increasingly likely to be interactive allowing viewers to control where they want to go. Viewers are attracted to multimedia as it is more interactive and multi-sensory. They can explore at their own pace, experiment and receive immediate feedback.

Some examples of the use of multimedia for marketing communications are:

(a) promotional material – products can be demonstrated, annual reports made more interesting, can be viewed on home PCs

(b) customer interaction – eg in car showrooms to avoid feeling pressured by sales people, multimedia kiosks can be accessed directly by customers who can view models from different angles, design their own cars and have their questions answered

Definition

> **Multimedia kiosks**: free-standing stations where computer access is facilitated either using CD-ROMs/DVDs or linked to other computers. These kiosks may be located in retail outlets.

(c) staff training – advantages include ease of use, cost savings and effectiveness

The **ability to shop from home** and choose items directly with the use of scanners can be integrated with direct advertising. **Infomercials** (which combine information with a commercial) which the consumer has chosen from a databank will be relayed directly to the home down cable links. These may take the form of recipes, DIY hints, car repairs and so on. Consumers will also be able to purchase the necessary ingredients or parts simultaneously, simply by pointing a mouse on a computer screen at the desired goods and clicking its buttons.

It is, however, difficult to predict how successful and how big the market for home shopping will become in the UK. It appeals to consumers within the United States because many people live in remote parts, some distance away from a main shopping centre. Within the UK however, the vast majority of people live within easy reach of a shopping centre or out-of-town complex. The speed of adoption will depend upon how readily the British public accept and use the new technology and to what extent they will be deterred from actively browsing around the shops.

(a) Advantages of interactive systems

- Saving time spent in shopping visits.
- Saving use of cars and car parking.
- Reduction in congestion and pollution.
- Greater variety of products to choose from.
- Ability to watch demonstrations from the comfort of one's home.
- Ability to browse.
- Ability to interrogate, get technical advice.
- Getting bank balances immediately.
- Transferring funds between accounts.
- Paying bankers orders.
- Access to directories of suppliers.
- It may be possible to closely segment markets.
- The specific needs of individual customers could be met.
- The costs of stockholding could be reduced.

Home shopping in America is a £1 billion business and is growing at the rate of 20% per annum. These shopping channels are increasingly being used by professionals without time to wander around department stores. The amount of broad band multimedia will accelerate the process, first, by increasing the number of channels available, and secondly, by increasing the interactivity. Instead of having to ring up to order, viewers will be able to punch in a code on their handset and pay by swiping their credit card through a slot in the set top box.

(b) Limitations of interactive systems

There are limitations to such interactive systems, which may be related to the state of the technology or to ingrained social and cultural habits.

- There are inevitably high set up costs.
- There is a lack of knowledge of the system.
- Some people suffer from technophobia.
- There is a lack of personal contact.
- Expectations of quality may not be realised.
- It is necessary to touch, feel, smell or taste some products.
- Shopping for some people has social benefits.
- Existing shopping centres may be destabilised.

9.11 CD-ROM/DVD

CD-ROM stands for compact disk – read only memory. DVD stands for digital versatile disk. Both are thin plastic disks covered with a coating onto which digital data has been encoded. The read only aspects refers to the fact that once the information is recorded on a disk it can only be used to retrieve information.

A single CD-ROM can hold around 200,000 pages of text, making it a very size and cost efficient means of storing data. DVDs are able to store and retrieve significantly more data so that it is possible to view an entire feature-length film from disk.

DISCUSSION

The interactive nature of the internet creates opportunities for data gathering. It is acceptable for this data to be used for further promotional and marketing activities.

9.12 Micromarketing

Segmentation, as part of target marketing, looks certain to play an even more crucial role in the marketing strategies of consumer organisations in the years ahead. The move from traditional mass marketing to **micro marketing** is rapidly gaining ground as marketers explore more cost-effective ways to recruit new customers. Micromarketing means marketing to a very small number of people. This has been brought about by a number of trends.

(a) The ability to create large numbers of product variants without the need for corresponding increases in resources is causing markets to become overcrowded.

(b) The growth in 'minority' lifestyles is creating opportunities for niche brands aimed at consumers with very distinct purchasing habits.

(c) The fragmentation of the media to service ever more specialist and local audiences is denying mass media the ability to assure market dominance for major brand advertisers.

(d) The advance in information technology is enabling information about individual customers to be organised in ways that enable highly selective and personal communications, for example database marketing and the internet.

Such trends have promoted the developments in benefit, lifestyle and geodemographic segmentation techniques outlined. Consumer market segmentation has developed so much in the last few years that the vision of multinational marketers accessing a PC to plan retail distribution and supporting promotional activity in cities as far apart as Naples, Nottingham and Nice is now a practical reality.

Micro-marketing is made possible by **mass customisation**. Mass customisation enables the combination of:

(a) The huge economies of scale of mass production
(b) The tailoring of products precisely to the customer's requirements

New manufacturing technology makes this possible. There is less need for a 'standard' or 'average' product if people's individual preferences can be catered for.

Chapter roundup

- The prime aim of marketing communications is to influence consumers' buying behaviour.
- Selective attention, distortion and recall can contribute to a message not being received.
- The structure of the promotions industry is a relatively complex one, with many thousands of companies.
- Types of agency include in-house, one-stop shop, creative hot shops, media independents and a la carte and virtual agencies.
- The agency selection process involves a credentials shortlist followed by a pitch.
- Agency remuneration can be by commission, mark ups, fee payment or performance related.
- All marketing communications should be legal, decent, honest and truthful.
- Self regulatory codes of practice are issued by the bodies representing the marketing communications industry in order to establish standards for members to follow.
- The Advertising Standards Authority deals with complaints from the public and commercially interested parties.
- Some 80% of the internet activity in the UK is business to business.
- Developments in telecommunications, electronics and computing are combining to form a new era of marketing communications opportunities.
- Successful websites should attract visitors, facilitate participation, encourage return visits and allow for two-way information sharing.
- Digital TV is likely to have a significant impact on video-on-demand, home shopping and home banking services.
- Micro-marketing is made possible by mass customisation.

Quick quiz

1 What are the key elements of the communications model?

2 Define what is meant by the term noise when referring to communications.

3 What are the main activities of agencies?

4 In the UK what medium accounts for the greatest advertising expenditure?

5 What is a virtual agency?

6 When selecting an agency, what criteria can be considered?

7 What are the agency advantages of performance related remuneration schemes?

8 What is the basic remit of the 1968 Trade Descriptions Act?

9 What does ASA stand for?

10 Give two examples of ITC and RA unacceptable product categories.

11 Who are the PRCA?

12 What is the internet?

13 What is an ISP?

14 What can multimedia communications be used for?

15 What does micromarketing mean?

Answers to quick quiz

1 Parties (sender and receiver), communication tools (message and media) functions (encoding, decoding, response, feedback). (See paragraph 1.2)

2 Those distortions created in the encoding or decoding process that can result in inaccurate interpretation of meaning. (para 1.2)

3 Planning, creative work, scheduling and buying media, promotional integration, administration, implementation, monitoring and evaluation of campaigns. (para 3)

4 Press. (para 2.2)

5 A term used to describe a selection of specialist individuals from different agencies or from within an agency who work together. (para 3.1)

6 Services offered, agency size, quality of work, relevant experience, competing accounts, cost, location and reputation. (para 4.3)

7 Can compete better on price and breakdown costs accurately; allows for individual performance evaluation; a successful campaign would generate higher returns; might motivate the agency and so improve the client relationship. (para 4.7)

8 This act prohibits any person, in the course of trade or business, from applying a false description to goods, or from supplying or offering to supply any goods with a false trade description. (para 7.2)

9 Advertising Standards Authority. (para 6.3)

10 Tobacco products and guns. (para 6.5)

11 The Public Relations Consultants Association. (para 8.2)

12 The internet is the name given to the technology that allows any computer with a telecommunications link to send and receive information from any other suitably equipped computer. (para 9.1)

13 Internet Service Provider. (para 9.4)

14 Promotional material, customer interaction and staff training. (para 9.10)

15 Marketing to a very small number of people. (para 9.12)

Answers to activities

1 The answer will depend on the advertisements you have identified.

2 SMART
Specific
Measurable
Actionable
Reasonable
Timescaled

PEST
Political
Economic
Social
Technological

SLEPT
Social
Legal
Economic
Political
Technological

Fmcg – Fast moving consumer goods eg bread, newspapers

3 The answer will depend on what you have uncovered in the relevant magazines.

4 There is no specific answer to this activity.

5 There is no specific answer to this activity.

6 There is no specific answer to this activity.

Chapter 13 :
ADVERTISING

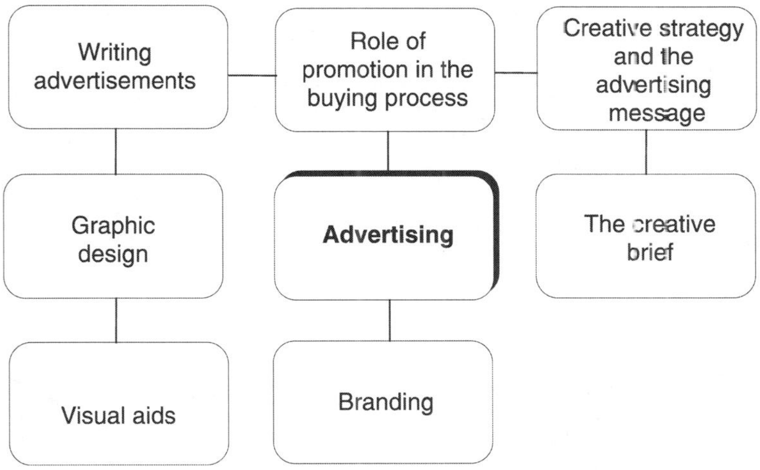

Introduction

This chapter will provide an understanding of advertising as just one element of the marketing communications mix. It is important to recognise this as many individuals use the word advertising when referring to all forms of promotional activity.

Branding will be discussed, as branding is not just a case of placing a symbol or name onto products to identify the manufacturer. A brand is a set of attributes, that have a meaning, an image and produce associations when being considered by a consumer.

The creative aspects of advertising will be considered in terms of strategy and the advertising message and the importance of the development of a clear creative brier.

The last part of this chapter will introduce the operational aspects of advertising, some guidelines for writing advertisements, principles of graphic design and finally the use of visual aids.

Your objectives

In this chapter you will learn about the following:

- (a) the role of advertising
- (b) the aspects of brand management
- (c) the importance of creative strategies
- (d) the function of the creative brief
- (e) guidelines for writing advertisements
- (f) the principles of graphic design
- (g) the main issues in using visual aids in advertising communications

1 ROLE OF PROMOTION IN THE BUYING PROCESS

The simple model below shows clearly the four flows that occur in an exchange process between the marketing company and the customer.

Model of the exchange between the marketing company and customers

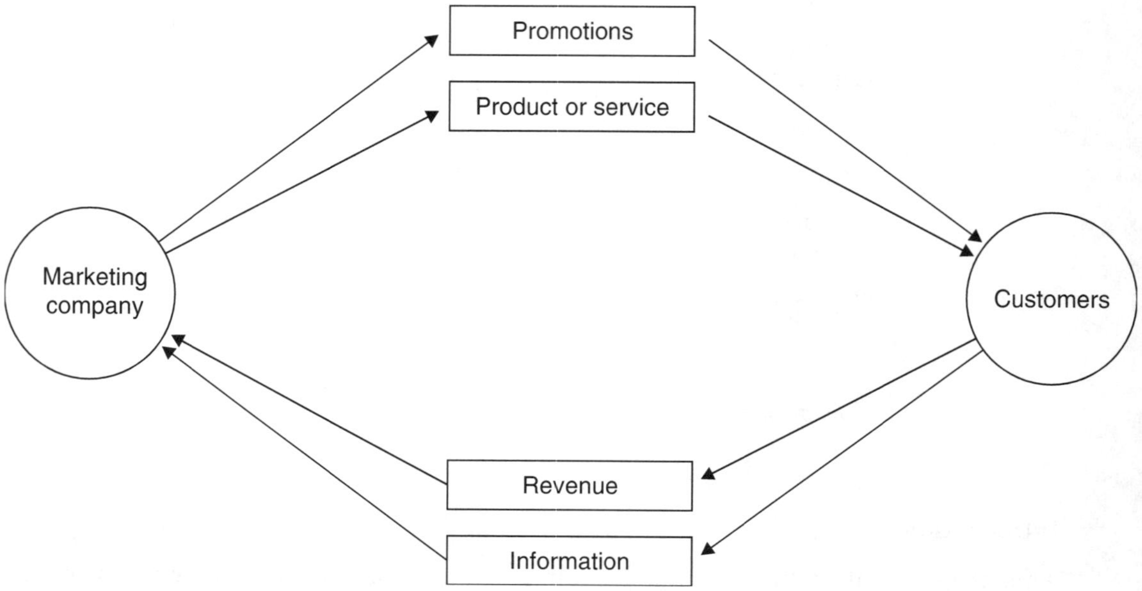

This model shows the importance of promotion in influencing the customer to buy a product or service.

Unit 18 requires you to cover buyer behaviour. Go back to Chapter 1 to learn about models of buyer behaviour. Below we discuss some of the issues particularly relevant for advertising.

1.1 The role of advertising

Definition

> **Advertising** is any paid form of non-personal presentation and promotion of ideas, goods or services by an identified sponsor.

It is an impersonal communications tool. Advertising is a means of reaching large audiences in a cost-effective manner. Personalised feedback from an advertising message is not usually obtained.

The purpose of advertising is to achieve set objectives. These objectives will vary depending on the product or service to be advertised; the stage it has reached in its life cycle; the marketplace in which it operates and the role advertising is to play.

It is *not* the purpose of advertising to win awards for creativity (though winning any sort of award is good publicity). In this chapter we are concerned with the practicalities of arranging for advertising to be used as a promotional tool.

1.2 Advertising objectives

The following are examples of advertising objectives, couched in broad terms.

(a) To support sales increases
(b) To encourage trial
(c) To create awareness
(d) To inform about a feature or benefit
(e) To remind
(f) To reassure
(g) To create an image
(h) To modify attitudes
(i) To gain trade and sales staff support

Advertisers will be expected to express objectives in 'SMART' terms. The broad objectives in (a) to (i) above should always be worked up into Specific, Measurable, Achievable, Relevant, Timed terms. Here are some examples.

(a) To support a sales increase on product X from 400,000 units to 500,000 units over the next 12 months.

(b) To raise awareness of service A amongst its target audience from its current level of 30% to 50% by the end of 1995

(c) To reinforce retailer Z's image as a company who offer a good range of basic food products at value for money prices.

Advertising is targeted at specific audiences segmented by demographic, geographic, behavioural or lifestyle variables.

FOR DISCUSSION

Classified advertisement columns are usually tightly packed with limited opportunity for individual advertisements to create impact. How can they then be effective?

Activity 1

Over the next week, note down one example of an advertising campaign from each of the following categories of advertising;

(a) Consumer goods
(b) Durables
(c) Retail
(d) Business to business
(e) Services
(f) Charity or not for profit

Try to analyse the advert, working backwards from the creative execution. Answer these questions:

(a) Who were the target market(s)?

(b) What were the advertising objectives?

(c) In your judgement, did the campaign succeed in meeting its objectives? Give reasons for your answer.

1.3 Principal benefits of advertising:

- reach mass audiences
- effective targeting
- low unit cost
- economical, efficient and effective at reaching large audiences
- successful at brand maintenance

1.4 Response hierarchy models

Response hierarchy (or hierarchy of effects)models attempt to predict the sequence of mental stages that the consumer passes through on the way to a purchase. Some of the major response hierarchy models are

(a) The AIDA model:

(b) The adoption model;

(c) DAGMAR (Defining Advertising Goals for Measured Advertising Response);

(d) Lavidge and Steiner's model.

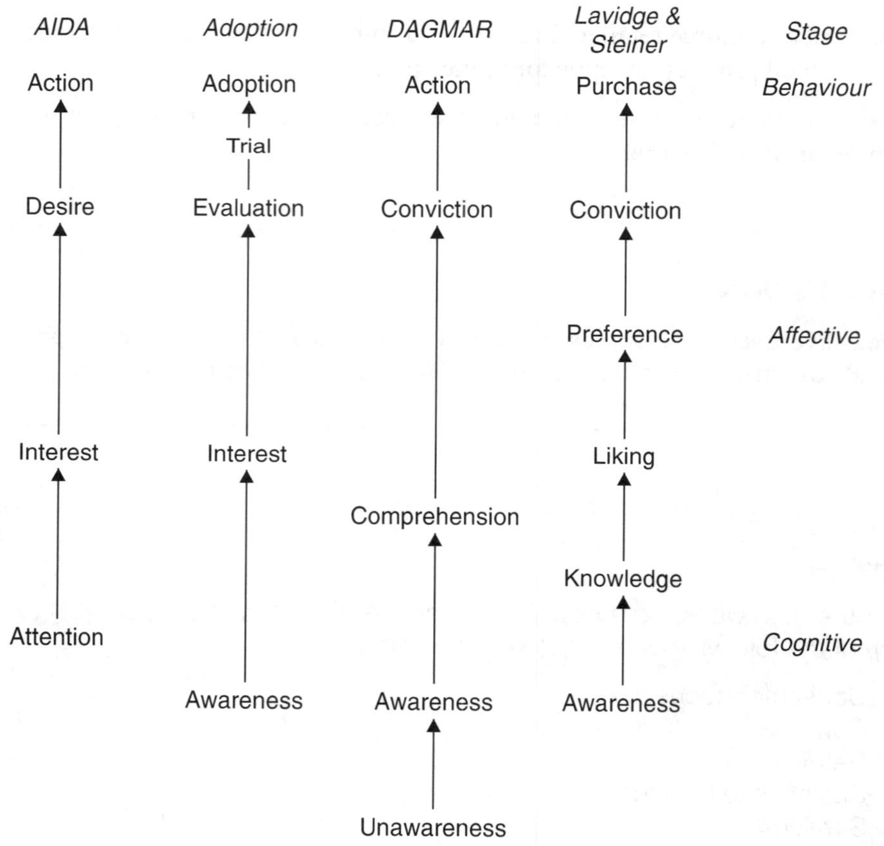

Source: *Adapted from PR Smith, Marketing Communications (1993)*

These models are useful in the sense that they attempt to **prioritise the communication objectives at various stages of the buying process**.

(a) These objectives can be classified into three main areas - cognitive, affective or behavioural. **Cognitive objectives** are concerned with creating knowledge or awareness in the mind of the consumer.

(b) **Affective objectives** are concerned with changing the consumer's attitude to the product as a whole or a specific aspect of the product.

(c) Behavioural objectives are concerned with getting the consumer to act in some way (buy the product).

These models have some drawbacks, as identified by Smith, *Marketing Communications: An Integrated Approach* (1993). As has been said, the core model of buying behaviour is most applicable to complex buying behaviour. In other situations the consumer may not go through the staged process of information search and evaluation of objectives before the purchase decision. Indeed, some of the stages might occur simultaneously, as in the case of an impulse purchase. Buyers may also bypass the hierarchy of stages. For example, during the evaluation stage a buyer may go back to the information search stage in order to obtain more information before making the decision to buy.

However, AIDA and similar 'Hierarchy of Effects' models, are now considered to be too rigid, inflexible and an inappropriate explanation of the communication process.

1.5 Sales, persuasion, involvement and saliency

The **Sales, Persuasion, Involvement** and **Saliency** frameworks (Hall and O'Malley) are considered by some to be more acceptable.

Sales	Advertising works on the basis that affects sales directly, and nothing else is worth considering.
Persuasion	Advertising works by persuading people to act (to buy products and services) in ways that they might not have acted had they not seen/heard the advertising message. For example, Ronseal (wood staining and preservatives), Pantene.
Involvement	Advertising works by drawing people into an advertisement and making associations between the advertisement and the product/brand. For example, Nescafe Gold Blend, Yellow Pages.
Saliency	Advertising works by standing out and being different from other advertisements, especially those in the same category. For example, Pot Noodle or Tango.

Activity 2 **(10 minutes)**

Find two further examples for each of the persuasion involvement and saliency interpretations of advertising.

Underpinning many of these views is the notion that advertising can persuade people to purchase products.

1.6 The ATRN model

Definition

Ehrenberg counters this view with an **ATRN (Awareness, Trial, Reinforcement and Nudge)** model, which interprets advertising as a 'Weak Force'. This says that advertising reinforces previous purchase decisions and serves to defend them and maintain market share.

NOTES

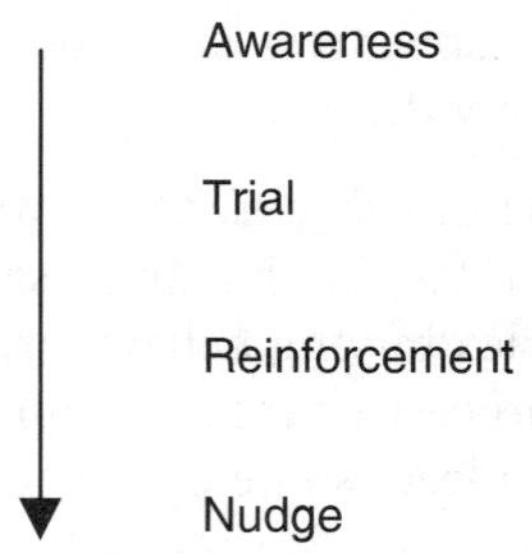

The ATRN model of advertising (after Ehrenberg 1997)

Both models accept that **awareness is a necessary prerequisite** for purchase, although it may not always be through advertising. Ehrenberg argues that there is no evidence that consumers feel anything like desire when they buy toilet cleaning products or coffee or tinned tomatoes. If a potential purchaser shows some interest in a product, perhaps because it is new or significant to them at that particular time, then they might try or **experiment** with the product. If this is successful then a repeat purchase may be made. With reinforcement, the purchaser might be encouraged to add the product to their repertoire or evoked set (a small cluster of brands in each product category from which purchase decisions are made, as loyalty to a single brand is rare).

Advertising can assist any of these stages and can nudge people into buying one particular brand from their repertoire.

There is no fixed model of advertising. However, research suggests that advertising might be more effective when combined with brands, so that potential purchasers are enabled to develop links or associations between a brand and its advertising and related communications. IMC has a significant role to play in assisting the development of co-ordinated messages in order to help develop this brand/advertising association.

1.7 The promotion mix

Kotler identifies four **categories of promotional activity**

Promotional	Comment
Advertising	Any **paid** form of non-personal presentation and promotion of ideas, goods or services by an identified sponsor.
Sales promotion	Encourage through incentives, over a short-term period, the purchase of the good or service.
Personal selling	The oral presentation of the goods or services, either to make a sale, or to create goodwill to improve the prospects of sales in the future.
Public relations	Unlike advertising, publicity cannot be bought and it might be thought of as unpaid advertising. Although organisations will spend large sums of money on publicity, they do not formally buy space in a newspaper or time on television or radio. Nor do they usually control the content of the publicity message, and so some publicity can be bad rather than good. However, they often try to manage publicity through the use of public relations.

Marketing communications convey information about the product and the company. Recently, the trend is towards **integrated marketing communications**. In other words, the marketing communications should be integrated with the business strategy, the other elements of the marketing mix, and with each other. Few organisations practise an integrated communications approach in any systematic way. The various tools of marketing communications have traditionally been the exclusive preserve of different groups within the organisation.

Promotion is the element of the mix most under control of the marketing department. Piercy suggests that, as far as managers are concerned, there are a number of issues which must be considered strategically for each form of communication.

Issue	Comment
Role	**Each form of communication has a different target.** Media advertising is direct to the end user, whereas personal selling may be preferred for distributors.
Objectives	Each form of communication needs specific objectives: • Advertising: raising awareness, repositioning • Public relations: favourable press exposure • Personal selling: sales targets, client relationships • Sales promotion: sample rates
Process management	This covers relationships with external suppliers, budgeting, recruiting and personnel
Integration	The elements of the mix should be integrated so that all customers get the appropriate message, and the different elements of the mix do not conflict with each other.

Key strategic developments in promotion

Development	Consequence
Database marketing and data mining	This enables targeting of promotional messages.
Digital TV, many channels	It will be harder to reach a single audience: rather like the trade magazine sector, fragmentation may cut advertising rates.
Internet	Internet advertisements are generally **sought** out by 'surfers' , possibility of interactive marketing, concerns about junk e-mail, concerns about low profitability of Internet firms.
Call centres	Telephone call centres are mushrooming over the country. They provide sales and customer support activity. They tend to be rigid and bureaucratic in style.
Sponsorship	Sports and cultural organisations are seeking sponsors. Like all forms of activity, the sponsor has objectives to fulfil. This can be a difficult relationship. Sponsorship is not intrusive.
Personal advice and loyalty	As service industries develop, there will be greater scope for personal service such as financial services.
Lobbying	Some decisions regarding product standardisation and safety will be taken at EU level. Expertise in this area is necessary.

2 BRANDING

As the choices available to the consumer becomes ever wider and products themselves become ever more similar in terms of the benefits and quality they offer, organisations are realising that they will only be able to compete effectively if their product has a distinctive 'voice', that helps consumers to single out their product above the noise made by competitors. In marketing this voice is called the **brand.**

A brand comprises 'intangible values created by a badge of reassurance'. The terminology perhaps makes the BMW badge leap to mind, together with reassurances about quality, performance and technological excellence that amount to status in the mind of the consumer.

Activity 3 **(15 minutes)**

What beliefs and expectations do you have about the following brands? How far are these due to promotion as opposed to personal experience?

(a) Fairy Liquid
(b) Persil washing powder
(c) HSBC bank
(d) Your own company's brand
(e) Land Rover
(f) Aldi

You might find it easier to focus if you compare the brands listed with other brands of the same product.

Definition

Brand – the totality of what the consumer takes into consideration before making a purchase decision.

2.1 Branding strategy

A brand can identify one item, a family of items or the seller. There are four main branding strategies.

1. Corporate umbrella – eg Heinz
2. Family umbrella – an organisation has a corporate brand and a separate brand for its products, eg Marks and Spencer's St Michael brand
3. Range branding – a number of related products are grouped together under one brand name, eg Weightwatchers
4. Individual branding – each product is branded separately, eg Penguin biscuits

Since the mid 1980s, the competitive balance of power has gradually shifted from manufacturers to retailers. This has resulted in retailers using proprietary own-label brands as strategic weapons against competitors.

Definition

Own-label brand – product that carries the name of the resellers – wholesalers or retailers – rather than the manufacturer's, and is sold exclusively through the resellers' outlets.

Euromonitor (1986) defined six main types of own-label branding.

1. Using a different name, eg Marks and Spencer's St Michael
2. Using the reseller's own name
3. 'Super' own labels, eg Sainsbury's Novon range
4. 'Exclusive' own label, eg Tesco's luxury range
5. Generics, eg Tesco's Value range
6. Surrogates which are manufacturers' brands that are exclusive to a chain of stores

2.2 Consumer and brand owner brand benefits

	Key benefit	Component
Consumer	Identification	simplifies improved
	Risk assessment	guarantees consistent quality
	Representation	embodies values, eg luxury, VFM
Brand owner	Price premium	increased profits
	Brand loyalty	reduced threat of price war
	Growth	NPD
	Barriers to entry	competitors find less attractive
	Legal device	protect from counterfeiting and look-a-likes

2.3 Brand equity

There are two contrasting views of brand equity. From the financial perspective, the brand is viewed as an asset. As such, greater brand equity can be expected to result in greater market shares, opportunities for premium pricing, reduced promotional costs, and increased trade leverage. For example, Proctor and Gamble recently asserted that their brands are valued at some £8 billion.

Definition

> **Brand equity** – the strength, currency and value of the brand ... the description and assessment of the appeal to all the target audiences who interact with it.

The alternative is the marketing view of brand equity. In essence, this views the situation from the perspective of the consumer. Those brands which have achieved substantial equity are those which can sustain a platform of premium quality, differentiated clear imagery and a uniqueness of proposition.

Definition

> **Unique selling proposition** (or point) (USP) – a term coined by Rosser Reeves to suggest that advertising strategy (and by implication other marketing communications) works best if there is a single, clear and unequivocal selling proposition.

There are a series of important components of brand equity:

- perceived quality - correlates closely to sales performance, price sensitivity and company value
- salience - indicates the proportion of people who have a perception of brand equity
- association - with positive images
- customer satisfaction - and therefore loyalty is an indicator of market success
- repeat purchase - and also willingness to recommend
- price premium potential - extent to which a brand can command a premium

Definition

> **Salience** – the term given to represent the degree of relevance a brand may have to a consumer. The concept of salience recognises that it will vary between customers, and that brand values are not determined in terms of there being a single best brand.

> **Activity 4** **(5 marks)**
>
> Ford own Jaguar. Given the means, why are you unlikely to be able to buy a product called a 'Ford Jaguar'?

2.4 Promotion and branding

Promotion cannot create a brand on its own. Obviously a pricing brand needs an appropriate price. A Rolex watch needs to be a product made of real gold. You might not want to be seen in an Armani suit if you could buy one in Asda. The whole of the marketing mix plays a part in establishing the personality of the brand.

The term brand 'personality' (or brand 'image') is revealing, though. What a product says to you, what is said about it, how it looks and where it is seen are all aspects of *communication*. A *name* and a *symbol* are key constituents in many definitions of the brand.

We shall be looking at the contribution that promotional tools such as advertising, sales promotion, public relations and so on make in communicating the brand image in Chapter 14. The key concept to take with you as you proceed is consistency: all of the tools must be integrated and work together to communicate a single consistent message.

DISCUSSION

The major world advertisers each spend millions of pounds worldwide. Their products are already widely known so that there can be little need to raise awareness levels. If this is so, what is the main purpose of advertising for such advertisements?

---

3 CREATIVE STRATEGYAND THE ADVERTISING MESSAGE

One of the crucial elements in the communication process is the creative stance taken by the advertising agency when designing commercials for television and the artwork for posters and press. The creative aspects may well be the vital ingredient for success. They may equally be the undoing of a carefully planned marketing strategy.

(a) A **generic strategy** is one which is based upon straight facts and does not attempt to make any distinguishing claims between one product and the next.

(b) **Pre-emptive strategy** is used where there are only limited differences between the products within a given product class. A pre-emptive strike attempts to say something about the product, which other competitors would be reluctant to adopt, in case they were labelled as blatant imitators. The constant battle between Procter & Gamble and Unilever in the soap detergent war is a good example of this kind of strategy.

(c) A **unique selling proposition** (USP) relates to the ability of a company to establish and communicate a distinct product benefit which competitors cannot make or refuse to make.

(d) **Brand image** is concerned more with psychological rather than physical differences between products. The aim is to associate the product with symbols and characters who relate to the potential target audience.

(e) **Positioning** attempts to define in the consumer's mind the comparisons between one product and the next. The task is to identify weaknesses in competing products and strengths in your own which can be reinforced so as to gain a competitive edge. (Stella Artois beer is 'reassuringly expensive'.)

(f) A **resonance strategy** is one which 'strikes a cord' with the consumer. The intention is to portray a life style orientation which is synonymous with the target group and one which is easily recognisable. The type of advertisements with which this is associated are typically the 'Is this you' scenario.

(g) **Affective strategy** is currently widely adopted by companies wishing to play on, as much as play to, the emotions of the consumer.

(h) **Informational strategy** is based on the view that an important element of the creative theme is to convey information, eg drug awareness campaigns.

Some of the more successful advertising strategies will integrate two or more of the above, so as to create maximum impact.

DISCUSSION

Creativity can be applied to all aspects of marketing communications.

3.1 Balance of the message and audience involvement

Our understanding of the **level of involvement** that may exist in the target audience can be used to determine the **overall balance of the message**.

(a) If there is **high involvement** then interested members of the target audience will **actively seek information**. Messages therefore tend to be rational, proclaiming product benefits and the key attributes.

(b) Where there is **low involvement** the audience are not really interested and **need to be drawn to the communication message**. In these cases, image-based appeals tend to be more successful and the use of emotion rather than logic predominates.

HIGH INVOLVEMENT	RATIONAL APPEALS BASED ON PRODUCT ATTRIBUTES INFORMATION PROVISION + BENEFIT CLAIMS
LOW INVOLVEMENT	EMOTIONAL APPEALS BASED ON IMAGERY SOCIAL, EGO AND HEDONIC ORIENTATION

If integration and consistency is to be achieved then adherence to an emotional or rational approach has to be maintained throughout all the promotional tools.

There are a number of ways in which the rational and image based messages can be presented to audiences. These are referred to as message appeals and some of the more common approaches are rational based appeals and image based appeals.

3.2 Rational based appeals

Issue	Comment
Factual	The benefits are presented using reasoned, factual arguments (eg nicotine patches).
Slice of Life	Allow the target customer to identify with the characters and a common problem. Brand X is then perceived as a suitable solution (eg washing powders).
Demonstration	Show the audience how the product solves a problem (eg floor cleaners, before and after use).
Comparative	Through comparison it is possible to achieved enhanced status and superiority (eg credit and charge cards).

3.3 Image based appeals

Issue	Comment
Fear	The suggestion of physical danger or social rejection might be alleviated through use of the brand (eg car safety; acne cream).
Humour	Attention and mood can be maintained by relaxing the target audience (eg Boddingtons).
Animation	For low interest products/services, animation can attract attention and convey complex products/issues in a novel manner (eg Clover, Tetley Tea Bags).
Sex	Used primarily to attract attention and to be salient (eg Diet Coke, Wonderbra, Citroen Xsara).
Music	Provides campaign continuity and a degree of differentiation through recognition (eg Ford Cougar, Peugeot 406).
Fantasy	Used to engage an audience and to encourage the question 'what is going on here?' (eg Silk Cut, Ericsson).

4 THE CREATIVE BRIEF

4.1 Instructions

Briefs are 'informative' in the sense that they equip people with information that they can use to perform various tasks - but this is a different function from the brief which acts as an **instruction**: guidance and specification for performance.

The main points about a creative brief is that it should be:

(a) Clear
(b) Sufficient

for the agency to proceed to fulfil the instructions to your satisfaction.

Definition

Creative brief – document that provides an outline of the creative task and the basis for creatives to develop their solutions.

A complete and detailed brief may include the following elements.

(a) Desired outcomes or results, including:

- (i) The standard to which they should be achieved
- (ii) The criteria on which successful performance will be judged
- (iii) The time-scale within which the task or project must be completed
- (iv) Resources available; financial targets and budgets set; payments agreed and so on

(b) Definition of all relevant terms, to minimise misunderstanding.

(c) A breakdown of the task or project into logical components, and their:

- (i) Context
- (ii) Requirements
- (iii) Resource budgets (if relevant)
- (vi) Methods (if required) - don't try to teach the experts their job
- (v) Relevant background.

(d) Information required to understand and carry out the task ('briefing' in the other sense).

Definition

Creative theme/concept – the basic or fundamental creative idea to be conveyed.

4.2 Advertising agency brief

Purpose: To instruct agency/copy writer on which products the client wishes to push, and when and how

To analyse/interpret the market of the product for the agency

To give relevant information about the features and benefits of the product

Audience: May not have technical knowledge/awareness of product

May not know the market for the product as you do
Need something to go on: 'shots in the dark' are expensive

4.3 Suggested structure

	Notes
Purpose/objectives of task (i) What it sets out to achieve. (ii) Where ad will be placed (if known). (iii) Deadlines. (iv) Budget (if known).	(i) eg to counter competitor demand, or launch new products. Be as specific as possible. eg a main launch ad plus 3 follow up ads at around half the price of the launch ad. (ii) Media choice may be part of the task.
Information about the market (i) Who are the audience/potential buyers? (ii) Constraints and opportunities. (iii) Buying habits and patterns. (iv) Important features of the market.	(i) Audience tastes, habits, age/sex etc. (ii) Restrictive legislation, competitor activity, new technology etc. (iii) Seasonal demand, tendency to buy through main/retail outlets etc. (iv) Any features of the market that you (and your competitors) take into account: price sensitivity, technology etc.
Information about the product (i) USP (unique selling proposition). (ii) Benefits to consumers. (iii) Price. (iv) Nearest competition. (v) Other features that might inspire the agency.	(i) Any 'edge' your product has over competition. (ii) Why would the consumer *want* to buy?
Information about the client (i) Corporate history and culture. (ii) Customer relations.	Ads should reflect what the organisation feels about itself: the client is in any case unlikely to accept a proposal which is uncongenial to its culture and image.

The 'background' information may, as you can see, be extensive. It may be helpful to provide product brochures and so on. However, a specifically-targeted brief such as the above will highlight the most usable factors, from the agency's point of view: audience characteristics, USP, benefits and so on. A simple **briefing digest** or aid may be prepared by the copywriter from a less helpfully structured brief: or may be provided by the briefing organisation. Here is an example.

(a) *The brief*

The task is to launch a new portable printer for a firm producing small-size office electronics for the home-user and small business. The ad is to appear in national press in February. The printer (the X40) is the first cordless portable on the market. It offers a choice of typestyles, a colour option, and various paper sizes. It costs £210.

The target audience is people who work from home, and people who travel in the course of their work and need printing facilities.

(b) *Briefing aid*

Task: Press advertisement

Media: National press

Deadline: February

Product: X40

Price: £210

USPs:		*Benefits:*
1 First ever cordless	→	1 Will operate anywhere
2 Compact, lightweight	→	2 Easy to carry
3 Choice of typefaces	→	3 Professional presentation
4 Colour option	→	4 Good for graphics
5 Various paper sizes	→	5 Versatile

Market: Freelance writers/journalists
Small businesses
Home use
Sales executives

Much the same structure will be usable for other briefing situations, such as:

(a) Briefing an artist or designer to prepare artwork for ads or sales literature

(b) Briefing a research agency (or staff) to design a questionnaire and research programme to find defined market/customer information

(c) Briefing an employee to:

(i) Prepare a report
(ii) Conduct an interview

EXAMPLE: ARTIST/DESIGNER BRIEF

	Notes
Purpose/objectives of task (i) What task needs to achieve (ii) Media with size/colour requirements (iii) Deadlines (iv) Budget	(i) Purpose, method of campaign. Place of task in campaign (if only one element) (ii) eg A5 6 pp brochure in 4 colours, or A4 black and white ad (iv) Including artist's fee + printing costs: a constraint on the artist's imagination
Information about the market and medium (i) Audience composition and tastes (ii) Media style and constraints	(i) Verbally/visually inclined? What images? etc (ii) Glossy magazine, or tabloid. Paper quality, colours, space size etc.
Information about the product and message (i) Priorities (ii) Features (iii) Content	(i) Which are the important items that need emphasising in the design. (ii) What features should be reflected in the design style? (iii) Are there photographs/ drawings/text to be incorporated: if so, of what type, how big? etc.
Information about the client (i) House 'style' (ii) Culture	(i) Logotypes, house style for design or layout etc. Does this task need to match other output? (ii) Is the organisation design-oriented? Modern or old-fashioned? etc.

Activity 5 **(30 minutes)**

Undertake an analysis of marketing communications materials – packaging, press advertisements, posters, direct mailings, exhibition stands etc – to assess the creative treatments used.

Identify the creative themes adopted and compare competitor approaches. Try to place the strategies adopted into one of the earlier listed categories.

5 WRITING ADVERTISEMENTS

Advertisements may, of course, be oral and visual as well as written. The advantage of a **written** advertisement is that it can increase the length and frequency of the recipient's exposure to the advertising message: it can be perused slowly and carefully, and more than once - unlike a radio or television advertisement, which 'goes by'. This enables the advertiser to put **more content** into the advertisement, if he wishes or needs to. Indeed in some contexts, such as advertising in railway stations, trains and newspapers, the length and complexity of the content may add to the audience's motivation and attention: they are attracted to text they can read while waiting for a train.

Written advertisements can be placed in a wide variety of media.

Media can be classified and appraised according to:

(a) **Editorial contents** (news, general interest, special interest, trade/profession)

(b) **Circulation** size (net sales), area (local, national, regional) and type (subscription, bought or free)

(c) **Type of reader**, or 'quality' (socio-economic class, background, special interests, age, profession etc which imply motivation and ability to spend money on the advertised product)

(d) **Frequency** of publication (daily, weekly, monthly, annual)

(e) **Production** (colour or black and white, 'glossy' or newsprint, loose-leaf or bound, size etc)

(f) **Cost of advertising space**, usually calculated as cost **per** page, **per** thousand readers (including extra expenses of colour, special positions etc)

5.1 Selecting the 'right' medium

(a) Identify the target group of people you wish to reach and influence.

(b) Identify media which they read frequently and dependably.

(c) Select, from these media, those which give you:

- (i) **The widest coverage of your target group** (ie wide circulation **and** relevant readership profile)
- (ii) **With the greatest frequency** (not just frequency of publication, eg daily newspapers, but frequency of reference: weeklies like the **Radio Times** are referred to several times)
- (iii) **With the greatest credibility** (where the editorial content is congenial, authoritative and relevant to the target group's motives and interests)
- (iv) **At the lowest cost**

Activity 6 **(20 minutes)**

(a) What media do *you* read regularly? List them.

(b) Classify them according to each of the factors mentioned in Paragraph 5, (a)-(f).

(c) If you wanted to advertise to people like yourself, which would you choose?

NOTES

DISCUSSION

Advertising is used extensively in industrial and business to business settings and not just for consumer promotions.

5.2 The advertising message

The general purposes of all advertisements are as follows.

(a) **Attract the attention**. You cannot expect - or instruct - people to read your message: you have to gain their attention, in competition with other messages and distractions.

(b) **Hold the attention**. In the words of H C Carter *(Effective Advertising)* you have to 'entice reluctant, busy eyes to scan your message and decide to read on. If, after that, the reader is disturbed by [various distractions], he or she must be sufficiently interested in your advertisement to make a point of returning to it.'

(c) **Persuade the reader**, so that:

(i) Desire (in some form) is aroused, so the reader is 'motivated'.

(ii) An **action or decision** is taken in your favour: whether proactively (the reader calls, sends a coupon, goes out to purchase) or reactively (the reader sees the product in the shop, or is offered the product by a salesman, and - recollecting the positive response to the ad - accepts it).

5.3 The selling theme or 'angle'

An effective advertisement will have a main theme or angle, within which selling points can be conveyed. The selling points will support and build the persuasive argument, but the main theme will hold them together in a single, more powerful message.

Step 1. Start with a list of the product's features.

Step 2. Highlight those features which are new and particularly those which differentiate your product from its competitors in the market. These are your main selling points.

Step 3. Identify those features which are relevant to the purpose and audience (their motives/attributes etc) of the ad: discard those that are negative, or irrelevant, and cannot be 'turned around' in order to be made positive.

Step 4. Now consider what exactly is 'in it' for the customer: how can each selling point or feature be seen as a **benefit** by the customer? Express each selling point and feature as a benefit.

Step 5. Select the selling point/feature/benefit(s) that will **most effectively** persuade the customer to buy the product. Price? Quality? Convenience? Reliability? Prestige? Effectiveness? Environment-friendliness? This will be your **selling proposition**, or **main selling theme**.

Example

Product: BPP HND Coursebooks

Audience: HND students and tutors

Audience motives: Desire for exam success
Need for confidence
(syllabus changes etc)
Fear of risk

Features: (*possible selling points)	→ *Benefits:*
Comprehensive coverage*	Little wasted effort in studying (ease)
Relevant coverage	Reduces uncertainty
Activities	(confidence: success)
Regularly updated*	Reduced risk of outdated knowledge (success)
Easy to use style and features	Makes studying easier (ease)

Main selling themes

You can be confident of exam Success	- combining 2 major benefits, meeting needs
- comprehensively prepared	- utilising selling point 1
- this year and every year	- utilising selling point 2
(And though it won't be easy, we'll make it as painless as possible.)	- adding third relevant benefit

5.4 The 'copy'

Having already listed all the product's features, expressed them as benefits, selected those most relevant to the prospective buyer, and thereby decided on the main selling theme, you have all the ammunition you require to write your text or **copy**.

(a) Draft a few simple statements to outline your selected propositions and benefits.

(b) Discard any 'extra' benefits - however interesting in themselves - that only dilute your argument, or do not fit into your primary theme.

(c) Find the words which will express your remaining statements most powerfully.

(d) Discard unnecessary words and ideas and use their 'space' to repeat, enliven and highlight the main ideas.

Activity 7 **(30 minutes)**

Pick a product you know a bit about, and have a go at writing an advertisement, using the procedure set out above.

Definition

Knocking copy – text that offers negative or disparaging comments about someone or something else.

5.5 Ten Commandments for advertising copy

Carter puts forward a number of rules which he believes are essential to success in all forms of advertising. We have adapted them as 10 Commandments, as follows.

1 **Be simple**

Avoid technical and exclusive vocabulary.

Use short, easy sentences where possible.

Avoid complex reasoning: keep logical progression and links obvious and simple, so an averagely intelligent person can follow you.

2 **Be interesting**

Attract attention: make the reader look - then engage.

Use vivid words, enthusiastic tone, congenial images ('cosy home' for 'comfortable house', say).

Arouse curiosity, where possible: use questions and surprises.

Focus on benefits to the consumer; he will rarely be interested in the product features as such.

3 **Be brief**

Get to the point quickly: be direct.

Small areas of text are easily scanned and so attract the reader.

Leave out unnecessary 'padding' (sentences **and** words).

Prune ruthlessly: retain only what is necessary for sense, style and rhythm.

4 **Be positive**

Convert warnings and negatives ('Don't miss out on') to positive encouragement ('Take advantage of').

Use positive motivations, generally, rather than negative (eg: desire for success, not fear of failure).

5 **Be factual**

Keep to the 'real world' of the product and consumer, unless the need for colourful presentation really requires imaginative fantasy.

6 **Be honest**

The Advertising Standards Authority Code of Practice bans extravagant or misleading claims, indecent copy or illustration, and illegal statements. Besides, dishonest claims get found out (causing disappointment and loss of credibility) and titillating images are generally 'seen through' as the last resort they often are.

7 **Be original**

Original 'angles' and unusual use of design or words create impact.

Don't be too clever: you may lose the sense or credibility of the message.

8 **Be emphatic**

Reduce the number of points or themes to a minimum. Then you can repeat, emphasise and illustrate those points, for impact and recall. Use variation, vividness and humour to disguise repetition and avoid boredom.

9 **Be instructive**

State strongly, frequently and clearly: why, where, when and how to order/ purchase/enquire etc (eg: 'Call us now for details'. 'In all good bookshops now'. 'Send the coupon today: no stamp required'.) Reinforce with incentive if necessary (eg discount for early order, free gift for first order).

10 **Be self-contained**

Avoid direct comparison with competitors by name; it merely gives them free publicity and implies that you are worried by their product/performance: the reader may investigate.

> **Activity 8** **(30 minutes)**
>
> Get hold of a convenient newspaper journal or magazine. Pick an advertisement that you find interesting.
>
> (a) Why did that particular ad attract your eye?
>
> (b) Evaluate its adherence to each of the 'rules' give above. (If it did not obey them, did that make the ad less effective, in your opinion - or did the copy writer achieve the desired effect in an original way?)
>
> (c) Repeat the exercise with a number of other ads: develop your awareness of advertisers' techniques (good and bad).

5.6 Advertising style

As you can see from the above, advertising style is brief, simple, and 'intense' - packing emphasis, repetition and interest into the small number of chosen points. Applying what we have already said about persuasive style, you should consider the following.

(a) **Emphasis** - by repetition, graphic design (emboldening, underlining, isolation in space, size etc), and sentence/paragraph structure.

(b) **Pace and fluency** - by varying sentence/paragraph lengths, and connecting sentences using logical links. (In advertising, it is considered acceptable to start sentences - actually clauses - with 'and', 'but', 'because' and so on).

(c) **Informality** - by using colloquial language and the kind of style you would use to explain the proposition or describe the product to a friend.

(d) **Appeal to audience motivations.** Words like 'now', 'free', 'new', 'save', 'value', 'quality', 'care' or 'family' - trite though they may seem - have powerful associations with consumers' needs for security, success, and belonging (and related fears) and perceptions of what they want from a product or organisation.

(e) **Credibility and congeniality**. Especially if the product is expensive, the reader will need to trust and relate to the ad before being persuaded - just as in face-to-face selling. So do not exaggerate, bully or patronise. Make sure that the ad is as well-presented, error-free and as helpful as possible.

(f) **Presentation**. We will be looking at graphic design later in this chapter. You should be aware of the use of:

- (i) **Space** - to attract attention, and make reading easy.
- (ii) **Typestyle** - and variation of it: to attract attention and convey impressions.
- (iii) **Illustration** - line drawings, photographs, colour illustrations, symbols etc: to attract attention, add information, or add interest. Consider whether the effect is clear, relevant, in tune with the style of the whole ad, and worthwhile enough to justify the use of space.
- (iv) **Colour** - for visibility, and to convey impressions or moods.
- (v) **Shape and texture** - to attract attention and enhance credibility.

(g) **Headlines and slogans**. Your aim is to attract attention by use of curiosity, or interesting language, or relevance to the audience's needs/wants/interests/ attitudes, or (ideally) all three. A headline should be a statement of the advertisement's main theme or proposition, put as pithily and attention-grabbingly as possible. Use:

(i) Puns, verbal or visual (referring to an illustration). Use carefully - they need to be subtle, yet easy to 'get'.

(ii) Questions.

(iii) Adaptations of well-known phrases or sayings.

(iv) Balanced phrases or word patterns.

(v) Controversial statements.

(vi) Appeals to powerful motivators like greed/loyalty/security/ambition/friendship.

(vii) Curiosity. ('Teaser' headlines do **not** sum up the selling proposition, but draw the reader into the copy - where the selling proposition should be **immediately** introduced).

(viii) Humour. The words need not be humorous in themselves, but may interact in a witty way with a picture.

Activity 9

Needless to say, you should study magazines, newspapers and posters to see all of these points in action.

The same advice applies even if you are writing and laying out a simple advertisement for the notice board at your college or workplace. The function of such an advertisement will be primarily to inform. Originality, creativity and competitive attention-grabbing will not be required to the same extent as in a press advertisement, especially if the topic of the ad is relevant to your fairly small, fairly familiar target audience.

5.7 Gaining attention

Here are 35 ways of gaining attention in advertisement.

1 Humour
2 Real life dramatisations
3 Slices of life
4 Testimonials
5 Guarantees
6 Comparisons
7 Problem solving
8 Characters
9 Talking heads
10 Recommendations
11 Reasons why
12 Facts
13 News
14 Emotion
15 Cartoons
16 Animation
17 Charts
18 Computer graphics
19 Claymation
20 Music
21 Symbols
22 Animals
23 Contests
24 Offers
25 Exaggeration
26 Glamour
27 Personalities
28 Spokespersons
29 Freephone numbers
30 The product alone
31 The product in use
32 Different uses of the product
33 Effects of not using the product
34 Before and after
35 The package as the star

6 GRAPHIC DESIGN

6.1 Principles of graphic design

There are no hard and fast rules in graphic design. It is best to be flexible, since appropriateness to the specific context is the most important thing - and the unexpected and unusual can be very effective, too.

6.2 Qualities of good design.

(a) *Suitability*

As ever, consider your purpose and your audience. Graphic elements should be appropriately related:

(i) To your message
(ii) To their surroundings

(b) *Consistency*

Allowing for variety and contrast, you should be consistent within each page and within the communication as a whole. Design elements such as margins, headlines, borders, straight or ragged line ends, indentation of new paragraphs and so on should be consistently handled. Even typestyle and size should not be changed unless there is a positive effect to be gained.

(c) *Tension*

Balance - equally sized elements, symmetrically arranged - can be satisfying to the eye as a whole picture. However, it can lead to boredom, indecision and interrupted eye movement when it comes to reading. Tension - created by unequal left/right or top/bottom balance - provides visual interest and 'movement' on the page, and is helpful in pulling the reader onwards through the text. The balance of a page can be altered by focusing interest off-centre: having a larger illustration towards one side, or towards the top or bottom, or using white space to unbalance text (eg by having columns of unequal length.)

Balance

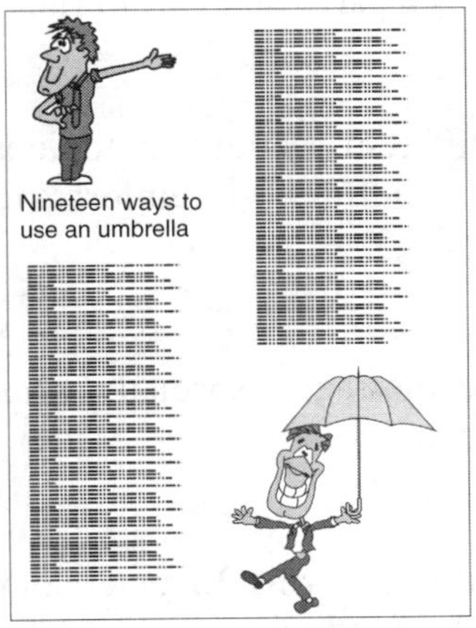

Tension

(d) *Continuity*

Balance on the page can create interrupted eye movement, as the eye attempts to see the whole picture, rather than following the line of meaning through the text. In a more obvious way, if your text is broken up with lots of devices and illustrations, the sense will be interrupted at each one: you risk losing the reader at each point.

(e) *Unity*

Just as a short message should have one dominant idea, and not more than three or four main points, so a page should be kept simple in order not to confuse the reader. There may be a rich variety of visual detail, but the design should give one dominant impression, and ideally have one dominant visual feature: a focal point to which the reader's eyes can be drawn, and on which they can rest, before beginning to move over the page. The dominant element may be:

- A headline
- A large photo or illustration
- A headline and illustration together
- A block of text, surrounded by white space

and so on.

Unifying headline

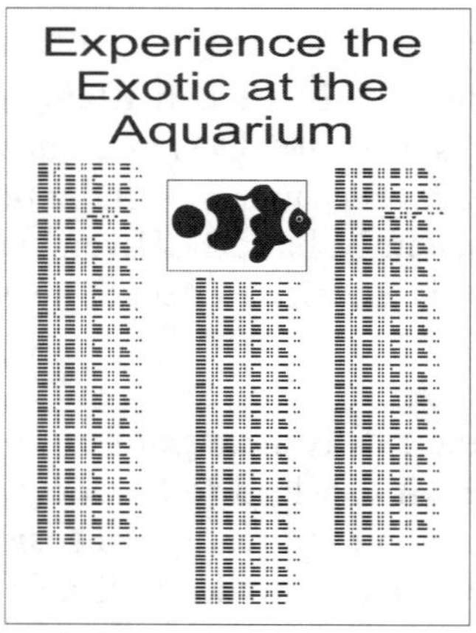

Unifying illustration

6.3 Colour

(a) Impact and interest.

(b) Emphasis.

Colour may be a means of highlighting a particular part of the page.

(c) Organisation

Different colours can be used for different sections or topic areas. Colour can be used on borders, rules or headlines to reinforce the message's structure for ease of reading.

(d) Meaning.

Colour can reflect or reinforce the message, especially where there are cultural norms about particular colours.

(e) Mood

Again, this tends to be a matter of cultural norms. In general, bright colours convey excitement, while subdued colours add dignity.

(f) Realism

Black and white pictures can be highly contrasted and textured, and so make a strong impression, but colour photographs offer a more accurate image of reality as we see it.

6.4 Typestyle

A huge selection of typestyles is now available in word processing packages, and. 'Typefaces' or 'Fonts', as they are called, vary widely in several areas.

(a) Ease of reading

(i) **Serif** type, like the text typeface used here, is characterised by small 'feet' or cross-lines at the ends of the main letter strokes. These draw the eye through letters and from one letter to another and make the face very easy to read: serif faces are often used for the body of text.

(ii) **Sans-serif** (without-serif) type, like the face used in our headings and subheadings, is more simple in appearance. It has great clarity, in small doses, and is ideal for headers, sub-headers, captions and writing for children.

(b) 'Personality' or mood.

(c) Emphasis and impact.

Different typefaces have different 'weights'. They may be **thick** (or 'bold') or thin ('light'). Bold typefaces in a small area highlight that area, altering the balance of the page, while light typefaces have an 'airier' appearance, especially where lines of text are also fairly widely spread.

In general, type size should be chosen according to:

(a) **Readability**. Consider your audience. Type size for an outdoor poster size will obviously be different to that in a letter or report: either way, the words should be legible without strain, particularly if the message is lengthy; and

(b) **Emphasis**. Consider balance, tension and unity (see Paragraph 2.1 above) and choose the relative proportions of your type elements accordingly. By and large your main header will be larger than your secondary headers, which will be larger than your sub-headers and so on.

7 VISUAL AIDS IN ADVERTISING COMMUNICATIONS

Visuals can certainly be:

(a) Clearer
(b) More impactful
(c) More memorable

than blocks of figures or text, because they are simplified, patterned and concrete (allowing lengthy or repeated perusal).

On the other hand, visual images are symbols - like language. They only communicate precisely and effectively if they are **shared** by the viewer and the communicator.

(a) **Visuals may be given a common meaning by consensus** - like the road signs used in the Highway Code, safety symbols, scientific and mathematical symbols.

(b) **Visuals may be given a meaning by the communicator**. In this case, he needs to inform the viewer of the meaning he attaches to the symbols he uses, unless it is extremely obvious.

(c) **Visuals may be given a wide range of meanings through association or resonance**. The associations evoked by a given image will be different according to the knowledge, experience, education, perceptions and expectations of the viewer. Symbols such as a cross or a heart have emotional and imaginative resonances beyond the simplicity of the image, because of the powerful associations built up in them over history.

7.1 The need for visual support

Visual aids should not be regarded as decoration or planned as features for their own sake. Visual aids are graphical symbols used to aid or support the main message. The type of visual support required should be clear, if you have properly defined your **purpose** in communicating, and the potential and problems offered by your **audience**.

If you are trying to persuade your audience that your washing powder washes whiter, for example, you might consider the following.

(a) If you are trying to persuade an audience of **chemists**, your aim will be information, explanation and evidence. You might choose to use diagrams of the chemical structure of whatever special ingredient your power contains, or a graph showing that lower water temperatures do not significantly reduce the powder's ability to kill bacteria.

(b) If you are trying to persuade an audience of **consumers**, your aim may be more to do with attitude change. You might use images of clothes before and after using the powder, to emphasise the after-wash whiteness. Or you may choose to show happy, active people in sparkling white clothes to accompany a verbal assertion that the powder washes whiter.

7.2 Diagrams

A diagram is basically a drawing or plan demonstrating the form or workings of something.

Diagrams have the following advantages for explaining and clarifying information.

(a) They show complex relationships and processes in a single image which can be perused at the reader's own pace, **unlike**:

   (i) A demonstration, which must be 'followed' as the events occur, with a danger of losing track or falling behind.

   (ii) A narrative description, which requires the reader/listener to remember and visualise each stage.

(b) They simplify and stylise the elements of the process or object, removing complicating or irrelevant factors.

In general, drawings are used to support **description**, since they convey appearance and to add visual **interest**, where a photograph would be difficult to obtain or reproduce. Photographs are generally more impactful, but drawings have the advantages of simplification, clarity and cleaner reproduction (where print quality or the surface of the paper may distort subtleties of shading in a photo). Compared to diagrams, illustration is less effective at conveying relationships and processes, but if you wished to show how each stage of a process **looked**, or to encourage reader identification by showing people **doing** whatever-it-was, an illustration would be more helpful: descriptive and 'human'.

7.3 Cartoons and animation

Cartoons are a variant on illustration: they are typically line drawings achieved with the greatest possible simplicity. They are generally associated with the use of humour, either in the images themselves, or in the juxtaposition of images and accompanying words. If you are fairly sure that the joke - or the style of humour generally - will be accessible to your audience, humour is an attention-grabbing and congenial method of emphasising a point, or encouraging the audience to look at something in a new way - to gain an insight into the topic. If humour is not shared by the audience, or is inappropriate to the situation, it may be confusing and /or damaging to the user's credibility as a source.

EXAMPLE

Many TV ads use animated cartoons to tell a story or capture the attention, or provide a readily recognisable symbol. An example is Felix the cat or even Hector (the Inland Revenue man).

7.4 Photographs

Photographs, whether black and white or colour, can be very impactful if well reproduced, and have a major advantage when it comes to implying realism, if required to 'prove' an event or situation. Photographic images may contain elements irrelevant to the main feature and message, but this can be avoided, or the viewer's attention can be suitably directed.

The main disadvantages to using photography are if the photographs are poor in quality (clarity, colour, exposure, composition and so on) or cannot be reproduced cleanly (if printing or paper quality is poor). In addition, you should consider whether the meaning and effect are worth the extra costs involved.

7.5 Balancing illustration and text

It is easy to get carried away with visual aids, especially if they seem more interesting, impactful or understandable than the accompanying text. However, visuals cannot contain and convey the same amount of information, with the same precision, as words can. A visual needs to be extremely impactful or significant to justify occupying space on a page that could be used for a number (often a large number) of words.

7.6 Digital imaging

Many graphic projects begin with analogue images such as 35mm slides, transparencies or reflective art. To produce a digital image, these elements are converted to digital files which can be manipulated on a computer system. This step is usually accomplished by scanning the analogue image. The scanner measures reflected or transmitted light from the analogue image, assigning numerical values to the colours or tones in the image to create a digital copy.

With the image translated into a series of numbers, the information can be stored on a computer hard disk or other electronic media such as a removable drive, photoCD or magnetic tape. Once the image has been converted to numbers, it can be transferred from one computer to another or sent electronically.

Definition

Analogue – data stored in a continuous form.

Digital – data processed using binary numbers via a scanner.

Scanner – an input device that digitises images, creating bit-mapped copies that can be manipulated electronically.

Chapter roundup

- Advertising is a means of reaching large audiences in a cost-effective manner.
- The purpose of advertising is to achieve set objectives.
- Response hierarchy models attempt to predict the sequence of mental stages that the consumer passes on the way to a purchase.
- The promotional mix can be defined as advertising, sales promotion, personal selling and public relations.
- A brand comprises intangible values created by a badge of reassurance.
- Own-label brands have been used by retailers since the mid 1980s as strategic weapons against competitors.
- Brand equity can be viewed from a financial perspective in terms of an asset or from a marketing perspective in terms of the customer perspective.
- Components of brand equity include perceived quality, salience, association, customer satisfaction, repeat purchase and price premium potential.
- Creative strategies will vary depending on the client, the product and the target market.
- A creative brief is used to equip an agency with the information needed to create communications.
- Media selection criteria include coverage, frequency, credibility and cost.
- Guidelines for advertising copy include being simple, interesting, brief, positive, factual, honest, original, emphatic, instructive and self-contained.
- Graphic design, use of colour and typestyle all make an important contribution to effective advertising.
- Visuals are used in advertising as they can be clearer, more memorable than text and create more impact.
- Many images are converted to digital format to facilitate computer manipulation.

Quick quiz

1. How can advertising be defined?
2. Give some examples of advertising objectives.
3. What are the principal benefits of advertising?
4. Name four response hierarchy models.
5. What does Ehrenberg's ATRN model stand for?
6. What is a brand?
7. What are the four main branding strategies?
8. What is meant by the term own-label brand?
9. What are the main brand owner's benefits of branding?
10. What is brand equity?

11 What is meant by the term salience?

12 List eight creative strategy options.

13 What is a creative brief?

14 What is meant by the term knocking copy?

15 What are the five key qualities of good design?

16 Why might analogue images be converted to digital?

Answers to quick quiz

1 Any paid form of non-personal presentation and promotion of ideas, goods or services by an identified sponsor. (See paragraph 1.1)

2 Increase sales, encourage trial, create awareness, inform, remind, reassure, create an image, modify attitudes, gain trade and sales staff support. (para 1.2)

3 Reach mass audience, effective targeting, low unit cost, economical, efficient and effective at reaching large audiences, successful at brand maintenance. (para 1.3)

4 AIDA, Adoption, DAGMAR, Lavidge and Steiner.(para 1.4)

5 Awareness, Trial, Reinforcement and Nudge. (para 1.6)

6 A brand is the totality of what the consumer takes into consideration before making a purchase decision. (para 2)

7 Corporate umbrella, family umbrella, range branding and individual branding. (para 2.1)

8 An own-label brand refers to a product that carries the name of the reseller, wholesaler or retailer – rather than the manufacturer. (para 2.1)

9 Price premium opportunities, increased brand loyalty, growth and increased barriers to entry. (para 2.2)

10 Brand equity refers to the strength, currency and value of the brand. (para 2.3)

11 Salience is the term given to represent the degree of relevance a brand may have to a consumer. (para 2.3)

12 Generic, pre-emptive, USP, brand image, positioning, resonance, affective and informational. (para 3)

13 A creative brief is a document that provides an outline of the creative task and is the basis for creatives to develop their solutions. (para 4.1)

14 Knocking copy is text that offers a negative or disparaging comment about someone or something. (para 5.4)

15 Suitability, consistency, tension, continuity and unity. (para 6.2)

16 So they can be manipulated by a computer system. (para 7.6)

Answers to activities

1 Here is the sort of thing that is required. Question (c) is a matter for you to judge.

Example: Full-page EuroDisney advert from Sunday magazine supplement

The advert features a full colour drawing of families enjoying EuroDisney train and boat rides through Storybook Land, "a miniature land on a grand scale, where everyone's favourite fairy tales come to life."

(a) Target markets

(i) ABC1 adults with children or grandchildren under 12 years.

(ii) Families with children living within a 150 mile radius of the Channel ports

(iii) Existing UK theme park users

(iv) Short break holidaymakers

(b) Advertising objectives

(i) To inform about a new feature attraction within EuroDisney

(ii) To create an image of EuroDisney as a theme park which takes the visitor away from reality to an exciting fairytale world.

(iii) To remind the holidaymaker about the potential of EuroDisney as a holiday venue

(iv) To reassure travel agents and potential visitors of EuroDisney's continuing presence in the packaged event holiday market, following adverse publicity during re-financing deals.

2 There is no specific answer to this activity.

3 The answer to this activity hinges on your own tastes and perceptions.

4 The two names represent very different sectors of the car market; Jaguar are at the luxury end and Ford produce mass-market cars. The Jaguar marque would arguably be compromised by association with the Ford name.

5 There is no specific answer to this activity.

6 There is no specific answer to this activity.

7 There is no specific answer to this activity.

8 There is no specific answer to this activity.

9 There is no specific answer to this activity.

Chapter 14 :

OTHER TOOLS OF THE PROMOTIONAL MIX

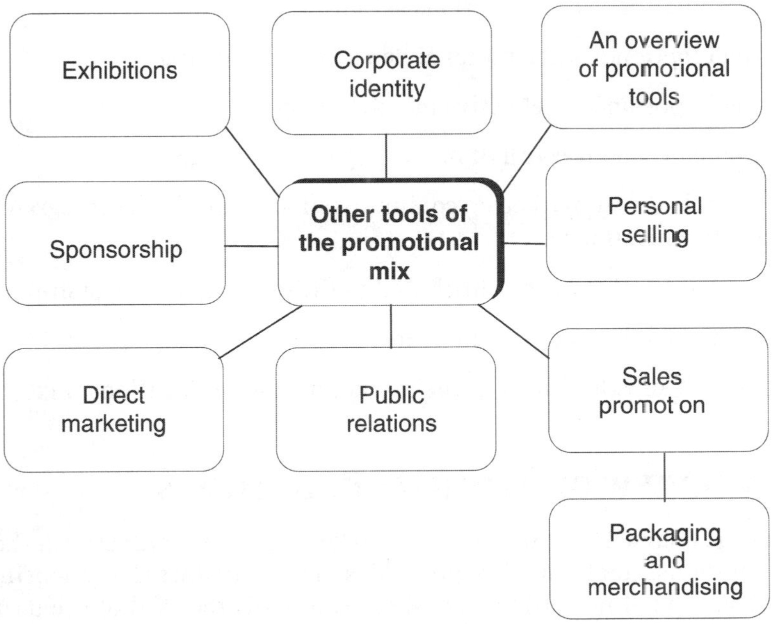

Introduction

This chapter will begin by providing an overview of promotional tools and stressing the importance of personal selling as an integral part of marketing communication. Personal selling is one of the principal areas identified in most descriptions of the promotional mix. Not only is the salesforce an important part of external marketing communications, the salesforce is also an important target group for internal marketing communications to ensure that its members are fully briefed to undertake the marketing communications and selling task they do.

The next section will discuss developments in sales promotions, which is a growth area in the marketing communications mix. Sales promotion's importance to the marketing communications mix should not be underestimated as it adds an extensive range of effective tools to the marketing communications armoury. Packaging will be discussed next as it is widely thought of as the visual identity of the brand and so embodies brand values and differentiates one brand from others.

Merchandising has been included in this section as it incorporates a range of sales promotions activities intended to ensure that products are easily available and prominently and attractively displayed at point of sale.

Public relations follows next and this can be defined as the planned and sustained effort to establish and maintain goodwill and mutual understanding between an organisation and its public. Direct marketing is a marketing system based on individual customer records held on a database, and new developments in database technology have revolutionised the effectiveness of this sector.

Sponsorship is one of the most rapidly growing elements of the marketing mix and yet, while it is one of the most widely used, it is also one of the least well understood. Corporate identity is the means by which corporate personality is projected and this will be evaluated alongside the role of exhibitions.

Your objectives

In this chapter you will learn about the following:

(a) an overview of personal selling

(b) the range of sales promotions activities

(c) the functional and emotional benefits of packaging

(d) the importance of effective merchandising

(e) the scope and breadth of marketing public relations

(f) the role direct marketing communications plays in the integrated marketing communications mix

(g) the factors that have contributed to the growth of sponsorship

(h) the principles of corporate identity

(i) the role of exhibitions in the marketing communications mix

1 AN OVERVIEW OF PROMOTIONAL TOOLS

In this part of the course book, the aim is to make you more familiar with the very broad range of promotional tools and to provide some guidelines for choosing the most appropriate promotional mix. Like any other set of tools the skill of the user is to select and apply the right tool for the particular task in hand. With promotional tools this is not an easy job because usually it is not just one tool that is required but a combination. Indeed, several different combinations could probably achieve the same result.

Having chosen a suite of promotional tools and even allocated them as either primary or supporting, it is important to be able to integrate them into a comprehensive and effective whole. As we shall see, this area of *integrated marketing communications* is becoming more important because of the need to achieve the desired end result cost-effectively.

1.1 The range of promotional tools

The range of promotional tools continues to grow. The variety of media that can be used for above the line campaigns has expanded, both in the printed advertising field and in the broadcast field. There are literally thousands of publications aimed at different target groups. In the personal computer field alone there are hundreds of magazines. In the broadcast field the number of television stations steadily increases through satellite, cable and digital television and the number of commercial radio stations has also grown considerably.

The diagram below shows the range of tools that can be used to influence a customer or potential customer.

NOTES

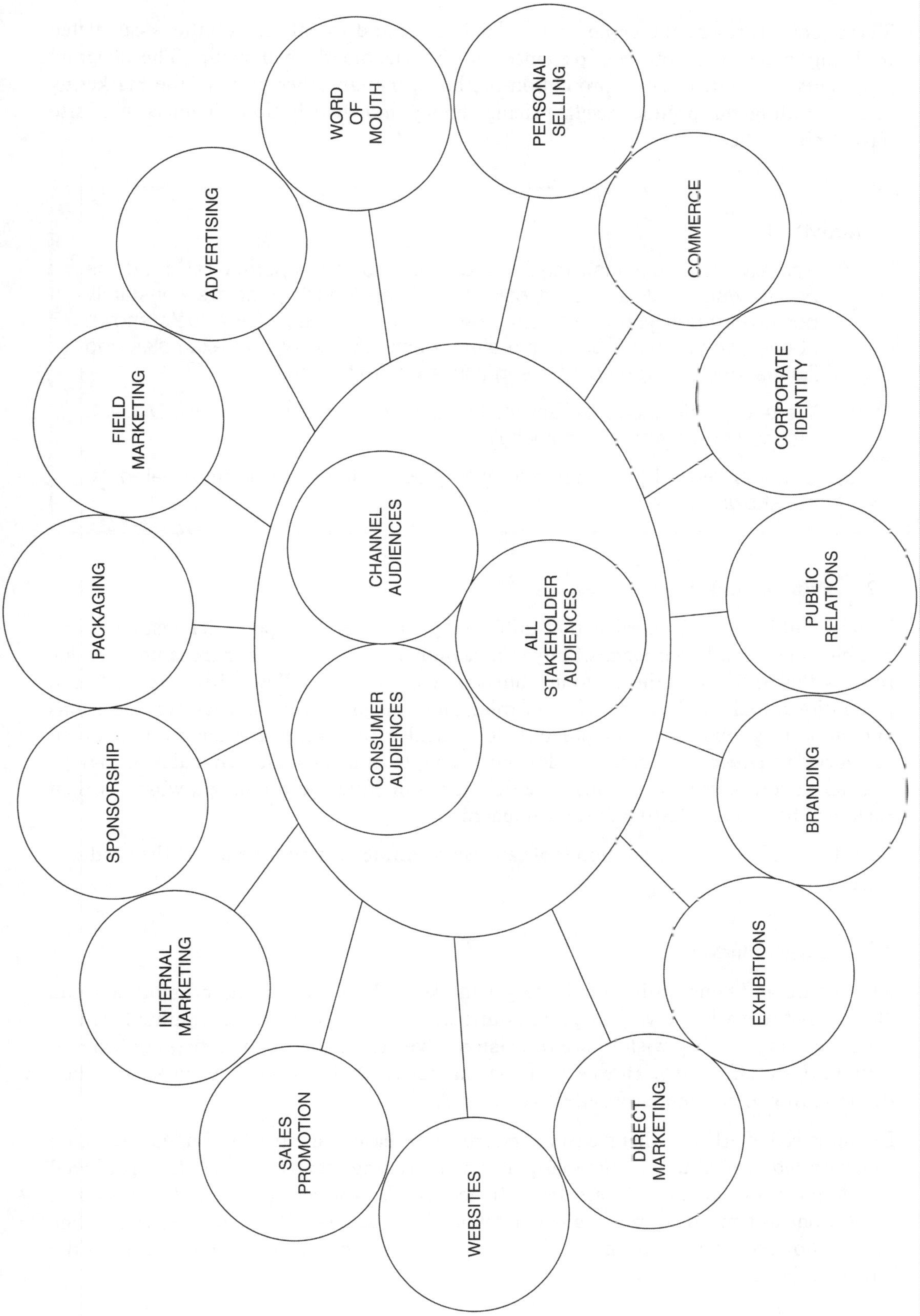
ALL STAKEHOLDER AUDIENCES
CHANNEL AUDIENCES
CONSUMER AUDIENCES
ADVERTISING
WORD OF MOUTH
PERSONAL SELLING
COMMERCE
CORPORATE IDENTITY
PUBLIC RELATIONS
BRANDING
EXHIBITIONS
DIRECT MARKETING
WEBSITES
SALES PROMOTION
INTERNAL MARKETING
SPONSORSHIP
PACKAGING
FIELD MARKETING

These tools represent the deployment of deliberate and intentional methods calculated to bring about a favourable response in the customer's behaviour. The diagram represents the most obvious promotion methods, though other parts of the marketing mix, including the product itself, pricing, policy and distribution channels, will also have decisive effects.

Activity 1

(a) Actually read your junk mail, wander around the supermarket, read the paper, watch TV, and start collecting those leaflets that are constantly posted through your letterbox. How many examples of the tools shown above can you find? Be on the alert constantly for real-life examples and illustrations that you could use in your examination answers.

(b) Were you influenced by any of the examples that you found? Did you respond? Can you work out why?

(c) Can you think of (or better, find examples of) any other promotional tools, not shown above?

1.2 Primary and support roles

What should already be clear is that influencing customers and potential customers is a complex business. Discussions of buyer behaviour have shown that there is not just one process that influences the customer but a whole series. It follows therefore that each promotional tool will have a variety of roles. In terms of making management decisions and allocating budgets it is possible to consider promotional tools in two broad categories of *primary* and *support* roles. For example in a consumer campaign it may be that television is used as the main vehicle for launching the campaign, which is then sustained by a longer-lasting poster campaign.

The choice of primary promotion tool can also be influenced by the stage of the product life cycle.

1.3 Target markets

The nature and constitution of the target market will also affect the promotional mix chosen. If the market is very large and quite dispersed in terms of geographic location, then the company may wish to use **television advertising** and national press in order to communicate effectively. However, if the market is small and widely dispersed, then **direct mail** will be a more cost effective method.

In industrial markets, where customers are more easily identifiable but utilise more concentrated distribution channels, personal selling tends to be the preferred communication method. A greater reliance is also placed upon trade press and exhibitions as a means of making contact with the widest possible audience. From time to time however, companies may utilise television as a means of communicating to the target audience.

EXAMPLE

Hewlett Packard have utilised television advertising as a means of communicating in the business-to-business markets. In an attempt to promote their office systems to corporate clients, they realised that the majority of the users of such systems would be office staff

NOTES

and junior managers who could be reached by television. The objective was to build awareness in the minds of this target audience who would then demand these systems within their own companies. Simultaneously, Hewlett Packard were utilising sales personnel, exhibitions and on site demonstrations to target the main influencers of the buying decision-making process within companies.

1.4 Product characteristics

The *attributes* of the product will determine the type of promotional strategy which is employed. If the product is highly technical in nature, then it will require a high degree of personal selling, where potential customers have the opportunity to ask detailed questions about the product. Personal selling will also be utilised to the full when introducing a new product to the market, in attempting to gain adequate distribution and dealer support.

The *price* of the product and its associated image will affect the choice of promotion used. Rolex watches for example, as well as using specified dealers (an example of exclusive distribution), concentrate upon high quality magazines and direct mail to communicate with their existing and potential target groups. There is also an emphasis upon personal service, since the expenditure on such an item is considerable, together with the necessary after sales back-up

> **Activity 2** **(15 minutes)**
>
> What types of promotional activity will be employed for a product at each stage of the product life cycle? Compare and contrast the differing methods for a consumer product and an industrial product.

2 PERSONAL SELLING

Personal selling has been defined as 'the presentation of products and associated persuasive communication to potential clients, which is employed by the supplying organisation. It is the most direct and longest established means of promotion within the promotional mix' (Baron *et al*, *Macmillan Dictionary of Retailing* 1991).

Definition

> **Transactional selling:** where the emphasis is simply placed on achieving the sale and following the steps proposed to a successful sale.

All organisations have employees with responsibility for contacting and dealing directly with customers and potential customers with a view to selling the company's products. These employees, known as the sales force, provide a vital function to the organisation as they form a direct link to the buyers.

An organisation has a choice as to how it organises itself for selling.

(a) Employ a direct (or company) sales force, consisting of full or part-time paid employees who work exclusively for the company. This type of sales force may, in turn, consist of two groups: inside sales personnel who conduct their business from the company premises via the telephone, or field sales personnel who travel and visit customers.

(b) In contrast, an organisation could employ a contractual sales force, which could comprise sales agents, dealers or brokers who are paid a commission on the sales they generate.

Irrespective of the type of sales force a company may use, the sales force needs the support of other groups within the organisation if it is to operate efficiently and effectively. Kotler (1991) identifies the following groups whose activities impact upon the effectiveness of the sales force.

(a) **Top management** who can be increasingly involved in the selling process, particularly with big orders or key accounts.

(b) **Technical sales personnel** who supply technical information and service to the customer before, during or after the sale of the product.

(c) **Customer service representatives** who provide installation, maintenance and other services to the customer.

(d) **Office staff** including sales analysts, administrators and secretarial staff.

Indeed, Kotler maintains that selling should increasingly be regarded as a team effort involving all these groups.

DISCUSSION

Probably the most significant change in thinking over recent years is the move to recognising the importance of developing longer-term customer relations and improving customer retention.

2.1 The tasks in the selling process

Personal selling is probably the area of the promotional mix that has the most stereotypes attached to it. The image of the 'travelling salesman' is an enduring one. However, this masks the reality that the term sales representative covers a broad range of positions, which vary tremendously in terms of tasks and responsibilities.

Role	Comment
Order collector	The salesperson's job is predominantly to deal with routine orders normally through telemarketing.
Order taker	The salesperson passively takes orders from the customer. This can be further divided into *inside* order takers, such as shop assistants, or *outside* order takers, such as those salespeople who call on regular customers to take an order periodically. The customer has already been persuaded to use the product, or has been using the product in the past.
Pre-Order caller	The salesperson is not expected or permitted to take an order but is expected to build goodwill or educate the customer in the use of the product. Medical representatives from pharmaceutical companies may fall into this category.
Order supporter	The salesperson's main skill is the application of his technical knowledge relating to the product.

Role	Comment
Order getter	The salesperson has to stimulate demand and creatively sell tangible or intangible products.

The 'degree of difficulty' of the salesperson's tasks increases the nearer the person gets to being an Order Getter. However, the art of 'selling' in its narrowest sense is only one of a number of tasks that the salesperson could perform. A salesperson could perform as many as seven different activities.

Activity	Comment
Prospecting	Gathering additional prospective customers in addition to sales leads generated by the company on his behalf.
Communicating	Communicating information to existing and potential customers about the company's products and services can take up a major proportion of the salesperson's time.
Selling	'The art of salesmanship', encompasses approaching the customer, presenting, answering objections and closing the sale.
Servicing	A salesperson may provide various services to the customer, such as consulting about their problems, rendering technical assistance, arranging finance and expediting delivery.
Information gathering	The salesperson can be a very useful source of marketing intelligence because of his or her links with the end customer. Many salespeople are responsible for supplying regular reports on competitive activity within their particular sales area.
Allocating	The salesperson may assist in evaluating customer profitability and creditworthiness, and may also have to control the allocation of products to customers in times of product shortages.
Shaping	An increasingly important role is to help build and sustain relationships with major customers.

While a salesperson may engage in all these tasks from time to time, the mix of tasks will vary according to the purchase decision process, company marketing strategy and the overall economic conditions of the time. For example, with regard to the influence that the buying decision process may have on the salesperson's mix of tasks, the skills needed for a straight rebuy situation (where the customer has bought the same product under the same conditions of sale in the past) will be totally different from those required to develop a new account.

Sales force activity must also be undertaken within the context of the organisation's overall marketing strategy.

(a) For example, if the organisation pursues a 'pull' strategy, relying on massive consumer advertising to draw customers into the premises of marketing intermediaries to ask for the brands, then the role of the sales force may primarily be a servicing one, ensuring that retailers carry sufficient stock, allocate adequate shelf space for display and co-operate in sales promotion programmes.

(b) Conversely, with a 'push' strategy, the organisation will rely primarily on the sales force to sell the brands to the marketing intermediaries who will then assume the main responsibility for selling on the brands to the end customer.

The mix of a salesperson's tasks may vary with the prevailing economic conditions. For example, in times of product shortage the art of selling may not be as important and one could argue that the sales force are redundant. However, such a view neglects the other roles of the salesperson that will be of greater importance in such circumstances, such as allocating, counselling customers, communicating company policy to customers and perhaps selling other products that are not in short supply.

DISCUSSION

Not only does the salesforce act in the capacity of salespeople, in an indirect way so do other employees.

---

3 SALES PROMOTION

Definition

> The Institute of Sales Promotion (ISP) defines **sales promotion** as 'a range of tactical marketing techniques, designed within a strategic marketing framework, to add value to a product or service, in order to achieve a specific sales and marketing objective.'

(a) Sales promotion encompasses a range of techniques appropriate for targeting consumers, for instance via price reductions, competitions or gifts with purchases. However, trade and sales force incentives are also implied under the general heading of sales promotion. It typifies what is generally thought of as below-the-line.

(b) Sales promotion is viewed by the ISP as a tactical promotional tool. The majority of companies will use sales promotion as a means of achieving a short-term objective, for instance to gain short-term sales volume or to encourage trial and brand switching by a rival manufacturer's consumers.

(c) Although it is used as a tactical tool, sales promotion works within a strategic marketing framework. Sales promotion should not start with a good idea that came to the Sales Director while in the bath, but with due regard to the strategic objectives for the brand, and the synergies that can brought about through a carefully designed promotional activity.

(d) Sales promotion always seeks to add value to a product or service. Thus consumers are offered something extra for their purchase, or the chance to obtain something extra.

Sales promotion includes the notion of both sales pull and sales push techniques. As we have seen, sales pull techniques incentivise the consumer to buy, thus pulling sales through the chain of distribution via consumer demand. Sales push techniques either encourage the sales force to sell products, or prompt the trade intermediary to buy, ensuring the distribution pipeline is well loaded, and sales are pushed through the distribution chain.

NOTES

Definition

Below-the-line communications – marketing communications that make use of the non-commissioning paying media.

Be aware of the potential for confusion between the terms promotion (used as a synonym for communication techniques in general) and sales promotion (which is a specialist term reserved for the specific techniques described in this chapter). In examinations some candidates read the question paper very quickly and mistake a question on sales promotion for one on promotional techniques in general. This unfortunate slip can result in a candidate scoring virtually no marks for a question.

DISCUSSION

The advertising to sales promotion ratio (30:70) suggests that more money is spent on sales promotion activities than on all forms of advertising.

3.1 Sales promotion objectives

Examples of consumer sales promotion objectives.

(a) Increase awareness and interest amongst target audiences.

(b) Achieve a switch in buying behaviour from competitor brands to your company's brand.

(c) Incentivise consumers to make a forward purchase of your brand, thus shutting out competitor purchase opportunities.

(d) Increase display space allocated to your brand in store.

(e) Smooth seasonal dips in demand for your product.

(f) Generate a consumer database from mail-in applications.

Sales promotion objectives will link into overarching marketing and marketing communications objectives.

Marketing objective	To increase brand X market share by 2 percentage points in the period January to December 1997
Marketing communications objective	To contribute to brand share gain of 2% in 1997 by increasing awareness of X from 50% to 70% among target consumers.
Sales promotion objective	To encourage trial of brand X among target consumers by offering a guaranteed incentive to purchase.

Activity 3 **(30 minutes)**

Tesco and Sainsbury both now issue a type of loyalty card which shoppers present when they reach the check-out. Points are awarded for sums spent over a minimum amount and these are added up each quarter. Money-off vouchers to be used against future grocery bills are sent to the shopper's home. Compare and contrast these schemes.

3.2 Sales promotion activities

There is a vast array of possible activities that can be classified as sales promotion. These include:

Consumer

- sampling
- couponing
- premiums
- money off
- bonus packs
- loyalty schemes
- branded packs
- contests
- cause related
- merchandising
- point of sale
- information

Trade

- consumer promotions
- allowances
- contests and incentives
- point of sale material and merchandising
- sampling
- gifts and free merchandise
- information

4 PACKAGING AND MERCHANDISING

Packaging is a marketing tool that combines graphic design with marketing concepts to create an identity for the brand. An ideal package is one which brings to the customer's mind the essence of what the brand is all about whenever and wherever it is seen. It can be effectively used to influence customer choice at the point of sale in terms of reducing the uncertainty and risk inherent in product choice and it acts as a tangible reminder at the point of sale.

4.1 The benefits of packaging

Packaging comprises a number of physical or functional benefits including the storage of the product, the extension of the product's shelf life, the facilitation of physical storage, the protection of the product during distribution, the communication of usage information and the assurance of consistent quality.

Emotional and psychological benefits of packaging include:

(a) a communication tool to express brand values
(b) aesthetically pleasing
(c) strong visual impact
(d) a living expression of what the brand represents
(e) adds value from a consumer's perspective
(f) a reminder
(g) provides cues to express loyalty
(h) creates an emotional link with the target audience

4.2 Packaging features

To achieve visual impact, packaging should attract the eye through colour and design. Listed below are the most important features of packaging:

Feature	Description
Colour	Powerful emotional signals, symbolic, eg Cadbury's purple is associated with luxury
Typography	Communicates the product image, eg ornate script implies tradition and sophistication
Logo	Signifies the brand's individuality and unique image, eg Coca-Cola and Kelloggs
Type/material	Recyclable, biodegradable, eg boxes, cartons, bags, bottles, tubes, cans, jars etc
Shape and structure	Used to attract attention, eg Jif's yellow lemon and character children's yoghurt
Label or mark	Varies with types and materials of packages, can be printed on the package or other materials
Size	Encourage product usage

DISCUSSION

How can packaging impact on a consumer's perceptual process?

4.3 Sales promotion and packaging

Packaging is normally used with sales promotion, in the special or non-routine events when a brand is needing a boost, eg seasonal, sale. Seven types of promotional packages are described below.

Package	Characteristic
Money-off pack	Announced on-pack
Bonus size pack	Standard price but additional content
Coupon pack	Packed into the container itself
Pack-on premium	New outer case or shrink wrapping to include for example a smaller version
Pack-in premium	Eg, a free mug with coffee
Self-liquidator	Buying the product at a reduced price by sending in labels, tokens or receipts

Activity 4 **(10 minutes)**

Select a fast moving consumer good package and associated press advertisement. Do the packaging components reflect/enhance the brand's image? If so, how?

4.4 Merchandising

Merchandising can be defined as the range of sales promotions activities intended to ensure that products are easily available, and prominently and attractively displayed at point of sale. It is also used to describe the activity of making promotional products available, such as those associated with new film releases, eg calendars, figurines, novelty items etc.

Many organisations employ merchandisers whose task it is to develop displays and ensure that products are appropriately displayed. Most retailers use planograms to assist in shelf display and layout. They are especially important if retailers wish to ensure consistency of display in all stores.

Definition

> **Planogram** – diagrams or plans showing store and shelf layout.

As was mentioned earlier, a phenomenal growth area in merchandising has been that associated with new film releases. This is especially so for the Disney Company who have extensive merchandising experience. Examples of films which have developed merchandise include Star Wars, The Lion King and Titanic.

DISCUSSION

The release of merchandise items to coincide with film releases has resulted in a multi-billion pound industry.

> **Activity 5**
>
> Visit a local supermarket and identify merchandise being used. Consider a selection and evaluate their effectiveness.

5 PUBLIC RELATIONS

Definitions

> The Institute of Public Relations has defined **PR** as 'the planned and sustained effort to establish and maintain goodwill and mutual understanding between an organisation and its publics'.

The Public Relations Consultants Association (PRCA) says that:

> Public relations is the name given to the managed process of communication between one group and another. In its purest form it has nothing to do with marketing,

NOTES

advertising or 'commercialism'. It will, however, often promote one group's endeavours to persuade another group to its point of view and it will use a number of different methods, other than (although often alongside) advertising to achieve this aim.

5.1 Public relations

The problem faced is invariably one of definition in terms of the aims and activities that PR encompasses. These embrace many groups of people known as publics and extend from:

- advice and counselling
- relations with employees during redundancy and closure
- relations with the local community and interest groups
- lobbying
- developing goodwill among all publics
- monitoring public opinion

to:

- publicity
- sponsorship and donations
- dealing with negative publicity and crises
- the preparation of press releases and publications
- helping to develop and maintain corporate image
- arranging events

Definition

> **Publics** – refers to the many target audiences that communications may be focused towards, eg customers, influencers, media, employees, pressure groups etc.

EXAMPLE

Brent Spar

An excellent example is provided by the public outcry that followed Shell's abortive attempts to dump the Brent Spar oil platform on the ocean floor. Announcing the reversal of the decision in June 1995 Shell UK's managing director stressed the huge amount of research that had gone into selecting what the company had thought was the best option for disposal of Brent Spar. Shell took the view that it merely needed to respect the voluminous laws and conventions governing dumping at sea. However, environmental pressure groups led by Greenpeace were outraged and, realising that the oceans and the atmosphere are hugely emotive issues for the general public, the German and Danish governments joined the protest. Shell caved in to the pressure, but at the time the Institute of Public Relations said that a U-turn was 'almost the worst thing you can do' in such a situation, and that it would take years for Shell to rebuild its environmental credibility.

Shell have learnt their environmental lesson well: at one point during a press conference in January 1997 unveiling new ideas for the disposal of the oil platform, a spokesman commented that one option for moving it 'was no longer being considered because the energy consumed was too great'.

From the list of activities above it can be seen that the scope of **public relations activity**, if implemented effectively, should **embrace the whole organisation.** A number of criteria have been put forward in an attempt to define what constitutes 'excellent' public relations within an organisation, many of which relate to the role and position of the public relations department within the organisation.

(a) Programmes should be managed strategically.

(b) There should be a single integrated public relations department.

(c) Public relations managers should report directly to senior management.

(d) Public relations should be a separate function from marketing.

(e) The senior public relations person should be a member of the organisation's dominant coalition.

(f) Communication should adhere to the 'two-way symmetrical model'.

5.2 Four models of PR

This last factor relates to the way in which public relations is practised. Given the diversity of the role of PR as emphasised above, it is logical to consider different ways in which PR could be practised. A framework for considering this has been propounded by Grunig and Hunt, *Managing Public Relations* (1984), who suggest that there are four models of public relations practice. Each model will be considered in turn.

5.3 Press agency/publicity

The role of PR is primarily one of **propaganda**, spreading the faith of the organisation, often through incomplete, half-true or distorted information. Communication is one-way, from the organisation to its publics: essentially telling the publics the information the organisation wants them to hear.

5.4 Public information

In this model the role of PR is the dissemination of **information**, not necessarily with a persuasive intent. As Grunig and Hunt state, 'the public relations person functions essentially as a journalist in residence, whose job it is to report objectively information about his organisation to the public'. Like the first model, this type of communication is one-way, but it does differ in the fact that public information specialists feel obliged to present a complete picture of the organisation they represent, whereas the press agency specialists do not. The public information model of PR is typified by government information promotions for such issues as health, crime prevention and education.

5.5 Two-way asymmetric

Grunig and Hunt describe the main function of the two-way asymmetric model as scientific persuasion, using social science theory and research about attitudes and behaviour to persuade publics to accept the organisation's point of view and to behave in a way that supports the organisation. The aim is to achieve the maximum change in attitudes and behaviour. However, while the **communication is two-way** in that there is a flow of information back to the organisation from the publics, this flow is asymmetric because the response to this feedback from the publics is to improve the effectiveness of the outgoing communication rather than to stimulate a change in the message *content*, reflecting change within the organisation.

Definition

Two-way asymmetric communications – communications from a sender to a receiver with little or delayed feedback, producing a non-direct dialogue.

NOTES

5.6 Two-way symmetric

In the two-way symmetric model the **PR practitioner serves as a mediator between the organisation and its publics** with the aim of facilitating mutual understanding between the two. The communication is therefore more of a dialogue than a monologue. If persuasion occurs it is as likely to persuade the organisation's management to change its attitude as it is to persuade the publics to change theirs. In an ideal situation, both management and publics will change their attitudes or behaviour, but if the PR function has brought the two sides together, and as long as both sides communicate well enough to understand the position of the other, then the PR effort will have been successful.

Definition

Two-way symmetric communications – direct dialogue between a sender and receiver of communications.

Grunig and Hunt suggest that the model used varies depending on the type of organisation concerned.

PR model	Area of practice	% of organisations practising
Press agency/publicity	Sports, theatre, product promotion	15%
Public information	Government and non-profit organisations	50%
Two-way asymmetric	Competitive business and PR agencies	20%
Two-way symmetric	Regulated business agencies (water, electricity)	15%

The two-way symmetric model is seen as the ideal that should be aspired to, but Grunig and Hunt recognise that only a minority of companies will achieve it.

Public relations is, therefore, the **management of an organisation's reputation with its publics** and this management involves a close consideration of the relationships involved. The organisation can be either reactive or proactive in its management of these relationships.

(a) **Reactive PR** is primarily concerned with the communication of what has happened and responding to factors affecting the organisation. It is primarily defensive, with little or no responsibility for influencing policies that may change the perceptions of the organisation among its publics. The publics with which the PR function communicates are largely those with whom it is in direct contact and the scope of PR activities is relatively narrow, with the emphasis on media relations and publications.

(b) In contrast, **proactive public relations practitioners** have a much wider role and thus have a far greater influence on overall organisational strategy. They will communicate with a broad range of publics, not only those with whom they are in direct contact but also those who have the potential to influence the future plans of the organisation. The scope of the activities of the PR function is much wider, encompassing communications activities in their entirety, counselling and strategic planning.

DISCUSSION

Publicity can create greater credibility than other forms of promotion.

5.7 Classification of techniques

Inevitably some techniques will be more appropriate in certain circumstances with certain types of publics than others. It is possible, therefore, to classify the different types of techniques or media according to the type of project areas in which they appear to be most effective. The most frequently used techniques are as follows.

(a) Consumer marketing support area techniques

- Consumer and trade press releases
- Product/service literature
- Promotional videos
- Special events (in-store competitions, celebrity store openings
- Consumer exhibitions
- In-house magazines for sales staff, customers and/or trade
- Salesforce/distributor incentive schemes
- Sport, and to a lesser extent, arts sponsorships
- Advertorials

Definition

> **Advertorials** – advertisements that are designed to look as thought they are editorial.

(b) Business-to-business communication area techniques

- Corporate identity design
- Corporate literature
- Corporate advertising
- Trade and general press relations, possibly on a national or international basis
- Corporate and product videos
- Direct mailings
- Sports and arts sponsorships
- Trade exhibitions

(c) Internal/employee communications area techniques

- In-house magazines and employee newsletters
- Employee relations videos
- Formal employee communications networks and channels for feedback
- Recruitment exhibitions/conferences
- Speech writing for executives
- Company notice boards
- Briefing meetings

(d) Corporate, external and public affairs area techniques

- Corporate literature
- Corporate social responsibility programmes, community involvement

- Trade, local, national and possibly international media relations
- Issues tracking
- Management counselling
- Local or central government lobbying
- Industrial lobbying
- Facility visits
- Local/national sponsorships

(e) Financial public relations area techniques

- Financial media relations on both a national and international basis
- Design of annual and interim reports
- Facility visits for analysts, brokers, fund managers, etc
- Organising shareholder meetings
- Shareholder tracking research

While this is not a comprehensive list it does give an indication of the many types of PR techniques that can be used in various circumstances and how certain techniques will re-occur in various settings. Media relations, for example, is used in virtually all areas of activity.

DISCUSSION

Public relations should not only be thought of in the context of corporate promotions, it has a role in product promotions too.

EXAMPLE

Lobbying

The following cases are found on the website of a leading PR consultancy.

'Companies often come to Charles Barker for political intelligence to enable them to stay one step ahead of the game. Others require a comprehensive strategy in order to amend or oppose a proposed government initiative. Yet others wish to promote a policy or business initiative. In all cases, we work closely with our clients to ensure that their viewpoint is expressed at all appropriate occasions during consultative periods and to all relevant political and official audiences.

Faciltiy visits

Sellafield Nuclear Plant run by British Nuclear Fuels Limited has a visitors' information centre. This plays an important role as part of its promotional and PR activity.

Media conferences

When painkiller, Tylenol was deliberately contaminated with a poison by an extortionist, Johnson & Johnson, the manufacturer, held a media conference as a means of maintaining confidence and quickly and effectively conveying how it was handling the situation. Despite potentially catastrophic consequences, the company was praised for its actions.

6 DIRECT MARKETING

Theodore Levitt once stated that 'The sole purpose of a business is to create and keep a customer'. In brief, the aims of direct marketing are to acquire and retain customers. Here are two further definitions.

Definitions

> The Institute of Direct Marketing in the UK defines **direct marketing** as 'The planned recording, analysis and tracking of customer behaviour to develop relational marketing strategies'.
>
> The Direct Marketing Association in the US define direct marketing as 'An interactive system of marketing which uses one or more advertising media to effect a measurable response and/or transaction at any location'.

Definition

> **Database** – collection of data, usually on computer, stored to provide useful, convenient and interactive access to information.

It is worth studying these definitions and noting some key words and phrases.

Response	Direct marketing is about getting people to send in coupons, or make telephone calls in response to invitations and offers.
Interactive	It is a two-way process, involving the supplier and the customer.
Relationship	It is in many instances an on-going process of selling again and again to the same customer.
Recording and analysis	Response data are collected and analysed so that the most cost-effective procedures may be arrived at. Direct marketing has been called 'marketing with numbers'. It aims to take the waste out of marketing.
Strategy	Direct marketing should not be seen merely as a 'quick fix', a 'one-off mailing', a promotional device. It should be seen as a part of a comprehensive plan stemming from clearly formulated objectives.

Direct marketing helps create and develop direct relationships between you and each of your prospects, between the consumer and the company on an individual basis. It is a form of direct supply, embracing both a variety of alternative **media channels** (like direct mail), and a choice of **distribution channels** (like mail order). Because direct marketing removes all channel intermediaries apart from the advertising medium and the delivery medium, there are no resellers, therefore avoiding loss of control and loss of revenue.

Definition

> **Relationship marketing** – view that emphasises the importance of the relationships developed between an organisation and other parties (including customers, partners, suppliers and the trade).

EXAMPLE

This campaign won the Gold Award for Direct Marketing in 1998.

Following the launch of Cable and Wireless Communications an acquisition programme was devised. Nine advertisements were developed to promote three key product benefits. The first was a price promise (cheaper than BT or double the difference back) a 50p call cap on weekend national calls and 100 minutes of free local calls.

Rather than use direct mail it was decided to use DRTV, based on TV regions which correlated with cable franchise areas and where telephone revenue is higher. Heavy use was made of off-peak spots which in turn yield lower costs per response. With the cost per response falling below £5, DRTV now accounts for a third of all Cable and Wireless Communications' acquisitions, with a response level of 80 for every 100,000 viewers, near double the industry average. The acquisition programme itself generated 180,000 responses against a target of just 100,000.

Source: Adapted from the 18th DMA/Royal Mail Direct Marketing Awards 1998.

DISCUSSION

Direct marekting communciations is not restricted to direct mail. Potentially all media can utilise a direct function, eg direct response TV advertising, direct response radio advertising, internet communciations, direct response billboards.

6.1 Components of direct marketing

Direct marketing encompasses a wide range of media and distribution opportunities.

- Television
- Radio
- Direct mail
- Direct response advertising
- Telemarketing
- Statement stuffers
- Inserts
- Take-ones
- Electronic media
- Door to door
- Mail order
- Computerised home shopping
- Home shopping networks

In developing a comprehensive direct marketing strategy, organisations will often utilise a range of different yet complementary techniques.

Direct mail tends to be the main medium of direct response advertising. It has become the synonym for it. The reasons for this is that other major media, newspapers and magazines, are familiar to people in advertising in other contexts. Newspaper ads can include coupons to fill out and return, and radio and TV can give a phone number to ring (DRTV is now very common). However, direct mail has a number of strengths as a direct response medium.

(a) The advertiser can target down to **individual level**.

(b) The communication can **be personalised**. Known data about the individual can be used, while modern printing techniques mean that parts of a letter can be altered to accommodate this.

(c) The medium is good **for reinforcing interest stimulated by other media** such as TV. It can supply the response mechanism (a coupon) which is not yet available in that medium.

(d) The opportunity to use **different creative formats** is almost unlimited.

(e) **Testing potential is sophisticated**: a limited number of items can be sent out to a 'test' cell and the results can be evaluated. As success is achieved, so the mailing campaign can be rolled out.

The cornerstone upon which the direct mailing is based, however, is **the mailing list**. It is far and away the most important element in the list of variables, which also include the offer, timing and creative content.

DISCUSSION

Be wary of 'average response rates'. Response rates vary widely by industry sector, mailing list, creative and offer.

EXAMPLE

Database applications

Computers now have the capacity to operate in three new ways which will enable businesses to operate in a totally different dimension.

'Customers can be tracked individually. Thousands of pieces of information about each of millions of customers can be stored and accessed economically.

Companies and customers can interact through, for example, phones, mail, E-mail and interactive kiosks. ... for the first time since the invention of mass marketing, 'companies will be hearing from individual customers in a cost-efficient manner'.

Computers allow companies to match their production processes to what they learn from their individual customers - a process known as 'mass customisation' which Peppers explains as 'the cost-efficient mass production of products and services in lot sizes of one'.

There are many examples of companies which are already employing or experimenting with these ideas. In the US Levi Strauss, the jeans company, is taking measurements and preferences from female customers to produce exact-fitting garments. The customisation is currently limited to one line of jeans but ... the approach 'offers the company tremendous opportunities for building learning relationships'.

The Ritz-Carlton hotel chain has trained staff throughout the organisation to jot down customer details at every opportunity on a 'guest preference pad'.

The result, he says, could be the following: 'You stay at the Ritz-Carlton in Cancun, Mexico, call room service for dinner, and request an ice cube in your glass of white wine. Months later, when you stay at the Ritz-Carlton in Naples, Florida, and order a glass of white wine from room service, you will almost certainly be asked if you would like an ice cube in it.' (*Financial Times*)

DISCUSSION

In direct marketing communications, the creative approach, although important, has less effect on response rates than the targeting, the offer and incentive and the media utilised.

6.2 Telemarketing as an integrated marketing activity

Role of telemarketing

(a) **Building, maintaining, cleaning and updating databases.** The telephone allows for accurate data-gathering by compiling relevant information on customers and prospects, and selecting appropriate target groups for specific product offerings.

(b) **Market evaluation and test marketing**. Almost any feature of a market can be measured and tested by telephone. Feedback is immediate so response can be targeted quickly to exploit market knowledge.

(c) **Dealer support.** Leads can be passed on to the nearest dealer who is provided with full details.

(d) **Traffic generation**. The telephone, combined with postal invitations, is the most cost effective way of screening leads and encouraging attendance at promotional events.

(e) **Direct sales and account servicing**. The telephone can be used at all stages of the relationship with the prospects and customers. This includes lead generation, establishing buying potential for appropriate follow-up and defining the decision-making process.

(f) **Customer care and loyalty building**. Every telephone contact opportunity can demonstrate to customers that they are valued.

(g) **Crisis management**. If, for example, there is a consumer scare, immediate action is essential to minimise commercial damage. A dedicated hotline number can be advertised to provide information and advice.

Activity 6

Look out for example of programme sponsorship on TV and radio and product placement in the cinema, on TV and radio. Identify how they are being used and how appropriate their use seems to be. How effective do you think your examples of programme sponsorship and product placement are and in what ways do you think the sponsors have benefited?

Definition

Outbound telemarketing is where calls are made to customers.

Inbound telemarketing is concerned with receiving calls from customers.

6.3 Media choice

A framework known as AIMRITE has been developed to help organisations make consistent media choices.

Audience	- the desired target
Impact	- to get through clutter
Message	- clearly communicated
Response	- is this easy
Internal management	- enhancing efficiency
End results	- cost/benefit

Activity 7 (20 minutes)

Collect a direct response press or magazine advertisement or a piece of direct mail. Using the AIMRITE framework, critically appraise the media choice made. How could the communication be improved?

7 SPONSORSHIP

Sponsorship can be defined as a contribution to an activity or organisation by another. Although sponsorship may be purely altruistic, it is normally undertaken with the expectations of achieving benefit for the sponsor, eg in achieving corporate or marketing objectives.

7.1 Growth of sponsorship

The growth of sponsorship as a form of marketing communication can be attributed to a number of factors. These include:

(a) concern over traditional promotional methods, ie media fragmentation and clutter

(b) creation of favourable associations

(c) overcome linguistic/cultural barriers

(d) wide/multiple target audience appeal

(e) overcome legal barriers

(f) selective targeting

DISCUSSION

Where legal constraints prohibit the promotion of products (eg tobacco) using other forms of marketing communications, sponsorship can be used to overcome some of their limitations.

7.2 Benefits and risks of sponsorship

One of the benefits attributed to sponsorship is that it can be more efficient than other forms of marketing communication because it can generate both audience appeal and link the values of the sponsored entity to the sponsor.

Other benefits may include community image building where a small business may sponsor a local football team by providing their strip emblazoned with their logo. Sponsorship also appeals to corporations as a marketing communications medium because it can be tied to other marketing activities, eg providing a free sample of a sports energy drink at a sponsored event. Corporate sponsorships of many art and cultural events and sports such as Wimbledon are frequently used for corporate hospitality opportunities

---

DISCUSSION

It is important to select the appropriate sponsorship deal to ensure synergy between the sponsor and the sponsored. Sponsorship deals, particualrly with individuals, can go wrong due to unforeseen circumstances.

The potential risks associated with sponsorship include negative associations where perhaps a sports team does not perform well. Clutter is a particular issue in sports such as Formula 1 where a vehicle may have a number of different corporate names. Sponsorship is also risky because any benefits are difficult to evaluate.

DISCUSSION

Increasingly, popular sponsored activities are becoming overcrowded with marketing communications mesasges.

7.3 Sponsorship developments

Three aspects of sponsorship which have grown markedly in recent years are broadcast sponsorship, product placement and cause-related marketing.

A programme is deemed to be sponsored if any or part of its costs of production or transmission is met by an organisation or person, other than the broadcaster or producer. This is exemplified by Cadbury's £10m sponsorship of Coronation Street and more recently, the sponsorship of ITV's Cold Feet by United Airlines. Radio sponsorship has also increased and one of the largest radio programme sponsorships is the Pepsi Network Chart Show.

Product placement is defined as the inclusion of, or reference to, a product or service within the programme in return for payment or other valuable consideration to the programme maker. Both the ITC and BBC are finding it increasingly difficult to control and hard to prove.

DISCUSSION

Product placement is prohibited in the UK.

Organisations have a long history of giving to charitable causes. This type of sponsorship (sometimes referred to as CRM – cause related marketing), involves a firm aligning itself to a particular charitable cause or foundation, and supporting it either financially, or donating staff time and/or product. CRM allows firms to portray themselves as caring.

7.4 Ambush marketing

Ambush marketing involves a firm, often a competitor, attempting to deflect attention from another sponsor onto itself.

Definition

> **Ambush marketing** is the term used to refer to a company's intentional effort to weaken or ambush its competitor's official sponsorship by engaging in promotions or advertising that seek to confuse the buying public as to which company really holds official sponsorship rights.

There are various ambush strategies that a firm can employ. The first is to sponsor the media coverage of the event but not the event itself. Secondly they could sponsor a sub-category within a particular event, eg a horse race on Gold Cup day and then heavily market the association. They could sponsor an individual such as a footballer and then run advertisements during the main event. Finally, a company could run an advertisement campaign that features the type of activity being sponsored but not the actual event.

DISCUSSION

There is no overarching regulation that controls sponsorship although it is still subject to professional codes of practice and the general law of the land.

---

8 EXHIBITIONS

Exhibitions and trade shows provide a temporary forum for sellers of a product category to exhibit and demonstrate their products to prospective buyers. Some exhibitions exist as marketplaces where buyers and sellers meet, other exist purely as promotional vehicles, eg London Motor Show. Some exhibitions are open to the public, eg BBC Good Food Show, while others are business-to-business vehicles, eg Concrete Today. These events can take many forms from in-store tasting demonstrations, to conferences, to very large international trade and consumer shows like the International Spring Fair at the National Exhibition Centre in Birmingham.

DISCUSSION

A significant proportion of promotional expenditure can be used in exhibiting, the value being in excess of many of the higher profile promotional actvities and media.

8.1 Reasons for exhibiting

One important role of exhibitions and trade shows is to increase sales either directly on the stand or through follow-up activity. Other reasons include:

(a) enhance company image
(b) interact with customer
(c) promote existing products
(d) launch new products
(e) obtain competitor intelligence
(f) enhance personal morale
(g) interact with distributors

DISCUSSION

Prospects made via exhibitions are generally recognised to be less expensive than field contacts.

8.2 Planning exhibitions

Although exhibitions can be expensive activities, many firms do not put adequate time and effort into planning. Here are the recommended stages:

1. Set objectives
2. Select which exhibition to attend
3. Plan for staffing the stand
4. Plan support promotions
5. Decide stand layout and currents
6. Plan follow-up activities
7. Plan the project-logistics
8. Evaluate and follow up

DISCUSSION

Exhibitions and trade shows are a good place to launch new products.

Activity 8

Visit an exhibition. Carefully observe and evaluate all the activities that are going on. Consider the organisation of the exhibition as a whole; the number of stands, layout, visitor attendance, exhibitor attendance, promotional materials, atmosphere and all supporting services, eg catering. Evaluate the event from a visitor's perspective.

9 CORPORATE IDENTITY

The situation analysis may have uncovered issues concerning the way the organisation is perceived by a range of stakeholders, or **negative attitudes** towards the organisation, perhaps as a result of an **ethical issue or crisis that struck the company** and the associated **media comment**. In these circumstances part of the objectives of the marketing communications strategy will be to correct or adjust the perception or attitude influential stakeholder audiences have of the organisation.

EXAMPLE

Brand: North West Water
Client: John Drummond

Agency: BDH-TBWA
Authors: Belinda Miller
Katherine Dinwoodie

Despite the fact that key stakeholders (customers, employees, community groups, opinion leaders, and the company's most hostile critics, the press) attacked the company for high costs, research revealed extreme ignorance of actual prices. The brief was to achieve measurable improvements in customer satisfaction, ensuring that North West Water was repositioned as a customer orientated company that delivered value for money services. The campaign highlighted the range of services provided, at an average daily cost of 60p.

As a result of the campaign:

- Over a third of customers became aware of the 60p figure
- Value for money perceptions increased by 22%
- Customer satisfaction reached 78%
- Loyalty increased – 75% of customers claimed they couldn't switch
- 75% of key stakeholders viewed the company as socially responsible
- Agreement that 'community expectations are met-exceeded' increased from 54% to 70%
- Employees were optimistic in the belief that customer perceptions would improve further
- Levels of job satisfaction increased by 10%
- 87% of customers believed that bills should remain the same or rise.

Source : Reproduced with kind permission of IPA

A Profile Communication Strategy therefore addresses the needs of how the corporate entity is perceived by a range of stakeholder audiences. For example, it is quite common for an organisation to develop a communications campaign that is targeted at the Financial markets and the Stock Market in particular. This is referred to as Investor Communications. This happens because the company feels the share price undervalues the organisation or fails to reflect the true worth. It may be that the company wants to inform the financial markets of profit results, changes in senior management or prepare the way for merger and acquisition activities, all of which can seriously affect a companies standing unless handled in the appropriate way.

EXAMPLE

Standard Life are a well known provider of financial services products in its native Scotland but lacks strength of presence elsewhere. 85% of Standard Life's business is generated through independent financial advisors. However, the market conditions are changing and with the emergence of stakeholder pensions customers will go out and buy pension products themselves. This means that top of mind awareness will become crucial and that there is a need to create a corporate brand identity to facilitate direct selling.

With this background context Standard Life embarked on a profile strategy, mainly TV-led campaigns, to increase awareness. Having achieved the awareness objectives it then sought to communicate factual information to build understanding and credibility. Consequently, recent campaigns presented information about size, financial strength and performance.

However, the challenge was not to appear patronising or dull when attempting to educate and entertain its target audiences. To avoid this problem they used a 14 month baby who appears to be talking eloquently with his father about Standard Life. Through the use of graphics and computer morphing techniques it was possible to superimpose an older child's voice and mouth movements onto the baby's.

Source : Adapted from McLuhan, Robert, (1998) Standard Life finds its Voice, Marketing, 29 October, p24

9.1 Corporate identity, corporate image

Corporate identity and **corporate image** are two different facets of the profile development strategy. Increasingly organisations are adopting the phrase corporate branding as a substitute for Corporate identity.

Corporate identity is about the way an organisation communicates with its audiences. There are two main forms of communication, those that are planned and pre-determined by the organisation, and those that are unplanned and unexpected

The individual communication methods that make up these Planned and Unplanned communications are referred to as cues. Examples of planned cues are letterheads, logos, signage, product quality and the behaviour and level of knowledge of its employees. Examples of unplanned cues are media comment, the cleanliness of the company's vehicles and any actions taken by competitors and consumer groups that may reflect or directly relate to the organisation.

Activity 9 **(30 minutes)**

Identify three corporate communication campaigns and the cues used by each to communicate with the different audiences.

The way in which these cues are perceived frames the way an individual sees and understands an organisation and helps form the image they have of an organisation. Monsanto developed a strong corporate campaign in order to raise the social and scientific arguments related to genetically modified foods. This attempt at being perceived as fair minded and concerned about these issues was articulated using two-sided arguments and invited comment and discussion.

Corporate identity therefore is about how an organisation presents itself. Corporate image is the what an audience believes an organisation to be as a result of their understanding of the cues. Sometimes the perception of these cues is correct and sometimes they are not correct. This may be because corporate communications are good or because corporate performance is not good.

Corporate reputation is an extension of corporate image. Corporate reputation refers to the individual's reflection of the historical and accumulated impacts of previous identify cues, whether or not they have been influenced by transactional experiences. (Marwick and Fill, 1997)

9.2 Corporate communication strategy

As well as communicating about its individual products and services, the company may wish to pursue a corporate communication strategy. This can take either of two forms. Firstly it can be a simple corporate communication campaign aimed at improving the company's identity and subsequently its image. Secondly, it may be a campaign whereby the company associates itself with a current and topical social issue.

Activity 10 **(30 minutes)**

Identify two major companies who have developed corporate campaigns related to social issues. What do you consider to be the benefits and potential problems associated with such a strategy?

9.3 Crisis communications

Closely allied to corporate identity is the field of crisis management (communications). Company image and reputation can be severely tarnished or even ruined if a response to a crisis is deemed inappropriate.

EXAMPLE

Mercedes

The initial response by Mercedes when its then prototype vehicle the A-Class turned over when driven by journalists was to deny that there was a problem. That denial, which lasted eight days, turned into a crisis as 3,000 orders were lost and the media refused to let go of the problem. The reputation of Mercedes was dented or challenged for the first time in a long time and only the acceptance of the problem and a public statement on the actions the company was to take with regard to production and design, alleviated the pressure on the company.

Some crises can be anticipated perhaps because of the nature of the business environment in which an organisation operates. For example, hospitals can plan for bed shortages due to epidemics or local rail/traffic accidents. Airlines plan meticulously to cope with air accidents although their incidence is relative rare. However, the kidnapping of a senior executive cannot be anticipated with such clarity and neither can product sabotage and other seemingly unprovoked attacks on an organisation.

Chapter roundup

- Choice of promotional tool can be affected by factors such as time available, budget constraints, stage of the product life cycle, target market and the product or service's characteristics.
- The sales force provide a vital function to the organisation as they form a direct link to buyers.
- Not only does the salesforce act in the capacity of salespeople, in an indirect way so do other employees.
- Sales promotion encompasses a range of techniques appropriate for targeting consumers, trade and the sales force.
- Below the line communications make use of non-commissioning paying media.
- Sales promotion objectives can include increasing awareness, encouraging brand switching, giving incentives to consumers, increasing display space and developing a consumer database.
- Packaging is a marketing tool that encompasses graphic design with marketing concepts to create an identity for the brand.
- Merchandising can be defined as the range of sales promotions activities intended to ensure that products are easily available and prominently displayed.
- Public relations is defined as the planned and sustained effort to establish and maintain goodwill and mutual understanding between an organisation and its publics.
- PR embraces a range of activities including advice, employee relations, community and interest group relations, lobbying and monitoring public opinion.
- Four PR models exist and the ideal one is the two way symmetric one.
- PR techniques can be utilised to communicate with consumers, other businesses, employees, external publics and finance.
- Direct marketing is the planned recording, analysis and tracking of customer behaviour to develop relational marketing strategies.
- Relationship marketing is a view that emphasises the importance of the relationships developed between an organisation and other parties including customers, partners, suppliers and the trade.
- Sponsorship is a contribution to an activity or organisation by another, usually with the expectation of achieving benefit for the sponsor.
- Sponsorship can be more efficient than other forms of communication as it can generate both audience appeal while linking the values of the sponsored entity to the sponsor.
- Ambush marketing involves a firm, often a competitor, attempting to deflect attention from another sponsor onto itself.
- A profile communication strategy addresses the needs of how the corporate entity is perceived by a range of stakeholder audiences.
- Corporate identity is about the way an organisation communicates with its audiences.
- Exhibitions and trade shows provide a temporary forum for sellers of a product category to exhibit and demonstrate their products to prospective buyers.

Quick quiz

1. Define personal selling.
2. What roles can the salesforce be involved in?
3. What activities can the salesforce be involved in?
4. Define sales promotion.
5. What is the advertising to sales promotion ratio?
6. List four consumer and four trade sales promotions activities.
7. What are the potential emotional and psychological benefits of packaging?
8. What are the key packaging features?
9. What is a planogram?
10. What are publics?
11. What are the four models of PR?
12. Define two way symmetric.
13. What is a database?
14. List four direct marketing media.
15. What factors have contributed to the growth of sponsorship?
16. What are the potential risks associated with sponsorship?
17. What are the three main developments in sponsorship?
18. What does AIMRITE stand for?
19. List four reasons for exhibiting.
20. What are the two main forms of communication concerned with corporate identity?

Answers to quick quiz

1. The presentation of products and associated persuasive communication to potential clients, which is employed by the supplying organisation. (See paragraph 2)
2. Order collecting, order taking, pre-order caller, order supporter and order getter. (para 2.1)
3. Prospecting, communicating, selling, servicing, information gathering, allocating and shaping relationships. (para 2.1)
4. A range of tactical marketing techniques, designed within a strategic marketing framework, to add value to a product or service, in order to achieve a specific sales and marketing objective. (para 3)
5. 30:70 (para 3)
6. Consumer: coupons, money off, loyalty schemes, merchandising
   Trade: allowances, contests, sampling, free gifts. (para 3.2)
7. Aesthetically pleasing, expression of brand values, visual impact, added value, a reminder, loyalty cues and creation of an emotional link. (para 4.1)

8 Colour, typography, logo, type/material, shape and structure, label or mark and size. (para 4.2)

9 Diagrams or plans showing store and shelf layout. (para 4.4)

10 Refers to the many target audiences that communications may be focussed towards, eg customers, influencers, media, employees, pressure groups etc. (para 5.1)

11 Press agency/publicity, public information, two way asymmetric and two way symmetric. (paras 5.2-5.6)

12 Direct dialogue between a sender and receiver of communications. (para 5.6)

13 A collection of data, usually on a computer, shared to provide useful, convenient and interactive access to information. (para 6)

14 TV, radio, direct mail, telemarketing. (para 6.1)

15 Media fragmentation, favourable associations, overcome linguistic and cultural barriers, wide appeal, overcome legal barriers (eg tobacco) and allows for selective targeting. (para 7.1)

16 Negative associations, clutter and evaluation difficulties. (para 7.2)

17 Broadcast sponsorship, product placement and cause-related marketing. (para 7.3)

18 Audience, Impact, Message, Response, Internal Management and End results. (para 6.3)

19 Enhance company image, interact with customers, promote existing products and obtain competitor intelligence. (para 8.1)

20 Planned, ie pre-determined by the organisation and those that are unplanned and unexpected. (para 9.1)

Answers to activities

1 The answer to this activity will depend on the items you have chosen

2

Stage in the PLC	Promotional Activity
Introduction	High profile activities to raise awareness and encourage trial eg TV and poster campaigns as well as sampling (either door drops or in-store)
Growth	Need to build brand preference and loyalty using promotions such as competitions and free offers as well as advertising to create long term image
Maturity	A high degree of customer understanding so need to encourage greater consumption by reminding and reinforcing through print media and mass advertising
Decline	Need to attempt to control the rate of decline by rewarding loyalty through promotional activities which are low cost

3 You will need to research the answer to this activity yourself, by obtaining the relevant literature.

4 The answer to this activity will depend on the items you have chosen

5 The answer to this activity will depend on the items you have chosen

6 There is no specific answer to this activity.

7 The answer to this activity will depend on the items you have chosen

8 The answer to this activity will depend on the items you have chosen

9 The answer to this activity will depend on the items you have chosen

10 The answer to this activity will depend on the items you have chosen

Chapter 15 :
MARKETING COMMUNICATIONS

Introduction

Planning is the process by which one establishes objectives, strategy and tactics. This chapter will begin by considering the purpose and process of marketing communications planning. Objectives are necessary for planning operations at all levels of business, and marketing communication objectives typically refer to the goals the marketing communications have in affecting the mind of the target audience.

The third section will consider the factors that have encouraged the development of integrated marketing communications as well as the associated barriers. Tactics refers to the individual actions that combine to achieve the promotional objectives. The relative advantages and disadvantages of key media are discussed when reviewing the media planning process.

The chapter concludes with a section on budgeting approaches and a final section is concerned with the tools and techniques of marketing communications evaluation.

Your objectives

In this chapter you will learn about the following:

(a) the role of planning in developing successful marketing communications

(b) the importance of devising SMART objectives to facilitate evaluation

(c) the factors which have contributed to the increasing recognition of the benefits of integrated marketing communications

(d) an overview of action planning and the development of tactics

(e) the importance of effective media planning

(f) the principles underlying the key budgeting approaches

(g) the range of effectiveness measurement methods and tools

1 THE MARKETING COMMUNICATIONS PLANNING PROCESS

1.1 Overview

It is important to realise at the outset that the planning of marketing communications is an integral part of much wider and more comprehensive business planning and marketing planning processes.

Integration of business and promotion planning

Definition

> **Marketing communications plan**: document that summaries the main issues and details of marketing communications activities, including relevant background information and marketing communications decisions.

NOTES

Activity 1 **(30 minutes)**

For your own organisation, or an organisation of your choice, set out your understanding of how business planning, marketing planning and promotion planning are carried out and integrated.

It may be necessary to consult your own managers or other senior managers to get them to describe the process.

It will be useful to chart the process.

Suggest ways in which the process might be improved.

All planning at what ever level may be summed up as a process of answering three basic questions.

(a) Where are we now?
(b) Where do we want to go?
(c) How do we get there?

These are powerful questions and indicate the dynamics of planning; that is the answers should enable a firm sense of direction to be established and a number of specific steps defined to take an organisation forward.

Whilst these questions are powerful it is necessary to build a more comprehensive and structured process that can be easily understood, easily remembered and easily applied both in practice and also in examination situations. Paul Smith in his book *Marketing Communications: An Integrated Approach*, suggests a process based on a mnemonic.

SOSTT

+ 4Ms

These letters then provide the standard elements of a promotions plan.

Situation	(Where are we now?)
Objectives	(Where do we want to go?)
Strategy	(How do we get there?)
Tactics	(Details of strategy)
Targets	(Target markets/audiences)
+	
Men	(and women required to do the job)
Money	(financial resources/budget)
Minutes	(timetable of activities)
Measurement	(monitoring effectiveness)

The order of the letters represents the logical order of the planning process.

NOTES

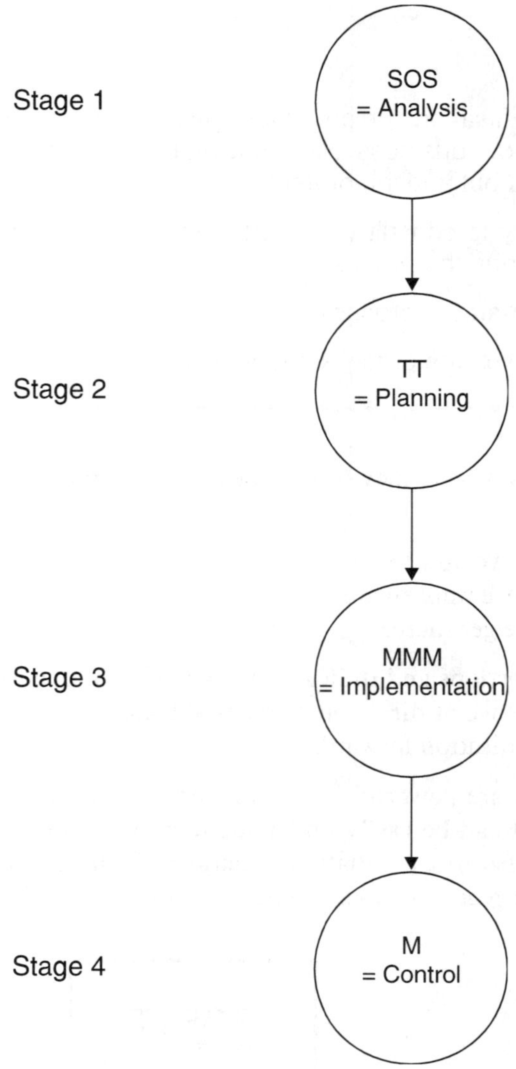

1.2 Audit

The 'situation analysis' is sometimes called a 'marketing audit' and occasionally an 'environmental analysis'. It is worth repeating that what we are concerned with is primarily promotional planning but this must be seen within the broader context of business and marketing planning.

For discussion of the overall marketing audit, go to Chapter 7.

2 DEFINING OBJECTIVES

Having arrived at a comprehensive and structured list of strengths, weaknesses, opportunities and threats it is now possible to set about the key task of defining marketing communications objectives. Again it is very important to remember that communications objectives cannot be generated in isolation as they are part of a hierarchy of objectives.

Definition

Objective: the goal or aim or end result that one is seeking to achieve.

Hierarchy of objectives

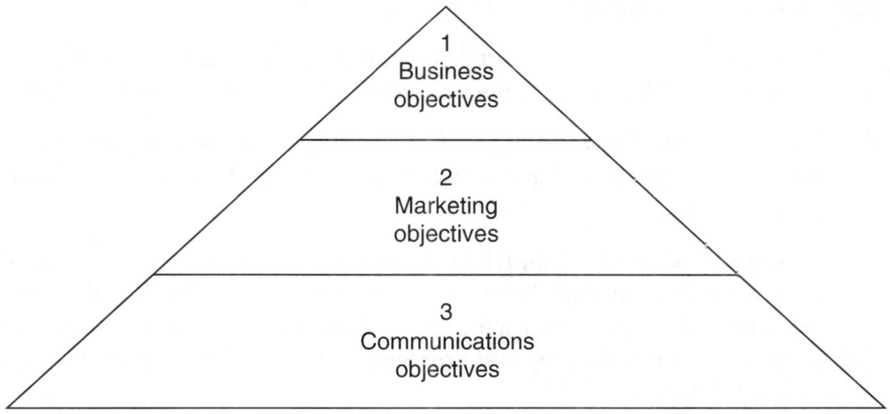

Business objectives are typically concerned with profitability growth and organisation improvements and will normally be of a longer-term nature. **Marketing objectives** are typically concerned with increasing sales, increasing market share and with all the elements of the extended marketing mix: the twelve P's. Of the extended marketing mix only one P is devoted specifically to promotion. However communications can have an important impact on many if not all of the other elements.

An alternative powerful way of generating communications objectives is to consider the individual elements of one of the communication models such as AIDA.

(a) **Awareness**. Promotion is almost always designed to increase the awareness of an organisation's products or services among its target audiences.

(b) **Interest**. Besides generating awareness, promotional strategies, and therefore objectives, must also be concerned with creating specific interest.

(c) **Desire**. Though valuable precursors, awareness and interest objectives are not in themselves sufficient. Other promotion objectives must be established with a view to increasing the desire for an organisation's products or services.

(d) **Action**. The final stage is getting the customer or potential customer to purchase the company's products or services. Therefore promotion objectives must be concerned with bringing about these actions.

Communications objectives like business objectives and marketing objectives are not simple wish lists but are concrete examples of a determination to succeed. They provide milestones against which to judge future performance and they are also the key to the integration of business activities. The characteristics of objectives can usefully be defined using the mnemonic SMART. Thus all communications objectives must be SMART.

Specific	Promotion objectives must relate to specific end results and not be so generalised as to be useless.
Measurable	Promotional objectives must, wherever possible, be quantified and therefore capable of being measured.
Achievable	If objectives are not capable of being reached they can be demotivating. They should be challenging but also achievable.
Relevant	All business objectives are about making choices between priorities in the use of resources. It is therefore important that the chosen promotion objectives are relevant to the overall marketing strategy.
Timed and targeted	To measure whether an objective has been achieved it is necessary to set agreed timescales. The T also refers to the need to target objectives at particular groups of customers or market sectors.

Some specific examples may be helpful. These are mainly taken from articles in the marketing press. (Details of timescale and measurability are not generally explicit, though there is no reason why they should not be.)

(a) 'BBC 2 is mounting an advertising campaign for the first time in its history *to boost its profile among a younger, less middle-class, more female audience*'.

(b) ' ... *to promote Stella Artois's Belgian heritage and premium ingredients* ... last year's campaign aimed *to persuade consumers that it was worth splashing out for a Stella Artois*.'

(c) 'Late-night slots on Channel 4 are the best way *to reach 17-year-olds. We want to intrigue them so that they will call in*, and from there decide whether De Montfort is right for them. The University needs *to stand out in an increasingly competitive environment*, and *to confront historic prejudices against the former polytechnics*.'

3 INTEGRATING THE PROMOTIONAL TOOLS

3.1 What is integration?

Strategy must be communicated in such a way that the messages are consistent through time and targeted accurately at appropriate stakeholder audiences. Each organisation must constantly guard against the transmission of **confusing messages,** whether this is through the way in which the telephone is answered, the impact of sales literature, the way sales persons approach prospective clients or the transparency of an organisation's overall corporate activities.

Marketing communications is about the promotion of both **the organisation** and its **products and services.** An increasing number of managers recognise the growing role the organisation plays in the marketing process and the impact that organisational factors can have on the minds of consumers.

It appears logical to conclude therefore that, if there are different audiences, many of them exist inside and outside the organisation, and some of them actively contribute to the source of some communications (eg marketing communication agencies). It is **important to bring corporate and business strategy together with marketing strategy** so that at some point, in some way, all these elements can be integrated, as is necessary if communication, marketing communication, is to be effective.

A dictionary definition says that integration is 'combining parts into a whole'.

Definition

Immediately it can be seen that **integration** of marketing communications is possible at three levels.

(a) Integration with business strategy
(b) Integration with marketing strategy
(c) Integration of the promotional tools

NOTES

DISCUSSION

For integrated marketing communications, more than one creative treatment – message or image – may be used, but where more than a single treatment is employed, they should be mutually consistent.

EXAMPLE

Renault

The end of the long running Renault campaign featuring Papa and Nicole was signalled by her television marriage in 1998. This featured comedians Reeves and Mortimer but prior to the ceremony 3,000 wedding invitations were sent out to the national and local press, requesting that journalists join Papa at the wedding of beloved daughter, Nicole, on Friday 29 May on ITV at 7.40pm. They were also invited to a pre-wedding breakfast at the Savoy the day before, where the advertisement of the marriage was shown.

The story appeared in every national newspaper (except the Independent and the Financial Times).

Source: Adapted from Gray, Robert (1999) 'Turning ads into talking points', Marketing , 1 April, p29.

Integrated marketing communications (IMC) means different things to different people, but is more likely to occur when organisations attempt to enter into a co-ordinated dialogue with their various internal and external audiences.

Definition

> **Marketing Communications** is 'a management process through which an organisation enters into a dialogue with its various audiences. To accomplish this the organisation develops, presents and evaluates a series of co-ordinated messages to identified stakeholder groups.
>
> The objective of the process is to (re)position the organisation and/or their offerings, in the mind of each member of the target audience in a consistent and likeable way. This seeks to encourage buyers and other stakeholders to perceive and experience the organisation and its offerings as solutions to some of their current and future challenges (Fill, 1999).

The word dialogue is used deliberately. Communication theory tells us that feedback is important. Of course, it is important to use feedback constructively and good marketing communications allows for the development of a circle of information between an organisation, its customers and interested stakeholders. Promotional messages should encourage target audiences to respond to organisations (or products/brands). This response can be immediate through, for example, purchase behaviour, registering on a website, using customer care lines or even through storing information in memory (or a file or desk) for future use. Creating and maintaining a dialogue therefore is a critical aspect of marketing communications.

The communication tools used in this dialogue and the messages conveyed should be **internally consistent with an organisation's strategies**. The target audiences should perceive the communication and associated cues as coordinated, likeable and timely. In

NOTES

addition, members of the target audience(s) should, at some time, be sufficiently motivated to want to respond to the communication and encourage future messages.

The word **positioning** is used in the definition as well. The manner in which an organisation (product or brand) is perceived relative to other competing products can be important to the level of success an organisation might enjoy. Therefore, the way in which a product is perceived by its various audiences is influenced by the marketing communications (stimuli) that are received by the audience.

Management pursuit and development of IMC involves the totality of an **organisation and all those with whom it interacts**. Because of the range of activities, the customer/audience focus, the breadth of the organisation and cultural shift involved in developing IMC, this concept is regarded as a strategy. This is important as IMC is too often depicted as just the co-ordinated impacts of the tools of the promotional mix.

DISCUSSION

Where integration is not applied, there are potiential dangers of marketing communciation dysfunction in which the activities and effort become counter-productive.

3.2 The development of IMC

There are a number of reasons why organisations are seeking to establish IMC. The following table sets out some of the drivers behind this growth (Fill, 1999).

Organisational Drivers for IMC

- Increasing profits through improved efficiency
- Increasing need for greater levels of accountability
- Rapid move towards cross-border marketing and the need for changing structures and communications
- Co-ordinated brand development and competitive advantage
- Opportunities to utilise management time more productively
- Provide direction and purpose

Market Based Drivers for IMC

- Greater levels of audience communications literacy
- Media cost inflation
- Media and audience fragmentation
- Stakeholder's need for increasing amounts and diversity of information
- Greater amounts of message clutter
- Competitor activity and low levels of brand differentiation
- Move towards relationship marketing from transaction based marketing
- Development of networks, collaboration and alliances

Communication Based Drivers for IMC

- Technological advances
- (Internet, databases, segmentation techniques)
- Increased message effectiveness through consistency and reinforcement of core messages
- More effective triggers for brand and message recall
- More consistent and less confusing brand images
- Need to build brand reputations and to provide clear identity cues

As with any new development or attempt to advance an organisation, there will inevitably be those who wish to resist any change to their accepted pattern of life and understanding of their world. IMC is resisted for many reasons. Failure to establish IMC as a total concept may be for one or other of the following reasons.

- Financial structures and frameworks
- Reluctance to change
- Traditional hierarchical management and brand structures
- Attitudes and structure of suppliers and agencies
- Perceived complexity of planning and coordination
- Lack of experience

Overcoming these different forms of resistance can be tricky and partly because of the enormity of the task, especially in global organisations, there are few examples of truly rooted IMC. Here are some of the ways in which the restraints can be overcome.

- Adopting a customer focused philosophy
- Using training and development programmes
- Appointing change agents
- Planning to achieve competitive advantage
- Developing an incremental approach

The diagram below sets out a model of IMC and demonstrates the way in which the different elements of an organisation's activities need to be brought together if IMC is to flourish (Fill, 1999).

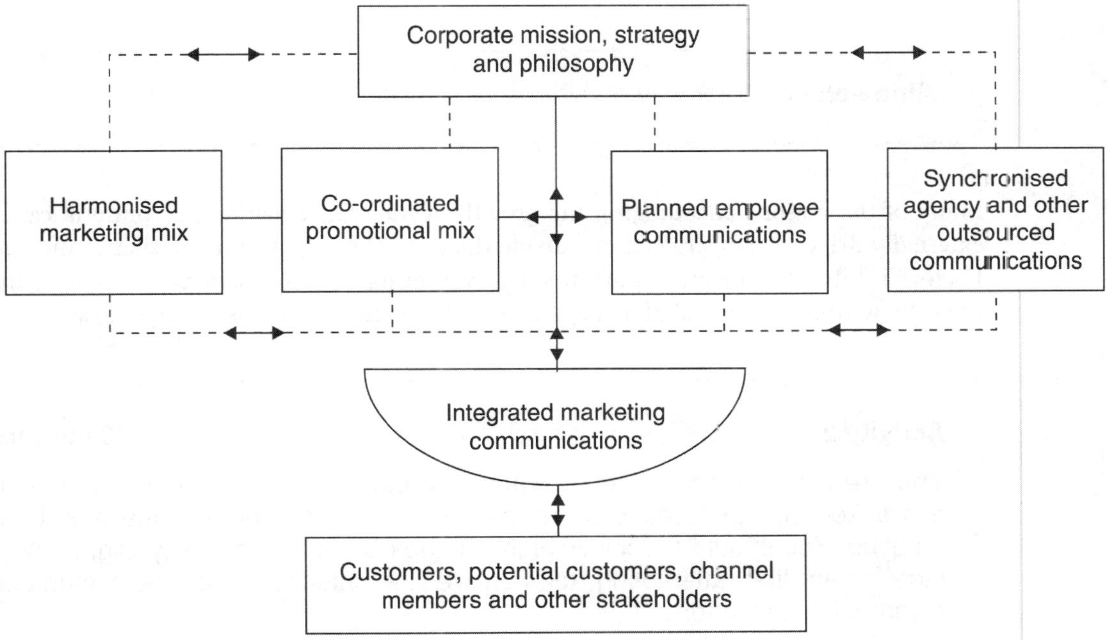

3.3 Benefits of integrated marketing communications

The principal benefit derived from the integration of marketing communications is synergy. By bringing together the various facets of marketing communications in a mutually supportive and enhancing way then the resulting 'whole' is more than the simple sum of its parts.

Benefits of integrated marketing communications include:

- creative integrity
- consistent messages
- unbiased marketing recommendations
- better use of media
- greater marketing precision

- operational efficiency
- cost savings
- high calibre consistent service
- easier working relations
- greater agency accountability

3.4 Barriers to integrated marketing communications

Integration is not easily achieved and while the associated problems are not insurmountable, they are significant for a variety of reasons. These include:

(a) mind set
(b) taxonomy and language
(c) structure of organisations
(d) elitism
(e) magnitude of task
(f) adequacy of budget
(g) manager ability
(h) agency remuneration systems
(i) dimensions of integration

Definition

Mind set: particular way of thinking or view held.

Many of the reasons encouraging the growth of integrated marketing communications are externally driven - they are factors outside the control of organisations, clients and agencies. Factors inhibiting integration are frequently internally, organisationally driven which are typically within the control of management to overcome, if there is a will to do so.

Activity 2 **(30 minutes)**

You are a newly appointed marketing executive and your marketing director has asked you to produce a report that can be presented at the next board meeting. You should succinctly highlight the issues the company might have to face when first attempting to improve the integration of their marketing communications effort.

4 TACTICS AND ACTION PLANNING

Having decided the promotional objectives and the broad promotional strategy it is now necessary to decide the individual actions to be undertaken (tactics). This requires a great deal of creativity on the part of the marketing team, their advertising agencies and other supporting agencies. A number of steps can be taken in deciding actions, including the following.

(a) **Review the conclusions of the situation analysis,** and consider how to build on strengths, overcome weaknesses, grasp opportunities and avoid weaknesses.

(b) **Consider the achievement of promotional objectives.** What promotional methods are most appropriate?

(c) **Evaluate the promotional tool kit.** Evaluate each of the promotional tools, above the line methods and below the line methods, to see which can make a contribution.

(d) **Consider the promotional budget.** The size of the promotional budget may eliminate the more expensive promotional media such as television advertising.

(e) **Integrate together into a schedule.** Having decided the most appropriate and cost efficient forms of promotion it is necessary to weld them together into an overall schedule of activities.

It will be extremely useful to construct an overall promotions plan and timetable, usually expressed in the form of a Gantt chart, as shown below. This serves to focus the minds of the planners on the contribution of each promotional element and how they may be integrated. It also provides a method of communicating the plan effectively and can be used for monitoring actual achievement against that planned and budgeted.

Timetable for a promotions plan

Activities	Jan	Feb	Mar	Apr	May	Jun	Jul	Aug	Sep	Oct	Nov	Dec	Cost £000s
1 Initial research	■	■											30
2 Corporate design			■	■									50
3 Trade advertising					■	■							700
4 Launch event						⊗							100
5 Editorial coverage						■	■						50
6 Special promotions								■	■				100
7 Consumer advertising									■	■	■		1000
8 Monitoring effectiveness												⊗	20

Total cost £2.05 million

5 MEDIA PLANNING

The concept of segmentation, which leads on to targets and positioning, is an essential part of marketing theory and practice. Segmentation is the process of dividing up large heterogeneous markets with similar needs. The ultimate, of course, would be to address the needs of every individual customer directly and specifically. This may become possible in future with the growth of electronic home shopping using the telecommunications superhighway.

Variable	*Example*
Geographic	Continent (Europe) Country (United Kingdom) Region (South East) County (Lancashire) Town (Manchester) Postcode (WA14)
Demographic	Age (over sixty) Sex (male, female) Status (married) Family size (3,4,5) Income (under £20,000) Occupation (lecturer) Education (degree) Religion (Protestant)
Psychographic	Social class (A B C1 C2 D E) Lifestyle (upwardly mobile) Personality (ambitious)
Behavioural	Benefits required (quality, service, price) Usage rate (light, medium, heavy) Loyalty status (strong)

Definition

Psychographic segmentation: based on psychological dimensions such as values, lifestyles, attitudes, interests and opinions.

Once the market has been divided into segments it is necessary for the marketing manager to make the correct target decision. Three broad options are possible: undifferentiated marketing, differentiated marketing and concentrated marketing.

(a) **Undifferentiated marketing.** Segments can be ignored and one marketing strategy offered to all customers. There are certain cost advantages to this approach and perhaps the most famous example is that of Henry Ford who introduced the Model T Ford in any colour you wanted as long as it was black!

(b) **Differentiated marketing.** A company can operate in two or more segments and offer a unique marketing mix to each. This is quite common among larger companies who may employ several different brands in the same market.

(c) **Concentrated marketing.** In undifferentiated marketing the whole market is attacked and in differentiated marketing, marketers go for two or more segments. In *concentrated* marketing the concentration is on a single market sector, for example Rolls Royce in the luxury car market.

Next it is necessary to select a strategy to position the product or service in the minds of the consumers of the selected segments. *Positioning* can be undertaken using one of the segmentation bases.

(a) By benefit or attribute
(b) By price and quality
(c) By use or application
(d) By product user
(e) By competition

Definition

> **Positioning:** the relative perceptual position of one brand compared with competing brands.

5.1 Media planning concepts

There are a number of concepts associated with media planning and an understanding of these (and the jargon) will help you to appreciate some of the strategic issues associated with this important aspect of the communication process.

Reach

When a new product is launched or a new variant introduced to the market, the communications objective is very often to generate high levels of awareness. The complementary media strategy is called a reach (or coverage) strategy. This means ensuring that as many people in the target audience have an **opportunity** to see/hear the message during the relevant time period/campaign.

Frequency

The ability of people to retain (and of course forget) information varies widely. In view of this, **advertising messages need to be repeated**.

Definition

> **Frequency** is used to refer to the number of times a person is exposed to the message, within a particular campaign or period of time.

DISCUSSION

Frequency is important because promotional messages usually have to be seen more than once to create a meaningful efffect.

The word exposure in the preceding paragraph is important. Calculations in media planning are based upon an individual's **opportunity to see** (OTS) the advertisement. This means seeing the media vehicle (Marie Claire, FHM) which, of course, is not the same as actually seeing or reading a particular advertisement.

The relationship between reach and frequency is important. All campaigns need to generate a certain number of OTS and these are determined and measured by what are referred to as ratings (or Gross Rating Points). Ratings are the multiple of reach and frequency.

Reach × Frequency = Ratings (in television these are known as TVRs)

Definition

> **TVR – television rating points** – an estimate of the audience for a TV advertisement and are determined through BARB data. They are in effect index numbers that represent the proportion of the potential viewing audience.

One of the important tasks of the media planner is to determine the number of times the target audience should be exposed to the message. This is referred to as the **level of effective frequency**. There is no set answer and a debate about whether it should be 1, 2 3 or 10 times in any one purchase interval, continues. Without wishing to trivialise an important issue there appear to be two main views.

(a) Effective Frequency state that the answer is three.

(b) Recency Planning argue that one exposure per purchase interval is all that is necessary.

You need to be aware of the issue and be able to justify your media schedule when preparing a marketing communication plan.

5.2 Developing the media plan

Many of the initial considerations in media planning will be identical to those which apply when starting communications planning.

Market background

Market size, shares and trends must all be taken into account. If a client is trying to break into a highly competitive marketplace, such as washing powder, perfumes or confectionery, then heavyweight multi-media advertising may be the only way of making a presence felt. On the other hand, if a small advertiser is trying to establish himself in the market for a highly specialised service (for example genealogical research services for the family historian), a tightly targeted campaign through a specialist medium will probably suffice.

EXAMPLE

For the large advertiser trying to track competitive media expenditure, Register MEAL provides a useful reference point. Advertising expenditure levels across a wide variety of product and service groupings are monitored and published quarterly. Figures are calculated using ratecard prices published by the different media, or by using industry benchmark estimates. As most advertisers do not usually pay ratecard prices, accuracy for specific campaigns can be questionable. However, it is a helpful guide to relative levels of expenditure within an industry or product grouping.

Although some advertisers are forced into specific media choices in order to mirror and offset the actions of their competitors, other advertisers may choose a little-used medium in order to capitalise on 'stand out value'.

Media must be able to deliver the target market required. Some audiences are more difficult to deliver than others, owing to their media viewing habits. Young adults tend to be light television viewers and may be best targeted with cinema advertising. Mass media will rarely deliver niche audiences, special interest magazines being a more appropriate media vehicle.

Activity 3 **(15 minutes)**

Suppose you work for a cinema chain. What information might it be useful to collect to help potential advertisers decide when and whether to use some or all of your cinemas as an advertising medium?

Product/service background

The role which advertising is to play for the product or service will to some extent dictate media strategy. If the campaign's objective is to ensure that the audience is constantly **reminded** about the product being advertised, then media may be used continuously in a low key manner. If the objective is to inform about a new product or service, then a mass media launch will be more suitable.

Budget

Clients should always specify the amount of money that they intend to spend on *media*, as opposed to the production budget for a campaign.

The budget can prove to be a media constraint. A budget of £100,000 would tend to dictate a campaign that runs on a local basis only, or a national campaign which utilises only one medium (for example, a national press campaign with a limited number of titles). A budget of £2m would allow for a national campaign across a mix of media. As previously stated, you should try to get a feel for this by reading the marketing press.

Media characteristics

Media choice is also governed by a number of factors arising from the different properties of the various media options.

The nature of the medium in its own right is an important consideration. People purchase magazines for their entertainment value, or because they serve as an information source.

The **positioning of adverts within television, radio or cinema contexts** can make a difference to how they are perceived. An advert scheduled in the middle of a TV game show will deliver an audience with a different mind set from one scheduled in the centre break of a documentary. Take notes next time you watch either on commercial TV.

Another consideration is **how people use media**. For instance, many popular radio stations are used as a background to other activities (driving a car, talking to friends, carrying out activities at work or in the home). People are generally unlikely to be giving their main attention to listening to the radio (unless it is 'talk radio').

The amount of time spent with the medium can be a factor. Daily newspapers are a relatively quick read in the busy environment of the working week.

Booking and production lead times may rule out the use of certain media. Magazine space is generally booked months in advance. Television and cinema commercials with high production values will take months to prepare, film and edit.

As well as taking into account the inherent features of each medium, **media channels must be evaluated quantitatively** for their ability to deliver against criteria such as coverage, frequency and cost.

Coverage (also called reach or penetration) is a measure of the percentage of a particular target audience reached by a medium or a whole campaign. Frequency is the number of times the target audience has an opportunity to see (or hear) an advertising message. Cost will not only be measured as an absolute, but also in terms of the cost per thousand contacts of the target audience.

Media planners will use recognised media research sources such as the National Readership Survey, Target Group Index and BARB to calculate media efficiency.

Definition

BARB – Broadcasters' Audience Research Board. This body is jointly owned by the BBC and ITV and is responsible for producing information on TV viewing activity. Electronic meters and diaries from over 4,400 nationally representative households are used to record the information.

Client preferences

Clients may have their own specific reasons for dictating or declining the use of specific media options. One company booked a poster site directly opposite one of their main competitor's head offices on an 'until cancelled' basis. Every morning and evening, employees were greeted with the sight of their rival's latest advertising campaign.

Media scheduling

As the media planner works through the available choices, a media schedule begins to evolve. This is the formal listing of which adverts are to appear where. Media schedules can be constructed for short term campaign bursts or for a whole year's advertising cycle.

Budget will be a major determinant in the seasonality of advertising. A very small budget may dictate that advertising is limited to certain key times of the year (eg pre Christmas; peak sales periods). A large budget that allows for year round advertising is usually allocated in one of two ways.

Definitions

(a) A **burst campaign** concentrates expenditure into promotional bursts of three or four weeks in length.

(b) A **drip campaign** allows for a continuous but more spread out presence.

NOTES

Example media schedule

	September 5	12	19	26	31	October 3
Supplements						
Observer	•	•	•			
Independent				•	•	•
S. Times		•	•	•		
Telegraph		•	•	•		
You	•	•	•			
Women's mags						
Vogue	September issue		•			
Tatler	September issue		•			
Elle	September issue		•			
Marie Claire	September issue		•			
Cosmopolitan	September issue		•			
Television						
Granada	◄------	------	------►			
Central	◄------	------	------►			
Yorkshire	◄------	------	------►			

DISCUSSION

Media planning requires that consideration is given to target audiences beyond the target market.

5.3 Key media characteristics

Medium	Advantages	Disadvantages
Newspapers (daily metropolitan/ national)	• 'Mass' medium: large audience in single exposure • Targeted sections (auto, home, computers etc) • Reader navigation: seeking news, information • Short lead time for production: accept ads 24-48 hours before publication • Flexibility of ad size • Tangibility of ad (can be torn out and kept) • Multiple readers/users • Allows detailed information (prices, phone numbers etc) • Allows (still) images	• Circulation does not mean readership: wasted circulation paid for • Print/image reproduction of variable quality • No exclusivity: ad may be next to competitor's • Costs loaded for preferred positions • Short life-span of news

BPP PUBLISHING

NOTES

Medium	Advantages	Disadvantages
	• Allows response mechanisms (eg captions)	
Newspapers (local/free)	• Low cost • Geographical targeting • High local readership • Special sections (especially local real estate, entertainment etc)	• Circulation of free papers/weeklies not always monitored/audited • Variable editorial content • Subject to weather and junk mail rejection if letterbox dropped
Magazines	• High circulation (major titles) • Targeted audiences (special) • High quality reproduction (colour photography etc) • Potential high prestige (vogue, time etc) • Reader motivation (selection, subscription) • Long shelf life and multiple use/readership • Tangibility, detail, images, response mechanisms (see newspapers)	• High costs of production • Hyper-segmentation (by interest and geography, may be insufficient circulation to support local outlets) • Long lead times: copy/artwork required 1 – 3 months before publication, can be inflexible
Television	• 'Mass' medium: large audience at single exposure, almost universal ownership/access • Detailed monitoring of exposure, reach, viewer habits • Allows for high degree of creativity • Realism: impact of sound + sight + movement • High-impact visual images reinforce retention • Allows demonstration • Flexibility as to scheduling • Allows association with desirable products	• Most expensive of all media costs • High production costs • Lack of selectivity (except via programming) of audience • Lack of opportunity/: does not reach commuters/workers • Long lead times for booking and production: penalties for withdrawal: inflexibility • Passive, unmotivated audience: 'zapping' by video fast-forward and remote controls erodes reach
Radio	• 'Mass' medium: wide coverage/access • Audience selectivity (local/regional) programme style/variety/content) • Opportunity: radio is portable – in-home, in-car, on public transport, shops, offices – even jogging	• May be passive 'background' noise: low attention, retention • May be 'cluttered' by announcers/DJ promotions • Sound only: no tangibility (pressure on retention of message), no shelf-life or 'pass on' circulation, no demonstration, no coupons, limited details etc

NOTES

Medium	Advantages	Disadvantages
	• Function: high usage for morning news, home 'companionship', background • Personal (+ potential for participation through talk-back) • Highly competitive costs of air time and production • Can be backed by personal DJ promos	
Outdoor media (poster sites bus stops, buildings etc)	• Flexible: sites, duration of lease • Comparatively low cost • Opportunity: exposure to commuters, shoppers	• Difficulty of verification of exposure/response • Subject to weather • Opportunity: site specific • No audience selectivity (except by site)
Cinema	• Glamorous • High impact (large size, highly visual, loud sound, high quality) • Captive audience (no TV 'zap' factor) • Can segment by local area	• High cost • Opportunity: site/time specific • Poor verification of response • Limited number of people reached per exposure

The following bar chart compares the media actually used most to advertise different products, suggesting that consumers look to different media for information about different products – or that advertisers (perhaps, your competitors) think they do.

Media used for different products

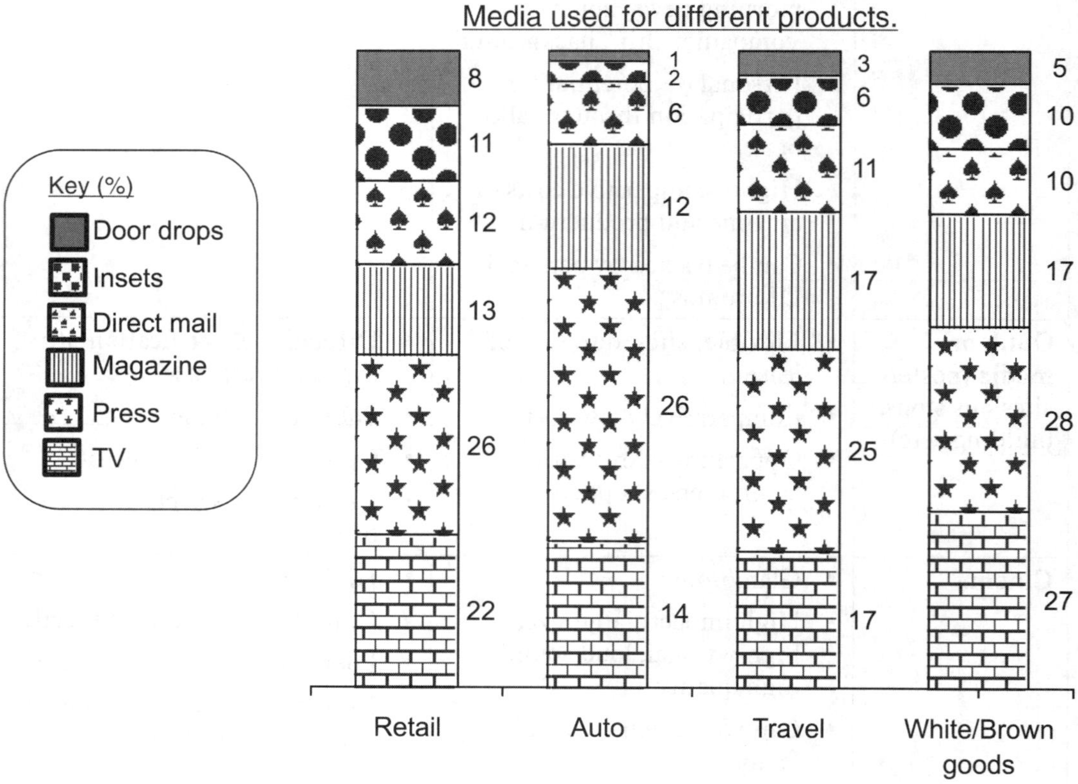

(Source: Direct Mail Information Service (DMIS) Intelligence Sector Report, 1997)

The following is a broad SWOT analysis comparing major media.

Medium	**Applications**	**Targeting**	**Testing**	**Cost per contact**	**Response speed**	**Response %**	**Response volume**
Press	– Lead generation – Direct sales – General awareness – Support for other activities – Boost store traffic	Medium	Medium	V low	Fast	Low	High
Radio	– Awareness – store and event traffic boost – lead generation (high ticket business-to-business)	Medium to poor	Poor	High	Medium	V Low	Low
TV - general	– Awareness – Store traffic boost	Medium to poor	Poor	High	Fast	Low	Low

Medium	Applications	Targeting	Testing	Cost per contact	Response speed	Response %	Response volume
TV – direct response	– Lead generation (high ticket items) – Direct sales (low ticket items) – Support for other activities	Medium	Poor	Low	Fast	Low	Medium
Posters	– Awareness – Store traffic boost	Poor	Nil	V low	Slow	Nil	Nil
Inserts	– Lead generation – Direct sales (especially non cash-with-order sales	Good	V Good	Low to medium	Fast	Medium to low	High
Direct Mail	– All (weakest where prospects 'cold', no suitable list available)	V Good	V Good	V High	Medium	High	Medium

The principal task in using media is to reach the right people, the right number of times, with greatest effect, with the least waste, at least cost, without distorting the message. The watchwords in media are reach, frequency, impact, economy, efficiency and effectiveness.

6 BUDGETS

6.1 How to decide budgets

There is no one uniform method of deciding what to spend on marketing communications. This is not so surprising. The following are some of the considerations that can affect the amount of expenditure.

(a) What variety of marketing communications is to be used?
(b) What tasks are to be undertaken?
(c) How competitive is the market place?
(d) How well known is the organisation?
(e) Are there any special requirements?

Costs to be budgeted

(a) Air time and broadcast media
(b) Space and printed media
(c) Production costs
(d) Staff salaries
(e) Overheads and expenses

DISCUSSION

Marketing communciations expenditures should be thought of as investments not expenses.

6.2 Theoretical approaches to budgeting

Theoretical approaches to setting budgets, for example by marginal costing approaches, have not found favour in industry because the effects of **any marginal increase on**

NOTES

expenditure are likely to be swamped, or at least hidden, by many other marketing variables. Therefore, we must still **rely a great deal on our judgement**. This in itself is not easy: the effects of any expenditure will have both long-term and short-term effects, as the following diagram shows. It can be seen that if investment is stopped then measured by brand recall its effects decrease with time. It is worthwhile emphasising the view here that **marketing communications should therefore be treated as an essential long-term investment**.

EXAMPLE

After deregulation of the UK optician market, optician practices were allowed to undertake unrestricted marketing communications. The optical industry was initially characterised as a low-spend sector until the retail trade was revolutionised by the mass media approach of new entrants such as Vision Express. Vision Express used their high promotional budgets to experiment with intensive and successful TV campaigns.

A similar approach was adopted by new homes builder Barratts who re-positioned their media communications by adopting high profile TV commercials. The result was that Barrett Homes became instantly recognisable to all new home buyers, beating all other building firms in spontaneous recall tests.

Methods of deciding budgets have, however, been developed over a period of time and, in the absence of clearer guidance, are useful in approaching a budget decision for the first time. After several years' operations it is possible to use experience to make decisions. One, or a combination of more than one, of the following methods can be used to approach the problem.

- Completely arbitrarily
- All you can afford
- Historical basis
- Matching the competition
- Percentage of sales
- Experiment and testing
- Modelling and simulation
- Objective and task method

Recent research has indicated a growing trend towards database methods and especially favours the objective and task method.

Completely arbitrarily

There are many examples of budgets being set in an apparently **arbitrary way by senior management**. There may be a link between the **personality** of the **decision maker and the level of expenditure**. This link may not be obvious to people elsewhere in the organisation. Subsequent arbitrary *cuts* in expenditure if trading becomes difficult and the profit margins begin to suffer are more worrying. Again, evidence from previous recessionary periods show that those companies which *do not* cut marketing communication expenditure in times of difficulty benefit in the long term by holding on to market share.

All you can afford (usually a minimum)

This often applies to a new company starting up or to an existing company advertising for the first time. The conscious decision has to be taken to forgo immediate profits or to forgo an investment in another area in favour of an investment in marketing communications. It is natural in these circumstances to act cautiously. This often means investing at a minimum level. This will necessarily limit the scope of the work, however, and limit the results to be achieved. It can be argued that **in many cases there is a threshold over which it is necessary to spend to obtain useful results**.

NOTES

DISCUSSION

When using the affordable method, extra care has to be exercised in particular situations such as when launching a new product or operating with declining sales.

Historical basis

We have already indicated that with experience managers are able to form their own judgement of the effectiveness or otherwise of particular expenditure levels and different promotional methods. Year-on-year figures provide the basis for following trends and making decisions accordingly.

(a) The **danger of inertia**: a temptation just to keep it the same, in which case all the elements of the environment and the costs associated with the task facing the organisation are ignored.

(b) A slight improvement is to use a media multiplier, which at least recognises that media rate card costs may have increased.

Matching the competition

In many cases an organisation is trying to reach exactly the same customers through exactly the same channels. In order to obtain a certain market share it is then necessary to match the competition and particularly the market leader.

Percentage of sales method

The percentage of sales is a commonly used method of determining a marketing communications budget because:

- It is easy to calculate
- It is precise
- It can be quickly monitored
- It can be varied in progressive steps
- It appears logical
- It is financially safe

However, the percentage chosen should be conditioned by all the variables listed earlier (not least by whether the market is a consumer or industrial one) and it should be dependent upon how competitive the market is. The following figures are suggested based on experience of different accounts.

Percentage of sales on total communications budget

State of competition	*Consumer markets*	*Industrial markets*
No competition	1%	0.5%
Little competition	2%	1%
Average competition	5%	2%
Heavy competition	10%	3%

DISCUSSION

Two primary decisions have to be made in setting budgets using the percentage of sales method – what percentage to use and what sales period to use.

Activity 4 **(30 minutes)**

Use the above table to determine the approximate marketing communications budget for a number of market situations with which you are familiar. Include consumer and industrial markets.

Experiment and testing method

This method involves selecting a set of matched markets. Different final promotional budgets can be set for each of these markets and the results carefully monitored. The resulting levels of awareness and sales delivered can be compared. For example this method can be used to evaluate alternative media schedules. Problems associated with this method include:

- The cost of conducting the experiment
- The time it takes to get results
- The premature informing of competitors
- The fact that markets can never be completely matched

Modelling and simulation method

With advancing use of computer databases and more precise promotional media it is possible to build models to forecast the likely performance of different media schedules. There are likely to be an increasing number of PC based modelling programs available which will allow a number of business variables to be examined including:

- Sales levels
- Purchase frequency
- Awareness levels
- Profits achievable

Problems associated with modelling include time and cost and the validity of the chosen model. 'Garbage in will give garbage out'.

The objective and task method

The objective and task method is probably the one which is most logical and appropriate to the complex situation found in planning marketing communications programs. Basically the logic of the method is as follows.

Determine the marketing communications objectives

↓

Determine tasks necessary to achieve these objectives

↓

Determine the cost of cash element

This approach is simple to understand and it embodies some elements of the marginal cost approach but this time in conjunction with carefully considered and linked objectives and tasks. It is necessary to be realistic about the objectives and accurate in the costing of the tasks. This an extremely difficult process in reality because of the large number of unknowns.

Activity 5 **(30 minutes)**

To demonstrate the logic and difficulty of this method choose a marketing communications problem with which you are familiar.

(a) Define the precise marketing communication objectives.
(b) Determine the tasks necessary to achieve these objectives.
(c) Cost out the problem both in terms of the individual tasks and in total.

A systematic approach to applying the objective and task method will pay dividends because of its rigorous nature. Although it will not necessarily produce perfect results it will lead to disciplined thinking and provide an excellent communication and decision device.

Ten steps in applying the objective and task method

Step 1.	Define marketing and promotion objectives
Step 2.	Determine the tasks to be undertaken
Step 3.	Build up expenditure by costing the tasks
Step 4.	Compare the results against industry averages
Step 5.	Compare the results as a percentage of sales
Step 6.	Reconcile differences between steps 3, 4 and 5
Step 7.	Modify estimates to meet company policies
Step 8.	Specify when expenditures are to be made
Step 9.	Maintain an element of flexibility
Step 10.	Monitor actual results against these forecasts

DISCUSSION

It is difficult to operationalise the objective and task method because it is not possible to guarantee that by undertaking a particular marketing communications task, or combination of tasks, a specified outcome will be achieved. Nor is it possible to know if the tasks were conducted in the most efficient way. There could be significant over-spending as a result of being over-cautious in using this method.

Activity 6 **(15 marks)**

Compare the advantages and disadvantages of the various methods that can be used to determine the appropriate levels of marketing communication budgets.

6.3 Advertising to Sales Ratios (A/S Ratios)

One of the important factors that always needs to be considered is the amount spent on communications by competitors. It can be difficult determining the amount spent by competitors on below-the-line activities, although accurate guesstimates can often be made by those actively involved in the market.

Above-the-line activities can be measured (data bought from various marketing research agencies) and can be used to gain an insight into possible strategies.

The A/S ratio for an industry provides a benchmark against which it is possible to determine how much should be spent or stimulate consideration of why certain amounts have been spent.

Definition

> The **A/S ratio** is different for each market sector. It is calculated by working out the total amount spent on advertising (usually at rate card cost) as a proportion of the sales in the market. Therefore, if sales in a market are valued at £150 million per year and the amount spent on advertising is £14 million then the A/S ratio is said to be 9.33%.

Part of the strategic decision is to decide whether an individual company's A/S ratio should be higher or lower than, or the same as (at equilibrium with) the industry average.

(a) **Reasons to spend more** might be that a **new product or variant** is being introduced to the market so greater effort is require to **develop awareness** (reach) and then perhaps knowledge and or establish brand values.

(b) **Reasons to underspend** the industry average might include trying to maintain an established market position or **directing spend to other products** in the portfolio or deciding to **put more work below-the-line**.

6.4 Share of voice

Definition

> **Share of voice.** Within any market the total of all advertising expenditure (adspend), that is, all the advertising by all the players, can be analysed in the context of the proportions each player has made to the total.

If one advertiser spends more than any other then more of their messages will be received and therefore stand a better chance of being heard and acted upon. If a brand's **market share (SOM)** is equal to its **share of voice (SOV)** an equilibrium can be said to have been reached.

It is possible that organisations can use their advertising spending either to maintain equilibrium (SOV = SOM) or to create disequilibrium.

The following matrix (Shroer, 1990) shows how different spending strategies are appropriate depending on your competitors' share of voice and your own share of market.

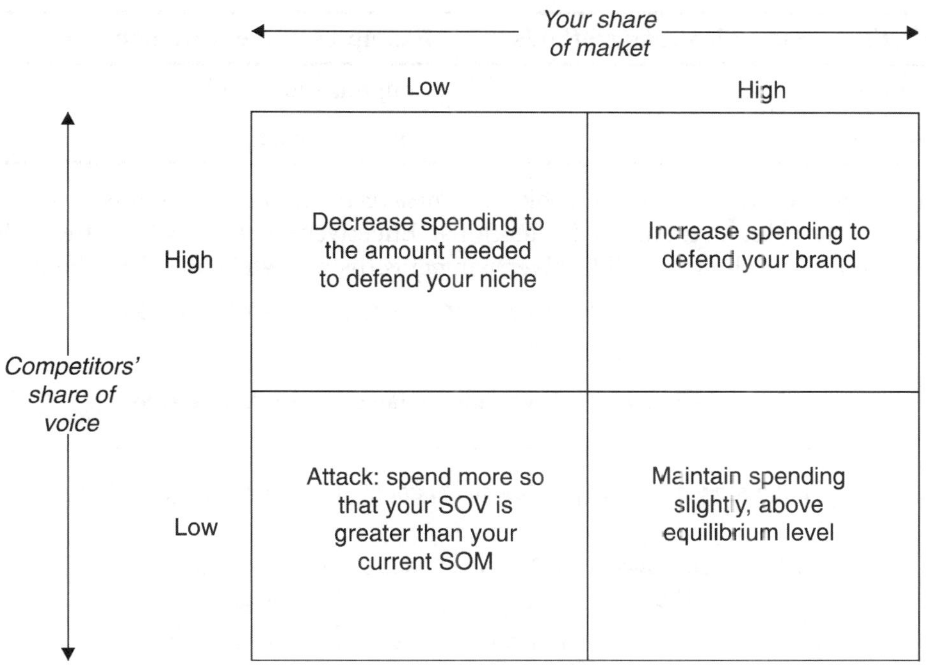

Note that careful monitoring of the fortunes of competitors is needed: if you know that a competitor is spending large sums on restructuring, say, they may not be in a position to retaliate to a sudden advertising burst by your company.

6.5 Controlling the budget

Marketing communication budgets may be very substantial and have a major effect on profitability. Controlling the effectiveness of the budget may be difficult if not impossible. What *is* possible is to use normal budgetary control techniques in marketing expenditure and to review its effectiveness regularly even if this is only by means of informed judgement. A simple way of representing this twin track is shown below.

Controlling the budgets and effectiveness

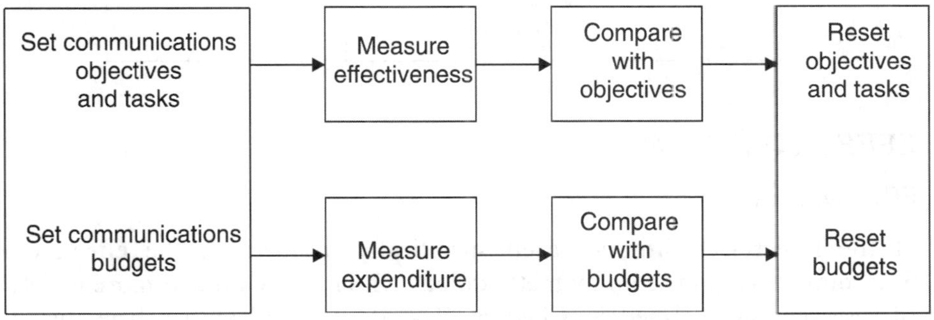

The difficult part is measuring the effectiveness of the marketing communications process. The following are some possible techniques.

Marketing communications methods	Examples of measurement
Personal selling	Sales targets
Public relations	Editorial coverage
Direct marketing	Enquiries generated
Advertising	Brand awareness

Marketing communications methods	Examples of measurement
Sales promotion	Coupons redeemed
Exhibitions	Contacts made

Engel, Warshaw and Kinnear's book on *Promotional Strategy* contains a substantial chapter on the 'Measurement of Promotional Effectiveness' from which the following table is taken. This shows possible advertising effectiveness and control methods.

Classification of advertising effectiveness measures

Type of Measure	Advertising related	Product related
Laboratory measures (Respondent aware of testing)	*Pretesting panels* • Consumer panels • Portfolio tests • Readability tests • Physiological measures eg eye movements	*Pretesting* • Theatre tests • Hall tests • Laboratory scores
Real world measures (Respondent unaware of testing)	*Pretesting* • Dummy advertising • Inquiry tests • On air tests *Post testing* • Recognition • Recall tests • Association measures	*Pre and post procedures* • Sales tests • Test markets

7 EFFECTIVENESS

7.1 Effectiveness

Most of the research techniques used specifically to measure the effectiveness of marketing communications employ methodology which is used much more widely in all kinds of research (as outlined in Chapters 2 – 4). As such only a brief list will be discussed.

- sampling
- questionnaires (and so analysis)
- ad hoc and continuous research
- panels and audits
- pre and post testing

7.2 Performance measures for advertising

(a) **Exposure**. Exposure can be measured in terms of frequency (eg the number of times a TV advertisement is screened) and the number of potential customers reached. One TV advertisement might reach two million people; by repeating the advertisement, the intention would be to reach people who missed the advertisement previously, but also to reinforce the message through repetition to people who have seen it before.

(b) **Awareness**. Awareness of the existence of a product, or awareness of certain particular features of a product. Awareness could be measured by recall tests or recognition tests.

(c) **Sales** (volume and/or revenue). Advertising is often intended to increase sales, the effect of advertising on sales is not easy to measure. Why?

  (i) Advertising is only one part of a marketing mix. Other factors influencing sales might be price changes, whether intermediaries have stocked enough of the products to meet an increase in demand, and competitors' actions.

  (ii) Advertising might succeed in **maintaining** a firm's existing market share, without actually increasing sales.

(d) **Profits**. The difficulties of measuring the effect of an advertising campaign on profits are therefore the same as those described in (c) above. Breakeven analysis might be used to calculate the volume of extra sales required to cover the (fixed) costs of the advertising. In monitoring the effects of a campaign, management might be able to judge whether this minimum increase in sales has or has not, in all probability, been achieved. However, advertising might be necessary to 'build' a brand or for management to 'invest' in it.

(e) **Attitudes**. The aim of a campaign might be expressed in terms of 'x% of customers should show a preference for Product A over rival products'.

(f) **Enquiries**. Advertising might be aimed at generating extra enquiries from potential customers. Where possible, enquiries should be traced to the advertisement. For example, a customer reply coupon in a magazine advertisement should be printed with an identification number or label, identifying the magazine and date of its issue.

It is difficult to measure the **success of an advertising** campaign, although volume of sales may be a short-term guide.

(a) A campaign to launch a new product, however, may have to be judged over a longer period of time (ie to see how well the product establishes itself in the market).

(b) Advertising's main purpose in the communication mix is to create **awareness** and **interest**.

(c) The effectiveness of advertising is therefore usually measured by marketing researchers in terms of **customer attitudes** or **psychological response**. Most of the money is spent by agencies on **pre-testing** the given advertisement or campaign before launching it into national circulation. Relatively less tends to be spent on **post-testing** the effect of given advertisements and campaigns.

Post-testing involves finding out how well people can **recall** an advertisement and the product it advertises, and whether (on the basis of a sample of respondents) attitudes to the product have changed since the advertising campaign.

EXAMPLE

New financial service brands including Virgin Direct and Goldfish are failing to convert high levels of awareness into new business.

'The brands, supported by estimated ad budgets of about £5m and £10m respectively and featuring Richard Branson and Billy Connolly, were ever-present on TV at the end of 1996, with Goldfish securing 30 per cent brand awareness for its credit card and Virgin 13 per cent for its products. But neither converted that awareness into new business, according to exclusive research on new financial service and loyalty schemes conducted by the RSL Strategic Initiatives Monitor.

Its survey showed that less high-profile brands such as MBNA's credit card, which had an awareness of only ten per cent, achieved a holding of two per cent - outstripping its higher spending rivals.

Significantly the reasons for changing suggest that credit card holders are looking for immediate benefits rather than the promise of rebates in the future from their cards. Over a third of new cardholders mention low APR (annual percentage rate - broadly, interest rate) and a quarter 'no annual fee' as reasons for taking new cards. In contrast only six per cent were attracted by points or tokens offered, while five per cent claim to have switched because they banked with the card issuer.

7.3 The effectiveness of sales promotions

There is often a direct link between below-the-line advertising (sales promotions) and short-term sales volume.

(a) The **consumer sales response** to the following is readily measurable.

- Price reductions as sales promotions (for example introductory offers)
- Coupon 'money-off' offers
- Free sendaway gifts
- On-pack free gift offers
- Combination pack offers

(b) It might also be possible to measure the link between sales and promotions for industrial goods, for example special discounts, orders taken at trade fairs or exhibitions and the response to trade-in allowances.

(c) However, there are other promotions where the effect on sales volume is **indirect** and not readily measurable, for example sponsorship, free samples, catalogues, point-of-sale material and inducements.

(d) Promotions may go hand in hand with a direct advertising campaign, especially in the case of consumer products, and so the effectiveness of the advertising and the sales promotions should then be considered together.

A manufacturer can try to control sales promotion costs by:

(a) Setting a **time limit** to the campaign (for example money off coupons, free gift offers etc must be used before a specified date).

(b) **Restricting the campaign** to certain areas or outlets.

(c) Restricting the campaign to **specific goods** (for example to only three or four goods in the manufacturer's product range, or only to products which are specially labelled with the offer).

7.4 Channels of distribution

Some organisations might use channels of distribution for their goods which are unprofitable to use, and which should either be abandoned in favour of more profitable channels, or made profitable by giving some attention to cutting costs or increasing minimum order sizes.

It might well be the case that an organisation gives close scrutiny to the profitability of its products, and the profitability of its market segments, but does not have a costing system which measures the costs of distributing the products to their markets via different distribution channels.

A numerical example might help to illustrate this point. Let us suppose that Biomarket Ltd sells two consumer products, X and Y, in two markets A and B. In both markets, sales are made through the following outlets.

- Direct sales to supermarkets
- Wholesalers

Sales and costs for the most recent quarter have been analysed by product and market as follows.

	Market A			*Market B*			*Both markets*		
	X	*Y*	*Total*	*X*	*Y*	*Total*	*X*	*Y*	*Total*
	£'000	£'000	£'000	£'000	£'000	£'000	£'000	£'000	£'000
Sales	900	600	1,500	1,000	2,000	3,000	1,900	2,600	4,500
Variable production costs	450	450	900	500	1,500	2,000	950	1,950	2,900
	450	150	600	500	500	1,000	950	650	1,600
Variable sales costs	90	60	150	100	100	200	190	160	350
Contribution	360	90	450	400	400	800	760	490	1,250
Share of fixed costs (production, sales, distribution, administration)	170	80	250	290	170	460	460	250	710
Net profit	190	10	200	110	230	340	300	240	540

This analysis shows that both products are profitable, and both markets are profitable. But what about the channels of distribution? A further analysis of market A might show the following.

	Market A		
	Supermarkets	*Wholesalers*	*Total*
	£'000	£'000	£'000
Sales	1,125	375	1,500
Variable production costs	675	225	900
	450	150	600
Variable selling costs	105	45	150
Contribution	345	105	
Direct distribution costs	10	80	90
	335	25	360
Share of fixed costs	120	40	160
Net profit/(loss)	215	(15)	200

This analysis shows that although sales through wholesalers make a contribution after deducting direct distribution costs, the profitability of this channel of distribution is disappointing, and some attention ought perhaps to be given to improving it.

EXAMPLE

Some of the most familiar ways to market consumer goods are proving to be costly failures (extracts from *The Economist,* 14 March 1998).

Recent research has begun to tell the makers of consumer goods which types of marketing actually work. Marketing is not about to become a science, but it will henceforth be easier to tell one half of the marketing budget from the other.

One surprise concerns price cuts. Packaged-goods firms spend some $70 billion a year on various promotions. Among marketing men, however, price cuts remained as popular as ever. It is an article of faith that they both reward loyal customers and woo new ones. Now even this is in question.

Chapter roundup

- The planning of marketing communications is an integral part of much wider and more comprehensive business planning and marketing planning processes.
- Marketing communications objectives should be specific, measurable, achievable, relevant, timed and targeted.
- In its simplest form, integrated marketing communications is concerned with the integration of all elements of the marketing communications mix across all customer contact points to achieve greater brand coherence.
- The development of IMC has been encouraged by factors such as lack of real growth in advertising expenditure, a growth in media independents and a growth in international communications.
- Failure to establish IMC may be down to financial structures, reluctance to change and lack of experience.
- Positioning can be undertaken by benefit, price and quality, use or application, product user or competition.
- When developing a media plan a number of different factors need to be taken into consideration. These include market background, product/service background, budget, media characteristics and scheduling.
- Media planning requires that consideration is given to target audiences beyond the target market.
- The watchwords in media are reach, frequency, impact, economy, efficiency and effectiveness.
- Budgets are both a resource and a constraint and increasing emphasis is being placed on being able to justify them in the light of marketing communications performance.
- In determining budgets it is important to clearly identify what they are to be used for because what is included and excluded varies between companies.
- A variety of basic budgeting methods are available but there is no single best method.
- Performance measures for advertising include exposure, awareness, sales, profits, attitudes and enquiries.

Quick quiz

1 What should be included in a marketing communications plan?

2 What does the SOSTT + 4Ms mnemonic stand for?

3 What does AIDA refer to?

4 Define marketing communications.

5 How can IMC be encouraged within an organisation?

6 Name four key benefits of IMC?

7 Define psychographic segmentation.

8 What is meant by the term reach?

9 What does TVR stand for?

10 What do BARB do?

11 What are the three key disadvantages of magazines?

12 Name three advantages of using outdoor media.

13 Why is the percentage of sales the most commonly used method of setting a budget?

14 Define the term share of voice.

15 List five types of research that could be undertaken to determine effectiveness.

Answers to quick quiz

1 It should summarise the main issues and details of marketing communications activities, including relevant background information and marketing communications discussions. (See paragraph 1.1)

2 Situation, Objectives, Strategy, Tactics, Targets + Men, Money, Minutes and Measurement. (para 1.1)

3 A communications model concerned with Awareness, Interest, Desire and Action. (para 2)

4 Marketing communications is a management process through which an organisation enters into a dialogue with its various audiences. (para 3.1)

5 Adopting a customer focused philosophy, using training and development programmes and developing an incremental approach. (para 3.2)

6 Benefits include creative integrity, consistent messages, better use of media and cost savings. (para 3.3)

7 Psychographic segmentation is based on psychological dimensions such as values, lifestyles, attitudes, interests and opinions. (para 5)

8 A measure of how many members of the target audience are reached by a medium or collection of media used in a campaign. (para 5.1)

9 Television rating point. (para 5.1)

10 The Broadcasters' Audience Research Board is responsible for producing information on TV viewing activity. (para 5.2)

11 High production costs, hyper-segmentation and long lead times. (para 5.3)

12 Flexibility (of sites and lease duration), comparatively low cost and opportunities to see. (para 5.3)

13 Ease of calculation, ability to be precise, can be quickly monitored, appears logical and is low risk from a financial perspective. (para 6.2)

14 Within any market the total of all advertising expenditure can be analysed in the context of the contributions each player has made to the total. (para 6.4)

15 Sampling, questionnaires, ad hoc and continuous research, panels and audits, pre and post testing. (para 7.1)

Answers to activities

1 This will depend on the organisation you have chosen.

2 Notes for a report highlighting the issues the company might have to face when first attempting to improve the integration of its marketing communication effort:

- the development of clearly defined marketing objectives which are consistent with other organisational objectives
- a planned approach which covers the full extent of marketing communications activities in a coherent and synergistic way.
- identify a range of target audiences – not just confined to customers or prospects but include all selected target audience groups
- the management of all forms of contact which may form the basis of marketing communications activity
- effective management and integration of all promotional activities and people involved
- incorporate all product/brand and corporate marketing communications efforts
- range of promotional tools/messages/media need to be consistent

3 Number of screens
Policy on screen usage: are some always eg used for children's films?
Foyer facilities: café or bar available
Type of customer: local or from a wide area
Type of film shown eg very cultural, or just mainstream
Foreign language films shown

4 This will depend on the organisation you have chosen.

5 This will depend on the organisation you have chosen.

6 **Arbitrary method;**

Advantages: uses experience
Disadvantages: based on intuition and so not recommended

Affordable method:

Advantages: relatively easy to undertake

Disadvantages:	product rather than marketing orientated as not based on market analysis
	Not useful for new products where little may be considered to be 'left over' for promotion
	Lacks flexibility and an appreciation of situations such as declining sales

Competitive parity method:

Advantages:	useful to recognise competitor activities so could be useful in conjunction with other methods
Disadvantages:	need to consider a number of factors including size of the competitor and its market position
	Looks at averages and so does not appreciate industry variations
	Cannot react to competitive activity, nor differing objectives

Objective and task method:

Advantages:	based on objectives
Disadvantages:	need to ensure that objectives are appropriate and this can be problematic
	Difficult to implement

Percentage of sales method:

Advantages:	most popular approach
	Links marketing communications expenditure directly to levels of sales
	Flexibility in that it can be based on future sales, historic or averaged sales
Disadvantages:	need to ascertain what percentage to set and how turnover should be determined

PART D: UNIT 20

SALES PLANNING AND OPERATIONS

Chapter 16 : SELLING AND THE PROMOTIONAL MIX

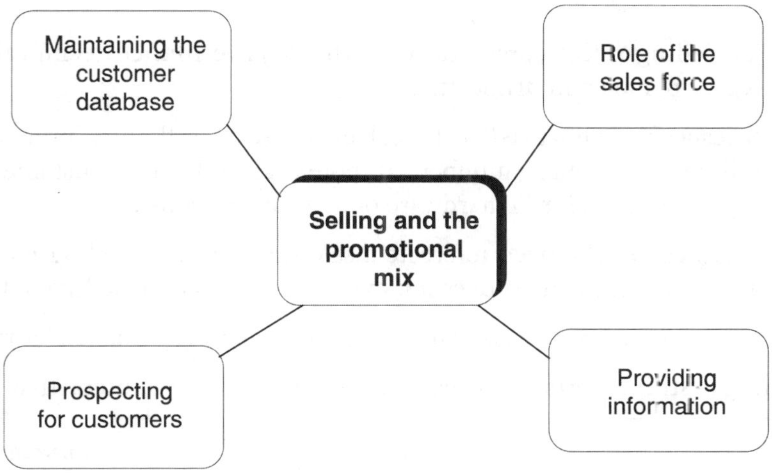

Introduction

Personal selling is part of the overall promotional mix, but is more relevant to some activities and products than others. This chapter will cover the role of selling and how it fits into the marketing mix, how information is gathered to help in sales planning and prospecting for customers and the importance of maintaining an effective customer database.

Your objectives

In this chapter you will learn about the following:

(a) The role of personal selling in the communications mix

(b) The components of the selling task

(c) The importance of information gathering by and for sales personnel

(d) How customer databases can be managed

The Unit details describe the role of selling in the promotional mix. The overall promotional mix, and the need for integration were described in Chapter 14. Review that chapter if you feel you need content.

Similarly, this unit covers buyer behaviour. This has been extensively covered in Unit 17, including the nature of the decision making unit.

1 THE ROLE OF THE SALES FORCE

1.1 Personal selling

Each individual probably has his or her own ideas of the 'typical' salesperson, but it is interesting to consider the wide range of face to face sales activities which exist. Types of selling include:

- Delivery people who also sell (eg a milkman).
- Salespeople within the premises of the sales organisations (eg a shopkeeper or store assistant).
- Travelling sales representatives, who require limited technical knowledge (eg soap, food and drink, etc).
- Salespeople who need technical expertise to sell their product, probably selling to a small number of potential industrial customers (eg sales representatives for IT hardware or software systems).
- Salespeople who need to create a sale through their selling methods where an established market does not exist (eg door-to-door selling of Cable TV).
- Sales people acting as consultants to consumers (eg financial services).

Personal selling is still important because it is both personal and interactive

	Personal?	*Interactive?*
Advertising	No	No
Sales promotion	No	No
Public relations	No	No
Selling	Yes	Yes
Internet selling	No	Yes

Activity 1 (10 minutes)

Take note of the next time you have an encounter with a sales person. How much advice did they give you, how interactive was the process?

Advertising is a message directed to customers in aggregate. Sales promotion is driven by the consumer. Selling is the only activity that is genuinely personal although customer care – post purchase – should also be personal.

The reasons why an organisation might decide that a personal sales element in the communication mix is worthwhile are likewise diverse. They include the following.

(a) The need to **demonstrate** a technical product (especially in the sale of industrial goods). Retailers may employ store assistants with some technical knowledge of the products on sale, but a manufacturer's own sales force is likely to be given specialised product training.

(b) The need to **explain a complex product** or service.

(c) **A lack of active selling by intermediaries and the desire to improve sales**. Wholesalers and retailers will try to sell; all the products they handle, and will not favour one manufacturer's products. Even dealers are sometimes lethargic in trying to sell their products.

(d) An **inability to persuade intermediaries** to accept products (there is often resistance by wholesalers and retailers to new products).

(e) **High intermediary profit margins** affecting the final sale price to customers. These costs of intermediate stages in the distribution channel mean that direct selling in some cases will be cheaper.

(f) A **small market** with only a few target customers may make direct selling cheap (and a dealer network impracticable).

EXAMPLE

Business to business marketers in technical markets, such as computers or specialist machinery, will take the time to explain the product benefits or be involved in the design of the product (or service, such as computer software) with the client.

(g) As a means of maintaining **good relations with end customers**, and obtaining feedback (ie market research information) about what the customer likes and does not like about the current products, or what new product developments the customer would wish to see happening.

1.2 The task of selling

Even in an organisation with a market orientated philosophy, there will be a need for a persuasive sales force. The need to convince the customer will arise because the customer's needs are unlikely to be **satisfied** exactly by any one product on offer. The sales task is to offer the most suitable product. For instance customers might need some reassurance that they are getting what they want. For example, a customer for a domestic household appliance might want to be certain that it can do everything he or she wants it to, and customers in DIY stores or garden centres often seek similar 'technical' advice from sales assistants. Another reason is that it may not be economically or technologically feasible to satisfy a customer's needs exactly. This is especially true in mass production industries. Customer tastes might have changed since the decisions about designing a product were first made, or expertise may be needed, for example in financial services so selling is a very important element of the promotional mix.

FOR DISCUSSION

Selling an intangible service such as life assurance is difficult, as benefits of the service are difficult to communicate

---

The task of selling involves:

(a) Communicating the advantages of a product to the customer

(b) Securing a sale

(c) Prospecting for additional customers. This involves searching for prospective customers, perhaps visiting them several times, and then making a sales 'pitch'.

(d) After-sales service. Queries and complaints will arise and must be dealt with to the customer's satisfaction, in order to win repeat sales.

(e) Gathering information about what the customer wants. 'The sales force can and should be the eyes and ears of the marketing organisation ... The sales force's fingers are on the market's pulse.' (P. Bennett *Marketing*)

EXAMPLE

Many holiday companies will send or give a customer a questionnaire after the holiday. This can be used to assess customer satisfaction and to gather important market research information that can be used by sales staff.

The detailed tasks involved can and do vary substantially but have been listed to include:

(a) Product delivery (eg the milkman);

(b) Order taking inside the seller's store

(c) Order taking 'outside' by a field sales force;

(d) Order taking by telephone

(e) Building up goodwill (eg merchandising work)

(f) The provision of technical or engineering advice to customers, perhaps in helping a customer to draft specifications for a product

(g) 'Creative' selling of tangible products

(h) 'Creative' selling of intangible products (eg people involved in the sale of services such as banking, or insurance)

(i) Recommending credit

(j) Collecting payment and avoiding bad debts

(k) Researching the market providing new prospects and up to date information for management

Given that the term 'salesperson' covers such a wide range of selling activities, it may be apparent that the desirable personality of the salesperson is likely to vary from one type of selling to the next.

Activity 2 **(5 minutes)**

Professional services such as medical services can also be marketed. What characteristics would a sales person in this market need?

Making sure that the right person is selected for the right sales job is an important element of the sales management task. Successful selection and recruitment starts with a thorough and careful analysis of the job description.

Salespeople can be required to have many skills besides the obvious ones of presentation, communication and negotiating competence. They may be required to speak other languages, drive and have technical expertise as well. It is important that all these necessary attributes are recognised and built into the job description.

On many occasions, personal selling is used in combination with other aspects of the marketing and promotional mix. We discuss this in the next section.

For the most effective use of the sales resource, it has **to be supported by other activities in the organisation, particularly marketing. The external focus** of the sales team, their apparently independent **work** culture and some misplaced envy for the travel and entertaining (often an integral part of the sales role) can easily lead to a 'them and us' attitude developing between sales personnel and their colleagues in other departments.

Management have an important task in preventing such barriers developing. They need to ensure the sales staff are recognised as being at the sharp end of a team effort a position which can often be both uncomfortable and lonely. Support provided from the centre not only makes the salesperson's task easier, it makes the whole team effort more effective.

The role of the sales support activities should be to:

(a) Maximise the proportion of sales time spent in face to face client contact

(b) Provide direction, and to ensure sales resources are targeted at the market segments and leads offering the greatest potential

(c) Provide the necessary backup to help the sales person ensure an continuing relationship with a satisfied customer

Sales promotion activities are temporary changes in the marketing mix, used to achieve tactical objectives. They can take many forms like free gifts and competitions, temporary price offers or, as we have already indicated, extra volume.

Sales promotions can be designed to influence three distinct groups.

(a) The **sales team** themselves, where promotions are incentives to encourage extra effort in promoting a new or sluggish product line etc.

(b) **Intermediaries**, like wholesalers or retailers, where promotions are designed usually to encourage some brand loyalty in their recommendation to the customer, to win extra shelf space or to encourage increased volume sales.

(c) To the **end user**, where promotions are designed to create interest or remind the customer of the product and its benefits.

Sales promotions need to be devised to meet specific objectives. These can be to help sell more in a quiet sales period, eg the January post Christmas store sales. Sales promotions can be used to encourage trials of a new product, like smaller sizes, test period offers, demonstrations etc. A product positioned in a competitive growth market needs promotions to encourage brand loyalty and repeat purchases. Collect six box tops for a free gift would help to achieve this. Mature products rely on promotions like competitions to generate interest. Promotions of products in decline are used to clear end of line stocks.

The distributor and supplier have a shared interest. Both will benefit from increased sales. The intermediary, however, is unlikely to be concerned about **which** brand customers choose to buy. Either way a sale is made. The distributor may actually make a higher margin on another brand, perhaps an 'own' brand.

1.3 Converting awareness to action

Sales and marketing have to be co-ordinated in the joint objective of **easing customers through the decision making process from awareness to action.**

One role of marketing is to provide sales with a flow of **qualified leads**. These should represent potential customers who are aware of the company and/or product, are already interested in it and who have or have begun to have a positive attitude to its purchase.

(a) The conversion rate of contacts already this far down the decision making process is likely to be higher than if the buyer has to be introduced to the product or company by the salesperson.

(b) The salesperson can concentrate on the action stage of selling, where it is particularly effective. This reduces the amount of non-selling time spent generating leads etc.

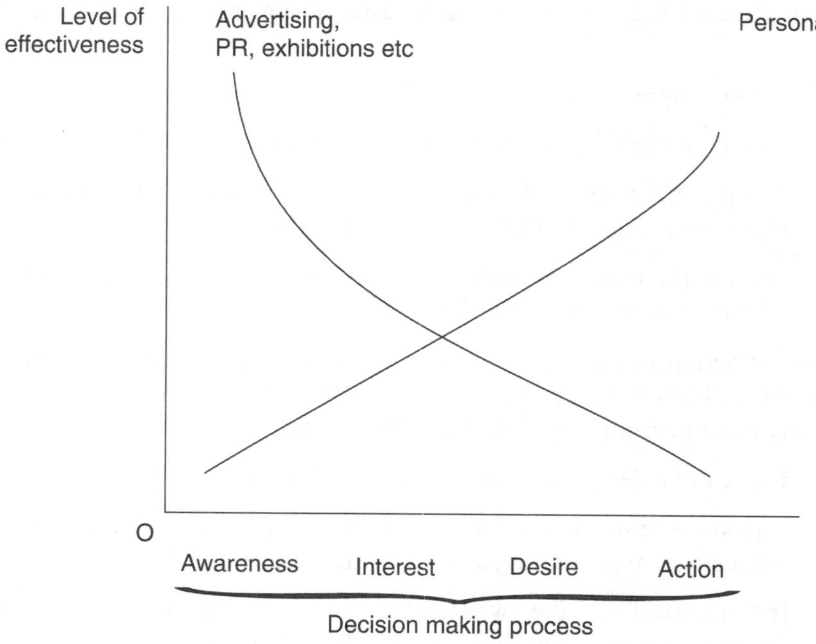

As we have already seen each of the promotional tools of marketing have their own particular strengths and weaknesses.

(a) **Advertising and public relations** are good at generating awareness and interest, but poor at action.

(b) **Personal selling** on the other hand is too labour intensive and expensive to be very good at generating awareness and interest, but it is very good at building **desire, changing attitudes and converting this to sales.**

Used in combination, the promotional tools ensure the maximum number of customers are moved through the decision making process at the minimum cost.

Communication objectives should therefore be written and results measured, in specific terms. Advertising should not be judged in terms of actual sales, but in terms of awareness or attitude. The advertising may be working, generating awareness and interested but if they are not being converted to sales by the sales team, then this is the element of the communication mix which needs reviewing.

The precise combination of marketing activities used to generate quality sales leads will vary from industry to industry. In consumer markets media advertising, offering brochures may be a means of identifying precisely those who are interested. In industrial markets the exhibition may be a more appropriate means of generating qualified leads. Direct mail and telephone selling are also likely to be used to provide the sales team with qualified sales leads.

NOTES

FOR DISCUSSION

Collect examples of direct mail. Discuss/evaluate how effective they are at generating sales.

Whatever combination of communication tools is used, the contribution of each to achieving eventual sales must be quantified and evaluated. Marketing managers need to recognise that it is often more cost effective to increase the conversion rate of interested contracts into sales, than to increase the numbers of people who are aware of the product. Getting the balance right between the selling effort and other promotional support is critical to the effectiveness and efficiency of the overall marketing effort.

2 PROVIDING INFORMATION

The support activities need to provide the sales team with information to make the sales activity more effective. In turn, the sales team should be providing a stream of information and feedback about the customers and the marketplace. This information will aid managers in their future marketing and sales decision making.

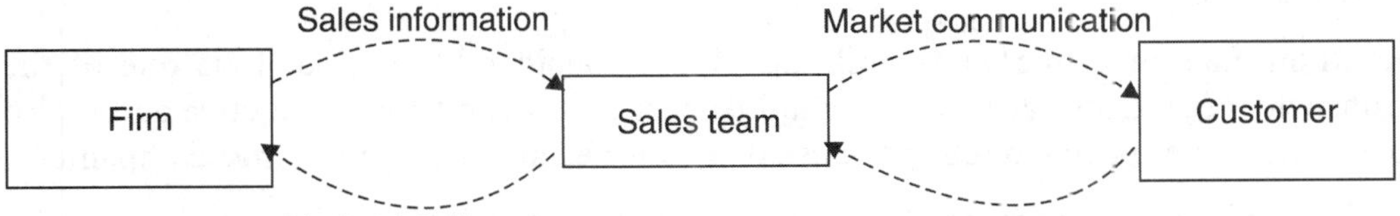

The sales team can be seen to hold a special place in the flow of information and communication between the firm and its customers. It is clearly important that the sales personnel have the skills to perform these functions accurately, without distortions and omissions.

FOR DISCUSSION

Sales personnel need training to be effective information gatherers.

Providing the sales force with adequate technical and functional training to perform their role is one way management can support the sales effort.

2.1 Sales research

Information is often an undervalued resource within the organisation. Yet it can provide considerable competitive advantage if managed and used well. In the context of selling, good information can both reduce sales costs and help to increase sales revenues generated by the same sales team.

Feedback information can be analysed by sales managers to enable them to **diagnose weaknesses** in the sales activity and identify the most rewarding targets.

(a) Profiling the 20% of customers who generate 80% of the business provides segmentation information, which means more customers of the same type can be identified and targeted.

(b) Analysis of the sales effort enables managers to give advice about:

  (i) The most profitable balance of new to old calls
  (ii) The most effective call rate per day
  (iii) The best use of presentations and demonstrations etc in a sales call
  (iv) The most effective frequency of sales calls

When it is recognised that the average sales person often spends less than 10% of his or her time in direct customer contact, it can be seen that any improvements either in the amount of effective selling time or the effectiveness of the selling process, can generate significant improvement in performance. Information provides the clues which enable managers to facilitate these incremental improvements.

The salesperson's perspective of the market place is perhaps unique. Of all people in the organisation the salesperson is most likely to see the company as the customer sees it - from the outside in. Others look at the business from the inside out. This different perspective should not be undervalued. It can contribute to both sales forecasting and business planning, but the flow of information needs to be encouraged and nurtured.

2.2 Customer and competitor intelligence

Good salespeople are ones who know their customer's business. This means not only knowing who they are competing with for the contract, but also who their customers are competing with.

This knowledge of a market is built up over a considerable period. It is one of the reasons why organising sales forces by industry or sector can be very effective and it also explains why sales people often specialise in a sector even when they change companies.

Now it is only necessary to reinforce the importance of building up and maintaining a good database of intelligence about both customers and competitors. Communicating this information to the sales force is the second but equally important step in this process.

New technology provides the systems to both store and retrieve rapidly such information. Sales teams should be able to access an up to date record on a company, immediately before a sales visit. This should record:

(a) Sales contacts made, including those made by other sales teams from the company

(b) Orders received, value, frequency etc

(c) Current financial standing, including overdue accounts

(d) Any intelligence on changing personnel in the company, new business won, contracts signed, plans announced etc

This information would supplement the sales persons own personal records and would provide a more macro view of the client company.

Knowing what your competitors are up to is of course a continuing concern for the marketer. As already indicated, the sales team may be an important early warning system in this respect. Equally, providing the sales teams with early information about proposed special offers, or new products being launched by competitors, helps the salesperson be better prepared when negotiating with a customer.

FOR DISCUSSION

Both information and intelligence are only of value if they are shared and used.

2.3 Measuring sales potential

Both specific sales information about calls and sales actually made, and market intelligence about customers and competitors, provide managers with an insight into sales potential.

If the sales resource is regarded as both valuable and scarce, it must be used with care. Maximising its value to the organisation means using it in areas where the sales potential is perceived to be greatest. This analysis of potential would then be a matter of policy, which would be implemented to guide the salesperson's allocation of effort and time.

Whilst it is possible to identify a number of factors likely to influence sales potential, it should be remembered that sometimes the greatest opportunities are not the most obvious and the customer who seems to offer they least potential may in fact offer the greatest. Too narrow an approach, prescribed by managers, may hinder the salespersons ability to identify new sales opportunities.

Sales potential can be affected by a number of issues, as indicated below.

(a) **Competition**. It can be more profitable to concentrate activities on a part of the market with a lower total potential because there is less competition. This is the concept of **niche marketing**. It is often harder to win a small share of a big cake than to gain a larger share of a small one:.

(b) **Future forecasts.** Sales potential should not be judged only on a short term basis, but should also be assessed on a forecast of the longer term future. A company in a mature industry wishing to place a very large order now, may offer a lower potential in the long term than a smaller company operating in a growth market, which today only requires a small order.

(c) **External factors**. All business is influenced by its external environment. Suppliers should assess the both factors which affect their business, but also those which affect their customers.

Activity 3 **(20 minutes)**

What factors have increased the mobile phone market over the past few years? How does this affect the sales function in mobile phone companies?

(d) **Marketing strategy.** The company decision about product range, service levels and pricing policy will all have an impact on the sales potential of an area or customer. It is worth remembering that sales revenue can be increased either by:

(i) increasing the number of customers or by
(ii) increasing the average spend of the existing client base.

The strategies to support either of these approaches will influence the effectiveness of the sales activity.

Market forecasts and business plans need to be informed by consumer information. Their basis can usually be found in forecasts of sales and market potential.

(a) Market potential data usually comes from the market researchers' assessment of a particular market segment.

(b) Sales potential estimates (the amount of expected sales which can be achieved profitably within the market segment) will be provided by the sales department.

When evaluating the sales potential of an area or territory it should be recognised that not all clients will be of equal value or potential. Looked at in terms of a life cycle it can be seen that the salesperson's portfolio of clients will be made up of:

(a) New customers with low current value but high potential;

(b) Growing customers with greater current value but only limited future growth potential;

(c) Mature clients with significant current value but no growth potential;

(d) Declining clients with only the potential of diminishing sales, but whose current value may still be worthwhile.

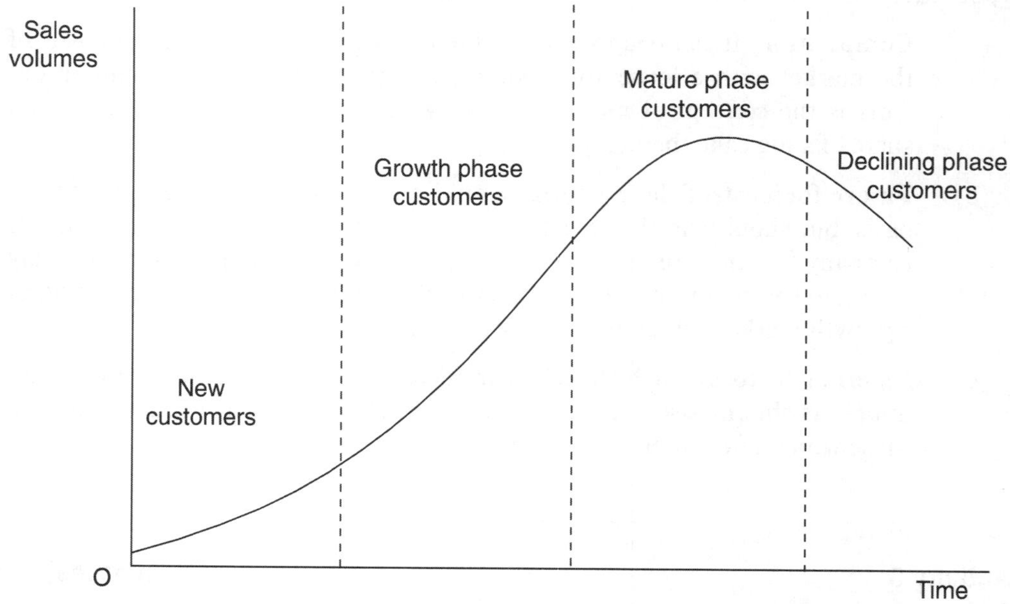

This analysis shows how it is possible for 20% of customers to generate 80% of sales, because their sales values are not equal.

FOR DISCUSSION

Sales effort is often concentrated on new customers to the detriment of existing customers.

The dilemma for the sales team its the trade off between current sales value and future sales potential. How much time should be allocated to the declining customers whose orders are still valuable and how much to the currently less valuable new accounts?

3 PROSPECTING FOR CUSTOMERS

3.1 Need for new

Whatever the organisation, the need for new customers is ever present. This does not just apply to profit earning producers of goods and services. Political parties require new supporters, charities new contributors and celebrities new fans and sponsors. This means that prospecting for new customers is an ever present part of the job for all those involved in selling.

New customers are needed for two reasons.

(a) To facilitate the growth and expansion plans of the organisation.

(b) To replace 'lost' customers who, through retirement, death, liquidation, take-over, or who have moved to a competitor, cease buying.

Successful sales staff are those who are always aware of the need for expanding their list of qualified prospects. The ability to locate new prospects is therefore a fundamental sales skill.

Definition

> Defining what is meant by the term **prospect** is quite important. A list of possible customers not screened in any way, for example, taken from a phone book or a list of visitors at an exhibition are known as **leads.** Leads may be potential prospects.
>
> When leads have been screened or assessed against specific criteria, like their need for a product, ability to pay for it or interest in it, then they are qualified prospects.

It is then possible for the sales team to qualify leads according to their potential value and the likelihood that they might make a purchase. This approach means priority can be given to the strongest leads or prospects and it is an important procedure for ensuring the most effective use of the sales resources.

3.2 Locating new leads

The professional sales person is always on the look out for potential new clients and leads, but there are a number of sources which can help in this process.

From the marketing effort

In a marketing orientated organisation other elements of the marketing and communication mix will be active in generating awareness and creating interest amongst new potential clients and customers. For example, an advertising campaign or direct mail drop, with a freephone number or an offer of further sales information or brochure, will generate a list of interested clients. Similarly an exhibition stand should also generate a list of qualified prospects.

From other parts of the company

Where the organisation has several divisions or the sales force activity is organised around products rather than customers, it is likely that potential prospects may already be contacts of the organisation.

(a) The mail lists and customer details from other sections and sales teams will consist of people who already have a relationship with the organisation.

(b) Similarly lists of past clients may also be capable of being reactivated.

(c) Service engineers are often well aware of clients who may be in the market for a new product. They are not always trained to sell, but they can be encouraged to pass on these qualified leads to the sales team.

Networking for leads

The best leads are often those which come along with a personal recommendation from an existing client. This adds the powerful dimension of word of mouth communication to the formal sales approach. Seeking and obtaining such leads from current customers and forming a network of clients, perhaps within the same business or area, can be very useful.

Leads from an industry

Becoming an industry watcher is also an invaluable source of leads. Trade journals and associations provide names of key decision makers, news of moves and new strategies can all be monitored and responded to proactively. It is also possible to purchase mail lists of key personnel in specific industries. The problem with such purchased lists is that they may be out of date and they are unqualified leads.

Leads from other firms

The activities of competitors can also be tracked by observation, informal meetings at industry events like trade fairs and trade association meetings, and through the industry press. It is also worthwhile striking up relationships with the sales staff of noncompeting firms. They will know the key decision makers and policies of their clients and exchanging such information can benefit both sales teams.

Cold call canvassing

Despite all the sources of qualified prospects and the support provided by the rest of the marketing activity, cold calling for new leads is still important in many sales departments. The use of telephone books, newspapers, membership lists, or just knocking on doors in an area, are all well established methods of cold calling. Often firms will provide telephone sales support to their representatives in order to undertake the cold calling more cost effectively and **qualify leads** to ensure that sales staff contacts the person who:

- is the key decision maker with the authority to pay
- has a need for the product
- is able to pay.

This preparation ensures that the sales time spent giving a presentation is not wasted.

It is worth the sales team remembering that, a sale is only a book entry until payment has been received. Getting credit references about prospective clients is best done before sales effort is expended on the lead and many firms have departments or access to credit rating services like Dunn & Bradstreet who can undertake this routinely.

NOTES

4 MAINTAINING THE CUSTOMER DATABASE

Definition

In theory, a database is simply a coherent structure for the storage and use of data. It involves the centralised storage of information, which provides:

(a) **Common data** for all users to share

(b) Avoidance of **data duplication** in files kept by different users

(c) **Consistency** in the organisation's use of data, and in the accuracy and up-to-dateness of data accessed by different users, because all records are centrally maintained and updated

(d) **Flexibility** in the way in which shared data can be queried, analysed and formatted by individual users for specific purposes, without altering the store of data itself

Such structure could be fulfilled by a centralised file registry or library, or a self-contained data record like a master index card file. In practice, however, large scale databases are created and stored on **computer systems,** using **database application packages** such as Microsoft Access.

4.1 Features of databases

Computer database packages allow data to be stored in a coherent structure in one place.

(a) **Data** are the raw components of information: names, dates, item descriptions, prices, colours, addresses and so on.

(b) **Fields** are the labels given to types of data. (The book *Access for Dummies* refers to them as 'places for your data to live'.) A customer database, for example, might include fields such as: title (data = Mr), first name (data = Joseph), last name (data = Bloggs), Company (data = Anon Ltd), Address, Phone Number, Fax Number, Contact Type (data = customer), interests (data = widgets) and so on.

(c) **Records** are the collection of field relevant to one entry. (*Access for Dummies* suggests 'all the homes on one block'.) So all the above data fields for a particular customer (Mr Bloggs) make up one customer record.

(d) **Tables** (or database files) are collections of records that describe similar data ('all the blocks in one neighbourhood'). All the customer records for a particular region or product may be stored in such a file.

(e) **Databases** (catalogues) are collections of all the tables (and other formats which can be created from them) relating to a particular set of information. ('A community of neighbourhoods'.) So your customer database may include tables for various regions, customers, product customers, customer contacts and so on, plus various reports and queries that you use to access different types of information.

Basic features of database packages

(a) **Find particular records,** using any data item you know

(b) **Sort records alphabetically,** numerically or by date, in ascending or descending order

(c) **Filer records**, so that you 'pull out' and view a selection of records based on specified criteria (all addresses in a certain postcode, for example, or all purchasers of a particular product)

(d) **Interrogate records**, generating the selection of records based on a complex set of criteria, from one or more linked tables. (For example, you might specify that you want all customer records where the field 'City' equals London or Birmingham and where the field 'Product' equals Widget and where the field 'Purchase Date' is between January 1999 and January 2000. The query would generate a table consisting of customers in London and Birmingham who purchased Widgets in 1999.)

(e) **Calculate and count** data entries. (For example if you wanted to find out how many customers had purchased each product, you could run a query that asked the database to group the data by the field 'product' and then count by field 'customer ID' or 'last name': it would count the number of to 'sum' or add up all the values in a field: total number of purchases, or total purchase value.)

(f) **Format** selected data for a variety of uses, as reports, forms, mailing labels, charts and diagrams

Activity 4 **(30 minutes)**

Find out what type(s) of database your organisation (or college) uses, and for what applications. If possible, get access to the database and browse through the index, directory or switchboard to see what databases/catalogues contain what database files or tables, queries, reports and forms, with what fields. If you can't get access to a database at work, try the local library, where you may find that the 'index card' system has been computerised as a database. Or use an Internet search engine or browser to interrogate some on-line databases. This is not really something you can learn from books - have a go!

Our interest in databases is simply a user interest, because databases can provide valuable information to sales personnel.

(a) Computer databases make it easier to collect and store more **data/information.**

(b) Computer software allows the data to be **extracted** from the file and **processed** to provide whatever information management needs.

(c) Developments in information technology allow businesses to have access to the databases of **external organisations**. Reuters, for example, provides an on-line information system about money market interest rates and foreign exchange rates to firms involved in money market and foreign exchange dealings, and to the treasury departments of a large number of companies.

(d) The growing adoption of technology at **point of sale** provides a potentially invaluable source of data to both retailer and manufacturer.

(e) Increased **sales and/or market share** (due to enhanced lead follow-up, cross-selling, customer contact)

(f) Increased **customer retention** (through better targeting)

(g) Better use of **resources** (targeting, less duplication of information handling)

(h) Better **decision-making** (from quality management information)

4.2 Building a database

A comprehensive customer database might include the following.

(a) **Customer titles**, names, addresses and contact (telephone, fax, (e-mail) details

(b) **Professional details** (company; job title; responsibilities), especially for business-to-business marketing

(c) **Personal details** (sex, age, number of people at the same address, spouse's name, children, interests, and any other relevant data known, such as newspapers read, journals subscribed to)

(d) **Transaction history** (what products/services are ordered, how often, how much is spent)

(e) **Call/contact history** (sales or after sales service calls made, complaints/queries received, meetings at shows/exhibitions)

(f) **Credit/payment history** (credit rating, amounts outstanding, aged debts)

(g) **Current transaction/details** (items currently on order, dates, prices, delivery arrangements)

(h) **Special account details** (membership number, loyalty or incentive points earned, discount awarded), where customer loyalty or incentive schemes or valued customer cards are used.

Each of these items will be in a separate field (and, in a relational database, perhaps separate tables) in your database.

Contacts databases

As well as a database of existing customers, the organisation may wish to build a database of sales leads, prospects and other contacts as a **mailing list**.

(a) **Contact titles**, names, addresses and contact (telephone, fax, (e-mail) details

(b) **Professional details** (company name, address, contact details, job title) in a business-to-business context

(c) **Contact 'type'** - exhibition visitor, referral, engineer, 'cold' contact, bought-in list

(d) **Contact's interests** in a particular product/service area

(e) **Contact history** (whether called/mailed, whether responded, whether followed up, whether purchased)

EXAMPLE

Sources of contact or mailing list information

(a) Recommendation and referrals from customers (whether spontaneous or through 'introduce a friend' schemes or referral requests)

(b) **Enquiries** for further information, in response to advertising, promotion and PR (via telephone, mail, 'hits' on web site)

(c) Enquiries compiled at exhibitions and fairs

(d) **Leads** brought back by salespeople, not yet converted into sales

(e) Details provided in response to **promotional competitions**, prize draws and incentives. Every 'send in for your chance to win' or 'send in to claim your discount' coupon should be a vehicle of capture of mailing list data: this will often be their primary purpose

(f) Relevant **secondary sources**

(g) Specialist **mailing list suppliers**. Lists can be hired or bought from commercial list owners: they can often be appropriately segmented (we discuss this further below)

(h) The **in-house database** of non-competing organisations in the same market, who may be willing to swap or rent lists. If you buy anything by post, you end up on a mailing database, and are often given the opportunity to receive, or decline to receive, information on related products.

4.3 Maintaining the database

If the customer database is linked to **on-line transaction processing** (for example, via EPOS), purchase data will automatically be updated with each new transaction. However, a typical contacts database will have to be regularly and systematically **maintained**.

(a) Contacts who become customers should be transferred to the customer database and deleted from the contacts database in order to avoid duplicated mailings.

(b) Any up-dated or altered information should be entered in the database such as changes of address or customer status.

(c) Additional information obtained from contacts should be added to the relevant records.

(d) New names and records should periodically be added to the database, and names which have received no response should be deleted.

(e) 'Undeliverable' items are returned to the sender, often marked with reason for non-delivery. If the mailing list has been bought or rented, any undeliverables should be returned to the owner or broker so they can update their database. If the mailing was based on an in-house list, addresses and names should be checked (common errors include misspelt names, missing lines of the address, wrong company name) and if no error can be readily identified, the record should be erased.

(f) Requests from customers or members of the public to have their details erased from the database should be honoured.

(g) New fields can be added to the database design as new types of information become available.

A customer database which allows purchase frequency and value per customer to be calculated indicates to the marketer who the potential heavy users are, and therefore where the promotional budget can most profitably be spent.

By tracking purchases per customer (or customer group) you may be able to identify:

(a) **Loyal repeat customers** (who cost less to retain than new customers cost to find and attract, and who therefore need to be retained

(b) **'Backsliding'** or lost customers, who have reduced or ceased the frequency or volume of their purchases (These may be a useful diagnostic sample for market research into declining sales or failing customer care.)

(c) **Seasonal** or local purchase patterns (heavier consumption of soup in England in winter, for example)

(d) **Demographic purchase patterns**. These may be quite unexpected. Grey Advertising carried out studies in the US in 1987 which showed that many consumers behave inconsistently to the patterns assumed for their socio-economic groups. Lower income consumers buy top-of-the-range products, which they value and save for. Prestige and luxury goods, which marketers promote largely to affluent white-collar consumers, are also purchased by students, secretaries and young families, which have been dubbed 'Ultra Consumers' because they transcend demographic clusters.

(e) Purchase patterns in response to **promotional campaigns** (Increased sales volume or frequency following promotions is an important measurement of their effectiveness.)

4.4 Identifying marketing opportunities

More detailed information (where available) on customer likes and dislikes, complaints, feedback and lifestyle values may offer useful information for:

(a) **Product** improvement

(b) **Customer care** and quality programmes

(c) New **product development,** and

(d) **Decision-making** across the marketing mix: on prices, product specifications, distribution channels, promotional messages and so on

Simple data fields such as 'contact type' will help to evaluate how contact is made with customers, of what types and in what numbers. Business leads may be generated most often by trade conferences and exhibitions, light users by promotional competitions and incentives, and loyal customers by personal contact through representatives.

Customers can be investigated using any data field included in the database: How many are on e-mail or the Internet? How many have spouses or children? Essentially, these parameters allow the marketer to **segment** the customer base for marketing purposes.

EXAMPLE

Hallmark salespeople in the US have laptop computers which allow them to analyse the mix of greeting cards sold at individual stores, in order to create a merchandising package tailored to capitalise on the strengths of each store customer.

Compaq Computers has a similar program, with sales people linked by computer to the headquarters' databases providing information on every product and every client. In the first two years of the programme, it reduced its sales force by a third - and doubled its sales volume.

4.5 Using database information

The following is a summary of the main ways in which database information can be used.

(a) **Direct mail** used to:

   (i) Maintain customer contact between (or instead of) sales calls
   (ii) Generate leads and 'warmed' prospects for sales calls
   (iii) Promote and/or sell products and services direct to customers
   (iv) Distribute product or service information

(b) **Transaction processing**. Databases can be linked to programmes which generate order confirmations, despatch notes, invoices, statements and receipts.

(c) **Marketing research and planning**. The database can be used to send out market surveys, and may itself be investigated to show purchasing patterns and trends.

(d) **Contacts planning**. The database can indicate what customers need to be contacted or given incentives to maintain their level of purchase and commitment. A separate database may similarly be used to track planned and on-going contacts at conferences and trade shows and invitation lists to marketing events.

(e) **Product development and improvement**. Product purchases can be tracked through the product life cycle, and weaknesses and opportunities identified from records of customer feedback, complaints and warranty/guarantee claims.

(f) The **Data Protection Acts 1984 and 1998** provide that data users (organisations or individuals who control the contents of files of personal data and the use of personal data) must register with the Data Protection Registrar. They must limit their use of personal data (defined as any information about an identifiable living individual) to the uses registered.

4.6 Data mining

With a good database of information, companies undertake **data mining** for information that can be used for marketing purposes. (See the example of Intelligent Miner given later in this chapter). Data mining can identify target customers for appropriate campaigns. The term **on-line analytical processing (OLAP)** is often used now to describe the analysis of huge amounts of data by **data warehouses**, creating a major source of information for marketing decisions.

EXAMPLE

(a) 'Dialogue marketing is the term for involving the consumer in the route from brand awareness to sale by providing information only in response to requests, and tailoring it to the individual. It is most suitable for buying decisions that are deliberate rather than impulsive – as in business-to-business marketing or large personal purchases – and is on the increase in many countries.

At one level it sounds a straightforward way of moving seamlessly from mass market advertising to clinching a sale with one customer. Along the way it includes making sure the brand is considered by the customer, through marketing that reflects the consumer's concerns, and creating a preference for the brand by providing incentives.

But dialogue marketing is possible only through the use of sophisticated technology both to create a detailed database and then to use it to respond to individual customers.

Advances such as the internet have been important in its development as they offer more varied ways to communicate with potential customers. These new methods, for example clicking on a company's web site, have the benefit of leaving consumers feeling more in control of the exchange of information than conventional forms of contact such as telemarketing, which can seem intrusive.

Allan Steinmetz, director of marketing at Arthur D Little, the consulting firm, says the core requirement for effective dialogue marketing is a good database where the information can be readily "harvested".

'If you try to do this with index cards, it is not going to work,' he says. 'Consumers have to feel that you are talking to them as individuals – if you're ever addressed as "Dear customer", forget it.'

Sophisticated technology is needed far more than just getting the name right in the initial communication: once someone has asked for information, any response that fails to provide an answer, or which appears mass-produced, will alienate rather than enthuse.

Mr Steinmetz says the two areas where the use of dialogue marketing is most developed are the financial services sector, particularly in promoting products such as credit cards, and the motor industry. In order to open contact, for example, Korean car maker Daewoo once asked people to reveal their worst experiences about dealing with the motor trade, providing the incentive of a car to drive for a year for those sending in the best stories.

Companies in these two sectors have access to detailed information about their customers' lives, and have become adept at using this information in communicating with them. Mr Steinmetz cites American Express, which recently launched a programme linking the rewards to the customers' own spending patterns.

Other areas in which the use of dialogue marketing is developing are healthcare – particularly in the US – and utilities, such as power and water companies. This is most notable in countries where these companies are starting to face competition and so are coming under increasing pressure to make more use of the extensive information they hold."

(b) A major photographic processing house surveys its customer base by self-completed questionnaires, responses being motivated by a free film on receipt of the questionnaire. This is done three times a year. All respondents are asked if they would like to become members of a customer panel. This panel now comprises a customer database of over 6,000 people (who regularly engage in photography) into which the company can dip when required. In addition, the company has generated feedback from some 23,000 'occasional' customers, giving data on lifestyles, customer perceptions of quality, customer requirements, and so forth. The resulting database, which given its size is statistically very powerful, has a cost of under £1 per respondent.

(c) Heinz use a magazine both to put across brand messages and to build up a database of customers.

'The vehicle for these messages about value, product range and new lines is the Heinz 'At home' magazine-format mailing which is sent out quarterly to about 4m households. The database, built up from an original 1m names of consumers who had taken part in promotional offers, contains an extraordinary array of individuals' details, derived from questionnaires in 'At Home'. To continue receiving the magazine, recipients have to fill in the questionnaire; as an extra incentive, Heinz provides a prize draw.

Questions cover which grocery brands are bought, where the shopping is done, who does it and whether they have access to a car. Income, occupation, marital status, children's birthdays, credit card and housing details are all covered. Consumers complete details of the make and age of their car, and tick activities and interests from a list of 59 options including golf, bingo and stocks and shares.

The magazine itself contains product information, recipes .... and, very important, tear-out money-off coupons. Each coupon is personalised with a barcode and the recipient's name, enabling Heinz to tell exactly who has used their coupons for what.

Several versions of the magazine are produced, targeting, for example, families with children and "healthy eating" consumers.' *Financial Times*

As well as providing invaluable information about its customers, Heinz claims that market share increases were immediately apparent after the first mailing.

(d) There are numerous other examples.

(i) Helena Rubenstein, the cosmetics company, has begun to build a database to promote a closer relationship with users.

(ii) Unilever is centralising the customer data amassed by its British subsidiaries.

(iii) Kraft (the food division of America's Philip Morris) have a database of the addresses of 30 million customers who have replied to free sample offers and other promotions.

(iv) American Express uses its customer database to tailor offers, such as a special sale at Harrods, to small groups of cardholders according to their spending patterns.

(v) Procter & Gamble uses its database to market Pampers disposable nappies: 'individualised' birthday cards are sent to babies and customers are sent reminder letters to move up to the next nappy size.

(e) Charities often have extremely comprehensive and effective databases.

'Since recruitment [of donors] was the most expensive and difficult part of the equation, charities with long-term commitment and sufficient finance built databases of supporters, so they did not maintain the continuous search for new donors.

It was soon obvious that some donors gave more generously or more frequently than others. These people were therefore worth mailing more often. Thus, donor-base segmentation was conceived. Donors are split into groups depending on the 'recency', 'value' and 'frequency' of gifts.

This is why database segmentation, relationship marketing and customer (donor) care, the buzzwords in today's direct marketing industry are old friends to many of Britain's household-name charities.'

Marketing Business

Chapter roundup

- Personal selling is an important aspect of the communications mix.
- The task of selling involves communication, securing a sale, prospecting for potential customers, after sales service, information gathering.
- Sales personnel are in an important position in the flow of information between the customer and the organisation.
- Sales people are useful in gathering information on customers and competitors.
- Information about sales, customers and competitors can be used to give an indication of sales potential.
- The Product Life Cycle (PLC) can be evaluated in terms of sales potential and customer characteristics.
- Prospects are potential customers who have been screened or assessed.
- Managing customer databases is an important and growing area of sales management
- Database information can also be used strategically, for example to give indications on product improvements and customer care programmes.

Quick quiz

1. Why might an organisation decide to incorporate personal selling in its communications mix?
2. What type of information can sales personnel gather?
3. In terms of the PLC, who makes up a sales person's clients?
4. Where might a sales person get new customer leads from?
5. What type of information might an effective customer database include.
6. Selling is important because it is both personal and interactive. True or False?
7. Is personal selling good for raising awareness of products?
8. How can sales revenue be increased?

Answers to quick quiz

1. To demonstrate a technical product, explain a complex product, improve sales, to persuade wholesalers and retailers to stock products, if it is a small market or if direct selling may be cheaper. (See paragraph 1.1)
2. Sales, consumer characteristics, competitor information. (para 2)
3. New customers, growing customers, mature customers and declining customers. (para 2.3)

4 From marketing efforts (eg advertising, direct mail), from within the company (eg lists of past customers, mailing lists), from networking, from industry sources, other firms or cold calling. (para 3.2)

5 Customer titles, professional details, personal history, transaction history, contact and payment history, current transactions and special account details. (para 4.2)

6 True (para 1.1)

7 Usually advertising is better to raise awareness; personal selling is too expensive and labour intensive. The exception may be if the market is specialised and small. (para 1.3)

8 By either increasing the number of customers or increasing the spending of existing clients. (para 2.3)

Answers to activities

1 There is no specific answer to this activity.

2 Knowledge and understanding of the profession.

Professionalism
An 'unpushy' approach
Technical excellence
Good communication skills

3 Reductions in price
3rd generation licences; greater accessibility
Fashion and popularity
Better technology; internet access etc
Better technology; smaller handsets

It is currently very 'easy' to sell mobile phones, especially eg at Christmas. The sales function is probably of lesser importance at the moment, although there is a greater level of competition.

4 There is no specific answer to this activity.

Chapter 17 :
THE SELLING PROCESS

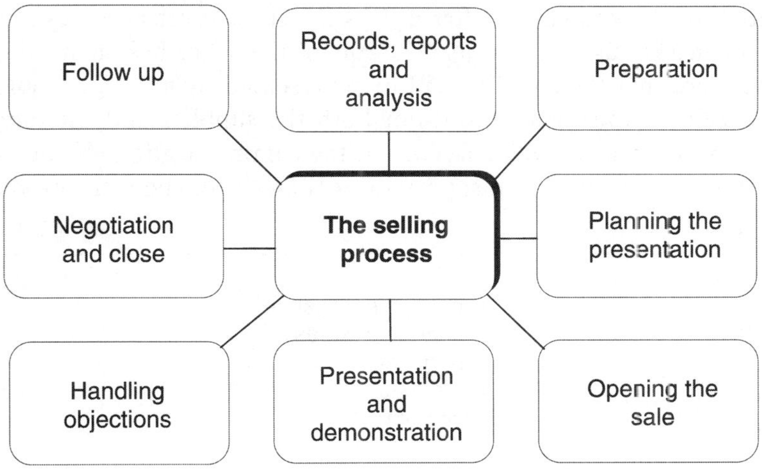

Introduction

This chapter will describe the selling process and the stages for effective selling. This includes planning and preparing the presentation, how to present the offer, handling objections and closing the sale. Follow up and record keeping are also of importance to the sales function and are discussed in this chapter.

Your objectives

In this chapter you will learn about the following:

(a) The importance of having a process of selling.

(b) How to plan and conduct a presentation or demonstration.

(c) Ways of dealing with objections.

(d) The process should continue with follow up procedures necessary after the close of a presentation.

1 PREPARATION

As with so many activities, the key to success in selling lies in the preparation and planning. In this chapter we will examine the groundwork which the professional salesperson needs to do in terms of sales preparation before embarking on the sales call.

1.1 The role of the seller

Today's sales representatives need much more than a bag of product samples and a well 'rehearsed' pitch of the company's offering. As the sales effort becomes more and more integrated with marketing activities, so the role of the seller has changed. Expectations amongst buyers are that the supplier will be represented by an 'expert' able to diagnose problems and help in their resolution. For both the supplier and the buyer, then, the sales person represents a very valuable link in the communication channel - responsible for transmitting much more than just promotional messages about the product.

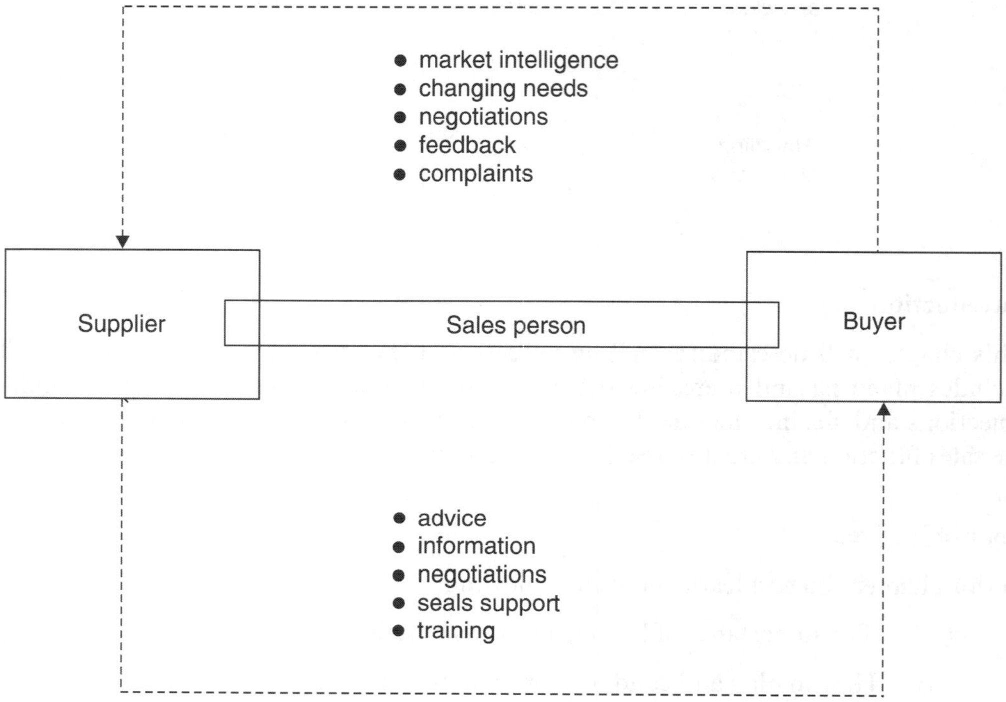

The salesperson facilitates a two way flow of communication and information between buyer and supplier. The value of that information is enhanced by adequate planning and training for the sales team.

As expectations of the sales team increase, their customers become increasingly sophisticated and educated and the products being sold more complex. The need for preparation becomes ever more important, as expectations of sales teams increase. Customers needs become more sophisticated, customers' education is enhanced, and products themselves become more complex.

The well prepared sales person needs to know:

- About the company or organisation
- About the industry and competition
- About the products
- About the customers.

NOTES

Activity 1 **(10 minutes)**

Before moving on jot down a list of the ways in which you think information about the above might help in the selling situation.

1.2 What you should know about your employer

To the customer, the salesperson personifies the company, although in fact he or she only **represents** it. The well informed sales representative needs to be aware of company policy, key personnel and be able to answer any questions with confidence. The following is not an exhaustive list of what the sales team should know, but it is a starting point.

(a) The history and current company organisation. How long has the firm been in operation? Why, when and how did it originate? What new or unusual products has it been involved with, has it done anything especially worthy of note, for example awards, prizes etc?

(b) What is the standing of the firm in the industry? What is its reputation? market share? standing in the stock market, if it is a listed company? How many employees does it have? What countries does it operate in?

(c) Who are the senior managers in the firm? Who are the non-executive directors? Are any of them well known for other activities?

(d) What are the general policies of the firm? (Policies reflect the culture of the organisation and can be important.) How does the firm stand on equal work opportunities? Does it employ disabled people? What is it doing to promote environmentally friendly production methods? How does company policy promote customer satisfaction? policy on refunds, guarantees and warranties etc?

(e) Does the company operate within politically sensitive areas, for example trading with developing economies? What are its policies for such activities?

(f) Specific policy areas which are likely to be of direct interest to buyers include:

(i) policy on pricing and discounts;
(ii) the granting of credit facilities and the basis of contracts;
(iii) delivery promises;
(iv) periods of notice and basis for termination etc.

The sales staff must not only be familiar with these specific issues, but also be able to interpret their implications for a particular customer.

Although much of this information will be provided through induction and sales training, keeping up to date and extending the base of company knowledge will often be the individual's responsibility. Annual reports are a useful source of background information as are staff newsletters and other sources of internal briefing. A sales person working away from base for much of the week has to make a special effort to keep up with changes in personnel, new policies and the firms projects within the community.

Activity 2 **(60 minutes)**

In your organisation (or one you are familiar with) gather the type of information above that it would be useful for sales personnel to know.

1.3 What you should know about the industry and competition

Knowing what share of a market your firm controls is important, but it is equally important to know about the industry as a whole.

(a) What is its history? what developments are forecast? What is the size and standing of the industry when compared to other industries?

(b) What type of customers typify the industry? How are they changing?

(c) Who are the key suppliers in the industry? Who are the closest competitors? What are their strengths and weaknesses?

(d) Are there any likely newcomers to the industry? If so who are they? Who are the key players in overseas markets and are they likely to compete with you in the future?

(e) How are products and services distributed and promoted within your industry?

Information about the industry and competitors can be found in a number of places. Trade associations and industry publications can provide valuable background information.

Activity 3 **(15 minutes)**

Answer the questions above for an industry of your choice.

(a) They are a useful source of updates on new developments, and forecast changes.

(b) Company reports and surveys are also useful as they indicate in broad terms a company's strategy, and its financial health.

(c) Customers may also be in regular contact with competitors sales teams.

1.4 What you should know about the product

The sales representative is expected to know about the company's products, what and, how they are made, what they can do, why they are different or better than the competitors. What really is a product though?

To the customer, the product is a tool for solving a problem. It is the package of benefits which the supplier is offering as a solution to that problem. The 'product' is therefore more than simply a bundle of physical attributes, it also features the intangible elements of its image, and reputation, the after sales service promise, and the price.

EXAMPLE

Endowment policy and pensions providers have recently faced criticism that they have on many occasions sold policies that are not suitable for clients.

1.5 How much benefit is on offer, and at what price?

The salesperson needs to know how to present the product's features in such a way that the product provides the buyer with relevant and valuable benefits. This requires extensive knowledge of both the product and all its attributes, possible uses and varieties. A retail salesperson requires extensive knowledge of the alternative products available and their relative strengths, weaknesses and attributes.

Particularly in industrial markets, it is increasingly the case that the complexity of the product requires the expert knowledge of a technical sales force. In these markets the process of gaining credible product knowledge is likely to take years, so instead of training the sales staff about the product, technical experts such as engineers are given sales training.

1.6 What you should know about the customers

Customer knowledge is essential to the sales preparation process. In general terms it is useful as has already been indicated, to know about the type of firms who are buyers from your industry. It is also helpful to know about their activities and how these are changing.

Specific customer information can hardly be too extensive. Prior knowledge of a client's business, organisation and interests demonstrates good customer care and interest. Information which indicates the customers current supplier, and the value of potential sales is particularly useful as it assists sales staff in assessing the priority each prospect should be given.

Customer information can also be obtained from published sources as indicated above. Trade associations and publications as well as annual reports provide a good basic framework of customer data. To this can be included in-house and industry market research surveys which may have profiled typical customers and their buying behaviour and any customer data base information available to the company.

Across a number of sectors and industries the increased availability of computerised information systems is providing more and better data on past and present customers. Sales teams need to make use of these new sources of up to the minute market intelligence.

2 PLANNING THE PRESENTATION

Preparation for a sales call requires much more that knowing about your company and products and identifying who you are going to visit. Planning how you will approach the client, what benefits you need to present and the best approach for communicating them, are all essential elements of the preparation process.

2.1 Deciding an approach

Sales presentations are like any other form of communication. To work, there must be a number of elements in place. Preparation of these elements is key to success.

The sales representative

As has already been said, the sales representative personifies the supplier. The degree of preparation undertaken will indicate the professionalism of the organisation and the importance and seriousness with which the customer is credited. Preparation for a sales visit includes not only the background and homework as indicated earlier in this chapter, but also preparation of approach and of course personal preparation.

Knowing the objectives

Finding the right approach and effective preparation is dependent on clarifying the sales visit objectives. Objectives can vary widely according to the nature of the product, requirements of the supplier and the relationship with the customer. Certainly different objectives will be best achieved with different approaches. Objectives could be:

(a) Get a meeting and arouse the clients interest, or to win the opportunity of making a sales presentation

(b) Come away with an order for new business or a commitment to put you on a shortlist of suppliers

(c) Win a routine reorder or to simply ensure awareness of a new product

(d) Fulfil any number of secondary objectives, for example collecting feedback on product performance or attitudes to a competitors recent initiative?

FOR DISCUSSION

A different approach needs to be made to companies depending on the sales objective.

The buyer

The buyer may be representing others, the family in the case of a consumer purchase, or a company in a business to business market. However, before making a sales presentation to him or her, you have to first attract the buyer's attention.

Appointments

Ensuring you have the attention of the buyer is often easier if you have arranged an **appointment**. This is particularly the case if the sales presentation requires concentration and the undivided attention of the audience.

The problem with asking for an appointment is that it invites the opportunity of being turned down. Getting through the front door, past battalions of gatekeepers in the form of receptionists, telephonists, secretaries and assistants can be a daunting task. Using the right approach can increase the chances of success.

Gaining an appointment depends on quickly attracting interest, which means:

(a) Introducing yourself and your company
(b) Briefly outlining the benefits you and your product can offer to the company
(c) Ask for a specific appointment date and time.

This formula can be more easily guaranteed by letter. There are no interruptions but of course it is more difficult to ensure a letter will reach its intended audience and there has to be a follow up call to confirm the arrangement for an appointment.

EXAMPLE

Some attention grabbing approaches include the following.

(a) **Solution approach**
Mrs Holmes, this is Jo Seller of XYZ Company. Our recently launched Gold system has been designed to halve the administrative paperwork of companies your size. I am in the area on Thursday next week, would it be convenient to show you how this saving can be made, or would Friday be better?

(b) **Endorsement approach**
... We have recently installed our new system at WXZ Company and they are delighted with the results. Their Mr Smith thought you would find the system a great benefit to your operation ...

(c) **Congratulations approach**

... Mrs Law, congratulations on the forthcoming wedding of your daughter which I saw announced in the paper today. Our special brides wedding service can take the headache out of the arrangements and save you money ...

Whichever approach you use, whether by phone or letter make sure it is:

- Personal
- Clear
- Positive
- Concise
- Interesting

It is not always practical to make appointments in advance (eg when selling door to door). However, you have to be prepared for the customer to be out or too busy to deal with you. In some sectors, customers may be happy for the sales representative just to 'pop in'. However most people resent time wasting so only call if you have a clear purpose and objective, something new to offer or discuss.

Increasingly, as the real cost of selling is recognised, making the most of sales time is also being given a higher priority. Appointments help to ensure sales time is spent with contacts who are genuinely interested, reduces the 'waiting time' to see buyers and increases the 'quality' of sales time by reducing the number of interruptions.

Whether a sales presentation is made as the result of an appointment or not, it is important to remember that sales communication can only be effective if it is made to the right audience and that listener is receiving the message clearly.

2.2 The message

A message's clarity can be adversely affected by a variety of factors including an audience which does not listen properly, and also by the way the message is constructed and communicated (ie encoded).

Preparation is important in this stage and depends on knowing the audience. Using technical jargon to a non-specialist buyer is unlikely to have a positive impact, but neither is talking down to an expert. Concepts which are hard to express verbally may be easily communicated with an illustration or diagram.

Successful sales messages are those which are based on identified customer needs and clearly present **relevant user benefits**. Then the message appears relevant and is much more likely to be acted upon.

Standard or variable messages?

One way of controlling what salespeople say is to encourage them to deliver a standard or set sales presentation. This is often the case for telephone selling.

(a) The 'word perfect' sales pitch, more suitable for delivery by phone (when the buyer's cues to interrupt can be more easily ignored) is much less common today than in the past.

NOTES

(b) It fails to maximise the real value of the salesperson, - the ability to respond to customer needs and worries, and to judge the mood of the sales negotiation. It takes away the benefit of *two way* sales communication and turns the salesperson into another media for delivering a standard message *just like the TY or radio*. Such an approach cannot really provide for individual customer needs, and is unlikely to maximise sales opportunities.

EXAMPLE

Some companies such as McDonalds have scripts that sales personnel follow when dealing with members of the public. Business to business markets are much less likely to have scripts as negotiations are usually two way.

Providing sophisticated sales aids which present key product features and benefits is a less rigid approach to standardising the sales presentation. Visual presenters, short videos and computer and slide presentations can enhance the professional image of the presentation and can help to communicate fundamental aspects of the product or service.

The sales representative planning a structured sales presentation is aware of the need to take the buyer through the stages of the AIDA decision process.

Awareness
Interest
Desire
Action

The **action** stage should not necessarily be seen as making a sale. It needs to be considered in the context of the original objectives - if that was to be invited to make a full presentation, then that is the action to be targeted.

EXAMPLE

Toshiba have developed an interactive 3D animated laptop presentation for their medical sales market (CT and MRI scanners) with video clips and testimonials from satisfied customers.

2.3 The formal presentation

In some industries the 'interested' customer will invite the supplier to make a formal proposal or presentation of what they can offer. In industries like computers, consultancy and advertising this formal presentation may well be at the end of a detailed evaluation of the clients needs and present position. It can take the form, as in the advertising world, of specially produced multi media presentations. It can involve many individuals on both sides and can be very expensive to mount. It is worthwhile only when the potential business is substantial and should only be undertaken on the basis of the most thorough preparation.

A good presentation will display the following attributes.

- It should be flexible - able to be adapted to the interests, needs and wants of the prospect.

- It should be clear
- It must be credible and relevant
- It should clearly describe the product or service and the *benefits* it offers the prospect
- It should arouse and maintain interest
- It should motivate the prospect to action, set by the sales objective.

2.4 The unspoken message

Sales professionals have to pay attention not only to their preparation of the spoken selling message, but also the unspoken one. Body language is the term given to the visual clues, which we are all expert at picking up and often translate at a subconscious level, eg a salesperson lacking in the confidence to look a buyer in the eyes may be perceived to be dishonest and untrustworthy. The professional seller must become a skilled communicator both spoken and unspoken messages.

2.5 Feedback

The final element in sales communication is feedback. If the advantage of selling is its ability to be a two way communication channel, then the 'receive' button on the sales person has to be tuned in!

3 OPENING THE SALE: AWARENESS AND INTEREST

The actual sales interview is often the culmination of hours or even weeks of preparation and planning. How long it lasts is not important, it is the **outcome** that matters.

Every word and action will have a bearing on the eventual outcome, and on the long term relationship between the two.

3.1 First impressions count

The buyer will begin to assess the seller before a word has been spoken. The manner in which the interview was set up, the appearance, posture and body language of the sales person will all contribute to vital first impressions.

(a) The approach phase has a clear responsibility in this structure - to gain and hold the attention of the buyer. Most sales professionals consider this **initial phase** as being the most **crucial** of a successful sales visit. It is the first moments which set the tone for the whole meeting.

(b) The worst first impression can be made by keeping the customer waiting. Appointments made must be kept punctually. That means allowing adequate time between sales calls and knowing in advance where you are going and how to get there. Unavoidable delays must be communicated as soon as possible to the prospect.

The sales person has a number of points which need to be covered in the approach phase of the interview.

(a) Personal introductions should reinforce the buyer's conviction that it is worth spending time on this meeting.

(b) The sales person therefore has to **sell himself** or **herself** before anything else. They must convince the prospect of their credibility. They can then move on to selling **their products** and **their organisation**.

(c) Gain and retain the prospects' interest and win their trust so they will enter into a dialogue about their needs., problems, concerns etc.

The first minutes of a meeting are really about selling the rest of the interview.

Activity 4

Set yourself a project related to a major purchase you are planning/hoping to make in the future. This might be a new washing machine, car or stereo system, a holiday in the sun, or a new camera. Take the time to identify a range of potential suppliers and then approach them for information about the product you are considering. Pay particular attention to the approach the sales staff use and their presentation or demonstration of the product.

- Which sales person was best?
- Why?
- If you were responsible for training the sales staff you encountered what suggestions would you make for improving each individual's effectiveness?

4 PRESENTATION AND DEMONSTRATION: INTEREST AND DESIRE

The stage of presentation and demonstration should be designed to help change the attitude of potential customers from 'not purchasing' towards a conviction 'to purchase'.

Showing or demonstrating the product, its features and benefits is particularly useful in maintaining the buyer's interest because it involves the buyer's **other senses in addition to hearing**. They are no longer just listening to the seller, they are looking at the visual aids or trying out the product.

4.1 Questions

During this second stage the salesperson will continue to ask questions and listen to answers which will build a more and more complete picture of the customer's needs and requirements.

(a) **Open questions**

Using open questions like who, when, why, how and what, are good for encouraging the customer to enter discussions and reveal preferences and buying motives.

> For example:
>
> Q: Do you like this red model?
> A: No
>
> A better question is:
>
> Q: What colour do you like best?

(b) **Focus**

Questions can **help focus the buyer's attention** on an issue he or she had not previously considered or a problem not yet recognised.

> Q: Have you considered how much heat is lost in a typical flat roofed factory?

(c) **Involvement**

People **become more involved** when they are asked questions. Questions are part of the whole process and satisfactory answers provide further evidence of the product's benefits.

(d) **Clarify**

Questions can also be used to **check understanding** and encourage the customers to clarify or answer their own objections.

> Q: Are you clear how this system works?
>
> Q: Have you any questions about the products performance?
>
> Q: What don't you like about this new lever operated mechanism?
>
> Q: Why do you prefer the old style?

Although anyone can ask questions, it takes a well trained and professional sales person to:

- Ask the right question
- Listen to the answers
- Interpret their implications in terms of the sales situation.

4.2 Turn features into benefits

The object of the exercise is to present the product in a way which is meaningful for the prospective buyer. It is worth reiterating the concept we saw much earlier - of the product as a tool for solving a customer's problem. Without a need, there will be no purchase.

The process the sales person has to go through can be illustrated as:

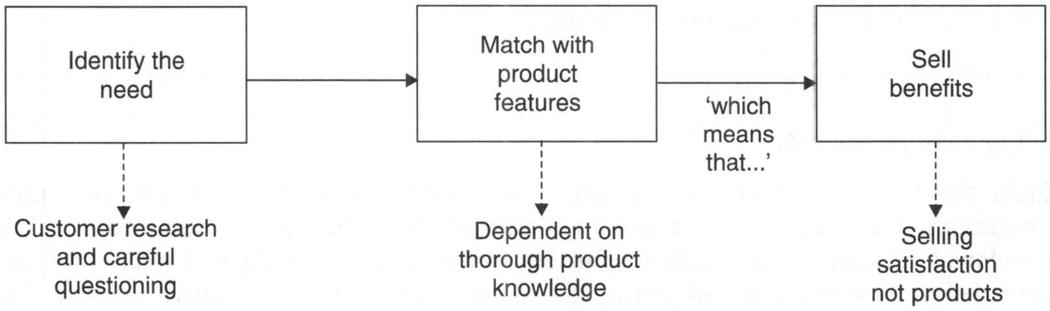

Firms develop specific features to give them a competitive position in the market place, but features belong to the product (product orientation). Customers buy benefits not features (ie what those features will do for them). Turning features into benefits demonstrates a customer-orientated approach. This is easy to do by taking the feature and adding the phrase - '... which means that ...'.

Feature		*Benefit*
This model has five doors	*which means that ...*	... it is very easy to load shopping and children!

NOTES

Feature		*Benefit*
The compact design of this model	*means that ...*	... it is very easy to park.

The benefit offered should be relevant and important to the customer. **This is why the preapproach research and questioning are so important.**

An effective sales presentation will:

- Be complete
- Be clear and concise
- Highlight features and benefits relevant to the prospective buyer
- Cover and eliminate as many questions and objections as possible
- Handle the question of competition and thorny issues like price.

The process of making a sale is not simply a matter of routinely going through a series of rehearsed stages and steps. It actually requires motivating the customer to want to buy. This process requires skill and patience and depends on:

(a) Customers recognising, accepting or convincing themselves they have a need;

(b) Customers believing that the benefits being offered satisfy their buying motives;

(c) Customers believing that the potential benefits/value of the product justifies its price, in other words, that there is nothing better to buy with the same money. (*Note*. This is not just **direct** competition, but also indirect competition from other types of product or service, eg a family may buy a new car **or** have a special holiday abroad. The family might have a finite amount of resources, and a variety of choices.)

FOR DISCUSSION

People buy people first and products second.

4.3 Using sales aids

Sales aids have already been mentioned in the previous chapter. Extended and highly programmed aids can risk making the sales person redundant to some extent, but developed creatively and designed for flexible use, they can do just what they are intended to do which is to **aid selling.** Sales aids in the form of brochures, presentation kits and demonstration models can help to:

(a) Add tangibility to a service or product not available for demonstration at the point of sale

(b) Add interest and variety to the sales presentation

(c) Make it easier to explain key selling points or complex products

(d) Show the products in use and customers benefiting from them

4.4 The role of training

The sales person's success in selling is very dependent on the skills demonstrated throughout the sales presentation. Questioning techniques to uncover needs, handling different types of customers and presenting products can all be enhanced by training, particularly the use of role play scenarios.

The ability to highlight the various attributes of a product offering, in the light of revealed customer needs, is only developed with practice.

5 HANDLING OBJECTIONS

5.1 Objections are a good thing

Buyers can object to the product or its price, the company or the timing of the offer. Objections should not be seen as negative.

(a) **They indicate the buyer is actually considering the sales proposition** and objections represent the vocalisation of anxieties, obstacles and issues which stand in the way of making a decision to buy. Objections give the sales person the opportunity of finding out more about the buyer and the buyer's needs.

(b) Buying a new product or service often involves change from tried and trusted methods or brands or well known suppliers. It is human behaviour to resist change and to feel more comfortable with the idea of change if convinced and reassured by the sales person. Sales staff should remember that they are in the business of modifying behaviour and changing attitudes - processes which require a raft of motivational and persuasive skills.

5.2 Ways of overcoming objections

Experience and training will provide the sales person with a toolbox of techniques for handling objections. An appropriate approach can then be selected to suit the specific situation and objection.

(a) All these techniques have one thing in common - they must evolve from **careful listening**. Listening is important to convey to the buyers that their views are important and to reduce any resentment from 'being sold to'.

(b) It helps the buyer feel more involved in the process and eventually will lead to him or her owning (taking responsibility for) the purchase decision. At the end of the process the buyer should be able to say '**I bought** this from you' rather than '**You sold** this to me'.

Common techniques for handling objections

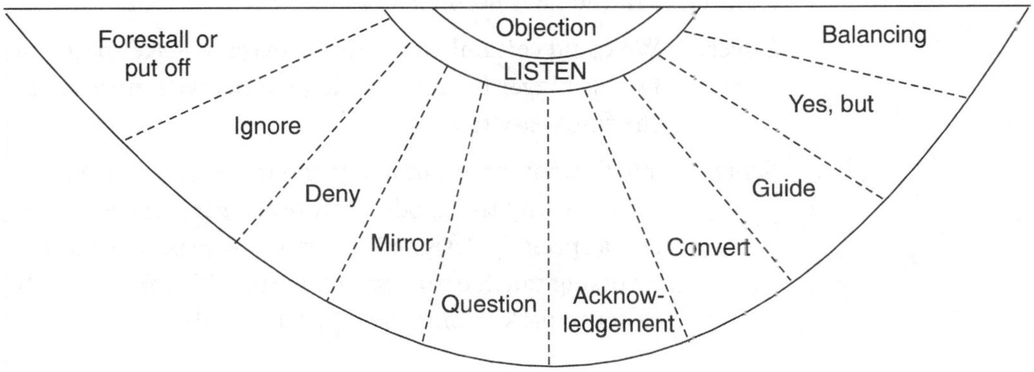

Technique	Comment
Forestall or put off	**Anticipating objections** and building the answer into the earlier part of the sales presentation is known as forestalling. Putting off handling an objection until later is valid, if you feel it is better dealt with after more of the product's benefits have been demonstrated.
Ignore	This is certainly a technique some sellers use, but it is not to be recommended or used regularly. It can only be valid if the objection is felt to be very weak.
Deny	Denying has to be done tactfully and politely as it can be interpreted as an aggressive response - but if the buyer is claiming something definitely untrue, for example 'your company insists on payments in fourteen days or it imposes a penalty charge', then a direct polite denial would be appropriate.
Mirror	Mirroring is a technique used to give the buyer the chance to consider their own objection as well as an opportunity to clarify your understanding of it. • Your main concern then is • ... Are you saying • ... If I understand you ...
Question	Asking for details of the basis of the objection can provide specific instances or examples which can make the objection seem less serious, eg: Buyer: My experience with your company is that they cannot deliver on time. Seller: I am very sorry you have got that impression. Can I ask specifically what problems you have had? Buyer: During the bad weather last winter deliveries were late etc.
Acknowledge	Acknowledging an objection can be seen in the seller's first statement in the example above. It shows the buyer that the objection has been noted sympathetically, recognised but its validity has not been accepted.
Convert	Turning objections into **selling features** is one of the most powerful techniques in the sales persons tool kit. Buyer: We could certainly do with the extra luggage space offered by this bigger fivedoor model, but my wife must have a car she finds easy to park. Seller: That's what we found many of our customers needed, which is why this model features power assisted steering, and a specially designed rear window making visibility for reversing much easier, which means this car is actually easier to park than many smaller models.

Technique	Comment
Guide	Guiding is a technique by which the sales person provides a framework to 'guide' the buyer to make their own conversion. It is best used when the buyer has made both positive and negative comments about the product. Buyer: I can see the benefits of this cleaner system, but our old one is still working and I am not sure it is worth the cost of changing. Seller: Have you calculated the weekly costs of the extra cleaning your current system requires? How many hours of production are lost each month whilst cleaning is done? What benefits do you think a cleaner working environment would give to your staff?
Yes, but	The yes but or yes however approach is based on an agree and neutralise technique. Agreeing shows understanding and sympathy with the objection, whilst providing the chance to demonstrate why the objection is unfounded. Like the 'deny' technique, this can cause offence if not handled with care. Buyers do not like to be contradicted or proven wrong!
Balancing	Visualise the pros and cons of the product offering using a simple list technique. This demonstrates the balance of advantages very clearly. *Pros*: • Quicker delivery • Less stockholding • More durable • Compatible with existing units *Cons*: • Initial start up costs • Heavier weight

Handling objections is an essential part of the selling role. Experience of customer objections will help the seller be better prepared for future objections, but even the most experienced sales representative can expect two to six objections in a typical sales interview.

5.3 Summarising the key steps in objection handling

- Welcome objections
- Put yourself in the buyers shoes
- Listen carefully
- Acknowledge and repeat or rephrase the objection
- Investigate any hidden objections
- Ask more questions: what, why and when?
- Choose a technique for handling the objection - but be **tactful**.

Although the sales person must be prepared to meet and respond to new or specific objections it is possible to identify a number of categories or sources of likely objection. Thinking through possible objections means the sales team will be better prepared to handle them and provides the chance to forestall many of those most likely to come up.

NOTES

DISCUSSION

The customer is always right.

EXAMPLE

Ford has launched a website (Fordjourney.com) to sell cars direct to customers who want 'haggle-free' prices. (Marketing Week October 26 2000)

Activity 5 **(5 minutes)**

Role play a scenario with a friend where one plays a sales person and the other a prospective customer at a car showroom

6 NEGOTIATIONS AND CLOSING THE SALE

Changing the customer's attitude towards a product is an important step in the selling process, but by itself achieves nothing tangible. The sales person is ultimately looking for a sale or an order and so the sales interview has to build up to the point at which the sales person asks for the business - the **close**.

Convincing and persuading customers is the job of the sales team and it starts with their own positive attitude and the expectation that they will make the sale.

6.1 Timing of close

There is no single moment when a sale can be closed. It is a mistake to think that all the stages of the sales sequence which we have outlined in this chapter have to be complete before a sale can be confirmed. Sellers must be alert for 'buying cues' or signals throughout the meeting. These are the signals that the buyer is committed to a purchase and they appear at any point.

EXAMPLE

Seller: I wanted the opportunity of showing you the improved features on our model xyz.

Buyer: Yes, I've heard about this model, I think we will need ten.

Seller: Let me demonstrate how it works

Or:

Buyer: Are easy credit terms available?

Seller: I am sure you will enjoy the benefits of the remote control feature.

Buying signals can be an expression of interest either verbal, physically or facially communicated. Whatever form they take the salesperson should attempt a trial close as soon as they are recognised.

NOTES

DISCUSSION

A trial close loses nothing and acts as a test of the buyer's responsiveness.

There are many techniques for closing a sale. The following table indicates some of the main ones.

Approach	Example
1. **Ask for the order** (Its surprising how many forget to!)	Shall I wrap this one up for you?
2 **Either/or?** (Choice technique)	Would you prefer the green or the blue model? Do you prefer to pay by cash or cheque or credit card?
3 **Assumption** (Based on the belief you will get the order)	As you obviously prefer this model shall I arrange for delivery next week?
4 **Testimonial close** (Using others indirectly as influencers and advisers by listing or showing the orders from other impressive clients)	You know ABC Ltd had their second delivery of this product only last week.
5 **Tip the scales** Following a summing up of all the relevant benefits and selling points	In view of this attractive offer is there anything stopping you from placing an order now?
6 **Why not close**	You still seem uncertain, is there any reason why you should not buy now?
7 **Emotional appeal** (For use when the purchase decision is likely to be based on emotion or impulse. Insurance can be sold on fear, new cars on pride and charitable giving on guilt)	You look very fashionable in that colour.
8 **Conversion close** (As seen earlier this takes the customers objection and turns it into a benefit)	Buyer: I can't really afford it this quarter. Seller: At this special low introductory price can you really afford to wait?
9 **Concessions close** (Provide a final incentive to help the buyer over the final decision making hurdle - it can be based on the fear of a loss or the chance to make a gain)	I cannot guarantee these prices next month. If you order now I can offer a special discount.

Buyer incentives devised and developed by marketing to support the sales activity can help at the close of the sale. They need to appeal to the buyer and be designed to achieve specific objectives, eg a new product trial or an increase in average order size.

Promotions can take many forms like special terms, advertising support, extra product or seasonal packaging or gifts. Like all promotions they must be ethical and legal and in line with all relevant codes of practice.

6.2 Negotiation of terms

Even when a sale is almost certain, its close can often be determined by the detailed negotiation of the terms of business. As can be seen from above, the sales person may use the flexibility of terms like price or delivery to help close the sale.

Negotiating can take many forms from a minor 'haggling' over price to a major round the table exchange of legal contracts.

The sales team must be well briefed as to the extent of their authority to negotiate terms. The size of discounts acceptable and the ability to deliver service promises should all be known in advance of the sales interview. Confirming availability and delivery dates for products is an important part of the preparation stage of selling.

The degree of autonomy the sales team has in such negotiations is clearly a matter of policy.

- Too much freedom can have considerable impact on the profitability of new business.
- Too little and sales opportunities may be missed simply because of the salespersons inability to move a little on terms.

6.3 Negotiations on price

It is the area of price discounts that causes the greatest concerns for managers. A sales team, with authority to offer discounts, is often suspected of giving these away, perhaps unnecessarily - certainly too easily. The fear is that it becomes too easy to offer inducements. The sales team will use discounts rather than persuasion to motivate a purchase.

Certainly selling on price is a minefield. Lower prices today tend to lead to an expectation of similarly low prices in the future. In consumer markets particularly, price is taken to be the guide to quality, and lowering price can directly impact on product image. Ideally it is preferable to sell added benefits rather than to lower prices and this needs to be borne in mind.

6.4 Agreeing the terms

Marketing is concerned not with simply selling the product but with developing a continuing relationship with the customer. It is increasingly referred to as relationship marketing in industrial sectors and brand loyalty in consumer markets. The measure of success in marketing terms is not simply making the sale, but in ensuring the customer is satisfied.

Negotiating and clarifying all the relevant terms of business are essential first stages in establishing a positive future relationship. Misunderstanding about payment terms, delivery dates or quality of product can all lead to dissatisfaction and lost future business.

It is fundamental to ethical and professional selling that an order is not signed on the basis of 'pie in the sky' promises or unclear terms. Getting it right at this stage is the foundation of good future relations.

6.5 Improving negotiation skills

Negotiation is the process of bringing the buyer and seller together. The objective is straightforward enough: to ensure that both parties are satisfied by the exchange.

EXAMPLE

A report in *Marketing Business* in March 1998 showed that although promotional activity accounts for the majority of marketing budgets, the expenditure may not be very effective. The glut of price promotions, loyalty cards and long-term low pricing strategies has disorientated customers, and not led to the desired results.

In the newspaper industry for example *The Times*, *Independent* and *Daily Telegraph* have all experimented with price-cutting strategies. However opinion in the industry is divided about the effectiveness of this strategy. It can be argued that many people buy the same paper for many years, and if they do change, having changed once they are more likely to change again.

Many stores now have loyalty cards. There are approximately 150 loyalty card schemes in operation. Research suggests that most consumers carry between five and ten loyalty cards, but only use one or two on a regular basis. Stores could be doing more to establish relationships with individual cardholders by for example reminding them of how they can use their loyalty card points.

There is also evidence that stores are not using the information on cardholders to the best effect. They should be trying to identify more precisely how consumers react to promotions. Research suggests some consumers are loyal to brands and not to stores, some are loyal to stores and not to brands, some get a thrill out of taking advantage of promotions, some will take advantage of promotions to hoard and stockpile, and some consumers are totally oblivious to promotions, remaining both brand and store loyal. Stores should be trying to identify what type of consumer predominates in their own customer base and target their promotional activity accordingly.

Negotiating and clarifying all the relevant terms of business are essential first stages in establishing a positive future relationship. Misunderstanding about payment terms, delivery dates or quality of product can all lead to dissatisfaction and lost future business.

Activity 6 **(10 minutes)**

You have been asked to advise a colleague who is about to embark on a negotiation with a key client about a continuation of contract. How should she prepare?

A basic '**win-win' approach** to negotiating is as follows.

(a) Map out, in advance, what the needs and fears of both parties are. This outlines the psychological and practical territory.

(b) **Define your desired outcome** and estimate the worst, realistic and best case scenarios. ('If I can pay £500, it would be ideal, but I'd settle for £600. Above £700, it's just not worth my while.') Start with the best case and leave room to fall back to the realistic case. Keep your goal in sight.

(c) **Look for mutual or trade-off benefits.** How might you both gain (for example, by getting a higher discount in return for longer or pre-booked series of ads or providing camera ready copy)? What might be cheap for you to give that would be valuable for the other party to receive, or vice versa?

(d) **Spell out the positive benefits** to the other party and support them in saying 'yes' to your proposals by making it as easy as possible. (Offer to supply information or help with follow-up tasks, for example.) Emphasise areas of agreement and common ground.

(e) **Overcome negativity** by asking questions

- What will make it work for you?
- What would it take to make this possible?

(f) **Overcome side-tracks** by asking questions such as: ' How is this going to get us where we want to go?'

(g) **Be hard on the problem but soft on the person.** This is not personal competition or antagonism: work together on problem solving (eg by using flip chart or paper to make shared notes). Show that you have heard the other person (by summarising their argument) before responding with your counter argument.

(h) **Be flexible**. A 'take it or leave it' approach breaks relationships. (However, saying 'no' repeatedly to sales people is a good way of finding out just how far below the list price they are prepared to go!) Make and invite reasonable counter offers.

(i) **Be culturally sensitive**. Some markets thrive on 'haggling'. Some cultures engage in a lot of movement up and down the bargaining scale (eg Asian and Middle Eastern), while others do their homework and fix their prices (eg German). In the former cultures, much emphasis is placed on building relationships and extending hospitality before getting down to terms.

(j) **Take notes,** so the accuracy of everyone's recollection of what was proposed and agreed can be checked.

(k) Summarise and **confirm the details** of your agreements to both parties (by memo, letter, contract) and acknowledge a mutually positive outcome.

Experience, knowledge and **expertise** count in negotiation: they add up to bargaining power, which is important even in a win-win approach. If there is someone in your department who has experience in a particular field (such as advertising sales), or your organisation retains an agency or consultancy, be prepared to let them handle negotiations for you.

NOTES

Activity 7 **(30 minutes)**

Get together with fellow students (or friends) in pairs or teams to prepare and role-play a negotiation. *Either*:

(a) You are looking to purchase advertising space in (any appropriate) magazine for a colour advertisement for your product. You have not previously advertised in this magazine, but have identified it as one which is targeted for your market and high circulation: it could be the key to your up-coming campaign. The copy deadline for the next issue is approaching and the magazine had an unsold colour page which it needs to fill. Rate card price for the colour page is £2,000 (£2,800 for the inside front cover, £2,500 for the inside back cover highly contested positions), which you would love to secure. Standard discounts include 10% media buyer's commission, 10% for a series of six ads. You pay 5% extra for bleed colour (running off the page edge). You and the magazine representative(s) should separately (without telling each other) decide what your necessary outcomes are: you should decide what you have to spend from your space budget, and how many ads you think you will need; the magazine rep(s) should decide that the minimum price they will accept, given their need to see space filled. Negotiate a deal!

or

(b) You want to go on holiday with the whole family to a coastal resort this summer. Your (role-play) partner wants to have some quiet time at home redecorating the bathroom, knowing that the two teenage (role-play) kids are keen to spend time with friends. These projects are important to both (or all four) of you. Negotiate!

If you really can't find role-play partners, make notes on the possible strategies, win-win potential, and best-realistic-worst positions for all participants.

7 FOLLOW UP

Understanding about the need for and the value of sales follow up requires recognition that:

(a) The sales effort is not simply a short-term tactical activity aimed at winning a one off sale

(b) The selling process is expensive representing a considerable investment of company resources which is unlikely to be paid back on the basis of just one order

(c) Even a sale which was not made can be followed up and represents a qualified lead for future business

It is important that sales staff do not feel that the signing of an order is the end of the sales process. **In many respects it should be seen as the beginning of the seller-buyer relationship.**

7.1 Thank the customer

Thanking the buyer for the order should be done at the end of the sales interview, but it can be reinforced by a phone call or letter. If the sales call has resulted in something other than a firm order, for example the opportunity to submit a proposal or estimate, then the follow up in writing is important to confirm the details of the brief or agreement. The simple act of thanking the client for the order or opportunity to compete for work is a courtesy, but people do like to feel their business is appreciated and important.

7.2 Check the order has been fulfilled

Checking the order has been fulfilled is the next vital stage in the follow up. With products, this means a phone call on the day of delivery to ensure the order has arrived. With a service or installation, it is important to check at an early stage that work is under way and the client is satisfied with both progress and performance.

(a) The **client** should be contacted, not the seller's operations or delivery staff, as the customer may have a problem of which they are unaware.

(b) The process of checking directly has positive PR benefits. It the client feels you are interested, it presents an image that the seller and the supplier are concerned and it continues the dialogue, making future sales calls easier. The feeling that the sales representative will take direct personal action to correct any errors or mistakes is very reassuring to a new customer. It has the effect of reducing the risk perceived in both the current and future purchases.

(c) It can lead to an increased order of extra fitments, additional supplier etc.

(d) It provides a solid basis for a long term relationship.

(e) It represents a proactive approach to heading off possible future complaints.

(f) It represents an ideal opportunity to ask for referrals, contacts and colleagues who might also appreciate the benefits offered by your product.

(g) The easiest sales come from satisfied customers.

8 SALES REPORTS, RECORDS AND ANALYSES

8.1 Paperwork

Paperwork of all types represents non-productive selling time and as such is often resented and avoided wherever possible by the sales personnel. This same lost sales time should cause sales management to think carefully about what paperwork they really need and what their objectives are in requesting it.

However, despite streamlining, computerisation and rationalisation, it has to be appreciated that the selling job is fundamentally about communication. Communication does not stop at the meeting or interview, but has to be followed up, confirmed and acted upon by communication in writing. This includes order forms and internal paperwork as well as correspondence with the client.

As we have seen, the sales professional is a medium for communication between the company and the customer. The details of feedback, comments, complaints, offers and selling messages all have to be passed accurately between the two parties. Written records and reports are essential to this process.

8.2 Sales reports

Substitute for supervision

In many organisations the report is treated as a means of controlling the sales staff, on the assumption that if you get staff to put in writing what they were doing, when and where, they must have been using their time productively.

Reports are seen as a substitute for close supervision over staff who are working independently.

Seen in this way the process of reporting is both unproductive and demotivating. It is unlikely to result in effective use of sales efforts and will almost certainly fail to provide managers with a stream of valuable market intelligence and feedback.

Control cycle

Controlling the sales activity is nontheless a responsibility management has to undertake. But control can only be meaningful if it is preceded by thorough planning. Likewise sales plans are only of use if their outcomes are monitored and controlled. The essential ingredient of plans is of course that they contain quantified objectives or targets, which can be used as a basis for monitoring performance.

Once objectives are established, the function of the report can be seen as providing evidence of performance against set targets, (weekly or monthly etc) and providing information which enables management to analyse any variances between planned and actual results.

Management get sales information from visiting sales staff in the field, from sales results and call reports. Sales results, recording actual sales made, do not necessarily provide very useful insights. A particularly large order, or regional economic fluctuations can distort the underlying sales patterns.
Typically the report should contain the information below.

Who?	• New or existing customer? • Name of the contact • Details of the lead source.	
What?	• The objective of the visit • What happened during the visit • Past sales history with the client • Results achieved	
Next	• Any action to be taken	- by sales person - by others
Other	• Details of time spent in sales interview • Mileage and expenses incurred.	

8.3 Sales records

Records enable the salesperson to keep track of contact details, (eg when, where and who). They ensure that important personal contacts and details are not lost or forgotten.

The record system of the sales person might be a database from which sales activities can be planned. A well maintained customer record system helps ensure the sales person maximises potential business from existing clients.

Organisations often have to take positive steps to ensure they too have access to the **customer database**. Otherwise when a sales person leaves the company not only is there the risk of the clients following the representative, there is also the danger of losing potential business through lack of contact with the existing client database.

8.4 Sales analysis

If information is not going to be used, there is little point in collecting it. Both the sales professional and the sales manager should be analysing information for the same reason - to improve efficiency and performance.

Analysis of the selling activity can be both qualitative and quantitative.

8.5 Qualitative analysis

Qualitative measures are much more subjective than quantitative ones, and are likely to involve an assessment of both the sales techniques and process. This would, for example, form the basis of a field appraisal following a manager's field sales visit. Its role is to provide on the job training which is effective and ongoing as well as motivation and control.

The individual sales person can undertake **qualitative analysis**. This involves a review and analysis of his or her own sales performance, particularly when sales were not made. Critical and routine reflection can help to highlight strengths which can be developed and weaknesses which can be improved. This process of personal improvement is of considerable importance to sales staff, particularly those remunerated in part by commission payments.

8.6 Quantitative analysis

Quantitative analysis provides the objective basis for comparing sales performance of

- The individual over time
- Products within a range
- sales within a region

There are a number of ways in which results can be assessed. Typically, the ratios which might be considered include:

(a) Sales call ratio (ie the number of calls made to produce one sale)
(b) Costs per order
(c) Average order value
(d) Proportion of repeat/new orders
(e) Sales calls per day.

Chapter roundup

- Sales personnel need to know about
  - the organisation they represent
  - the industry
  - the competition
  - the products/services
  - the customers
- Sales calls need to be prepared for and the objective of the call needs to be understood.
- Sales messages have to be constructed and communicated (encoded).
- Awareness and interest in the company's product needs to be developed in the sales presentation, hopefully followed by desire.
- A dialogue between the client and sales person should be developed, asking questions and presenting benefits.
- Objections can be handled with experience, training and techniques.
- Sellers must be alert to 'buying curves' throughout the sales meeting.
- Follow up should include confirmation that the order has been fulfilled.
- Sales reports should be seen as a means of retaining control and imparting information.

Quick quiz

1 Give three internal sources of information that sales personnel could use to obtain information about an organisation.

2 Should sales personnel make appointments or cold call?

3 How can a salesperson make a good first impression with a client?

4 Give examples of sales aids.

5 What are the benefits of sales aids to the sales persons?

6 Give three ways in which a sales person can overcome objections.

7 What negotiations should be undertaken before closing the sale?

Answers to quick quiz

1 Could include induction, training, annual reports, staff newsletters etc. (See paragraph 1.2)

2 It is usually better to make appointments. (para 2.1)

3 Be on time, take care with appearance, personal introduction, and listening. (para 3.1)

4 Brochures, presentation kits, demonstration models, videos, computer generated images etc. (para 4.3)

5 Add interest, add tangibility, show products in use and make it easier to explain key selling points. (para 4.3)

6 Forestall or put off, ignore, acknowledge (para 5.2)

7 Terms and price. (paras 6.2, 6.3)

Answers to activities

1 *Company/organisation:* to understand the company ethos and communicate it.

Industry and competition: put the company and its products into perspective.

Products: to focus on the sellable or 'good' points.

Customers: to target the intended purchasers and gear the marketing towards them.

2 There is no specific answer to this activity

3 There is no specific answer to this activity

4 There is no specific answer to this activity

5 There is no specific answer to this activity

6 Find out details of current contract
What has the client liked?
What has the client disliked?
How to remedy what the client has disliked?
Does the client want to change any aspect?
Do we need to be armed with good ideas for a change?
Is price a factor?
Can we offer a discount?
Do we need a change of personnel on the account?

7 There is no specific answer to this activity

Chapter 18 :

ORGANISING THE ACHIEVEMENT OF SALES OBJECTIVES

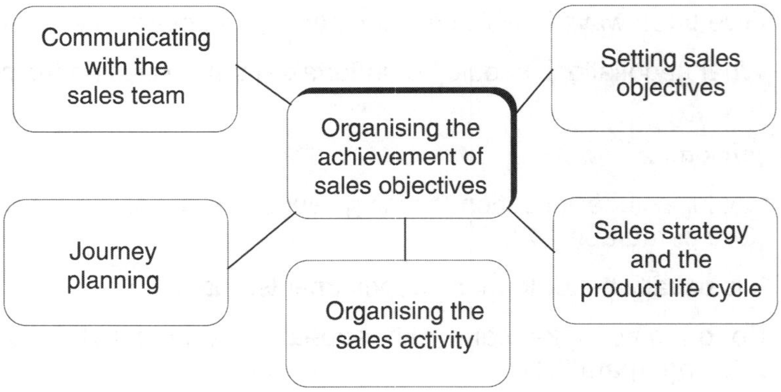

Introduction

This chapter looks at sales strategy in the context of the organisation's overall strategy and the product life cycle (PLC). This is followed by aspects of how management organises the sales function and how this can be maximised in terms of effort and time with careful journey planning, and how management can communicate policies and strategies to their sales force.

Your objectives

In this chapter you will learn about the following:

(a) How sales objectives fit into overall corporate and marketing objectives.

(b) The impact of the PLC on sales strategies.

(c) How the sales function can be organised by management.

(d) The importance of careful journey planning.

(e) The ways in which management can communicate with the sales force.

NOTES

1 SETTING SALES OBJECTIVES

1.1 Level of objectives

Sales objectives are – or should be – set in the wider context of the marketing mix.

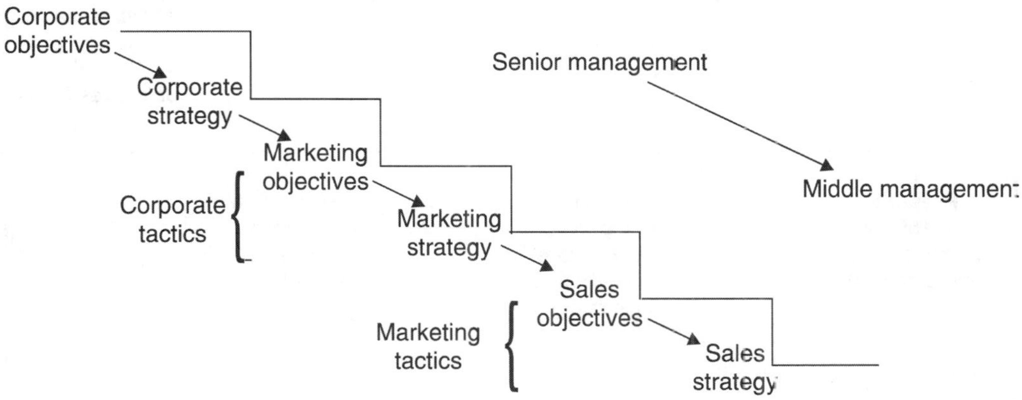

EXAMPLE

A Bank wants to increase profits.

(a) **Business objective:** grow profits.

(b) **Strategy:** Increase revenue per customer.

(c) **Tactics:** increasing revenue per customer might not be possible unless customers buy other services form the bank (eg insurance).

  (i) The **critical success factor** will be the number of extra services sold to each customer.

  (ii) A **key task** might involve developing a **customer database** so that the firm can target customers with information about other services more effectively.

  (iii) The **resources needed** might include the services of a system analyst, hardware etc and increased sales force

---

1.2 Marketing objectives

To take an example, let's say that middle managers have been faced with a corporate objective of increasing profitability by x% over three years.

(a) In pursuit of this, **production** could cut costs, reduce stockholdings and trim back production levels.

(b) **Marketing** could be implementing strategies to increase revenue, through higher sales. These two departments would clearly be working **against each other**, although both aiming to contribute to the stated corporate goal.

It is only when armed with clear, quantified corporate objectives and the co-ordinating influence of a corporate strategy that unit managers can develop their own functional plans. The first step is to generate unit objectives.

We can outline a hierarchy as follows.

BPP PUBLISHING

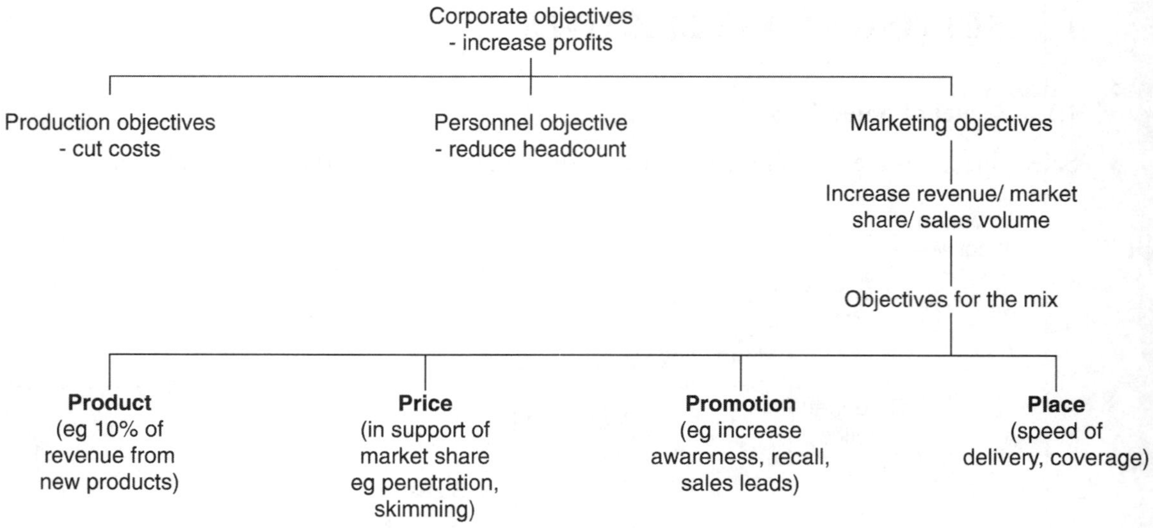

DISCUSSION

The most important aspect of the marketing mix is ensuring that it is integrated, ie that the market place is not getting conflicting messages.

EXAMPLE

Marketing objectives are often expressed in **sales terms**, for example, market share or revenue or sales volume.

(a) For example A Ltd wishes to increase **market share** to 43% by 2007

(b) This objective can then be further developed by the sales manager who can forecast that 43% in 2007 will equal 1 million cases. In turn the sales manager can then develop the next level of objectives into terms which mean something to those in the sales team: to sell 1,000 more cases per month by 2007

(c) The individual sales targets or objectives can be set from this. With a salesforce of 20, each salesperson needs to be selling 50 extra cases per month by 2007

Objectives can be set for other elements of the mix and for marketing activities.

Mix element	Comment
Product	Although 'marketing' deals with products and markets, marketing objectives for products require the co-operation of the production department and R&D. Marketing can suggest that a percentage (eg 10%) of revenue should come from **new products.**
Pricing	**Distribution** pricing has market share implications (eg penetration or skimming pricing). Distribution can be considered a marketing tool - an objective might be to reduce the time from when the order is received to when the goods are delivered: 'By March 2007, reduce delivery lead times from 5 to 3 days'.

NOTES

Mix element	Comment
Promotion	Advertising and promotion objectives can be set to shape customer awareness and expectations of the product as well as to generate sales leads. • Recall: How many remember an ad? • Awareness • Interest (eg % of people replying to a mailshot) • 'Share of voice' (compared to other companies' promotions)
Service marketing mix	• People - staff training • Processes - efficiency • Physical evidence (cleanliness of sites).
Customers	• For many firms, repeat business is more profitable than new business - this is the justification behind **relationship marketing**. • A firm might **reposition** its offer to attract a new segment.

EXAMPLE

Reebok are involved not only with selling to retailers, but also with working closely with them in terms of point of purchase displays.

Activity 1 **(10 minutes)**

The American tobacco company Philip Morris advertised scientific studies which revealed that the dangers of passive smoking (ie inhaling other people's cigarette smoke) have been much exaggerated.

This campaign was widely controversial. Allegedly, the tobacco industry funded the research, but importantly, other research studies contradicted its conclusions. Most people don't understand the niceties of a scientific procedure and are unaware of much of the material on the topic.

What do you think the objective of the campaign was, in terms of the firm's wider strategy?

2 SALES STRATEGY AND THE PRODUCT LIFE CYCLE

The sector of business in which a firm operates is likely to have a significant impact on the role of selling within the marketing strategy. Likewise there are a number of situations where the sales activity may be particularly challenging or important. Of particular relevance is the product life cycle. This was introduced in the previous chapter and will be developed in the next section.

2.1 Selling across the product life cycle

Definition

You will probably already be familiar with the concept of the **product life cycle** (PLC). It provides managers with a broad picture of how sales might change over the life of the product, from introduction to decline. Its real value to marketing lies in the awareness that at the various stages of the PLC, the condition of the market, characteristics of the customer and nature of the competition all change and so marketing strategies need to be developed and modified.

Just as the marketing approach needs to change, the various stages represent specific selling situations which the sales person might meet and have to deal with. Although in this section we will examine the roles of sales throughout the PLC it needs to be remembered that in many circumstances the sales person will be offering not just a single product but a portfolio of products at different stages of the PLC.

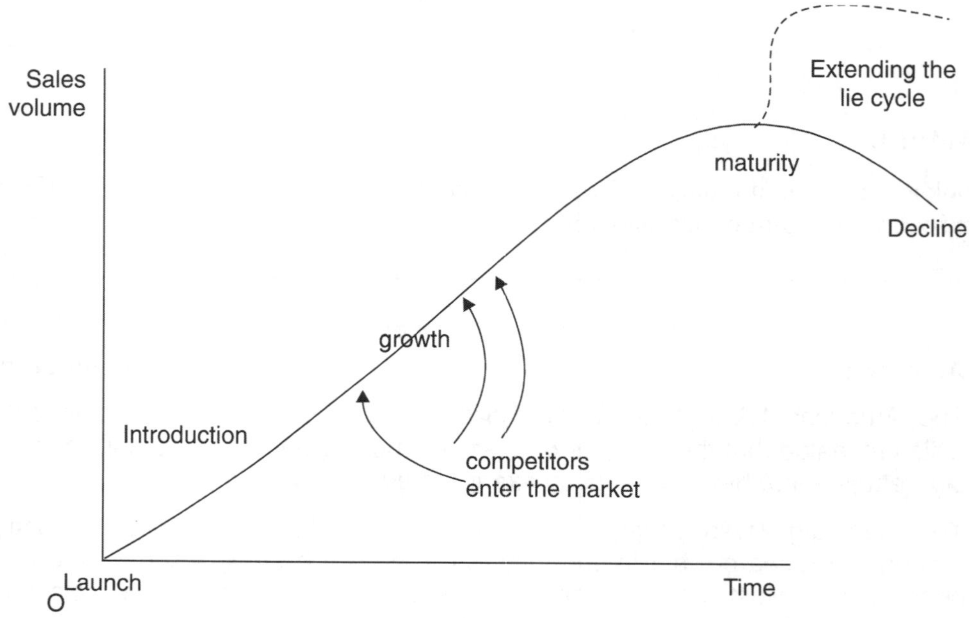

The sales team need to be aware of the changing market situation in which they are operating. The marketing support which is provided is also likely to change reflecting the changing needs of potential customers.

DISCUSSION

The PLC is a self fulfilling prophecy if not used with care, and products can be deleted before the market is ready.

2.2 Selling a new product: achieve a trial

The launch of a new product is the most critical time of its life. Despite rigorous testing and screening at the new product development stage, a very high proportion of products launched still fail to become successful mature products.

The task of the sales force will to some extent depend on the exact situation. Is this a new generic product, or simply an improved model or innovation to a well established range? Is the target market made up of existing customers or new ones? Despite these variations the objective in all cases will be to generate awareness and interest, as quickly as possible, in the target market.

For a really innovative new product, the end users of the product may not be the target group who will be the **main users** once it has been established. Identifying these 'innovators' and influencing the relevant opinion leaders is very important.

The salesperson must make sure that the product is stocked by distributors whose customer profile includes such adventurous clients.

The sales person needs to recognise that **from the customer's point of view, a new product is a risky option**. The greater the perceived risk the more complex and drawn out the decision making process is likely to be. A number of tactics can be used to counter the **risk factor**.

(a) Free trials or tests to demonstrate functional performance.

(b) Guarantees and warranties provided, to 'insure' the continuing performance.

(c) The backing of the company endorsing the product with its image and reputation for:

- innovation
- reliability
- performance
- quality etc

(d) **The advice and recommendation of the salesperson.** This can be very valuable is there is an established relationship of trust between the client and sales representative. The long term integrity of the individual can be a valuable asset when launching a new product.

(e) In the **resell market**, commitment to a major advertising and promotional launch for a new product, will help convince retailers that the product line will be profitable.

(f) Special offers on **after sales service,** like training and technical support will reduce the perceived risk.

(g) A lower **introductory price** is a strategy which may be adopted to ensure rapid penetration of the market.

Activity 2 **(5 minutes)**

You work for a shampoo manufacturer who has developed a new line of organic hair products. Give examples of how you could make retailers stock your product and examples of how you could encourage end users to try your product.

2.3 Selling in the growth phase: forestall competitors

Selling when sales volume is expanding rapidly is probably the **easiest stage in which to be working**. The new product is by now established and proven, so there is less risk involved in the purchase and more awareness and interest in the product generally.

NOTES

However, in this stage, new competitors enter the market place, and so marketing activities to ensure brand or company loyalty are likely to be implemented. For the sales team, growth in sales is likely to be depends on reaching the customer before competitors do. It is important therefore, to make a priority of visiting potential customers and to plan sales journeys in a way which fulfils this objective. The growth stage can be protracted or fairly short lived. The nature of the business tends to indicate the likely length each stage of the PLC will last. However, at some point, the growth in sales will level off as the **market reaches saturation.**

EXAMPLE

Mobile phone usage has taken off rapidly and service providers have got away with customer service not acceptable in other industries.

2.4 Selling a mature product: account maintenance

At this stage there are few if any new customers and as most sales will be repeat purchases, there is unlikely to be any overall increase in the market size.

(a) The mature stage is usually the longest stage of the life cycle and the sales person's role becomes one of **account maintenance**. Ensuring customer loyalty by providing good quality customer care, easy re-ordering and regular sales contact is the key to maintaining sales at this stage. The sales function at this stage requires a different set of skills than the creative development of 'new' sales at earlier stages of the PLC. Some companies recognise this and the development of new business is the job of a separate sales team to the group who maintain existing accounts.

(b) Alternatively, selling will 'be devoted towards increasing market share.

2.5 Selling to new markets

At the mature stage of the PLC the company may decide to adopt a strategy developed to extend the product life cycle. These modification strategies can be based on the following.

(a) The **product**. Modifications to features and performance are used to:

  (i) Attract a more rapid replacement purchase from existing customers, for example, in the car market; or

  (ii) Gaining competitive advantage with 'new improved' versions of the product.

  This strategy may win a few new sales, and can retain interest and protect existing market share.

(b) The **market**. The product is presented to a new group of customers. **Selling to new markets is a difficult challenge to the sales team**. They will have little knowledge of the market, its needs or key decision makers. This information needs researching and the network of contacts, company reputation and profile will need establishing from scratch. Initially sales visits may be 'cold' calls to people with little awareness of the company or what it can achieve. Again the risks involved for the buyer are high and a supportive strategy needs to be developed to reduce the risk. Publicity and press coverage of the firm's move to the market, advertising, and promotional activities can all be used to generate awareness and interest in the sales call.

(c) **Modify the marketing mix**. This can also result in new customers for the product, for instance:

(i) if price is lowered enabling a different segment of the market access to the product for the first time;

(ii) changing the product's availability can have a similar effect.

Any such strategy needs developing with care as it will reposition the product and may alienate existing customers. The sales team are likely to be the most aware of how customers respond to any such changes.

> **Activity 3** **(10 minutes)**
>
> Think of examples that fall under (a), (b) and (c) above.

2.6 Selling in the decline stage

Once sales start to decline it is usually means that customers are switching to a new product. This may be a product offered by the same company and so being presented by the same sales team. In this case orchestrating the switch from one to another can be achieved if management provide sales teams with a clear targets and priorities. In such a case resources can be reallocated gradually to the new product, in line with the shifting patterns of demand.

As products enter the decline stage, decisions have to be made about their future. The sales team will be a valuable source of customer feedback and should help to inform managers about the feasibility of withdrawing the product. It may be that, although less profitable, it is seen to be an important core of the range offered, and its existence indirectly encourages sales elsewhere.

The sales person's task if a product is withdrawn is to maintain the business and loyalty of the customer. Handling worries about servicing and spares for existing purchases and helping customers find alternative products are all critical parts of the sales task at this stage.

3 ORGANISING THE SALES ACTIVITY

3.1 Sales force size

Provided that an organisation has sufficient resources to increase its output and distribution, the sales force's size could be increased up to the point where the marginal costs of extra sales effort begins to exceed the marginal revenue from the incremental sales. Effectively, however, the overall size of the sales organisation is restricted by the resources available to the company and by company policy, and by the balance in the communications mix between personal and non-personal selling.

Every organisation will have some idea about what it can afford to spend on selling. A useful example might be as follows.

(a) Selling expenses should not exceed, say, 10% of sales.

(b) If a salesperson, with selling expenses and commission etc, costs, say £30,000 per annum, then turnover of £300,000 per annum would be required to support one salesperson.

(c) If a company budgets annual turnover of, say, £6 million, then the total sales force should not exceed 20 employees.

These figures are hypothetical, but should indicate to you about how a rule of thumb judgement can be made about the maximum economic size of a sales force, based on annual turnover and selling costs. Obviously, a complex sales force organisation would be inappropriate for a firm with only a relatively low sales turnover!

EXAMPLE

With more efficient sales management techniques and the use of Information Technology, sales forces in many industries have been reduced substantially over the past few years. For example IBM has halved its sales force in the US over the last decade.

3.2 The selling organisation

The type of selling organisation will be influenced by various factors.

(a) The **intensity of competition**, and possibly the structure of a competitor's selling organisation, will affect a company's own sales organisation structure. If, for example, specialisation appears to give a marketing advantage to a rival product, a company might need to use specialised selling itself.

(b) If it is decided that personal selling by salespeople is the most efficient way to sell, the quantity and quality of the sales force will reflect this decision (ie low dependence on advertising may result in a greater reliance on personal selling).

(c) Wherever possible, specialisation of the sales force should be introduced (whether by function, product, type of customer, outlet or market) but it must be economically justified.

(d) All organisation should be based on functions, not personalities.

(e) Because of the possible social bridge between a 'low status' salesperson and the 'high status' of the buying representative of a potential customer (perhaps its managing director, production or financial director), it may be necessary to use sales management executives to deal with these special cases, (ie to use management as sales people).

(f) The extent to which dealers are used will affect organisation. If a company sells only to a limited number of multiple stores and wholesalers, a small sales organisation will be sufficient.

(g) Generally, there is direct selling for industrial goods but sales are often confined to a few customers, so that the number of orders is small but their value high, and consequently:

(i) the **number** of orders/size of sales force ratio is low; but
(ii) the **value** of orders/size of sales force ratio is high.

DISCUSSION

Speculation of the sales force is usually undertaken for hihg-tech industrial goods.

BPP PUBLISHING

NOTES

3.3 Territorial design

Eventually, all large sales organisations involve a territorial breakdown. Where there is no specialisation, the sales organisation may be based entirely on geographical divisions.

(a) There may be a **pyramid organisation** structure with top management at head office, sales supervisors controlling the sales force in a region, and a salesperson or sales force for each territory in a region.

(b) The span of **control of a sales supervisor** is influenced by:

- (i) The amount of work to be done.
- (ii) The physical conditions under which it is done (eg how much travelling).

(c) The amount of supervision required depends on:.

- (i) The initiative which individual salespeople are allowed (if salespeople can arrange delivery dates, price and production possibilities, they must have easy communication access back to their immediate superiors).
- (ii) The size of sales commission will determine how much salespeople are willing to work without the need to be supervised.

(d) The size of each sales territory should be such that the amount of time wasted by salespeople in travelling is not excessive; there should be a good 'frequency of call' rate.

The purpose of a territorial sales force

(a) Reduce travelling time and costs.
(b) Enable the salespeople to get to know their customers and sales areas.
(c) Motivate salespeople by giving them autonomy over their area.
(d) Give salespeople an equal workload or equal sales potential.
(e) Keep the organisation and administration simple.

It is most suited therefore, to the sale of products in a homogeneous range (ie it is important for the salespeople to know their products as well as their customers). If the range of products is wide, and technically complex, it is unlikely that an individual salesperson will be able to learn enough about them to sell them effectively.

EXAMPLE

An example of territorial selling in the UK is Reebok. A sales person (account manager) will represent all Reebok's products in a geographical area.

The size of the sales area will depend on the expected workload for each salesperson, or the sales potential of any area. An organisation might need several sales areas in South East England whereas the whole of Scotland might be a single area.

DISCUSSION

With new technology, geographical territories are not as important.

3.4 Specialised selling organisation structures

Specialisation may be introduced into a sales organisation, and may take any of the following forms (or combination of several).

(a) **Specialisation by function:** eg advertising group, market research group, new production group, sales/production liaison group, sales training and personnel section. This **functional specialisation** is more relevant to the marketing and selling department as a whole rather than to the sales force itself.

(b) **Specialisation by the nature of goods:** the more complex the nature of the goods to be sold and the more knowledgeable the customer, the more it is necessary to employ salespeople with a skilled knowledge of the product.

(c) **Specialisation by the range of goods**

(i) If a company manufactures a range of goods, its salespeople may specialise in a section of the range, for example, in the sale of a range of office equipment some salespeople may specialise in calculators and others in document copiers.

(ii) It is also possible to employ product managers who specialise in a product or range of products and who advise the sales force, who sell the entire range without specialising. This type of organisation has drawbacks because it may be difficult to decide how far product managers should be advisers and how much authority they should be allowed over sales activities.

(iii) Salespeople must know their products; therefore if their company's product range is broad and complex, product specialisation may be desirable. Several salespeople would be required to cover the same sales area. Disadvantages of product specialisation are as follows.

(1) Travelling time and expenses are higher than with a territorial sales organisation.

(2) One customer buying two different products from the same company might have to deal with two different salespeople.

(d) **Specialisation by range of market:** ie by market segments. Examples of specialisation by market segment are as follows.

(i) Home and overseas sales.
(ii) Industrial and non-industrial sales.
(iii) Male and female markets (eg clothiers).

The advantage of market specialisation is that salespeople get to know the needs of a particular market segment. The disadvantages of market specialisation are as follows.

(i) Travelling time and costs.

(ii) Potential problems for product designers when different market segments begin to show differing requirements.

(iii) The potentially complex organisation structure; eg possible problems of identifying boundaries between one segment of the market and another, especially when new market segments are evolving.

(e) **Specialisation by range of customers:** in selling industrial goods, a specialised sales force should be organised so that each salesperson deals with a small number of potential customers in order to foster a better

NOTES

understanding of the motivation of the customers. This could be vital for securing large or valuable industrial orders.

The advantages of specialisation by types of customer are as follows.

(i) The sales force will be more alert to the specific needs of each type of customer.

(ii) In selling industrial goods, knowledge about the customer's industry and needs might be crucial in winning sales over the bids of competitors.

(f) **Specialisation by range of outlets:** with changing patterns of consumer and wholesale buying, eg the growth of multiple stores and superstores - specialisation by salespeople in dealing with different types of outlet may improve a manufacturer's selling efficiency.

A combination of these different types of sales force designs can be used. Salespeople might specialise in a type of customer or type of product within a sales area or they might specialise in a type of product for a restricted number of potential customers etc.

EXAMPLE

Here might be the possible organisation of a sales force for a company manufacturing and marketing upholstered furniture.

The following points can be made about this example.

(a) **Specialisation by product type is probably unsuitable,** because in the case of upholstered furniture there is little or no technical difference between one product and another. Specialisation by product serves no purpose if all products are basically the same, since salespeople will not acquire differences in technical expertise and know-how.

(b) On the other hand, customers for upholstered furniture can probably be divided into distinct categories. Alternatively, distinct market segments might exist.

A possible analysis of customers might be as follows.

Those buying directly, for their own use	*Those buying in order to resell*
Companies (office furniture)	Department stores
Hotels, Theatres, Shipping lines	Retail furniture shops
	Mail order businesses
	Wholesalers
	Discount houses

The total number of potential customers might be quite large, (eg independent retailers, department stores, companies etc); even so, each type of customer might have certain particular characteristics or requirements or buying habits, so that specialisation by customer type would be an appropriate form of sales force organisation.

Some customers might be buyers in bulk, in which case individual salespeople should be given a number of large accounts to handle.

We do not have enough information about market segments to suggest a form of sales force organisation based on market specialisation, and so a suggested organisation might be as follows.

(a) **Key accounts**. A number of key account salespeople (perhaps two or three) each dealing with several large customers, and responsible to senior sales

NOTES

executives at head office. A territorial organisation would probably be unnecessary, although it might be convenient to divide key account customers by geographical area, depending on how many of them there are.

(b) If it is considered potentially useful, the rest of the sales force could specialise by customer type, divided between:

   (i) those selling to direct users;
   (ii) those selling to resellers, including exporters.

Given the large number of potential customers, a territorial sales force organisation would still be necessary. Since furniture is not a high-volume product, a UK territorial division might be into two or three regions, without the need for sub-division into areas.

Individual salespeople would report to regional managers as follows.

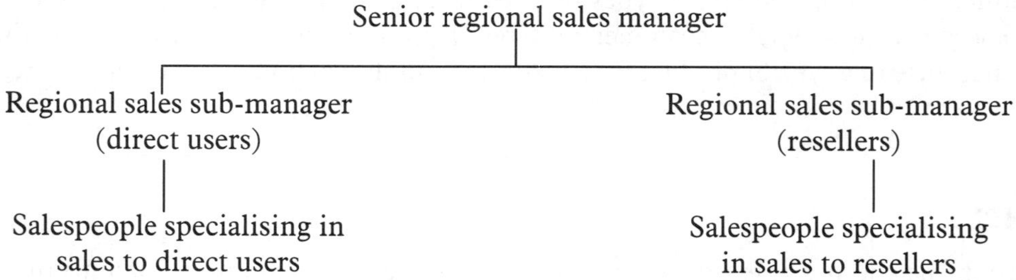

However, if the volume of sales does not justify employing a large sales force, specialisation of the sales force by customer type would be inappropriate, because its costs would outweigh the benefits obtained.

As with any aspect of marketing and selling, it is the job of marketing management to organise resources so as to maximise the efficiency of selling (and thus to reduce the costs of selling).

Activity 4 **(20 minutes)**

For the organisation you work for or one you have knowledge of (perhaps the management of your college) find out who supplies to the organisation and how they are organised.

3.5 Selling and information technology

Personal selling and management of the selling tasks are expensive activities for an organisation. Information technology is changing the way sales are organised and operationalised. The buying process can sometimes eliminate personal selling using the internet or computerised buying. However, information technology can also be used to make personal selling more efficient and effective. Some applications are as follows.

(a) **Telecommunications**

The use of pagers and mobile telephones means that the sales force can be in constant contact with the head office or clients. Working from home with the use of telecommunications and e-mail is on the increase with less time spent inefficiently travelling. Video conferencing is also possible, although has been relatively slow to progress.

(b) **Data handling**

Database management has been an important growth area for organisations. It has meant more effective segmentation and targeting of consumers. The effectiveness of various promotional methods can be tracked. Specifically the effectiveness of sales personnel can be assessed more easily. Customer records can be easily kept up to date with personal details stored in the system. Contacts and follow ups can be alerted 'automatically'. In general, if customer information is used effectively then there can be an increase in customer care levels.

(c) **Customer presentations**

The use of IT to tailor presentations to customers and to visually display benefits of the product/service is one of the most exciting developments of IT and marketing. Presentation 'slides' can be tailored and shown on a computer as can product designs.

EXAMPLE

A sales person for a bedroom furniture manufacturer may have software that can show prospective customers what the furniture would look like in their room in a 3D computer generated image. Designs, colours etc can all be changed to give the customer the best possible idea of what the product would look like in their own setting.

(d) **Management of the sales force**

Sales persons' individual performance can be analysed along with the sales force function to assess effectiveness. Spreadsheets can be used to plan sales force activities. Again video conferencing is an area that can be used here and looks to increase with the development of web cams. This means that meetings can be attended without taking time out to travel to a central location.

A further aspect of sales territory design is sales call planning. Given that a sales area must have adequate sales potential and work-load, it should be possible to plan the number of calls a salesperson should be able to make over a period of time. 'Standards' should exist for the average number of calls per day, or average miles travelled per day; and by planning the salesman's work load, it should be possible to prevent time lost through inefficient routing, or spending too long with difficult or reluctant customers etc, we will be looking at sales planning in more detail in a later chapter. We cover this in the next section.

4 JOURNEY PLANNING

The sales resource is both valuable and scarce. Planning how to get the most from it and the best out of the sales hours available is an important element in the preparation process.

The nature of selling makes it not only possible, but actually easy to waste both time and effort.

NOTES

- Time can be wasted in waiting to see prospects
- Time is spent travelling between appointments
- Time and energy is wasted visiting prospects with little or no likelihood of buying
- Time and energy is wasted visiting existing clients unnecessarily.

4.1 Effective use

Management decisions can have enormous impact on how effectively the salespersons time will be used.

(a) **Geography**. Decisions on sales organisation and sales territories will determine the proximity of **sales prospects and clients to each other**. Journey times between sales visits can represent a very large percentage of the representative's day.

(b) **Other tasks.** Management makes demands on sales staff to undertake **other routine tasks**, for example, administrative duties, report writing and marketing research. All these reduce the available 'real' selling time. Managers need to be sure that these additional responsibilities are best done by the sales team and are the best use of their time.

(c) **Sales report.** The sales support provided by management can significantly alter the proportion of time the sales personnel can spend with clients. Providing telephone sales support to identify potential prospects, research to screen them and provide background on them and administrative support to make appointments and travel arrangements can all free the sales team from routine and time consuming aspects of their work.

(d) **Objectives.** Managers should provide clear objectives and guidelines to help channel selling activities in a way consistent with overall objectives or strategy. They may produce guidelines on percentage of calls which should be made to potential new clients or the number of times per year existing clients should be visited.

Preparation enables for well designed journey plans and an organised approach to the sales activities. Set times for being in the office, for example on a Monday morning and Friday afternoon or every day before l0am and after 5pm allows queries and callers to be given precise information as to when the sales representative will be available and able to return their call. Now, with the use of e-mail and mobile phones, sales personnel can be contacted much of the time.

Activity 5 **(5 minutes)**

How can administrative support help the sales person make more effective use of his/her time.

4.2 Call frequency

Sales people, looking to build strong relationships with customers, need to think through the frequency with which they call them, either in person or by telephone:

(a) **too often** and they will be perceived as a nuisance and 'hard seller';

(b) **too infrequently** will allow potentially valuable contacts to lapse and future business opportunities diminish.

Well planned sales activities are based on organised and **regular cycles of calls and visits**. In some situations the sales management will fix a very rigid journey cycle, with the sales team being allocated a list of customers to be contacted each week. Where sales staff are left to manage their own territory, the journey plan is likely to be based on the desired call frequency.

4.3 How often a customer should be visited.

(a) **Importance of the customer?** (usually in terms of sales value or potential sales value).

(b) **Rate of stock turn and stock levels held by the customer**. Stock turnover and levels will directly influence the order frequency, although where this is a regular occurrence reordering may be done routinely by telephone. The more regularly purchases are made, the more regular the sales contact should be. Products with long life expectancy like capital equipment may be bought infrequently, but a regular if infrequent contact ensures the sales person is well placed to benefit from any expansion plans etc.

(c) **What the buyer wants**. Buyers may specify when and how often they wish to see sales representatives. This may be the case for example with GPs and medical sales staff.

Each customer can be given a rating indicating the frequency with which they should be visited. In this scheme the most time to elapse between calls is six months. By quantifying how many customers the sales person has in each category it is possible to quantify the scale of the journey cycle required.

Customer type	*Frequency*	*Number*	*Calls in six months*	*Total calls*
Category A	Monthly	20	6	120
Category B	Two months	50	3	150
Category C	Three months	90	2	180
Category D	Six months	150	1	150
Existing customers				600

In this example, the salesperson needs to make 600 calls in six months, ie 100 a month. To this total we must add new customer targets. In this case, if we assume management requires each sales person to call on 20 new prospects each month this adds a further 120 calls to the total.

(a) The sales person needs to make 720 calls in six months, 120 calls a month, 30 calls a week (a 4week month), 6 calls a day.

(b) It is also possible to see that in every month the seller needs to visit:

20 Category A
20 New prospects
25 Category B
30 Category C
25 Category D

4.4 Time

Considerations of location need to be added to this analysis of call targets.

(a) Location indicates how much travelling time needs to be allowed between calls, but simple distance is not an adequate consideration. The degree of congestion, ease of parking and type of road links all need to be taken into account.

(b) A large scale map with key customer categories indicated by different coloured markers helps the sales representative to see at a glance the possible clients who can be visited in any one day. By breaking the whole sales territory down into smaller segments it is possible to ensure that the whole territory is covered and customers within each area seen in a logical and cost effective way.

(c) There is a final dimension which needs to be considered before determining the number of appointments to be made for each day and that is the length of time each sales visit might take. Some will be quick and routine, in others it may be necessary to visit several people or usual to be kept waiting.

4.5 Costing each sale

Once sales activity has been planned out it is possible to assess actual performance against the plan and make modifications to ensure all the targets set are met.

It is also possible to quantify the cost per sales call and the cost per order. If a sales person's salary plus expenses etc costs the firm £1,000 per week and:

(a) He or she makes 20 calls a week each sales call costs £50;

(b) If in an average week he or she takes £10,000 of orders then the sales costs are equal to 10% of sales value.

These sorts of performance analysis provide the basis for setting new performance targets and for measuring the effectiveness of training or new sales aids.

5 COMMUNICATING WITH THE SALES TEAM

The final link in our communication chain is between the **firm** and its **sales force**.

5.1 Role of management

The role of management in maintaining not just routine communication, but informative, supportive, persuasive and effective communication, is key to successful sales operation.

(a) The reality is that weaknesses in this area of management activity will show up more quickly and visibly in a sales term than anywhere else.

(b) The sales job is peculiar often isolated and difficult, yet performance can be measured and monitored by the success or not of yesterday's sales calls.

(c) The communication task facing the sales manager is made more difficult by another characteristic of the sales team. They are trained communicators and so likely to see through any insincere messages. If the manager does not believe targets are really achievable, however he or she dresses it up, the sales team are likely to recognise the lack of confidence.

(d) Their performance will reflect the expectation to fail. Attitude effects results and performance and positive communication can change both.

E-mail, mobile phones and video conferencing all have improved day to day communications between head office, clients and the sales force.

5.2 Sales manuals

Sales manuals and sales bulletins do not represent ideal examples of communicating with the sales team. This is because they represent written communication - one way not two way processes. It is difficult to ensure that messages in the written form are correctly decoded, or interpreted.

Sales manuals can be useful **reference documents** for the sales team, providing detailed information of products and procedures. However, these should be used to support other forms of staff briefing and training. Written documentation provides a formal record of communication, but it does little to guarantee either that it has been read or understood.

5.3 Sales bulletins

Sales bulletins can be seen as more immediate communication, useful when staff are not in regular contact with managers. They provide a means of keeping staff up to date on relevant issues between sales meetings. Information on product availability, promotional activity or price changes can all be communicated quickly in this way.

When presented as a **newsletter**, inclusion of positive success stories and achievement can build up team spirit and contribute towards positive motivation. Stories and pictures of themselves and friends increase the chance of a bulletin being read and other information being absorbed.

5.4 Sales meetings

Using face to face communication, these approaches have the advantage of offering two way communication opportunities. Feedback allows managers to assess attitude and monitor responses from their teams.

Sales meetings can take many forms; on a one to one basis; with a team; formally or informally; in the field, the office or an outside venue. When they are formal and involve a large number of sales staff, they are likely to be classified as a sales conference.

Meetings take time, and so their cost, not only in terms of staff time, but also lost sales opportunities can and often are calculated. As with all aspects of business, it is management's task to make sure that sales meetings are worthwhile; in other words that the benefits they generate exceed the costs of holding them. Effective meetings are those which are called for a specific reason - they have a clear objective.

There can be many reasons or objectives for a sales meeting ranging from motivating, to informing, planning and training to discussing and reporting.

The important thing is to make sure sales meetings work. They need planning and later evaluating. Venues, time and frequency of meeting needs careful consideration to minimise disruption to other sales activities and to ensure maximum support.

Objectives need to be translated into a clear agenda, with plenty of opportunity for participation from all those attending.

Results and outcomes need to be reviewed and analysed. Training inputs may need to be repeated and messages reinforced in other ways. Managers should avoid the temptation of holding fewer meetings but cramming more in. Keeping to a single or simple theme, but repeating and reinforcing the messages is much more likely to have a positive impact.

5.5 Sales conference

Sales conferences are often much more elaborate affairs, and seen as more social than normal sales meetings. Venues are often external, even glamorous or exotic and partners may be invited. Participants are still expected to work, attending presentations on training activities. They are an important occasion for developing a sense of corporate belonging and loyalty, networking with colleagues and being motivated by the latest products or plans proposed by the company.

As with any sales meeting the conference must not turn into an anti-sales event. A positive approach by management will become a positive view by the sales teams and positive results for the company. This positive push is a sales presentation to the sales force. They are being 'sold' on what they can achieve. The preparation for this pitch must be as thorough as for any other if it is to be effective.

Chapter roundup

- Sales objectives should be set in the context of the marketing strategy, which should also be set in the context of corporate objectives.
- The sales strategy varies dependant on the stage in the PLC of the product.
- If it is a new product the goal may be to get people to try the product, in growth to combat competitors, in maturity to maintain sales or look for new markets and in decline to analyse if it is still worthwhile to be in the market.
- Sales forces have to be organised in terms of sales force size, nature and territory design.
- Territories are geographic groupings of sales areas. Advantages include:
  - low travel time and costs
  - close customer relationships
  - autonomy gives motivation to sales person
  - equality
  - simple to organise
- The sales force may be organised instead by specialisation, for example by function, the nature of goods sold, the range of goods sold, the market, customers or outlets
- Time and effort can be saved by careful journey planning
- Communicating with the sales team is now much easier with e-mails, mobile phones and video conferencing
- Formal communications between the firm and the sales force include sales manuals, sales bulletins, sales meetings and conferences

Quick quiz

1. Marketing objectives should be set in the context of sales objectives. True or false?
2. What is usually the main aim for sales staff in the introductory phase of the PLC?
3. How might sales personnel selling in a mature market ensure customer loyalty?
4. A company in the mature stage for a product might decide to try to sell to new markets to extend the PLC. In what ways could it do this?
5. What input might the sales force have to management in the decline stage of the PLC?
6. Give some examples of specialised selling organisation structures by market segments.
7. How can time and effort be wasted if sales journies are not adequately planned?

8 Are there any rules on how often a customer should be visited?

9 In what ways can management communicate with the sales team?

Answers to quick quiz

1 False. Sales objectives should be set in line with overall marketing objectives. (See paragraph 1.2)

2 To get customers to try the product. (para 2.2)

3 Effort in terms of customer care, ease of reordering and relationship building. (para 2.4)

4 (i) With product modifications (ii) To a new market eg overseas (iii) Modification to other aspects of the marketing mix. (para 2.5)

5 As they are close to the customer they can advise management about decisions to withdraw the product and the impact in terms of switching products. (para 2.6)

6 Could include, UK and overseas, industrial and non industrial, customer characteristics such as demographics (eg male/female hair salons). (para 3.4)

7 Time wasted waiting to see prospects, travelling between appointments, poor potential prospects and visiting unnecessarily. (para 4)

8 Not really but management have to consider the importance of the customer, stock levels of the customer and what the buyer's requirements are. (para 4.2)

9 Telephone (mobile), e-mail, sales manuals, bulletins, meetings and conferences. (para 5)

Answers to activities

1 The objective was to alleviate to some extent the adverse reputation of the tobacco industry, and attempt to narrow the perceived area of risk from smoking.

The firm's wider strategy is to maintain levels of cigarette sales and minimise negative publicity.

2 Price concessions
Free salon equipment
Mention specific salons in advertising
Free samples
Samples inside magazines
Television advertising

3 Examples could include:

(a) 'New improved' washing powders, additional features on a personal computer, additional features on a mobile phone.

(b) Expanding overseas, such as financial services institutions, selling to a new segment or group of customers eg satellite TV selling.

(c) Selling at a cheaper price eg an offer on double glazing to gain new customers. Advertising to gain a 'new' group eg children for a fruit drink such as Sunny Delight.

4 There is no specific answer to this.

5 By enabling them to concentrate on communicating with customers, rather than engaging in administration.

Chapter 19 :
MANAGING THE SALES TEAM

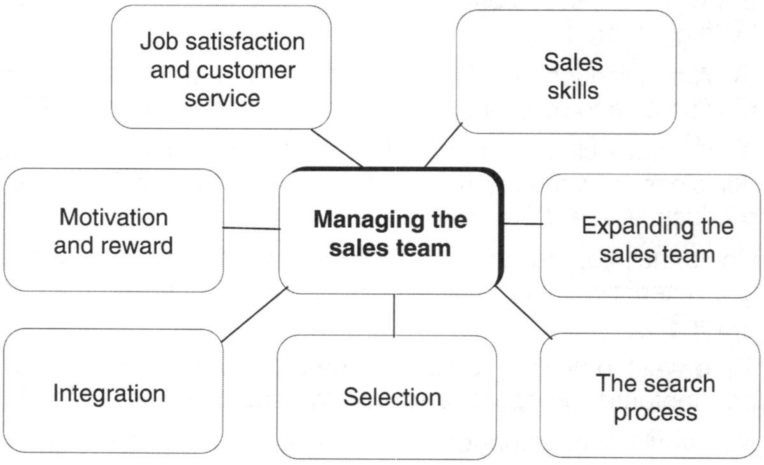

Note. Recruitment and selection processes are covered in detail in Unit 14 of the HND/HNC qualification, Managing People.

Introduction

This chapter will look at the skills that a good sales person requires. It will then concentrate on the recruitment process and how candidates for sales positions can be recruited and selected and fit into an existing sales team. Aspects of employee motivation are then discussed along with how job satisfaction - and increased customer service levels - can go hand in hand.

Your objectives

In this chapter you will learn about the following:

(a) The key personal skills a good sales person needs

(b) How sales employees can be recruited

(c) What might motivate sales staff

(d) How customer service can be a key to job satisfaction

1 SALES SKILLS

1.1 The characteristics of a salesperson

The qualities and characteristics which make up a good salesperson are many and varied.

The role of a salesperson is not a particularly easy one. Often working alone, it is easy to become isolated and the need to be a **self-motivator** is essential. Contact with clients requires patience and tenacity and a sense of humour is likely to be a valuable commodity too. Although it is possible to develop some of the skills with training, and good management: support can reduce the impact of working alone, provide motivations.

- Enthusiasm (and an ability to be a 'self-starter')
- Intelligence
- Reliability
- Commitment
- Initiative and creativity
- Self-confidence
- Courtesy
- Sensitivity

Characteristic	Comment
Enthusiasm	for the **product and company** is likely to mean the person will be a good ambassador. Enthusiasm for the **job** will help provide the energy necessary for the self motivator.
Intelligence	The salesperson is to be a credible troubleshooter for the company and problem solver for the client. This intelligence does not necessarily need to be certificated by academic qualifications. It is more a natural wit and common sense which enables the individual to assess new people and situations, and react positively. Being able to communicate at different levels of seniority and modify the message according to its audience is also a reflection of a level of intelligence.
Reliability	Salespeople often work alone and are unsupervised. They have to be relied on to undertake their functions thoroughly and as briefed. Equally important is the client's perception of the company - late arrival for meetings and agreements which are broken, generate the image of an unreliable company as well as an unreliable salesperson.
Commitment	Commitment ensures that sales targets are pursued with determination, whilst commitment to the customer ensures their needs and problems are dealt with diligently. Commitment also encompasses a sense of loyalty to the firm. It is easy for a salesperson to fall into the trap of 'blaming head office'. A sense of loyalty and commitment to the rest of the team is an important anchor for the salesperson working alone.
Initiative and creativity	A salesperson will seldom be in the same situation twice. As the needs of the customer and market place vary, so there are new opportunities which need to be recognised and developed. This required both initiative and creativity. Developing new contacts and new avenues for business will be unlikely if the sales approach is routine and narrow.

Characteristic	Comment
Self-confidence	Constantly meeting new people and travelling to new places requires a confidence in oneself and also in the company and the products being represented. Not all potential buyers are pleasant and morale can take a considerable hammering if the individual is not of a resilient and confident nature.
Courtesy	'The customer is always right', is an easier philosophy to preach than it is to always follow. As sales staff are likely to be at the front line of dealing with customer complaints, their tact, integrity and customer care training will determine whether or not the customer remains loyal to the company, despite the lapse in product or service quality.
Sensitive	In order to pick up the behavioural signals and messages and interpret them effectively, the sales person needs a degree of sensitivity.

Activity 1 **(20 minutes)**

Using the above table, assess yourself against these characteristics – be honest!

2 EXPANDING THE SALES TEAM

It will often be necessary to bring new people into the team.

- To fill an identified skills gap
- To replace staff who have been promoted or who have left
- Because the work of the team has expanded

The process of recruitment is very important. Getting the wrong person can cause problems within the existing group, and the person will require either extensive training and development, or will require replacing, with all the attendant disruption this involves.

The overall aim of the recruitment and selection process is to obtain the employees required by the human resource plan. This process can be broken down into three main stages:

(a) **Definition of requirements**, including the preparation of job descriptions and specifications.

(b) **Recruitment.** The identification and attraction of potential applicants, inside and outside the organisation.

(c) **Selection**. Selection is the part of the employee resourcing process which involves choosing between applicants for jobs: it is largely a 'negative' process, eliminating unsuitable applicants.

A sales manager may have the help and support of **human resources (HR) specialists** during the process but in smaller organisations, he or she will be responsible for all aspects of the search and selection process. Many firms outsource the early stages of the process to consultants or agencies.

2.1 An approach to recruitment and selection

If not approached systematically, the process of recruitment and selection can become costly and time-consuming. A methodical approach will probably involve the following stages:

(a) Detailed **human resource planning,** defining what resources the organisation needs to meet its objectives. At sales team level, this activity would require an analysis of the future sales skills needed.

(b) **Job analysis,** so that for any given job there are three things.

- **A job description** giving a broad statement of the nature of the job
- **A job specification** giving detail of the job's responsibilities
- **A person specification** describing the ideal candidate for the job

(c) An identification of **vacancies,** from the requirements of the human resources plan or by a **job requisition** from the section needing a new post holder.

(d) Evaluation of the **sources of labour,** which should be in the HR plan. Internal and external sources, and media for reaching both, will be considered.

(e) **Advertising** has three functions.

- To attract the attention and interest of potentially suitable candidates
- To give a favourable (but accurate) impression of the job and the organisation
- To tell candidates how to apply

(f) **Processing applications** and assessing candidates

(g) **Notifying applicants** of the results of the selection process

Activity 2 **(30 minutes)**

Find out what the recruitment and selection procedures are in your organisation and who is responsible for each stage. A procedures manual might set this out, or you may need to ask someone - perhaps in the Personnel or Human Resources department. In your own experience, what part does the manager play in these procedures? Get hold of some of the documentation your company uses.

- The job description for your job
- The personnel specification (if any) for your job
- If your firm is currently recruiting, a full set of the paperwork including the job ad

Before the search process can begin managers have a great deal to do. When the need for a new member of the team is recognised, a careful review should be undertaken to ensure that an extra full time post is justified by the contribution the person is expected to make.

Particular care is needed when the **vacancy is due to a team member leaving.** Simple replacement is not always appropriate. During the sales person's time in the job, he or she may have developed particular relationships with clients or expertise. These clients may feel concerned at the loss of their 'champion' within the organisation.

2.2 Job analysis and job specification

Job analysis is 'the determination of the essential characteristics of a job' (British Standards Institute) - that is, the process of examining a job to identify its component parts and the circumstances in which it is performed.

Information elicited from a job analysis includes both task-orientated and worker-orientated details.

(a) **Initial requirements** of the employee include aptitudes, qualifications, experience and training required.

(b) **Duties and responsibilities** include physical aspects, mental effort, routine or requiring initiative, difficult or disagreeable features, consequences of failure, responsibilities for staff, materials, equipment or cash and so on.

(c) **Environment and conditions** include physical surroundings, with particular features (eg temperature, noise, hazards), remuneration, other conditions such as hours, shifts, travel, benefits, holidays, career prospects, provision of employee services (eg canteens, protective clothing).

(d) **Social factors** include size of the department, teamwork or isolation. The sort of people dealt with (eg senior management, the public), the amount of supervision and job status.

A job analysis may cause some concern among employees from fear of standards being raised, rates cut or redundancy imposed. The job analyst will need to gain confidence; this can be done in a variety of ways.

- Communicating (explaining the process, methods and purpose of the analysis)
- Being thorough and competent in carrying out the analysis
- Respecting the work flow of the department, which should not be disrupted
- Giving feedback on the results of the appraisal, and the achievement of its objectives

2.3 Recruitment process

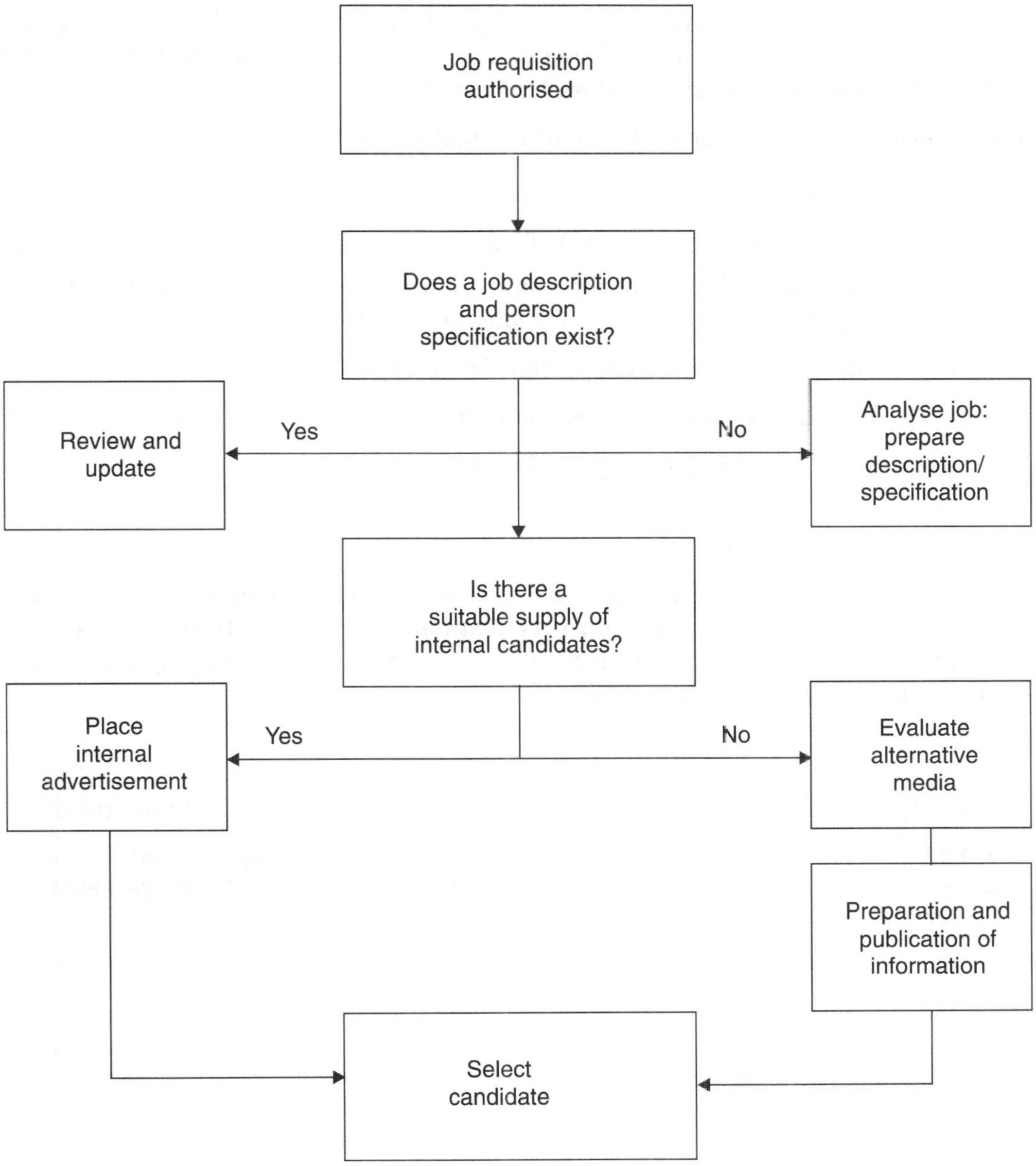

The product of the job analysis is usually a **job specification.** This is defined by *Bennett* (*Dictionary of Personnel and Human Resource Management*) as 'a detailed statement of the physical and mental activities involved in a job and (where appropriate) a description of the environment in which work is undertaken. Job specifications are usually expressed in terms of **what the worker has to do and the knowledge and judgements required** for successful completion of duties.'

EXAMPLE

Some companies tie some of their human resource requirements to the **product life cycle.** Armstrong states that 'Texas Instruments believes that it is necessary to match management style to product life cycle. As a product moves through different phases of its life cycle, different levels of management skills become dominant. It could be disastrous, for instance, to put risk taking entrepreneurs in charge of mature cash flow businesses'.

2.4 Job description

A **job description** is prepared from the job analysis. It is a broad statement of the purpose, scope, duties and responsibilities of a job. It describes the content of a job; and its relative importance in comparison with other jobs.

The job description states the principal details of the job.

- Job title/summary
- Location of the job (department, place)
- The relationship of the job to other positions such as who the job holder is responsible to and who are the job-holder's subordinates
- The main duties and responsibilities of the job
- The limits to the job holder's authority
- Any equipment for which the job holder is responsible

2.5 Person specification

Once the job has been clearly defined, the organisation can decide what kind of person is needed to fill it effectively. A **person specification** identifies the **type of person** the organisation should be trying to recruit - his or her character, aptitudes, qualifications, career aspirations, special abilities and experience.

Activity 3 **(30 minutes)**

Do you have a job description? (If you don't, draw one up.) Determine a person specification for the job. How far do you match the ideal requirements of your job?

NOTES

EXAMPLE

	JOB DESCRIPTION
1 Job title	Area sales representative
2 Location	Northern sales office
3 Job summary	To develop the sales and customer base within this area
4 Job content	Typical duties will include: (a) prospecting for new customer contracts; (b) presenting new products to existing customers; (c) providing merchandising support to customers; (d) taking orders and dealing with customer queries.
5 Reporting structure	Marketing manager Northern area │ Sales Manager (North) │ Area Sales representatives
6 Experience/ education	Two 'A' levels, experienced negotiator, clean driving license; experience of retail sales
7 Training to be provided	Induction and initial product knowledge training
8 Hours	40 per week, or as required
9 Personal characteristics required	Well motivated, good communicator, reliable and 'honest', prepared to travel
10 Objectives and appraisal	Sales targets set monthly in conjunction with sales manager. Annual appraisal
11 Salary	£25,000 plus car and commission
	Job description prepared by: Head office HR department Date: March 20X2

3 THE SEARCH PROCESS

The objective at this stage of the process is to identify candidates who are likely to be most suited to the vacancy. It is an exercise in segmentation and promotional targeting which marketers are well trained to manage.

3.1 Tapping unused labour resources

Older workers are a possible labour market. Some companies in the retail sector have targeted older workers (over-45s) for customer service positions. They bring important qualities.

- Skills and experience
- High regard for customer service
- Stabilising influence on younger staff
- Contribution to better staff retention rates

Women returners. There are a number of factors determining a woman's return to work.

(a) **Child care facilities**. If these are easily obtainable, a mother is likely to use them. Employers can provide them. Private child care is expensive. Some organisations, which do not wish to provide child care facilities themselves, might offer **child care vouchers**.

(b) **Career break schemes** have been introduced in particular in the financial services sector. Women are allowed to take time off for a few years to have children and return to the same job. Some organisations require a 'satisfactory performance record'. Other factors affecting retention include equal opportunity training schemes and assertiveness courses.

EXAMPLE

Women are frequently cited as having many of the skills attributed to a good sales person - empathy, listening and following up. There is also evidence that they are better than men at 'building trust'.

(Sales and Marketing Management Jan 1995)

Activity 4 **(10 minutes)**

What would be the benefits of attracting an internal candidate? What would be the possible problems?

3.2 Internal recruitment

Internal candidates can be considered before advertising outside or they can be included in the process as candidates. It is worth remembering, though, that an internal candidate who fails to be offered a post requires much more sensitive handling, as there will be a strong sense of rejection and this can sour an otherwise happy team. The individual may resent the successful candidate and be unco-operative. In the worst case you might even lose what is otherwise a key member of the team, thereby creating a new search and selection problem.

EXAMPLE

Personnel Management (December 1994) reported an innovative approach to **internal recruitment** at computer company Logica. As part of a more flexible and international approach (including performance-related pay, appraisal and training), Logica is implementing a global 'resource management system' in which a central database of employees' skills and experiences is being established. 'As well as holding employees' CVs, this will be the first medium to advertise vacancies on a global basis within the company.'

3.3 Job advertisements

Despite these options, in the end many posts will be advertised. The advertisement is, in a way, already part of the selection process, because it will be placed where suitable people are likely to see it, and will be worded in a way that further weeds out people who would not be suitable for the job (or for whom the job would not be suitable). Obviously, for marketing posts, the advertisement is the recruit's first sight of the firm's marketing communications.

DISCUSSION

In specialist markets sales people from competitors will know each other. What are the advantages and disadvantages in recruiting in such markets?

In order for this pre-selection to be effective, the advertisement will have to contain details of the organisation and the job.

- Employer's **location** and **business**
- **Rewards**: the salary or wage benefits, training
- **The job**: title, main duties and responsibility, special factors
- **Career prospects**
- **Qualifications and experience required**/preferred, other aptitudes
- **How to apply**

It will have to present an attractive image, but also an honest one, so as not to disillusion successful applicants.

Preparation of the job information requires skill and attention in order to fulfil its objectives of attraction and preselection. It should meet a number of criteria.

(a) It should be **concise**, but comprehensive enough to be an accurate description of the job, its rewards and requirements.

(b) It should be **targeted** to attract the attention of the maximum number of the right sort of people.

(c) It should be **attractive**, conveying a favourable impression of the organisation, but not falsely so.

(d) It should be **relevant** and appropriate to the job and the applicant. Skills, qualifications and special aptitudes required should be prominently set out, along with special features of the job that might attract or deter applicants, such as shiftwork or extensive travel.

The way in which a job is advertised will depend on the type of organisation and the type of job. A factory is likely to advertise a vacancy for an unskilled worker in a different way from a company advertising vacancies for clerical staff. Managerial jobs may merit national advertisements, whereas semi- or unskilled jobs may only warrant local coverage, depending on the supply of suitable candidates in the local area. Specific skills may be most appropriately reached through trade, technical or professional journals, like *Marketing Week*.

The choice of **advertising medium** will depend upon three considerations.

(a) The **cost** of advertising. It is more expensive to advertise in a national newspaper than on local radio, and more expensive to advertise on local radio than in a local newspaper.

(b) The **type and number of readers** of the medium, and its suitability for the number and type of people the organisation wants to reach.

(c) The **frequency** with which the organisation wants to advertise the job vacancy. A monthly magazine or weekly newspaper are probably only useful for advertising a vacancy once. This is probably sufficient for a specialist or professional, or for a senior management position, since those who are interested will be on the look-out for vacancies advertised in certain magazines or newspapers.

Activity 5 **(10 minutes)**

What is the most usual type of medium used to advertise job vacancies in your field (or the field you would like to work in). Assess the medium in terms of the above criteria.

Methods and media for advertising jobs.

- In-house magazines and notice-boards
- Professional and specialist newspapers or magazines, such as *Personnel Management*, *Marketing* or *Computing*
- National newspapers, especially for senior management jobs or vacancies for skilled workers, where potential applicants will not necessarily be found through local advertising. Local newspapers would be suitable for jobs where applicants are sought from the local area
- Local radio, television and cinema. These are becoming increasingly popular, especially for large-scale campaigns, for large numbers of vacancies
- Job centres. On the whole, vacancies for unskilled work (rather than skilled work or management jobs) are advertised through local job centres, although in theory any type of job can be advertised here
- School and university careers offices
- The Internet, especially for IT professionals and to attract candidates internationally
- Employment agencies and recruitment consultants for unusual or specialist posts

4 SELECTION

4.1 Application forms

Applicants who reply to job advertisements are usually asked to fill in a job application form, or to send a letter giving details about themselves and their previous job experience and explaining why they think they are qualified to do the job. An application form should elicit sufficient information to screen candidates into two groups.

- Those obviously unsuitable for the job
- Those who might be of the right calibre, and worth inviting to an interview

Application forms have two important aspects.

(a) An open-ended element, which will enable a candidate to give information about his or her abilities and achievements, including academic qualifications, work experience, activities and interests, career expectations and why the candidate thinks he or she is suitable.

(b) The closed element is much more structured. In this case the candidate is required to answer detailed questions (eg basic biographical information) which are posed in a restricted format (eg tick boxes). This element of an application form enables easier comparison between candidates.

4.2 The selection interview

The selection interview is the next stage of the selection process. Interviewing is a crucial part of the selection process.

The interview has a three-fold purpose.

(a) To find the best person for the job.

(b) To ensure that applicants understand what the job is and what the career prospects are. They must be allowed a fair opportunity to decide whether or not they want the job.

(c) To make applicants feel that they have been given fair treatment in the interview, whether they get the job or not. Current applicants may still be future employees or customers.

The interview must be prepared carefully, to make sure that the right questions are asked, and relevant information obtained to give the interviewers what they need to make their selection.

(a) The **job description should be studied** to review the major demands of the job.

(b) The **person specification should be studied and questions should be planned** which might help the interviewer make relevant assessments of the applicant's character and qualifications. The interview may concentrate on the following aspects:

- Confirming and expanding factual knowledge about the candidate. This means, for example, asking about the major problems the candidate faced in previous jobs
- Gauging the candidate's level of knowledge
- Judging how quick the candidate is to respond to questions
- Finding out likes and dislikes

- Establishing a trend in his or her thinking

(c) Each application form should be carefully studied, in order to decide on questions or question areas for the individual applicant.

The interview should be conducted in such a way that the information required is successfully obtained during the interview.

(a) The **layout of the room** and the number of interviewers should be planned carefully. Most interviewers wish to put candidates at their ease, and so it would be inadvisable to put the candidate in a 'hot seat' across a table from a large number of hostile-looking interviewers. However, some interviewers might want to observe the candidate's reaction under severe pressure, and deliberately make the layout of the room uncomfortable and off-putting.

(b) The **manner of the interviewers**, the tone of their voice, and the way their early questions are phrased can all be significant in establishing the tone of the interview.

(c) **Questions should be put carefully**. The interviewers should not be trying to confuse the candidate, but should be trying to obtain the information that they need.

(d) It is necessary to ask relevant questions, but the time of **the interview should be taken up mostly with the candidate talking,** and not with the interviewers asking questions. The more a candidate talks, the easier it should be to assess their suitability for the job. As a rule of thumb, the candidate should be talking for 70% of the time.

(e) **The candidate should be given the opportunity to ask questions.** Indeed well-prepared candidates should go into an interview knowing what questions they may want to ask. The choice of questions might well have some influence on how the interviewers finally assess them.

(f) Similarly the interviewer should be aware of the questions candidates are likely to ask. Candidates may well try to probe behind the statements made about the business, by asking for example why the interviewer chose or has remained with the organisation. Some candidate questioning may be a sign that the interviewer has failed to impart key information - for example the candidate's likely role within the organisation or the opportunities for advancement.

Activity 6 **(5 minutes)**

Role play with a friend or colleague an interview situation for a job you are relatively familiar with.

After each interview has been completed, notes should be made and, if more than one interviewer was present, impressions compared. Each candidate should be evaluated against the criteria for appointment. There are then three possible outcomes for each candidate.

(a) A job offer, possibly subject to conditions.

- Taking up references
- Obtaining evidence of educational and professional qualifications
- Medical examination

NOTES

(b) An invitation to a **second interview**. Some organisations have a two-stage interview process, whereby first stage interview candidates are reduced to a short-list for a second stage interview. The second stage of the interview might well be based on a group selection method (see below). In many instances, the recruitment consultant might carry out the first stage interview.

(c) Rejection.

Interviews have often been criticised because they **fail to select suitable people** for job vacancies.

(a) **Assessment may be unclear**. The opinion of one interviewer may differ from the opinion of another. They cannot both be right, but because of their different opinions, a suitable candidate might be rejected or an unsuitable candidate offered a job.

(b) **Interviews fail to provide accurate predictions** of how a person will perform in the job.

(c) **The interviewers are likely to make errors of judgement** even when they agree about a candidate. There are several reasons for this.

(d) The candidate may be adept at being interviewed. Many will have received training, including video debriefs, in presenting themselves.

FOR DISCUSSION

What assumptions might an interviewer make about **you**, based on your:

(a) accent, or regional/national variations in your spoken English
(b) school
(c) clothes and hair-style
(d) stated hobbies, interests, 'philosophies'
(e) taste in books and TV programmes.

To what extent would any of these assumptions be fair?

For objectivity, you might like to conduct this exercise in class. What assumptions do you make about the person sitting next to you?

It might be apparent from the list of limitations above that a major problem with interviews is the **skill and experience of the interviewers themselves**. Any interviewer is prone to bias, but a person can learn to reduce this problem through training and experience. Inexperienced interviewers have other problems as well.

- **Inability to evaluate** properly information about a candidate
- **Inability to compare** a candidate against the requirements for a job or a personnel specification
- Bad interview planning
- A **tendency to talk too much** in interviews, and to ask questions which call for a short answer
- A tendency to act as an inquisitor and make candidates feel uneasy.

To some extent the problems can be overcome with training.

BPP PUBLISHING

4.3 Selection testing

In some job selection procedures, an interview is supplemented by some form of selection test. The interviewers must be certain that the results of such tests are reliable, and that a candidate who scores well in a test will be more likely to succeed in the job.

There are four types of test commonly used in practice.

(a) **Intelligence tests** aim to measure the applicant's general intellectual ability.

(b) **Aptitude tests** are designed to predict an individual's potential for performing a job or learning new skills.

(c) **Proficiency tests** are perhaps the most closely related to an assessor's objectives, because they measure ability to do the work involved. An applicant for an audio typist's job, for example, might be given a dictation tape and asked to type it.

(d) **Psychological tests** may measure a variety of characteristics, such as an applicant's skill in dealing with other people, ambition and motivation or emotional stability.

Sometimes applicants are required to attempt several tests (a **test battery**) aimed at giving a more rounded picture than would be available from a single test.

This kind of testing must be used with care as it suffers from several limitations.

(a) It was mentioned above **that there must be a direct relationship between ability in the test and ability in the job**. One way of assessing a test is to try it on existing employees whose capabilities are already known. It is very unlikely that tests alone will be sufficient to assess an applicant's suitability. They should be supplemented by other information, such as that derived from interview.

(b) **The interpretation of test results is a skilled task**, for which training and experience is essential. It is not something a marketing manager would undertake.

(c) Particular difficulties are experienced with particular kinds of test.

(d) It is difficult to exclude **bias against racial and ethnic minorities** from these tests.

4.4 References

References provide further confidential information about the prospective employee. This may be of varying value, **as the reliability of all but the most factual information must be in question.** A reference should contain:

(a) straightforward factual information confirming the nature of the applicant's previous job(s), period of employment, pay, and circumstances of leaving

(b) opinions about the applicant's personality and other attributes, which should obviously be treated with some caution.

4.5 The offer

Once a selection is made the candidate should be approached with a formal offer. It is best not to notify a suitable second choice until the candidate has accepted. Unsuccessful candidates should be notified as quickly as possible.

The organisation should be prepared for its offer to be rejected at this stage. Applicants may have received and accepted other offers. They may not have been attracted by their first-hand view of the organisation, and may have changed their mind about applying; they may only have been testing the water in applying in the first place, gauging the market for their skills and experience for future reference, or seeking a position of strength from which to bargain with their present employers. **A small number of eligible applicants should therefore be kept in reserve.**

FOR DISCUSSION

Some companies have run into trouble from disgruntled employees because the companies have given them poor references. Certain companies have therefore tried to deal with this situation by giving references along the following lines: 'You will be lucky to have this person working for you.'

What are the potential problems with that reference?

EXAMPLE

Instead of using their own sales representatives, many companies are recruiting field marketing agencies to work for them, finding it cheaper and more efficient. When Mars launched 'Celebrations' an agency was used to persuade wholesalers to stock the new product.

---

5 INTEGRATING NEW MEMBERS INTO THE TEAM

Giving someone the job does not magically convert that person from an acceptable or good fit for the post to an ideal one. Action to fill the gaps with training or even to modify the job is needed.

The manager should be sensitive to potential problems and take action to help new team members settle in quickly and make a positive contribution. They might need new skills or knowledge and experience for the job, or their existing skills might need developing.

Once an applicant for a job is offered the job and accepts it, he or she has to be introduced to the job. This is **the process of induction**. If you are examined about the induction process, you should be able to draw on your own experience on first starting work. From the first day in a job, a new recruit must be helped to find his or her bearings. There are limits to what any person can pick up in a short time.

Good induction should set out performance targets and encourage quality work. It should also maintain the motivation of starters and develop a commitment to the company.

Induction starts before the first day with **joining instructions**. These should tell the joiner where, when and to whom to report, and also the documentation they need to bring in with them.

On the first day, a senior person should welcome the new recruit. The seniority of this manager is likely to vary according to the size of the organisation, and the size of the section where the recruit will be working. In smaller organisations a recruit is more likely to see a manager in a more senior position than in larger organisations. The manager might discuss in broad terms what is required from people at work, working conditions, pay and benefits, training opportunities and career opportunities and should then introduce the new recruit to the person who will be the recruit's immediate manager.

The immediate line manager should then take over the **continuing process of induction and development**. This involves a number of tasks.

(a) Pinpoint the **areas that the new staff member will have to learn** about **in order to start** his or her job. Some things (such as detailed technical knowledge) may be identified as areas for later study or training. A list of learning priorities should be drawn up so that the recruit and the manager are clear about the rate and direction of progress required.

(b) Explain first of all the **nature** of the job, and its **goals, in the context of the department as a whole**. This will help the recruit to work to specific targets and to understand how his or her tasks relate to the organisation as a whole.

(c) Explain the **structure** of the department - and introduce those who will be working with or for the new team member. He or she should meet all the members of the immediate work team. One colleague may be assigned to a recruit as a **mentor** for his or her first few days, to keep an eye on him or her, answer routine queries and 'show the ropes'.

(d) Plan and implement an appropriate **training programme** for whatever technical or practical knowledge is required. The programme should have a **clear schedule and set of goals** so that the recruit has a sense of purpose, and so that the programme can be efficiently organised to fit in with the activities of the department. Training should cover general information about the business and also the specific skills that the employee will need to perform properly.

(e) **Coach and train** the recruit; check regularly on progress. **Feedback** information on how he or she is doing will be essential to the learning process, correcting any faults at an early stage and building the confidence of the recruit.

(f) **Integrate** the recruit into the **culture** of the organisation. Much of this may be done informally to reinforce commitment by rewarding evidence of loyalty, hard work and desired behaviour.

6 MOTIVATION AND REWARD

Definition

> **Motivation** is simply reasons for behaviour. People at work display varying degrees of motivation to achieve the goals set by management. It is an important task of managers at all levels to enhance the individual's motivation to work effectively.

Managers can provide the team with the opportunity and resources to work, but without motivation, little effective work will result. Motivation is the magic ingredient or catalyst which the manager has to add to the work situation to generate results.

6.1 Why is motivation important?

It could be argued that a person is employed to do a job, and so will do that job and no question of motivation arises. A person who does not want to do the work can resign.

The point at issue, however, is the **efficiency** with which the job is done. It is suggested that if individuals can be motivated, by one means or another, they will produce a better quality of work. Sales personnel, in particular, need to be motivated.

6.2 Motivators and motivation

In the most basic terms, an individual has **needs** which he or she wishes to satisfy. The means of satisfying the needs are **wants**. For example, an individual might feel the need for power, and to fulfil this need, might want money and a position of authority. Depending on the strength of these needs and wants, she/he may take action to achieve them. If successful in achieving them, she/he will be satisfied. This can be shown in a simple diagram.

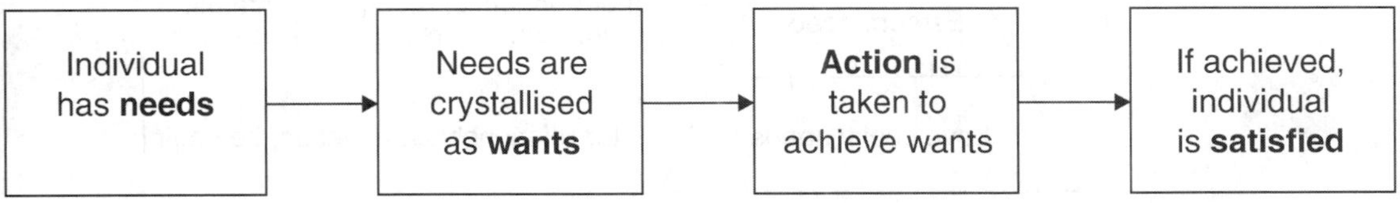

Motivators can be established which act as the wants of the individual. For example, the position of sales director might serve as a want to satisfy an individual's need for power, or access to the senior executive's dining room might serve as a want to satisfy a need for status. **Motivators may exist which are not directly controllable by management;** for example, an individual might want to be accepted by work mates, to satisfy a need for friendship and affiliation with others, and might therefore choose to conform to the norms and adopt the attitudes of the work group, which are not necessarily shared by the organisation as a whole.

Management has the problem of creating or manipulating motivators which will actually motivate employees to perform in a desired way.

6.3 Motivation theories

What we believe motivation is and what can be done with it will influence all our attitudes to individuals in organisations and to our management style.

(a) Some suggest that a **satisfied** worker will work harder, although there is little evidence to support the assumption. Satisfaction may reduce labour turnover and absenteeism, but will not necessarily increase individual productivity. Some hold that people work best within a compatible work group, or under a well-liked leader.

(b) There is a common assumption that individuals will work harder in order to obtain a desired reward. **Incentives** can work if certain conditions are satisfied.

- The individual perceives the increased reward to be worth the extra effort
- The performance can be measured and clearly attributed to that individual
- The individual wants that particular kind of reward
- The increased performance will not become the new minimum standard

6.4 Maslow's hierarchy of needs

In his motivation theory, Maslow put forward certain propositions about the motivating power of people's **needs**.

(a) Every person's needs can be arranged in **a hierarchy of relative strength**.

(b) Each **level of need is dominant until satisfied;** only then does the next higher level of need become a motivating factor.

(c) A **need which has been satisfied no longer motivates** an individual's behaviour. The need for self-actualisation can never be satisfied.

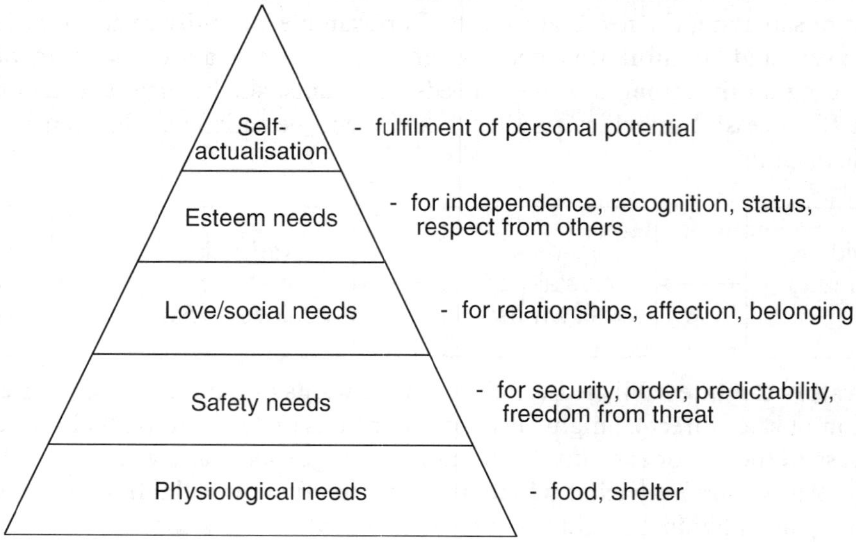

FOR DISCUSSION

What aspects of the sales job do you think relates to Maslow's need hierarchy?

6.5 Vroom's expectancy theory

Victor Vroom suggested that the strength of an individual's motivation to do something will depend on the extent to which he **expects** the results of his efforts to contribute towards his personal needs or goals, to reward him or to punish him. Put another way, expectancy theory states that people will effectively decide how much they are going to put into their work as a result of two considerations.

(a) The **value** that they place on the expected outcome, whether the positive value of a reward, or the negative value of a punishment. Vroom called this '**valence**'.

(b) The strength of their **expectation** that behaving in a certain way will in fact bring out the desired outcome. Vroom called this **expectancy**.

> **E**xpectancy x **V**alence = **F**orce of motivation.

This may be relevant to selling staff, if money is typically a reward.

6.6 Methods of improving motivation and job satisfaction

There are various ways in which managers can attempt to increase the motivation of their subordinates.

(a) Herzberg and others recommended better **job design**, in terms of content, and extent methods

(b) Various writers have suggested that subordinates' **participation in decision making** will improve motivation through self-realisation and **empowerment**.

(c) **Pay and incentive schemes** are frequently regarded as powerful motivators.

We shall discuss each of these ways in turn.

The objectives of the job design process are to improve productivity, efficiency and quality and to satisfy the individual's needs for interest, challenge and accomplishment. The process begins with job design.

Job enrichment is planned, deliberate action to build greater responsibility, breadth and challenge of work into a job. A job may be enriched in a variety of ways.

- Giving it greater variety (although this could also be described as job enlargement)
- Allowing the employee in the job greater freedom to decide how the job should be done
- Encouraging employees to participate in the planning decisions of their superiors
- Ensuring that the employee receives regular feedback on his/her performance, comparing actual results against personal targets

Job enrichment alone will not automatically make employees more productive. If jobs are enriched, employees will expect to be paid fairly for what they are doing. It might be more correct therefore to say that **job enrichment might improve productivity through greater motivation, but only if it is rewarded fairly**. 'Even those who want their jobs enriched will expect to be rewarded with more than job satisfaction. Job enrichment is not a cheaper way to greater productivity. Its pay-off will come in the less visible costs of morale, climate and working relationships'.

Job enlargement is frequently confused with job enrichment. **Job enlargement is the attempt to widen jobs by increasing the number of operations in which a job holder is involved.**

This has the effect of lengthening the cycle time of repeated operations; by reducing the number of repetitions of the same work, the dullness of the job should also be reduced. Job enlargement is therefore a horizontal extension of an individual's work, whereas job enrichment is a vertical extension. For most knowledge workers, like marketing staff, this may be less useful than job enrichment.

Aspects of well-designed jobs

- Scope for the individual to set work standards and targets
- Individual control over the pace and methods of working
- Provision of variety by allowing for inter-locking tasks to be done by the same person
- Opportunity to comment about the design of the product, or job
- Feedback to the individual about performance.

Job rotation

Job rotation may take two forms:

(a) An employee might be transferred to another job after a period of, say, two to four years in an existing job in order to give him or her a new interest and challenge, and to bring a fresh person to the job being vacated.

(b) Job rotation might be regarded as a form of training. Trainees might be expected to learn a bit about a number of different jobs, by spending six months or one year in each job before being moved on. The employee is regarded as a 'trainee' rather than as an experienced person holding down a demanding job.

No doubt you will have your own views about the value of job rotation as a method of training or career development. It is interesting to note Drucker's view: 'The whole idea of training jobs is contrary to all rules and experience. A person should never be given a job that is not a real job, that does not require performance from him'.

FOR DISCUSSION

Good sales people do not necessarily go on to managerial positions. How would **you** go about motivating a sales person through job enrichment or enlargement? Is it realistic?

6.7 Pay and incentive schemes

Pay as a motivator

Employee need income to live. The size of that income will affect the standard of living, and although they would obviously like to earn more, they are probably more concerned about two other aspects of pay.

- That they should earn **enough**
- That pay should be **fair in comparison** with the pay of others both inside and outside the organisation

Limitations to the use of money as a form of motivation

Rates of pay are perhaps more useful as a means of **keeping an organisation adequately staffed** by competent, qualified people, rather than as a means of getting them to work harder.

In most large companies, salary levels and pay levels are usually structured carefully so as to be 'equitable' or fair. Managers and workers will compare each other's pay and will be dissatisfied if the comparison is unfavourable. Pay is therefore more likely to be a hygiene factor than a motivator.

When employees expect a regular annual review of salary, increases in pay will not motivate them to work harder. Indeed, if the increase is not high enough, it may be a source of dissatisfaction.

6.8 Incentive schemes

Pay as a motivator is commonly associated with commission or incentive schemes, where a salesperson's pay depend on sales targets. If pay increases do not immediately follow improved performance, or completed tasks, they lose their 'connection' with results.

All incentive schemes are based on the principle that people are willing to work harder to obtain more money. However, the work of Mayo has shown that there are several constraints which can nullify this basic principle.

(a) The average employee is generally capable of influencing the timings and control systems used by management.

(b) Employees remain suspicious that if they achieved high levels of output and earnings then management would alter the basis of the incentive rates to reduce future earnings.

(c) Often, employees conform to a group output norm. The need to have the approval of their fellow workers by conforming is more important than the money urge.

(d) High taxation rates would mean that workers do not believe that extra effort produces an adequate increase in pay.

A short-term incentive scheme involves a direct observable link between personal or team efforts and the reward gained. However a long-term scheme such as a profit sharing scheme, has a less personal relevance and a slower pay-back.

Common types of short-term incentive schemes

Individual payment by results, such as a sales bonus over and above a basic wage ('day rate') for achieving set standards of sales over a prescribed period. There is thus a direct link between performance and earnings for each individual so the motivating effect is strong. However, it has its disadvantages.

(a) The system is complex and expensive to administer.

(b) If quantity of sales is the relevant index, margins may suffer as sales staff negotiate lower prices to make sales.

(c) Employees may manipulate sales, because of fears that high sales will become a new 'norm', with a reduction in the pay incentive.

(d) Employees outside the scheme may resent the wages levels of those inside: pay differentials may be eroded. It has been known for top sales people to earn more than the Managing Director.

(e) Employees may worry about losing pay because of illness, holidays and so on.

EXAMPLE

The role of commission in selling is significant, but there are important 'profile interest' issues to consider as well.

For example, pensions and endowment policies mortgages were sold in the 1980s and 1990s, but many policy-holders now claim that pensions were sold on poor advice and are claiming compensation.

The financial services ndustry – wher personal sellng is particularly important – has been hit by claims of unethical sales practices, based on the fact that many financial advisers were motivated by commission.

---

7 JOB SATISFACTION AND CUSTOMER SERVICE

7.1 Accountability

Many organisations now use **competency frameworks** in preference to person specifications, and **accountability profiles** in preference to job descriptions.

Whereas job descriptions conventionally consist of a comprehensive list of the various **tasks** and **activities** to be performed by the job-holder, accountability profiles focus on **results** and **outcomes**. The performance of tasks and activities is meant to contribute to the achievement of some desired result or other, so tasks and activities are not ends in themselves.

EXAMPLE

The significant difference between **doing** and **achieving** can be illustrated in the following (imaginary) conversation between a supermarket manager and one of his customer checkout staff.

Manager:	What are you paid for?
Checkout operator:	I'm a checkout operator
Manager:	That's your title. What are you paid for?
Checkout operator:	I'm paid to pass customer purchases in front of the barcode scanner, and then take the customer's money.
Manager:	Those are activities - the things you do. I still want to know what you're paid for.
Checkout operator:	Now that you mention it, I haven't a clue

It would be relatively straightforward to say to the checkout operator (as one UK supermarket company has already done) that her **principal accountability**, her key role is:

To make the customer want to come back

Against this principal accountability, everything the checkout operator does has a meaningful purpose.

All jobs can be outlined in this way, with a principal accountability defined as an **added-value output**, not simply as a summary of some key activities. It is important, too, that the principal accountability is kept simple, brief and straightforward.

Once the principal purpose (or 'mission') for any given role has been determined, it then becomes possible to identify up to six **Key Performance Areas** some companies call them Key Accountabilities or Key Performance Indicators, which represent the principal ways in which the role occupant will be measured. Note that KPAs are not the same as competencies: KPAs refer to the results which should be achieved within the occupational role, whereas competencies describe the attributes of the individual job-holder. When discussing recruitment and selection, we often talk of finding the right 'peg' (person) for the 'hole' (the job): KPAs are part of the 'hole', and competencies represent a way of describing the 'peg'.

EXAMPLE

The following are Key Performance Areas used within front-line customer service roles for a major UK water utility. Note the combination of KPAs which are concerned with day-to-day performance plus others which focus on 'added-value' outcomes like change and continuous improvement.

The effective performer will:

(1) Provide immediate, positive and constructive responses to all customer contact.
(2) Provide excellent customer service to all our customers.
(3) Demonstrate a flexible attitude to the requirements of a changing business.
(4) Achieve required performance levels (quality and quantity).
(5) Supply a multi-functional service.
(6) Highlight CUSTOMER service opportunities.

7.2 The position of customer service

If, strictly speaking, people in organisations are not employed to **do** anything, but are employed in order to **achieve** something, then what is customer service meant to achieve?

Customer service used to be something done by reactive people who waited for complaints, were shouted at, then put things right and organised compensation. In many organisations, service is still like that: it's seen as a ragbag, poorly-resourced residual department, an unpleasant necessity, an overhead, a refuge for staff whose performance is only marginally acceptable, rather than a marketing tool and an investment.

The Bain research (*The Future of Customer Service*, published by the Institute of Customer Service, 1998) shows that in the opinion of the major service-industry players, customer service will be a powerful ingredient for **competitive advantage** and **corporate survival** in the years ahead.

Andy Grove's 1996 book, *Only the Paranoid Survive*, argues that **strategic leaders are often remote** from their customers: in some organisations the people at the top may not have encountered customers for more than ten years. Their ideas about customers may not have kept up to date, and they may be out of touch with customer aspirations. As Grove points out, 'snow melts first at the periphery' - in other words, a company begins to fail at the point where it **interfaces** with the customer.

7.3 Developments in customer care

A major development in terms of customer care is Total Quality Management (TQM). This is the fulfilment of corporate objectives alongside the satisfaction of customer needs. TQM looks into the following areas to develop an effective customer care strategy.

- Quality
- Availability
- Service
- Support
- Reliability
- Value for money

Relationships need to be managed between the organisation and customers. Relationship marketing occurs where a long term view of the customer's value to the organisation is developed. The main aim is to build customer loyalty. This approach can be used in both consumer and business markets, but is perhaps more well developed in business markets. Sometimes this is combined with specific delivery requirements such as Just in Time (JIT) systems, where stock is not held by the manufacturer in bulk. Purchasing agreements involve stock being ordered and supplied at short notice.

EXAMPLE

At the Nissan car plant in Sunderland the carpets for the cars are only ordered 42 minutes before they are fitted *(Lancaster and Jobber: Selling & Sales Management 1994)*

7.4 Customer related competency models

Increasingly popular in organisations - not always connected to the requirement for improved customer service - are **competency frameworks** which list the standard of behaviour required in any given job.

Competency frameworks can be used for **many purposes:** human resource planning, recruitment, selection, induction, training, development, performance appraisal, and promotion. They may consist simply of a collection of **defined and classified behaviours,** or they may be prioritised between the 'Essential' and the 'Desirable'.

It cannot be expected that the precise behaviours associated with any given competency will be the same at all levels of the organisation and within all functions. Look at the following example, which can be visualised as part of the competency framework for people working in a retail or financial services operation.

Key result areas are the following.

- Creating value through customers
- Creating value for the business
- Working with others
- Working smarter
- Managing change

We expand upon the result area of 'creating value through customers' in the box below.

EXAMPLE

Competences linked to creating value through customers

- Providing excellent customer service
- Managing the customer relationship

Core behaviours linked to providing excellent customer service

- Always keeps promises
- Develops excellent understanding of customer needs and concerns
- Takes personal responsibility for resolving all customer issues
- Strives to exceed customer expectations
- Consults regularly with customers to secure performance feedback
- Tries to anticipate customer needs and act accordingly

Role-specific behaviours linked to providing excellent customer service

Directors and senior executives

- Establishes clear criteria to measure customer satisfaction
- Identifies new opportunities to create competitive advantage through customer service
- Reinforces a commitment to customer service excellence in self and others

- Seeks to understand trends and developments elsewhere, with a view to adopting them for the company's use
- Takes 'best practice' ideas/solutions and makes them work for the company

People managers and team leaders

- Reinforces key messages about customer service to all staff and team members
- Assists staff and team members to meet/exceed customer service standards by creating the right working environment
- Encourages, motivates, trains and coaches others in the assimilation of a customer-focused culture

Front-line customer service

- Treats each contact with customers as an opportunity to impress them with the service offered by the business
- Acts as the key ambassadorial interface between the business and its customers

Core behaviours linked to managing the customer relationship

- Builds rapport by taking a real interest in customers
- Builds customer trust by meeting their needs and fulfilling all promises
- Regularly seeks customer feedback and takes action accordingly
- Presents a positive image of the company to customers
- Listens sensitively to customer communications
- Remains polite, tactful, courteous and friendly towards customers

Role-specific behaviours linked to managing the customer relationship

Directors and senior executives

- Defines policies which enable all staff to understand the value of individual customer relationships
- Differentiates the services and products offered by the business from those of competitors
- Influences the external perception of the organisation and its brand(s) by raising the profile of the company

People managers and team leaders

- Makes the management of customer relationships a regular agenda item for team meetings, coaching session, and performance reviews
- Focuses attention on those customer relationships which are especially crucial in terms of their commercial significance
- Personally makes periodic contact with selected customers in order to retain expertise in the management of customer relationships
- Seeks out customers' views to establish realistic service level agreements (principally so far as internal customers are concerned)

Front-line customer service

- Collects and disseminates relevant information about customers
- Sensitively reacts to customer concerns and responds accordingly, with restitution if necessary
- Takes the heat out of what might otherwise be confrontational scenarios involving customers

7.5 Competency frameworks for personal learning and development

We have already discussed the benefits of competency profiling for recruitment, selection and appraisal. Several organisations majoring on customer service as a source of competitive advantage have begun to use competencies for purposes of **self-appraisal, self-learning** and **self-development.**

Once a competency framework has been developed, individual employees may score themselves against each element within the system; they can also assess the relative importance of each competency.

(a) The competencies which deserve attention will be those

  (i) Where current achievement is unsatisfactory.

  (ii) Where improvement is essential if the individual is likely to achieve career progression.

(b) The questions to be asked in the self-evaluation process should include:

  (i) Which competencies within the competency framework do I already display, and in what measure?

  (ii) Which of the components do I really need in order to do my present job satisfactorily?

  (iii) Which of the competencies do I need to concentrate on in order to prepare myself for predicted changes to my current role?

  (iv) Which of the competencies do I need to concentrate on in order to prepare myself for a career move?

  (v) Which of the competencies do I need to address in relation to my current performance?

Here is an example of some learning activities linked to a customer focus competency.

(a) Select up to five named individuals as customers for your services.

(b) Consciously initiate a customer feedback programme in which you seek assessments from each of these five customers about their perceptions of what you supply for them, which areas could be improved, and which aspects are perceived to be either particularly important or relatively insignificant.

(c) Produce an action plan for personal customer-service improvement, with a timetable for measuring progress.

(d) Identify a '**benchmark**' customer-service performance comparison, and seek to apply the lessons to be learned.

Chapter roundup

- Characteristics of a good sales person include enthusiasm, intelligence, reliability, commitment, initiative, creativity, self-confidence, courtesy and sensitivity.
- Recruiting new people into the sales function may be necessary if there is a gap in the skills of the existing sales force, to replace staff or to increase the sales force because the work has expanded.
- The recruitment and selection process starts with a definition of requirements.
- Job analysis involves the examination of the essential characteristics of the job. The product of a job analysis is usually a job specification followed by a job description and person specification.
- In searching for new sales personnel, companies may use internal recruitment (recruiting perhaps from other departments) and/or job advertisements.
- Selection is usually based on the written application, interview and in some cases tests.
- The induction process should help new staff become effective members of the sales team. It should involve welcoming the staff, explaining about the organisation and pinpointing additional training requirements.
- Sales personnel will respond to different aspect of motivation.
- Incentives are often used in sales force management.
- Job enrichment can be used as a motivator where a job is changed to have greater responsibility, interest and challenge.
- Job enlargement occurs where jobs are widened by increasing the number of operations in which a job holder is involved.
- Incentive schemes can include pay or monetary rewards such as commission and bonuses.
- Reward can also be expressed in terms of job satisfaction and personal responsibility for good customer service.

Quick quiz

1. List three characteristics of a good sales person.
2. Give an outline of the recruitment and selection process.
3. What information should be gathered in job analysis?
4. What basic elements should be on a job description?
5. What important qualities might recruiting older employees bring?
6. Are there any problems in internal recruitment?
7. What considerations should a company take into account when deciding on an advertising medium for job vacancies?
8. What are aptitude tests used for?
9. Is pay a good motivator?
10. Sales people are often at the front line of customer service. This puts them in a unique position - why?

Answers to quick quiz

1 Could include 3 of enthusiasm, intelligence, reliability, commitment, initiative, creativity, self confidence, courtesy or sensitivity. (See paragraph 1.1)

2 Human resource planning - job analysis - vacancies - sources of labour - advertising - process applications - notifying applicants. (para 2.1)

3 Initial requirements, duties and responsibilities, environmental conditions and social factors. (para 2.2)

4 Job title, location, accountability (who reports to who), and main duties. (para 2.4)

5 Skills and experience, regard for customer service, stabilising influence and better staff retention. (para 3.1)

6 Yes, if an internal candidate does not get the job there could be resentment towards the successful candidate and a sense of rejection on the part of the unsuccessful internal candidate. (para 3.2)

7 The cost, type and number of readers or users of the medium, frequency. (para 3.3)

8 To try to predict an individual's potential for performing a job or learning new skills. (para 4.3)

9 It can be, but there are some problems. (para 6.7)

10 They can react to customer concerns, give and receive information about service and can handle problems and manage the client - organisational relationship. (para 7.4)

Answers to activities

1 There is no specific answer to this activity.

2 There is no specific answer to this activity.

3 There is no specific answer to this activity.

4 *Benefits*

Existing knowledge of the business
Existing contracts
No learning curve
Continuity

Problems

Lack of a refreshing approach
Resentment among other employees
Loss of an opportunity to bring in new talent

5 There is no specific answer to this activity.

6 There is no specific answer to this activity.

Chapter 20 : SALES OUTPUT

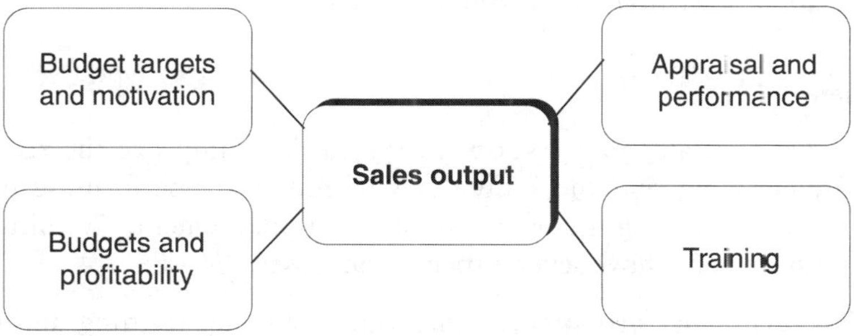

Introduction

This chapter will look at some of the outputs of the sales function. It will explore how appraisal systems can be put into place and made effective and aspects of staff training. Finally this chapter will concentrate on the role of budgets in terms of both profits and as an employee motivator.

Your objectives

In this chapter you will learn about the following:

(a) Different types of appraisal systems

(b) The need for up to date relevant training

(c) The link between budgets and profitability

(d) How the budget process can affect sales force motivation by the use of targets

1 APPRAISAL AND PERFORMANCE

Motivation is concerned with attempts to improve the performance of groups and individuals. Appraisal is a systematic approach to providing that feedback and for putting praise and criticism in context.

It also provides an assessment of current performance against which future improvements can be measured and training needs established.

1.1 Overview

The general purpose of any staff assessment system is to improve the efficiency of the organisation by ensuring that the individuals within it are performing to the best of their ability and developing their potential for improvement. Within this overall objective, staff assessments have several specific purposes.

- To review **performance**, to plan and follow up training and development programmes; and to set targets for future performance
- To review **potential**, as an aid to planning career development by predicting the level and type of work the individual will be capable of in the future
- To increase **motivation by providing feedback**
- To review **salaries**: measuring the extent to which an employee is deserving of a salary increase as compared with peers

Features of a typical system

- **Identification of criteria for assessment**, perhaps based on job analysis, performance standards and person specifications
- The preparation by the subordinate's manager of an **assessment report**
- An **appraisal interview**, for an exchange of views about the results of the assessment and targets for improvement
- **Review of the assessment by the assessor's own superior**, so that the appraisee does not feel subject to one person's prejudices. Formal appeals may be allowed, if necessary to establish the fairness of the procedure
- The preparation and implementation of **action plans** to achieve improvements and changes agreed
- **Follow-up**: monitoring the progress of the action plan

There may not need to be standard forms for appraisal (and elaborate form-filling procedures should be avoided) as long as managers understand the nature and extent of what is required, and are motivated to take it seriously. Most systems, however, provide for assessments to be recorded, and report forms of various lengths and complexity may be designed for standard use, A written record of some form is essential to prevent doubts and uncertainties at a later date.

1.2 The assessment report

The basis of assessment must first be determined. Assessments must be related to a **common standard**, in order for comparisons to be made between individuals, and of a particular individual's progress over time. They should also be related to meaningful performance criteria, which take account of the critical variables in each different job.

1.3 Techniques of appraisal

(a) **Overall assessment** is the simplest method, simply requiring the manager to write in narrative form judgements about the appraisee, possibly with a checklist of personality characteristics and performance targets to work from. There will be no guaranteed consistency of the criteria and areas of assessment, however, and managers may not be able to convey clear, effective judgements in writing.

(b) **Guided assessment** requires assessors to comment on a number of specified characteristics and performance elements, with guidelines as to how the terms (eg 'application', 'integrity', 'adaptability') are to be interpreted in the work context. This is a more precise, but still rather vague method.

(c) **Grading** adds a comparative frame of reference to the general guidelines, whereby managers are asked to select one of a number of levels or degrees to which the individual in question displays the given characteristic. These are also known as **rating scales**, and are much used in standard appraisal forms. Their effectiveness depends to a large extent on the **relevance** of the factors chosen for assessment and the definition of the agreed standards of assessment.

(i) Numerical values may be added to ratings to give rating 'scores'. Alternatively a less precise **graphic scale** may be used to indicate general position on a plus/minus scale, for example:

Factor: job knowledge

High ———————————— Average ———————✓———————— Low

(ii) The principal drawback of such schemes is that the subordinate may not agree with the precise ratings given. This may lead to the subordinate questioning the judgement of the appraiser. The appraisal may degenerate into an argument about the appraiser's use of the grading system rather than what the assessment tells the subordinate about his or her performance.

(d) **Results-orientated schemes.** The above techniques will be concerned with results but are commonly based on behavioural appraisal. A wholly results-orientated approach (eg Management by Objectives) sets out to review performance against specific targets and standards of performance agreed in advance by manager and subordinate together. This scheme has a number of advantages.

- The subordinate is more involved in appraisal because success or progress is measured against specific, jointly agreed targets.
- The manager is relieved, to some extent, of the role of **critic**, and becomes a **counsellor**.
- Learning and motivation theories suggest that clear and known targets are important in modifying and determining behaviour.

(e) **Self-appraisals,** where the individuals carry out their own self-evaluation, can be an alternative to management/subordinate appraisals. They have the advantage that the system is evidently aimed at the needs of the individual. Self-appraisal schemes can also be combined with training schemes where the individuals decide on the training they require.

Activity 1 **(20 minutes)**

What type of appraisal scheme does your organisation have? How effective do you think it is? If you are not employed, which appraisal scheme would you prefer to be appraised by?

The effectiveness of any scheme will depend on the realistic and clear statement of targets; and the commitment of both parties to make it work. The **measurement of success or failure is only part of the picture**: **reasons** for failure and opportunities arising from success must be evaluated.

Managers will need guidance, or perhaps training to help them make a relevant, objective and helpful report. Most large organisations with standard review forms also issue detailed guidance notes to aid assessors with the written and discussion elements.

1.4 Appraisal interview

The report may be shown to the appraisee and thus form a basis for discussion. Some organisations, however, do not show the report to the employee; this is likely to lead to resentment and anxiety about the correctness or otherwise of its contents.

Approaches to appraisal interviews

Approach	Comments
The **tell and sell** method	The manager gives details of the assessment to the subordinate and then tries to **gain acceptance** of the evaluation and the improvement plan. This requires unusual human relations skills in order to convey constructive criticism in an acceptable manner, and to motivate appraisees to alter their behaviour.
The **tell and listen** method	The manager gives the assessment and then **invites response**. The manager no longer dominates the interview, and there is greater opportunity for **counselling**. The employee is encouraged to participate in the assessment and the working out of improvement targets and methods. Managers using this method will need to have good listening skills.
The **problem solving** approach	The manager abandons the role of critic altogether, and becomes a counsellor and helper. The discussion is centred not on the assessment, but on the employee's work problems. The employee is encouraged to think solutions through, and to commit to the recognised need for personal improvement.

Many organisations waste the opportunities for **upward communication** embedded in the appraisal process. In order to get a positive contribution from employees, the appraisal interviewer should ask positive and thought-provoking questions. Here are some examples.

- What parts of your job do you do best?
- Could any changes be made in your job which might result in improved performance?
- Have you any skills, knowledge, or aptitudes which could be made better use of in the organisation?

Follow-up procedures

- Having the report agreed and counter-signed by a more senior manager
- Informing appraisees of the final results of the appraisal, if this has been contentious in the review interview
- Carrying out agreed actions on training, promotions and so on
- Monitoring the appraisee's progress with agreed actions
- Taking necessary steps to help the appraisee for example by guidance, providing feedback or upgrading equipment

1.5 The effectiveness of appraisal

In practice, the system often goes wrong.

(a) There may be a divergence between the subordinate's and interviewer's perceived and actual needs. The subordinates may **want** praise, they may, however, **need** constructive criticism. The interviewer may wish to concentrate on criticising, whereas the appraisal could be used to give feedback on management practice.

(b) Appraisal interviews are often **defensive on the part of the subordinate**, who believes that any criticism will bring sanctions. There may also be some mistrust of the validity of the scheme itself.

(c) Interviews are also often **defensive on the part of the superior**, who cannot reconcile the role of judge and critic with the 'human relations' aspect of the interview. As a result there may be many unresolved issues left at the end.

(d) The superior might show **conscious or unconscious bias** in the report. Systems without clearly defined standard criteria will be particularly prone to the subjectivity of the assessor's judgements.

(e) The general **level of ratings** may vary widely from manager to manager.

(f) There may be **bias** resulting from the personal interaction between appraiser and appraisee.

(g) Appraisals may deal with specific problems which should have been dealt with at the time they arose by counselling. Appraisals ought to concentrate on ongoing matters that are important to career development.

(h) Appraisals may be seen merely as a bureaucratic form-filling exercise or as no more than an annual formality.

DISCUSSION

An appraisal process that is simply a once a year bureaucratic exercise is a wasted opportunity for both sales staff and management.

1.6 Upward appraisal

A notable modern trend, adopted in the UK by companies such as BP, British Airways TV and others, is upward appraisal, whereby **employees are not only rated by their superiors but also (or instead) by their subordinates.** The followers appraise the leader.

- Subordinates tend to know their superior better than superiors know their subordinates.

- As all subordinates rate their managers statistically, these ratings tend to be more reliable - the more subordinates the better.
- Subordinates' ratings have more impact because it is more unusual to receive ratings from subordinates.

Problems with the method include fear of reprisals, vindictiveness, and extra form processing. Some bosses in strong positions might refuse to act, even if a consensus of staff suggested that they should change their ways.

1.7 Peer rating

An alternative approach to individual appraisal (which also removes the link between past performance and reward) is **peer rating** in which an individual is judged and counselled by workmates or colleagues. It has been argued that peer rating will be devoid of mistrust and fear of missing promotion and will therefore be more honest and constructive, thus aiding the individual to develop in his job. It may be a useful strategy amongst professionally qualified staff.

1.8 360-degree appraisal

A final variant on appraisal schemes is the 360 degree appraisal. In this case, effectiveness is appraised by all the people with whom the subject has dealings - superiors, subordinates, customers and suppliers, internal and external.

EXAMPLE

(a) At BA, managers will have measurable performance targets based on customers' perceptions of service: 'the manager of the cabin crew on an aircraft will be judged, for example, on how many customers think staff were warm and friendly.' The internal customer is not forgotten, either. 'In the case of departments that do not deal directly with passengers, such as engineering, those who use their services within the airline will be asked to evaluate them.'

(b) Burger King has an appraisal scheme for some of its regional managers - the outlets are asked to give feedback on individual managers' performance.

Advantages of 360-degree feedback

- It **highlights every aspect** of the individual's performance, and allows comparison of the individual's self-assessment with the views of others.
- Feedback tends, overall, to be **balanced**, covering strengths in some areas with weaknesses in others, so it is less discouraging.
- The assessment is based on the normal work environment and circumstances. The feedback is thus felt to **be fairer and more relevant**, making it easier for employees to accept.

Potential pitfalls of 360-degree feedback

- **Negative emphasis**. Feedback on weaknesses should be balanced by positive feedback on strengths and potential, to encourage the employee to develop.

- **'Flavour of the month approach'**. The technique and its results are seen as interesting but no thought has been given to follow-up action.
- **Lack of confidentiality**. Respondents must be anonymous, or they may fear to tell the truth in an assessment.
- **Poor communication about the purpose of the exercise**. It can be daunting, and employees need to understand that it is not a political exercise, or a rod to beat anyone.
- **Lack of action and support**. The organisation must support the employee in the development suggested by the feedback.

2 TRAINING

Procuring the most appropriate human resources for the task and environment is an on-going process. It involves not only recruitment and selection, but the training and development of employees prior to employment, or at any time during their employment, in order to help them meet the requirements of their current, and potential future job.

2.1 The contribution of training

The increasingly dynamic nature of modern business (changes in technology, products, processes and control techniques) and the need for planned growth mean that a working organisation's competitiveness depends more and more on the continuous reassessment of training needs and the provision of planned training to meet those needs.

Training can certainly contribute, given the following provisos:

(a) It must be the correct tool for the need: it cannot solve problems caused by faulty organisation, equipment or employee selection.

(b) Reasons for neglecting training must be overcome: these include cost, inconvenience, apathy and an unrealistic expectation of training in the past.

(c) Limitations imposed by intelligence, motivation and the psychological restrictions of the learning process must be understood.

Activity 2 **(10 miuntes)**

Make a list of the training you have received (if any) in your current post. Do you still have some training needs?

2.2 On-the-job training (OJT)

OJT is very common, especially when the work involved is not complex. For example a new recruit can accompany a senior sale executive to the customer.

Coaching

Coaching is a common method of OJT; the trainee is put under the guidance of an experienced employee who demonstrates how to do the job and helps refine the trainee's technique.

All forms of training require the commitment of the organisation to the learning programme. It must believe in training and developing employees, and be prepared to devote both the money and the time. The manager will largely dictate the department's attitude to these things.

DISCUSSION

What are the problems of relying on 'on the job' training?

A training programme

Training is often concerned with teaching a person how to do a particular job, or how to do it better. Many firms have structured training programmes.

A systematic approach to training

- **Identify areas** where training will be beneficial.
- **Establish learning targets**. The areas where learning is needed should be identified and specific, realistic goals stated, including standards of performance.
- Decide on the **training methods to be used**.
- **Plan a systematic learning and development programme**. This should allow for practice and consolidation.
- **Identify opportunities for broadening the trainee's knowledge and experience** such as involvement in new projects, extending the job or greater responsibility.
- **Take into account the strengths and limitations of the trainee**. A trainee from an academic background may learn best through research-based learning like fact-finding for a committee; whilst those who learn best by doing may profit from project work.
- **Implement** the scheme in full.
- **Exchange feedback**. The manager will want performance information in order to monitor the progress, adjust the learning programme, identify further needs and plan future development.
- **Validate the results** to check that the training works and benefits exceed costs.

EXAMPLE

Brann Contact is a direct marketing agency who run a call centre for Fiat. Fiat have spent a great deal of time and money training call centre operators. They also use cars as an incentive - if operators have done well they can take a car home for the weekend.

(Marketing Week Sept 14 2000)

2.3 Analysis of training needs

Training needs can be identified by considering the **gap** between **job requirements**, as determined by job analysis, job description and so on, and the **ability of the job holder**, as determined by testing or observation and appraisal.

The training department's management should make an initial investigation of the problem. Even if work is not done as well as it could be, training is not necessarily the right answer. We have seen that poor working standards might also be caused by other factors.

Objectives

If the training department concludes that the provision of training could improve work performance, it must analyse the work in detail in order to decide what the requirements of a training programme should be. In particular, there should be a training objective or objectives. These are tangible, observable targets which trainees should be capable of reaching at the end of the course.

The training objectives should be clear, specific and measurable, for example: 'at the end of a course a trainee must be able to describe ..., or identify ..., or list ..., or state ..., or distinguish x from y ...'. It is insufficient to state as an objective of a course 'to give trainees a grounding in ...' or 'to give trainees a better appreciation of ...'. These objectives are too woolly, and actual achievements cannot be measured against them.

EXAMPLE

In addition to in-house training, there are a number of independent training companies that specialise in sales courses.

2.4 Training methods

Having decided what must be learned and to what standard of achievement, the next stage is to decide what method of training should be used.

2.5 Course training methods

(a) **Lectures**. Lectures are suitable for large audiences and can be an efficient way of putting across information. However lack of participation may lead to lack of interest and/or failure to understand by most of the audience.

(b) **Discussions.** Discussions aim to impart information but allow much greater opportunities for audience participation. They are often suitable for groups up to 20 and can be a good means of maintaining interest.

(c) **Exercises**. An exercise involves a particular task being undertaken with pre-set results following guidance laid down. They are a very active form of learning and are a good means of checking whether trainees have assimilated information.

(d) **Role plays.** Trainees act out roles in a typical work situation. They are useful practice for face-to-face situations. However, they may embarrass some participants and may not be taken seriously.

(e) **Case studies.** Case studies identify causes and/or suggest solutions. They are a good means of exchanging ideas and thinking out solutions. However trainees may see the case study as divorced from their real work experience.

(f) **Programmed learning** can be provided on a computer terminal, but it is still associated with printed booklets which provide information in easy-to-learn steps. The booklet asks simple questions which the trainee must answer. If they are answered correctly, the trainee is instructed to carry on with more learning. If the questions are answered wrongly, the booklet gives an alternative set of instructions to go back and learn again. Programmed learning has a number of advantages.

EXAMPLE

Sainsbury's run food fairs at which marketing services and call centre staff are invited to test products and find out how they are made. *(Marketing Week Sept 14 2000)*

DISCUSSION

Have you used any computer aided learning packages. What did you think of them? Would you (or did you) find it easier than more traditional methods?

- Trainees can work through the course in simple stages and continually checks their progress. Misunderstandings are quickly put right.
- Trainees are kept actively involved in the learning process because they must keep answering questions put to them in the booklet.
- Giving correct answers immediately reinforces the learning process.
- Trainees can work at their own pace.

2.6 Cost/benefit analysis of training

The training course should only go ahead if the **likely benefits are expected to exceed the costs** of designing and then running the course. **Costs** include training materials, the salaries of the staff attending training courses, their travelling expenses, the salaries of training staff and training overheads. **Benefits** might be measured in a variety of ways.

- Quicker working and therefore reductions in overtime or staff numbers
- Greater accuracy of work
- More extensive skills
- Improved motivation

As you will appreciate, the **benefits are more easily stated in general terms than quantified in money terms**. Indeed, it is often difficult to measure benefits such as increased identification with business objectives and increased cohesion as a team, but these benefits may nevertheless be significant.

2.7 Implementation and evaluation of training

When the training course has been designed, **a pilot course may be run**. The purpose of the test would be to find out whether the training scheme appears to achieve what it has set out to do, or whether some revisions are necessary. After the pilot test, the scheme can be implemented in full.

Implementation of the training scheme is not the end of the story. The scheme should be validated and evaluated.

(a) **Validation** means observing the results of the course, and measuring whether the training objective has been achieved.

(b) **Evaluation** means comparing the actual costs of the scheme against the assessed benefits which are being obtained. If the costs exceed the benefits, the scheme will need to be re-designed or withdrawn.

Validation methods

(a) **Asking the trainees** whether they thought the training programme was relevant to their work, and whether they found it useful. This is rather inexact and does not measure results for comparison against the training objective.

(b) **Measuring what the trainees have learned** on the course, perhaps by means of a test at the end of the course.

(c) Studying the **subsequent behaviour of the trainees** in their jobs to measure how the training scheme has altered the way they do their work. This is possible where the purpose of the course was to learn a particular skill.

(d) Finding out whether the training has affected **the work or behaviour of other employees not on the course**. This form of monitoring would probably be reserved for senior managers in the training department.

(e) Seeing whether training in general has contributed to the **overall objectives of the organisation**. This too is a form of monitoring reserved for senior managers and would perhaps be discussed at board level in the organisation.

DISCUSSION

Training is one of the aspects organisations cut back on in hard times.

EXAMPLE

An article in *Marketing Business* in March 1998 highlighted recent trends in marketing training, particularly its interaction with the rest of the organisation. This reflects a change in emphasis in the role of marketing in many companies, away from product management and towards anticipating and supplying customer needs.

Companies are supplying increased marketing training to operating departments in topics such as brand awareness and are giving marketing departments training which consists of two parts. The first part focuses on normal technicalities such as research and promotional techniques. The second gives marketers a wider perspective on the rest of the company, focusing on issues such as systems, distribution, customer service and financial management. Motivating operating departments to become more innovative and centred on the customer is seen as being very important.

2.8 Personal development plans

Definition

> **Personal development plans (PDPs)** are essentially action plans for people's career development. It is the individuals responsibility to seek and organise training.

'Organisations no longer feel they can take prime responsibility for the future careers and development of their employees, and the PDP approach clearly places the development ball in the employee's court'. (*People Management)*

The most popular PDP schemes take account of people's wider needs and aspirations, rather than focusing simply on skills required to do their current job better. Such schemes are undoubtedly popular because of the changes in the employment market. Most people believe they need to obtain skills and experiences which will be of benefit should they move jobs. **As a result people are better able than companies to assess their training requirements**. They will choose courses, where the form and content assist their personal development, and will avoid courses which are of no value to their personal development.

This trend is also reflected in employee development programmes (EDPs), company-run schemes which offer employees a wide range of development opportunities, not necessarily related to the job. The effect of such schemes is to develop a culture in which learning and adaptability are valued as well as to enhance employee satisfaction and morale. Expense has hitherto confined EDPs to large companies such as Ford, Unipart and Rover.

The importance of personal development plans

Managers have to take responsibility for their own learning. Personal development needs to be considered and managed by the individual, working, where possible, in partnership with the employer.

- The habit of setting personal development targets should be a long-term commitment for the successful manager.
- In the examination you will be able to draw upon your experience of setting personal goals and the problems of achieving them.
- As a manager, you are likely to be faced with helping others with their personal development. Your personal experience of the process will be of some help then.
- The plans can be part of a **learning contract**, whereby targets are agreed with the employer, and their attainment is monitored.

2.9 Learning contracts

Definition

A **learning contract** is an agreement between:

(a) the person undergoing the training or education or experience; and

(b) the provider or the sponsor of the training, education or experience.

The learning contract will normally detail three things.

- The type of **learning process** involved
- The expected **achievement** (in terms of the increase in skills)
- The **timescale** required

The learning contract is a way for the individual to get a commitment out of the firm.

Activity 3 **(30 minutes)**

Look back at Activity 2. Did you identify any training needs? Develop these into a learning contract.

3 BUDGETS AND PROFITABILITY

Definition

> A **budget** is a quantitative statement for a defined period of time which may include planned revenues, expenses, assets, liabilities and cash flows.

3.1 The purpose of budgets

Communication, coordination and control are general objectives of budgetary control systems: more information is provided by an inspection of specific objectives.

(a) **To ensure the achievement of the organisation's objectives**

Objectives for the organisation as a whole, and for individual departments and operations within the organisation, are set. Quantified expressions of these objectives are then drawn up as targets to be achieved.

(b) **To compel planning**

This is probably the most important feature of a budgetary planning and control system. Planning forces management to look ahead, to set out detailed plans for achieving the targets for each department, operation and each manager and to anticipate problems.

(c) **To communicate ideas and plans**

A formal system is necessary to ensure that each person affected by the plans is aware of what he or she is supposed to be doing.

(d) **To coordinate activities**

The activities of different departments of the organisation need to be coordinated. This concept of coordination implies, for example, that the production budget should be based on sales expectations. Although straightforward in concept, coordination is remarkably difficult to achieve, and there is often conflict between departmental plans in the budget.

(e) **To provide a framework for responsibility accounting**

Budgetary planning and control systems require that managers of budget centres are made responsible for the achievement of budget targets for the operations under their control.

(f) **To establish a system of control**

Control over actual performance is provided by the comparisons of actual results against the budget. Departures from budget can then be investigated and the reasons divided into controllable and uncontrollable factors.

(g) **To motivate employees to improve their performance**

The interest and commitment of employees can be retained via a system of feedback of actual results, which lets them know how well or badly they are performing.

In order to achieve these various objectives, budgets should be broken down into relevant business segments. These should naturally fit both the products and the markets in which the company operates. This will be set in the context of the **overall marketing plan**.

3.2 The budgeting process

In overall terms the budget tries to put into a **financial framework** the predicted result of all the activities that will achieve the overall corporate objectives.

Data for the budgeting process

Internal information available.

(a) **Marketing and sales information** on, for example, performance, revenues, market share and distribution channels

(b) **Production and operational information** on, for example, manufacturing capacities and capabilities and lead times

(c) **Financial information** on, for example, how much cash it has in the bank, how much it could borrow, profits, costs, cash flows and investments

(d) **Research and development information** on, for example, new products and developments

(e) **Personnel information** on, for example, labour skills, labour availability and expected wage increases

External information available

(a) **Market and competitors.** The organisation must assess its competitors. It should analyse its market (and any other markets that it is intending to enter) to identify possible **new opportunities**. This subject is covered in Part D of this Study Text.

(b) **Economic conditions**. The state of the world must be considered. Is it in recession or is it booming? The organisation should gather information on forecasts for growth, inflation, GDP and so on and the effect of developments such as the European Community single market.

(c) **Industrial structure**. The organisation should determine whether a process of rationalisation or concentration is taking place within the industry, whether there are any privatisation issues to take into consideration and whether many new firms are entering the industry.

(d) **Political factors**. Any political instability, especially in overseas markets, and any significant political decisions, should be assessed.

(e) **Technological change**. Information on any new technology of which the organisation might be able to take advantage should be collected.

(f) **Demographic trends and social factors**. The organisation should assess the effects of any changes in the population structure, the age profile of customers, family patterns, and attitudes to consumption and savings.

Activity 4 **(30 minutes)**

You work for a company within the mobile phone industry. Conduct an analysis of the above external information needs.

The master budget

An overall **master budget** consists of the following.

(a) A **budgeted profit and loss account**. The total profit and loss account budget will often be sub-divided into departmental budgets (a budgeted profit and loss account for each department, division or other profit centre in the organisation).

(b) A **cash budget**. A business needs to make sure that it will have enough cash to continue operating, or that an overdraft facility is available with a bank to cover the expected need.

(c) An end-of-period **budgeted balance sheet**.

Preparing the sales budget

Since the sales budget is usually the budget from which cost budgets and the budgeted profit and loss account are developed, it is obviously very important that sales in the budget should be **reasonable and realistic**.

It is not easy to assess potential sales with any degree of accuracy. All that a business can do is put as much care as possible into preparing the sales budget.

(a) An organisation might produce a large number of products or services, and sell them in a wide geographical area. In such cases, sales budgets should be prepared for each **product or product group** and for each region.

(b) For many organisations, sales have seasonal peaks and troughs. **Seasonal variations** in sales should be recognised in the budgets.

DISCUSSION

What is meant by 'reasonable' and 'realistic' in terms of sales budgets?

Preparing other resource budgets

Budgets for **marketing and administration costs** must be prepared. Many cost items will be fixed, although there may be some variable costs (for example sales commission). Some of the marketing budget will have to be prepared in conjunction with the sales budget since the level of sales anticipated will rely on marketing support. The balance of the budget may well be determined by the activity anticipated from new products which may be launched during the year.

3.3 The nature of selling costs

Management's job is to ensure that:

(a) the sales effort is used efficiently and effectively; and
(b) its cost are controlled.

Selling costs can be considered in terms of their fixed and variable elements.

(a) **Fixed sales costs** are those which would have to be paid even in a week when the salesperson was inactive. Salary, employer's contributions to pension schemes and National Insurance, cost of leasing and maintaining a car and the person's share of sales administration, support and management costs are all likely to be considered as fixed costs.

(b) **Variable sales costs** are those which change with the volume of sales. They would include commission payments and sales expenses.

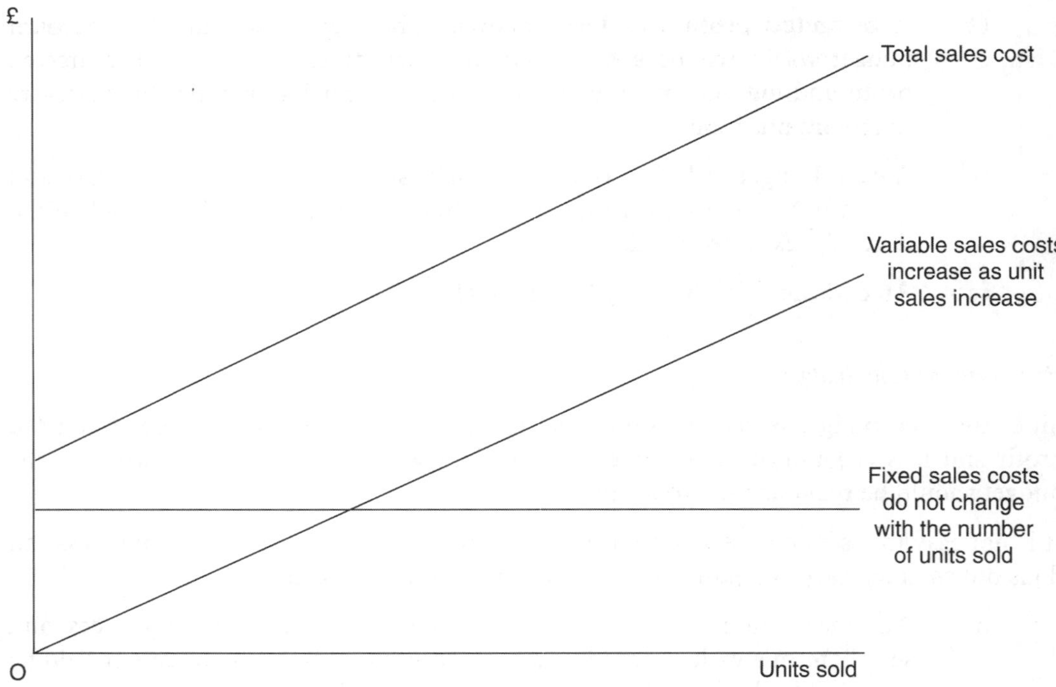

Total sales costs are the sum of the variable and fixed costs elements.

The proportion of fixed to variable costs varies according to the nature of the business and the terms and conditions under which the salesperson is employed. In some sales activities, for example in door to door selling of products like cosmetics, the sales personnel are self employed agents, earning commission only and paying their own sales expenses. In this case the variable cost element would be very high, with sales costs directly linked to sales success. In other sectors, particularly where the sales activity emphasises the non sales elements of the sales task, staff may be salaried with no commission. In this case the fixed cost element of sales is very high.

Management decisions can have a significant impact on sales costs. In particular, territory design and the organisation of the sales force can alter both the expenses incurred in selling and the travelling time between sales calls eg when the sales force is organised by product rather than geography, it is possible to have two sales people, both travelling the length and breadth of the country to visit customers. A different basis for territory design may increase the call rate and reduce the sales expenses.

3.4 Allocation of resources in sales budgets

Budgets can be analysed in a variety of ways. The sales budget reflects the estimated sales costs and forecast sales revenues for the department as a whole. But in turn these need to be further split by:

(a) Product/(to help operations planning)
(b) Market/customer group
(c) Sales area

Budgets need to be allocated in a manner which is **both meaningful to the way the department is organised** and **easy to administer**.

(a) If the sales force is organised on a geographic basis, then that is how the sales budget should be sub-divided. If the sales force is organised on a product basis the system of budget allocation should be based by product, too.

(b) The budget's allocation of resources also needs to take into account **variations in the potential of sales areas**, products or customer groups. Simply dividing the forecast sales by the number of products in the company portfolio takes no account of differences in their sales potential, the stage of the product life cycle or the sales objectives for each product. Likewise, each sales area may have a different sales forecast because of economic or cultural variations influencing demand.

(c) Once analysed, it should then be broken down further so that it becomes possible to generate sales targets for the individual members of the sales team. If everyone achieves their targets, within cost, the overall sales budget will also be met.

(d) Sales **targets** are supposed not just to be reached but perhaps exceeded. The sales **budget** is not like this; it is used to coordinate the resources of the organisation. An excess of sales orders might put a strain on operations and possibly the organisation's cash flow.

The administration of the budget must be up to date if it is to be of value. The ability to know about the current position to assess the variance between planned and actual activity levels, is necessary to give managers the maximum opportunity to take corrective action. The contribution of management accountants to this process is very important.

3.5 Sales activities and their impact on profitability

Every salesperson should be interested in the profitability of the organisation and should fully appreciate the impact of their performance and actions on that **profitability**. Sales personnel sometimes naturally look to revenue – but profitability is as significant.

Revenue impact. The success of the sales team is influenced by:

(a) The number of customers they contact
(b) The sales:call conversion rate
(c) The average order value.

Effectiveness of effort

Equally the sales team can improve **profitability** by selling more without increasing selling costs or by selling the same volume but at a lower cost. The individual sales person needs to appreciate the impact of their expenses on profitability and take responsibility for controlling these costs.

Many sales staff will have the flexibility and authority to negotiate with customers. It is very easy to give profit away with generous discounts. If the organisation's costs are 80% of revenue, a case of products with a selling price of £100 represents £20 profit. A discount of £5 reduces the profits earned by 25%.

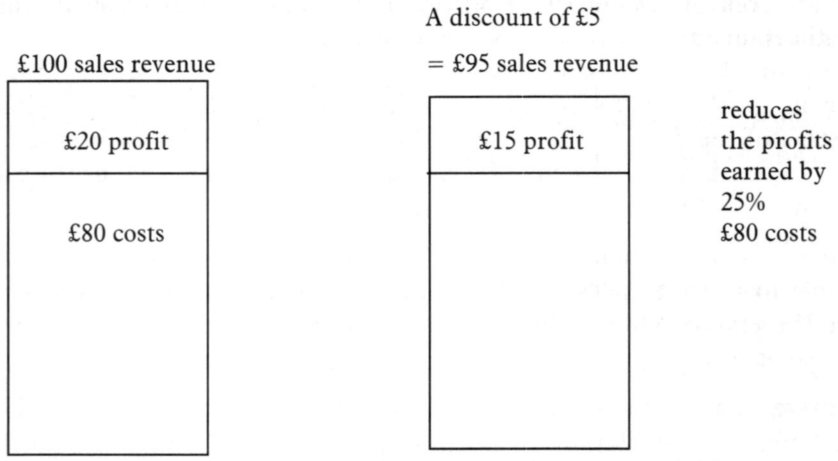

The salesperson has to sell another £25 worth of product at the original profit margin to make up the difference.

It is also possible to see that the value of discount to the customer is just £5. Providing £5 additional product instead would give the customer the same perceived value, but would only cost the firm £4.

4 BUDGET TARGETS AND MOTIVATION

The purpose of a budgetary control system is to assist management in planning and controlling the resources of their organisation by providing appropriate control information. The information will only be valuable, however, if it is interpreted correctly and used purposefully by managers *and* employees.

The correct use of control information therefore depends not only on the content of the information itself, but also on the behaviour of its recipients. This is because control in business is exercised by people. Their attitude to control information will colour their views on what they should do with it and a number of behavioural problems can arise.

(a) The **managers who set the budget** or standards are **often not the managers** who are then **made responsible for achieving budget targets.**

(b) The **goals of the organisation as a whole**, as expressed in a budget, **may not coincide with the personal aspirations of individual managers.**

(c) **Control is applied at different stages by different people.** A supervisor might get weekly control reports, and act on them; his superior might get monthly control reports, and decide to take different control action. Different managers can get in each others' way, and resent the interference from others.

4.1 Motivation and budgets

Motivation is what makes people behave in the way that they do. It comes from individual attitudes, or group attitudes. Individuals will be motivated by personal desires and interests. These may be in line with the objectives of the organisation, and some people 'live for their jobs'. Other individuals see their job as a chore, and their motivations will be unrelated to the objectives of the organisation they work for.

It is therefore vital that the goals of management and the employees harmonise with the goals of the organisation as a whole. This is known as **goal congruence**. Although obtaining goal congruence is essentially a behavioural problem, **it is possible to design**

and run a budgetary control system which will go some way towards ensuring that goal congruence is achieved.

Management should therefore try to ensure that employees have positive attitudes towards **setting budgets, implementing budgets** (that is, putting the organisation's plans into practice) and feedback of results (**control information**).

Poor attitudes when setting budgets

If managers are involved in preparing a budget, poor attitudes or hostile behaviour towards the budgetary control system can begin at the **planning stage.**

(a) Managers may **complain that they are too busy** to spend much time on budgeting.

(b) They may **build 'slack' into their expenditure estimates** or be too conservative in their sales estimates.

(c) They may argue that **formalising a budget plan on paper is too restricting** and that managers should be allowed flexibility in the decisions they take.

(d) They may set budgets for their budget centre and **not coordinate** their own plans with those of other budget centres.

(e) They may **base future plans on past results,** instead of using the opportunity for formalised planning to look at alternative options and new ideas.

Poor attitudes when putting plans into action

Poor attitudes also arise **when a budget is implemented.**

(a) Managers might **put in only just enough effort** to achieve budget targets, without trying to beat targets.

(b) A formal budget might **encourage rigidity and discourage flexibility.**

(c) **Short-term planning** in a budget **can draw attention away from the longer-term consequences** of decisions.

(d) There might be **minimal cooperation and communication** between managers.

(e) Managers will often try to make sure that they **spend up to their full budget allowance, and do not overspend,** so that they will not be accused of having asked for too much spending allowance in the first place.

It has been argued that participation in the budgeting process will improve motivation and so will improve the quality of budget decisions and the efforts of individuals to achieve their budget targets (although obviously this will depend on the personality of the individual, the nature of the task (narrowly defined or flexible) and the organisational culture).

There are basically two ways in which a budget can be set: from the top down (imposed budget) or from the bottom up (participatory budget).

4.2 Top down budgeting

In this approach to budgeting, **top management prepare a budget with little or no input from operating personnel** which is then imposed upon the employees who have to work to the budgeted figures.

Times when imposed budgets are effective

- In newly-formed organisations
- In very small businesses
- During periods of economic hardship
- When operational managers lack budgeting skills
- When the organisation's different units require precise coordination

There are, of course, advantages and disadvantages to this style of setting budgets.

(a) **Advantages**

- Strategic plans are likely to be incorporated into planned activities.
- They enhance the coordination between the plans and objectives of divisions.
- They use senior management's awareness of total resource availability.
- They decrease the input from inexperienced or uninformed lower-level employees.
- They decrease the period of time taken to draw up the budgets.

(b) **Disadvantages**

- Dissatisfaction, defensiveness and low morale amongst employees. It is hard for people to be motivated to achieve targets set by somebody else.
- The feeling of team spirit may disappear.
- The acceptance of organisational goals and objectives could be limited
- The feeling of the budget as a punitive device could arise.
- Managers who are performing operations on a day to day basis are likely to have a better understanding of what is achievable.
- Unachievable budgets could result if consideration is not given to local operating and political environments. This applies particularly to overseas divisions.
- Lower-level management initiative may be stifled.

4.3 Bottom up budgeting

Definition

> **Participative/bottom-up budgeting** is 'A budgeting system in which all budget holders are given the opportunity to participate in setting their own budgets'. (CIMA *Official Terminology*)

In this approach to budgeting, **budgets are developed by lower-level managers who then submit the budgets to their superiors**. The budgets are based on the lower-level managers' perceptions of what is achievable and the associated necessary resources.

When participative budgets are effective

- In decentralised organisations
- In well-established organisations

- In very large businesses
- During periods of economic affluence
- When operational managers have strong budgeting skills
- When the organisation's different units act autonomously

Advantages of participative budgets

- They are based on information from employees most familiar with the department.
- Knowledge spread among several levels of management is pulled together.
- Morale and motivation is improved.
- They increase operational managers' commitment to organisational objectives.
- In general they are more realistic.
- Co-ordination between units is improved.
- Specific resource requirements are included.
- Senior managers' overview is mixed with operational level details.
- Individual managers' aspiration levels are more likely to be taken into account.

Disadvantages of participative budgets

- They consume more time.
- Changes implemented by senior management may cause dissatisfaction.
- Budgets may be unachievable if managers are not qualified to participate.
- They may cause managers to introduce budgetary slack.
- They can support 'empire building' by subordinates.
- An earlier start to the budgeting process could be required.
- Managers may set 'easy' budgets to ensure that they are achievable.

4.4 Negotiated style of budgeting

Definition

A **negotiated budget** is 'A budget in which budget allowances are set largely on the basis of negotiations between budget holders and those to whom they report'. (CIMA *Official Terminology*)

At the two extremes, budgets can be dictated from above or simply emerge from below but, in practice, different levels of management often agree budgets by a process of negotiation. In the imposed budget approach, operational managers will try to negotiate with senior managers the budget targets which they consider to be unreasonable or unrealistic. Likewise senior management usually review and revise budgets presented to them under a participative approach through a process of negotiation with lower level managers. **Final budgets are therefore most likely to lie between what top management would really like and what junior managers believe is feasible.** The budgeting process is hence a **bargaining process** and it is this bargaining which is of vital importance, **determining whether the budget is an effective management tool or simply a clerical device**.

4.5 Budgetary slack

Definition

Budgetary slack is the difference between the minimum necessary costs and the costs built into the budget or actually incurred.

In the process of preparing budgets, managers might deliberately overestimate costs and underestimate sales, so that they will not be blamed in the future for overspending and poor results.

In controlling actual operations, managers must then **ensure that their spending rises to meet their budget**, otherwise they will be 'blamed' for careless budgeting.

After a run of mediocre results, some managers deliberately overstate revenues and understate cost estimates, no doubt feeling the need to make an immediate favourable impact by promising better performance in the future. They may merely delay problems, however, as the managers may well be censured when they fail to hit these optimistic targets.

4.6 The use of budgets as targets

Once decided, budgets become targets. As targets, they can motivate managers to achieve a high level of performance. But **how difficult should targets be**? And how might people react to targets of differing degrees of difficulty in achievement?

(a) There is likely to be a **demotivating** effect where an **ideal standard** of performance is set, because adverse efficiency variances will always be reported.

(b) A **low standard of efficiency** is also **demotivating**, because there is no sense of achievement in attaining the required standards, and there will be no impetus for employees to try harder to do better than this.

(c) A **budgeted level of attainment** could be 'normal': that is, the **same as the level that has been achieved in the past**. Arguably, this level will be **too low**. It might **encourage budgetary slack**.

It has been argued that **each individual has a personal 'aspiration level'**. This is a level of performance in a task with which the individual is familiar, which the individual undertakes for himself to reach. This aspiration level might be quite challenging and if individuals in a work group all have similar aspiration levels it should be possible to incorporate these levels within the official operating standards.

Some care should be taken, however, in applying this.

(a) A salesperson's tendency to achieve success is stronger than the tendency to avoid failure, budgets with targets of intermediate levels of difficulty are the most motivating, and stimulate a manager to better performance levels.

(b) A salesperson's **tendency to avoid failure might be stronger than the tendency to achieve success**. (This is likely in an organisation in which the budget is used as a pressure device on subordinates by senior managers). Managers might then be discouraged from trying to achieve budgets of intermediate difficulty and tend to avoid taking on such tasks, resulting in poor levels of performance, worse than if budget targets were either easy or very difficult to achieve.

It has therefore been suggested that in a situation where budget targets of an intermediate difficulty *are* motivating, such targets ought to be set if the purpose of budgets is to motivate; however, although budgets which are set for **motivational purposes** need to be stated in terms of **aspirations rather than expectations,** budgets for planning and decision purposes need to be stated in terms of the best available estimate of expected actual performance. The **solution** might therefore be to have **two budgets.**

(a) A **budget for planning and decision making based on reasonable expectations.**

(b) A second **budget for motivational purposes,** with **more difficult targets of performance** (that is, targets of an intermediate level of difficulty).

These two budgets might be called an '**expectations budget**' and an '**aspirations budget**' respectively.

FOR DISCUSSION

What do you think the impact of demanding targets are on:

(a) A field sales force
(b) A customer service centre in a call-centre?

Chapter roundup

- An appraisal system is designed to be a systematic approach to provide feedback and to review performance and potential. Sometimes it is also designed to review salaries.
- Usually an appraisal system will have criteria for assessment, an assessment report, an appraisal interview, a review of the assessment, action plans and follow up.
- In practice, appraisal systems are often seen not to be working effectively.
- Training is very important for sales personnel; however it needs to be carefully planned and executed. Structured training programmes may be beneficial.
- Training methods can be on the job, or more formal such as lectures, discussions, exercises, role plays and case studies.
- Individual action plans can be called personal development plans. This approach gives an individual the responsibility for their own training needs.
- A learning contract can be formally drawn up between the sales person and the organisation and is often used to get commitment from the organisation.
- Budgetary control systems are used to ensure communication, coordination and control.
- Sales budgets should be reasonable and realistic.
- Allocations of sales budgets can be divided by product, market/customer group and/or sales area.
- Budgets can have a major impact on employees of an organisation and their motivation.
- Budget setting can either be top down, bottom up or negotiated.

Quick quiz

1. Why are appraisals linked to motivation?
2. What is a results orientated appraisal scheme?
3. Give some examples of how the appraisal system can go wrong.
4. What types of appraisal system are there?
5. How can training needs be identified?
6. What advantages are there to programmed learning?
7. What should a learning contract include?
8. Give some examples of the use of budgets in the selling function.
9. Total sales costs is equal to ....costs plus .... costs.
10. What is meant by a 'negotiated budget'?

Answers to quick quiz

1. Appraisals are the systematic approach to providing feedback as a tool for motivation. (See paragraph 1.1)
2. An approach that reviews performance against specific targets agreed in advance by the appraisee and appraisor. (para 1.2)
3. Divergence of needs
   Subordinate is defensive
   Risk of bias
   Different ratings from different managers
   Perceived as a bureaucratic exercise (para 1.5)
4. Downward, upward, peer rated, 360 degree. (paras 1.6, 1.7, 1.8)
5. By research by the training department, by individuals or by the appraisal system. (para 2.3)
6. Trainees can monitor their progress, they can learn interactively and at their own pace. (para 2.5)
7. The type of learning process, expected achievement and timescale. (para 2.9)
8. To make sure objectives and plans are set and met, to communicate plans, to establish a system of control and to motivate sales staff. (para 3.1)
9. Fixed and variable. (para 3.3)
10. A budget that is set largely on the basis of negotiations between budget holders and those to whom they report. (para 4.4)

Answers to activities

1. There is no specific answer to this activity.
2. There is no specific answer to this activity.
3. There is no specific answer to this activity.
4. Your answer should be structured around the headings in the text.

Chapter 21 : SELLING IN DIFFERENT ENVIRONMENTS

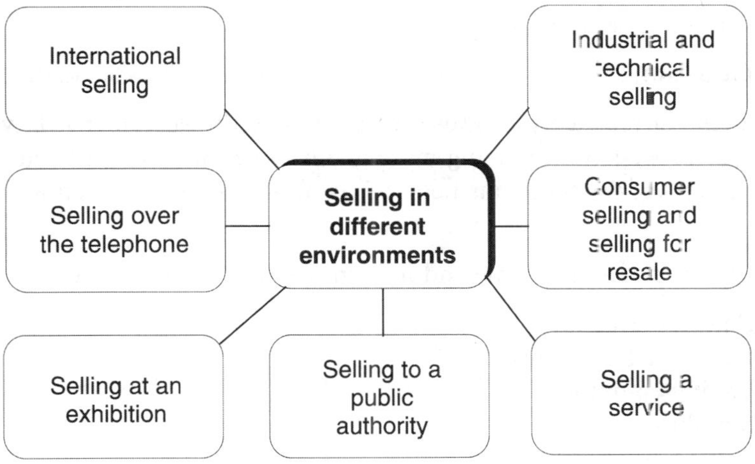

Introduction

As we have already seen, the many variables influencing a sale makes every purchase in its way unique. The situation in which the sale occurs plays an important part in influencing the process by which decisions are made and affects the moods and motives of the buyer.

The salesperson needs to appreciate these differences and be able and willing to vary the sales approach to the selling activity in different sectors.

The frequency, cost and risk involved in purchases in each of these categories varies and so the DMU (Decision Making Unit) and DMP (Decision-Making process) will also vary significantly. It is, however, possible to identify a number of characteristics likely to typify industrial markets and which provide important background for the salesperson.

Your objectives

In this chapter you will learn about the following.

(a) The differences between industrial and consumer selling

(b) The implications of selling a service

(c) The characteristics of public authorities

(d) Uses of telephone selling and attendance at exhibitions

(e) The selling decisions which organisations have to make when selling overseas

1 INDUSTRIAL AND TECHNICAL SELLING

Demand levels in business to business markets are directly influenced by the demand for the client's products. (The term, borrowed from economics, is **derived demand.**) Sales levels and potentials are directly tied to the business climate experienced by the customer. Business confidence is an important factor when forecasting sales in this section. It can be helpful for the salesperson to known about the client's industry, anticipated changes in demand, new competitive activity and emerging opportunities.

As demand is derived, the pattern of demand (for example for raw materials, parts or supplies), will reflect the pattern of demand for the client's products.

1.1 Characteristics

Industrial markets are made up of those sectors where the customer is buying products to be used in the process of producing more goods or services. Because customers are in fact firms, we often use the term 'business to business marketing', when working in these sectors.

Industrial goods are not all the same and in turn they can be classified into:

- Raw materials
- Fabricated materials
- Capital equipment
- Supplies

Distribution channels are typically short

This gives the industrial supplier control over the marketing of the product, but also increases the costs of providing the distribution services. As many industrial suppliers work directly with their clients, the salesperson can be critical in taking care of many of the distribution services from order processing, assistance with installation to collecting payment. The sales element in the industrial communication mix is usually particularly important.

The DMU in these sectors is often complex, difficult to identify and hard to access. At the same time the decision making process can be protracted. Even supplies like office stationery may be provided on a contract basis and so only negotiated and reviewed periodically. Therefore, once a client's custom has been won, there is a move towards **relationship marketing** where suppliers work in partnership with clients to help solve the client's problems. Client loyalty therefore develops in time.

As a result, repeat business is commonly automatic once the initial order is secured - providing that after sales service and all aspects of quality remain satisfactory. Industrial sectors are thus often characterised by inertia in the decision making unit. Making decisions is a time consuming, often very involved process. A manager's life is made easier if the manager chooses to stick with the known supplier, unless there are very positive reasons for change.

1.2 Large orders

Because of the size of contracts and orders the average value per purchase is substantially greater than in a consumer market, and for large capital purchases a single order can be worth millions of pounds. This has the following implications

(a) The average marketing spend per enquiry or sale is likely to be high leading to a special need for careful monitoring and control.

(b) Negotiations which lead to 1 or 2% off the price can have a large impact on a firm's profitability.

(c) Agreements to sell only a few per cent more to a large client can have major implications for increasing production capacity.

(d) Losing a client can be a serious business.

1.3 Price sensitivity

It is a traditional belief that buyers in industrial markets behave 'rationally'. This does not necessarily equate with buying the cheapest.

It is a fallacy that industrial markets are particularly price sensitive. Quality, reliability and performance are much more likely to influence purchase decision than price. Management's overriding needs are equipment and materials which help their jobs run smoothly!

In industrial markets, the individuals who make up the DMU are likely to be specialists and expert in their particular areas. This places added pressures on the salesperson who:

(a) must have complete product knowledge; and

(b) where necessary, be able to call on the support of in-house specialists within the company to assist in negotiations

Industrial buyers will themselves be trained in the process of negotiation and so represent a further test of the salesperson's selling skills.

Although the background and experience necessary varies according to the particular category of industrial products being sold, increasingly in the component and capital goods sectors, sales teams are being drawn from the ranks of qualified engineers and technicians who have the necessary product knowledge. These staff need to be trained in a customer orientated approach.

DISCUSSION

Industrial buyers are more price sensitive and rational than consumer buyers.

1.4 Technical selling

When the sales staff are themselves technical experts, the sales activity may be referred to as **technical selling**. In these cases, the product's features and functions are usually complex, and so expert product knowledge is needed for the required sales function to be performed. Computer systems are an example, where the sales person needs the necessary technical qualifications to recommend an appropriate system, and, possibly, to help the client during installation and staff training.

In this close working relationship, the salesperson becomes almost a consultant to the client, and might even be seconded to work with the customer for a period of time. The resulting relationship between sales staff and client can become very strong. Maintaining a strong sense of loyalty to the employer, not the customer can become difficult in situations where the sales team build up these close working partnerships. Good management and communication is essential to ensure the sales team does not become estranged from each other and from management.

2 CONSUMER SELLING AND SELLING FOR RESALE

Owing to the greater number of potential customers and their geographic distribution, consumer goods are less likely to be supplied directly from manufacturer to customer.

NOTES

The channels of distribution which characterise this sector include retailers, wholesalers and other middlemen. As a result, in these industries, manufacturers have tended to develop the non-personal elements of the communication mix, such as advertising and sales promotion techniques to get their messages direct to the consumer.

Despite using predominantly **advertising pull** strategies to encourage the consumer to seek out brands and literally pull then through the distribution channels, **selling push** does still have an important role to play in these markets.

Personal selling features strongly in two possible areas of consumer product marketing:

- Ensure distribution for the products - selling for resale;
- The retail interface with the customer.

2.1 Selling for resale

The manufacturer's use of personal selling is likely to be limited to the sales effort necessary to ensure **distribution**, by selling the products to middlemen. Availability is an essential element in the marketing mix. Without access to the final customer the product is unlikely to be successful. So the manufacturer is likely to adopt two distinct communication strategies:

(a) An advertising based mix to attract customers to the brand;

(b) A sales push strategy designed to take the product to the distributors and encourage them to stock it.

The potential distributors are relatively few in number, and are easy to identify and access. This is particularly true in the fast moving consumer goods (fmcg's) markets selling convenience categories of products. However, even in the more fragmented markets for consumer durables, distribution is likely to be controlled by a fairly small number of key wholesale chains and distributors.

Distributor's positioning

There is however, an important difference in selling to these markets. The retail **customer** is not the **end** user. The retailer is acting as an indirect adviser in the DMU of the final consumer. Supermarkets select, on behalf of their customers, four or five brands of toothpaste, soap powder, coffee etc, which they believe will satisfy customer needs. By endorsing a brand, (ie by stocking it), the retailer is in effect recommending it. Ultimately therefore, distributors only stock products which they believe will be attractive to their customers. The **product's positioning** has to match the **distributor's positioning,** so Harrods would be unlikely to stock 'value for money' discount products and Kwik Save unlikely to offer premium priced ranges of speciality delicatessen products.

EXAMPLE

There have been efforts by perfume manufacturers to ban the sale of their products in stores such as high street chemists and supermarkets. They feel it is not in keeping with their high class image. They have at present been unsuccessful in trying to stop the stores stocking their products.

Opportunity cost

Sales staff must find out the type of customer shopping at a particular retailer, to ensure that the products being offered reflect the benefits likely to be attractive to that market segment. Products will only win and retain shelf space if it can be demonstrated that they are worth that space. That means achieving an earnings per square foot of shelf space which is acceptable to the distributor. The retailer is looking for the best use of his/her limited resource - space. Therefore the **opportunity cost** of stocking product A is the revenue which would have been generated by stocking product B, so product A must generate more than B to be acceptable.

Both manufacturer and distributor share the same goal, which is to encourage the customer to buy. Bad selling lines may never be re-ordered, but once placed, the distributor will normally take legal title to the goods and so will have a vested interest in helping to sell them. Stock turnover is essential to the financial health of a middleman.

Distribution needs

The manufacturer must consider the distributor's need throughout the development of the marketing mix.

(a) Products should be attractive to the end users, but they must also be easy to handle, stock and distribute (eg packaging has to be stable on the shelves).

(b) In any pricing strategy, the price to the end user will have to include the distributor's margin and this must be carefully assessed.

(c) Brands backed by strong promotional campaigns are likely to be more attractive to the retailer. Whilst merchandising and sales promotion activities encourage sales, they should be designed to be easy to handle and implement on the shop floor.

With the increased sophistication of retail information systems provided by electronic point of sale devices, the distribution function has up to the minute information on stock turnover, sales value and fluctuations in demand for any product line stocked. In the past, the manufacturer would have had much more detailed sales information from delivery data etc. The big multiples which supermarket chain operate centralised distribution systems for themselves now tend to have a much fuller picture of sales patterns than the producer. This imbalance in information can disadvantage the sales person during negotiations.

The balance of power rests firmly with those who are the gatekeepers to the consumers. Negotiations over price levels and promotions support have, over recent years, tended to go in favour of the retailer. The manufacturer's sales staff have to be very skilled at developing long term relationships with clients, so that increasingly they can work together to develop new products for emerging market opportunities.

Activity 1 **(30 minutes)**

Interview someone from the purchasing department of an organisation you are familiar with (you could interview someone at college or a small retailer if you do not have other contacts). Ask them about who sells to them and find out if anyone acts as gatekeepers. Ask also about the purchasing process and who is involved in purchase decisions.

2.2 Selling in the retail environment

In the markets for convenience goods, the retail sales assistant has in the main been replaced by self service systems, but in many markets for shopping and specialist goods, the retail sales activity is an important element in the communication mix.

These purchases are less frequently made, cost more than convenience goods and the purchase entails more perceived risk for the customer. From shoes to lounge furniture, electrical goods to motor cars, product features and performance are likely to be the most important factors influencing consumer demand. The DMP will take longer and the DMU will typically involve more people.

The retail salesperson will most likely be employed by the distributor, not the manufacturer and so has no real brand loyalty.

(a) The role is to ensure the customer is satisfied with the retailer by:

  (i) helping the customer solve his or her problem;
  (ii) therefore ensure a sale.

(b) Retail sales staff often are important 'advisers' in the DMU.

The task of the retailer has not become any easier over recent years.

(a) Customers are more knowledgeable and demanding.

(b) Their behaviour is less easy to predict than in the traditional male dominated household of the past.

(c) Product choice has been extended.

(d) Products have become functionally more complex requiring considerable product knowledge on the part of the retailer.

FOR DISCUSSION

How have changes in retailing made consumers behave differently?

Activity 2 **(30 minutes)**

Consider a family holiday that is purchased with input from different members of the family. Gather some brochures and look at whether there are different messages for different members of the family. Consider what would appeal to different family members.

Manufacturers of these products need to ensure that retail staff fully understand features and benefits of the products they sell by providing training support and/or good sales support literature. Many will consider incentives which encourage the retailer to promote their brand, eg joint promotions, sales incentives to the staff etc.

3 SELLING A SERVICE

In marketing we often include services under the umbrella of products assuming both are treated similarly from the marketing standpoint. Certainly marketing a service is not fundamentally different from marketing a product. In essence services are simply products with no shelf life they are intangible and this characteristic makes working with services more difficult than working with products.

The dimensions of services which make them very different from products are given below.

(a) **Intangibility** means that services cannot be stockpiled to meet peaks in demand.

(b) Intangibility means that customers have to **buy on trust**, unable to try out a service before a purchase.

(c) **Services are frequently produced, distributed and consumed in one place**. The distribution staff are also often the producers of a service. They have all to be skilled in customer care and sales techniques, because they are often involved directly with customers.

FOR DISCUSSION

Intangibility means that it is difficult to see, taste, smell, touch etc the product before purchase. Think of examples that are purely intangible and some that are attached in some way to physical products.

Customer services

As most of the staff involved in service provision have direct contact with customers, most of them need to have some sales training. Hotel receptionists, restaurant waiters, airline staff and service engineers all have the opportunity to increase company revenue by encouraging additional customer purchases and repeat business. However, service industries employ staff with a more exclusive sales brief and title, and so we would probably classify them as service sellers (eg insurance sales representatives and sales teams from commercial service providers).

Selling role

Because of the intangibility of a service, the sales staff are even more likely to be perceived to represent and personify the company. Those employed in the service sector are more likely to wear uniforms, in order to provide users with a sense of security. The quality and cut of those **uniforms** will be taken as indicative of the quality of the whole service.

EXAMPLE

Over the last ten years, banks and other financial institutions have tried to make their services more tangible by using branch design, the use of colour, physical evidence and staff uniforms.

Within the overall title of services it must be recognised that some sales activity will be focused in the industrial sectors, others in the public and consumer markets. In each of these, the basic characteristics of the DMU and DMP of the market will still be relevant and need to be taken into account when developing the sales and marketing strategy.

> **Activity 3** **(10 minutes)**
>
> What implications will there be for an accounting firm selling its services both to organisations and members of the public (eg tax returns)

4 SELLING TO A PUBLIC AUTHORITY

The public sector still represents almost half of the total spending undertaken in the UK economy, making the government to largest customer for many businesses. Suppliers for defence, health and education are amongst those who must be able to sell to the public sector.

Characteristics

(a) **Public sector organisations do not primarily exist to make a profit.** Their objectives are therefore more likely to involve providing satisfactory service levels and constrained by the available budget. However, they are likely to be cost conscious.

(b) **Decision making will be influenced by political considerations** and suppliers need to take these into account when presenting product benefits to public sector decision makers. More importantly changes in the political climate at local, regional, or national levels can occur quickly and these need to be considered when forecasting future demand and developing marketing strategy for these sectors.

(c) **Public sector employees are not usually the decision makers in the DMU**. These are normally some sort of elected representatives for example, school governors, local authority councillors, government ministers etc. These people are harder to identify and access than even industrial decision makers. Unravelling the DMU from the bureaucracy of public sector organisations is a particular challenge for the sales person.

DISCUSSION

It is difficult for an art supplier (not already involved in the organisation) to become accepted as a supplier in the public sector.

The development of executive agencies may mean that there is less central control.

Contractors working in partnership for example providing cleaning and catering services for the health services, will be at the forefront of developing 'relationship marketing'. The role of the sales contract will increasingly be to monitor performance, negotiate standards of service delivery and tackle management problems jointly with the public sector clients.

5 SELLING AT AN EXHIBITION

Most sales representatives and managers are likely at some point, to find themselves in the situation of selling at an exhibition or trade show. These are unusual buying situations, artificially created to bring together buyers and sellers, with a shared area of interest.

Exhibitions and trade fairs (for example, the Ideal Home Exhibition, the Boat Show or the London Book Fair) offer several opportunities.

(a) **Public relations** (both to visitors and via media coverage, taking advantage of the interest generated by the exhibition organisers).

(b) **Promoting and selling** products/services to a wide audience of pre-targeted potential customers, particularly where demonstrations (eg of technical innovations) or visual inspection (eg clothes or motor cars) are likely to influence buyers.

(c) **Networking** within the industry and with existing clients.

(d) **Testing the response** to new products.

(e) **Researching competitor products** and promotions.

(f) **Researching suppliers' products** and services and making contacts along the supply chain.

DISCUSSION

The key to successful exhibitions is to know who will be attending - both visitors and other exhibitors.

5.1 Considering exhibiting

Most industries are catered for by at least one annual or bi-annual exhibition in the UK, as well as internationally. The events themselves are set up by **exhibition organisers** who are responsible for booking and preparing the venue, registering participants and organising seminars and events, issuing catalogues of stand-holders and events, providing stand construction services, organising lounges, amenities and catering facilities, access and parking, power and lighting, promotion and press coverage.

At the time of booking a stand or space, you will have to decide on several issues.

(a) The **size** of your site.

(b) The **location** of your site.

(c) The **design** and **construction** of your site.

(d) The **information** you will provide for the exhibition catalogue, press pack and signage.

5.2 Planning and preparation

Exhibitions can be a huge logistical exercise. They require planning well in advance – and then compress a lot of activity all at once into a very hectic period.

There are a number of areas in which **advance planning** will pay off.

(a) **Stand design, display and services.** As we mentioned above, specialist stand contractors can set up the structure, fixtures and fittings of a stand to your specifications, but you need to have considered what your needs for display and facilities will be.

(b) **Stand staffing**

Trade show networking and selling is hectic, intense and tiring. You will need to arrange for a **rotating roster** of stand staff, including a Stand Manager to organise the stand and liaise with exhibition organisers, reception staff, sales staff, technical staff (if the product requires expert demonstration or advice) and multilingual export staff.

(c) **Accommodation and transport for personnel**

A large exhibition can absorb available transport and accommodation even in a major city. If you are outside your home area, ensure that you have booked transport to the exhibition city, hotel or other accommodation and also any hire cars required, well in advance.

(d) **Pre-arranged meetings and visits**

In order to maximise your return on investment, ensure that you hit as many of your target audience as you can. Make a 'hit list' of key customers, suppliers and agents (from your database or from the pre-circulated list of exhibitors and attendees).

5.3 At the exhibition

During the **set-up** period before the exhibition, you will work with contractors and your own staff to check that all the structures, fixtures, fittings and services associated with the stand are in place and functioning correctly.

Day-to-day **administration** of the stand

- Appointment making, communications, offering refreshments
- Providing information, screening and routing 'serious' prospects
- Distributing leaflets or running competitions
- Recording all visits and sending visitors away with information

---

EXAMPLE

Websites have been said to be taking over from exhibitions. However evidence suggests that instead of posing a threat IT is actually boosting exhibition efficiency and making it more rewarding. It can be used to extend the life of an exhibition. Stand displays can use IT to illustrate styles and colours.

5.4 After the exhibition

Once an exhibition is finished, the stand will need to be dismantled, and its various components sent back where they came from.

The most important stage of the exhibition is **follow-up**.

(a) The contact information gained needs to be input to the organisation **database** and immediately utilised, even if it is only an e-mail to thank the contact for the visit.

(b) All promises made during the show (to send out literature or make a sales call) must be fulfilled as soon as possible.

5.5 Exhibiting is expensive.

- Site fees, stand construction and display (estimated 66% by the Exhibition Industry Federation)
- Staff costs, including opportunity cost of staff being withdrawn from their normal sales work (22%)
- Promotion and entertainment of visitors (12%)

A **budget** should be drawn up to cover all costs associated with going to the show/exhibition. This should be compared with forecast revenue from the show in order to assess the show's viability. After the event, the show's **profitability** can be evaluated in the same way.

However, it should be recognised that your objectives for a particular show may not solely be sales revenue. You may want to find a **distributor** in a new international market, or to **raise awareness** of your brand with the trade press, or to **introduce your product** to a new market. Such achievements may take time to 'ripen' into confirmed sales. In the Exhibition Industry Federation survey, the average time to convert an exhibition lead to a sale was seven months, and in some cases, two years or more.

5.6 Exhibition checklist

- Book space and pay direct
- Draft and supply catalogue/signage information
- Design stand/lighting/fixture and fittings
- Order lighting, flooring, furniture, shelving, and storage
- Order water, power, heating, telecom, drainage
- Order fire extinguisher, check safety regulations
- Insure stand and exhibits
- Organise products/brochures/display materials for exhibit
- Arrange delivery/export of large items, and return
- Contract for stand cleaning, plant/flower supply and maintenance, security
- Plan staffing of stand
- Plan VIP appearances
- Arrange transport and accommodation of staff, VIP's
- Design and prepare promotional literature, signage, incentives to visitors
- Gather stationery and equipment for use on stand
- Invite customers/prospects, arrange meetings
- Arrange for photography, prepare press releases
- Order stand catering/refreshments
- Brief stand personnel; prepare task lists, rotas

5.7 The view of the sales team

The poorly motivated or badly trained sales team may take a fairly jaundiced view of an exhibition. They may well be seconded to staff a stand. A number of factors may reduce the sales person's enthusiasm of the event.

(a) It takes him or her away from normal weekly activities and duties, which may not be undertaken by anyone else. The members of sales team return to overflowing in-trays.

(b) Sales targets and quotas may not be modified to take account of time spent at an exhibition.

(c) They may resent lost selling days, which reduce commission opportunities and therefore average pay.

(d) Contacts made at an exhibition may have to be referred to a colleague because of the way the sales organisation is structured. It can lead to a 'what's in it for me?' feeling, if the colleague gets the commission.

(e) The sales situation at an exhibition is very enclosed, formal and public, very different to the normal sales environment of a representative. Some do not like the change.

(f) Following up exhibition leads may be seen as added work and so not undertaken effectively.

The attitude and motivation of the staff working on an exhibition stand is critical to the success of the event. Management's job is to recognise the problems of those involved and ensure they are overcome (eg with special incentive schemes for leads handed over to colleagues, bonus payments to ensure earnings are maintained etc).

Activity 4

If you have not been involved in exhibition selling make a point of attending an exhibition over the next few months. There are often smaller 'business to business' exhibitions run by the Chamber of Commerce or you could visit a work related event or a big consumer show like the Motor Show or Ideal Home. Take a note of the selling done at this event. Critically evaluate the stand management and try to identify the objectives. If staff are not too busy try and talk to them about the process of exhibition selling.

6 SELLING OVER THE TELEPHONE

6.1 Uses of telephone selling

The telephone is a very important tool in the salesperson's toolbox. Like any other tool the effective use of telephone selling depends on the appropriate situation, and the skill of individuals who have learned the techniques of selling by phone.

The single biggest advantage of using the telephone is that it provides person to person contact at a much lower cost than a sales visit. It can therefore be used to:

(a) Maintain contact with existing customers, taking repeat orders etc;

(b) Generate a list of interested contacts, to increase the sales conversion rates from sales visits;

(c) Create awareness of special offers, new products etc;

(d) Make the sale by phone.

Definition

Telemarketing can be defined as a marketing communication system using ained personnel to conduct planned, measurable marketing activities by phone hich are directed at targeted groups of customers.

6.2 The benefits of using the phone

The telephone provides the seller with a number of positive advantages.

(a) **Quick response**

- Prospects receive immediate information about your product/service.

- Sellers get immediate response (feedback) from consumers and vice versa.
- Selling is speeded up - no tea, no coffee, no telephone calls or indeed visitors to delay or interrupt discussions.

(b) **Interaction**

- Although both parties (buyer and seller) do not see each other, telephone provides the fastest person-to-person contact with two way traffic of information and instant personal reaction.
- A successful telephone conversation can result in an appointment to visit or even a sale.

(c) **Accessibility**

- It is often possible to gain access to individuals who would never agree to an appointment.
- Little preparation is needed to access your target audience.
- It enables access to large number of potential customers in a very short time period.

(d) **Easy assessment**

The telephone allows the seller the opportunity to assess the individuals willingness or readiness to buy. If out of every group of 50 people you could expect to sell to five, the telephone allows those prospects with the greatest potential to be assessed quickly and easily.

(e) **Cost**

- Although telephone contact is still labour intensive, it allows personal contact to be made without the expense of travel. This is particularly important in geographically diverse markets.
- Used in preparation of personal visits it can ensure the most effective use of sales time with appointments established prior to the visit etc.

6.3 Limitations and problems with the telephone

The telephone does have its limitations and it needs to be used with care to avoid problems.

(a) Unsolicited calls can cause annoyance, particularly amongst householders when calls can be intrusive or received at an inconvenient time.

(b) Calls may be disguised as research or other information-generating activities, and so are therefore misleading.

(c) Sales calls leave an intangible record. Without support literature, the buyer or seller may misunderstand the communication and verbal contracts negotiated by phone are difficult to prove. In the business sectors, the increased availability of fax machines to be used in conjunction with or instead of direct telephone selling does offer the chance for instant tangibility of messages.

(d) Telephone selling provides no opportunity to judge body language, making negotiation by phone much more difficult than face to face contact.

(e) There is equally no chance to demonstrate or show samples thus increasing the buyer's risk unless the seller is already known.

(f) Many consumers are hostile to unsolicited 'cold' calls anyway, and might be less inclined to buy if they feel they are put under pressure.

EXAMPLE

Telephone selling: good practice. The Office of Fair Trading is to publish guidelines for the use of telephones in selling.

(a) Callers should ask whether the timing of the call is convenient. If it is not they should offer to ring back at a more convenient time. Calls should not be made after 9.00pm

(b) The caller's name and that of the company responsible for the call should be given at the start of the call and repeated at any time if requested.

(c) The purpose of the call should be made clear at the start, and the content of the call should be restricted to matters directly relevant to its purpose. Calls should never be made under guise of market research, nor combined with the offer of unrelated goods and services.

(d) Callers should not mislead, be evasive, exaggerate or use partial truths and they should answer any questions honestly and fully. Companies should accept responsibility for statements made by their sales staff or agents and take appropriate disciplinary action if breaches of these guidelines occur.

(e) The caller should always recognise the right of the person called to terminate the telephone conversation at any stage and should accept such a termination promptly and courteously.

(f) The caller should provide the person called with a clear opportunity to refuse any appointment or offer.

(g) If the caller makes an appointment for someone to visit the consumer's home, he or she should provide a contact point in order to facilitate possible cancellation or alteration of the visit by the consumer.

(h) Unsolicited calls should not be made to people at their place of work.

(i) Callers should ensure that they do not obtain information or appointments or orders from minors and that they do not call unlisted telephone numbers.

(j) Consumers should be sent copies of all relevant documents, including agreements, contracts and statements of their legal rights if they place an order. A cooling-off period of at least seven days should apply following receipt of such papers during which the consumers could, if they wished, cancel their order and be entitled to a refund of any payment which they may have made.

Managers need to ensure that they establish clear policy when staff are engaged in telephone selling and they must be thoroughly trained to ensure the medium is not abused.

Taking on board these possible problem areas, it is possible to still make effective and positive use of the telephone as part of the sales process.

Activity 5 **(20 minutes)**

Think about the last time someone called you at home or at work to try and sell you something. Did they abide by the code of conduct? Did you purchase anything? How happy were you with the call?

6.4 Incoming sales calls

When used in conjunction with advertising and direct mail, interested customers can be encouraged to phone enquires in. This allows queries to be handled, quotations to be given, appointments made or orders taken.

Using Freephone numbers

When encouraging incoming sales enquiries a Freephone number is highly recommended. It is your objective to make it as easy as possible for the enquirer to contact you. A Freephone number:

(a) Prevents individuals being put off by the cost of a call - which may affect the household sector.

(b) Means that customers do not have to remember a phone number. This is particularly helpful when using the radio or TV as an advertising medium, where individuals may not have a pen and paper with them.

DISCUSSION

Call centres have expanded hugely over the past few years. Some are now both physically remote (even located in other countries) and service a number of suppliers.

6.5 Outgoing sales calls

Outgoing sales calls are generally unsolicited from the customer's point of view. They are however, particularly valuable as a means of keeping in contact with existing customers and giving them information about special offers etc.

Used in conjunction with other marketing tools, it does provide a quick and easy method for identifying prospects which can increase the effectiveness of limited sales resources.

6.6 Sales research and the phone

The telephone can be used to gain information very rapidly, either in preparation of a sales strategy or a specific sales visit. Sales research in this context can help the sale team assess the viability of various target markets or identify the DMU in a particular organisation.

Activity 6 **(20 minutes)**

Find out how the telephone is used in the selling process of your company or one you are familiar with. Could it be used more effectively?

7 INTERNATIONAL SELLING

Exporting is the easiest, cheapest and most commonly used route into a new foreign market.

NOTES

(a) The principal benefit is that exporters are able to concentrate production in a **single location**, giving economies of scale and consistency of product quality.

(b) Firms lacking the **know-how and experience** can try international marketing on a small scale.

(c) Exporting enables firms to **develop and test** their plans and strategies.

(d) Exporting enables firms to minimise their **operating costs**, administrative overheads and personnel requirements.

Although exporting requires a **low involvement** in the overseas market, this does not necessarily imply that only low investment is needed. Exporting requires investment in **market research, strategy** formulation and careful **implementation of the marketing mix**. The initial success of Japanese car firms in the USA and Europe was based on research and strategic planning that was both extensive and costly.

7.1 Indirect exports

Indirect exporting is where a firm's goods are sold abroad by other organisations. There are four ways of indirect export.

- Export houses
- Specialist export managers
- UK buying offices of foreign stores and governments
- Complementary exporting

Export houses

Export houses are firms which facilitate exporting on behalf of the producer. There are three main types of export house.

(a) **Export merchants** act as export principals. They buy goods from a producer and sell them abroad.

(b) **Confirming houses** also act as principals. Their main function is to provide credit to customers when the producer is unwilling to do so.

(c) **Manufacturers' export agents** are based at home, but sell abroad for the producer. An agent will usually cover a particular sector or industry, (eg pottery). Remuneration is by commission.

Advantages of export houses

(a) The producer gains the benefits of the export house's market knowledge and contacts.

(b) Except in the case of export agents the producer is relieved of the need to do the following.

- **Finance** the export transaction
- Suffer the **credit risk**
- Prepare **export documentation**

(c) The producer does not bear the **overhead costs** of export marketing.

(d) In some cases export merchants receive preferential treatment from foreign institutional and organisational customers.

BPP PUBLISHING

(e) Where export agents are used, the producer retains considerable **control** over the market.

Disadvantages of export houses

(a) Ultimately, it is not the producer's but the merchant's decision to market a product, and so a producer is at the merchant's mercy.

(b) Any goodwill created in the market usually benefits the merchant and not the producer.

(c) As with all intermediaries, an export house or merchant might service a variety of producing organisations. An individual producer cannot rely on the merchant's exclusive loyalty.

(d) Export houses are not normally willing to enter into long term arrangements with a producer.

Specialist export managers

Specialist **export management firms** (SEMs) offer a full export management service. In effect, they perform the same functions as an in-house export department but are normally remunerated by way of commission.

(a) Advantages of using a specialist export manager are the same as those for export houses. In addition, the manufacturer (or service provider) immediately gains its own export department without incurring overheads, retains full market control and can normally expect a long term relationship with the export manager.

(b) Disadvantages do exist however.

    (i) As the export manager is an independent organisation, it can leave the producer's service and the producer will have gained **no in-house exporting expertise.**

    (ii) As the producer does not learn from the experience of exporting, this may adversely affect future options by restricting those available.

    (iii) The SEM may not have sufficient knowledge of all the producer's markets.

UK buying offices of foreign stores and governments

Many foreign governments and foreign companies (eg department stores) have buying offices set up permanently in the UK. In addition, other foreign companies send representatives on buying expeditions to the UK.

Complementary exporting

Definition

> **Complementary exporting** ('**piggy back exporting**') occurs when one producing organisation (the **carrier**) uses its own established IM channels to market the products of another producer (the **rider**) as well as its own. The carrier may act as:
>
> (a) a simple transporter, using spare capacity in its distribution network;
> (b) an agent, selling the rider's goods for commission;
> (c) a merchant, buying and selling the rider's goods.

Advantages of complementary exporting

(a) The carrier earns increased profit from a better use of distribution capacity and can sell a more attractive product range.

(b) The rider obtains entry to a market at low cost and low risk.

Turnkey contracts may also provide opportunities for complementary exporting. A single firm engaged on a particular project overseas (eg construction and civil engineering projects in the Middle East) will often acquire products and services from other firms in the home country for the project.

7.2 Direct exports

Direct exporting occurs where the producing organisation itself performs the export tasks rather than using an intermediary. Sales are made directly to customers overseas who may be the wholesalers, retailers or final users. Sales may increasingly be made via e-commerce on the Internet.

Sales to final user

In this case there are clearly no intermediaries. Typical customers include industrial users, governments or mail order customers. Marketing in this environment is similar to marketing in the domestic market, although there are the added problems of distance, product regulations, language and culture.

Overseas agencies

Strictly speaking an **overseas export agent** is an overseas firm hired to effect a sales contract between the principal (ie the exporter) and a customer. Agents do not take title to goods; they earn a commission. In practice, however, the phrase is often understood to include distributors (who do take title). Some agents merely arrange sales; others hold stocks and/or carry out servicing on the principal's behalf.

Advantages of overseas agents

(a) They have extensive knowledge and experience of the overseas market and the customers.

(b) Their existing product range is usually complementary to the exporter's. This may help the exporter penetrate the overseas market.

(c) The exporter does not have to make a large investment outlay.

(d) The political risk is low.

Disadvantages

(a) An intermediary's commitment and motivation may be weaker than the producer's.

(b) Agents usually want steady turnover. Using an agent may not be the most appropriate way of selling low volume, high value goods with unsteady patterns of demand, or where sales are infrequent.

(c) Many agents are too small to exploit a major market to its full extent. Many serve only limited geographical segments.

(d) As a market grows large it becomes less efficient to use an agent. A branch office or subsidiary company will achieve economies of scale.

As with all intermediaries, the use of an agent requires careful planning, selection, motivation and control.

7.3 Distributors/stockists

Distributors are customers with preferential rights to buy and sell a range of a firm's goods in a specific geographical area. Distributors earn profit, not commission. They differ from wholesalers only in that their selling and marketing activities on behalf of a producer are restricted geographically.

Stockists are distributors who receive more favourable financial rewards than distributors as they normally undertake to carry at least a certain minimum level of stock. The advantages and disadvantages of distributors and stockists are similar to those associated with overseas agents.

EXAMPLE

In some markets, such as Japan which has a complicated distribution system of retailers, a knowledgeable local distributor is essential. Tie-ups with Japanese partners and expensive marketing are necessary before discussions can start.

7.4 Company branch offices abroad

A firm can establish its own office in a foreign market for the purpose of marketing and distribution.

Advantages

(a) When sales have reached a certain level, branch offices become more effective than agencies.

(b) Sales performance will improve, as the commitment and motivation of a producer's own staff should be more effective than those of an agent.

(c) The producer retains complete marketing control.

(d) The producer should be able to acquire more accurate and timely market information.

(e) Customer service should improve. Intermediaries are notorious for poor performance in this respect.

Disadvantages

(a) Higher investment, overhead and running costs are entailed.

(b) There can be a political risk, particularly expropriation of assets.

(c) The firm will be subject to local employee legislation (eg minimum number of local staff, dismissal, trade union membership) which it may not welcome.

7.5 The export sales team

Export selling is an opportunistic, toe in the water approach, frequently as a reaction to an overseas enquiry. In this instance the same product as the home market is provided, often with little modification to the domestic marketing mix. In these scenarios, the sales team is often expected to handle negotiations with little specific training or background understanding of the market place, with probably minimal knowledge of the buyer's language, customs and culture.

This sort of 'hit and miss' introduction to overseas markets, places the sales team at a considerable disadvantage. They will be working away from home, will be very isolated in cultural terms and will not receive adequate marketing support. Sales opportunities are unlikely to be maximised in such situations and the cost of winning and servicing customers can be high when compared with the domestic market. Companies with twenty representatives working in the UK will appoint one person for Southern Europe, say, and this unsophisticated targeting is unlikely to deliver realistic marketing objectives in terms of market share, turnover, profit or awareness.

To summarise, international selling would appear to be poorly supported, poorly managed and is really the 'poor relation' of its domestic base. Where management are not fully committed to developing overseas markets they would be better off remaining in their domestic market only and developing it further.

Some companies, having identified a market opportunity abroad, set about developing it in a proactive customer-orientated way. This requires evaluating the potential markets available and deciding on priorities.

Distribution is often the key factor in international markets and decisions here will determine the extent of the **selling** role. Joint ventures or agents often represent the quickest route into a market. In this way the overseas partner provides local knowledge, contacts and sales effort and the domestic sales role may be limited to management and co-ordination of the process.

Where selling is direct to the customer, for example in industrial markets, a sales organisation may need to be established.

(a) This may take the form of **regional sales office**, or include warehousing and finishing processes close to the internal customer base.

(b) It is likely that both the product and its marketing mix are likely to have been modified to meet the needs of this new target market (for example sales literature provided in the user's language, advertising approaches modified to be culturally effective and perhaps to meet legal requirements of the market).

(c) Eventually the sales team may be drawn from the export market, as they might be more effective at selling than expatriates. However, it should be noted that as many customers are also becoming more global or at least European in their operations, so it is less acceptable to organise the sales force on a geographic basis.

7.6 Organising sales teams for export marketing

Sales teams organised by country are likely to remain isolated units with little communication across the teams.

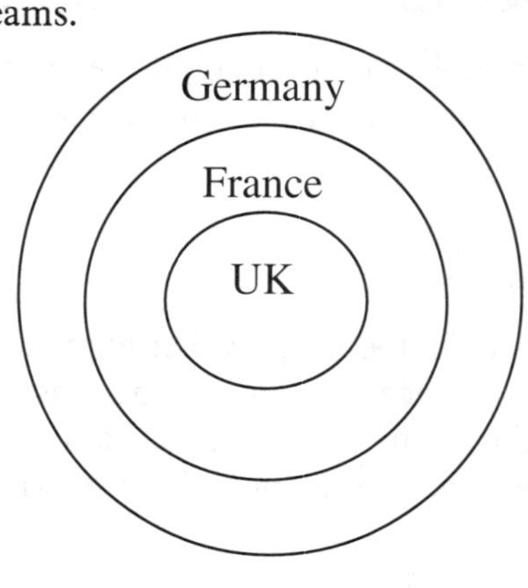

As the needs of for example European firms becomes more similar so specialisation by sector across country, as a matrix organisation structure becomes more attractive.

As the needs of for example European firms becomes more similar so specialisation by

Over time the cultural difference and barriers between European countries will begin to diminish and selling across Europe will be no different than selling across America. Of course each region will have its particular characteristics, but these will be recognised and accommodated. Until then, or whilst operating in countries outside Europe, the sales team has to recognise the cultural differences and their implications on negotiating and the selling process.

7.7 Expatriates or locals?

For an international company, which has to 'think globally' as well as act 'locally', there are a number of problems.

- Do you employ mainly **expatriate staff** to control local operations?
- Do you employ **local sales personnel**, with the possible loss of central control?
- Is there such a thing as the **global manager**, equally at home in different cultures?

Expatriate staff are sometimes favoured over local staff.

(a) Poor **educational opportunities** in the market may require the 'import' of skilled technicians and managers. For example, expatriates have been needed in many western firms' operations in Russia and Eastern Europe, simply because they are familiar with the meaning of profit'.

(b) Some senior managers believe that a business run by expatriates is easier to **control** than one run by local staff.

(c) Expatriates might be better able than locals to **communicate** with the corporate centre.

(d) The expatriate may **know more about the firm** overall, which is especially important if he or she is fronting a sales office.

The use of expatriates in overseas markets has certain disadvantages.

(a) They **cost** more (eg subsidised housing, school fees).

(b) **Culture shock.** The expatriate may fail to adjust to the culture (eg by associating only with other expatriates). This is likely to lead to poor management effectiveness, especially if the business requires personal contact.

(c) A substantial training programme might be needed.

(i) **Basic facts** about the country will be given with basic language training, and some briefings about cultural differences.

(ii) **Immersion training** involves detailed language training, simulation of field experiences etc. This is necessary to obtain an intellectual understanding and practical awareness of the culture.

Employing local managers raises the following issues.

(a) A '**glass ceiling**' might exist in some companies. Talented local managers may not make it to board levels if, as in many Japanese firms, most members of the board are drawn from one country.

(b) In some cases, it may be hard for locals to assimilate into the corporate culture, and this might led to communication problems.

(c) They will have greater local knowledge - but the difficulty of course is to get them to understand the wider corporate picture, but this is true of management at operational level generally.

Those firms which export sporadically might employ a home-based sales force. Their travel expenses will of course be high, and it might not always be easy to recruit people willing to cope with the pace.

7.8 Management effectiveness

A problem is that there are often severe cultural differences as to what constitutes 'management' in the first place. Are **management** principles universally applicable? The marketing function needs awareness of effective management approaches in different cultures.

Two American writers, Gonzalez and McMillan, suggested after a two-year study of management in Brazil that no general conclusions on management principles can be arrived at, and that different principles will apply in different cultures. It even opens up the possibility that general management principles may not be applicable throughout a large country such as the United States because of the variety of sub-cultures that may exist.

Koontz, O'Donnell and Weihrich (KOW) on the other hand have argued that apparent differences between management **principles** in different countries are actually differences of **application**, and that this distinction has been blurred by careless use of terminology. Their idea is that certain universal **fundamentals** of management exist, which may be applied in different ways depending on the local culture.

R N Farmer and B M Richman emphasise the importance of the external environment in which an organisation operates. They developed a model to illustrate the distinction between the management process and the environment of managing.

7.9 Human resources management

Definition

> **Human resources management** involves recruitment and selection, training, appraisal systems and such like, in other words the organisation's relationship with its employees. From management's point of view, HRM is designed to get the best possible performance from employees.

Relevant issues to keep in mind are these.

(a) **Recruitment and training**. In countries with low levels of literacy, more effort might need to be spent on basic training.

(b) **Career management**. Can overseas staff realistically expect promotion to the firm's highest levels if they do well?

(c) **Appraisal schemes**. These can be a minefield at the best of times, and the possibilities for communications failure are endless. For example, in some cultures, an appraisal is a two way discussion whereas in others arguing back might be considered a sign of insubordination.

(d) **Communications**. HRM tries to mobilise employees' commitment to the goals of the organisation. In far-flung global firms, the normal panoply of staff newsletters and team briefings may be hard to institute but are vital. Time differences also make communication difficult.

   (i) **E-mail** and satellite linkages between branch offices can be used for routine messages: e-mail is especially useful, as it allows swift access to a person's electronic mailbox.

   (ii) Major conferences are also necessary.

   (iii) Firms with many subsidiaries face additional problems of **language.** What language should be used for business communications? Some multinational firms have decreed English the language of official internal communications, even if they are not headquartered in the English speaking world.

Chapter roundup

- There are characteristics of industrial or business markets that make buying processes and decision making different from consumer markets.
- Essentially these characteristics can be listed as short distribution channels, large orders, price sensitivity and technical selling.
- In consumer markets although advertising pull strategies are predominant, selling does have an important role - mainly in terms of selling products to distributors and the retail-customer interface.
- Services can also be marketed and 'sold'. There are particular characteristics that make it different and sometimes more difficult to sell in these markets.
- Selling to the public sector (whether it is services or goods) has additional special characteristics especially in terms of the decision-making process and who is involved in the decision-making unit.
- Exhibitions are unique selling situations for sales persons and require specific skills and planning.
- Telephone selling and call centres are used increasingly but have pros and cons.
- There are specific implications and decisions to make in terms of selling in international markets. This is both in general strategic terms and in recruitment terms.

Quick quiz

1 How can industrial goods be classified?

2 What implications are there for sales people in industrial markets selling technical products?

3 What two types of strategies do sellers to a retailer market use to communicate their products?

4 How should the manufacturer consider the distributor in packaging design?

5 What are the implications of intangibility of a service to the sales person?

6 What characteristics of public authorities make them different to sell to?

7 What opportunities do exhibitions and trade fairs present to organisations?

8 What benefits are there to telephone selling?

9 What is the difference between indirect and direct exporting?

Answers to quick quiz

1 Into raw materials, fabricated materials, capital equipment, supplies. (See paragraph 1.1)

2 They have to have specialist product knowledge and be as technically aware as the customer. (para 1.4)

3 (i) Advertising to attract end customers and/or (ii) sales push to encourage distributors to stock the product. (para 2.1)

4 Packaging should be attractive to end users but also has to be stable on shelves, easy to handle, stock and distribute. (para 2.1)

5 They represent the company so their appearance is of importance. They also have to appear to be trustworthy and professional to customers. (para 3)

6 They (i) do not exist primarily to make profits. (ii) Decision-making may be political (iii) Employees may not have much influence/involvement in the DMU. (para 4)

7 Opportunities in public relations, promoting and selling, networking, testing new products, researching competitors and researching suppliers' products. (para 5)

8 A quick response, interaction, accessibility, easy assessment and cost. (para 6.2)

9 Indirect exporting occurs where a firm's goods are sold abroad by other organisations; direct exporting occurs where an intermediary is not used. (paras 7.1, 7.2)

Answers to activities

1 There is no specific answer to this activity.

2 There is no specific answer to this activity.

3 *Costs:* organisations will be willing to bear a higher cost than an individual

Work: will be of a different nature, eg corporation tax vs personal tax.

NOTES

Staff: need staff to be able to cope with both.

Different advertising media will be needed

4 There is no specific answer to this activity.

5 There is no specific answer to this activity.

6 There is no specific answer to this activity.

ASSIGNMENTS

UNIT 17

Assignment 1 **(2 hours)**

BUYER BEHAVIOUR AND CUSTOMER SATISFACTION

This is an open book assignment and so any relevant materials can be used. However, you are not permitted to bring in any other materials or study notes after the assignment has begun.

All tasks carry equal weighting.

Introduction

The purpose of this assignment is to provide the student with the opportunity to demonstrate an understanding of buyer behaviour and customer satisfaction concepts and their practical application.

Scenario

You have been invited to an interview for a post as marketing assistant at Bargain Airlines. The company has provided you with the following information.

- In 1999 a market survey revealed that few travellers named Bargain Airlines as their first choice because they considered them to be unproven.
- Following this survey, Bargain Airlines introduced a promotion offering to match any competitor's fare on its eight main routes.
- Although Bargain Airlines was successful in attracting passengers, the number of them paying full fare dropped to 30%.
- In early 2000 the company acquired another low cost airline as a means of expanding their service offering, and their market share increased accordingly.
- The company is endeavouring to engender loyalty by offering attractive schemes for frequent flyers.
- No customer satisfaction research has been undertaken.

Task 1

You are asked to prepare a memo to the Marketing Director:

(a) Indicating what role you think modelling could have played in the diffusion of innovative low cost airlines

(b) Developing and describing a sequence of behaviours for purchasing and using airline services.

Task 2

Develop a 20 minute presentation with slides and explanatory notes for the interview panel on the following.

(a) An evaluation of the techniques that could be used to assess customer satisfaction.

(b) How to design a customer satisfaction survey.

Assignment 2 (2 hours)

COMPETITIVE ANALYSIS AND MARKET RESEARCH

Introduction

The purpose of this assignment is to provide the student with the opportunity to demonstrate an understanding of market research and competitive analysis techniques.

Scenario

You are a marketing assistant in the shampoo department of a major toiletries manufacturer. You have a new marketing director who has come from the dental care sector and as such has very limited knowledge about your sector.

Task 1

You are required to write a report which will establish the competitive environment in which your organisation operates.

(a) Identify the number of manufacturers making shampoo and, if possible, the market share of each

(b) Visit a retailer and record the price of the various products

(c) Examine the degree of price competition that exists in the shampoo market

(d) Identify the ways in which non-price competition takes place

Task 2

Your manager has expressed an interest in targeting the more mature (50+) female customer and has asked you to investigate.

(a) Identify sources of secondary data which may help to understand the size and behaviour of this sector

(b) Design a marketing research plan to obtain relevant information which cannot be found via secondary sources

The answer should be in report form.

NOTES

UNIT 18

Assignment 3 (3 hours)

ADVERTISING AND PROMOTIONS

Introduction

The purpose of this assignment is to give the student an opportunity to consider the link between target markets, advertising and below the line communications.

Scenario

You are the newly appointed Marketing Communications manager at Champagne Chanson in the UK. The company details are as follows.

- The second largest market share in the UK champagne market
- Increased production is not an option and so the focus is on activities to support the premium pricing policy
- TGI data indicates that indicates that adult penetration is at 7%
- The market is made up of three sectors: off trade, such as wine merchants and selected outlets, on trade, such as hotels and restaurants and finally areas such as corporate hospitality
- Bulk purchasing is made on the basis of price and personal contacts
- Personal purchasers are more brand sensitive
- The company image is stylish and carefully understated
- Recent research has indicated that consumers associate champagne with romance and special occasions
- You have a budget of £7 million for below the line promotions

Tasks

(a) Discuss the role of models to assess the impact of communications on customer behaviour

(b) Develop a set of marketing communications objectives for a below the line campaign

(c) Set out a rationale for the adoption of an integrated marketing communications approach and an indication of the range of promotional techniques which could be used

(d) Show the selection, justification and recommendations for the implementation of two promotional techniques which you feel could be used to achieve your promotional objectives

(e) Set out your proposals for the evaluation which might be appropriate for the measurement of the campaign against the objectives

Your findings should be presented in the form of a report to the Marketing Director comprising around 1,500 words maximum. It should be supported by appendices containing any evidence used in the completion of this report. There should be a bibliography correctly cited and referred to in the report.

NOTES

Assignment 3 (continued)

Guidelines for completion

The organisation used in this case is a fictitious one and as such no attempt should be made to research it. You should consider the particular characteristics of the champagne market, and to that end students are encouraged to undertake appropriate desk research.

You should consider the importance of the target market and their key segmentation variables.

You should remember the importance of SMART objectives as those you develop in part (b) will need to be capable of evaluation for part (e).

Part (c) asks only for an indication of the range of promotional techniques which could be used to support this product. A bullet point list would suffice.

Attention should be paid to the synergy between the objectives, the chosen techniques and the overall campaign budget.

Assignment 4 **(3 hours)**

THE PROCESS OF ADVERTISING

Introduction

The purpose of this assignment is to give the student an opportunity to demonstrate an understanding of the nature of fmcg advertising.

Scenario

You are an account executive at a medium sized advertising agency. You have been asked to present a one hour lecture, with supporting materials, to a group of first year higher education students. They are particularly keen to hear about real life advertising, campaigns and are interested in the advertising process.

Task

You are required to undertake research and develop a minimum of 20 slides with accompanying notes.

The specific topics are as follows.

(a) explain the structure of the communications industry's key players

(b) discuss the agency selection process

(c) explain and illustrate how advertising can help to stimulate consumer response in two situations

(d) identify current trends in marketing communications and use two products/services to illustrate.

Your findings should be presented in the form of slides with associated explanatory text. This should be appropriately bound and should be supported with appendices containing any evidence gathered in the completion of this assignment. There should be a bibliography correctly cited and referred to in the document.

Guidelines for completion

The key to this assignment is effective and contemporary research. You should be referring to publications such as *Campaign* and *Marketing Week.*

You should consider using illustrative examples from both product and service sectors.

You should also consider the requirements of the audience in terms of relevant information.

The request for an evaluation of current trends should include reference to technological developments.

UNIT 19

Assignment 5 **(2 hours)**

MARKETING PLANNING

Background

You left college two years ago after completely a business and computing course. Since then you have been working as a freelance web page designer. You share a rented house with two friends and work from home. Recently you have had a great deal of work and you have subcontracted some work to another friend who was on your course. You have managed to save almost £10,000 from the business. However, you are now in a position where you think the business could be expanded perhaps formally to employ another two full time designers and administrative help. You are also considering having office premises and registering as a company with an associated company name. You have not conducted any market research or promotional activities but instead have relied on informal contacts and word of mouth. Most of your customers are small/medium sized local firms.

You need some backing from the bank if you are to expand your business. They have asked for some more information on your business and a proposed marketing plan for the next five years.

Tasks

(1) Conduct a SWOT analysis for your business.

(2) Design a draft marketing plan for the business.

(3) Report briefly how you will ensure your product/service will keep up to date with competitors.

NOTES

Assignment 6 **(2 hours)**

ECOTOURS

Background

EcoTours are a small specialist travel company. They organise educational visits for small groups to environmentally interesting areas, and working holidays on environmental projects. Tours are both UK based and overseas, ranging from working holidays in Wales clearing rhododendrons from native woodlands, to tours of a Malaysian National Park to look at orang-utans.

The types of holidays are therefore very diverse and rely on local guides and organisers. UK holidays have specific tour representatives. Overseas representatives will not work for EcoTours solely but will work for a number of organisations, and often groups will be of mixed tour operators.

The present mission statement aims 'to provide our customers with value for money, informative, and enjoyable holidays/visits with an environmental theme'. Their customers are usually upper middle class and fall into a younger age group of 20-25 year olds and an older group of 45-55 year olds. There are also groups such as interest groups or small charity groups who are customers, as are some educational establishments who take groups of students on field trips organised by EcoTours. Some group visits/holidays are therefore tailor made to the client's requirements.

EcoTours has a small marketing department of six people. They issue feedback forms to all customers when they are issued with their itineraries. Promotion is usually concentrated on specialist magazines and repeat business is very important to EcoTours. There is however growing competition in the sector as even some traditional package tour operators are offering more specialist holidays. Prices are set competitively with discounts for group booking.

Recently Bob Evans, the managing director of EcoTours, went to an environmental tourism conference where he was very interested in the concept of 'societal marketing'. Although the company is in the environmental sector he would like to know whether it does practice societal marketing, and what he can do to make the company practice good business ethics.

You are a new recruit to the Marketing Department, and Mr Evans has asked for you to take a look at the company operations to see if it is operating ethically and what further research may be needed to assess marketing ethics for the company.

Tasks

You have been asked to provide a report to Mr Evans covering the following.

(1) How the societal marketing concept can be applied to the company.

(2) A review of the marketing mix (7Ps) to analyse societal marketing applications and any corresponding further information that is needed.

(3) A re-assessment of the mission statement in the light of the societal marketing concept.

UNIT 20

Assignment 7 **(2 hours)**

MEDISERVE CASE STUDY

Background

Mediserve is a company which manufactures and supplies medical products to hospitals and clinics (private and NHS) throughout the UK. Their main products are feeding products which include specialist baby feeding products, food replacement high nutritional value drinks and entereal feeding products (via drips).

Mediserve's sales personnel are organised into geographical areas and each representative will serve all clients in their area. Personnel are usually graduates in one of the sciences or have some background in medicine, such as nursing.

Decision making units in the health sector are complex. They could include:

INITIATORS	Administrators, nursing staff, doctors
USERS	(in this case would not be the consumer) Doctors, nurses
INFLUENCERS	Administrators, management, specialists, doctors
BUYER/NEGOTIATOR	Management/administrator
FINANCIER	Management/administrator
DECIDER	Management
GATEKEEPER	Administrators, secretary

Tasks

(1) Mediserve at present relies mainly on personal selling. Give examples of how other elements of the communication mix can be used effectively alongside selling to improve communication.

(2) Discuss how the selling process can help sales representatives in Mediserve.

NOTES

Assignment 8 **(1½ hours)**

GROUP ROLE PLAY EXERCISE

This exercise is to be conducted in groups of 3 - 4.

You are part of a sales team which works for an advertising agency. A potential client has asked for a presentation from your company. The client is a manufacturer of soft drinks and they are launching a new product aimed at the teen market. They have called the new drink PowR. It is to be targeted at both the male and female 13 - 18 year age group. It is a drink with added vitamins, minerals and herbal extracts that is supposed to give health and energy. The client wants a high profile mass media campaign to launch the product and has asked for your ideas.

You can name your agency as you wish. The client has asked for a 20 minute presentation on your ideas for the advertising campaign. Your task is to make a sales presentation to the client, with all members of the sales team contributing, and using visual aids as appropriate. Other members of your class or your tutors should act as the clients and ask questions/raise objections etc.

ANSWERS TO ASSIGNMENTS

Answer to Assignment 1

To achieve a **Pass** grade a student must:

- explain the role modelling could play in the diffusion of innovation in this market
- develop and describe a sequence of behaviours for purchasing in this market
- include an evaluation of customer satisfaction measurement techniques
- design a customer satisfaction survey

To achieve a **Merit** a student must in addition:

- complete all tasks to a level which demonstrates a good level of understanding of relevant concepts
- display a satisfactory knowledge of buyer behaviour and customer satisfaction concepts
- show well written answers and conform to the specified response formats
- communicate findings using appropriate technical terms in a coherent manner

To achieve a **Distinction** a student must in addition:

- complete all tasks to a high standard while demonstrating full and comprehensive responses
- display a comprehensive knowledge of buyer behaviour and customer satisfaction concepts
- demonstrate creativity in the execution of work
- communicate findings that comprehensively support conclusions reached

Answer plan to Assignment 1

Report format for task 1 and presentation format for task 2

(a) Discussion of the diffusion of innovation model using appropriate illustrations

(b) Relate the model to the specified industry

(c) Discussion of at least two models of consumer behaviour and their associated influencing factors

(d) In-depth evaluation of at least two customer satisfaction measurement techniques indicating why they were selected and how they relate to the specified industry

(e) An effective and comprehensive customer satisfaction survey relating to the airline industry

Answer to Assignment 2

To achieve a **Pass** grade a student must:

- identify shampoo manufacturers
- discuss relative retail prices
- evaluate the level of price competition

- identify non-price competitive activities
- report on relevant secondary data for the selected target market
- develop a marketing research plan to identify segment characteristics and behaviour

To achieve a **Merit** a student must in addition:

- complete all tasks to a level which demonstrates a good level of understanding of competitive and market research concepts
- display a satisfactory knowledge of those concepts using appropriate technical terms in a coherent manner
- show well written answers and conform to the specified response formats

To achieve a **Distinction** a student must in addition:

- complete all tasks to a high standard while demonstrating full and comprehensive responses
- display a comprehensive understanding of competitive and market research concepts
- demonstrate creativity in the planning of work
- communicate findings that comprehensively support the conclusions reached

Answer plan to Assignment 2

Report format

(a) identification of competitors

(b) evaluation of competitor prices and the degree of price competition

(c) discussion of non-price competition activities with appropriate examples to illustrate

(d) explanation of the secondary data located on the chosen segment with an indication of pertinent information gaps

(e) development of a marketing research plan to address the gap identification

Answer to Assignment 3

Assessment notes

To achieve a **Pass** grade a student must:

- identify consumer models and promotional techniques
- develop communications objectives and associated evaluative methods
- evaluate the role of IMC

To achieve a **Merit** a student must in addition:

- complete all tasks to a level which demonstrates a good level of understanding of relevant concepts
- display a satisfactory level of knowledge of promotional techniques

- communicate findings using appropriate technical terms in a coherent manner

To achieve a **Distinction** a student must in addition:

- complete all tasks to a high standard, demonstrate full and comprehensive responses
- display a comprehensive understanding of promotional techniques
- demonstrate creativity in the planning of work and execution of that plan
- communicate findings that comprehensively support conclusions reached

Answer plan to Assignment 3

Report format for the attention of the Marketing Director

(a) Brief discussion of at least two models with illustrative diagram, where appropriate. Evaluation of how understanding these can help explain customer behaviour in the context of the champagne market

(b) A minimum of four objectives which all adhere to the requirements of the SMART approach

(c) A discussion of the development and potential benefits of IMC. A bullet point list of possible techniques for the champagne market

(d) In-depth discussion of two of these techniques, indicating why they were selected and how they relate to the objectives detailed in part (a)

(e) Evaluation of how the objectives can be measured

Brief summary and conclusion

Answer to Assignment 4

Assessment notes

To achieve a **Pass** grade a student must:

- explain the industry structure and the agency selection process
- explain and illustrate the relationship between advertising and consumer behaviour
- evaluate and illustrate current advertising trends

To achieve a **Merit** a student must in addition:

- complete all tasks to a level which demonstrates a good level of understanding of relevant concepts
- display a satisfactory level of knowledge of advertising
- communicate findings using appropriate technical terms in a coherent manner

To achieve a **Distinction** a student must in addition:

- complete all tasks to a high standard, demonstrate full and comprehensive responses
- display a comprehensive understanding of the role and function of advertising

- demonstrate creativity in the planning of work
- communicate findings that comprehensively support conclusions reached

Answer plan to Assignment 4

Slides and associated text in bound format for the attention of first year students

(a) Discussion of the organisation of the industry. This should cover advertising agencies, media owners, types of agency, eg full service, a la carte, media independents and hot shops

(b) Evaluation of the agency selection process including briefing, short listing and pitching

(c) Explanation of influences on consumer behaviour with relevant examples to illustrate

(d) Current trends should refer to media fragmentation, micro-marketing and new media such as the internet

Answer to assignment 5

Answer guide

(1) Some elements of a SWOT you could include are as follows.

Strengths	*Weaknesses*
Good reputation Solvent Has some capital Has technical skills Has some business education Business contacts	Limited capital No company name No premises Unprofessional way of subcontracting
Opportunities	*Threats*
Growing market Customers do not have internal skills to do themselves Web pages need regular updating	Internal staff will develop their own skills Limited geographical area Market may become saturated

(2) Your draft marketing plan should have the following sections.

(a) Analysis – a brief summary of your answer to question one

(b) Mission/objectives. An attempt to draft some objectives for the next five years

(c) Strategies in terms of segmentation and product-market analysis

(d) Operational plan. That corresponds with the strategies outlined in the previous section. As this is a service it should look at the extended marketing mix of product, price, place, promotion, people, physical evidence and processes

NOTES

(e) Budgets and control aspects

(3) Here you should discuss how you will manage the innovation process and whether you will have any formal new product/service development strategies.

Answer to Assignment 6

Assignment answer guide

The assignment should be in report format. Your college may have a preferred house style you should follow.

(1) The societal marketing concept is 'a management orientation that holds that the key task of the organisation is to determine the needs and wants of the target markets and to adapt the organisation to delivering the desired satisfactions more effectively and efficiently than its competitors, in a way that preserves or enhances the consumers' and society's well being'.

In many respects it is easier for companies that are already in a sector that is aiming to be socially and/or environmentally aware such as EcoTours. The employees have chosen to work for a company in this sector, so should need no convincing as to its importance. The important distinguishing feature of the societal marketing concept from the basic marketing concept is the last part 'preserving/enhancing customers' and society's well being'. You should consider ways in which EcoTours could audit that they are doing this, and control mechanisms to monitor activities.

(2) You could include issues around:

Product/service. Are the actual holidays at all environmentally damaging, do they support sustainability, are they using environmentally friendly transport systems where possible? As overseas holidays are contracted to local suppliers, what control mechanisms and safeguards should be put in place?

Price. Making sure customers are getting what they pay for: again this may be more problematic overseas. It could include aspects such as local guides charging to take photographs or additional charges for tours which customers were expecting to be included.

Promotion. Checks that it is truthful, honest and legal.

Place. In this industry 'place' is very closely related to 'product', so again checks on local suppliers and their use of power.

Processes. Are there any implications for service delivery processes, eg customer details – are they passed on to any third parties?

Physical evidence. Whether any aspect of the tangible evidence is ethical. Some aspects of transportation are inherently damaging to the environment and may have to be accepted (eg air travel). Brochures and stationery could use recycled materials.

People. Essentially making sure that all employees and overseas representatives understand that EcoTours aims to be ethically sound.

(3) The mission statement needs some form of specified ethical content. It is suggested that you try to make the revised mission statement more detailed and specific to EcoTours as at present it could be applied to many suppliers.

BPP PUBLISHING

Answer to Assignment 7

(1) You could use any aspect of the communications mix here, for example:

Advertising - specialist/trade press advertising may be effective, however mass media advertising would be too wasteful.

Sales promotion may not be a logical choice as special offers are unlikely to be effective; however, bulk purchasing with discounts might be useful.

Public relations can be used but has to be targeted towards medical services. If you use the example of advertising, adverts can be placed in specialist publications which could be medical management journals, nursing publications such as Nursing Times or clinical journals. In addition, leaflets and brochures could be produced to leave with hospital staff.

More imaginative aspects of communications that don't fit particularly well in the communications mix headings could also be discussed. This could include attendance at medical exhibitions, and sponsorship of events. A useful way of getting your name known is to have merchandise printed with the Mediserve name. This could include stationery, calendars, pens etc that hospital staff would use everyday.

(2) The sales process is:

(a) Preparation
(b) Planning the presentation
(c) Opening the sale
(d) Presenting and demonstration
(e) Handling objectives
(f) Negotiations and close
(g) Follow up
(h) Records, reports and analysis

Each of these should be discussed with implications for Mediserve. In terms of preparation they would need to know about the organisation, the industry, competition, products and customers (ie DMU). When planning the presentation sales objectives need to be clear, appointments made and the presentation prepared. Opening the sale: consideration should be made of appearance and introduction. The actual presentation should try to turn product features into benefits. In handling objections, experience will count for the sales representative. Negotiations may then continue on terms and price. Follow up should therefore then be instigated by the representative who should check that any orders have been received. Finally reports and paperwork on the sale and who is involved in the DMU of the organisation should be kept.

Answer to Assignment 8

You should concentrate on the sales process and presentation techniques rather than on the creative aspects of the campaign. You should go through the process of preparation, planning, opening, presenting, handling objections, negotiation and close.

INDEX

NOTES

BPP PUBLISHING

NOTES

BPP PUBLISHING

NOTES

BPP PUBLISHING

NOTES

NOTES

BPP PUBLISHING

NOTES

NOTES

BPP PUBLISHING

ORDER FORM

Any books from our HNC/HND range can be ordered in one of the following ways:

- Telephone us on **020 8740 2211**
- Send this page to our **Freepost** address
- Fax this page on **020 8740 1184**
- Email us at **publishing@bpp.com**
- Go to our website: **www.bpp.com**

We aim to deliver to all UK addresses inside 5 working days. Orders to all EU addresses should be delivered within 6 working days. All other orders to overseas addresses should be delivered within 8 working days.

BPP Publishing Ltd
Aldine House
Aldine Place
London W12 8AW
Tel: 020 8740 2211
Fax: 020 8740 1184
Email: publishing@bpp.com

Full name: ____

Day-time delivery address: ______________________________

____

______________________________ Postcode ______________

Day-time telephone (for queries only): ____________________

Please send me the following quantities of books:

Core

		No. of copies	Price	Total
Unit 1	Marketing (8/00)		£7.95	
Unit 2	Managing Financial Resources (8/00)		£7.95	
Unit 3	Organisations and Behaviour (8/00)		£7.95	
Unit 4	Organisations, Competition and Environment (8/00)		£7.95	
Unit 5	Quantitative Techniques for Business (8/00)		£7.95	
Unit 6	Legal and Regulatory Framework (8/00)		£7.95	
Unit 7	Management Information Systems (8/00)		£7.95	
Unit 8	Business Strategy (8/00)		£7.95	

Option

Units 9-12	Business & Finance (1/2001)		£10.95	
Units 13-16	Business & Management (1/2001)		£10.95	
Units 17-20	Business & Marketing (1/2001)		£10.95	
Unit 21-24	Business & Personnel (1/2001)		£10.95	

Other Material

	Workbook (3/00)		£9.95	

Sub Total	£

Postage & Packaging

UK :	Course book £3.00 for first plus £2.00 for each extra, Workbook £2.00 for first plus £1.00 for each	£
Europe : (inc. ROI)	Course book £5.00 for first plus £4.00 for each extra, Workbook £2.50 for first plus £1.00 for each	£
Rest of the world :	Course book £20.00 for first plus £10.00 for each extra, Workbook £2.50 for first plus £1.00 for each	£

Grand Total	£

I enclose a cheque for £____________ (cheque to BPP Publishing Ltd) or charge to Access/VISA/Switch

Card number: ☐☐☐☐☐☐☐☐☐☐☐☐☐☐☐☐☐☐☐

Issues number (Switch only): ____________

Start date: ____________ Expiry date: ____________

Signature ____________

BPP PUBLISHING

REVIEW FORM & FREE PRIZE DRAW

We are constantly reviewing, updating and improving our Course Books. We would be grateful for any comments or thoughts you have on this Course Book. Cut out and send this page to our Freepost address and you will be automatically entered in a £50 prize draw.

Jed Cope
HNC/HND Range Manager
BPP Publishing Ltd, FREEPOST, London W12 8BR

Full name: ____

Address: ____

____

__________________________________ Postcode ______________

Where are you studying?

Where did you find out about BPP range books?

Why did you decide to buy this Course Book?

Have you used our texts for the other units in your HNC/HND studies?

What thoughts do you have on our:

- Introductory pages
- Topic coverage
- Summary diagrams, icons, chapter roundups and quick quizzes
- Discussion topics, activities and assignments

The other side of this form is left blank for any further comments you wish to make.

BPP PUBLISHING

Please give any further comments and suggestions (with page number if necessary) below.

FREE PRIZE DRAW RULES

1. Closing date for 31 July 2001 draw is 30 June 2001. Closing date for 31 January 2002 draw is 31 December 2001.
2. Restricted to entries with UK and Eire addresses only. BPP employees, their families and business associates are excluded.
3. No purchase necessary. Entry forms are available upon request from BPP Publishing. No more than one entry per title, per person. Draw restricted to persons aged 16 and over.
4. Winners will be notified by post and receive their cheques not later than 6 weeks after the relevant draw date.
5. The decision of the promoter in all matters is final and binding. No correspondence will be entered into.

BPP PUBLISHING